Reading, Thinking, and Writing About

Multicultural Literature

Edited by Carol Booth Olson

UCI/California Writing Project
University of California, Irvine

ScottForesman

A Division of HarperCollinsPublishers

EDITORIAL OFFICES: Glenview, Illinois
REGIONAL OFFICES: Sunnyvale, California • Tucker, Georgia
• Glenview, Illinois • Oakland, New Jersey • Dallas Texas

ISBN: 0–673–36296–5
Acknowledgments for quoted matter are included in the text credits section on pages
685–686. The text credits section is an extension of the copyright page.

23456789-WC-04030201009998

Ahana

Africanos, Hispanos
Asians, and Native Americanos
in the back seats
on the back burners,
how well we are represented
in the front lines
in the cages
of the amply dying
colored ephemera
of the wars of our worlds!

Now we are the clamoring flowers,
the second spring,
the new majority aborning.
No more killing time,
you of the lowered eyes.
Lift up your hearts, not shamed
into some tired old melting pot,
for we are wonderful
as we were
as we are.

Be called by your names,
AHANA, you
men and women of the dark eyes
of the sloe eyes
of the bright wings. Now
we will fashion our word
quicken our metaphor
fly like eagles
father in tomorrow.

César A. González-T.

We are grateful to César González for contributing this poem to our manuscript. The term AHANA (Africano, Hispano, Asian, and Native American) was first brought to Mr. González's attention by Luis Alberto Urrea at Massachusetts Bay Community College.

Contents

Poetry

Short Story

Research and References

Preface

Orange County, California, is in the midst of a wave of immigration that is dramatically transforming its cultural makeup. What was once a primarily white community is changing rapidly in its racial and ethnic diversity.

As the chart indicates, while the white population increased only slightly over the last decade, Orange County experienced an influx of African American, Asian and, particularly, Hispanic residents. "Orange County is no longer a predominantly white community," according to Rusty Kennedy, Executive Director of the Orange County Human Relations Commission. "It's a rapidly growing multi-ethnic urban community with a large Latino population." (*Orange County Register*, 1991) Since Orange County has been identified by the U.S. Bureau of the Census as one of the major intended destinations of future immigrants, its population is predicted to become increasingly diverse by the year 2000 (*Journal of Orange County Studies*, Spring 1990).

	1980	1990	1980–1990 Increase/Decrease
White	1,382,975	1,544,501	+ 12.4%
Hispanic	286,339	564,828	+ 97.3%
Black	25,287	39,159	+ 54.9%
American Indian, Eskimo & Aleutian	12,951	8,584	– 33.7%
Asian & Pacific Islander	86,893	240,756	+ 177.1%

Source: U.S. Bureau of the Census, 1990

As *Crossing the Schoolhouse Border*, a 1988 report by *California Tomorrow* states so well, "California's changing face is visible in the workplaces, streets and communities of the state. But nowhere is California's changed population more prevalent than in the public schools—and nowhere is the need to acknowledge the changes more critical." This is especially true of Orange County where, across all twenty-seven districts, white students now comprise just 48% of the population. This percentage is on the decline while the percentages of Hispanic students (35%) and Asian students (14%) are dramatically on the rise (Orange County Department of Education, 1993). In Orange County's largest school district, Santa Ana Unified (48,500), the student population is now 95% ethnic minority and 67% limited English proficient (LEP). In another large district, Garden Grove Unified, the ethnic minority population (66%) and the percentage of LEP students (36%) are also growing rapidly. Given that Orange County's teachers are primarily white (81%) and, more often than not, monolingual, these changing demographics pose major challenges for our school system (Orange County Department of Education, 1991). As the *Los Angeles Times* noted in a 1992 article, "In a county that is accustomed to homogeneity and classrooms filled with students who speak English fluently, educators are being forced to come to grips with the language barrier and the frantic pace of ethnic changes in their classrooms."

The situation we face in Orange County is by no means unique. In fact, it is often a surprise to people outside our service area that what is often considered to be an "upscale" community mirrors very closely the demographics of California. Statewide, white students comprise roughly 42% of the K–12 population. The Hispanic student population is slightly larger than Orange County's at 37% and the Asian/Pacific Islander/Filipino student population is somewhat smaller at 11%. Black students statewide represent almost 9% of the population and Native Americans comprise less than 1% of the students in California schools *(California Basic Educational Data System,* 1993*)*. Although California has seen the most dramatic demographic shift in the last ten years, the entire nation has felt the impact of immigration. The most comprehensive report which addresses trends toward diversity, *The Road to College: Educational Progress by Race and Ethnicity* (The College Board and the Western Interstate Commission for Higher Education, 1991), projects that non-white and Hispanic student enrollment will skyrocket from its current percentage (23%) to 70% of our nation's school enrollment by the year 2026. As Richard Figueroa and Eugene Garcia point out, "In 2026, we will have the exact inverse of student representation as we knew it in 1990 when white students made up 70 percent of our enrolled K–12 student body" (*Multicultural Education,* Fall 1994).

Compiling statistics is one thing. Meeting the needs of an increasingly diverse student population on a day-to-day basis is another. As we acknowledged the "changing face" of California and the nation in the changing faces in our class-rooms, we began to ask ourselves: How can we, as teachers, be responsive to these changes and responsible about finding ways to recognize, validate and motivate all of the children whom we serve? To that end, a group of UCI Writing Project Teacher/Consultants, under the leadership of Brenda Borron, formed a special interest group in 1987 to explore ways to achieve this goal. Early on in their efforts, they reported informally to other Writing Project colleagues that experiments with infusing multicultural literature into the curriculum at a variety of grade levels were yielding positive results in their classrooms.

As Diane Pollard states, "We need to honor pluralism. We need not only to recognize the existence of other cultures but also to incorporate them into the classroom everyday. Non-European cultures must be presented not just as an adjunct to the 'regular' classroom but as a part of the total curriculum present-ed to the child. This is necessary in classrooms that are culturally heteroge-neous but also in classrooms composed primarily or solely of white students" (*Educational Leadership,* October 1989). Because literature is the stock in trade of the English/language arts teacher, it seemed like one of the most natural vehicles for Writing Project teachers to "honor pluralism" in their classrooms. Accordingly, in 1989, the UCI Writing Project—along with partners Garden Grove, Irvine, Santa Ana, and Saddleback Valley Unified School Districts and Orange Coast College—applied to the California Academic Partnership Program (CAPP) to develop curriculum materials that respond to the California

Department of Education's call for the "diversity of American society" to be "reflected in the literature program" (*Model Curriculum Standards,* 1985); to provide staff development training to help teachers enhance their understanding and use of multicultural literature in the classroom; and to conduct teacher research to determine what impact both our curriculum materials and in-service training might have on student learning.

CAPP's funding of our grant proposal not only enabled us to work collaboratively toward a professional goal but also afforded us an opportunity to enrich ourselves by reading a wide array of impressive and memorable works by writers from a range of culturally diverse backgrounds—writers we were not taught when we were in school and that few of us included in our own current syllabuses. Instantly recognizing what we had been missing out on all these years, many of us who were less well-read than some other colleagues have become bookstore junkies, scouring the shelves for the newest releases of many of the authors included in this book, and more, eagerly collecting the newest anthologies of multicultural literature, and searching for more accurate translations of speeches and other nonfiction documents we have used in the classroom.

Our goals in developing the materials in this book are both cognitive and affective. Cognitively, we wish to enhance the reading, thinking, and writing ability of all students—but particularly, to provide support to linguistic and ethnic minority students. The lessons are based upon the UCI Writing Project's Thinking/Writing model, which blends learning theory, composing process research, and the practical strategies of the National Writing Project in a scaffolded approach to fostering critical thinking through writing. One of the key questions we are currently exploring is: *Do lessons that are carefully scaffolded to foster thinking and writing positively affect student performance?* Much of the literature we have selected is sophisticated and the thinking/writing tasks quite challenging. Our experience thus far has been that if the literature is relevant and engaging, students will rise to the occasion. As Jane Bruckler, an English teacher from Saddleback High School in Santa Ana Unified School District who participated in one of our research studies, noted, "I've discovered that my students can have much stronger analytical faculties than I was previously aware of. We've all learned and are more aware, and hopefully, more sensitive Jane's colleague, Connie Mayhugh, at Century High School, echoed this st ment: "I was surprised that their [my students'] insight can oftentimes intense and so deep."

Affectively, we wish to foster in our students both cultural a*ay or* One of the research questions we have been exploring is: *What their own culture encourage students to engage more inter r fine* This question grows out of the hope that by infusin literature into the curriculum—not just as a nod Asian-American Studies Week—but as an o constitutes a quality English/language art

arts program, students who have normally felt excluded in school will feel more connected to the learning environment. In recalling his own education, Professor César González from Mesa College notes,

> The school for me was a foreign land to which I traveled each day and in which I was made expert by academic degrees. This lack of inclusiveness must continue to change. My students continue to be profoundly moved when they see *nuestra cosas,* our things in literature. There, they live, they will abide, and others will come there to see *nuestras cosas,* our humanity.[1]

Our experience in piloting our materials thus far reinforces what González has noticed in his college classrooms. As Christine Lammers, an English teacher from Saddleback High School observed, "I will definitely teach more ethnic lit—my students ate it up! . . . Students have gained self-esteem about their own cultures. . . . Those students of a particular group were especially proud when we read of their heritage."

Our goal to foster cultural and personal pride within our students is coupled with an equal commitment to foster cultural awareness, tolerance, mutual respect, and understanding among students from diverse backgrounds. Psychologist Thomas Parham has pointed out, "It is only through the constant study of history and culture that our children will come to know, understand and appreciate their own cultural values and traditions." We were especially pleased to see students of diverse backgrounds learning important lessons, not only from the authors who share their cultural heritage, but also from those who do not, as well. The following excerpts from the students' metacognitive logs demonstrate how they successfully crossed cultural barriers to embrace an idea that resonated for them:

"The Esperanza [lesson] helped me to appreciate my own culture. Writing about my own name helped me to understand that my culture has reasons for doing everything that it does. ... Chinese name has ...ing behind it."

Lan Huynh

"The lesson of 'Everyday Use' helped me appreciate another culture because of the way that they lived. Even though they had nothing, they had their pride and their culture."

Angelina Ramirez

(About "The Moon Lady" lesson . . .) "I can tell you that it is good to believe in your culture's way but you should also believe in yourself and your own ideals. If you keep your desires hidden away and don't talk about them, no one will really know who you are as a person."

Ofelia Valencia

... are excerpted from a videotaped interview that is part of artists ...nchez's piece, "La Reconquista: A Post-Columbian New World."

Ultimately, we wish not only to celebrate and validate the uniqueness of each individual and culture but also to surface the commonalities that unite us all as Americans and human beings. Kristi Kemp, an English teacher from Bolsa Grande High School in Garden Grove Unified School District, noted of her students, "I know my students became emotionally involved with the stories from the lessons because they felt a common human link, even if the culture was different. . . . I will be more inclined to seek out literature from other cultures in my teaching." Perhaps Jimmy Santiago Baca, author of *Martin & Meditations on the South Valley,* says it best:

> It's much better to celebrate and acknowledge one's culture than to censor and ignore. One's culture is part of the seasons of America. They make America blossom. It is truest democracy, giving to future generations its most important gift via language through literature and poetry. Literature is the tree through which we pass on the most important fruits of culture, nourish the soul, and give it sustenance to dream of a world more humane and loving.

It is in the spirit of engendering "a world more humane and loving" that we embarked upon this project and offer you this book. As a group composed almost exclusively of white teachers, we were not without concerns about proceeding with this project. Would it be considered presumptuous of such a group as ours to seek to make accessible to other teachers and to students works of literature from cultural backgrounds we do not personally share? After much reflection, we decided to venture into what for many of us was unfamiliar territory because we hoped to give other teachers in California and the nation the courage and conviction to make changes in their curriculum. Regardless of our cultural backgrounds, those of us in the teaching profession share one thing in common: *we care about kids.* And while we may not be able to understand every cultural nuance of Sandra Cisneros or Alice Walker or Amy Tan any more than we can pretend to have an insider's understanding of James Joyce, as teachers of literature we can empower our students to construct their own meaning from texts, to make personal connections between their own lives and the literary works they read, to approach literary works from other cultures with respect, and to bring forward the universal themes that connect us all. By expanding our own horizons, we can enable our students to broaden theirs.

We hope our work enhances your awareness of the rich potential for infusing multicultural literature into the classroom and that you will find the experience as rewarding as we have.

Carol Booth Olson
University of California, Irvine

Acknowledgments

This book is the result of the collaborative effort of a group of Teacher/Consultants from the UCI Writing Project—many of whom have come back to the University of California, Irvine, campus every summer since 1982 to continue to develop their professional expertise and to work together as a community of learners. It is the commitment of this group to recognize, validate, and motivate the students of culturally diverse backgrounds that they interact with every day in their classrooms that is the driving force behind this manuscript. Although the lessons in this book have individual by-lines, they are the product of a whole group process.

These colleagues include:

Virginia Bergquist
Teacher
Meadow Park Elementary School
Irvine Unified School District

Brenda Borron
Instructor of English
Irvine Valley College

Bill Burns
English Teacher
Sonora High School
Fullerton Joint Union HSD

Chris Byron
English Teacher
Thurston Intermediate
Laguna Beach USD

Pat Clark
English Teacher
Century High School
Santa Ana USD

Susanna Clemans
Instructor of English
Cerritos College

Catherine D'Aoust
Coordinator of Instructional
Services, K–12
Saddleback Valley USD
Co-Director, UCI Writing Project

Scott Edwards
English Teacher
La Habra High School
Fullerton Joint Union HSD

Sue Ellen Gold
Former English Teacher
Irvine High School
Irvine USD

Cristan Greaves
English Teacher
Valley View High School
Moreno Valley Unified School District

Todd Huck
Instructor of English
Rancho Santiago College

Jerry Judd
English Teacher
Irvine High School
Irvine USD

Mifanwy Pat Kaiser
English Teacher
Costa Mesa High School
Newport-Mesa USD

Sheila Koff
Instructor of English
Orange Coast College

Erline Krebs
Student Teacher Supervisor
School of Education
Chapman University

Shari Lockman
Resource Specialist,
Learning Handicapped Program
Saddleback High School
Santa Ana USD

Mindy Moffatt
English/History/Technology Teacher
White Hill School
Ross Valley School District

Michael O'Brien
Language Arts Department Chair
Allan Hancock College

Glenn Patchell
English Teacher
Irvine High School
Irvine USD

Maureen Rippee
English Teacher
Wilson High School
Long Beach USD

Meredith Ritner
English Teacher
Aliso Viejo Middle School
Capistrano USD

Esther Severy
Assistant Principal
McFadden Intermediate
Santa Ana USD

Julie Simpson
English Teacher
Sunny Hills High School
Fullerton Joint Union HSD

Dale Sprowl
Former English Teacher
Irvine High School
Irvine USD

Susan Starbuck
English Teacher
Long Beach Polytechnic High School
Long Beach USD

Lynne Watenpaugh
English Teacher
White Hill School
Ross Valley School District

Sue Rader Willett
English Teacher
Capistrano Valley High School
Capistrano USD

Special Thanks

Special thanks to the UCI/CAPP Research and Curriculum Development Team—Brenda Borron, Pat Clark, Sue Ellen Gold, Jerry Judd, Glenn Patchell, Esther Severy, and Julie Simpson—for their leadership of this project and to Bob Land, Senior Researcher at the UCLA Center for the Study of Evaluation, for serving as our CAPP Project Internal Evaluator.

UCLA Professor Raymond Paredes has noted that "in order to educate effectively present and future generations of students in Southern California, we teachers need to re-educate ourselves dramatically and continuously" (*CAIP Quarterly*, Winter 1990). We would like to express our deepest gratitude to the following scholar/authors for helping us to "re-educate" ourselves, for generously sharing their expertise, and for their support and encouragement:

Paul Apodaca, Curator of Native American Art, Bowers Museum.

Jimmy Santiago Baca, author of *Working in the Dark* and *Martin and Meditations on the South Valley*. (Note: Although we did not work directly with Mr. Baca as a group, he was kind enough to visit the classroom of one of our Teacher/Consultants and to work with her students.)

Lindon Barrett, Assistant Professor of English and Comparative Literature, University of California, Irvine.

Juan Bruce-Novoa, Professor of Spanish and Portugese, University of California, Irvine; author of *Chicano Poetry: A Response to Chaos.*

Nan Cano, Teacher, Agoura High School, Las Virgenes School District; Teacher/Consultant, UCLA Literature Project.

Marilyn Colyar, English Teacher, San Marino High School, San Marino USD; Teacher/Consultant, California Literature Project.

Winn Cooper, Co-Director, San Diego Area Writing Project, University of California, San Diego.

Manuel Gomez, Associate Vice Chancellor, Academic Affairs, University of California, Irvine.

César González, Professor of Chicano Study, Mesa College; author of *Rudolfo Anaya: Focus on Criticism.*

Kris Gutierrez, Assistant Professor of Education, Graduate School of Education, University of California, Los Angeles.

Maria Herrera-Sobek, Professor, Spanish and Portugese, University of California, Irvine; author of *Beyond Stereotypes: The Critical Analysis of Chicana Literature.*

Carol Jago, English Teacher, Santa Monica High School, Santa Monica USD; Director, UCLA Literature Project.

Kamchung Luangpraseut, Director, Southeast Asian Programs, Santa Ana Unified School District.

Jean Molesky-Poz, Lecturer, Department of English, University of California, Berkeley.

Thomas Parham, Director, UCI Counseling Center and Career Planning and Placement Center; co-author of *The Psychology of Blacks: An African American Perspective.*

David Peck, Professor of English, California State University, Long Beach; author of *American Ethnic Literatures.*

Amelia Ramirez, Teacher/Consultant, UCLA Writing Project.

Helena Viramontes, author of *The Moths and Other Stories.*

Sherley Anne Williams, Professor of American and African-American Literature, Department of English, University of California, San Diego; author of *Dessa Rose.*

Mitsuye Yamada, Poet and Lecturer; author, *Camp Notes and Other Poems* and *Sowing Ti Leaves: Writings by Multicultural Women.*

Richard Yarborough, Associate Professor of English, University of California, Los Angeles; contributing editor, *The Heath Anthology of American Literature.*

Many of these people were kind enough to contribute original quotations to this manuscript.

About the Demonstration Lessons

The demonstration lessons in this book are based upon the UCI Writing Project's Thinking/Writing model. Blending learning theory, composing process research, and the practical strategies of the National Writing Project, the lessons recognize the importance of thinking about what you write and writing about what you think. Depth and clarity of thinking enhance the quality of writing. At the same time, writing is a learning tool for heightening and refining thinking.

Based upon works of multicultural literature, the lessons:

- identify specific thinking and writing skills to be fostered;
- offer practical ideas for implementing each stage of the writing process—prewriting, precomposing, writing, sharing, revising, editing, and evaluation;
- provide suggestions for extension activities—many of which tie in with supplementary readings.

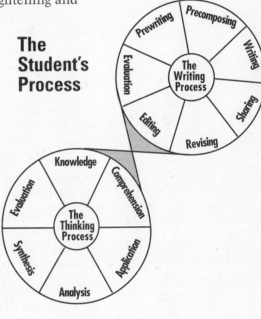

Some of the lessons have completely opened-ended tasks; others are more structured. Almost all are built upon a strong experience base.

Our goals in developing our multicultural literature-based curriculum are both cognitive and affective. Cognitively, we wish to enhance the reading, thinking, and writing ability of all students—but particularly, to provide support to ethnic and linguistic minority students. One of the key questions we have been exploring is: *Do lessons that are carefully scaffolded to foster thinking and writing positively affect the performance of ethnic and linguistic minority students?*

The notion of "instructional scaffolding" comes from the work of Arthur Applebee and Judith Langer (168). In a scaffolded approach, the teacher analyzes the language task to be carried out by the students, determines the difficulties that task is likely to pose, and then selects and provides guided practice in strategies that enable students to approach and complete the task successfully. Just as a real scaffold is a temporary structure that holds workers and materials while a building is under construction, the ultimate goal of instructional scaffolding is to gradually withdraw the teacher-guided practice when students demonstrate that they have internalized the strategies and can apply them independently.

Underlying the concept of scaffolding as it is used in the Thinking/Writing model are a number of fundamental premises about thinking that have informed our teaching of writing.

- *Writing* is a mode of *thinking*. In order to produce a composition, writers must generate ideas, plan for both the process of writing and for the written product itself, translate thought into print, revise what they have articulated, and evaluate the effectiveness of their efforts. In short, in moving from conception to completion, writers tap all of the levels of Bloom's taxonomy of the cognitive domain (201–207).

- *Thinking* is *progressive*. As Piaget observed, the mind is better able to make cognitive leaps when learning moves from the concrete to the abstract. Individual thinking/writing tasks should begin by focusing on something tangible and/or concrete. For example, students who observe a seashell are encouraged to explore analogy by creating similes about the seashell. An overall writing curriculum should also move progressively. Such a progression might take the form of sequencing the domains of writing from descriptive to narrative to expository, or it might involve moving from known to unknown audiences.

- *Thinking* is *cumulative* and *recursive*. All thinking experiences build upon one another. However, the pathway to more complex thought is not a linear one. Researchers have noted that writing, in particular, is a recursive process. Writers often go back in their thinking in order to move forward with their writing. Therefore, teachers who use a stage process model of composition that moves from prewriting to writing to revising and editing should continually invite students to think about their thinking and their writing by revisiting what they have written. So too, a writing curriculum should be scaffolded in such a way that students must go back to prior learning in order to move forward to the next task.

- *Thinking* is *not taught* but *fostered*. Thinking is an innate capacity that can be enhanced through the act of writing. Hilda Taba concludes that "how people think may depend largely on the kinds of 'thinking experience' they have had" (12). The teacher, then, plays a crucial role by providing students with thinking experiences that facilitate cognitive growth. Writing is one of the most complex and challenging thinking experiences the teacher can provide.

- Ultimately, the key to independent thinking and writing is *practice*. Teachers must provide students with the guided practice in a range of thinking and writing tasks that will enable them to develop and internalize a repertoire of problem-solving strategies that they can apply with confidence to future thinking and writing challenges.

In developing the Thinking/Writing model, we have turned to Bloom's taxonomy of the cognitive domain as a way of identifying the thinking skills to be fostered in the lessons. The chart on the next page defines the levels of Bloom's taxonomy and offers "cue words" that one might use in developing a writing prompt.

Thinking Levels

Level	Cue Words		
Knowledge			
Recall Remembering previously learned material	Observe Repeat Label/Name Cluster Outline (format stated)	Memorize Recall Recount Sort	Record Define Match List
Comprehension			
Translate Grasping the meaning of material	Recognize Locate Identify Restate Document/Support	Report Express Explain Review Summarize Precis/Abstract	Tell Describe Cite Paraphase
Application			
Generalize Using the learned material in new and concrete sistuation	Select Test out/Solve Manipulate Sequence Imagine (information known)	Show/Demonstrate How to Apply Dramatize Use	Frame Imitate Illustrate Organize
Analysis			

Break Down/Discover
 	
Breaking down material into its component parts so that it may be more easily understood
	Examine
	Outline
	  (no format given)
	Interpret
	Characterize
	Compare/Contrast
	Relate To
	Distinguish/
	  Differentiate
		Question
		Research
		
		Classify
		Refute
		Map
			Analyze
			Conclude
			
			Debate/Defend
			Conclude
			Infer

Synthesis			
Compose Putting material together to form a new whole	Propose Plan Compose Imagine/Speculate	Construct Emulate Formulate	Design Invent Create
Evaluation			
Judge Judging the value of material for a given purpose	Compare Pro/Con Prioritize/Rank Judge Decide Rate	Criticize Argue Justify Convince Persuade	Value Predict Assess Evaluate

Though many of us perceive the levels in Bloom to be more fluid and overlapping than static and hierarchical, we do find the concept and the chart useful in identifying the key cognitive task within a writing prompt, whether it be to recall, describe, analyze, speculate, or persuade, etc.

While our adaptation of Bloom's taxonomy can serve as a useful tool in examining what it is we are asking students to do when they undertake a particular writing task, the stage process model of composition defined below—which serves as the backbone of the demonstration lesson format—can provide a framework for sequencing activities and allowing the necessary think time to help students move from conception to completion:

Demonstration Lesson Format

Title	
Overview	A brief description of the final writing assignment
Objectives	THINKING: Specific skills from Bloom's taxonomy
	WRITING: Specific writing skills utilized in the writing

The Process	
Prewriting	Activities and experiences that capture students' attention and promote students' confidence in themselves as writers, that generate ideas—setting the stage for the prompt, that give practice in higher level thinking skills
Prompt	A specific writing task
Precomposing	Activities and experiences that promote the development of a plan for writing to a particular prompt and provide practice in the skills taught in the lesson
Writing	The first draft—aims for fluency, for rapid, rough completion, for discovery of content rather than refinement of thought
Sharing	Writing being read by another that allows for input to be refined by the writer
Revising	Reexamining, rethinking, reformulating the content and clarity of the first draft, incorporating the sharing
Editing	Proofreading the surface of the writing to ensure that it conforms to standards of correctness
Evaluation	Judging the writing to determine whether it satisfies the writer and reader as well as fulfills the requirements of the prompt

Linda Flower and John Hayes have observed in "The Dynamics of Composing" that the stage process model can make composing sound as if it can be accomplished in a "tidy sequence of steps," like baking a cake or filling out a tax return. In actuality, "a writer caught in the act looks like a busy switchboard operator," juggling "constraints" and working on "cognitive overload" (33). However, we have found that although there is no one description of *THE writing process*, the stage process model can serve as a teaching tool that provides students with a language with which to talk about writing, and which builds in "think time" for ideas and expression to evolve.

As Flower and Hayes have also observed in "Plans That Guide the Composing Process," "Writing is among the most complex of all human mental activities" (39–40). One of our objectives in using the Thinking/Writing model is to reduce the "constraints" that affect student writers, such as the knowledge they must have to construct and express meaning, the language they must have to communicate what they know, the awareness of audience and purpose for writing, and the context in which writing occurs (Frederiksen and Dominic, 19–20). In designing our approach, we have been influenced by George Hillocks's description of the *environmental method* of teaching composition (122). According to Hillocks, the environmental mode is characterized by the following: 1) clear and specific objectives; 2) materials and problems selected to engage students with one another in specific activities related to the writing task; and 3) high levels of peer interaction in small-group problem-centered discussion and activities. Hillocks notes that "although principles are taught" in the environmental method, "they are not simply announced and illustrated. Rather, they are approached through concrete materials and problems, the working through of which not only illustrates the principle but engages students in its use" (122).

As we designed the lessons, we consciously aimed to build in scaffolded activities that would reduce the following constraints on student writers:

- *Cognitive Constraints* (the knowledge the student brings to the task)
  To reduce the *cognitive constraints* on student writers, we provided guided practice in the key cognitive task called for in the writing prompt—be it description, inference, comparing and contrasting, speculation, or prediction. Further, influenced by Howard Gardner's theory of multiple intelligences, in addition to creating oral and written brainstorming activities, wherever appropriate, to appeal to the diversity of learning styles within our classrooms, we brought music, art, movement, and problem-solving activities into the lessons.

- *Linguistic Constraints* (the language the student brings to the task)
  To reduce the *linguistic constraints* on student writers, we built in an array of language-generating activities such as clustering, mapping, and showing, not telling, which created in the classroom a language-rich environment for our limited English proficient students to draw upon.

- *Communicative Constraints* (the audience for whom the student is writing) To lessen the *communicative constraints,* we downplayed the role of the teacher as assessor and implemented peer partners and small group sharing to broaden the students' concept of audience.

- *Contextual Constraints* (the context in which the writing occurs) To alleviate the *contextual constraints* students usually face when they must produce a composition on demand, we expanded the time frame for writing (allowing up to three weeks for the completion of a final draft) and adopted a "less is more philosophy" which emphasized the *process* of writing multiple drafts that evolved over time rather than focusing exclusively on the finished *product.*

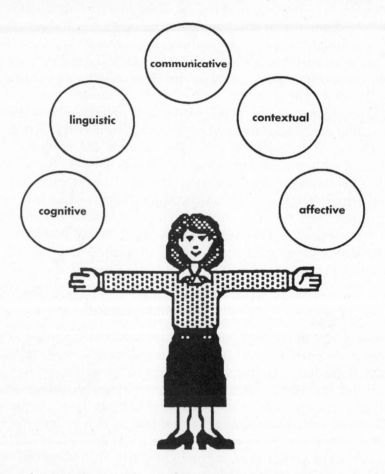

While researchers tend to zero in on the cognitive constraints that students "juggle" when they compose, we are also aware of the affective constraints they face when they do not find the tasks they undertake at school to be meaningful, relevant, or engaging. Accordingly, we have endeavored to choose high interest, challenging texts representing authors from a range of cultural backgrounds. Another research question we have been exploring is: *Does reading about their own culture encourage students to engage more interactively with texts?* The

Research Studies section of this book shares our findings, thus far, on the cognitive and affective impact of the use of these multicultural Thinking/Writing lessons in culturally diverse classrooms.

Each of the lessons has a side bar on the first page that will serve as a key to its contents.

Lesson Side Bar Explanation

Featured Literature

***Master Harold . . .
and the boys***
by Athol Fugard

Grade Level
For High School

Thinking Level
Synthesis

Writing Domain
Analytical/Expository
Imaginative/Narrative

Materials Needed
No special materials
required

**Suggested
Supplementary
Readings**
"We Are Many" by
Pablo Neruda

FEATURED LITERATURE indicates the work(s) of literature on which the lesson is based.

GRADE LEVEL indicates the ability for which the lesson is best suited.

THINKING LEVEL describes the key cognitive task that is called for in the writing prompt. Levels are identified according to those in Bloom's taxonomy in the chart on page 3.

WRITING DOMAIN describes the broad categories of writing or writing domain (or domains) into which the writing task falls. Theese domains include:

- sensory/descriptive;
- imaginative/narrative;
- practical/informative; and
- analytical/expository.

(Note: Please see the Glossary for a definition of the purpose of each domain.)

MATERIALS NEEDED Additionally, some lessons require special materials that are also noted on the side bar.

SUGGESTED SUPPLEMENTARY READING Additionally, some lessons require suggested supplementary readings that are also noted on the side bar.

We hope this side bar will be useful to you as you peruse the contents of this book.

Just as our ultimate goal in exposing students to Thinking/Writing lessons is to provide them with a repertoire of strategies that they can internalize and apply as autonomous learners to future Thinking/Writing challenges, our goal in providing you, as teachers, with these model multicultural, literature-based lessons is to offer you a point of departure for developing your own curriculum.

Note: For a more in-depth description of the Thinking/Writing model, please see *Thinking/Writing: Fostering Critical Thinking Skills Through Writing,* ed. Carol Booth Olson, (New York: HarperCollins Publishers, 1992).

References

Applebee, Arthur N., and Judith Langer. "Instructional Scaffolding: Reading and Writing as Natural Language Activities." *Language Arts* 60 (Feb. 1983): 168–75.

Bloom, Benjamin, ed. *Taxonomy of Educational Objectives—Handbook I: Cognitive Domain.* New York: David McKay Company, Inc., 1956.

Flower, Linda, and J. R. Hayes. "Plans That Guide the Composing Process." *Writing: The Nature, Development and Teaching of Written Communication.* Ed. Carl H. Frederiksen and Joseph F. Dominic. vol. 2. Hillsdale, NJ: Lawrence Erlbaum Associates, 1981. 39–58.

Flower, Linda, and J. R. Hayes. "The Dynamics of Composing." *Cognitive Processes in Writing.* Ed. L.W. Gregg and E.R. Steinberg. Hillsdale, NJ: Lawrence Erlbaum Associates, 1981. 31–40.

Frederiksen, Carl H., and Joseph F. Dominic. "Introduction: Perspective on the Activity of Writing." *Writing: The Nature, Development, and Teaching of Written Communication.* vol. 2. Hillsdale, NJ: Lawrence Erlbaum Associates, 1981. 1–20.

Gardner, Howard. *Frames of the Mind: The Theory of Multiple Intelligences.* New York: Basic Books, Inc., 1983.

Hillocks, George. "What Works in the Teaching of Composition: A Meta-analysis of Experimental Treatment Studies." *American Journal of Education* (Nov. 1984): 133–69.

Olson, Carol Booth, ed. *Thinking/Writing: Fostering Critical Thinking Through Writing.* New York: HarperCollins, 1992.

Taba, Hilda. *Thinking in Elementary School Children.* Washington, D.C.: U.S. Dept. of Health, Education, and Welfare, Cooperative Research Project No. 1574, 1964.

Multicultural Terms

In any collection of multicultural materials, the labels used to identify individuals of a particular racial, ethnic, or cultural heritage are problematic. To begin with, there is confusion about the terms *race, ethnicity, culture,* and *nationality.* These terms are often substituted for one another and often overlap. For example, when we are asked to indicate our "ethnicity" on forms by checking the appropriate box, the choices may include race based on color (white), ethnicity (African American), language (Hispanic), and geography (Pacific Islander). Moreover, political concerns about what is the "proper" label (is it American Indian or Native American?) and even generational differences (is it Chicano or Mexican American?) add to the confusion.

It is not a problem to identify a Korean writer, a South African writer, a Mexican writer. But when writers of different races and ethnicities within one country are identified, there is the problem of seeming to separate people based on their differences rather than recognizing their common nationality. Our purpose in this book is twofold: first, we want to provide some new views and resources for the teacher who is looking for material by writers other than white European Americans. Second, we want to celebrate the differences among us as one of our strengths as human beings, not as one of our weaknesses. Descartes said, "I think, therefore I am." An Ashanti (West African) proverb says, "I am because we are." These two statements certainly reflect different world views but they both agree on one thing: "I am." The literature within this book reflects those different but similar views. All cultures provide a design for living, a method to define reality. In the chart, we have chosen terms that identify the country or region of origin coupled, in most instances, with the term American (as in Mexican American.)

Overview of the Lessons

The lessons in this book can be categorized in three different ways:

1. Literary Genre
- Drama
- Nonfiction
- Novel
- Poem
- Short Story

2. Writing Type*
- Narration
- Personal Expression
- Persuasion
- Information

3. Culture Represented in the Literature
- African
- Mexican
- African American
- Mexican American
- Asian
- Native American
- Asian American
- South American
- European American

The chart on the following two pages lists the lessons and indicates where each one falls in these categories. In most cases, but not all, the culture represented in the literature reflects the cultural background of the author.

(California Learning Assessment System writing type terminology)

Lesson Title	Literary Genre					Writing Type	
	Drama	Nonfiction	Novel	Poem	Short Story	Narration	Persuasion
A Mother's Decision					▲		Interpretation
A Special Place		▲					
Be an Outcast				▲		Autobio. Incident	
Customs and Conflict	▲		▲				Interpretation
Fifth Chinese Daughter		▲				Autobio. Incident	
Getting in Touch with Your Family's Roots					▲	Autobio. Incident	
Growing Up: A Personal Reflection				▲			
Importance of Being		▲					Interpretation
Just Another Fool in Love					▲		Problem Solution
Living in Life's Shadow					▲		Interpretation
Loss of Innocence					▲		Interpretation
Many Voices, One Heart					▲	Poem	Interpretation
Memories and Metaphors					▲	Autobio. Incident	
Mercy or Death					▲		Controversial Issue
My Life Through Images				▲			
My Name, My Self					▲		
Native American Voices		▲		▲	▲		
Peopling Poems				▲			
Reflecting About Our Many Selves				▲			
Reflecting Upon Alienation		▲					
Round 1: Dramatizing the Argument Round 2: Resolving the Argument			▲			Story	
Speculating About Master Harold	▲						Speculation
Stories in Clay		▲				Story	
The Class Quilt		▲					
The Poet Within Us				▲			
The Rules of the Game	▲		▲				Interpretation
The Saturation Recall Paper		▲				Autobio. Incident	
What's Behind the Gift Horse's Mouth			▲			Autobio. Incident	
Writing a Persuasive Speech Using American Indians as a Model		▲					Controversial Issue

Culture Represented

Personal Expression	Information	African	African-American	Asian	Asian-American	European	European-American	Latin American	Mexican	Mexican-American	Native American
			▲								
Poem											▲
			▲								
						▲			▲	▲	
Personal Reflection					▲						
Personal Reflection							▲				
					▲						
							▲				
										▲	
					▲						
								▲			
Personal Reflection							▲			▲	
										▲	
		▲									
Personal Reflection						▲	▲			▲	
Personal Reflection										▲	
Personal Reflection							▲				▲
Poem			▲							▲	▲
Reflection								▲			
Reflection											▲
			▲								
Reflection		▲									
											▲
Report of Inform.							▲				
Poem					▲					▲	
				▲	▲						
			▲								
			▲								
											▲

11

Drama

Featured Literature

*Master Harold . . .
and the boys*
by Athol Fugard

Grade Level
For High School
and College

Thinking Level
Synthesis

Writing Domain
Analytical/Expository

Materials needed
No special materials
required.

**Suggested
Supplementary
Readings**
"We Are Many" by
Pablo Neruda

Speculating about Master Harold

by Julie Simpson

Overview

This lesson takes students into and through a reading and close analysis of Athol Fugard's play *Master Harold . . . and the boys*. Students look at the relationships of the characters and the motivations for their actions. The writing part of the lesson focuses on speculating about what Hally will do after the action of the play is over.

Objectives

THINKING SKILLS

Students will:

- *summarize* what happens in the play;
- *apply* a specific action to their own experiences;
- *analyze* how symbolism in the beginning of the play extends through the ending;
- *analyze* the significance of events and motives of the characters;
- *analyze* cause-effect relationships by breaking down and writing about characters' actions;
- *synthesize* the characters' ideas into a prediction of what Hally will do after the action of the play is over.

WRITING SKILLS

Students will write an analytical/expository piece in which they:

- *write* a speculation predicting Hally's future action once the events of the play are over;
- *support* the extended ending of the play with textual details and interrelated ideas from the play;
- *use* analytical/expository form (introduction, main body, conclusion);
- *follow* the conventions of standard written English.

The Process

Before beginning, you might want to warn your class that the play they are about to read contains some strong language and a brutal action. When the characters become upset, their language reflects their emotions. Select three boys to read the roles of Willie, Sam, and Hally. They should be willing to read the play beforehand, and mature enough to carry off the language in the play without causing the class to lose control. I usually allow only those three scripts out of the classroom.

 PREWRITING

Prewriting Step 1: *Class Discussion—Practicing Speculation*

Speculating about the effects of a character's action or decision necessitates interpreting the motives that led the character into his action. (In the play, Hally, who appears for the most part to care a great deal for Sam, suddenly turns on him, committing a racist act. Students can sometimes not understand why this happens, unless they have been interpreting motives for Hally's actions up to this point.) Practice in predicting actions from motives will help students pay attention to details in the play and prepare them for drawing inferences and making interpretations about those details.

They also need to see that the inferences a reader makes about a character depend to some extent on the values that reader brings to the literature; consequently, even though several students base their inferences on the same elements of a plot, each of their interpretations may differ.

Although the following problem does not parallel the situation of the play, it will offer students practice in making inferences about causes and predictions about effects—skills they will use throughout the lesson.

Pose the following problem:

Suppose the following students were in our class:
- Aimee —who doesn't like herself very much;
- Alex —who is currently experiencing serious problems at home;
- Sandy—who is just beginning to fall in love;
- Terry—who has just achieved great success in high school (ASB Vice President, basketball star, honors student), and has just been recruited into the college of his choice.

How do you suppose each of them would first respond to this new student:

Chas, frustrated by his strangeness and lack of friends, slouches in his desk, grumbling that this school is not as good as the last one and that he doesn't know why he has to be in this class, anyway. He already knows everything they're going to do.

To stimulate discussion, you might assign one character to each peer group to brainstorm various ways in which their character might react to Chas. Remind the groups that there could be lots of answers to "What does the character do?" The "why" questions that follow are also important because they infer the motives behind the actions. After discussing various possibilities, the groups are to decide on one kind of response to share with the class. Tell them that any response will be valid as long as the motives for it are clearly explained and sound logical.

Ask the groups to begin their discussions by answering the following:

- What do you think your character would first notice about Chas? Why? *(For example: Aimee might notice his sneer and envy him for being able to snub the people she wants to like her. Or, she might notice his sneer and be frightened by it. Alex might see his slouch and the sloppy clothes he wears as a sign of a rebel like himself.)*
- How long do you think it might take your character to notice him at all? Why? *(For example: Sandy might be so involved in planning what she is going to say to her new boyfriend that she doesn't notice him at all until days later when he is called out of class.)*
- Would your character want to get to know Chas? Why? *(For example: Terry might be so self-confident that he would automatically want to get to know him, just as he wants to get to know everyone. Or, he might take one look at him, see whether he looks like a jock or not, and let that determine whether or not he wants to get to know Chas.)*
- What do you think your character would do to meet (or to avoid meeting) Chas? Why? *(Bold Terry might just speak right out to him, across the room, never thinking that Chas might not respond. Quiet Aimee might conveniently arrange to walk out the door at the same time after class.)*

Ask a representative from each group to either share the group's predictions and/or volunteer to role-play a mock response to Chas.

Prewriting Step 2: *Showing Writing*

To give more practice in analyzing character motivation, have the class break into partners. Then present the following "telling sentence," and instruct each pair to use a class period to write a "showing" story to illustrate it. *(Note: See the Glossary for a definition of Showing, not Telling.)*

He took his frustrations out on his friends.

- Remind the class that their goal in creating this piece of "showing" writing is to present the character and his situation so clearly that the rest of the class will feel as if they were watching the story portrayed as a film.

To get them started, have them list or brainstorm the kinds of questions they will have to consider and show answers for in their stories:

- How did he look? What was his body language?
- What did he say?
- What did he think? How did he feel?
- What did he do?
- Could his friends understand?
- How did his friends—who only saw the outside—respond?
- What did they do? What did they say?

The next day, collect all the stories and randomly select a few (or ask for volunteers, if you have a comfortable class) to read aloud. Tell the class that they are going to listen for the following elements:

- How well can we understand what motivates this character?
- How do we gain our understanding?
- Could his friends understand why he acts as he does? Why or why not?
- Do you think they are going to stay friends?

Discussing each story in terms of these questions will give the class practice in the kinds of analytical skills they will use in discussing the play.

Prewriting Step 3: *Speculating About the Title*

To introduce the play, tell the class they are going to read a play about a 17-year-old boy who must deal with frustrations.

Write the title on the board (remember to write it exactly as Fugard did) and ask them to study it carefully, to observe as much as they can about these words and their possible meanings. You might ask these kinds of questions:

- What do you notice about the way the title is written?
- What do you suppose those three dots mean?
- What words are capitalized and what words aren't?
- Why do you suppose some important words are not capitalized?
- What can we infer about the relationship between the Master and the boys?
- What can you predict about the play from this title?

A class brainstorm might look something like this:

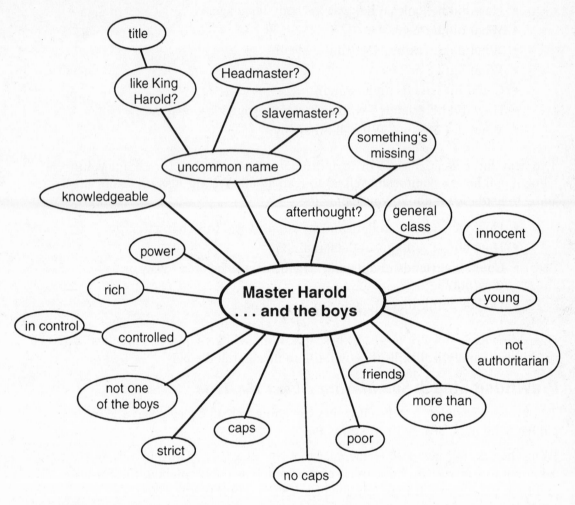

After the class has brainstormed, ask students to write a three-minute quick-write speculating on what they predict the play will be about. Share some of these in class.

A sample quickwrite is included below:

> It looks like the play is going to be about a stuffy British teacher in a boys school. I can tell he doesn't like his "boys" too well by the way the three dots show they are a kind of afterthought. I hope the boys do something to make themselves important enough to become capitalized at the end.

Inform the class that this play is written by a South African man. Ask if that information affects their predictions about the story. What do we know about South African culture that may affect our view of the play?

Prewriting Step 4: *Studying the Setting*

Read the introductory stage directions aloud to the class. Ask them to envision the scene as you describe it.

> The St. George's Park Tea Room on a <u>wet and windy</u> Port Elizabeth afternoon.
>
> Tables and chairs have been cleared and are stacked on one side except for <u>one which stands apart</u> with a single chair. On this table a knife, fork, spoon and side plate in anticipation of a <u>simple meal</u>, together with a pile of comic books.
>
> Other elements: a serving counter with a few <u>stale</u> cakes under glass and a <u>not very impressive display</u> of sweets, cigarettes and cool drinks, etc.; a few cardboard advertising handouts—Cadbury's Chocolate, Cocoa-Cola—and a <u>blackboard</u> on which an <u>untrained hand</u> has chalked up the prices of Tea, Coffee, Scones, Milkshakes—all flavors—and Cool Drinks; <u>a few sad ferns</u> in pots; a telephone; an old-style jukebox.
>
> There is an entrance on one side and an exit into a kitchen on the other.
>
> Leaning on the solitary table, his head cupped in one hand as he pages through one of the comic books, is SAM. A black man in his mid-forties. He wears the white coat of a waiter. Behind him <u>on his knees</u>, mopping down the floor with a bucket and a rag, is WILLIE. Also black and about the same age as Sam. He has his <u>sleeves and trousers rolled up</u>.

After reading the setting once, ask volunteers to call out words that stand out for them (like those underlined above) and that set the tone for the play. List those words on the board. Taking a look at all the words they volunteer, ask the class what they expect will happen in this room. Then, ask them to explain what makes them predict that.

Prewriting Step 5: *Reading and Analyzing the Play*

For the sake of this lesson, the play has been divided into eight scenes. Following are suggestions for questions and activities to help analyze each scene.

1. **Introduction to Sam and Willie** (ending with Willie singing, "I'd be lost without you.")

    In this scene, Willie is giving Sam advice about preparing for the ballroom dance contest. Either directly or by inference, he offers at least six pieces of advice to Sam As you read this section, look for these pieces of advice. List each one, phrasing it in general terms that could apply to living as well as dancing. (**Examples:** glide; look like you're enjoying yourself; make it look romantic; pretend if you have to; don't use violence to get your way; don't worry about the outside world).

2. Introduction to Hally (ending when Sam says "Okay.")

After reading this scene, ask the class to list facts and draw inferences about the relationship between Sam and Hally and about the relationship between Hally and his father.

Facts	Inferences
Hally whispers "conspiratorial[ly]" to Sam and Willie.	Seems like he looks forward to being with them.
Hally is "stopped short" when Sam says his dad is coming home.	Hally has a problem with his dad.
Hally spies the comic books for his father and calls them "mental pollution." Wants to be sure Sam hasn't read them, but says nothing about his father's reading them.	Father's hobby disgusts Hally. He wants to protect Sam from the bad habit.

Near the end of this section, Hally becomes "furious" with Willie and Sam. Ask in discussion: What causes this anger? Why do you suppose Hally's mood shifts so suddenly?

3. **Men of Magnitude** (ending when Hally says, "Tolstoy may have educated his peasants, but I've educated you.")

Before reading, explain the definition of "men of magnitude" that Hally and Sam discuss: men who "contributed greatly to some significant social reform."

As a class, discuss:

- What qualities do you think it would take for someone to earn this title?
- How many people do you think she or he would have to affect?
- For how long?
- Could someone earn this title in his or her own lifetime?
- Whom would you suggest as "men of magnitude?"

This section opens with Hally back in a good mood. As he begins to do his homework, he and Sam get into a discussion of "men of magnitude." Note the logical connections their discussion takes:

- Punishment—Hally's is on the "bum" and Sam's was with his pants down
- Progress is changing things
- Math book—magnitude qualities → using the word with social reformers
- History text—Napoleon and his theory of equality = social reform = man of magnitude
- Definitions of greatness = somebody who benefited all mankind
- Test out this theory on men of magnitude.

Have students fill out the following chart for each of the men discussed:

Man	Arguments For	Arguments Against	Inferences to Draw
Napoleon	Sam: saw everyone as equal	Hally: He lost the Battle of Waterloo	Hally thinks winning is most important

After studying this scene, write a two-minute quickwrite answer:

How does Hally teach Sam? How does Sam teach Hally?

A sample quickwrite follows:

Hally teaches Sam by discussing his homework with him and by defining words Sam doesn't know as they talk. Sam teaches Hally by getting him to do his homework and by making him explain his ideas and reactions.

4. **Memories of Childhood with Sam and Willie** (ending when Hally says, "It's got so bloody complicated since then.")

In this section, Sam and Willie reminisce with Hally about his childhood with them, when life was "just the right size" and it "wasn't so hard to work up a bit of courage" to face it. As the class reads the first part, have them answer these questions:

- Whom does Sam say he works for—Hally's mother or his father?
- What were the conditions Sam and Willie lived in?
- Hally excuses his cheating at checkers as "the mistakes of youth." Remember that he didn't accept Napoleon as a "man of magnitude" because he lost the Battle of Waterloo. What is Hally's attitude about losing?
- About playing fair—when does he think it's OK not to play fair?

After reading about the kite-flying incident, answer these questions to notice facts and make inferences:

- What kind of a day was it for Hally?
- Whose idea was it to make a kite?
- What were Hally's thoughts, reactions? Why did he feel this way?
- What made the kite flying seem miraculous to Hally? Why?
- How did Hally's reaction to the kite change when he was flying it?
- Sam says he left because he "had work to do." What are some other possible reasons for his leaving this miraculous moment? What in the play makes you think these are logical speculations?
- Hally thinks there was "no drama" in the ending of the incident. Do you agree? Explain your idea.
- Hally says it's time for another kite. Reread the rest of this scene and interpret what you think he means by that statement.
- What inferences are you making about Hally in your interpretation?
- What parallels could there be between Hally's kite flying and Sam and Willie's practicing for the dance contest?

5. **Hally's Present Problem with His Father** (ending when Sam says, "Okay, Hally, okay.")

   In this section, we see how Hally's life has become too large for him.

   Ask students to answer these questions:

   - What earlier inferences about Hally's relationship to his father are confirmed in this section?
   - What new inferences can you make about their relationship?
   - What details support those inferences?
   - In section 3, Hally said he oscillated "between hope and despair" for the world. How have the last two sections illustrated this idea?
   - What do you predict the next section will do?

6. **A World Without Collisions** (ending when Hally says, "What about 'Ballroom Dancing as a Political Vision?'")

   The focus shifts to Sam and Willie and the dance.

   When Sam and Willie talk about Hilda, ask:

   - Sam says, "Then you mustn't complain either." To what earlier statement does the "either" refer? *(Sam says this to Hally when he complains that people deserve what they get.)* How would you interpret this advice to Willie? *(Don't complain about the consequences of your own doing.)*
   - How is Willie's situation here similar to Hally's discussion when Sam gave him the same advice?

   When Sam is trying to convince Hally that the dance contest is art, ask:

   - What do you think art is? Could a dance contest ever be art?
   - What is Hally's definition of art?
   - From what you know of the dance contest and the lives Willie and Sam live, does the contest qualify as art?
   - From what you know of Hally's life, does the kite-flying episode qualify as art? Why do you or don't you think so?

   When Hally wants to know what the penalties are for doing something wrong, and Sam is aghast, ask:

   - Why do you suppose Hally cannot conceive of a situation with no penalties? What does he assume in asking his question?
   - Why do Sam and Willie laugh at the question?
   - What can you infer about the contest?

   As the scene ends, ask:

   - Explain in your own words Sam's vision of the purpose of the dance contest. How do you suppose it would be if we learned "to dance life like champions instead of always being just a bunch of beginners at it"?
   - What has the dance come to symbolize to Sam, Hally, and the whole play?

7. **Collisions** (ending when Willie says, "Long trousers now, but he's still little boy.")

Just as everything is going well, Hally is plunged back into despair.

Before beginning to read this scene, recap for the class the interpretive analysis this class has done: They've drawn inferences and speculated about Hally's relationship with his father, and they have looked at his relationship to Sam. Sam has clearly taken on some paternal traits that Hally's father couldn't offer him.

Allow students to get into peer groups and suggest that they discuss these questions:

- What are some of Sam's fatherly traits that Hally's real father lacks?
- Can you see any possible drawbacks or negative aspects to Sam's role with Hally?
- Look back to your original speculations about the play from the title. How appropriate were they? Are there any elements of your speculations that haven't been covered yet but might be later on in the play?
- Do you suppose a "a substitute" father could ever replace a real father in the eyes of the "son"? Explore your thinking.

After ten minutes or so, ask groups to share their ideas with the rest of the class.

Read through the phone conversation and stop. Ask:

- Why do you think Hally's tone is so different when he talks directly to his father than when he talks to his mother about his father?
- Which tone do you believe? Why?
- Have students discuss these questions in peer groups and report back to the class, adding any new information as one group moves to the next.

Read to the point where Hally is "suddenly appalled by how far he has gone" and ask:

- Why do you think Hally has become "reckless"?
- Why has Sam warned him: "Be careful, Hally"?
- Hally says he is telling the truth about life. Why do you suppose his truth is such a negative one at this point? What can you tell about Hally's maturity level and/or his psyche here?

Read through the initial argument where Hally vents his frustrations at Sam. Stop at the point that Sam says, "Just telling you what will happen if you make me do that. You must decide what it means to you." Ask the class to identify what it was that finally got Sam needled. What can we infer about Sam's view of Hally's father?

Ask the class to use the following chart to analyze Hally's choices at this point (now that he has insisted that Sam call him "Master Harold"):

Alternatives	Arguments in Favor of Each Alternative	Arguments Against Each Alternative
Hally can insist on his way	It might make him think he has power over Sam.	He might lose his only friend.
	He has to take his anger out on something; he can't do it on his dad.	He's abusing the wrong person.

Instruct the class to write: Which choice do you predict Hally will take? Why? Quickwrite for three minutes before reading more.

A sample quickwrite follows:

> Hally seems to be a pretty bull-headed kid when it comes to Sam. I think he'll insist on his way. He has to have power over something, and Sam is near. He's too stubborn to see what effect the action may have.

Read until Hally walks out of the tearoom. Ask the class to quickwrite for three more minutes to this question: Did Hally make the choice you predicted he would? Why do you think he did what he did? What are you learning about Hally's character from his choices?

Read the rest of the play and ask:

- What do you think has happened to Hally's hope?
- What does he mean when he says, "I don't know. I don't know anything anymore"?
- What does Sam mean when he says, "You know what that bench means now, and you can leave it any time you choose. All you've got to do is stand up and walk away from it"? What has that bench come to symbolize?
- What might happen to Hally's relationship with his father if he walked away from that bench? Explain your thinking.
- Why do you suppose Hally leaves without saying anything? What do you infer from this act?
- Why is the Sarah Vaughan song on the jukebox particularly poignant?

After brief discussion, ask students to do a five-minute quickwrite, formalizing their ideas about the end of the play in terms of the discussion.

PROMPT

In Athol Fugard's play *Master Harold ... and the boys*, Hally has lots of problems that cause him great frustrations. We've looked at his problems and how he has dealt with them. We've seen that he has had Sam to guide him—to teach him as well as to learn from him. When Hally becomes so frustrated by his father that he has to strike out, he strikes at this guide. Brutally, he insults Sam and turns on him.

In one sense, Hally has broken his ties with Sam and now is alone. Even though Sam has forgiven him, Hally walks out.

Why do you suppose he does this? Why can't he make up with Sam? Do you think he will want, or be able, to reestablish his relationship with Sam? What do you predict he will do? What do you know about him thus far that helps you make this prediction?

Write an essay in which you speculate about Hally's relationship with Sam after the curtain falls. Do you think he will be able to repair their friendship? Explain your prediction clearly and support it with a strong analysis of Hally and his past relationships (both to Sam and to his father), as well as his motivations for making the decisions he makes.

Approach writing speculation as you would any expository essay of argumentation. Begin your essay by stating your prediction and defining the context or situation from which your speculative claim arises. Your interpretation of Hally's character must be based on logical inferences about his motivations. The body of your essay must offer your analysis of Hally's motives—the reasons why he will act as you predict. The arguments for that analysis must be arranged in a logical and effective order. You must also provide adequate and logical backing for your arguments; the actual details and incidents from the play must support the analysis of your prediction. Any situations in the plot that might appear to work against your claim must be considered and explained. The tone of your speculation should be authoritative, convincing the reader that you have thought through the subject thoroughly.

Convince your readers that your ideas are plausible, and that you have seriously considered the question of Hally's potential for reconciliation with Sam. Write in analytical/expository form (introduction, main body, conclusion) and follow the conventions of standard written English.

 **PRECOMPOSING**

Precomposing Step 1: *Developing a Speculative Argument Chart*

To facilitate the analysis required in speculation, ask students to fill out a Speculative Argument chart like the one below.

Developing a Speculative Argument

Speculative Claim: What do you think Hally will do? *He will apologize to Sam and make amends.*

Arguments: Main Arguments in Favor of Claim	**Backing:** Past Actions to Support Claim	**References:** Textual Details to Show Backing
Sam is too important to Hally.	Sam has been Hally's main teacher. Hally has no other friends.	"That is why you started passing your exams. You tried to be better than me." (24)
Hally has to live with Sam.	Sam works in the cafe.	"If you make me say it once, I'll never call you anything else again." (54)
Sam has already given in.	He called Hally by his nickname.	"Hally...I've got no right to tell you what being a man means if I don't behave like one myself." (59)
Other Options: What Else Can Hally Do?	**Reservations:** Drawbacks to the Claim	**Response:** Refuting the Reservations
He can have Sam fired.	Hally has never apologized to Sam before.	He has never been in this serious a crisis before.
He can ignore the problem.	His pride is stubborn and gets in the way.	He can't just ignore the problem this time.

Precomposing **Step 2**: *Oral Presentations*

Put students into peer groups of four or five, matching like claims about Hally. Sample claims include:

- Hally will apologize to Sam and make amends.
- Hally will remain stubborn and sever his relationship with Sam.
- Hally will ignore his outburst and pretend nothing has happened.

Explain that each group should share the responses on their charts, and individuals may add to their own charts any new information they wish. Each group is responsible for formulating a full speculative argument to present orally to the class. One person from each group will serve as a spokesperson; however, everybody in the group may be allowed to contribute to the argument during the presentation. The presentation will take no more than five minutes per group. No one from other groups will be allowed to speak during another group's presentation.

During the presentations, give everyone another blank chart to fill out as the group speaks. This will aid students in the development of their own ideas.

Precomposing **Step 3**: *Substantiate or Rebut Speculation*

After the first round of presentations is given, allow groups about a half of a class period to come up with any new reservations, counterarguments, new arguments, or new textual backing to continue their speculative arguments or to rebut another group's argument. Allow an open discussion of the predictions for the rest of the class period. *(To avoid confusion and name calling, you might want to allow no group to speak unless recognized by the teacher.)*

Precomposing **Step 4**: *Feedback on Argumentation*

After all claims have been argued, ask the class for feedback on the process of argumentation: What have they learned about supporting a claim? What makes an effective argument?

Precomposing **Step 5**: *Planning the Introduction*

Now that students have the arguments for the bodies of their essays, the next step is to decide how to introduce their speculations. Explain: Your introduction must create the situation that sets the stage for your speculative claim. To prepare for writing your introduction, paraphrase what you take to be the central situation that creates the predicament Hally finds himself in at the end of the play. In a five-minute quickwrite, explain that situation.

Note: You may want to refer students to the packet on "Writing an Introduction to an Expository Composition," which is appended to the "Living in Life's Shadow" lesson and also to the guidelines on how to quote from the text.

 **WRITING**

Students write a draft of their essay at home, using the information they recorded on their Speculative Argument Chart and any notes and quickwrites that may help them argue their claim. When they return the next day, they should be allowed time with the texts to find more specific quotes to support their arguments.

 SHARING

Sharing Step 1: *Scoring Guide*

Pass out drafts of the scoring guide for Speculation. (See the Evaluation section of this lesson for the scoring guide.) Identify any unfamiliar terms and look at the characteristics of a strong 6 in contrast to a 3 or a 4.

Sharing Step 2: *WIRMI*

Before students exchange their papers with peer partners, have them write a WIRMI (What-I-Really-Mean-Is) statement, which they will keep and later compare with their partners' responses.

Sharing Step 3: *Sharing with Partners*

Ask students to get into groups of three.

- As one person reads his or her paper aloud, the other two listen for the characteristics of effective speculation.
- Ask the two partners to get together to fill in the following chart to help the writer to visually analyze the thinking in a speculative draft.

Situation	Speculative Claim	Argument Reasons/Evidence
1. In your own words, identify the situation that sets the stage for the speculative claim.	**1.** In your own words, explain the writer's claim.	**1.** List briefly each of the reasons or evidence offered in support of the speculative claim. • • • **2.** On the writer's draft put a + in front of each reason or piece of evidence that seems relevant to the situation as the writer presented it.
2. Do you need to know anything else about the situation? If so, what?	**2.** Does the claim follow logically out of the situation? If not, what does it need to account for?	**3.** On the writer's draft put an * in front of each argument that needs explanation in relation to the situation as presented. **4.** Is the sequence of arguments arranged in an effectively logical order? ❑ yes ❑ no If not, how might the idea be presented better ?

1. Studying the writer's draft carefully, answer each of the above questions on the chart itself.

2. Look again at the column of arguments in relation to the situation and speculative claim presented. Are there any other arguments you might suggest that would be relevant to the paper? List them here: _____

_____

3. Assume that you don't personally agree with the writer's speculative claim. Are the arguments sufficient to convince you that the writer has thought them through with a thorough awareness of the text? _____ If not, what suggestions do you have for the writer? _____

_____

4. Does the paper end in a satisfying manner?_____ If not, circle any of the following problems that might apply: the reader is left hanging; the conclusion is irrelevant to the speculation; other: _____

_____

 # REVISING

With input from response partners, writers revise first drafts at home. If a computer lab is available, this is a good time for students to enter their drafts into the computer.

 # EDITING

Editing Step 1: *Editing Read-Around*

To make these drafts into a final form, divide students into triads to edit for the conventions of standard written English. Label each group A or B. Remind students of the basic mechanics and usage elements that they are expected to have mastered. Depending on whether or not they have access to a word processing program, they may be able to check for things like spelling, apostrophes, and pronouns on their computers. Triads will be in charge of the following:

Triad A	Triad B
• Correct subject-verb agreement	• Clear pronoun references
• Correct use of apostrophes	• Complete sentences
• Correct capitalization	• Correct spelling

Each paper must pass through both groups within a class period, so no one can take more than about five to seven minutes on a paper. It is best to organize this session like a Read-Around, timing each reading so that no one takes too long.

Editors make corrections directly on the draft in various colors of ink. Each editor should sign off the paper when he or she finishes with it. If an editor cannot finish within the time period, he can sign the paper off as far as he got.

Editing Step 2: *Self-Correction*

Writers get their edited papers back to put any revisions and corrections into the computer in a final version.

 # EVALUATION

Score the papers against the Speculation Scoring Guide.

Speculation Scoring Guide

6   An exceptional paper presents the claim with a clear explanation of the situation from which it arises and strong insight into Hally's character. It defines and focuses the situation with an authoritative voice. Motives and reasons for the prediction are examined coherently and supported in a well-controlled argument. They often go beyond the predictable. Textual details are elaborated to connect to the argument presented. Potential conflicting ideas are considered, explicitly or implicitly; but they are offered only to convince the reader of the logic of the writer's stance. Paper has a strong introduction, well developed main body, and effective conclusion. There are few, if any, errors in the conventions of written English.

5   A commendable paper presents the claim clearly, but may define the situation with less sophistication than the 6 paper. Motives and reasons are examined coherently and with authority, but less effectively and with less continuity than in the 6 paper. They do still include more than the predictable. The argument presented is logical, but less controlled than in the 6 paper. Textual details are elaborated and well connected to the argument, although with less sophistication that in the 6 paper. Potential conflicting ideas are considered, explicitly or implicitly; but they are offered only to convince the reader of the logic of the writer's stance. There may be a few errors in the conventions of written English but none that interfere with the writer's message.

4   An adequate paper is more predictable. The claim is stated, but the situation surrounding the claim may be less focused. The writer may only paraphrase the information in the prompt rather than focus it through his own perspective. Motives and reasons for Hally's decision are clear in themselves but may not closely follow from the situation presented. Development of ideas and use of textual details begin to thin out in a 4 paper. Connections are not as explicit as in the better papers. Paper may have a few errors in the conventions of written English but none that interfere with the writer's message.

3   The 3 paper shows some evidence of achievement. It presents the claim clearly but may only briefly explain the situation—often more in summary than as an authoritative interpretation of Hally's predicament. Motives and reasons tend to be listed; explanation is limited. The paper does not always show connections between one motive and another. The paper lacks consistency in development of detail. The logical sequence of the arguments supporting the causes of the claim may be unclear. Some errors in the conventions of written English may interfere with the writer's message.

2   The paper shows a minimal understanding of the requirements of the prompt. It may read more like a summary of the play, with a prediction coming only at the end. Motives and reasons may be implied through the summary more than explicitly analyzed within the paper. If motives are singled out, their explanation may be rambling and unfocused, with no connections or elaboration. A 2 paper may merely list motives with no support. It has little or no semblance of expository form. There are frequent errors in the conventions of written English.

1   A 1 paper shows no clear understanding of the requirements of the prompt. Or, its attempt to offer a claim and reasons may be so superficial that the paper is difficult to follow.

EXTENSION ACTIVITIES

1. *Reflection Exercise*

Reflection   Why did Hally hurt Sam? Can you understand this act? Have you ever done anything like it? Why? What good did it do you? How did you feel afterward? Why do people behave this way? What can you learn about people (including yourself) from understanding why they behave like this?

2. *Compare Master Harold with the Poem "We Are Many"*

Evaluation   Who is better off as a human being—the speaker in Neruda's poem or Hally? Why? What are your standards for measurement and how does each fit in to your standard?

Analysis/ Interpretation   If Hally were to go to his closet of many selves, what kinds of humilities do you think he would find there? Analyze his character in terms of his "many selves."

Synthesis   Create similar metaphors after the fashion of Pablo Neruda that you think would apply to Hally's "many selves."

Character Analysis/ Interpretation   The speaker of Neruda's poem is very introspective. He has an image of himself that he feels he always falls short of. Do you think Hally also has an image of himself? If so, how would you identify it? If not, why not? How can he be going through life without an ideal image? What does he have instead?

Featured Literature

Like Water for Chocolate
by Laura Esquivel

Romeo and Juliet
by William Shakespeare

Grade Level
For High School
and College

Thinking Level
Analysis/Synthesis

Writing Domain
Analytical/Expository

Materials Needed
• Butcher paper
• Scissors
• Index cards
• Colored pens
• Transparencies

**Suggested
Supplementary
Readings**
• *Waves* by Bei Dao
• *West Side Story*
  by Arthur Laurents
• *Spring Snow*
  by Yukio Mishima
• *The House of Spirits*
  by Isabel Allende

Customs and Conflicts

by Maureen Rippee

Overview

After reading and analyzing the first chapter of Laura Esquivel's novel *Like Water for Chocolate: A Novel in Monthly Installments, with Recipes, Romances, and Home Remedies,* students will write an analytical/expository essay in which they compare the novel to the play *Romeo and Juliet* by: 1) discussing the role of "love at first sight" and marriage customs and traditions that lead to conflict; 2) contrasting characters; and 3) predicting how the conflict in *Like Water for Chocolate* might be resolved (based on their knowledge of the plot and ending of *Romeo and Juliet*).

Objectives

THINKING SKILLS

Students will:

- *analyze* the role of "love at first sight" in both texts;
- *examine* marriage customs and traditions that lead to conflict;
- *identify* the reasons why people marry;
- *dramatize* the subtle pressures and conflicts that are the result of marriage customs and traditions;
- *compare and contrast* literary characters;
- *predict* the outcome of a novel.

WRITING SKILLS

Students will:

- *use* standard analytical/expository form: introduction, main body, and conclusion, including transitions, sequencing, and rhetorical development;
- *support* their analysis with specific quotes from the texts;
- *follow* the conventions of standard written English.

The Process

This seven-to-ten-day lesson allows students to experience a variety of prewriting and precomposing activities that help them compare and contrast a similar theme in two genres of literature. It provides a strong example of how teachers can revitalize the study of core curriculum by infusing multicultural literature. This lesson can be taught as a companion piece for *Romeo and Juliet*, as an extension for a lesson on *Romeo and Juliet*, or as a way for students to re-examine a work to gain new meaning and insight.

Note: The amount of time is an estimate. Actual timing will depend upon such variables as grade level and ability, your experience with the writing process, and whether you are going to use this lesson as a companion to, extension of, or reexamination of Romeo and Juliet.

 PREWRITING

Prewriting Step 1: *Quickwrite*

Ask students to respond to the following question: Do you believe in love at first sight?

Give students approximately ten minutes to think about and respond in writing. Here are some typical student responses:

> No, I do not believe in love at first sight. However, a person may be attracted to someone else at first sight. I believe love comes from knowing and understanding the person personally. Love is not only an attraction to a person's looks, but also to that person's personality. How can a person love someone else without knowing who they are and what they are like?

> "Love at first sight" is an over-rated phrase. It probably is an attraction that may grow into love.

> *Gavin Morinaga (11th grade)*

> I think that sometimes "love at first sight" is overstated in life. Many books and plays are about characters that fall in love with each other the moment their eyes meet, but in real life that rarely happens. Most people have to get to know each other or at least spend time together before they know they are in "love." Sometimes some people have to hate each other before they actually fall in love. Although I wish that fairy tales would come true in real life, I believe a few hundred within a few thousand people maybe meet and fall instantly in love.

> *Miho Zaitsu (10th grade)*

Probably I do believe in love at first sight. It happened to Romeo and Juliet and there are a lot of situations similar to them, even today. I've seen it happen to some people, but I don't know if they usually last. I guess it should, but I don't know much about it. In my opinion, "love at first sight" is very weird, but it just happens and sometimes there is nothing you can do about it. I wonder if today it really lasts? For this question, I'm not sure of the answer 'cause I may need to find out myself.

Theresa Lee (10th grade)

I believe in "like at first sight." That's different than love. You can like a person for the way they walk, talk, eat, or look, but you can't automatically know a person in one glance. If you don't know a person, how can you love them? They could have a completely nauseating personality, and one look does not tell you that. Call me cold-hearted and unromantic, but I can't believe that one glance can show you the love of your life. If it happens to me and I change my mind, I'll keep you posted.

Annaliese Paul (10th grade)

Ask students to compare their quickwrite with a partner. After their discussion with a partner, ask students how many of them believe in love at first sight. (You might notice that the majority of students in your class will probably respond to this idea in a negative way by writing about how physical attraction, lust, and infatuation can be mistaken for "true love.")

Tell them that they will be comparing and contrasting two works of literature where love at first sight and traditional marriage customs lead to conflict.

Prewriting Step 2: *Discussion*

Hand out a copy of "Marriage Traditions and Customs: Do They Conflict with True Love?" (the handout on the next page) to each student. Have students read and discuss the information. Remind them that many of these traditions and customs are still followed in many cultures today.

Ask students if they know of any traditions and customs from their own culture that you can add to the list, and then have them save this information for further reference.

Marriage Traditions and Customs

Do they conflict with true love?

1. Arranged marriages (arranged by parents; by matchmaker; arranged for children; arranged at birth—matters of property, prestige, etc.)

2. Royal marriages as political alliances and a way of keeping blood pure—Hawaiian royalty married brother and sister

3. Marriage by capture (wife as slave) or purchase

   Aborigines: Kidnapping of bride, who, if pregnant when family catches up with the couple, is considered married

4. Oldest daughter must marry first

5. Youngest daughter can never marry, in order to take care of her mother

6. Being ostracized for marrying outside of your religion

7. Girl must be a virgin

8. In Africa, female circumcision ensures virginity

9. Girl must prove her fertility before she is worthy of marriage (Tahiti)

10. Mixed racial marriages against the law

11. Must have written parental consent for marriage (for underage; for marriage at any age in Japan)

12. Must prove marriage has been consummated

13. Brothers marry same woman (to ensure property rights)

14. A girl is married when she reaches puberty

15. Bridegroom must pay or work for father of girl to offset her loss to family (females regarded as possessions to be passed from father to son-in-law)

16. Mother acts as go-between by inspecting prospective women as they parade nude in public baths and then reports to son (Turkey)

(Information above compiled by Maureen Rippee based on newspaper and magazine articles and the curriculum for a Women and Men in Literature course.)

Prewriting Step 3: *Clustering*

NOTE: *To prepare for Prewriting Step 4: Role-Playing, you might want to first ask for student volunteers to participate in the role-playing that follows Step 3. While you are explaining the students' tasks to them and assigning the situations, have the rest of the class brainstorming with a partner or making up their own cluster on "reasons why people get married." This will give the volunteers the time they need to practice. See directions in Step 4.*

Ask a large group for choral responses to brainstorm and cluster the reasons why people get married. Write responses on the board, overhead, or butcher paper. A sample cluster might look like this:

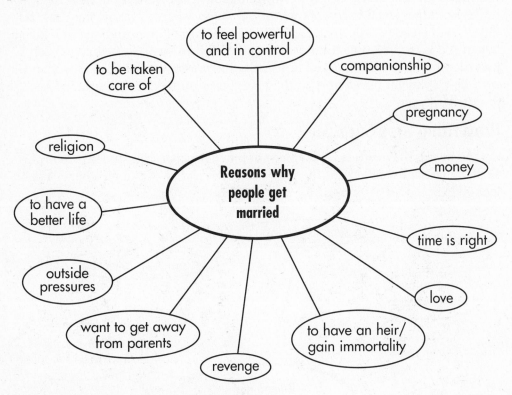

Prewriting Step 4: *Role-Playing*

Ask for approximately ten volunteers to participate in a role-play and give them one of the four situations below to present to the class. The gender combinations for each situation will depend on which students volunteer.

Volunteers should probably be given about fifteen minutes for private practice (see note above under Prewriting Step 3). The situations are:

1. A girl/boy telling her/his father that she/he is dating and wants to marry an individual from another race or culture.

2. A recent college graduate telling her/his wealthy parents that her/his romantic interest has decided upon a career with McDonald's.

3. Your mother wants you to date the son/daughter of her best friend, even though you already are involved in a serious relationship.

4. You want to marry someone who would take you away from your family and its traditions (Examples: physically moving away; practicing a different religion; spending holidays with your in-laws; etc.). Your parents refuse to listen to your arguments.

After all students who are presenting have had time to practice, introduce role-playing to the rest of the class by telling students that, in order to help them understand that, even in today's world, subtle pressures to follow marriage traditions and customs still exist, they will be observing four situations in which a boy or girl is feeling some kind of pressure. Tell them that at the end of each presentation, they will be asked to identify the pressures that each character in the role-play might have felt. List their responses on the blackboard, overhead, or butcher paper.

Prewriting Step 5: *Cluster*

On the board, the overhead, or a piece of butcher paper, ask students to brainstorm what they recall about the play *Romeo and Juliet*. A sample cluster might look like:

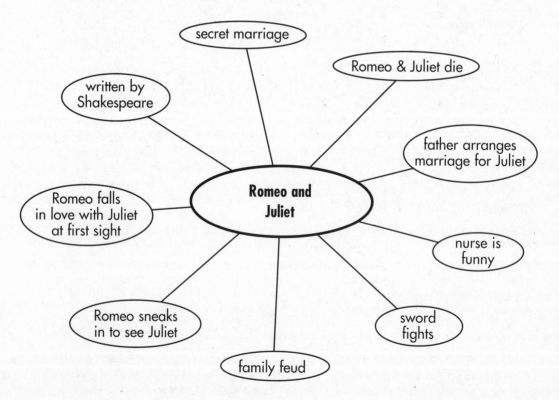

Prewriting Step 6: *Reading/Quickwrite*

At this time, students should read the first chapter of *Like Water for Chocolate : A Novel in Monthly Installments, with Recipes, Romances, and Home Remedies* (Bantam Doubleday Dell Publishing Group, Inc., 1992).

Featured Literature

Excerpt from Like Water for Chocolate
by Laura Esquivel

CHAPTER 1 January
CHRISTMAS ROLLS

Ingredients:

1 can of sardines	*oregano*
1/2 chorizo sausage	*1 can of chiles serranos*
1 onion	*10 hard rolls*

PREPARATION:

Take care to chop the onion fine. To keep from crying when you chop it (which is so annoying!), I suggest you place a little bit on your head. The trouble with crying over an onion is that once the chopping gets you started and the tears begin to well up, the next thing you know you just can't stop. I don't know whether that's ever happened to you, but I have to confess it's happened to me, many times. Mama used to say it was because I was especially sensitive to onions, like my great-aunt, Tita.

Tita was so sensitive to onions, any time they were being chopped, they say she would just cry and cry; when she was still in my great-grandmother's belly her sobs were so loud that even Nacha, the cook, who was half-deaf, could hear them easily. Once her wailing got so violent that it brought on an early labor. And before my great-grandmother could let out a word or even a whimper, Tita made her entrance into this world, prematurely, right there on the kitchen table amid the smells of simmering noodle soup, thyme, bay leaves, and cilantro, steamed milk, garlic, and, of course, onion. Tita had no need for the usual slap on the bottom, because she was already crying as she emerged; maybe that was because she knew then that it would be her lot in life to be denied marriage. The way Nacha told it, Tita was literally washed into this world on a great tide of tears that spilled over the edge of the table and flooded across the kitchen floor.

That afternoon, when the uproar had subsided and the water had been dried up by the sun, Nacha swept up the residue the tears had left on the red stone floor. There was enough salt to fill a ten-pound sack—it was used for cooking and lasted a long time. Thanks to her unusual birth, Tita felt a deep love for the kitchen, where she spent most of her life from the day she was born.

When she was only two days old, Tita's father, my great-grandfather, died of a heart attack and Mama Elena's milk dried up from the shock. Since there was

Customs and Conflicts

❈ DRAMA

no such thing as powdered milk in those days, and they couldn't find a wet nurse anywhere, they were in a panic to satisfy the infant's hunger. Nacha, who knew everything about cooking—and much more that doesn't enter the picture until later—offered to take charge of feeding Tita. She felt she had the best chance of "educating the innocent child's stomach," even though she had never married or had children. Though she didn't know how to read or write, when it came to cooking she knew everything there was to know. Mama Elena accepted her offer gratefully, she had enough to do between her mourning and the enormous responsibility of running the ranch—and it was the ranch that would provide her children the food and education they deserved—without having to worry about feeding a newborn baby on top of everything else.

From that day on, Tita's domain was the kitchen, where she grew vigorous and healthy on a diet of teas and thin corn gruels. This explains the sixth sense Tita developed about everything concerning food. Her eating habits, for example, were attuned to the kitchen routine: in the morning, when she could smell that the beans were ready; at midday, when she sensed the water was ready for plucking the chickens; and in the afternoon, when the dinner bread was baking, Tita knew it was time for her to be fed.

Sometimes she would cry for no reason at all, like when Nacha chopped onions, but since they both knew the cause of those tears, they didn't pay them much mind. They made them a source of entertainment, so that during her childhood Tita didn't distinguish between tears of laughter and tears of sorrow. For her laughing was a form of crying.

Likewise for Tita the joy of living was wrapped up in the delights of food. It wasn't easy for a person whose knowledge of life was based on the kitchen to comprehend the outside world. That world was an endless expanse that began at the door between the kitchen and the rest of the house, whereas everything on the kitchen side of that door, on through the door leading to the patio and the kitchen and herb gardens was completely hers—it was Tita's realm.

Her sisters were just the opposite: to them, Tita's world seemed full of unknown dangers, and they were terrified of it. They felt that playing in the kitchen was foolish and dangerous. But once, Tita managed to convince them to join her in watching the dazzling display made by dancing water drops dribbled on a red hot griddle.

While Tita was singing and waving her wet hands in time, showering drops of water down on the griddle so they would "dance," Rosaura was cowering in the corner, stunned by the display. Gertrudis, on the other hand, found this game enticing, and she threw herself into it with the enthusiasm she always showed where rhythm, movement, or music were involved. Then Rosaura had tried to join them—but since she barely moistened her hands and then shook them gingerly, her efforts didn't have the desired effect. So Tita tried to move her hands closer to the griddle. Rosaura resisted, and they struggled for control until Tita became annoyed and let go, so that momentum carried Rosaura's hands onto it. Tita got a terrible spanking for that, and she was forbidden to play with her sisters in her own world. Nacha became her playmate then. Together they made up all sorts of games and activities having to do with cooking. Like the day they saw a man in the village plaza twisting long thin balloons into animal shapes, and they decided to do it with sausages. They didn't just make real animals, they also made up some of their own, creatures with the neck of a swan, the legs of a dog, the tail of a horse, and on and on.

Then there was trouble, however, when the animals had to be taken apart to fry the sausage. Tita refused to do it. The only time she was willing to take them apart was when the sausage was intended for the Christmas rolls she loved so much. Then she not only allowed her animals to be dismantled, she watched them fry with glee.

The sausage for the rolls must be fried over very low heat, so that it cooks thoroughly without getting too brown. When done, remove from the heat and add the sardines, which have been deboned ahead of time. Any black spots on the skin should also have been scraped off with a knife. Combine the onions, chopped chiles, and the ground oregano with the sardines. Let the mixture stand before filling the rolls.

Tita enjoyed this step enormously; while the filling was resting, it was very pleasant to savor its aroma, for smells have the power to evoke the past, bringing back sounds and even other smells that have no match in the present. Tita liked to take a deep breath and let the characteristic smoke and smell transport her through the recesses of her memory.

It was useless to try to recall the first time she had smelled one of those rolls—she couldn't, possibly because it had been before she was born. It might have been the unusual combination of sardines and sausages that had called to her and made her decide to trade the peace of ethereal existence in Mama Elena's belly for life as her daughter, in order to enter the De la Garza family and share their delicious meals and wonderful sausage.

On Mama Elena's ranch, sausage making was a real ritual. The day before, they started peeling garlic, cleaning cells, and grinding spices. All the women in the family had to participate: Mama Elena; her daughters, Gertrudis, Rosaura, and Tita; Nacha, the cook; and Chencha, the maid. They gathered around the dining room table in the afternoon, and between the talking and the joking the time flew by until it started to get dark. Then Mama Elena would say:

"That's it for today."

For a good listener, it is said, a single word will suffice, so when they heard that, they all sprang into action. First they had to clear the table; then they had to assign tasks: one collected the chickens, another drew water for breakfast from the well, a third was in charge of wood for the stove. There would be no ironing, no embroidery, no sewing that day. When it was all finished, they went to their bedrooms to read, say their prayers, and go to sleep. One afternoon, before Mama Elena told them they could leave the table, Tita, who was then fifteen, announced in a trembling voice that Pedro Muzquiz would like to come and speak with her. . . .

After an endless silence during which Tita's soul shrank, Mama Elena asked.

"And why should this gentleman want to come talk to me?"

Tita's answer could barely be heard:

"I don't know."

Mama Elena threw her a look that seemed to Tita to contain all the years of repression that had flowed over the family, and said:

"If he intends to ask for your hand, tell him not to bother. He'll be wasting his time and mine too. You know perfectly well that being the youngest daughter means you have to take care of me until the day I die."

With that Mama Elena got slowly to her feet, put her glasses in her apron, and said in a tone of final command:

"That's it for today."

Tita knew that discussion was not one of the forms of communication permitted in Mama Elena's household, but even so, for the first time in her life, she intended to protest her mother's ruling.

"But in my opinion . . ."

"You don't have an opinion, and that's all I want to hear about it. For generations, not a single person in my family has ever questioned this tradition, and no daughter of mine is going to be the one to start."

Tita lowered her head, and the realization of her fate struck her as forcibly as her tears struck the table. From then on they knew, she and the table, that they could never have even the slightest voice in the unknown forces that fated Tita to bow before her mother's absurd decision, and the table to continue to receive the bitter tears that she had first shed on the day of her birth.

Still Tita did not submit. Doubts and anxieties sprang to her mind. For one thing, she wanted to know who started this family tradition. It would be nice if she could let that genius know about one little flaw in this perfect plan for taking care of women in their old age. If Tita couldn't marry and have children, who would take care of her when she got old? Was there a solution in a case like that? Or are daughters who stay home and take care of their mothers not expected to survive too long after the parent's death? And what about women who marry and can't have children, who will take care of them? And besides, she'd like to know what kind of studies had established that the youngest daughter and not the eldest is best suited to care for their mother. Had the opinion of the daughter affected by the plan ever been taken into account? If she couldn't marry, was she at least allowed to experience love? Or not even that?

Tita knew perfectly well that all these questions would have to be buried forever in the archive of questions that have no answers. In the De la Garza family, one obeyed—immediately. Ignoring Tita completely, a very angry Mama Elena left the kitchen, and for the next week she didn't speak a single word to her.

What passed for communication between them resumed when Mama Elena, who was inspecting the clothes each of the women had been sewing, discovered that Tita's creation, which was the most perfect, had not been basted before it was sewed.

"Congratulations," she said, "your stitches are perfect—but your didn't baste it, did you?"

"No," answered Tita, astonished that the sentence of silence had been revoked.

"Then go and rip it out. Baste it and sew it again and then come and show it to me. And remember that the lazy man and the stingy man end up walking their road twice."

"But that's if a person makes a mistake, and you yourself said a moment ago that my sewing was . . ."

"Are you starting up with your rebelliousness again? It's enough that you have the audacity to break the rules in your sewing."

"I'm sorry, Mami. I won't ever do it again."

With that Tita succeeded in calming Mama Elena's anger. For once she had been very careful; she had called her "Mami" in the correct tone of voice. Mama Elena felt that the word Mama had a disrespectful sound to it, and so, from the time they were little, she had ordered her daughters to use the word *Mami* when speaking to her. The only one who resisted, the only one who said the word without the proper deference was Tita, which had earned her plenty of slaps. But how perfectly she had said it this time! Mama Elena took comfort in the hope that she had finally managed to subdue her youngest daughter.

Unfortunately her hope was short-lived, for the very next day Pedro Muzquiz appeared at the house, his esteemed father at his side, to ask for Tita's hand in marriage. His arrival caused a huge uproar, as his visit was completely unexpected. Several days earlier Tita had sent Pedro a message via Nacha's brother asking him to abandon his suit. The brother swore he had delivered the message to Pedro, and yet, there they were, in the house. Mama Elena received them in the living room; she was extremely polite and explained why it was impossible for Tita to marry.

"But if you really want Pedro to get married, allow me to suggest my daughter Rosaura, who's just two years older than Tita. *She* is one hundred percent available, and ready for marriage. . . ."

At that Chencha almost dropped right onto Mama Elena the tray containing coffee and cookies, which had carried into the living room to offer Don Pascual and his son. Excusing herself, she rushed back to the kitchen, where Tita, Rosaura, and Gertrudis were waiting for her to fill them in on every detail about what was going on in the living room. She burst headlong into the room, and they all immediately stopped what they were doing, so as not to miss a word she said.

They were together in the kitchen making Christmas Rolls. As the name implies, these rolls are usually prepared around Christmas, but today they were being prepared in honor of Tita's birthday. She would soon be sixteen years old, and she wanted to celebrate with one of her favorite dishes.

"Isn't that something? Your ma talks about being ready for marriage like she was dishing up a plate of enchiladas! And the worse thing is, they're completely different! You can't just switch tacos and enchiladas like that!"

Chencha kept up this kind of running commentary as she told the others—in her own way, of course—about the scene she had just witnessed. Tita knew Chencha sometimes exaggerated and distorted things, so she held her aching heart in check. She would not accept what she had just heard. Feigning calm, she continued cutting the rolls for her sisters and Nacha to fill.

It is best to use homemade rolls. Hard rolls can easily be obtained from a bakery, but they should be small; the larger ones are unsuited for this recipe. After filling the rolls, bake for ten minutes and serve hot. For best results, leave the rolls out overnight, wrapped in a cloth, so that the grease from the sausage soaks into the bread.

When Tita was finishing wrapping the next day's rolls, Mama Elena came into the kitchen and informed them that she had agreed to Pedro's marriage—to Rosaura.

Hearing Chencha's story confirmed, Tita felt her body fill with a wintry chill: in one sharp, quick blast she was so cold and dry her cheeks burned and turned red, red as the apples beside her. That overpowering chill lasted a long time, and she could find no respite, not even when Nacha told her what she had overheard as she escorted Don Pascual Muzquiz and his son to the ranch's gate. Nacha followed them, walking as quieting as she could in order to hear the conversation between father and son. Don Pascual and Pedro were walking slowly, speaking in low, controlled, angry voices.

"Why did you do that, Pedro? It will look ridiculous, your agreeing to marry Rosaura. What happened to the eternal love you swore to Tita? Aren't you going to keep that vow?"

"Of course I'll keep it. When you're told there's no way you can marry the woman you love and your only hope of being near her is to marry her sister, wouldn't you do the same?"

Nacha didn't manage to hear the answer; Pulque, the ranch dog, went running by, barking at a rabbit he mistook for a cat.

"So you intend to marry without love?"

"No, Papa, I am going to marry with a great love for Tita that will never die."

Their voices grew less and less audible, drowned out by the crackling of dried leaves beneath their feet. How strange that Nacha, who was quite hard of hearing by that time, should have claimed to have heard this conversation. Still, Tita thanked Nacha for telling her—but that did not alter the icy feelings she began to have for Pedro. It is said that the deaf can't hear but can understand. Perhaps Nacha only heard what everyone else was afraid to say. Tita could not get to sleep that night; she could not find the words for what she was feeling. How unfortunate that black holes in space had not yet been discovered, for then she might have understood the black hole in the center of her chest, infinite coldness flowing through it.

Whenever she closed her eyes she saw scenes from last Christmas, the first time Pedro and his family had been invited to dinner; the scenes grew more and more vivid, and the cold within her grew sharper. Despite the time that had passed since that evening, she remembered it perfectly: the sounds, the smells, the way her new dress had grazed the freshly waxed floor, the look Pedro gave her . . . That look! She had been walking to the table carrying a tray of egg-yolk candies when she first felt his hot gaze burning her skin. She turned her head, and her eyes met Pedro's. It was then she understood how dough feels when it is plunged into boiling oil. The heat that invaded her body was so real she was afraid she would start to bubble—her face, her stomach, her heart, her breasts—like batter, and unable to endure his gaze she lowered her eyes and hastily crossed the room, to where Gertrudis was pedaling the player piano, playing a waltz called "The Eyes of Youth." She set her tray on a little table in the middle of the room, picked up a glass of Noyo liquor that was in front of her, hardly aware of what she was doing, and in front of her, hardly aware of the De la Garza's neighbor. But even that distance between herself and Pedro was not enough; she felt her blood pulsing, searing her veins. A deep flush suffused her face and no matter how she tried she could not find a place for her eyes to rest. Paquita saw that something was bothering her, and with a look of great concern, she asked:

"That liquor is pretty strong, isn't it?"

"Pardon me?"

"You look a little woozy, Tita. Are you feeling all right?"

"Yes, thank you."

"You're old enough to have a little drink on a special occasion, but tell me, you little devil, did your mama say it was okay? I can see you're excited—you're shaking—and I'm sorry but I must say you'd better not have any more. You wouldn't want to make a fool of yourself."

That was the last straw! To have Paquita Lobo think she was drunk. She couldn't allow the tiniest suspicion to remain in Paquita's mind or she might tell her mother. Tita's fear for her mother was enough to make her forget Pedro for a moment, and she applied herself to convincing Paquita, any way she could, that she was thinking clearly, that her mind was alert. She chatted with her, she gossiped, she made small talk. She even told her the recipe for this Noyo liquor which was supposed to have had such an effect on her. The liquor is made by soaking four ounces of peaches and a half a pound of apricots in water for twenty-four hours to loosen the skin; next, they are peeled, crushed, and steeped in hot water for fifteen days. Then the liquor is distilled. After two and a half pounds of sugar have been completely dissolved in the water, four ounces of orange-flower water are added, and the mixture is stirred and strained. And so there would be no lingering doubts about her mental and physical well-being, she reminded Paquita, as if it were just an aside, that the water containers held 2.016 liters, no more and no less.

So when Mama Elena came over to ask Paquita if she was being properly entertained, she replied enthusiastically.

"Oh yes, perfectly! You have such wonderful daughters. Such fascinating conversation!"

Mama Elena sent Tita to the kitchen to get something for the guests. Pedro "happened" to be walking by at that moment and he offered his help. Tita rushed off to the kitchen without a word. His presence made her extremely uncomfortable. He followed her in, and she quickly sent him off with one of the trays of delicious snacks that had been waiting on the kitchen table.

She would never forget the moment their hands accidentally touched as they both slowly bent down to pick up the same tray.

That was when Pedro confessed his love.

"Señorita Tita, I would like to take advantage of this opportunity to be alone with you to tell you that I am deeply in love with you. I know this declaration is presumptuous, and that it's quite sudden, but it's so hard to get near you that I decided to tell you tonight. All I ask is that you tell me whether I can hope to win your love."

"I don't know what to say . . . give me time to think."

"No, no, I can't! I need an answer now: you don't have to think about love; you either feel it or you don't. I am a man of few words, but my word is my pledge. I swear that my love for you will last forever. What about you? Do you feel the same way about me?"

"Yes!"

Yes, a thousand times. From that night on she would love him forever. And now she had to give him up. It wasn't decent to desire your sister's future husband. She had to try to put him out of her mind somehow, so she could get to sleep. She started to eat the Christmas Roll Nacha had left out on her bureau, along with a glass of milk; this remedy had proven effective many times.

Nacha, with all her experience, knew that for Tita there was no pain that wouldn't disappear if she ate a delicious Christmas Roll. But this time it didn't work. She felt no relief from the hollow sensation in her stomach. Just the opposite, a wave of nausea flowed over her. She realized that the hollow sensation was not hunger but an icy feeling of grief. She had to get rid of that terrible sensation of cold. First she put on a wool robe and a heavy cloak. The cold still gripped her. Then she put on felt slippers and another two shawls. No good. Finally she went to her sewing box and pulled out the bedspread she had started the day Pedro first spoke of marriage. A bedspread like that, a crocheted one, takes about a year to complete. Exactly the length of time Pedro and Tita had planned to wait before getting married. She decided to use the yarn, not to let it go to waste, and so she worked on the bedspread and wept furiously, weeping and working until dawn, and threw it over herself. It didn't help at all. Not that night, nor many others, for as long as she lived, could she free herself from that cold.

At the end of the reading, ask students to write a response to what they read. They should include their feelings about the plot and characters and conclude with a prediction about what they think might happen next in the story and how they think the story might end. Here are some typical student responses:

> The first chapter of *Like Water for Chocolate* conveyed that this family had strong feelings about tradition. The tradition of making the Christmas rolls and the more controversial tradition of the youngest daughter not being allowed to marry are examples of this. I got the feeling that this family would follow tradition no matter what.
>
> My prediction of what might happen next is while the family is planning the marriage of Pedro and Rosaura, Tita and Pedro secretly get married instead. As the story progresses, the secret marriage will cause quite a commotion when the family finds out. I predict that Tita and Pedro won't be able to handle the conflict and will decide to take their lives in the name of love.
>
> *Britt Nilsen (12th grade)*

> I was crying, screaming and laughing all at the same time as I read the first chapter of *Like Water for Chocolate*. I was disappointed when my journey through the novel was called to an abrupt halt and I can't wait to read the second chapter. The way the author introduces Tita makes you fall in love with her right from the start. The way she integrated the recipe to tie in with the events enhanced all the emotions that were swimming about in the chapter.

I predict that Pedro will still marry Rosaura, but love Tita secretly. Mama Elena will keep the lovers apart and in the end Tita will die of sadness and heartbreak. Pedro will be so overcome with grief that he will die too. Secretly, they will be buried together and will be happy in eternity.

Elizabeth Ahn (11th grade)

 # PROMPT

Writing Situation:

In the first chapter of *Like Water for Chocolate* and in the play *Romeo and Juliet*, traditions and customs stand in the way of true love and result in conflict.

Writing Directions:

Write an analytical/expository essay in which you compare and contrast this theme in these two works. Your essay should:

- address the role of love at first sight in both works;
- discuss marriage customs and traditions in each culture and the conflicts that result from adherence to these traditions;
- compare and contrast the characters of Tita and Juliet and Pedro and Romeo;
- include your predictions for how you think the conflicts will be resolved in *Like Water for Chocolate* by considering your recollections of the conflicts and results in *Romeo and Juliet*.

Your essay must have a clear introduction with an interesting hook, include textual references to support your ideas, contain a strong conclusion, and follow the basic standards for writing.

 # PRECOMPOSING

Precomposing Step 1: *Textual Analysis*

At this time, students should reread the first chapter of *Like Water for Chocolate*. Ask them to underline any words, lines, or phrases that reveal characterization, say something about love at first sight, and deal with conflicts that result from traditions and customs. Ask students to also make a list of any questions they have about the story. This step works well as a homework assignment.

Upon completion, you can brainstorm their textual analysis on an overhead, have students write them on the blackboard, or split the class into six groups, with two groups charting characterization, two groups charting love at first sight, and two groups charting conflicts that result from traditions and customs. Some samples of textual analysis might look like:

Words, Lines, or Phrases That Say Something About Love at First Sight

"the look Pedro gave her ... That look!" p. 16

"It was then she understood how dough feels when it is plunged into boiling oil." p. 16

"unable to endure his gaze she lowered her eyes" p. 16

"playing a waltz called *The Eyes of Youth*." p. 16

"But even that distance between herself and Pedro was not enough; she felt her blood pulsing, searing her veins. A deep flush suffused her face and no matter how she tried she could not find a place for her eyes to rest." p. 16

"His presence made her extremely uncomfortable." p. 18

Words, Lines, or Phrases That Deal with the Conflicts That Result from Traditions and Customs

"a look that seemed to Tita to contain all the years of repression that had flowed over the family" p. 10

"He'll be wasting his time and mine too. You know perfectly well that being the youngest daughter means you have to take care of me until the day I die." p. 10

"That's it for today." p. 11

"Tita knew that discussion was not one of the forms of communication permitted in Mama Elena's household," p. 11

"For generations, not a single person in my family has ever questioned this tradition, and no daughter of mine is going to be the one to start." p. 11

"Still Tita did not submit." p. 11

"It would be nice if she could let that genius know about one little flaw in this perfect plan for taking care of women in their old age." p. 11

"Had the opinion of the daughter affected by the plan ever been taken into account?" pp. 11–12

"In the De la Garza family one obeyed—immediately." p. 12

"His arrival caused a huge uproar, as his visit was completely unexpected. Several days earlier Tita had sent Pedro a message via Nacha's brother asking him to abandon his suit." p. 13

Words, Lines, or Phrases That Reveal the Characters

TITA

"Tita had no need for the usual slap on the bottom, because she was already crying when she emerged; maybe that was because she knew that it would be her lot in life to be denied marriage." p. 6

"Tita didn't distinguish between tears of laughter and tears of sorrow." p. 7

"It wasn't easy for a person whose knowledge of life was based on the kitchen to comprehend the outside world." p. 7

"Tita's soul shrank" p. 10

"Still Tita did not submit." p. 11

"The only one that resisted, the only one who said the word without proper deference was Tita," p. 13

"For the first time in her life, she intended to protest her mother's ruling." p. 11

PEDRO

"speaking in low, controlled, angry voices." p. 15

"No, Papa, I am going to marry with a great love for Tita that will never die." p. 15

"All I ask is that you tell me whether I can hope to win your love." p. 18

"I need an answer now: you don't have to think about love; you either feel it or you don't. I am a man of few words, but my word is my pledge. I swear that my love for you will last forever. What about you? Do you feel the same way about me?" p. 18

After students have shared their textual analysis or you have discussed their analysis on the overhead, ask students to brainstorm their questions as you write them on the overhead. Some sample questions might be:

- Is this a real tradition and is it still followed?
- How does this story end?
- How many chapters are in this book and do they all start with recipes?
- How do the recipes affect the action or plot?
- How is Tita going to live in the house with Pedro and Rosaura?
- Is the conflict between Tita and Mama Elena ever resolved?
- Will Pedro confess to Rosaura his real love for Tita?

Precomposing Step 2: *Comparison And Contrast Language*

In order for students to begin to make comparisons and contrasts, it might be necessary to review examples of comparison and contrast language. Ask students to copy the following chart off the board or overhead.

Words That Can Be Used to Compare Two Things		
like	*as*	*in the same way*
likewise	*also*	*similarly*
just as	*both*	*in comparison to*

Words That Can Be Used to Contrast Things		
unlike	*but*	*on the other hand*
however	*yet*	*even though*
otherwise	*still*	*in contrast*
although		

Precomposing Step 3: *Comparisons with* Romeo and Juliet

In order for students to compare *Like Water for Chocolate* and *Romeo and Juliet*, use the following excerpts to introduce examples from *Romeo and Juliet* that can be compared with "love at first sight" and traditions that lead to conflicts in *Like Water for Chocolate*. In addition to looking for comparisons for "love" and "conflicts," ask students to look for any comparisons between Tita and Juliet and Pedro and Romeo they find. After reading the excerpts, ask students to begin to make a chart outlining specific comparisons from excerpts.

Featured Literature

Excerpts from Romeo and Juliet

Compare these two examples from the play with the "love at first sight" description Tita gives in *Like Water for Chocolate*, and youngest daughter tradition that lead to conflict in *Like Water for Chocolate*.

Act I, Scene 5

Example of Romeo's reaction to "love at first sight"

ROMEO:
O, she doth teach the torches to burn bright!
It seems she hangs upon the cheek of night
Like a rich jewel in an Ethiop's ear—
Beauty too rich for use, for earth too dear!
So shows a snowy dove trooping with crows
As yonder lady o'er her fellows shows.
The measure done, I'll watch her place of stand
And, touching hers, make blessed my rude hand.
Did my heart love till now? Forswear it, sight!
For I ne'er saw true beauty till this night.

Act 3, Scene 5

Reflection of tradition of a father arranging a marriage without his daughter's input (a daughter was considered to be her father's property)

CAPULET:
God's bread! it makes me mad. Day, night, late, early,
At home, abroad, alone, in company,
Waking or sleeping, still my care hath been
To have her match'd; and having now provided
A gentleman of princely parentage,
Of fair demesnes, youthful, and nobly train'd,

Stuff'd, as they say, with honourable parts,
Proportion'd as one's thought would with a man—
And then to have a wretched puling fool,
A whining mammet, in her fortune's tender,
To answer "I'll not wed, I cannot love;
I am too young, I pray you pardon me"!
But, and you will not wed, I'll pardon you.
Graze where you will, you shall not house with me.
Look to't, think on't it; I do not use to jest.
Thursday is near; lay hand on heart, advise:
An you be mine, I'll give you to my friend;
An you be not, hang, beg, starve, die in the streets,
For, by my soul, I'll ne'er acknowledge thee,
Nor what is mine shall never do thee good.
Trust to't. Bethink you. I'll not be forsworn.

Note: Depending upon the level, the individual needs of the students and/or the availability of copies of Romeo and Juliet, *you can use also use a prose version of the play (Example: Lamb, Charles and Mary.* Tales from Shakespeare. *London: Chaucer Press, 1985, 242-261.) or clips from Zeffirelli's* Romeo and Juliet *(a movie produced by Paramount Pictures, 1968) to make comparisons.*

Next, give students approximately thirty minutes to analyze *Romeo and Juliet* for more comparisons to add to their chart, which might look like:

Romeo and Juliet	*Like Water for Chocolate*	**Comparative responses**
"Did my heart love till now? Forswear it, sight!" (Act 1, Scene 5)	"That look!" (p. 16)	Like Romeo, Pedro falls strongly in love at first sight.
My only love … enemy" (Act 1 Scene 5)	"It was then she understood how dough feels when it is plunged into boiling oil." (p. 16)	Both Juliet and Tita experience a strong reaction after seeing their loves for the first time.
"And you be mine, I'll give you to my friend;" (Act 3, Scene 5)	"You don't have an opinion and that's all I want to hear about it. For generations not a single person in my family has ever questioned this tradition." (p. 11)	Similar conflict are the result when Lord Capulet and Mama Elena force Juliet and Tita to follow tradition.
"I'll not wed, I cannot love;" (Act 3, Scene 5)	"For the first time in her life, she intended to protest her mother's ruling." (p. 11)	Juliet and Tita rebel in the same way against tradition.

Precomposing Step 4: *Word Walls: Bridges to Analysis*

These word walls extend those found in Karin Hess's *Enhancing Writing through Imagery* (Trillium Press, 1987) and should help students in textual analysis.

First, student groups of four to six use index cards (20–30 per group), butcher paper, scissors (one per group), and two different colored pens per group to write the following topics across the top of their butcher paper or on index cards taped at the top of the paper: 1) Love at First Sight and 2) Customs and Traditions. Second, students analyze their charts in Step 3 and report the lines, words, or phrases. Individuals will write those lines, words, or phrases in one color for Romeo and Juliet and the other for Like Water for Chocolate on cards and tape them under the appropriate topic on the butcher paper. (Students should cut cards into parts, depending on the amount of information to be written.) *Third,* students number each card and copy their group's wall. Fourth, a student from each group (or the entire group) introduces their wall. Students may add information from another group to their own walls. Post group work. An abbreviated group analysis might look like:

Love at First Sight	Customs/Traditions
1. "Did my heart love till now? Forswear it, sight!" (Romeo: **R&J,** Act 1, Scene 5)	**1.** Lord Capulet arranges marriage: "Still my care hath been to have her match'd" (**R&J,** Act 3, Scene 5)
2. Juliet asks Nurse to find out who Romeo is: "Too early seen unknown... My only love enemy" (**R&J,** Act 1, Scene 5)	**2.** "You don't have an opinion and that's all I want to hear about it. For generations not a single person in my family has ever questioned this tradition." (**LWFC,** p.11)
3. "That look!" (**LWFC,** p16)	**3.** "Pedro Musquiz appeared at the house, his esteemed father at his side, to ask for Tita's hand in marriage" (**LWFC,** p.13)
4. "It was then she understood how dough feels when it is plunged into boiling oil" (**LWFC,** p16)	**4.** Juliet worries about not following courtship etiquette (**R&J,** Act 2, Scene 2)
5. "O Romeo, Romeo . . ." (Juliet) "Do look kind upon me lady . . ." (Romeo: **R&J**, Act 2, Scene 2)	**5.** "a look that seemed to Tita to contain all the years of repression that had flowed over the family" (**LWFC,** p.10)
6. "Unable to endure his gaze she lowered her eyes" (**LWFC,** p16)	**6.** "He'll be wasting his time and mine too. You know perfectly well that being the youngest daughter means you have to take care of me until the day I die" (**LWFC,** p.10)
7. "Alike bewitched by the charm of looks; " (**R&J,** Act 2, Prologue)	

Precomposing Step 5: *Comparison and Contrast Sentences*

Ask students to formulate comparison sentences in addition to those they wrote in Precomposing Step 2 and also to write some contrast sentences. Ask volunteers to write their sentences on the overhead and instruct the other students to copy. Some sample sentences students might construct are:

- Both Juliet and Tita are repressed by their family's customs or traditions concerning marriage.
- Like Romeo and Juliet, Pedro and Tita fall in love without realizing that conflict will be the result.
- In the same way that Mama Elena refuses to listen to Tita, Lord Capulet will not permit Juliet to question his authority.
- In contrast to Romeo's secret marriage to Juliet, Pedro follows the tradition of officially asking Mama Elena for Tita's hand in marriage.
- Romeo and Juliet secretly marry, but Pedro and Tita cannot marry.
- Although Juliet worries about not following courtship etiquette, Tita questions her family's tradition.

Precomposing Step 6: *Venn Diagram*

Students may now compare and contrast characters by completing one Venn diagram like the following for Tita and Juliet, another for Pedro and Romeo.

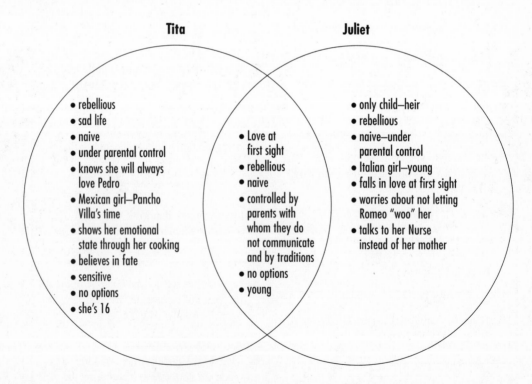

Tita   **Juliet**

- rebellious
- sad life
- naive
- under parental control
- knows she will always love Pedro
- Mexican girl—Pancho Villa's time
- shows her emotional state through her cooking
- believes in fate
- sensitive
- no options
- she's 16

- Love at first sight
- rebellious
- naive
- controlled by parents with whom they do not communicate and by traditions
- no options
- young

- only child—heir
- rebellious
- naive—under parental control
- Italian girl—young
- falls in love at first sight
- worries about not letting Romeo "woo" her
- talks to her Nurse instead of her mother

Precomposing Step 7: *Comparison and Contrast Sentences*

Using the Venn diagram as a guide, write comparison and contrast sentences for Tita and Juliet and Pedro and Romeo. You might want to list them on the board or overhead. Some sample sentences are:

- Tita and Pedro fall in love at first sight in the same way that Romeo and Juliet do.
- Both Tita and Juliet rebel against their parent's wishes.
- Tita is naive in the same way that Juliet is; both are unaware of the world outside their own environment.
- Like Tita and Pedro, Juliet and Romeo died in the end.
- Although Romeo is able to secretly marry Juliet, Pedro is forced to marry Rosaura in order to be near his true love, Tita.
- Even though Juliet is controlled by her parents, she is able to sneak out and marry Romeo. This is in contrast to Tita who is unable to escape her environment in order to run away with Pedro.

Precomposing Step 8: *Microtheme*

Note: In helping students construct a microtheme, you might want to refer to the examples of hooks in the "My Name, My Self" lesson and the Ways to Write an Introduction for an Expository Paper in the "Living in Life's Shadow" lesson (see Table of Contents). For a model of point-by-point and one-side-at-a-time develop-ment, please refer to Sheila Koff's lesson "A Rose-Colored Life by Any Other Name" in Thinking/Writing: Fostering Critical Thinking Through Writing *(ed. Carol Booth Olson, New York: HarperCollins Publishers, 1992).*

Students are now ready to organize all of their prewriting and precomposing ideas by synthesizing them into a writing plan or "microtheme." On a piece of notebook paper, have students write the categories—**Introduction, Main Body, Conclusion**. Under **Introduction**, ask them to write at least two "hooks" for beginning their paper.

Under **Main Body**, ask them to refer back to the prompt, their textual analysis and charts to brainstorm a list of main points they intend to make. Instruct them to note the specific references from the texts they will use to support either point-by-point or one-side-at-a-time comparisons and contrasts. Students can write the #'s that they put on the cards they taped on to butcher paper and on their individual charts instead of writing out complete quotes here.

Under **Conclusion**, suggest that they write their prediction of how the conflict will be resolved that they wrote in their freewrite and then end with a predomi-nant feeling, impression, or message that they would like to leave the reader of the essay with.

This microtheme should be viewed as a point of departure in writing or as a guideline for how students will communicate their ideas rather than an outline of precisely what they are going to say. (See the chart that follows.)

Microtheme

Introduction: I could begin my paper with one of the following hooks:

-
-

Main Body

Main points I want to make:	Specific References from the text to support my main point:	
	LWFC	**R & J**
• _____	• #_____	#_____
	• #_____	#_____
	• #_____	#_____
	• #_____	#_____
• _____	• #_____	#_____
	• #_____	#_____
	• #_____	#_____
	• #_____	#_____
• _____	• #_____	#_____
	• #_____	#_____
	• #_____	#_____
	• #_____	#_____
	• #_____	#_____

Conclusion: My prediction on how the conflict will be resolved is:

A predominant feeling, impression, or message that I want to leave my reader with is:

 WRITING

Students should now write their first drafts based on their prewriting and pre-composing activities. Depending upon students' level of readiness at this point, you might want to review the prompt and/or go over the Peer Response Sheet.

 SHARING

Have students choose two partners to jointly fill out the Peer Response Sheet. Writers should answer the questions asked in "Self-Reflection" before passing their essay and a Peer Response Sheet to each partner.

Optional: The author of each paper may want to fill out the Self-Reflection form on the next page and hand it to their response partners for review along with the blank Peer Response Sheet.

 REVISING

Students will use the suggestions on their two peer response forms and the critique of the model essay to revise their papers.

 EDITING

Students will also use the peer response forms as guides for editing. At this time, they will specifically correct for the conventions of standard English. They might want to confer with their response partners for any clarification necessary.

Self-Reflection Form

Name: _____

Author: What I meant to say in this essay is

Author: I would like you to specifically check for

Author: One part of my paper that bothers me is

Author: I feel the best part of my paper is

Peer Response Sheet

Peer Response Partner's Name:_____

This is in response to the first draft of _____ who will review my comments and ask questions so that he/she will be able to write a better paper during the revision process.

Your paper:	Very well done	OK	Needs some work
Includes a comparison of "love at first sight" from both texts			
Analyzes the traditions and how they lead into conflict in both texts			
Compares and contrasts the characters of Tita and Juliet			
Compares and contrasts the characters of Pedro and Romeo			
Includes your prediction for the resolution of conflicts in *Like Water for Chocolate*			
Is written in standard expository form: • Has a clear introduction with an interesting hook			
• Has a well-developed main body with good transitions and logical sequencing			
• Has a solid conclusion that reiterates essay rhetorically			
• Uses manuscript form			
Uses key lines, words, or phrases accurately as a means of support and characterization			
Uses sentences that are varied in length and structure			
Has few errors in the conventions of English			
Is interesting and keeps the reader engaged			

What I like best about your essay is

One thing you might want to work on in your revision is

EVALUATION

Use the student model appended to this lesson as a model draft to guide the evaluation process by putting it on the overhead. Have the class critique the model, using the holistic scoring guide below. Write students' comments directly on the transparency to help guide their cognition about how the model meets the criteria in the prompt.

After you have finished with the model essay, have students form groups to practice evaluation by scoring each other's papers, using the holistic scoring. Ask that each paper be scored by at least three different students.

Note: You might want to use Read-Around groups for evaluation. See the Glossary for a detailed description of the Read-Around process.

Holistic Scoring

6   *This is a paper that is clearly superior: well written, insightful, carefully organized, and technically correct. A 6 paper does most or all of the following well:*

- Carefully analyzes the traditions and how they lead to conflict in both *Romeo and Juliet* and *Like Water for Chocolate*.
- Includes a comparison of "love at first sight" from both texts.
- Offers insights into the characters of Tita, Juliet, Pedro, and Romeo.
- Predicts the resolution of conflicts in *Like Water for Chocolate*, demonstrating support from the text to support the prediction.
- Demonstrates mastery of standard written English and expository form: has a clear introduction with an interesting hook; has a well-developed main body with good transitions and logical sequencing; has a solid conclusion that reiterates the essay rhetorically; and uses manuscript form.
- Uses key lines, words, or phrases (quotes) when appropriate as a means of support and characterization.
- Uses sentences that are varied in length and structure.
- Has few errors (if any) in the conventions of written English.
- Is interesting and keeps the reader engaged.

5   *This is a strong paper that addresses all of the aspects of the assignment well. It is a thinner version of the 6 paper—still impressive and interesting, but less well-handled in terms of insight, analysis, organization, or language. A 5 paper will do all or most of the following:*

- Carefully analyzes the traditions that lead to conflict in both texts, but not quite as critically as a 6 paper.
- Offers a comparison of "love at first sight" from both texts, but comparison is not quite as insightful or profound as what is found in the 6 paper.
- Compares and contrasts the characters of Tita, Juliet, Pedro, and Romeo

- Predicts the completion in *Like Water for Chocolate* but does not use as strong of support as used in the 6 paper.
- Is written in standard expository form: Has a clear introduction with a "hook"; has a reasonably well-developed main body, adequate transitions, logical sequencing; has a logical conclusion; and uses manuscript form.
- Uses some appropriate quotes for support of ideas.
- Is interesting and keeps the reader engaged.
- Has a few errors in written English, but none interfere with the message.

4   *This solid paper meets most criteria of the assignment but does so in less depth than a 6 or 5 paper. A 4 paper may exhibit some of the following:*

- Analyzes the traditions in both texts but not as critically as a 6 or 5.
- Compares and contrasts "love at first sight" in both texts.
- Offers a fairly obvious comparison and contrast between the characters of Tita, Juliet, Pedro, and Romeo.
- Makes a prediction about the resolution of conflicts in *Like Water for Chocolate*; however, the support is weaker than in the 6 or 5 paper.
- Is written in standard expository form: Has a discernible introduction, but one that is not as clear or as well stated as the 6 or 5 paper or which does not have an interesting "hook"; has a less well developed main body with some weaknesses in transition and sequencing; has a conclusion that may simply restate the introduction rather than leaving the reader clear about what has been written; and uses manuscript form.
- Uses some quotes for support; however, there are some errors.
- Is less interesting or engaging interpretation than the 6 or 5 paper.
- Has some errors in the convention of standard English.

3   *This is a lower half paper that addresses the assignment superficially and is weak in organization and language. A 3 paper:*

- Superficially analyzes the traditions that lead to conflict in both texts.
- Begins to compare "love at first sight" but doesn't offer text support.
- Offers few insights into characters of Tita, Juliet, Pedro, and Romeo.
- Makes a prediction as to the resolution of conflicts in *Like Water for Chocolate* but doesn't support that prediction.
- Has weaknesses in the introduction, main body, and/or the conclusion.
- Has problems with transitions and/or sequencing.
- Uses manuscript form.
- Refers to few, if any, words, lines, or phrases (quotes) to support observations. Fails to interpret these references adequately.
- Interpretation is hard for the reader to follow.
- Has errors in the conventions of written English—some of which interfere with the reader's understanding of what is said.

2-1   *These scores apply to papers that fail to analyze traditions, "love at first sight", the characters, or say so little so poorly that the reader can't understand.*

EXTENSION ACTIVITIES

1. *Recipe Writing and Storytelling*

Have students write a practical/informative and imaginative/narrative essay that begins with a recipe that is special for them and/or reflects their culture. With *Like Water for Chocolate* as their model, have students begin with a practical/informative description of their recipe and how to prepare it. Next, they will write an imaginative/narrative story that reflecting the recipe.

Prewriting Step: Bring in a recipe and write the steps and ingredients on index cards and put the recipe together. This exercise can teach sequencing as well as preparation of a recipe. (Prewriting idea from Shari Lockman, UCI Writing Project Teacher/Consultant).

Student Model

Christmas Buñuelos

INGREDIENTS:

1 teaspoon salt	1 cup milk
1 teaspoon baking powder	1/4 cup butter
2 tablespoons sugar	Oil for frying
4 cups flour	Sugar and cinnamon mixture
2 eggs	

PREPARATION:

Carefully sift all the dry ingredients together. I say carefully because one Christmas (in fact, the first Christmas I was allowed to help my mom make buñuelos) I received quite a surprise. As I began to manipulate the strange contraption, I received a shower of the combined white and partially powdery substances from my hair to my knees. With quivering lips and wide eyes, I turned to my mother and, shaking her head, she helped me clean up my embarrassing appearance. Together, we started over and remeasured the dry ingredients. This time we were successful. Mom proceeded to masterfully beat the eggs and add the milk to them. To a five-year old, this action seemed rather cruel. I knew that at one point there were baby chicks inside the eggs and I wanted no part of their demise. In a pouting manner and with tears in my eyes, I covered my eyes with the rag that had been used to clean up my earlier catastrophe. After my mom promised me that there would be no more cruelty, I decided to unveil my eyes. She showed me how to combine the mixtures gradually and then add the butter. My mom turned this final combination on to a lightly floured board. She then instructed me to knead the dough gently. I was puzzled by this new word "knead," and I just stood there confused, looking at the dough, looking at my mother's back, and waiting for clarification. My mother turned around to see I hadn't even made a dent in the dough. Realizing my predicament, she began to show me the art of kneading. Together, we worked the dough into a large piece of smooth elastic. She told me that the way I kneaded the dough reminded her of the way my grandma did it. I assumed she meant we both had little hands. However, mom explained that it was because both my grandma and I had small, fragile-looking bodies that deceived the eyes of viewers that were strangers to our strength.

My mother and I both started to tear at the dough and form small balls. I felt really special when I my mom handed me the roller to flatten the balls. This was the final job I had in helping my mom make buñuelos.

I watched mom gently place the flattened balls into a greasy pan and heard them sizzle and pop. As they turned just the right color, Mom scooped them up and lay them on paper towels to drain. It seemed like hours before she said they were cool enough to sprinkle the cinnamon and sugar mixture, but finally they were ready. Watching her every move, I agonized over whether Mom would follow our standard rule about sweets or let me taste a buñuelo before dinner. She affectionately smiled down at me and handed the small, perfect pastry into my outstretched hand. I had never tasted anything so good in my life. I didn't remember them ever tasting so good. Was it because I had helped make them? I devoured my small buñuelo and licked the crumbs from my fingers. Later, as we ate our dinner, my mom told my father how I had helped as I continuously kept a proud and watchful eye over our dessert.

Every Christmas, I continue to help my mom make our traditional dessert. The Christmas buñuelos still taste as good as they did the first time I helped make them, and I enjoy making these treats that are symbolic of our culture and our family love.

Linda Torres (11th grade)

2. *Comparing and Contrasting the Book with the Movie*

Students can write an analytical/expository essay comparing and contrasting the novel *Like Water for Chocolate* with the movie version of the novel.

3. *Comparing and Contrasting Spanish and English Versions*

Students will translate the first chapters of the Spanish and English versions of *Like Water for Chocolate*. Then they can write an analytical/expository essay comparing/contrasting the two, or a practical/informative essay about Spanish words, phrases, and idioms not literally translated into English.

4. *Writing the I-Search Paper*

Students will write an I-Search paper about different marriage traditions.

Note: For a description of and a reference for the I-Search paper, see the Glossary. For an example of an I-Search lesson, see Carol Booth Olson's "Out of a Genuine Need to Know: Personalizing the Research Paper" in Thinking/Writing: Fostering Critical Thinking Through Writing, *ed. Carol Booth Olson (New York: HarperCollins Publishers, 1992).*

5. *Creating a Recipe for a Good Relationship*

Students will write a practical/informative essay that begins with an imaginative recipe and then supplements that recipe with practical information on how to have a good "love" relationship; or an imaginative/narrative essay that begins with a recipe and then supplements that recipe with a narrative example.

Prewriting Step 1: Cluster the qualities of a good relationship.

Note: See Extension Activity 1 for a more sequential development.

Student Model

Tradition and Tragedy

Are traditional customs concerning marriage always beneficial—even if two people are not attracted to each other? Or are traditions obstructions to true love? In Laura Esquivel's novel, *Like Water for Chocolate,* and William Shakespeare's play, *Romeo and Juliet*, both writers examine how traditions can conflict with true love. Esquivel shows this conflict through the "love at first sight" of Pedro and Tita conflicting with the custom of the youngest daughter never marrying in order to take care of her mother. Shakespeare shows through Romeo and Juliet how the Italian tradition of the father arranging his daughter's marriage without her consent can impede the growth of a relationship between two humans who fall in "love at first sight." Though the novel is set in Mexico during the time of Pancho Villa, and the play is set in Verona, Italy and was written in the 16th century, the conflicts are quite similar. Both sets of lovers can't be together because of traditional customs.

When the two characters in *Like Water for Chocolate,* Pedro and Tita, meet and when Romeo and Juliet meet, it is "love at first sight." Both the men and the women feel a heart-wrenching desire for one another. When Tita felt Pedro's gaze on her, "she understood how dough feels when it is plunged into boiling oil." As dough smolders in scalding oil, so does Tita's heart in Pedro's blistering stare. When Romeo first sees Juliet dancing at the party, he cries, "O, she doth teach the torches to burn bright!...Did my heart love till now? Forswear it, sight!" (Act 1, Scene 5). Romeo compares Juliet's appearance to a radiant flame that seems to have blinded him to all others. She is like a "dove trooping with crows" and he has forgotten about his infatuation with Rosaline and covets Juliet as his true love instead. With the images of oil boiling and torches burning, one can feel the heated passion that consumed the lovers when they first look at each other.

Not only do the stories parallel with the idea of "love at first sight," but also with the idea that both Tita and Juliet are unattainable because of traditional customs. According to the novel, in nineteenth century Mexico, the youngest daughter is unable to wed because of her responsibility to tend to her mother's needs. Since Tita is the youngest, she is bound by this tradition; therefore, Tita and Pedro can never marry. When Tita tries to challenge the set rules, her austere mother responds coldly, "For generations, not a single person in my family has ever questioned this tradition, and no daughter of mine is going to be the one to start." Even though this is the first time in her life that she protests the custom, her uncaring mother does not explain to her how important the tradition is, but instead, Mama Elena quickly scolds Tita for her disobedience. In comparison to Mama Elena, Lord Capulet will not deal with the disobedience of his daughter. After Juliet refuses to marry Paris, whom her father chose, Lord Capulet states in a definitive voice, "An you be mine, I'll give you to my friend" (Act 3, Scene 5). His statement reflects his attitude towards his daughter; he treats her as if she is a gift to be given away and not a person who could choose who to be given to. These examples of strict adherence to traditional customs lead to conflict and both daughters want to challenge their parents' control over them.

Both Tita and Juliet want to rebel against the tradition to which they are bound in order to marry the men they love. Tita "did not submit. Doubts and anxieties sprang to her mind...Had the opinion of the daughter affected by the plan ever been taken into account?" Tita again questions the tradition; however, this time in her mind and not out loud to her mother. Tita yearns to defy the custom because she sincerely loves Pedro and wants to be near him. Like Tita, Juliet's love for Romeo leads to the defiance of her family traditional custom. She would rather fake death rather than marry Paris since she is not allowed to question her father's plan.

Tita and Juliet have more in common that just their feelings of love and rebellion. However, they also have some differences. Both girls are segregated away from society; yet, they live in dissimilar surroundings. Tita lives on a Mexican ranch which is miles away from her nearest neighbor, while Juliet lives in the town of Verona in her father's home. Both are young girls who come from respectable families. Tita is the third daughter of a prosperous rancher, while Juliet is the only child and heir of a nobleman. Neither girl is raised by her mother. Tita is raised by the loving cook, Nacha; Juliet is nurtured by the affectionate Nurse. Both girls are under restrictive parental control and must obey their parents or suffer the consequences.

Like Tita and Juliet, Pedro and Romeo have their similarities and differences. When he first talks to Tita, Pedro professes, "I am a man of few words, but my word is my pledge. I swear that my love for you will last forever." Although both fall in love quickly, Romeo is more wordy and his speeches are full of foreshadowing. He promises to love Juliet by saying, "Better my life should be ended by their (the feuding families) hate, than that life should be prolonged, to live without your love." Both characters are very articulate and straightforward. They do not lie or play games, but are open and honest about their feelings. Both are well-brought up young gentleman. However, Romeo can't tell his family about his true love and Pedro can. Both make rash decisions when conflicts arise. Pedro decides to marry Rosaura in order to be close to Tita and Romeo marries Juliet immediately without letting his parents or friends know. This shows that both men are willing to sacrifice for love, but their rashness leads to unhappiness and tragedy.

At the end of *Romeo and Juliet*, Romeo sacrifices himself because he thinks that he can never be with Juliet and so life is not worth living. Juliet commits suicide to show that she can match Romeo's love. Because there are so many parallels between *Romeo and Juliet* and *Like Water for Chocolate*, a prediction for the novel must be tragic. Nine months after Pedro marries Tita's sister, Rosaura, she gives birth to a son. Pedro never grows to love Rosaura and secretly stays true to Tita and checks up on her without her or anyone else's knowledge. At a party held to celebrate the baby's birth, Tita is overcome with grief and loneliness. In the kitchen where she is so comfortable, she begins to cry into the food she is cooking and into the drinking water. Pedro comes into the kitchen but even though they are finally alone, they can't really express how much they hurt and yearn for each other. In between their few words, Pedro drinks a glass of water. Engulfed by pain and sorrow, Pedro falls to the ground and dies. Unable to deal with continuing to live without Pedro, Tita grabs a kitchen knife and stabs herself. Thus, the story ends in tragedy because the "star-crossed" lovers cannot be together.

In *Like Water for Chocolate* and *Romeo and Juliet*, Esquivel and Shakespeare show how traditions conflict with love and how these conflicts might lead to tragedy. The traditions hindered the development of relationships between people who truly loved each other. Unfortunately, the "star-crossed" lovers learned that "love doesn't conquer all." In these cases, it couldn't conquer tradition and customs, especially when it was up against a mother like Mama Elena, and a father like Lord Capulet.

Jayne Jung (Entering 11th Grade)

Featured Literature

Romeo and Juliet
by William Shakespere

Spring Snow
by Yukio Mishima

Grade Level
For High School
and College

Thinking Level
Application

Writing Domain
Analytical/Expository

Materials Needed
No special materials
required.

**Suggested
Supplementary
Readings**
The Sound of Waves by
Yukio Mishima

The Rules of the Game

by Michael O'Brien

Overview

After reading Shakespeare's *Romeo and Juliet* and Yukio Mishima's *Spring Snow*, students will use writing, drawing, close reading, and discussion in order to write an analytical paper exploring how "unwritten" rules for social behavior affect the young lovers in both works.

Objectives

THINKING SKILLS

Students will:

- *use* knowledge when they recall rules for social conduct;
- *apply* that knowledge when they draw out representations of how society can affect lovers;
- *use* analysis to examine the two works, exploring how the young lovers are affected by these "unwritten" social rules.

WRITING SKILLS

Students will:

- *write* in analytical/expository form with an introduction that grabs the reader's interest, a logically developed main body, and a conclusion that gives their analysis a sense of closure;
- *articulate* a clear thesis;
- *choose* a pattern of development to compare/contrast;
- *refer* to specific examples from the text (including direct quotations) to support their argument;
- *use* transition words to develop and link ideas and keep the paper flowing;
- *follow* conventions for standard written English: spelling, punctuation, grammar, sentence structure, and rules for quoting from the text.

The Process

This lesson is designed, first, to give students ways to connect with the lovers in the two works, lovers who live in the past and in cultures that are possibly alien to students. In making these connections, it is hoped that students will be able to bridge the gaps in time and culture, and to see that the lovers in literature face many of the same situations that contemporary couples face. Since reading literature is an activity that both leads the reader out into other worlds, as well as drawing the individual back into reflecting about the self, it is also hoped that this lesson will enable students to become more aware of how society shapes their behavior.

This lesson assumes that students have already read both Shakespeare's *Romeo and Juliet* and Mishima's *Spring Snow*. *Romeo and Juliet* is often taught in the ninth grade; *Spring Snow* would be best taught to mature juniors, seniors, or to college-level students. However, it would be rewarding for older students to go back to *Romeo and Juliet* in order to see some of the parallels with Mishima's novel. The lesson assumes that students are already familiar with how to write a comparison/contrast paper.

 PREWRITING

Prewriting Step 1: *Journal Jot List*

For a homework journal or class assignment, ask students to write down some rules they know for romantic relationships. Some examples:

- don't cheat on your partner
- keep parents in the background
- try to look nice for each other
- be on time for dates

Prewriting Step 2: *Small Group Collaboration*

Ask students to divide up into small groups of either males or females. *(I divide them according to gender because I have found that they are much more honest and open that way.)* Using their individual lists of rules from their journals, students will create a composite master list. A group recorder should make up this master list to be shared with the whole class, while the rest of the group writes down any rules they get from others that are not in their journals.

Prewriting Step 3: *Large Group Discussion*

After the groups have had sufficient time (about ten minutes), ask the group recorders to read their responses as you record them on the chalkboard or overhead projector. Depending on the time you have, this is an excellent opportunity to examine masculine versus feminine expectations for behavior. Since students eventually will be writing a comparison/contrast paper, practice comparison and contrast by creating a Venn diagram on the board. Use student input.

Example diagram

Rules for Both Genders

Women's Rules   **Men's Rules**

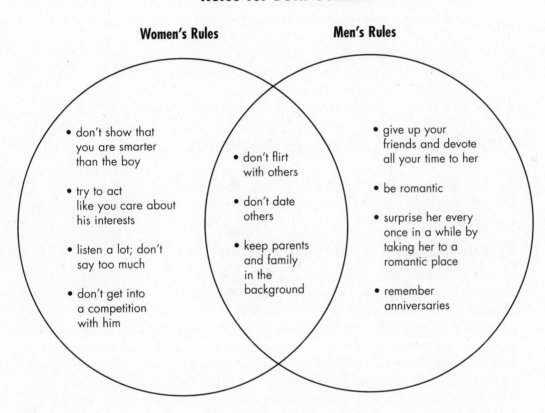

- don't show that you are smarter than the boy

- try to act like you care about his interests

- listen a lot; don't say too much

- don't get into a competition with him

- don't flirt with others

- don't date others

- keep parents and family in the background

- give up your friends and devote all your time to her

- be romantic

- surprise her every once in a while by taking her to a romantic place

- remember anniversaries

Regardless of whether the rules came from the women, men, or both genders, after the groups have all been polled, I point out that these are all spoken or unspoken rules for social behavior and that we probably knew a lot of them already, even though we may have not seen them written down before. Somehow, we learn these rules.

Prewriting Step 4: *Identifying Variations in the Rules*

Now, ask students to identify rules on the board that do not apply to them. If the class has done some work already on multicultural issues, they may be able to discuss how some rules may be different for different cultures. For example, in some cultures, a young woman may not ask out a boy for a date, while in other cultures this is permissible.

Prewriting Step 5: *Quickwrite*

The small group and whole group discussions of "unwritten" rules often take about fifty minutes. During the last five minutes of the period, ask the students to answer two questions in their journals:

1. Why do you think there are all of these rules?
2. What is one rule that has particularly affected you?

A sample quickwrite follows:

> The rule that has affected me most is the one about "don't get into competition with him." I've played tennis all my life and I was brought up to play to win. It's very hard to curb my own desire to come out on top. Why should I have to, anyway? It's just a game, right? But, then, why is it so important to me to win? Either way, if I win or let him win, I always feel funny afterwards. Why do Americans make sports so important? And why is the boy supposed to be better in sports than the girl?

Prewriting Step 6: *Sharing of Quickwrites*

The next session, have students share their responses to these questions, first in small groups, then with the whole class. Often, students bring up the idea that social rules are meant to protect people: sometimes the lovers themselves, sometimes their families.

Prewriting Step 7: *Dialectical Journal*

At this point I ask the students to do an assignment (as homework, if possible) that will begin to make connections between the students' own experiences and the two works of literature. They are to find places in both the play and the novel where the lovers' behavior is influenced by one of the unwritten rules for lovers of their respective cultures, or where the lovers are obviously breaking a rule. This may be made clear by something a character (either one of the lovers of someone in their society) has said or done. Once they find such passages, they are to record them in their journals, along with act, scene, and line, or, in the case of the novel, the page number. After each quoted passage, they are to explain in their own words what the rule is, as well as whether a similar rule exists in the student's own culture. Additionally, they should also record any similarities that they see in rules from both works of literature. (A sample dialectical journal is on the following page.)

Have students share their dialectical journals in small groups. Encourage them to add to their list of passages some of the passages noted by their peers. If time allows, have each group select one key passage from each work and report the unwritten rules of the respective cultures to the whole class.

Sample Dialectical Journal

Romeo and Juliet

Passage	What the Unwritten Rule Is	Similar Rules in My Culture
Juliet: Although I joy in thee,/ I have no joy of this contract tonight./ It is too rash, too unadvised, too sudden,/ Too like the lightning,...(II, ii, 116-119).	I think the unwritten rule Juliet is reacting to here goes something like, "You shouldn't let a relationship develop too quickly; things shouldn't go too far too quickly."	Yes, I think that this is still a rule in my culture, although many people break it. However, people who marry after a very short realtionship are sometimes joked about, and their marriage is regarded as one that may not last because they rushed things.

Spring Snow

Passage	What the Unwritten Rule Is	Similar Rules in My Culture
Tadeshina* says to Kiyoaki, "What do yo mean, young master? It's too late" (175).	Although she doesn't spell out the rule for Kiyoaki, she is letting him know that he is breaking a rule by asking to see Tadeshina's charge, Satoko, after Satoko has already been betrothed to another man.	This is certainly a rule in my culture. It is not proper for either a man or a woman to have a date with someone other than their betrothed.

* Note: Tadeshina plays a role somewhat like that of Juliet's nurse.

 **PROMPT**

Analyze how the unwritten rules for social behavior affect the young lovers in *Romeo and Juliet* and *Spring Snow*. In what ways do these rules of the game influence the lovers' actions and decisions? How are they punished for breaking some of the rules? Your paper should be written in standard analytical/expository form: introd uction, main body, conclusion. Open the paper in a way that grabs the reader's interest. Choose a pattern of development for the main body of your essay that lends itself best to the main points about the two works of literature you intend to compare and contrast. Be sure to refer to specific examples from each work and to quote from the texts to support your argument. Use transition words to logically develop your ideas and to keep the paper flowing. Include a final paragraph that gives your analysis a sense of closure.

Remember that a clear thesis, an interesting and thoughtful analysis, logically developed ideas, ample support, and a relatively error-free paper will help you convey your perceptions most effectively. The criteria upon which your paper will be evaluated will be provided for you before you begin writing your essay.

PRECOMPOSING

Precomposing Step 1: *Visually Representing Similarities*

This next step is valuable for the visual and kinesthetic learners in the class. Ask students to visually represent the relationship between the young lovers and their societies, and how the societies' rules affected them. *(I realize there are marked differences between Verona, 1594, and Tokyo, 1913, but I want them, at this point, to see the similarities. I am purposely vague about how they are to accomplish this, and I simply encourage them to be creative. There is no wrong way to do this assignment; the only way to fail is not to try. They still get frustrated that I won't tell them "exactly what I want," but I have to let them feel frustration at this point.)* Students end up doing drawings, flow charts, collages, even mobiles, as in the following example:

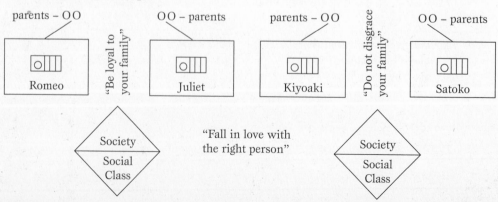

When the visual representations are due, ask students to share them with the class, explaining what they depict. Again, students not only learn from doing their own project, but also from seeing and hearing about the others. The concepts that the students come up with make excellent starting points for discussion, as well.

Precomposing Step 2: *Quickwrite*

When the presentations are done, I ask students to take five minutes and write down what they learned from this session. A sample quickwrite might look like this:

> Well, I can see that we're all affected. It's weird. Rules, rules, and more rules. Rules that we're not even aware of half the time. I wonder how these rules get communicated? No matter, it's clear that all societies have rules for relationships, and they're pretty strong. Break them and you're in deep trouble. But it gets to me how hypocritical the parents are in both of the works. It's like they lead rotten lives but they expect their kids to be perfect.

Precomposing Step 3: *Analyze Similarities, Differences*

Next, ask students to work in peer groups of three or four to look over their journal entries and share the information they have on "unwritten rules" in the two pieces of literature. Since they are going to be writing a paper on both works, they will need to compare and contrast. Thus, they will want to find rules that are important in both works, <u>and</u> they will want to show how differences in rules between the two societies make an important difference in the lives of the lovers. A sample list of similarities might look like this:

1. Don't show your emotions too openly, especially at first.
2. Don't get into a relationship that your parents would disapprove of.
3. Don't get overwhelmed by desire into doing something ill advised.
4. Avoid relationships that have to be maintained in secret.
5. Be honest with each other.
6. It's okay to seek help from a trusted adult.

Here is a small sample of some of the rules that are different between the two cultures:

1. In the Japanese culture, you should keep your emotions hidden and muted, whereas in Verona it's okay to be more open.
2. In the Japanese culture, your marriage should be made to give you a social advantage, whereas in Verona love can be part of the reason for marriage.

After they have shared similar or different rules as groups, ask students to individually choose the rules they want to focus on in writing their essays. Remind them that the better papers will explore fewer rules in depth.

Precomposing Step 4: *Microtheme*

In order to help students plan ahead, ask them to fill out the following microtheme sheet.

Microtheme

Introduction: Jot down two different ideas for opening your paper that will grab you reader's attention. Share these with a classmate and pick the more promising idea to develop.

         Idea 1   **Idea 2**

Main Body: Choose a pattern of development for your paper—Point-by-Point, One Side-at-a-Time, or Similarities/Differences. Then, use this space to generate the main points you will make, using that pattern of development and the supporting examples you will use to support those points.

      Main Points   **Supporting Details/Quotes**

-                •

                        •

-                •

                        •

-                •

                        •

-                •

Note: You may need to do a main points and supporting details list for both Romeo and Juliet *and* Spring Snow, *depending upon your selected method of development.*

Conclusion: Please do a ten-minute quickwrite to this question. What is the predominant message or impression that you would like your reader to get from your paper?

As they think of ways to write an introduction and grab their reader's attention, you may refer them to examples of hooks in the "My Name, My Self" lesson and the packet on *Ways to Write an Introduction for an Expository Paper* in the "Living in Life's Shadow" lesson. Both are elsewhere in this book.

As they are writing the main body of their essays, you may want to refer the students to the lesson "A Rose-Colored Life" by Sheila Koff in *Thinking/Writing: Fostering Critical Thinking Through Writing* (ed. Carol Booth Olson, New York: HarperCollins Publishers, 1992) to model Point-by-Point and One-Side-at-a-Time development. Additionally, the list of transitional words appended to this lesson may be helpful as students write this section of their essay. For rules for quoting from the text, see the guidelines appended to the "Living in Life's Shadow" lesson.

After students freewrite for their **conclusion,** ask them to consider whether the message with which they want to close reinforces a thesis they have asserted earlier in the paper or offers a new insight. Can they clearly point to the place in their paper where they advance their thesis?

 # WRITING

Review the prompt, and refer students to the criteria for evaluation on the scoring guide. Ask students to complete a rough draft, emphasizing the word *rough*. Urge them not to worry about mechanical errors at this point, and not to worry about the elegance of their style. The main thing is to make a start.

 # SHARING

Sharing Step 1: *Peer Group Critiques*

On the day that the rough draft is due, you may want to stamp the top of each paper as proof that the draft was turned in on time. (Students will attach all assignments to the back of the final draft in order to get full credit for the paper.) Ask students to get into peer response groups of their choosing (three to four per group). Before class, hand out the Peer Response Sheet on the next page.

In peer groups, they are to trade papers and to write their answers on the back of the drafts. Urge them to talk quietly to the writer if they need to, but push them along so that each paper ends up with three or four sets of comments.

Sharing Step 2: *Review the Critiqued Draft*

During the last five minutes, ask them to get their own papers back and to look over the comments, keeping in mind that some of the comments will be helpful, some will not. However, taken as a whole, the comments should give them direction when they revise. If they are not sure about any particular comment or are stumped about how to revise, then they are to see the teacher.

PEER RESPONSE SHEET

- Did the opening of the paper grab your interest? Why or why not?

- In your own words, describe the main point/thesis of this paper.

- Specifically what does the writer use to support the main point?

- For you, which was the most effective support? Why?

- What was something that the writer left out that might have made the paper more effective had it been included?

- What pattern of development did the author use for the main body of the paper?

- What comparisons did he/she make between the "rules of the game" in the two works?

- What "rules of the game" in the two works did he/she contrast?

- Please underline any parts of the paper that are either unclear or worded awkwardly.

- How logically developed was the argument?

- Does the conclusion establish a sense of closure for the essay?

- Do you have any other suggestions for improving the paper?

 **REVISING**

Students should revise their draft in light of the critiques of their peers. Before they turn in this draft, ask them to remove their name, replacing it with a four-digit number that they will quickly recognize (last four digits of their phone number, social security number, or their address, usually). As they turn in the revision, again stamp them, but this time do not return them directly to the writer; instead, redistribute the paper to other groups. Ask the groups to score the paper according to the rubric that was distributed at the time the students were given the prompt. (They will need to have the rubric out on their desks.) They are to write the score down on the back of the paper, then to write three text-specific comments (pointing to specific parts of the paper), and finally to sign their names. Remind them that they must be tactful, helpful, and legible in their comments. Again, push them along so that each paper gets evaluated by each person in the group.

As you collect the papers that have been evaluated by a group, skim over the scores and comments. If you find comments that are general or otherwise unhelpful, or if you find scores that vary widely, you may want to give the paper back to the group to improve the evaluation.

 EDITING

Editing Step 1: *Teacher Editing*

Instead of marking symbols to indicate errors on a final draft, I simply write the page number of the rule in the handbook. The student then has to look up the rule, write down the appropriate rule, and correct the errors on a final draft. *(I do not give credit on final drafts until the errors are corrected.)* If the student has lots of errors, I only mark the most serious ones. Therefore, when it is time to edit this comparison/contrast paper, I first have the student take out the final draft of an earlier assignment and look over the errors that he or she has corrected.

Editing Step 2: *Editing Groups*

Once students have reviewed previous drafts, ask them to form editing groups to help each other find those types of errors on the current paper.

If a student makes the same kinds of errors on the next paper, it will lower the grade. However, if the student has eliminated those errors, he or she will get a higher grade.

 **EVALUATION**

The following rubric may be used for self, peer, or teacher evaluation:

Rubric for Comparison/Contrast Paper

9–8   An excellent paper will have these qualities:

- a clearly stated thesis that relates to the assignment

- an opening that grabs the reader's interest

- comparison/contrast between the "rules of the game" in the two works that are important and relevant to the understanding of both works

- a body that contains several paragraphs and ample specific textual support, organized in a logical, coherent manner

- transitions wherever necessary

- a final paragraph that gives a sense of closure

- unusually perceptive understanding of the two works

- interesting, thoughtful analysis throughout

- generally free of editing errors (including no fragments, run-ons, comma splices, or errors in quoting from the text.)

7–6   This range will be used for a good paper that has a clear thesis, a good amount of support, and is well organized. It is distinguishable from a top-notch paper because it is less insightful, less interesting, or less readable (because of occasional editing problems.)

5–4   A paper in this range will have a clear thesis, and it will be organized well enough so that it can be read without significant confusion. However, the support, although present, is thin, so that the paper gives a sense of superficiality. Or, it may be an otherwise good paper that has too many editing errors.

3–2   A paper at this level will have significant problems in one or more of these areas:

- clear thesis

- organization

- support

- logical argument

- readability

- following the assignment

1   This score will be reserved for papers that are not written on the assigned topic.

EXTENSION ACTIVITIES

1. Comparing *The Sound of Waves* with *Romeo and Juliet*

Read Yukio Mishima's *The Sound of Waves*, another novel (this one short), which also has strong parallels to *Romeo and Juliet*.

2. Writing the Reflective Essay

Write a reflective essay exploring the sexism of the rules for the "game of romance" in either of the two literary works, or in the student's own culture.

3. Tracing "The Rules of the Game" to Modern Europe or Japan

Write a paper that traces the changes in the "rules of the game" (in Japan or in Europe) from the time in which *Romeo and Juliet* and *Spring Snow* were set to modern Europe or Japan.

Transitional Words

To mark an addition: *and, furthermore, next, moreover, in addition, again, also, likewise, similarly, finally, second, in the same respect, just as . . . so, concomitant with, interestingly*

To emphasize a contrast or alternative: *but, or, nor, neither, still, however, nevertheless, on the contrary, on the other hand, conversely, despite, aside from, although, even though*

To mark a conclusion: *therefore, thus, in conclusion, consequently, in consequence, as a result, in other words, accordingly, hence, subsequently, in summary, in the final analysis, finally, ultimately, in retrospect.*

To introduce an illustration or example: *for example, for instance, thus, hence, significantly, that us, again.*

Non Fiction

Featured Literature

"Letter to the U.S. Government"
by Chief Seattle

Grade Level
For Middle School

Thinking Level
Synthesis

Writing Domain
Sensory/Descriptive

Materials Needed:
• Paper for greeting cards
• Pens in 3 different colors
• Yellow highlighter pens

Suggested Supplementary Readings:
• *I Have Spoken: American History Through the Voices of the Indians* compiled by Virginia Irving Armstrong
• *Brother Eagle, Sister Sky a Message from Chief Seattle* with paintings by Susan Jeffers

A Special Place

by Mindy Moffatt

Overview

Using Chief Seattle's "Letter to the U.S. Government" as a point of departure, students write and illustrate a greeting card about a place that is special to them. Two points of view about the place are presented in the greeting card–that of the student who knows this place well, and the implied view of a person who has never been to this place and who, therefore, may not value it.

Objectives

THINKING SKILLS

Students will:

- *recall* places that are special and precious;
- *recognize* the unique qualities that any place might have and which make the place special to people;
- *describe* the special place clearly enough for readers to appreciate;
- *illustrate* a favorite place;
- *compare/contrast* images in the illustration with thoughts and/or feelings that others might have about the place;
- *speculate* what others, who do not know or value the special place, might think of the special place;
- *assess* the qualities of a special place so that others might also recognize how special the place can be.

WRITING SKILLS

Students will write an illustrated greeting card by:

- *creating* appropriate imagery to describe a place;
- *writing* a piece of found poetry;
- *composing* a personal note to the recipient of the card.

The Process

◈ PREWRITING/PREREADING

Prewriting Step 1: *Clustering*

As a whole class, cluster places that are special to people.

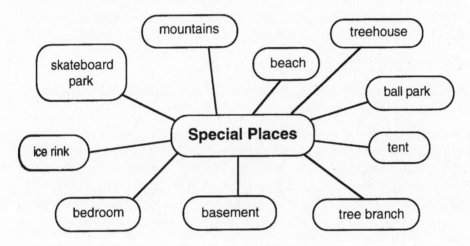

Prewriting Step 2: *Practice in Speculating*

Add offshoots to the cluster to speculate about how or why those places may be special to one person and not special to another.

After the class has clustered, students make their own clusters about favorite places. Then they freewrite about the places in their own clusters, explaining why each place is special.

 # WRITING/READING

Writing/Reading Step 1: *Oral Reading*

Provide each student with a copy of Chief Seattle's "Letter to the U.S. Government" (appended to this lesson) and read it to the whole class.

Writing/Reading Step 2: *Quaker Reading*

Instruct students to reread the letter silently and to underline words and/or phrases that they feel are significant.

Students read aloud any of their underlined words and/or phrases at random (without raising their hands to speak). Any part of the text may be read aloud and repeated. Continue this Quaker Reading until there is an extended pause that signifies most of the significant phrases have been read. *(Note: When middle school students do this activity for the first time, the Quaker Reading may take longer because of extended pauses between phrases. Once students are accustomed to this activity, only five to seven minutes is needed.)*

Writing/Reading Step 3: *Figurative Language*

Explain figurative language (similes and metaphors) to the class. Use examples from Chief Seattle's letter such as:

- "The perfumed flowers are our sisters; the deer, the horse, the great eagle, these are our brothers."
- "The shining water that moves in the streams and rivers is not just water but the blood of our ancestors."
- "He treats his mother, the earth, and his brother, the sky, as things to be bought, plundered, sold like sheep or bright beads."

Using two different colors, students find and identify metaphors and similes in Chief Seattle's letter by circling metaphors in one color and similes in another.

In small groups, students list the metaphors and similes they circled.

Writing/Reading Step 4: *Found Poetry*

In a third color of ink, have students underline other words and phrases in the text that create a sensory descriptive picture for them. Then, using their own underlined copies of Chief Seattle's letter, students each write a poem using the previously underlined words and phrases.

Students choose any words and phrases that reflect their thoughts and feelings and write them in any order or format. Students express their thoughts and feelings about the earth using Chief Seattle's words arranged in the students' individual ways. An example might be as follows:

(Note: The teacher should also write along with the students in order to use the teacher's work as a model for the class.)

> All things are connected
> Every
> shining pine needle
> Every
> sandy shore
> Every
> mist in the dark woods
> Every
> clearing and humming insect
> Holy, sacred
> Our sisters
> perfumed flowers
> Our brothers
> the deer, the horse, the great eagle
> The blood of our ancestors
> the shining water that moves in the streams and rivers
> The voice of my father's father
> the water's murmur
> Our mother
> the earth
> The same breath
> all things share
> The air shares its spirit with
> all the life it supports
> All things are
> connected
> Man did not weave the web of life:
> he is merely a strand in it, but
> remember
> Holy, sacred
> All things are connected.

Share found poems with the class by asking for volunteers to read their work aloud.

Writing/Reading Step 5: *Figurative Language Comparison Chart*

Chart the figurative descriptions in Chief Seattle's letter, using both the Chief's images and what he says are white man's images.

Item	Chief's Image	White Man's Image
earth	mother of the red man	enemy
flowers	sisters	
air	precious all of us share it	no notice of it
earth and sky	mother and brother	sheep or bright beads to be sold

Writing/Reading Step 6: *Drawing*

Ask students to draw a picture that symbolizes the opposing images on the chart as in the following picture.

In small groups, students share their drawings and evaluate the images that are the strongest. Discuss why some images are stronger than others.

PROMPT

You will write and illustrate a greeting card to another person, explaining why a favorite place is special to you. Images in your illustration must be related to the special place. Your writing will be in poetic free verse form and should include figurative language describing the special place. Speculate about thoughts of others who do not know or value the place. Include a personal note at the bottom of your card addressed to someone who might not value the place. Acknowledge that person's feelings and subtly persuade the person to rethink his or her position, using an appropriate tone.

Your writing should follow the conventions of standard written English, with particular emphasis on spelling and neatness. Because of the poetic nature of your writing, keep in mind that capital letters and punctuation affect the meaning of the poem.

PRECOMPOSING

Precomposing Step 1: *Student Clusters*

Each student returns to the cluster made about places that are special to them (from Prewriting Step 2).

Precomposing Step 2: *Drawing/Mapping*

Students choose one favorite place from their cluster and freewrite and draw a picture or map/drawing, of that place. Then, students label the picture, emphasizing the five senses. *(This drawing is a sketch of the place and will not be displayed on the final card. It is used to help the students remember as many details as possible about the place.)*

(See the example of the drawing/map on the next page of one student's memory of a vacant lot. This neighborhood playground became an exotic location in that student's imagination.)

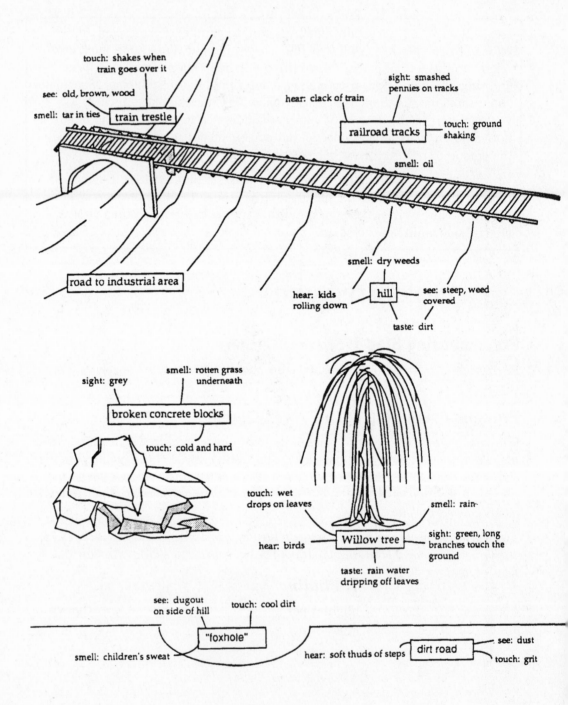

touch: shakes when
train goes over it

see: old, brown, wood

smell: tar in ties

train trestle

sight: smashed
pennies on tracks

hear: clack of train

railroad tracks

touch: ground
shaking

smell: oil

road to industrial area

smell: dry weeds

hear: kids
rolling down

hill

see: steep, weed
covered

taste: dirt

sight: grey

smell: rotten grass
underneath

broken concrete blocks

touch: cold and hard

touch: wet
drops on leaves

smell: rain

hear: birds

Willow tree

sight: green, long
branches touch the
ground

taste: rain water
dripping off leaves

see: dugout
on side of hill

touch: cool dirt

"foxhole"

hear: soft thuds of steps

dirt road

see: dust

touch: grit

smell: children's sweat

Precomposing Step 3: *Freewriting*

Students and teacher freewrite for ten to fifteen minutes about their own special place. *(Note: Instruct students to skip lines as they do their freewrite so that revisions will not demand that they rewrite their entire freewrite just to add more to their writing.)*

Precomposing Step 4: *Positive/Opposite Chart*

Students partially fill in the following chart about their special place. For each of the major items in their drawings, students think of a positive figurative image and also a quality or adjective to describe that image. Later, students think of what an opposite image might be and an opposite adjective or quality. However, have students leave the second two columns on their charts blank for the time being.

Example for drawing/map of vacant lot:

Item	Positive Image	Adjective	Opposite Image	Adjective
concrete blocks	Greek temple ruins	ancient		
willow tree	mother's arms	hugging		
railroad tracks	path	mystery		

Precomposing Step 5: *Revise Freewrites*

Students revise their freewrites, adding more sensory words, similes, and metaphors from their mapping and the partially completed positive/opposite chart.

Precomposing Step 6: *Finding Your Partner's "Golden Lines"*

With yellow highlighter pens, student partners share their freewrites with each other and highlight the "Golden Lines" in each other's writing. *(Golden Lines are those lines that a partner feels are significant and strong, thus "Golden.")*

Precomposing Step 7: *Finding Your Own Golden Lines*

With another color of highlighter pen (or a crayon or pen or pencil), the writer highlights his or her own Golden Lines.

 ## WRITING

Using found poetry techniques (as in the practice using Chief Seattle's letter), students write a poem found in their freewrites and Golden Lines.

SHARING/REVISING

Sharing/Revising Step 1: *Modeling*

Model how to manipulate the line breaks, punctuation, capitalization, etc., to make the free verse read poetically. *(The teacher can use his or her own found poem to demonstrate how moving the words and phrases can enhance the impact of the message.)*

Sharing/Revising Step 2: *Student Revision*

Students go back to their found poems and revise for emphasis, manipulating text for their desired impact.

Sharing/Revising Step 3: *Making the Greeting Card*

With hard stock paper (preferably legal size), fold the paper in half—top to bottom. On the outside front, students draw their special place or make a collage from magazine pictures. On the inside, students print their found poems.

At least five inches of space must be left open at the bottom of the text on the card.

Sharing/Revising Step 4: *Review Previous Cluster*

As a class, go back to Prewriting Step 2 to review the cluster to remember how a place that is positive to one person may be negative to another. Fill in a class chart about positive and negative images and adjectives.

Example:

Item	Positive Image	Adjective	Opposite Image	Adjective
mountain peaks	crown	shimmering	knife blade	cutting
trails	paths	welcoming	dusty paths to nowhere	exhausting
views	sights	panoramic	nightmare	treacherous

Sharing/Revising Step 5: *Adding to Positive/Opposite Chart*

Using their own incomplete positive/opposite chart, students complete the negative images and adjectives in the corresponding columns, thinking about what someone else might think of as the opposite images of each of the student's positive ones and adding that image in the opposite column along with an adjective to describe it.

Sharing/Revising Step 6: *Note Writing*

From the chart, model writing a note that acknowledges another person's point of view. After identifying an audience, subtly try to persuade the audience to rethink his or her opinion. (The teacher may use the following example or write a note based on the teacher's special place, using the positive/opposite chart that the teacher has filled out.)

Example:

Dear _____ ,

Although the mountains seem treacherous and hostile to you, they can also be peaceful and inviting. I know that you may feel that heights are things to be afraid of, with peaks shaped like knife blades that one can fall from. But the breathtaking scenery from a mountain peak can make your heart soar too. The trails to the top may seem like dusty paths leading nowhere, which can cause you to lose your way. But when you arrive at the top, you may actually "find" yourself. I hope my poem will help you see the mountains with new eyes.

On a piece of scratch paper *(not the greeting card),* students write their own note after identifying a specific audience. Students use their positive/opposite charts to pinpoint another person's opposite point of view.

 **SHARING**

Sharing Step 1: *Role-Play Response*

Students trade with a partner who plays the role of the audience. The partner writes back to the author to say whether the found poem and the note changed his or her perception.

Sharing Step 2: *Self-Revision Checklist*

Students take another look at their papers, using the following checklist.

SELF-REVISION CHECKLIST			
	Yes	No	Could Be Better
My greeting card has both illustrations and text that convey why a place is special to me.			
My found poem has strong sensory details and uses similes and metaphors to effectively convey feeling.			
The capital letters and line breaks add to, rather than detract from, the meaning of my poem.			
I have speculated about what someone who doesn't value my place would think and have written a note that anticipates his or her point of view and offers a counter point of view. My note has an appropriate tone.			
My card and note convinced my response partner to see my place with new eyes.			

REVISING

Taking both their partner's response and their own checklist into consideration, writers revise their greeting cards.

EDITING

In triads, students proofread each other's cards for:
- correct spelling;
- appropriate punctuation;
- appropriate use of capital and lower-case letters;
- correct sentence structure in the note.

EVALUATION

Rubric

5–6 This greeting card has both illustrations and text that convey why a place is special to one person. The found poem has strong sensory details and uses similes and metaphors effectively to convey feeling. The capital letters, line breaks, and punctuation add to, rather than detract from, the meaning of the poem. The note shows that the student has speculated about how someone who doesn't value his or her place would feel; the note antici pates the negative point of view and offers an alternative, positive view in an appropriate tone.

4 This greeting card has both illustrations and text that convey why a place is special to one person. However, fewer sensory details, images, and similes and metaphors are used and tone may not be appropriate. The capital letters, line breaks, and punctuation may confuse the reader to some extent. Also, speculation of what another may think of the place is not as strong as in a 5–6 paper.

3 This paper has text and illustrations; however they do not clearly convey why a place is special to one person. There are few sensory details, images, and metaphors and similes that tell us about the special place rather than show us the special place. The capital letters, line breaks, and punctuation confuse the reader. The speculation of what another may think of the place is weak or disconnected to the text. Tone may be inappropriate.

1–2 This paper needs more work with peer partners and the teacher to demonstrate knowledge of the writing and thinking techniques emphasized in this lesson.

POSTWRITING

After evaluation, mail cards to the audience. Allow time and opportunity in class to discuss responses to the cards, whether the responses are verbal or written. Recognize that responses may take time in coming back to students and that any class time may permit only one or two responses on any day.

EXTENSION ACTIVITIES

1. *Letter to the Editor*

Instead of a poem/card, students may write their text as a letter to the editor and send it in to a newspaper or magazine.

2. *Ecological Concerns*

Students may write about an ecological concern they have for saving the environment.

3. *Comparison/Contrast*

Note: The accuracy of the translation of Chief Seattle's letter used as the basis for this lesson (Prentice-Hall) has recently been brought into question. You might want to have students read a more faithful translation (from I Have Spoken*) and compare it with the version that is more widely anthologized and write an essay comparing and contrasting the two versions and speculating upon the reasons for the variations they find.*

Featured Literature

Letter to the U.S. Government
by Chief Seattle

"We are part of the earth and it is part of us."

How can you buy or sell the sky, the warmth of the land? The idea is strange to us.

If we do not own the freshness of the air and the sparkle of the water, how can you buy them?

Every part of the earth is sacred to my people.

Every shining pine needle, every sandy shore, every mist in the dark woods, every clearing and humming insect is holy in the memory and experience of my people. The sap which courses through the trees carries the memories of the red man.

The white man's dead forget the country of their birth when they go to walk among the stars. Our dead never forget this beautiful earth, for it is the mother of the red man.

We are part of the earth and it is part of us. The perfumed flowers are our sisters; the deer, the horse, the great eagle, these are our brothers.

The rocky crests, the juices in the meadows, the body heat of the pony, and man—all belong to the same family.

So, when the Great Chief in Washington sends word that he wishes to buy our land, he asks much of us. The Great Chief sends word he will reserve us a place so that we can live comfortably to ourselves.

He will be our father and we will be his children. So we will consider your offer to buy our land.

But it will not be easy. For this land is sacred to us.

This shining water that moves in the streams and rivers is not just water but the blood of our ancestors.

If we sell you land, you must remember that it is sacred and that each ghostly reflection in the clear water of the lakes tells of events and memories in the life of my people.

The water's murmur is the voice of my father's father.

The rivers are our brothers, they quench our thirst. The rivers carry our canoes, and feed our children. If we sell you our land, you must remember, and teach your children, that the rivers are our brothers, and yours, and you must henceforth give the rivers the kindness you would give any brother.

We know that the white man does not understand our ways. One portion of land is the same to him as the next, for he is a stranger who comes in the night and takes from the land whatever he needs.

The earth is not his brother, but his enemy, and when he has conquered it, he moves on.

He leaves his father's graves behind, and he does not care. He kidnaps the earth from the children, and he does not care.

His father's grave and his children's birthright, are forgotten. He treats his mother, the earth, and his brother, the sky, as things to be bought, plundered, sold like sheep or bright beads.

His appetite will devour the earth and leave behind only a desert.

I do not know. Our ways are different from your ways.

The sight of your cities pains the eyes of the red man. But perhaps it is because the red man is a savage and does not understand.

There is no quiet place in the white man's cities. No place to hear the unfurling of leaves in spring, or the rustle of an insect's wings.

But perhaps it is because I am a savage and do not understand.

The clatter only seems to insult the ears. And what is there to life if a man cannot hear the lonely cry of the whippoorwill or the arguments of the frogs around a pond at night? I am a red man and do not understand.

The Indian prefers the soft sound of the wind darting over the face of a pond, and the smell of the wind itself, cleaned by a midday rain, or scented with the piñon pine.

The air is precious to the red man, for all things share the same breath—the beast, the tree, the man, they share the same breath.

The white man does not seem to notice the air he breathes. Like a man dying for many days, he is numb to the stench.

But if we sell you the land, you must remember that the air is precious to us, that the air shares its spirit with all the life it supports. The wind that gave our grandfather his first breath also receives his last sigh.

And if we sell you our land, you must keep it apart and sacred, as a place where even the white man can go to taste the wind that is sweetened by the meadow's flowers.

So we will consider your offer to buy our land. If we decide to accept, I will make one condition: the white man must treat the beasts of this land as his brother.

I am a savage and I do not understand any other way.

I have seen a thousand rotting buffaloes on the prairie, left by the white man who shot them from a passing train.

I am a savage and I do not understand how the smoking iron horse can be more important than the buffalo that we kill only to stay alive.

What is man without the beasts? If all the beasts were gone, man would die from a great loneliness of spirit.

For whatever happens to the beasts, soon happens to man. All things are connected.

You must teach your children that the ground beneath their feet is the ashes of your grandfathers. So that they will respect the land, tell your children that the earth is rich with the lives of our kin.

Teach your children what we have taught our children, that the earth is our mother.

Whatever befalls the earth befalls the sons of the earth. If men spit upon the ground, they spit upon themselves.

This we know: the earth does not belong to man: man belongs to the earth. This we know.

All things are connected like the blood which unites one family. All things are connected.

Whatever befalls the earth befalls the sons of the earth. Man did not weave the web of life: he is merely a strand in it. Whatever he does to the web, he does to himself.

Even the white man, whose God walks and talks with him as friend to friend, cannot be exempt from the common destiny.

We may be brothers after all.

We shall see.

One thing we know, which the white man may one day discover—our God is the same God.

You think, now, that you own Him as you wish to own our land; but you cannot. He is the God of man, and His compassion is equal for the red man and the white.

This earth is precious to Him, and to harm the earth is to heap contempt on its Creator.

The whites too shall pass; perhaps sooner than all other tribes. Contaminate your bed, and you will one night suffocate in your own waste.

But in your perishing you will shine brightly, fired by the strength of the God who brought you to this land and for some special purpose gave you dominion over this land and over the red man.

That destiny is a mystery to us, for we do not understand when the buffalo are all slaughtered, the wild horses are tamed, the secret corners of the forest heavy with scent of many men, and the view of the ripe hills blotted by talking wires.

Where is the thicket? Gone.

Where is the eagle? Gone

The end of living and the beginning of survival.

"In our increasingly shrinking world, it is important we learn to celebrate our differences and rejoice in our similarities. Learning to accept and appreciate cultural diversity is of the utmost importance if we are to eliminate the ravages of racial and ethnic strife. The teaching of cultural diversity materials in the schools is a grand step toward achieving mutual respect among an ethnically and racially diverse population."

Maria Herrera-Sobek

Professor, Spanish and Portugese, University of California, Irvine; author of *Beyond Stereotypes: The Critical Analysis of Chicana Literature*

Featured Literature

The Keeping Quilt
by Patricia Polacco

Grade Level
For Middle School
(can also be adapted for
elementary and high
school level)

Thinking Level
Analysis

Writing Domain
Analytical/Expository

Materials Needed
• Construction paper
• Rulers
• Scissors
• Glue
• Crayons, pens, paints
• String, yarn, or ribbon
  If making quilt:
• 6 yards of cotton fabric
  in 4–5 coordinating
  fabrics
• Thread
• 1 package of batting
• 4 yards of cotton muslin
• Tacky glue

**Suggested
Supplementary
Readings**
A list of folk tales from
various cultures is
located at the end of
this lesson.

The Class Quilt:
A Multicultural Experience

by Dale Sprowl

Overview

After creating a class quilt which demonstrates their own unique family heritages and reading and discussing books which focus on quilts and folk-tales from their various cultures, students will analyze the diversity of their own class and draw conclusions about what people of all cultures have in common and how they are different.

Objectives

THINKING SKILLS

Students will:

- *describe* and *explain* symbols on their personal quilt square;
- *compare* and *contrast* what the student has in common with other students in the class;
- *compare* and *contrast* folk tales from their various cultures;
- *make generalizations* from specific facts and draw conclusions about how people the world over are alike and how each culture is different.

WRITING SKILLS

Each student will:

- *describe* and *explain* the significance of symbols on their quilt square;
- *logically develop* a three-part analytical/expository essay;
- *use* specific examples to support generalizations about various cultures;
- *use* transitional words to link sentences and paragraphs;
- *follow* the conventions of written English.

The Process

The idea for a class quilt comes from Marilyn Colyar at San Marino High School. *(See Extension Activities.)* Her idea of creating a quilt square with symbols that represent a student's family heritage is included in the prewriting section. This lesson will take about twenty hours of class time. Middle school and high school teachers might want to use this lesson as an "into" activity for Scott Edward's "A Mother's Decision" lesson elsewhere in this book, which is based on Alice Walker's story "Everyday Use."

 PREWRITING

Tell the class that they will be creating a quilt with each student contributing an individual square that represents his or her family's heritage.

Prewriting Step 1: *Clustering*

Cluster the word *quilt*. A sample cluster is shown on the next page.

Then, discuss any personal memories or anecdotes students may want to share about quilts.

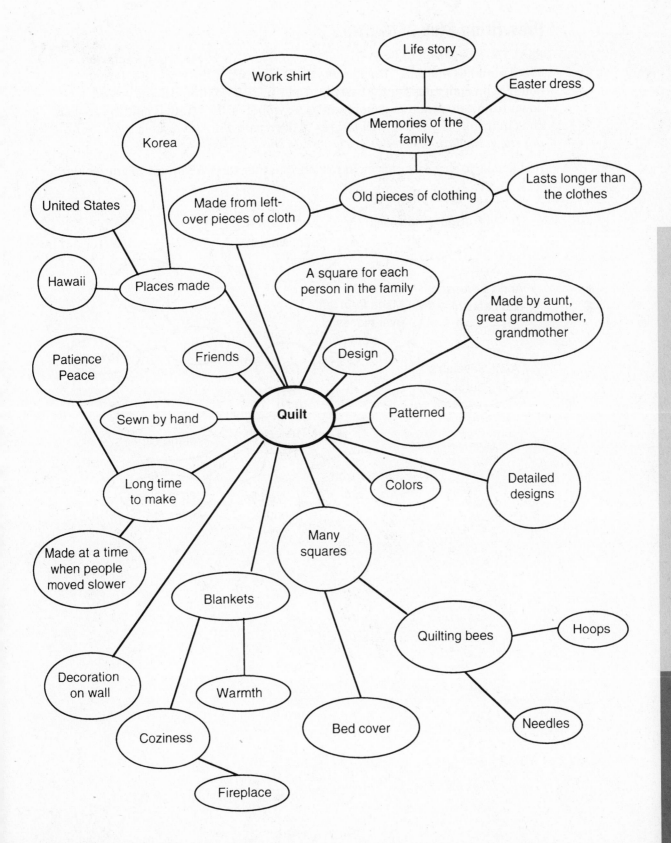

Prewriting Step 2: *Reading*

Read *The Keeping Quilt* by Patricia Polacco (New York: Simon and Schuster, 1988) aloud to the class. *The Keeping Quilt* chronicles the story of a Jewish family who emigrates from Russia to America and the quilt that is passed down from generation to generation as a symbol of the family's cultural roots and enduring love. (Note: *You may have to prepare older students to enjoy this story. Explain that children's books can speak to people of all ages.*)

Add details to the class cluster in response to the story. Additions might include:

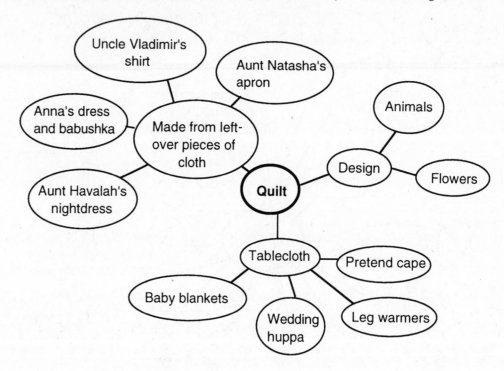

Note: Additional children's books focusing on quilts that you might want to share include:

The Patchwork Quilt by Valerie Flourney, New York: Dial Book for Young Readers, 1985. *(African American)*

The Quilt by Ann Jones, New York: Greenwillow Books, 1984. *(European American)*

The Josephina Story Quilt by Eleanor Coerr, New York: Harper & Row and Bruce Degan, 1986. *(Frontier American)*

Sam Johnson and the Blue Ribbon Quilt by Lisa Campbell Ernst, (New York: Lothrop, Lee and Shepard Books, 1983. *(Frontier American)*

Bizzy Bones and the Lost Quilt by Jacqueline Briggs Martin, New York: Lothrop, Lee and Shepard Books, 1988. *(Animal Story)*

The Quilt Story by Tony Johnston, New York: G.P. Putnam's Sons, 1985. *(Frontier American)*

Tar Beach by Faith Ringgold, New York: Crown Publishers, 1991. *(African American)*

Prewriting Step 3: *Keeping Quilt Family Tree*

In order to prepare students to create their own family tree, have them create a family tree for Patricia Polacco's family. A sample family tree might look like the following:

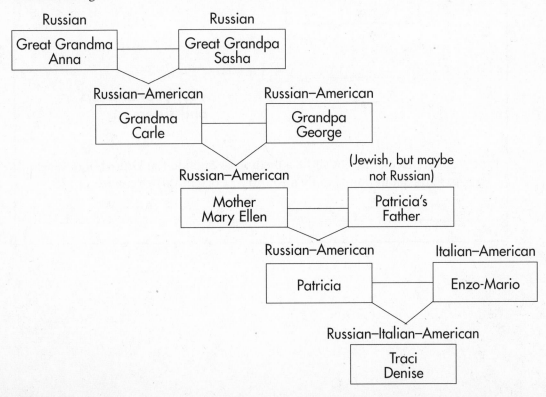

Prewriting Step 4: *Family Research*

Explain to the students that the class will be creating a quilt, with each square representing one student's family heritage. In order to accurately represent their own family backgrounds, they will need to do some research. The following activities will require help from their parents or grandparents:

- A Family Tree
- A Family Interest Inventory
- Discussion of Family Quilts and Other Heirlooms

Allow for an extended homework assignment so that students have time to interview their parents or other relatives in order to complete the following:

A. Family Tree

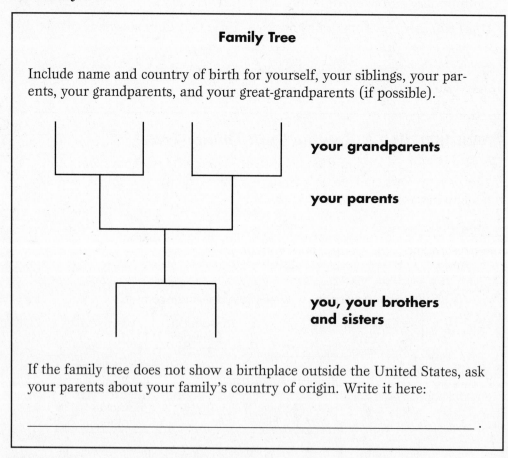

Family Tree

Include name and country of birth for yourself, your siblings, your parents, your grandparents, and your great-grandparents (if possible).

your grandparents

your parents

you, your brothers and sisters

If the family tree does not show a birthplace outside the United States, ask your parents about your family's country of origin. Write it here:

_____.

Student Model of Family Tree:

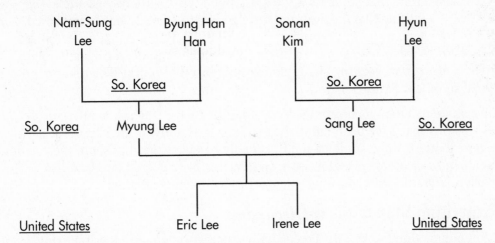

Note: *The Family Tree and Family Interest Inventory may bring up some sensitive issues relating to families. Teachers should use their discretion in deciding whether to use these activities or to adapt them for their students. An additional discussion that broadens the definition of what a family is might be appropriate.*

B. Family Interest Inventory

Family Interest Inventory

Use the information from your family to complete the following chart:

Family pet (name and type) _____

Favorite vacation spot _____

Favorite restaurant _____

Favorite special food _____

Family activity, hobby, interest and/or collection _____

_____

_____

Religion _____

Family tradition(s) _____

_____

_____

C. Family Quilts or Other Heirlooms

At the same time that students are researching their family backgrounds, they can ask if anything like the quilt in Patricia Polacco's family has been passed down from generation to generation in their family. Explain that other valued possessions, or heirlooms, passed down in a family might be a ring, a family Bible, a music box, rocking chair, photograph, or other object which has emotional significance for the family.

Give students an opportunity to share what they have learned about valued possessions that have been handed down in their family. If the parents feel secure about it, some students might actually be encouraged to share their own family quilt or other special possession in class. They should be asked to explain why this object has special significance for their family.

Prewriting Step 5: *Class Discussion*

After completing the Family Tree, Family Interest Inventory, and inquiring about family heirlooms, conduct a class discussion.

A. Family Tree

List on the board the countries of origin for each family in the class. If appropriate, identify the locations of countries on a map or globe.

> ### Sample List of Countries of Origin
>
> | | |
> |---|---|
> | Iran | Ireland |
> | Vietnam | Italy |
> | Korea | Philippines |
> | China | Poland |
> | Germany | Taiwan |
> | England | France |
> | United States (American Indian) | |

Have the class make some generalizations based on this list.

Examples:

- We have a well-rounded class.
- The students' families come from many different places.
- Some people from our class were born in other countries, such as Korea and Taiwan.
- Many people in our class were born in America.
- Many of our grandparents and great-grandparents immigrated from other countries.
- Many students' families originated in Asia.
- Many students' families originated in Europe.
- Some students' families originated in Africa.
- Two of our students are of American Indian origin.

Have students copy these models for their notes.

B. Family Interest Inventory

Tally the results of the Family Interest Inventory on the board. For example:

Family Pets	Vacation Spots	Restaurant/Foods
dog	Sun River	El Capitan
cat	Mammoth	Bullwinkles
fish	Palm Desert	hot dogs
bird	national parks	pizza
snake	beach	Kolbi
mouse	Las Vegas	egg rolls
hamster	San Diego	Chinese noodles

Activity/Sports/ Hobby/Collection	Religion	Traditions
snowskiing	Christian	presents Christmas morning
tennis	Jewish	money on New Year's
movies	Buddhist	special birthday cake
baseball	Bahai	special birthday candle
puzzles	Moslem	always plays volleyball on
games	Catholic	Christmas

Have a class discussion and make some generalizations based on this tally.

Examples:

- Most of the major religions of the world are represented in our class.
- Many families have a favorite food they enjoy.
- Most people like pizza.
- Many families take vacations to a special place together.
- Many families enjoy sports together.
- Most families have pet dogs or cats.
- Many families have a special tradition.
- A few families share a special collection.

Have students copy these model sentences for their notes.

Prewriting Step 6: *Library Research*

Schedule a library day so that students can find pictures of the flag(s) of the country(ies) of their origin. Recreate a flag by drawing, painting, or cutting construction paper. Students will have from one to four flags.

Prewriting Step 7: *Choosing Symbols*

After the class discussion of the family tree, the Family Interest Inventory, the discussion about family heirlooms, and the library flag research, have the students choose three to five things they would like to symbolize on their quilt squares. The flag could be one of the symbols. They can put an asterisk next to the items they have chosen on the Family Interest Inventory. Ask the class what choices Patricia Polacco would have on her quilt square, i.e., a gold coin, a loaf of bread, salt, a cup of wine, Russian and Italian flags, or a star of David.

Using the story *The Keeping Quilt,* model for the students on the overhead what Patricia Polacco might put on a quilt square.

On scratch paper, have students draw simple symbols for the things they have chosen. Tell them to keep the shapes simple, as it will be difficult to cut fabric in complicated shapes. Avoid words, except perhaps simple initials.

Prewriting Step 8: *Planning on Paper Squares*

Distribute thirteen-by-thirteen-inch construction paper squares. Have students use a ruler to draw a one-inch margin around the four edges of the square. This will allow a five-eighths inch margin plus a small margin for sewing fabric. Have students plan their quilt squares by cutting out paper symbols and gluing them in position.

Prewriting Step 9: *Small Group Sharing*

When paper quilt squares have been completed, have students work in small groups to explain each symbol in their quilt square, why they chose it, and why it is important.

Note: Several teachers have adapted this lesson and worked quite successfully toward a paper quilt as a final product rather than a cloth quilt. Holes can be punched in the corners of paper quilt squares that can then be tied together with yarn, string, or ribbon. A felt quilt is another option.

Before allowing students to begin fabric squares, the teacher should check each paper square, respond, and give suggestions on how to avoid possible problems:

- too crowded
- too detailed
- symbols in margin
- unbalanced symbols

Here are some examples of well-balanced quilt squares.

Quilt Square Examples

 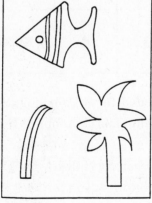 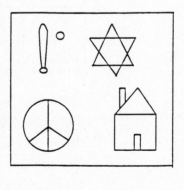

Prewriting Step 10: *Fabric Quilt Squares*

You will need a total of six yards of fabric in four to five coordinating fabrics (solids and small prints work best), which includes about one-half yard of each fabric to cut as scraps to make the symbols. This will allow for a rectangular quilt of thirty-five squares (13 x 13 inches). The teacher should plan the layout first. (Numbers indicate the same fabric for one possible plan.)

1	3	4	3	1
3	4	3	4	3
4	3	2	3	4
3	2	3	2	3
4	3	2	3	4
3	4	3	4	3
1	3	4	3	1

Materials Needed for a Fabric Quilt

Six yards of cotton fabric in four to five coordinating fabrics
thread
One package of batting (full-size bed)
Four yards of cotton muslin for backing
tacky glue

Distribute to each student a thirteen-by-thirteen-inch square with four to five coordinating scraps to each student. Have students cut and place their fabric symbols on their squares. Check the layout before allowing students to sew or glue *(use tacky glue)*. Be sure to remind them about the one-inch margin. Assign a due date to collect the squares. When they have been collected, sew the squares together (or get a parent to do so). For the backing you will need four yards of fabric *(to be pieced)* or a full-size sheet. Sew the quilt onto the backing, right sides together, as if it were a large pillowcase. Leave one side open. Then turn it right side out. Stuff with batting *(available at fabric stores)*. Sew the open end together turning in the cut edges. Hand stitch on corners of squares or machine stitch on some of the seams of the squares to keep the batting from slipping.

Prewriting Step 11: *Journal Entry*

Have students do a practical/informative journal entry entitled, "How I Planned and Made My Quilt Square." Before students write, elicit a list on the board of the steps taken to make a quilt square:

- Reading the quilt stories
- Making and discussing the family trees
- Listing the common interests of each family
- Discussing family heirlooms
- Doing library research on flags
- Choosing things to symbolize
- Drawing symbols
- Making the paper quilt square
- Cutting and applying the fabric to the square

Prewriting Step 12: *Transitional Words*

Instruct students in using transitional words such as *first, second, third,* and/or *then, next, following that, finally,* or *lastly.* Here is one example from a sixth-grade boy:

> The first step in planning the quilt square was making a family tree. We wrote down three generations of our family and where they originated. I learned most of the Chinese names in my family. Next, we listed our family's religion, sport, vacation place, restaurant, hobby etc. Then, we went to the library to research our flags. Following that, we chose items to symbolize. They had to be simple because we were putting them on our quilt square.

Prewriting Step 13: *Quilt Square I.D.*

When the quilt has been stuffed with batting and backed with a plain fabric, have the students complete a form with the following information. These forms can then be safety-pinned to the back of each student's square for future identification.

Name _____ Grade _____

School _____

Country(ies) of Origin _____

Favorite Recipe _____

Favorite Folktale _____

Symbols on My Quilt Square _____

Prewriting Step 14: *Read-Around of Folk Tales*

Go to the library and collect one to two folk tales from each of the countries represented in your class, Dewey Decimal 398.2 (or have students collect and bring their favorite folk tales). Tell your students that folk tales are another way to see how people the world over are united and how various cultures have both similarities and differences. Have students work in groups of three to five. Give each group one folk tale. Have one student read aloud the folk tale to the group. Allow approximately ten minutes to read one story. If a group finishes early, give them a short book to fill in the time. When most groups have finished, pass the books to the next group in rotation. Continue this procedure as long as students are interested (up to one hour). Each group will then have read at least six books. (Option: Read one folk tale aloud to the class each day during this unit.)

Prewriting Step 15: *Class Discussion of Folk Tales*

Ask students to compare and generalize about the folk tales they have read. List comments on the board, which students copy for their notes.

Examples:

- The Japanese story *Issunboshi* is a lot like Thumbelina.
- The book *In the Land of the Small Dragon* is just like Cinderella except it's from Vietnam.
- Some of the folk tales relate to a familiar story.
- It seems that all countries have folk tales.

Prewriting Step 16: *A Bibliography of Folk Tales*

See the list appended to this lesson.

PROMPT

We have examined similarities and differences among the people in our class by creating a class quilt and by reading folk tales from our various cultures.

Part I   Describe your quilt square and explain each of the three to five symbols that represent your family. Tell why you chose each symbol.

Part II   Our quilt shows that we are all part of the same class and that each person is special and unique but different from one another. Looking at the quilt, explain at least three general or specific ways that you are like the other people in our class. Explain at least three specific ways you are different. Include transitional words as you discuss both similarities and differences.

Part III   The research we have done on our own families and the folk tales we have read show that each country has its own special characteristics that make it distinct and that, at the same time, cultures have many things in common. On the basis of the class discussions we have had and the folk tales you have read, discuss at least three ways that entire cultures are alike and three ways that cultures are different. Use specific examples to support your generalizations and transitional words to connect sentences and paragraphs.

(Note: For younger students, it would be appropriate to introduce and write about each part of the prompt on a separate day.)

 PRECOMPOSING

Precomposing Step 1: *Class Discussion*

Display the quilt and discuss its symbols. Discuss each part of the prompt at length. Leave the quilt up during the remainder of the lesson.

A. Part I

Have students refer back to Prewriting Step 13 where they described how they made their quilt square. Have them use this freewrite as a model to describe their quilt square and explain its symbols.

B. Part II

Have partners or triads go to the quilt and discuss specific similarities and differences of their squares. From the class, elicit generalizations and specific examples for Parts II and write them on the board. Instruct students in how to use transitional words to give specific examples:

- *for example*
- *such as*
- *as follows*

Have students copy the model sentences for their notes.

Sample Generalizations with Examples:

- Most people in our class like sports such as soccer, baseball, and tennis.
- One of the ways I am different from the people in our class is that I like the piano and most people don't.
- One of the things I have in common with the people in our class is my religion. I am a Christian and so are many others. Some other religions in our class are Jewish, Moslem, and Bahai.
- Almost everyone in our class has a special vacation spot. My family travels to Sun River, whereas other families go to Palm Desert, Mammoth, Las Vegas, and San Diego.

C. Part III

Elicit generalizations and specific examples for Part III such as:

- Our class comes from many different cultural backgrounds. We come from twenty different countries in the continents of Asia, Africa, and Europe.
- I think students in various countries would have some sports in common, such as soccer. Some countries might like different sports.
- Another way we are alike is that most countries have schools.
- Many cultures in various countries have one main religion, while we have many.
- People in all cultures have families.
- People the world over have languages.
- Almost all young people go to school, but in China students start at the age of three.
- In France, young children drink wine. In other countries this is not legal.
- Most countries have folk tales. Many countries have a story similar to Cinderella.
- Most cultures have their own food, art, and music.

Precomposing Step 2: *Frames*

Have students use these frames to write several more ideas that they would like to include in their writing.

Part II: Most people in our class enjoy _(food)_ such as _(pizza)_, _(Mc Donalds)_, and _(Chinese food)_.

One thing I have in common with other students in our class is:

_____(I like sports.)_____

One way I am different from other students in our class is:

_____(I do not play a musical instrument.)_____

Part III: All people have _(family traditions)_; some people in _(China give money on New Year's)_, while others _(in Europe and America give presents on Christmas)_.

People the world over enjoy _(folk tales)_; many of them have similar themes or messages.

Almost all people have _(religions)_, but they may be different ones, for example, _(Christianity)_, _(Catholicism)_, _(Judaism)_, _(Buddhism)_, and _(Islam)_.

 ## WRITING

Before students write, allow them to compile all of their notes from the prewriting and precomposing steps. Be sure the quilt is displayed and the students have access to it while they are writing. It might be appropriate to write each of three sections on separate days.

 ## SHARING

If writing is done on separate days, have students share after each part. Each small group should complete the following response sheet after each student reads his or her paper.

Response Sheet

		Yes	No
Part I	Describes individual quilt square		
	Explains each of three to five symbols on square		
	Tells why each symbol was chosen		
	Includes transitional words		
Part II	Explains three ways you are like the other members of our class		
	Explains three specific ways you are different from the other members of our class		
	Includes transitional words		
Part III	Discusses three ways people the world over are alike		
	Discusses three ways various cultures are different		
	Uses specific examples to support generalization		
	Includes transitional words		

 REVISING

Allow students time to revise based on the feedback received in response groups. Have them share the Response Sheet with their parents and revise at home.

 EDITING

Before students submit the final draft for evaluating, they have a peer, parent, or teacher act as an editor/partner. They check for paraphrasing, spelling, grammar, punctuation, and sentence structure.

 EVALUATION

Teacher assigns one point for each of the items on the response sheet.

10–11 papers are excellent.
   9 papers are very good.
   8 papers are average.
   7 papers are fair.
   6 or below papers are below average.

Student Models

Part I Model: I chose to put a boogie board on my square because my family loves to boogie board. My boogie board is blue with black fins. My family goes to the beach a lot. Next, I put a Vietnamese flag on my square because my family came from Vietnam. I wouldn't want to go to that country, because it is not a free country. My family spends vacations in Hawaii a lot and loves it there. We always watch native dances. So, I put waves on my quilt square. My family goes to Maui. I like Maui the best because the waves are the best. My family will go to Hawaii and stay for 7 days. We will go to Hawaii and Waikiki.

Jimmy Nguyen—Grade 6

Part II Model: One thing our class has in common is that we come from places all over the world like Vietnam, Korea, Sweden, Holland, and many many more. It also seems like we have many religions such as: Christians, Catholics, and Jews. The list could go on and on. In addition, most of our class likes sports. I know that because there are symbols for skiing, badminton, tennis, baseball, football, and soccer. My quilt square shows that I am like the others because I play a sport and like to do things some other people like to do—like watching T.V and traveling. Even though we have different religions and different origins, we all share a religious background and cultural origin. We also have some of the same hobbies. Isn't that neat when we come from different places? Some of the differences I have apart from theirs are that I have a pet fish. Most people (well I think) don't have fish as pets. I originated in Vietnam. Most people in our class didn't originate in Vietnam. Finally, another difference is that I am me. Nobody else can be exactly like me.

Anh Bui—Grade 6

Part III Model: We all have religion. We also have different places we originally came from. Another thing we have in common is we all are human beings. We all have families and God loves us. We are not alike because we all have different races, different ways to celebrate holidays. Finally, each culture is different and special in different ways. For example, the Chinese culture and the American culture are very different. You see the Chinese believe in families, good education, respecting elders, and they talk a lot about food. They don't care about being fat. But Americans on the other hand, are independent. Most of them don't believe that strongly in education. They think a great deal about what they look like and they don't think as much as Chinese do about respecting elders.

Charlene Wang—Grade 4

EXTENSION ACTIVITIES

1. **Historical Study**
   Add a historical study of the immigrant experience in America to this unit *(See Marilyn Colyar's lesson, "New Americans: The Immigrant Experience in Literature and Media." Colyar is at San Marino High School in San Marino, CA)*. Use Oscar Handlin's *The Immigrants* for school readings.

2. **International Cookbook**
   Create an international cookbook. Have students bring a favorite recipe that is a part of their cultural heritage. Rewrite the recipe so that students of the same age could prepare it. Reproduce a class set. Have students prepare and share their recipes. Have a contest to create a cover.

3. **Passport to Peace**
   Use the Passport to Peace Program created by Paul Portner at the Riverdale School in the Garden Grove Unified School District. The students receive a "Passport to Peace" in the form of an actual passport. It contains twenty activities, such as writing a peace poem, writing a letter to the President, reading books about peace, learning to say hello in many languages, etc.

4. **Literature Share Day**
   Have students bring their own favorite literature selection from their cultural background. Have students share the literature or a synopsis and review with class-mates.

5. **The Quilters**
   This play is appropriate for high school students and could also be integrated into this lesson. For upper elementary and intermediate students, a story called *The Canada Geese Quilt* by Natalie Kinsey-Warnock could be used.

6. **Writing Folk Tales**
   Have students write folk tales individually or in cooperative learning groups. Illustrate and compile a class book.

SELECTED BIBLIOGRAPHY of Folk Tales

African Folklore
Aardema, Verna. *Rabbit Makes a Monkey of Lion.* New York: Dial Books for Young Readers, 1988.
Aardema, Verna. *Tales from the Story Hat.* New York: Coward-McCann, 1960.
Aardema, Verna. *Tales for the Third Ear.* New York: Dutton, 1969.
Arnott, Kathleen. *Dragons, Ogres, and Scary Things.* Champaign, IL: Garrard Pub. Co, 1974.
Arnott, Kathleen. *African Myths and Legends.* New York: H.Z. Walck, 1963.
Bernstein, Margery. *The First Morning: An African Myth.* New York: Scribner, 1976.

Bryan, Ashley. *The Cat's Purr*. New York: Atheneum, 1985.

Dayrell, Elphinstone. *Why the Sun and the Moon Live in the Sky*. Boston: Houghton, Mifflin, 1968.

Lexau, Joan M. *Crocodile and Hen*. New York: Harper & Row, 1969.

Phumla, and Carole Byard. *Nomi and the Magic Fish; A Story from Africa*. Garden City, New York: Doubleday, 1972.

Steptoe, John. *Mufaro's Beautiful Daughters*. New York: Lothrop, Lee & Shepard Books, 1987.

African American Folklore

Hamilton, Virginia. *The People Could Fly: The Book of Black Folktales*. New York: Knopf, 1985.

Harris, Joel Chandler, et al. *Brer Rabbit; Stories from Uncle Remus*. New York and London: Harper, 1941.

Hayward, Linda, et al. *Hello, House!* New York: Random House, 1988.

Lester, Julius, et al. *The Tales of Uncle Remus*. New York: Dial Books, 1987.

Lester, Julius, et al. *More Tales of Uncle Remus*. New York: Dial Books, 1988.

Lester, Julius. *The Knee-High Man, and Other Tales*. New York: Dial Press, 1972.

Lester, Julius. *Black Folktales*. New York: R.W. Baron, 1969.

Parks, Van Dyke, et al. *Jump Again! More Adventures*. San Diego: Harcourt Brace Jovanovich, 1987.

Parks, Van Dyke. *Jump! The Adventures of Brer Rabbit*. San Diego: Harcourt Brace Jovanovich, 1986.

Walt Disney's Brer Rabbit and His Friends New York: Random House, 1969.

Wolkstein, Diane. *The Cool Ride in the Sky*. New York: Knopf, 1973.

Arabian Folklore

Burton, Richard F. *The Arabian Nights Entertainments*. New York: Heritage Press, 1955.

Cohen, Barbara, et al. *Seven Daughters and Seven Sons*. New York: Antheneum, 1982.

Colum, Padraic. *The Arabian Nights, Tales of Wonder and Magnificence*. New York: MacMillan, 1953.

Dawood, N.J. *Tales from the Arabian Nights*. Garden City, New York: Doubleday, 1978.

Dolch, Edward W. *Famous Stories for Pleasure Reading*. Champaign, IL: Garrard, 1955.

Lane, Edward Will, et al. *Stories from the Thousand and One Nights*. New York: P.F. Collier, 1909.

Lang, Andrew, et al. *Arabian Nights*. Chicago: Childrens Press, 1968.

Lewis, Naomi, et al. *Stories from the Arabian Nights*. New York: H. Holt, 1987.

Mayer, Marianna, et al. *Aladdin and the Enchanted Lamp*. New York: MacMillan, 1985.

Noel, Bernard. *Sindbad the Sailor*. New York: Good Book Inc., 1972.

Riordan, James I., et al. *Tales from the Arabian Nights*. Chicago: Rand, McNally, 1985.

Chinese Folklore

Carpenter, France. *Tales of a Chinese Grandmother*. Rutland, VT: C.E. Tuttle Co., 1973.

Cheng, Hou-Tien. *Six Chinese Brothers: An Ancient Tale*. New York: Holt, Rinehart and Winston, 1979.

Demi. *A Chinese Zoo: Fables and Proverbs*. San Diego: Harcourt Brace Jovanovich, 987.

Demi. *Chen Ping and His Magic Axe*. New York: Dodd, Mead, 1987.

Kendall, Carol, et al. *Sweet and Sour: Tales from China*. New York: Seabury Press, 1979.

Morris, Winifred, et al. *The Magic Leaf*. New York: Atheneum, 1987.

San Souci, Robert, et al. *The Enchanted Tapestry.* New York: Dial Books for Young Readers, 1987.

Yolen, Jane, et al. *The Emperor and the Kite.* Cleveland: World Publishing Co., 1988.

Young, Ed. *The Terrible Nung Gwama.* New York: Collins and World in cooperation with UNICEF, 1978.

Ziner, Feenie, et al. *Cricket Boy: A Chinese Tale.* Garden City, NY: Doubleday, 1977.

Indian Folklore

Brown, Marcia. *The Blue Jackal.* New York: Scribner, 1977.

Brown, Marcia. *Once a Mouse...A Fable Cut in Wood.* New York: Scribner, 1961.

Demi. *The Hallowed Horse: A Folklore from India.* New York: Dodd, Mead, 1987.

Duff, Maggie, et al. *Rum Pum Pum: A Folk Tale from India.* New York: MacMillan, 1978.

Galdone, Paul. *The Monkey and the Crocodile.* New York: Houghton Mifflin/Clarion Books, 1969.

Gobhai, Mehlli. *The Blue Jackal.* Englewood Cliffs, NJ: Prentice-Hall, 1968.

Gobhai, Mehlli. *The Legend of the Orange Princess.* New York: Holiday House, 1971.

Haviland, Virginia. *Favorite Fairy Tales Told in India.* Boston: Little, Brown, 1973.

Kamen, Gloria. *The Ringdoves.* New York: Atheneum, 1988.

Mobley, Jane, et al. *The Star Husband.* Garden City, New York: Doubleday, 1979.

Quigley, Lillian. *The Blind Men and the Elephant.* New York: Random House, 1974.

Towle, Faith M. *The Magic Cooking Pot: A Folktale from India.* Boston: Houghton, Mifflin, 1975.

Italian Folklore

Basile, Giovanni, et al. *Petrosinella, a Neapolitan Rapunzel.* New York: F. Warne, 1981.

Bennett, Susan. *The Underground Cats.* New York: MacMillan, 1974.

Bowden, Joan. *The Bean Boy.* New York: MacMillan, 1979.

Cauley, Lorinda. *The Goose and the Golden Coins.* New York: Harcourt Brace Jovanovich, 1981.

De Paola, Thomas. *The Legend of Old Befana.* New York: Harcourt Brace Jovanovich, 1980.

De Paola, Tomie. *Strega Nonna.* Weston, Connecticut: Weston Woods, 1978.

De Paola, Tomie. *The Clown of God: An Old Story.* New York: Harcourt Brace Jovanovich, 1978.

Haviland, Virginia. *Favorite Fairy Tales Told in Italy.* Boston: Little, Brown, 1965.

Rockwell, Anne F. *Befana: A Christmas Story.* New York: Atheneum, 1974.

Japanese Folklore

Bang, Molly. *Men from the Village Deep in the Mountains.* New York: MacMillan, 1973.

Bartoli, Jennifer, et al. *The Story of the Grateful Crane.* Chicago: A. Whitman, 1977.

Bryan, Ashley, et al. *Sh-ko and His Eight Wicked Brothers.* New York: Atheneum, 1988.

Dolch, Edward, et al. *Stories from Japan.* Champaign, IL: Garrard Press, 1960.

Hirsh, Marilyn. *How the World Got Its Color.* New York: Crown Publishers, 1972.

Hodges, Margaret, et al. *The Wave.* Boston: Houghton, Mifflin, 1964.

Ishii, Momoko, et al. *Issun Boshi, the Inchling.* New York: Walker, 1967.

Kendall, Carol, et al. *Haunting Tales from Japan.* Lawrence, KS: Spencer-Museum of Art, University of Kansas, 1985.

Lifton, Betty J, et al. *The One-legged Ghost.* New York: Antheneum, 1968.

McDermott, Gerald. *The Stonecutter: A Japanese Folktale.* New York: Viking Press, 1975.

Mosel, Arlene, et al. *The Funny Little Woman.* Weston, CT: Weston Woods, 1973.

Naito, Hiroshi, et al. *Legends of Japan.* Rutland, VT: C.E. Tuttle Co., 1972.

Sakade, Florence. *Japanese Children's Stories.* Rutland, VT: Charles E. Tuttle, 1959.

Suyecka, George, et al. *Issunboshi.* Norfolk Island, Australia: Island Heritage, 1974.

Tabrah, Ruth, et al. *Momotaro: Peach Boy.* New York: J.Weatherhill, 1972.

Uchilda, Yoshiko. *The Magic Listening Cap.* New York: Harcourt, Brace and World, 1955.

Uchida, Yoshiko, et al. *The Two Foolish Cats.* New York: M.K. McElderry Books, 1987.

Yagawa, Sumiko, et al. *The Crane Wife.* New York: William Morrow, 1981.

Wolkstein, Diane. *Lazy Stories.* New York: Seabury Press, 1976.

Jewish Folklore

Ausubel, Nathan. *A Treasury of Jewish Folklore.* New York: Crown Publishers, 1948.

Brodsky, Beverly. *The Golem: A Jewish Legend.* Philadelphia: Lippincott, 1976.

Gershator, Philli, et al. *Honi and His Magic Circle.* Philadelphia: Jewish Publication Society of America, 1979.

Hirsh, Marilyn. *Could Anything Be Worse? A Yiddish Tale.* New York: Holiday House, 1974.

Hirsh, Marilyn. *The Rabbi and the Twenty-Nine Witches.* New York: Holiday House, 1976.

Hirsh, Marilyn, et al. *Joseph Who Loved the Sabbath.* New York: Viking Kestrel, 1986.

Singer, Isaac, et al. *Zlateh the Goat, and Other Stories.* New York: Harper and Row, 1966.

Singer, Isaac, et al. *When Shlemiel Went to Warsaw and Other Stories.* New York: Farrar, Straws and Giroux, 1968.

Suhl, Yuri. *Simon Boom Gives a Wedding.* New York: Four Winds Press, 1972.

Zemach, Margot. *It Could Always Be Worse.* New York: Farrar, Strauss and Giroux, 1976.

Korean Folklore

Carpenter, France. *Tales of a Korean Grandmother.* Garden City, NY: Doubleday, 1947.

Ginsburg, Mirra, et al. *The Chinese Mirror.* San Diego: Harcourt Brace Jovanovich, 1988.

Mexican Folklore

Aardema, Verna. *The Riddle of the Drum.* New York: Four Winds Press, 1979.

Baker, Betty, et al. *No Help at All.* New York: Greenwillow Books, 1978.

Czernecki, Stefan, et al. *Pancho's Piñata.* New York: Hyperion Books, 1992.

Kouzel, Daisy. *The Cuckoo's Reward.* New York: Doubleday, 1977.

Nicholson, Irene. *Mexican and Central American Mythology.* New York: P. Bedrick Books, 1985.

Singer, Jane, et al. *Folk Tales of Mexico.* Minneapolis: T.S. Denison, 1969.

Toor, Frances. *A Treasury of Mexican Folkways.* New York: Crown Publishers, 1947.

Whitehead, Barbara. *The Wonderful Chirrionera and Other Tales of Mexican Folklore.* Austin, TX: Heidelberg Publishing, 1974.

Wolkstein, Diane. *Lazy Stories.* New York: Seabury Press, 1976.

Soviet Union Folklore

Afanasev, A, et al. *Russian Fairy Tales.* New York: Pantheon, 1975.

Black, Algernon, et al. *The Woman of the Wood.* New York: Holt, Rinehart and Winston, 1973.

Brown, Marcia. *The Neighbors.* New York: Scribner, 1967.

Carey, Bonnie. *Grasshopper to the Rescue.* New York: Morrow, 1979.

Carpenter, France. *Tales of a Russian Grandmother.* New York: Doubleday, Doran, 1933.

Chroman, Eleanor, et al. *It Could Be Worse.* Chicago: Childrens Press, 1972.

Cole, Joanna. *Bony-legs.* New York: Random House, 1985.

Crouch, Marcus, et al. *Ivan.* Oxford: Oxford University Press, 1988.

Daniels, Guy, et al. *The Peasant's Pea Patch: A Russian Folktale.* New York: Delacorte Press, 1971.

Domanska, Janina. *A Scythe, a Rooster, and a Cat.* New York: Greenwillow Books, 1981.

Galdone, Paul. *A Strange Servant: A Russian Folktale.* New York: Knopf, 1977.

Ginsburg, Mirra. *The Night It Rained Pancakes.* San Diego: Harcourt Brace Jovanovich, 1980.

Ginsburg, Mirra, et al. *The Proud Maiden, Tungak and the Sun.* New York: MacMillan, 1974.

Ginsburg, Mirra, et al. *How Wilka Went to Sea, and Other Tales from West of the Urals.* New York: Four Crown Publishing, 1975.

Ginsburg, Mirra, et al. *The Lazies; Tales of the People of Russia.* New York: MacMillan, 1973.

Ginsburg, Mirra, et al. *One Trick too Many; Fox Stories from Russia.* New York: Dial Press, 1973.

Ginsburg, Mirra, et al. *Pampalche of the Silver Teeth.* New York: Crown, 1976.

Isele, Elizabeth, et al. *The Frog Princess.* New York: Crowell, 1984.

Jameson, Cynthia. *The Clay Pot Boy.* New York: Coward, McCann and Geohegan, 1973.

Jameson, Cynthia, et al. *Catofy the Clever.* New York: Coward, McCann and Geohegan, 1972.

Jameson, Cynthia, et al. *Tales from the Steppes.* New York: Coward, McCann and Geohegan, 1975.

Lowe, Patricia, et al. *The Tale of the Golden Cockerel.* New York: Crowell, 1975.

McCurdy, Michael. *The Devils Who Learned to Be Good.* Boston: Joy Street Books, 1987.

Morton, Miriam. *A Harvest of Russian Children's Literature.* Berkeley: University of California Press, 1967.

Polushkin, Maria, et al. *Bubba and Babba:* Based on a Russian Folktale. New York: Crown, 1976.

Prokofiev, Sergey, et al. *Peter and the Wolf.* Boston: P.R. Godine, 1980.

Ransome, Arthur. *The Fool of the World and the Flying Ship.* New York: Farrar, Strauss and Giroux, 1968.

Reesink, Marijke, et al. *The Magic Horse.* New York: McGraw-Hill, 1974.

Rudolf, Marguerita, et al. *Grey Neck.* Owings Mills, MD: Stemmer House, 1988.

Sherman, Josepha, et al. *Vassilisa the Wise.* San Diego: Harcourt Brace Jovanovich, 1988.

Shulevitz, Uri. *Soldier and Tsar in the Forest.* New York: Farrar, Strauss and Giroux, 1972.

Silverman, Maida, et al. *Anna and the Seven Swans.* New York: W. Morrow, 1984.

Singer, Isaac, et al. *Mazel and Shlimazel; or, The Milk of a Lioness .* New York: Farrar, Straus and Giroux, 1967.

Stern, Simon. *Vasily & the Dragon.* London: Pelham Books, 1982.

Titiev, Estelle, et al. *How the Moolah Was Taught a Lesson.* New York: Dial Press, 1976.

Wheeler, Post, et al. *Russian Wonder Tales.* New York: T. Yoseloff, 1957.

Zemach, Harve, et al. *Salt: A Russian Tale.* Chicago: Follett Publishing Co., 1965.

Zvorykin, Boris, et al. *The Firebird and Other Russian Fairy Tales.* New York: Viking Press, 1978.

Vietnamese Folklore

Kha, Dang Manh, et al. *In the Land of Small Dragon.* New York: Viking Press, 1979.

Taylor, Mark, et al. *The Fisherman and the Goblet.* San Carlos, CA: Golden Gate Jr. Books, 1971.

Vo, Dinh Mai. *The Toad Is the Emperor's Uncle.* Garden City, NY: Doubleday, 1970.

Fifth Chinese Daughter
by Jade Snow Wong

Grade Level
For Upper Elementary &
Middle School

Thinking Level
Analysis

Writing Domain
Analytical/Expository

Materials Needed
- Construction paper
- Marking pens

**Suggested
Supplementary
Readings**
"When I Was Growing Up"
by Nellie Wong

Fifth Chinese Daughter

by Meredith Ritner

Overview

After reading an excerpt from Jade Snow Wong's autobiography, *Fifth Chinese Daughter,* students will explore their values and identify similarities and differences between their lives and the life of Jade Snow Wong, in preparation for writing a comparison/contrast essay.

Objectives

THINKING SKILLS

Students will:

- *define* what a value is;
- *identify* and *prioritize* their personal values;
- *seek out* class members who share their primary values and create a graphic representation of their shared values;
- *classify* and *analyze* the similarities and differences between themselves and a character through a comparison/contrast essay.

WRITING SKILLS

Students will:

- *practice* syntactical structures for a comparison/contrast essay;
- *write* a comparison/contrast essay describing similarities and differences between their values, family life, and customs and those of Jade Snow Wong;
- *support* general statements with examples from the story and personal experiences;
- *use* analytical/expository form: introduction, main body, conclusion
- *follow* the conventions of standard written English.

The Process

The process described below has been specifically designed for English Language Development (ELD) students.

 **PREWRITING**

Prewriting Step 1: *Class Discussion*

Have students define what a value is in their own words.

Call upon volunteers to share their responses. Develop a class definition based upon student responses.

A sample definition might be as follows:

> *A value is a belief, idea, action, or possession that is important to you.*

Prewriting Step 2: *Clustering*

Have individual students cluster the many things a person might value. Create a whole-class cluster and have students add new ideas to their clusters.

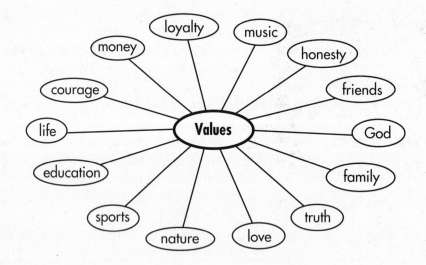

Prewriting Step 3: *Ranking Personal Values*

Have students rank their top five values. A sample ranking might look like this:

1. family
2. religion
3. education
4. friends
5. honesty

Have students do a quickwrite describing their values and explaining why they're important. A sample paragraph might look like this:

> There are many things in life that I value. If I had to choose the most important thing to me on this earth, it would be my family. I have three brothers and a sister. My family is always there for me when I need them. I also value God because He created me and everything on this earth. My family is Catholic and we go to church every Sunday. Education is important to me too. Without an education, it's difficult to get a job. If you can't read or write well, no one will want you to work for them. My friends are like my second family. We hang out together at school and sometimes we talk on the phone at night. Friends can also help you with problems. Finally, I value honesty. I always tell the truth. If someone isn't honest with you, you can't trust them. As you can see, I have many values. What do you value?

Prewriting Step 4: *Finding Similarities Amongst Peers*

Ask students to find two or three other people in the room who share at least two of their top five values and form a small group. For example, students who value family, religion, and education will collaborate with others who share those values.

Prewriting Step 5: *Creating a Graphic Representation*

Ask each group to choose whether they wish to focus on one shared value or a few. Have each group think up a symbol or artistic representation to illustrate their shared value(s). Then, ask them to write an explanation of their illustration and describe the importance of their value(s). Students may refer to their individual paragraphs. Next, students combine their art and their writing on a piece of construction paper to create a "Values Poster."

Ask groups to make an *informal* presentation of their poster to the class. A presentation might sound like this:

> The members of our group valued religion, life, and family. We chose to illustrate and explain why we value life. If you watch the news or read the papers, you know that there are many people who don't value life. Someone is always getting shot at or beat up. Also, we have many endangered species which are becoming extinct. We think that people should have more respect for the life of others and the animals on our planet. We value all living things—man, plants and animals. For our poster, we decided to draw a scene from the ocean because it has lots of life.

Prewriting Step 6: *Reading*

Read the excerpt from *Fifth Chinese Daughter* (below).

As you are reading, have students use a highlighter to highlight lines in which they notice similarities or differences between their lives and Jade Snow Wong's life. The vocabulary can be difficult for ELD students. However, challenging students to wrestle with the text produces worthwhile results. Ask students to identify similarities and differences as you are reading. Pause to allow students to record their observations in the margin.

For instance, as Chapter 1 opens, we learn that Jade Snow's family immigrated from China. Many of us have also immigrated from another country. Students should underline the specific area of text that pertains to them and then explain the similarity or difference in the margin.

Example: Jade Snows family immigrated from China to America in the early 1900's. However, my family immigrated to America from Mexico in the 1980s.

Prewriting Step 7: *Characteristics of Jade Snow Wong*

Create a whole class cluster on the board on the main character in the excerpt, Jade Snow:

Featured Literature

Fifth Chinese Daughter
Jade Snow Wong

Note: Although this story was written in the third person, it is an autobiography rooted in Chinese literary form. The missing I illustrates the cultural disregard for the individual.

Chapter One: The World Was New

Hugging the eastern slope of San Francisco's famous Nob Hill is one of the unique spots of this continent. A small, compact area overlooking the busy harbor at its feet, it extends only a few blocks in either direction. Above its narrow, congested streets, the chimes of beautiful Grace Cathedral ring out the quarter hours; and tourists and curio-seekers in a bare three minutes can stroll from the city's fashionable shopping district into the heart of Old China.

Chinatown in San Francisco teems with haunting memories, for it is wrapped in the atmosphere, customs, and manners of a land across the sea. The same Pacific Ocean laves the shores of both worlds, a tangible link between old and new, past and present, Orient and Occident.

To this China in the West, there came in the opening decade of this century a young Chinese with his wife and family. There they settled among the other Cantonese, and as the years slipped by, the couple established their place in the community.

I tell the story of their fifth daughter, Jade Snow, born to them in San Francisco.

Until she was five years old, Jade Snow's world was almost wholly Chinese, for her world was her family, the Wongs. Life was secure but formal, sober but quietly happy, and the few problems she had were entirely concerned with what was proper or improper in the behavior of a little Chinese girl.

Even at this early age she had learned the meaning of discipline, without understanding the necessity for it. A little girl never questioned the commands of Mother and Father, unless prepared to receive painful consequences. She never addressed an older person by name—it was always Older Brother, Oldest Sister, Second Older Sister, Third Older Sister (she had died at one month without a name, but still she held a place in the family), and Fourth Older Sister. Only her mother and father, or their generation of uncles and aunts, addressed them as Blessing from Heaven, Jade Swallow, Jade Lotus, or Jade Ornament. In short, a little girl was never casual with her elders. Even in handing them something she must use both hands to signify that she paid them undivided attention.

Respect and order—these were the key words of life. It did not matter what were the thoughts of a little girl; she did not voice them. She assumed that her mother must love her, because Mother made her bright silk Chinese dresses for holiday wear, embroidered with gold threads and bright-colored beads, and washed her, and cleaned her white, buckled sandals. Father must love her, because he taught her her first lessons from Chinese books and put her high on his shoulders above the crowds so that she could watch from unobstructed heights the Lion Dances on the streets at Chinese New Year's; and sometimes he took her downtown with him on business errands to that outside foreign American world.

But in spite of her parents' love, she must always be careful to do the proper thing. Failure to do so brought immediate and drastic punishment. Teaching and whipping were almost synonymous. Once, because in fun she had knocked Older Brother's hat off his head when she passed him on the stairs, Father whipped her with a bundle of tied cane; then he withdrew permission for her to go with Oldest Sister to visit the city zoo. Since she had never been to the zoo and had looked forward to this treat for a week, the disappointment and the shame hurt almost worse than the whipping.

Another time, when their neighbor's son spit on her as she was playing, she ran to tell Mother, who was sewing overalls in the factory which was also their home. Mother did not sympathize but reproved her, saying that she must have spit on her playmate first or he wouldn't have spit on her. She was told to bring a clothes hanger, and in front of all the other working women Mother spanked her. Again the shame was almost worse than the pain, and the pain was bad enough, for Mother usually spanked until the wooden hanger broke.

Thus, life was a constant puzzle. No one ever troubled to explain. Only through punishment did she learn that what was proper was right and what was improper was wrong.

At this time, Oldest Sister and Second Older Sister were already married, and Fourth Older Sister was living with Oldest Sister; Jade Snow scarcely knew them. At home, besides Jade Snow there were Father and Mother, Older Brother, who was about twelve, and three-year-old younger sister Jade Precious Stone.

Jade Precious Stone and Jade Snow were closest. They slept in the same room, dressed together, ate, played, cried, and got spanked together. They hardly ever disagreed. Jade Precious Stone was a delicate child, gentle and quiet. Because she was younger, she addressed her sister as Older Sister Snow, and she was taught to respect her Fifth Older Sister's judgment on all things. That meant that Jade Snow was responsible for any trouble they got into together.

The Wongs lived at the back of their father's overall factory on Stockton between Clay and Sacramento streets. The factory-home was huge. To the right on the street floor was a room containing ten or more sewing machines of various kinds. Also on the street floor, to the left, was the office. A forty-inch-wide cutting table ran the length of the room to the kitchen and dining room at the rear. Beyond was a door leading to the bathroom, one of the few in Chinatown at that time equipped with running water. What fun the children had in that bathtub, which served also for washing the family clothes!

On the second floor were the finishing machines and more long cutting tables where women sat all day examining the finished overalls before folding and tying them into bundles of a dozen each. In front were the family sleeping rooms: one for Mother and Father, one for the two younger daughters, and another for Older Brother.

Home life and work life were therefore mixed together. In the morning, Father opened the factory doors while Mother prepared a breakfast consisting of rice, a green vegetable or soup, a meat or fish, and steamed salted dried fish from China. For the rest of the day Mother was at a machine except when she stopped to get the meals or to do other housework.

The Wong daughters and the children of the workers played hide-and-seek around the high bundles of blue denim, rode on the pushcarts used for loading overalls, climbed onto the cutting tables to talk to the women as they worked. It was the Wong girls' responsibility not to quarrel with the employees' children, who were of guest status.

Instead of playing, Jade Snow often followed her father around as he saw to the placement and repair of the machines or the distribution of work. At first she asked questions, being curious. But her father did not like questions. He said that one was not supposed to talk when one was either eating or thinking, and when one was not eating, one should be thinking. Only when in bed did one neither eat nor think.

However, he seemed to understand a child's need to make noise. To satisfy this need constructively, he started to teach his daughter Chinese history. He would read aloud a sentence, "Wong Ti was the first king of China," and Jade Snow would repeat it after him word for word. So, while her father laid out material, or numbered and labeled the spools of thread, she would trail along near him, reciting the text over and over until she knew it without prompting.

It was not great fun to make a noise in this way, but Father said that all Chinese children in America should learn their ancestral language, and one did not dispute one's father if one were a dutiful little girl taught to act with propriety. From the first Chinese primer lessons of "Ding Dong; Ding Dong; the bell rushes me to attend school," and "Ding Dong; Ding Dong; the bell reminds me to leave school," Jade Snow was gradually advanced to "When Wellington was a boy he would not permit riders on horses to enter his father's fields of grain. . . ."

A primer lesson usually served as a text for a moral lesson too. Wellington, although a foreign Englishman, was an example of a small boy who followed absolutely the instructions of his father. He was told to guard the gate which opened into their grain fields, and he carried out the order to the point of defying a group of soldiers who wanted to take a short cut across these fields. He stood his ground with such determination that the cavalry would have had to trample him before they could trample the grain crop. Of course Wellington won out. Thus, duty to one's father came before duty to one's army.

The children could play out-of-doors if they stayed within their own block and did not cross any streets. They wore dark-blue denim coveralls which Father's seamstresses made, with bright red belt bands and red facings on the sleeves and on the square necklines, and buttoned drop-seats—a comfortable garment for climbing around. Sometimes they played in a nearby empty lot where it was interesting to explore all kinds of weeds and bugs. Only one other place in Jade Snow's early experience had any growing plants. That was the Presbyterian Home around the corner on Sacramento Street. She was told that women "in difficulties" sought refuge there, but curious stares yielded only disappointment, for the heavy red-brown brick building always stood in closed silence. Turning to go home she would pause to pick a little spray of yellow broom from its surrounding hedge and hold its delicate fragrance under her nose.

Her father and his bright red wheelbarrow provided Jade Snow with wonderful escapes to the world outside this block. While most Chinese women in San Francisco still had to conform to the Old-World custom of staying at home, her father believed that according to New-World Christian ideals women had a right to work to improve the economic status of their family. Because they couldn't come to the factory, Mr. Wong took their work to them, installed and maintained their sewing machines, taught them how to sew, and collected the finished overalls. On these trips, Jade Snow was his companion, for Younger Sister was still too small. When the wheelbarrow was loaded with materials, she had to run in quick little steps to keep up with her father's long strides, but after the wheelbarrow had delivered its burden she was privileged to sit inside while he pushed it easily up and down, clickety-clack, over the cobblestone hills of San Francisco. Her father was so strong! Looking around at the world, Jade Snow felt a burst of pride as she saw other children's envious wonder. At such times, she was very happy to have been born her father's fifth daughter.

There were other times when he had to go downtown to see his jobber boss and took Jade Snow with him. There she saw a completely different world which filled her with shyness and wonder. Pretty, strangely dressed foreign ladies with brightly colored faces and curled hair smiled at her and tried to make her speak to them in their language. They sat behind machines that made a clattering noise as they punched out figures which were repeated several times over by means of sheets of black paper. Jade Snow was always given a piece of this magic paper to take home, and very often the jobber boss gave her a booklet of bright cloth samples and a shining new nickel besides.

The nickel was always spent immediately at the corner candy store, which offered a choice among an ice cream cone, a "popsicle," and chewy Chinese toasted dried beef. For a penny one could buy four little packs of hot red ginger or three salty preserved olives twisted in rice paper, which were imports from China.

Lacking money for treats, Jade Snow would hope that the ice delivery truck might happen to stop and the iceman drop a small piece of ice from the big leather bag on his back. If her eyes were sharp she could dart over, pick it up, run home to wash it under the faucet, and enjoy its cool smoothness, sucking it and rolling it around her mouth. But she must never take pieces from the back of the truck while the iceman was momentarily gone, as she often saw other children do. To do this would be stealing, and her father had taught her a lesson in honesty she would never forget.

There had been an old, wrinkled, spectacled peddler, who was always a welcome visitor at the factory. Slovenly and with a white stubble which always needed shaving, he arrived carrying a big bundle whose contents varied from time to time. It might contain shoestrings, corsets, nightgowns, baby slippers, stockings, dish towels, or any number of miscellaneous things tempting to a woman.

Jade Snow had been aware of his visits ever since she could remember but had never paid much attention to his wares. Then one day the peddler's bundle revealed a riot of beautiful colors, for he was selling drapery samples. Jade Snow, hanging around her mother's skirt, gazed enraptured at the pretty posies on the chintz prints, shyly picked up a little square, and fingered it lovingly. The peddler called out, "Buy your girl a piece of material, ma'am. A penny is all I ask. I am almost giving it to her to play with, you can see. A penny, ma'am, a penny."

"Jade Snow, put that material back. Can't you see I am busy?"

Jade Snow looked wistfully at her mother, echoed her "No" by shaking her own head silently, and put the square of red and green back on the pile. Mother turned away, but the peddler followed, coaxing her to buy. Jade Snow looked at the square she had dropped. She wanted that colorful square for her very own!

But she had no penny. Why couldn't she have it? She was going to have it. So she quickly leaned down, picked up the square again, hid it in her pocket, and ran off.

She found a box in a corner of the factory and sat there, looking at her piece of material, counting the number of blossoms on it, studying the colors. She twisted it, turned it around, and rubbed it against her cheek. She didn't know how long she sat there, but suddenly she was jolted out of her enchantment by her father's firm voice:

"So there you are hiding. Where did you get that material?"

"I found it."

"Do not lie to me. Where did you find it? Things like that do not grow around here."

"I found it from the peddler's bag!"

"You mean you stole it from the peddler's bag! For shame, that a small girl of mine should begin to steal. I must teach you a lesson you will never forget. You may begin now with a small square, but the next thing will be a whole bolt of material. Go immediately and sit on the front step of our doorway with the material held prominently in your hand, so that when the peddler returns for it, he will find you and take it back. And whatever he does for punishment, you will deserve it."

Not until then did Jade Snow realize that she had committed a sin. She soberly took the material and sat on the front step. There she sat for minutes and then for hours. She grew hot in the afternoon sun. People coming in and out of the factory would ask, "Jade Snow, what are you doing here?" And she would reply miserably, "I am waiting for a man to come back for this material which I took."

She lost her interest in the material and began to dislike it. As she grew more uncomfortable, she hated it. But still the peddler did not return. She imagined the awful things that might happen to her. Perhaps they would put her in jail! She was terrified. She wished that he would come and get it over with. The sun went down; the evening bay breezes began to chill her. She was getting hungry as well as thirsty and cold. The workers all went home. Then her father came to bolt the front door.

"Do you remember that you are never to steal or be dishonest in any way?"

Jade Snow hugged her knees and looked up at the tall figure standing over her. "Yes."

"Very well, you may give the piece of material to me to put away until the next time the peddler visits our factory, and I shall return it to him."

During these years, the one older person who seemed most understanding of a little girl's failure to do the proper thing was Mother's mother. Grandmother was little and stooped and always wore a loose black Chinese coat and trousers. Her hair was fastened into a knot at the back of her neck by a gold brooch set with pretty jade stones. Sometimes she tucked a narcissus or a tuberose blossom into the edges of this knot. If Grandmother happened to be visiting when Mother spanked Jade Snow, she would always snatch the child away and scold Mother instead. To Jade Snow it was remarkable that she should have such power, especially since Grandmother was frail while Mother was strong. Yet her intervention was only mildly disputed.

Sometimes, Jade Snow and her sister were privileged to visit Grandmother's home. This was one small room in an old, dark, run-down building two blocks from the Wongs. In the corner facing the door a large bed was screened off in Chinese fashion; that is, a bamboo frame had been erected four-poster-wise, and draperies veiled it completely. The bed dominated the room, which also held a gas plate, a few chairs, a sewing machine, and an ancestral worship table. On the table, below the pictures or tablets bearing the names of Grandmother's forebears, were cups filled with wine, bowls of fruit and meat, and burning brown punk and red candles, arranged to feed and light their spirits, for Grandmother was not a Christian.

Whenever the sisters visited Grandmother, they knew that she would offer them a treat. On her window ledge she kept a glass jar filled with thick sweetened condensed milk. For child visitors she spread the sticky cream on thin salty soda crackers, as many as they wanted. Since their Chinese diet seldom included sweets, the children usually ate and ate. Sometimes Grandmother would offer instead dried lichees—that delicate-flavored fruit in its crisp, papery shell, which she kept in the sewing machine drawers. Or if she happened to be out of sweets, she would boil an egg for each visitor. But she always managed something.

There was one service Grandmother requested in return for all her kindnesses. She often asked Jade Snow and Jade Precious Stone to clench their fists and hammer her bent spine up and down. She said that the vibrations improved her circulation, that they were relaxing and felt good. Although the girls thought the exercise great fun, they found it hard to understand how their blows could make Grandmother feel better. They had tried the treatment on each other without experiencing any enjoyment.

A vivid memory Jade Snow was always to associate with Grandmother had to do with a live turkey her father brought home one American holiday week and tied to the leg of the dining table. He told his fifth daughter to go into the room alone and make her acquaintance with her first turkey.

Where was the bird in that dimly lighted room? The oilcloth on the table dropped almost to the floor, and the turkey must be hiding under it. Jade Snow lifted the cloth, and crawled in to see better this strange bird that her father had said was related to chickens. Only it was different, he said. . . . It was indeed different! Face to face with the ferocious creature, she sat petrified, seemingly imprisoned between the legs of the table with a bird which looked anything but friendly. Was it a bird? Those ugly blotches on his jerking head. . . . He was coming closer to her, closer, too close. Suddenly, though she could not seem to move, she found her voice and cried out with all her might. Whether such an uproar was proper or improper could not be helped. For the first time in her life Jade Snow was shaken with fright.

As a result, she became sick and insisted on sleeping with Mother, a thing she had never done before. She sweated; and for days and nights, whether she closed or opened her eyes, that turkey kept coming closer, and closer. . . .

The family conferred. It was Grandmother who reminded them that there was an established ritual which would "out the scare." The following evening, the entire family gathered in Grandmother's room, with Jade Snow the center of attention. Never before had she felt so important. The lights were turned off except for candles. Then Grandmother lit a fire in her bronze brazier and threw in a small lump of "Bok Fon," a white mineral with herbal properties. In the semidark room, she began to chant softly: "Out with the scare which is hiding in our Jade Snow. . . ." As she whispered the lines over and over rhythmically, she picked up the child and passed her back and forth above the glowing brazier. The candles flickered; the shadows of the family loomed like dancing giants on the walls. Jade Snow was frightened all over again. She did not like this silent, solemn, strange atmosphere. What were they doing to her? Still, it would not do to cry. Any outburst would surely have been improper at such a time.

It was confusing—that terrible turkey creature, the people quietly watching in the flickering light, Grandmother acting so unlike herself. Then the flames died down, and it was over. The grownups turned on the lights and gave the bewildered child something bitter and hot to drink. It was an herb tea brewed in a pot from which she saw Grandmother remove her jade pendant, a piece of gold ore, and a pearl brooch. The presence of the jewelry assured a "calming" and "precious" tea, they told her. Though the tea puckered her mouth, she felt relief for the first time since coming face to face with the turkey. That night, she slept alone peacefully for the first time in days.

The next day, Grandmother came, bringing the remains of the white substance that she had burned and left to cool overnight in the brazier. She showed it to Oldest Sister, who happened to be visiting but knew nothing of the turkey incident.

"What does this look like to you, Oldest One?" Grandmother asked.

Oldest Sister said unhesitatingly, "Why, that is a turkey."

Why did the "Bok Fon" which Grandmother bought at the herb store bear any relation to Jade Snow's scare? Why did that piece of white mineral burn to the shape of the object which had frightened her? The family did not seem concerned with questions. But although it was difficult to understand such things, Jade Snow remembered them.

Played hide-and-seek in factory

Spanked because boy spit on her and mother accused JSW of spitting first

Behind father's overall factory

Early 1900s

Discipline

Afraid of turkeys

Family immigrated from China

Family was her world

Chinatown

Lives in San Francisco

Jade Snow Wong

Never questioned mother or father

Respect

Ate ice from ice-truck

Closest in age to little sister

Must always behave properly

Jade Precious Stone

Called older brothers and sister by number, not name

Accompanied father on errands

Responsible for sister

Spoiled by grandmother

Stole square of fabric from peddler

Formal

Treats

Polite

Had to sit on step all day and wait for peddler to give punishment

Prewriting Step 8: *Interpreting the Text*

Have individual students respond to the following questions in writing:

- From what country is Jade Snow's family?
- What does Jade Snow do to show respect to her elders?
- What rules must Jade Snow follow?
- How does Jade Snow's father teach her a lesson?
- How does Jade Snow get along with her grandmother?
- Describe Jade Snow's first encounter with a turkey. How did she feel?
- How is Jade Snow expected to act when her family has company?

Note: See Extension Activity for Interpretive Question Game.

Prewriting Step 9: *Interviewing*

After students answer questions about Jade Snow, they will be answering questions about themselves. Have students pair off. They are going to interview one another, using the questions below. The purpose of the interview is to help students gather information about themselves.

Role-play an interview with a student and emphasize the need for the interviewer to probe for details and information. The interviewer's job is to elicit detailed responses from the interviewee and to write everything down. The interviewee's job is to give thoughtful responses. When the interview is over, the interviewee receives his/her answers and now has lots of information to assist him/her in writing to the prompt. Partners then switch roles.

- From what country is your family?
- How do you show respect to your parents, teachers, and other people in authority?
- What rules must you follow at home?
- Describe a time when one of your parents taught you a lesson.
- Describe a relative of yours who spoils you.
- Describe a time when you were frightened as a child.
- How are you expected to act when your family has company?

Prewriting Step 10: *Identifying Jade Snow Wong's Values*

Have students complete the following chart to assist them in identifying what Jade Snow Wong and her family value. Share the following examples to help students get started:

Jade Snow and her family value	I know this because
• Respect for elders	She is not allowed to address her older brothers and sister by name; she must call them by number—first older sister, second older sister, etc.
• Family	At a very young age, children are taught to respect their father and then their family above all else. Wellington is an example of a good son because he put his father above the army.
• Responsibility	Jade Snow was expected to be responsible for her younger sister. If her little sister does something wrong, Jade Snow gets in trouble.

Prewriting Step 11: *Identifying Individual Values*

Have students complete the following chart to assist them in identifying what their values are. Share the following examples to help students get started:

My family and I value	You can tell this about us because
• Education	My parents always ask me about school. I'm expected to complete my homework. My parents attend school activities.
• Helpfulness	I have chores that I do around the house. I babysit my younger brother.
• Health	We eat healthy foods and we're very active. My brother, sisters, and I always play sports.

Prewriting Step 12: *Common Attributes*

Play Common Attributes. Arrange the class in a circle and have each student remove a shoe and place it in the center of the circle. Explain that a common attribute is a similar feature. Select two shoes from the circle that have a common attribute (*i.e.*, stripes, black soles, fluorescent shoelaces, etc.). Have students guess the attribute. Whoever guesses correctly picks the next shoes.

Prewriting Step 13: *Practicing Syntactical Structures*

As you are playing, teach the structure of a sentence that makes a comparison by having students phrase their guesses with the correct syntactical format.

To make a comparison:

Both _____ and _____ have _____ .

Both _____ and _____ are _____ .

Both Ernie's shoe and Yen's shoe have stripes.

Both Ernie's shoe and Yen's shoe are black.

After students learn the game, teach the syntax needed for phrasing a contrasting sentence. Have students say "comma" so they learn its placement.

To contrast:

While _____ is/has _____ , _____ is/has _____ .

_____ is _____ ; however, _____ is _____ .

While Somaly's shoe has laces, Alex's shoe has Velcro. *(The words the student should say are, "While Somaly's shoe has laces **comma** Alex's shoe has Velcro.")*

Somaly's shoe has laces; however, Alex's shoe has Velcro.

 ## PROMPT

Writing Situation:

The excerpt we have read from Jade Snow Wong shows us that while the traditional Chinese culture has characteristics that make it distinct, it also has characteristics in common with your culture.

Writing Directions:

Recalling the class discussions we have had and using your story notes, your values charts, and your values poster, write a comparison/contrast essay showing how your culture is similar to Jade Snow Wong's and how your culture is different from Jade Snow Wong's.

Describe the similarities and differences between your values, your family life, and your customs, and the values, family life, and customs of Jade Snow Wong. Use examples from the story and your own life to show how your culture is similar to and different from Jade Snow Wong's.

Your essay must have an introduction, a body, and a conclusion. It must follow the basic conventions of standard written English (correct spelling, punctuation, sentence structure, etc.).

 ## PRECOMPOSING

Precomposing Step 1: *Venn Diagram*

Use the Venn diagram to help students delineate the similarities and differences between their culture and Jade Snow Wong's culture. They should refer to their values posters, highlighted text, and marginalia, as well as the charts in Prewriting Steps 7 and 9.

Example (based on student model at end of lesson):

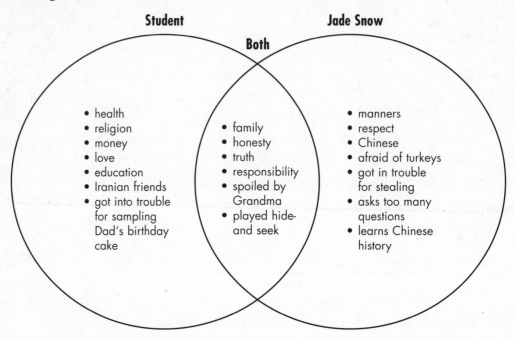

Student   Both   Jade Snow

Student:
- health
- religion
- money
- love
- education
- Iranian friends
- got into trouble for sampling Dad's birthday cake

Both:
- family
- honesty
- truth
- responsibility
- spoiled by Grandma
- played hide-and seek

Jade Snow:
- manners
- respect
- Chinese
- afraid of turkeys
- got in trouble for stealing
- asks too many questions
- learns Chinese history

Precomposing Step 2: *Practicing Sentence Structure*

Teach comparison/contrast sentence structures for students to practice. Have students create as many sentences of comparison and contrast as they can from their Venn Diagram. You might provide a few framing sentences and then challenge students to develop their own.

Potential sentence frames:

- Both Jade Snow Wong and I. _____.
- While Jade Snow Wong _____, I _____.
- Unlike Jade Snow Wong,_____.

- However, we do share_____.
- Jade Snow Wong _____; however, I _____.
- While Jade Snow Wong is/has _____, I am/have _____.
- Although Jade Snow Wong _____, we _____.

Some good examples look like this:

- Both Jade Snow Wong and I value our families.
- Unlike Jade Snow Wong, I do not spend my money on candy.
- However, I spend my money on video games at the 7-Eleven.
- Jade Snow Wong is Buddhist; however, I am a Catholic.
- While I am expected to have good manners, Jade Snow's family is more strict about politeness.
- Although Jade Snow Wong is Chinese and I am Iranian, both of our fathers carried us on their shoulders.

As students are working, walk around the room to praise and assist.

Precomposing Step 3: *Microtheme*

In order to prepare students to write their essays, ask them to do some brainstorming by creating microtheme notes on the form below:

Microtheme

Introduction: Jot down the background information about Jade Snow Wong that you wish to include in your essay. Brainstorm at least three pieces of information:

-

-

-

Main Body: List at least three values you will discuss in your essay. Note which details you will include from the story and your personal experience to show how you are similar to Jade Snow Wong and how you are different from Jade Snow Wong.

Value	How We Are Similar	Example	How We Are Different	Example

Conclusion: Now that you have studied your values and the values of Jade Snow Wong, explain what you have learned about yourself in relation to Jade Snow.

WRITING

Before students begin their comparison/contrast essay, they may need to analyze a model in order to see how a comparison/contrast essay is structured. Use the model at the end of this lesson (or write one of your own) and put it on the overhead. Discuss how this essay follows the microtheme. You might choose to have them complete a microtheme on the model "Hide-and-Seek and Shoulder Rides" to illustrate the organizational value of the microtheme. Then, have students write a first draft of their essays. Tell students to refer to their microthemes to assist them.

SHARING

Sharing Step 1: *Share Cards*

Use Share Cards to teach your class positive frames in which to structure their responses to each other's writing. Make construction paper "share cards" such as the ones that follow. Arrange your students in groups and give each group a share card.

title	background information	values	personal experience
something the writer has in common with Jade Snow	way in which the writer differs from Jade Snow	It would help me to understand better if ...	I like the way the writer ...
I need to know more about	A strength in this paper is...	A suggestion for the writer is ...	quotes

Sharing Step 2: *Getting Ready to Respond*

Tell your students that you are going to show them an example of an essay and that they are responsible for finding the item listed on their card. For example, if Group Three is holding the card "values," they will be required to identify the values discussed in the essay. Place the model of the essay that follows on the overhead and read aloud.

Model Essay

Hide-and-Seek and Shoulder Rides

In the biography, Fifth Chinese Daughter, the main character was named Jade Snow Wong. She lived on the steep streets of Clay and Sacramento, in the city of San Francisco, in a place known as Chinatown. In the early 1900s, the Wong family immigrated to this town from China. In this family, there were six daughters and one son. Jade Snow Wong was the fifth daughter. She and her family lived behind their father's overalls factory. Although Jade Snow Wong is Chinese and I am Iranian, we actually have a lot in common. I am the "Second Iranian Daughter." I have two older sisters and one younger brother. Both of our families expect us to be respectful, responsible, polite, and honest.

According to this story, the Chinese culture is very strict. Jade Snow Wong had to show respect to her elders. She couldn't even call her older brothers and sisters by name. She had to call them "Older Brother," "Older Sister," "Second Older Sister," "Third Older Sister" and "Fourth Older Sister." Once, she knocked her brother's hat off his head, just as a joke, and her father grounded her so that she couldn't go to the zoo. Although my family values respect for elders, my parents are not quite as strict. I'm supposed to call older people "Mr." or "Mrs." but I call my brothers and sisters by their real names.

Good manners and responsibility are important in both Jade Snow Wong's family and my family. While Jade Snow is responsible for her Younger Sister, Jade Precious Snow, I am responsible for my younger brother. If her younger sister got into trouble, Jade Snow was blamed because her parents expected her to be responsible. I also get blamed if my brother does something he's not supposed to. As you can see, both of our families value responsibility.

Like Jade Snow's family, my family also values good manners. When Jade Snow plays in the overalls factory with the other workers' children, she is expected to be extra polite and not argue because they are like guests. Whenever we have company to our house, I'm also supposed to be extra polite. My guest gets served before me and if we play a game, my guest gets to go first.

Both Jade Snow Wong's family and my family value honesty. This is why, when Jade Snow Wong stole a piece of fabric from the peddler, she got into big trouble. She and her father were on an errand. There was a man peddling fabric. Jade Snow thought that all of the colors were beautiful but she didn't have the penny she needed to buy some. As the peddler was leaving, he dropped a piece of the fabric. Jade Snow picked it up, but instead of returning it to the peddler, she kept it for herself. Her father was furious! As a punishment, Jade Snow's father made Jade Snow sit on the front steps of the overalls factory and hold the fabric so that all could see. He told her she would have to sit like that until the peddler she stole it from came back. Then the peddler could punish her however he wanted. Well, the peddler never came back, but she was embarrassed at having to sit on the steps all day and have everybody see her. Once, on my dad's birthday, I tasted part of my dad's cake before dinner. I just tasted some of the frosting, but my mom could tell that someone had tried some. When my mom asked me about it, I told her that I saw my brother eat some. I don't know how she knew I was lying, but she did. I had to apologize to my dad for ruining his cake, but I still got to eat some.

Although Jade Snow Wong's culture, family life, and customs are very different from mine, we share many of the same values. If you looked at Jade Snow Wong and me, you might think to yourself, these two girls are so different. It's true that we look different, but as you can see, our cultures are very similar. Not only are we respectful, responsible, polite, and honest, we also have fun in similar ways. Both Jade Snow Wong's father and my father used to carry us on their shoulders. Like Jade Snow Wong, I play hide-and-seek. Even though we come from different countries, and speak different languages, the values and activities that we have in common show that we are more alike than different. So the next time you see somebody and you think to yourself, that person looks different, think of Jade Snow Wong and me—you might be surprised to discover how much you have in common.

Sharing Step 3: *Practicing Responses*

Have groups take turns responding.

For example:

> Group One has a "title" card. Their response after listening to the essay is, "The title of this piece is Second Iranian Daughter ." *(Note: The group holding the title card might also make an alternate suggestion for the title.)*

> Group Five is holding "I would like to know more about . . . ." After listening to the essay, they might comment, "I would like to know more about the ways in which you and Jade Snow Wong differ."

This process enables you as the teacher to demonstrate how sharing should occur. It quickly teaches students valuable responses and the importance of positive frames in which to structure their responses. After turning their cards in, organize students into pairs and have them share their writing.

Sharing Step 4: *Sharing with a Partner*

Use the share sheet that follows. Now that you have demonstrated the sharing process, this activity should be more meaningful to your students.

Note: If you would like your students to practice this strategy with an essay that is not as complete, see the appended essay, "Jade Snow," by Ernie Gomez.

Share Sheet

Author's Name _____ Partner's Name _____

Directions: Read your partner's essay from beginning to end. When you are finished, respond to the items listed below. When you are finished, explain your responses to the author.

1. The title of this piece is:

2. Another title you might try is:

3. Some of the background information you include about Jade Snow Wong is:

4. The values you discuss in your essay are:

5. The personal experiences you include in your essay are:

6. Something you have in common with Jade Snow Wong is:

7. A way in which you differ from Jade Snow Wong is:

8. It would help me to understand better if:

9. I like the way you:

10. I need to know more about:

11. A strength in this paper is:

12. A suggestion for the writer is:

REVISING

Revising Step 1: *Revising the First Drafts*

Have students revise their first drafts based on the responses and suggestions from their partners.

Revising Step 2: *Showing the Changes*

Have students underline the parts they changed on their revision with colored pen or pencil.

EDITING

Editing Step 1: *Reading Aloud*

Have students reread their writing aloud, softly, to themselves. Reading aloud often helps them identify errors in punctuation and grammar as they notice where their voices naturally pause and are able to listen for what sounds right. Have them make any changes or corrections they want now because they will be sharing their piece in a few minutes. (Make dictionaries available.)

Editing Step 2: *Systematic Editing*

In groups of four, students will help each other edit. On the first pass to the left, students read for sentence punctuation. Each sentence must start with a capital and end appropriately. On the second pass to the left, students check for paragraph indentation, when appropriate, and punctuation. On the third and final pass, students check spelling, circling potentially misspelled words. Colored pens or pencils make this activity more interesting to the students and enable them to identify who marked what, should they wish to question an editor.

Note: Editing a sentence is not nearly as formidable as editing an entire essay. For this reason, I sometimes prepare my ELD students for editing by asking them to write their second draft sentence by sentence, one sentence per line. This is not meant to be busy work, although it does take some time. It is not recommended as a regular activity. However, it can work well with shorter pieces of writing—or even a paragraph. The process of breaking up the text into meaningful sentences is an enormous cognitive task for students who do not have a "monitor" for what a sentence is. It is also extremely helpful in teaching students to self-edit.

EVALUATION

Scoring Guide: Holistic

6   This paper is clearly superior in form and content. It demonstrates all or most of the following:

- contains examples of comparison and contrast with appropriate syntactical structure.

- includes introduction, main body, and conclusion as well as a discussion of family life, personal experiences, values and customs.

- pays careful attention to editing and correctness; minimal errors.

- demonstrates neatness and legibility in writing.

5   This paper is good to very good in terms of form and content. However, it will be a thinner version of the 6 paper. The writing is still impressive but the topic is less well handled in terms of organization, content, insight, and language.

4   The 4 paper is still in the upper-half category but is less well written than a 5, with less clarity of thought. A 4 paper exhibits some of these characteristics:

- includes similarities and differences but without the appropriate syntax.

- lacks examples from personal experience to support statements.

- shows a sense of organization but lacks cohesiveness.

- contains some errors in mechanics, usage, and sentence structure.

- is written legibly.

3   This paper is weak in content and form however but attempts to show similarities, and differences. It is weak in the qualities defined under the 6 paper. It:

- has no title.

- does not include examples from personal experience to support statements.

- fails to compare and contrast.

- lacks clarity and organization.

- contains serious errors in spelling, mechanics, usage, sentence structure.

2   This score applies to a paper that does not address the topic. The weaknesses in a 3 paper are compounded. A 2 paper is likely to exhibit the following characteristics in addition to the characteristics of a 3 paper:

- does not follow the directions in the prompt.

- does not develop ideas.

- has gross errors in the conventions of written English.

- is written illegibly.

1   This score is reserved for any response that ignores the topic.

EXTENSION ACTIVITY

Interpretive Question Game

Have students work together in their groups of four to answer the interpretive questions from Prewriting Step 8 as thoroughly as possible. Let them know that they are going to have an opportunity to earn points for their answers.

Ask the whole class one of the questions and allow them to rehearse the answer with their group members. Using numbered heads (where each student in the group has a different number from 1 to 4), call upon group representatives to answer the question. If the first group answers the question correctly, they earn five points. If another group can add meaningful information to the first group's response, they get two points. Sometimes, several groups get two points because they use details from the story to support their ideas.

This game encourages the ELD student to flesh out his or her responses with textual support. Because of the collaborative nature of the activity, the less fluent student has opportunities to become more familiar with the text.

Student Model

Jade Snow

There are several things that Jade Snow and I have different and in common. First, I am going to talk about the things we have different.

Well first, while she is Chinese, I am Mexican. Secondly, Jade Snow is a girl and I am a boy. Another thing, is that she is Buddhist, and I am Catholic. She is afraid of turkeys and I am scared of mud. I am scared of mud because my uncle used to get me dirty with mud and my mom gave me a bath and I hated baths.

We also have things that are the same. The first thing that we have the same is that we both have discipline. Secondly, Jade Snow and I are expected to be polite, honest, nice, and respectful. Both Jade Snow and I have learned a lesson. She learned that stealing is not nice. I learned a lesson about bedtime. One time, my dad told me to go to bed. I listened to him but when he went to sleep, I woke up and went to watch TV. My dad heard me and made me watch TV all night long so that I would listen to him better next time.

So, you see that we have more similarities than differences. You should learn not to think wrong about people. Don't judge them first. Get to know them.

By Ernie Gomez 6th Grade; ELD

Featured Literature

"Blue Winds Dancing"
by Thomas Whitecloud
From *Scribner's Monthly,*
103 (February 1938)

Grade Level
For High School and
College (may be adapted
for middle school)

Thinking Level
Synthesis

Writing Domains
Imaginative/Narrative
Analytical/Expository

Materials Needed
No special materials
required.

**Suggested
Supplementary
Readings**
• *Running Brave* (movie)
• "Indian Boarding School"
  by Louise Erdrich

Reflections on Alienation

by Shari Lockman

Overview

After reading "Blue Winds Dancing" by Thomas Whitecloud, students will write a reflective essay that explores the theme of alienation.

Objectives

THINKING SKILLS

Students will:

- *define* the concept of alienation;
- *describe* a time when they felt different from those around them;
- *compare* their experience with Thomas Whitecloud's in "Blue Winds Dancing";
- *comment on* the effects of alienation.

WRITING SKILLS

Students will:

- *use* sensory/descriptive and imaginative/narrative skills to enrich expository writing by incorporating personal experience into an analysis of theme;
- *use* analytical/expository skills to write a well-structured, reflective essay;
- *support* main points with textual and personal examples.

The Process

This five–to–seven–day lesson may be used as an introduction to or as part of a unit focusing on the theme of alienation. If taught along with an American Indian unit in a history class, it vividly illustrates the problems faced by American Indians today as they struggle to maintain their traditional values while living in the white world.

 PREWRITING

 Day 1 *Getting into the Story*

Prewriting Step 1: *Clustering*

As a way to introduce the theme of the lesson, cluster the word *alienation* on the board. Ask students to share any ideas, feelings, impressions, and memories that the word triggers. If students are reluctant to reveal themselves, share some of your own memories along with the feelings connected to the experience.

A sample class cluster might look like this:

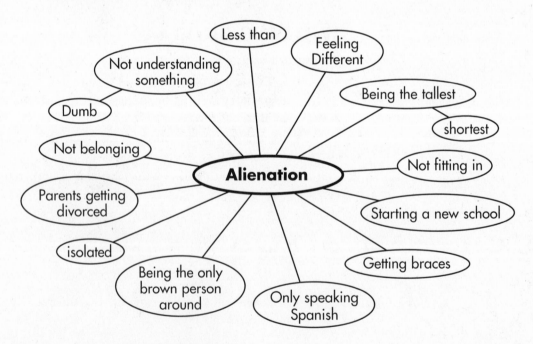

Prewriting Step 2: *Reading*

Read the story aloud to the students. To enhance the mood, you may want to play some American Indian background music as you read. (R. Carlos Nakai's *Canyon Trilogy* works well). See the bibliography at the end of the "Stories in Clay" lesson for more suggestions.

As they listen, have them underline the words, phrases, or sentences that appeal to them. *(Most students will be touched by the depth of emotion evoked by Whitecloud's vivid imagery.)* Give them time to share the images they selected in a class discussion, a Quaker Reading, or in small group discussions (whatever time permits).

Sample images might include:

- "clouds tipped with moonlight"
- "blue winds dancing over snow fields"
- "pine fighting for existence on a windy knoll"
- "winds come whispering through the forests"
- "soft lake waves wash the shores"

Writing a found poem at this point is also effective. *(See Glossary under "Found Poetry" for a description and see "Living in Life's Shadow" for a more detailed example of how to implement "Found Poetry.")*

Sample poems follow.

Student Models

The Journey

> Clouds tipped with moonlight
> Sunsets burst each evening over the lakes
> Going home
>
> The leaves change before the snows come
> The smell of rotting leaves
> Going home
>
> Chipmunks make tiny footprints on the limbs
> Squirrels busy in hollow trees, sorting acorns
> Going home
>
> Long forest wearing white
> Looking at dancing flames
> I am nearing home
>
> Snow clouds hang over the pines
> Designs of the track in the snow
> I am nearing home
>
> A small boy wandering away and he comes back
> Sharing some secret
> I am nearing home.

Night is beautiful
Music is beautiful
I am home

How to make each man his own songs
They know how to sing
I am home

I am happy
It is beautiful
I am home

Frank Chu —High School

Finding Freedom

Heavy mountains holding up
Night Sky
Home.
      Blue winds dancing over
      Snow fields
      Home.
Home and peace
The beat of drums
I should be at home.
      Fall rides in the valleys
      here .
      Winter never comes down the mountains
      here
      Trees grow in military row
      here
      The beauty of captivity
      is here
When snow crunches lightly beneath my feet,
When the pines are wearing white shawls
When a deer stands silhouetted on the rails
When white waving ribbons pulsate with the rhythm of
Drums
I am home then
I am free.

Melanie Langstaff—High School

Prewriting Step 3: *Charting Contrasting Images*

Reread the first section of the story aloud (up until the break before the actual journey starts). Then, to focus on the theme of alienation, have students chart the contrasting images that Whitecloud uses to show the differences between the Chippewa and white worlds.

A sample chart may look like the following:

White World

1. Fall hides in the valleys and winter never comes down from the mountains.

2. ...the trees grow in rows. The palms stand stiffly by the roadside and in the groves the orange trees line in military rows and endlessly bear fruit.

3. Driving to keep in a race that knows no ending and no goal.

4. Classes where men talk and talk, and then stop now and then to hear their own words come back to them from the students.

5. Hysterical preparing for life until that life is half over.

6. Always dissatisfied, getting a hill and wanting a mountain.

Chippewa World

1. The leaves change before the snow comes . . . Later when the first snow falls, one awakens in the morning to find the world white and beautiful and clean.

2. A pine fighting for existence on a windy knoll.

3. No hurry to get anywhere.

4. The ring of axes in deep woods, the crunch of snow beneath my feet . . . the smooth velvet of ghost birch bark. . . . the rhythm of the drums.

5. Knowing how to give—how to tear one's meat in two and share it with one's brothers.

6. How to make a thing of beauty from a piece of birch bark.

After charting the first part of the story together, have the students work in pairs or in groups of four *(Peer sharing groups work well for this activity.)* to chart the comparisons in the second half of the story. Have each group share their three most interesting sets of images from the contrast chart.

Reflections on Alienation

NONFICTION

Day 3 | *Going Beyond the Story*

Prewriting Step 4: *Clustering*

Review the class cluster on alienation and ask whether, after reading the story, students have any other words, ideas, or associations to add.

A sample addition to the original cluster may look like this:

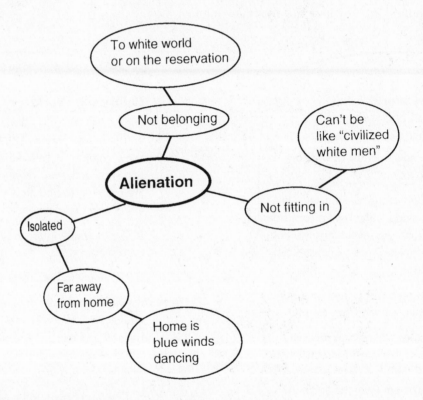

At this point in the lesson, introduce the prompt.

 **PROMPT**

Writing Situation:

In "Blue Winds Dancing," a college student compares his culture to the white world and discovers that his values differ from those around him. These differences make him feel alienated and alone. To achieve a sense of balance and belonging, he hitchhikes home at Christmas.

Writing Directions:

Write an essay in which you explore the impact of alienation on Thomas Whitecloud's life. Compare and contrast his experiences with a personal event from your own life—a time when you felt as if you didn't fit in or sensed a clash between your values and those of the people around you. Consider what both Whitecloud and you learned from your experiences and reflect about how alienation can affect human beings and human nature.

Your essay should have four parts:

Begin by exploring your own definition of alienation. Then discuss not only how but why Thomas Whitecloud comes to feel so alienated. In your discussion, you will need to show the reader, by using concrete examples and direct quotations from the text, the feelings, thoughts, and behaviors that exemplify Whitecloud's sense of alienation. Also, consider what Whitecloud does in an attempt to alleviate his feelings of alienation.

Next, compare and contrast Whitecloud's experience with one of your own. Begin by linking your experience to his with a transition sentence like:

- I can identify with Thomas Whitecloud because _____ .

- Like Thomas Whitecloud, I too experienced _____ .

- Unlike Thomas Whitecloud, I felt _____ .

Then, tell about a personal experience in which you felt a sense of alienation. Describe the circumstances that led you to feel this way, looking at both the **how** and **why** of the situation, as you did with Thomas Whitecloud's experience. In order for your readers to picture your thoughts, feelings, and actions, use concrete examples and vivid descriptive language as Whitecloud did in his story. Also, tell what you did to resolve your feelings or to overcome the situation. Throughout your narrative, be sure to compare and contrast your experience with Thomas Whitecloud's.

Feeling alienated can be a painful experience, but it can also be a learning process. In the final section of your essay, use Whitecloud's experience and your own to reflect upon what you have learned about how alienation can help us define ourselves as individuals or discover certain personal truths. You may also wish to consider how alienation can affect society as a whole. Remember, you are exploring your thoughts and reflections; you do not have to convince anyone that your ideas are "best" or "right."

NONFICTION

◆ PRECOMPOSING

Day 4 | *Planning the Reflective Essay*

Precomposing Step 1: *Clustering*

Have the students complete a series of clusters—one for each section of the prompt. Here are some sample clusters based on the student model, "Alienation: What Is It, and if I Catch It, How Can I Get Rid of it?"

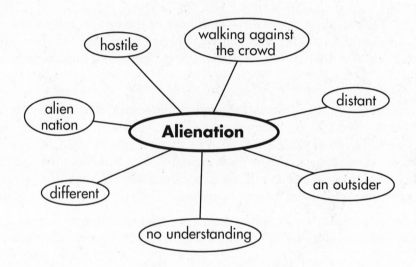

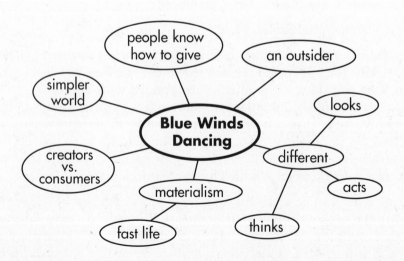

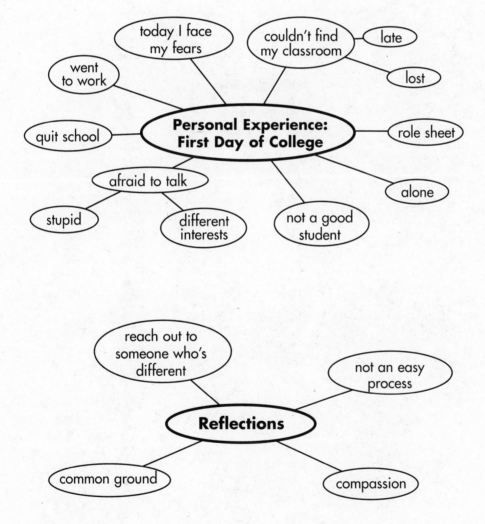

Precomposing Step 2: *Mapping*

After completing the clusters, some students will be able to write the first drafts of their essays. Others, especially younger or special-needs students, will need more precomposing activities in order to meet the demands of the prompt. Have these students make a map, which will constitute a more organized writing plan than the clusters. Students may choose to use the skeleton map (see previous page) or they may design a map of their own.

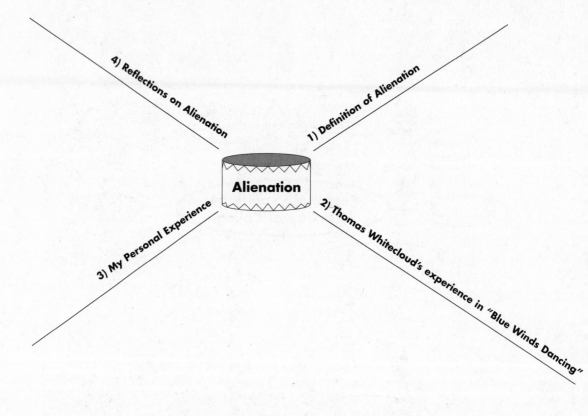

A sample map for the student model "Alienation: What Is It, and if I Catch It, How Can I Get Rid of It?" is as follows:

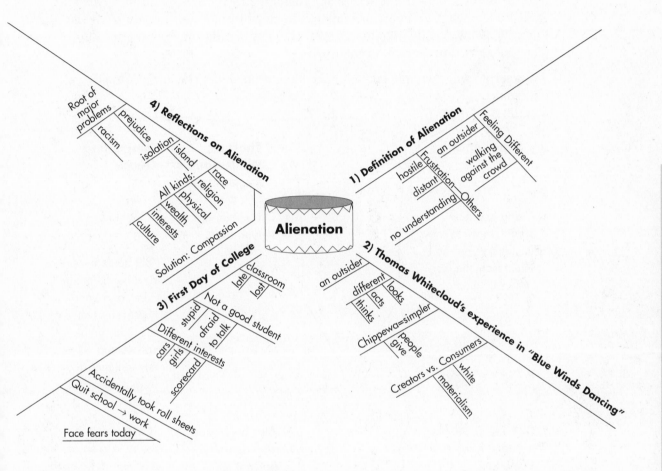

WRITING

Comparison Chart

Students should now be able to write the first drafts of their essays. Some younger or remedial writers may still have trouble weaving textual references into the fabric of their papers. Have them write the first section of their essays (the definition). Then, review with them the use of quotation marks. *(Refer to the "Quoting from the Text" handout appended to the "Living in Life's Shadow" lesson elsewhere in this book.)*

Next, have students complete another comparison chart, but this time they will compare their experience with Thomas Whitecloud's. Have them pick out two to three references from the text that parallel their experience and/or feelings. Actually seeing the comparisons laid out in chart form seems to help students linguistically weave the two ideas together. They should then be able to complete the reflection section on their own.

An excerpt from a sample chart for the student model, "Alienation," looks like this:

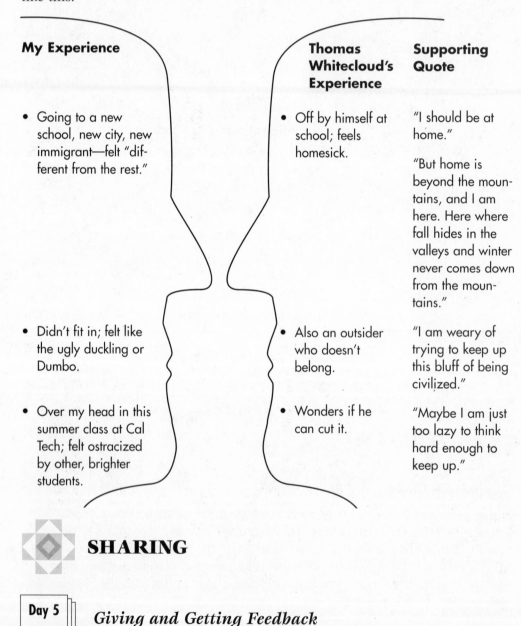

My Experience

- Going to a new school, new city, new immigrant—felt "different from the rest."

- Didn't fit in; felt like the ugly duckling or Dumbo.

- Over my head in this summer class at Cal Tech; felt ostracized by other, brighter students.

Thomas Whitecloud's Experience

- Off by himself at school; feels homesick.

- Also an outsider who doesn't belong.

- Wonders if he can cut it.

Supporting Quote

"I should be at home."

"But home is beyond the mountains, and I am here. Here where fall hides in the valleys and winter never comes down from the mountains."

"I am weary of trying to keep up this bluff of being civilized."

"Maybe I am just too lazy to think hard enough to keep up."

◆ SHARING

Day 5 | *Giving and Getting Feedback*

Working with partners or in peer response groups of four, have the students share their papers, using the following response sheet to provide written feedback:

Name _____

Sharing Sheet

Title of story that is being shared: _____

_____

Author: _____

Your Paper:

	Superb 4	Strong 3	Adequate 2	Needs Work 1
1. Includes a personal definition of alienation.				
2. Compares and/or contrasts your experiences to Thomas Whitecloud's.				
3. Makes good use of textual references and quotes correctly from the text.				
4. Describes a time when you felt alienated and tells how you resolved the situation.				
5. Includes the similarities and/or differences in your situation and feelings.				
6. Includes your personal reflections.				

7. Includes rich, descriptive language. These images work especially well for

me: _____

_____

8. One interesting point that you make about alienation is _____

_____

_____

9. I like the way you _____

_____

10. One thing you may want to work on in your revision is _____

_____

_____

REVISING

Students can revise their papers according to the responses they received on their sharing sheets.

EDITING

In pairs or peer response groups, students should edit their papers for correctness, paying particular attention to the rules for incorporating quotations into the body of a paper.

EVALUATION

The following guide may be used to score papers on a 1–4 point scale:

Scoring Guide

4   This paper is clearly superior. It is carefully organized, well written, insightful, and technically correct. A 4 paper does most or all of the following and does it well:

  • Offers a complete and insightful personal definition of *alienation*.

  • Compares and/or contrasts the writer's personal experience with Whitecloud's by considering the situations and feelings involved in both experiences.

  • Makes appropriate and correct use of references from the text when offering those comparisons.

  • Uses rich, descriptive language to describe a time when the author felt alienated and tells how the situation was resolved.

  • Includes thoughtful reflections about the nature of alienation in relation to self and to others.

  • Has few, if any, errors in the conventions of written English.

3   This is a strong paper that addresses all or most of the aspects of the assignment well. It is a thinner version of the 4 paper, but is less insightful, not as carefully organized, and may exhibit one or two errors in correctness. A 3 paper will do most of the following:

  • Offers a complete and reasonably insightful personal definition of *alienation*.

  • Compares and/or contrasts the writer's personal experience with Whitecloud's by considering the situations and feelings involved in both experiences.

- Makes appropriate and correct use of references from the text when offering those comparisons.

- Uses some rich, descriptive language to describe a time when the author felt alienated and tells how the situation was resolved.

- Includes reasonably thoughtful reflections about the nature of alienation in relation to self and to others.

- Has some errors in the conventions of written English but none that interfere with the writer's message.

2 This paper meets most of the criteria of the assignment but does so in less depth that a 4 or 3 paper. A 2 paper may demonstrate some of the following:

- Offers a two-to-three word definition of *alienation*.

- Compares and/or contrasts the writer's personal experience with Thomas Whitecloud's by describing the situation, but forgetting the feelings.

- Uses references from the text but does not use them correctly.

- Tells about a time when the author felt alienated and includes how the situation was resolved, but fails to use rich, descriptive language.

- Reflects upon the nature of alienation in relation to self and to others.

- Has errors in the conventions of standard written English that interfere with the writer's message.

1 This paper address the assignment superficially and is poorly organized. It fails to meet the demands of the assignment and has little impact on the reader.

EXTENSION ACTIVITIES

1. *Comparing/Contrasting* Running Brave *and "Blue Winds Dancing"*

Show the movie *Running Brave* (available at most video rental stores) to your students. The movie deals with Billy Mills's struggle to excel as a track star at the University of Kansas while still maintaining his traditional Lakota (Sioux) values. He, too, returns to the reservation to achieve a sense of balance and belonging—then goes on to win a gold medal at the Olympics. This movie parallels Whitecloud's experience and may help non-Indian students visualize life on a reservation (material poverty, but spiritual strength) while giving American Indian students a sense of pride in the accomplishments of their people. Have students use a Venn diagram to compare and contrast the two stories. *(Note: Another work of literature that has striking parallels to "Blue Winds Dancing" is the poem "Indian Boarding School: The Runaways" by Louise Erdrich.)*

2. *Freewriting Exercise*

Explain the American Indian belief that the drum is the heartbeat of the people. Look for references to this idea in "Blue Winds Dancing." Ask the students to complete a fifteen-to-twenty minute freewrite exploring the objects that represent the heartbeat of their culture.

3. *Metacognitive Questions*

As a way of providing closure to the unit, have students answer the following metacognitive questions:

Metacognitive Questions

- How did this lesson change or enrich your understanding of the theme of alienation?

- What did you learn from this story about American Indian culture?

- What did you learn from this story about your culture?

Student Models

Alienation: What Is It and If I Catch It, How Can I Get Rid of It?

What is alienation? Have you ever felt different, hostile, distant? Have you ever felt like an outsider, like you didn't fit in, like an individual walking against the crowd? Have you ever felt that no one understands you, that no one feels like you or thinks the way you do? If you have, then you've experienced alienation. Haven't we all felt alienated at one time or another? The very word alienation brings to mind the image of a nation of people from outer space; far from their own world, they look, act, and think differently than anyone from our world. I remember a time when I felt far from my own world... a time when I felt that I looked, acted, and thought differently than anyone else around me.

In my mind, I've been transported back to that time. It's an early Monday morning and I can't find my class. The campus is much bigger than my high school campus. By the time I find my class, I'm late. As I open the solid wood door, I feel like I've walked into a different world, a scary world. Though I'm surrounded by forty to fifty other students, I'm all alone. It's my first class... my very first day in college. I don't know anyone in any of my classes; there's not a friendly face to be found. I'm quiet and shy, afraid to begin a conversation with others in class. What do I say? I don't want them to think I'm stupid. I don't think I'm good at making conversation. I'm not a good student. I don't even know what major I want to pursue and I have no idea of what I want out of life. I'm not into cars, drinking or drugs, or locker room talk. I have no interest in talking about cars and "getting wasted," and I'm not impressed by guys who brag about how many times they've had sex. I'm different. Fear of what others will think about me has led me to say nothing. I sit quietly in the first row at the end of the classroom and pretend to pay close attention to the teacher. At the end of the day, the role sheet is passed around and we are to put out initials next to our names. I receive the role sheet last and, somehow, in my haste to get out of the class, I put the role sheet in my folder and take it home with me. At the beginning of class the next day, the teacher asks if anyone has the role sheet. As she's speaking, I'm opening my folder. When I see the role sheet, I immediately slam my folder shut, hoping no one has seen that I was the one who took the role sheet. Feeling really stupid, I withdraw even further into my own world. It wasn't long after this incident that I decided I wasn't ready for college, so I retreated to the work force. I don't regret this decision, though now I try not to let my fears get in the way of getting to know people and having wonderful experiences. I've made a great discovery—I'm not much different than everyone else. I have yet to meet anyone that I don't have something in common with.

In "Blue Winds Dancing," Thomas Whitecloud describes feeling like an outsider, an alien from another world. He's living in the white world, a world of people who look, act and think differently than he does. The white man is "always dissatisfied, getting a hill and wanting a mountain." They are concerned only with themselves and getting as much material wealth as they can... as fast as they can get it. In his world, people are content with simple things; "having work, a woman, and a place to hang their hats." They haven't been taught that if they want to be happy they need more. They are not consumers; they're creators. They make things of beauty with their own hands, and they share them with each other. They don't avoid eye contact; they truly see each other. They communicate without the need to talk. They can all share mood and enjoy being with each other. Living in a world where people "talk and talk, and then stop now and then to hear their own words come back to them," Thomas Whitecloud feels far from his Chippewa home. In this new world he lives in, he's taught that his people are inferior; they're less intelligent, and their gods have forgotten them—didn't even write them a book. Thomas Whitecloud responds to this alienation by running home. Is he running away from his feelings of alienation, retreating into the safe confines of his home, or is he going home to confirm in his mind that he's still an alien... an Indian who remains a part of that world? While it may appear that Thomas Whitecloud is running away from the alienation, he feels living in the white world, his real battle is the alienation he feels upon his re-entry into his own Chippewa world. But with the help of his people, "the invitation in the eyes of the old men," he overcomes these feelings. He's home at last.

Alienation not only affects each of our lives individually, but it has a great effect on our society and world as a whole. Alienation is a close relative of racism and prejudice. As it did with Thomas Whitecloud, it keeps people of different races, social class, and sometimes gender isolated, an island unto themselves. It keeps White, Black, Asian, and Vietnamese people from getting to know and understand each other; it separates Irish Protestants and Catholics, causing them to kill each other in their attempt to stay isolated from one another; it keeps young people and elderly folks from getting to know one another and learn from each other; it separates healthy people from those who have a mental or physical handicap; it keeps rappers, punk rockers, heavy-metalers, dweebs, nerds, jocks, brains, loners, and the in-crowd from discovering some kind of common ground they can build friendships on; it separates the rich and the poor, seeking to keep them both on their own side of the tracks; it imprisons most of them on their own side of the tracks; it imprisons most of us, confining us to a darkness we don't even realize is there; it restrains us from getting to know others who are different than us. How many of us have been used by it to cause someone else to feel alienated? How many of us, at one time or another, have made someone else feel inferior? How many of us haven't talked to someone because they were of a different race or religion or they weren't popular or good-looking? How many of us haven't taken the time to get to know someone just because they were a little bit different and that made us a little uncomfortable? Have we all caught alienation and passed it on to everyone around us? If we have caught it, how can we get rid of it? If you have ever made someone else feel alienated, then the solution begins with you.

You and I can get rid of alienation only by replacing it with some thing more powerful... something that will eject it from our bodies. What has the power to do this? Compassion. While alienation causes indifference, hostility, and distance, compassion causes one to identify with and understand the thoughts and feelings of another. If we begin to identify with and understand the thoughts and feelings of everyone who is different from us, do you think they will still feel alienated?

While this seems like a simple answer, it is not an easy process. There will be times when we don't feel like reaching out to someone who's different; there will be times when we feel like letting them reach out to us; there will be times when we feel extremely uncomfortable; there will be times when the crowd or our peers try to convince us that compassion is uncool; there will be times when we try to convince ourselves that we don't have time to be compassionate, a time when we feel that we have other things to do that are more important; there may be times when we feel that some groups of people don't deserve our compassion; there will be times when we reach out and we're not trusted, instead we're rejected, but if we can persevere and continue to show compassion for everyone who's different than we are, then we will have changed our world. We will have shown our world that people aren't much different no matter where they live or how different they appear... that it's possible to discover some common ground to build friendships on. We will have embraced into our society various multitudes of people who otherwise would have remained alienated and isolated.

Ted Becker—Community College

Alienation

Going to a new school; moving to a new city; a new immigrant; the ugly duckling; and Dumbo. Whether we are in a new environment, or different in appearance, or have huge ears that enable us to fly, we feel different from the rest—we don't fit in. At times we try our hardest to conform and mix in, but we just can't do it. Alienation is the feeling when an individual feels shunned or left out from the norms of society. It can result from something as trivial as using a different pen; or it can also be as severe as being a Puritan in Catholic England. Nevertheless, alienation is a part of all people because throughout our lives, we must continually strive to retain our individuality while simultaneously conforming to the existing standards of our ever-changing society.

Picture a baby being thrown in a pool full of water. As the baby flaps his arms and kicks his legs in desperation, he only sinks deeper. To complicate the situation, the water level begins to rise. This baby was me three summers ago. I had been "tossed head-first" into the summer science program at Caltech. Of course, I entered with the attitude that I would get an 'A' with relative ease, only to learn that I was shockingly wrong. I had signed up to take molecular biology and chemistry, both relatively general courses. When I entered, I noticed that everyone around me looked the same, except for a group of surfers in the front row. My initial scare was the reading assignment for which I was to be responsible in one night: 50 pages in my biology textbook. Furthermore, the textbook was designed for college sophomores who had a background in biochemistry.

But that was only the beginning. Next came the daily tests. My grade began to drop deeper and deeper into a chasm. Never before had I struggled so much just to pass my tests, much less get an 'A.' Never before had I needed to worry about just keeping my head above water. When grades were communicated among my classmates, I would shamefully hide my test in a notebook saturated with humility. Getting bad test grades wasn't the only problem I had to face. These grades were based on a curve, with me somewhere near or even at the bottom. I was desperate. I was drowning. Most of all, I was alone, ostracized by the academic excellence of my classmates.

Fortunately, I learned to swim. I began to realize that my biggest hindrance wasn't my inability to understand the Krebs Cycle or acid-base equilibria; nor was it the fact that I was in a class full of "the best of the best." My biggest hindrance was much closer to home—my attitude. When I realized that I wasn't at the top, but at the bottom, I felt alienated. Consequently, this alienation led me to feel angry, worthless, and lost.

In "Blue Winds Dancing," Whitecloud feels this alienation because he is half-American and half-Indian, living in the urban cities to which he is foreign. He feels lost in this world where "all the trees grow... in military rows and endlessly bear fruit." Realizing that he is uncomfortable and cannot successfully adapt to his new world, he longs greatly to return to his home. However, when he does return home, he feels awkward because he feels he does not fit in anywhere. As he says, "Nobody seems to notice me. It seems as though I were among a people I have never seen before." Thus, he is lost in a world in which he cannot adapt successfully. Indeed, he cannot change the circumstances he is in; however, only he is to blame for his helpless and pathetic attitude toward a future he can make better for himself.

When we are alienated, we feel extremely vulnerable. Unfortunately, this vulnerability can lead to unreasonable rationalizations, blaming others, and other various behavior that prevent us from making the best we can out of a difficult situation. After that summer, I looked at a challenge as something which could improve me and make me a better person—a tennis match, tough class, demanding teacher or difficult stage in life. We must learn to realize that alienation is a part of all of us. We all plead for affection and positive attention in some way, whether it's a job promotion or just a pat on the back. That is why when we don't receive this positive reinforcement, we are susceptible to feeling hurt, maybe even cheated. But in all things, we must learn not to let isolation and alienation blind our eyes, but to open them.

Jason Cheng—High School

Alienation

Alienation is the way you feel when people stare at you because you don't belong in that place. It makes you feel shy and afraid to talk to other people. Then other people don't talk to you and you feel alone. You feel different, like you don't fit in your surroundings.

Thomas Whitecloud felt different and alienated too. He was the only Indian in a white college. In school, he heard how his race was "behind on intelligence tests." He said, "It is terrible to sit in classes and hear men tell you that your people worship sticks of wood, that your gods are all false, that the Manitou forgot your people and did not write them a book." He must have felt ashamed and embarrassed to be an Indian. He felt better after he hitched home for a visit. Being with his people probably gave him the strength to try to go back to school again.

I remember a time when like Thomas Whitecloud, I felt like I didn't fit in at school. I entered a new school in Whittier, California. I was one of the only Mexican girls at the school. I didn't talk to other students because I was embarrassed about my accent. Almost everyone else was white and I felt different. They even put me in a beginning Spanish class when I have spoken Spanish since I was born. I felt like a little kid learning how to count all over again. I felt so different from the other students that I only talked to my teachers. After awhile, I stopped going to school because I couldn't handle feeling so different. Finally, I came back to school in Santa Ana where I feel like I fit in at school.

Alienation is the feeling you get when you don't fit in with the people around you. When people don't understand another race or culture, they think the things people do are stupid, when they're really not. If people would just understand and learn from each other, this world would be a better place to live.

Ana Lopez—Middle School

Featured Literature

Blue Winds Dancing

There is a moon out tonight. Moon and stars and clouds tipped with moonlight. And there is a fall wind blowing in my heart. Ever since this evening, when against a fading sky I saw geese wedge southward. Now I try to study, but against the pages I see them again, driving southward. Going home.

Across the valley there are heavy mountains holding up the night sky and beyond the mountain there is home. Home, and peace, and the beat of drums, and blue winds dancing over snow fields. The Indian lodge will fill with my people and our gods will come and sit among them. I should be there then. I should be at home.

But home is beyond the mountains, and I am here. Here where fall hides in the valleys, and winter never comes down from the mountains. Here where all the trees grow in rows; the palms stand stiffly by the roadsides, and in the groves the orange trees line in military rows, and endlessly bear fruit. Beautiful, yes, there is always beauty in order, in rows of growing things! But it is the beauty of captivity. A pine fighting for existence on a windy knoll is much more beautiful.

In my Wisconsin, the leaves change before the snows come. In the air there is the smell of wild rice and venison cooking; and when the winds come whispering through the forests, they carry the smell of rotting leaves. In the evenings, the loon calls, lonely; and birds sing their last songs before leaving. Bears dig roots and eat late fall berries, fattening for their long winter sleep. Later, when the first snows fall, one awakens in the morning to find the world white and beautiful and clean. Then one can look back over his trail and see the tracks following. In the woods there are tracks of deer and snowshoe rabbits, and long streaks where partridges slide to alight. Chipmunks make tiny footprints on the limbs; and one can hear squirrels busy in hollow trees, sorting acorns. Soft lake waves wash the shores, and sunsets burst each evening over the lakes, and make them look as if they were afire.

That land which is my home! Beautiful, calm—where there is no hurry to get anywhere, no driving to keep up in a race that knows no ending and no goal. No classes where men talk and talk and then stop now and then to hear their own words come back to them from the students. No constant peering into the maelstrom of one's mind; no worries about grades and honors; no hysterical preparing for life until that life is half over; no anxiety about one's place in the thing they call Society.

I hear again the ring of axes in deep woods, the crunch of snow beneath my feet. I feel again the smooth velvet of ghost-birch bark. I hear the rhythm of the drums... I am tired. I am weary of trying to keep up this bluff of being civilized. Being civilized means trying to do everything you don't want to, never doing anything you want to. It means dancing to the strings of custom and tradition: it means living in houses and never knowing or caring who is next door. These civilized white men want us to be like them—always dissatisfied, getting a hill and wanting a mountain.

Then again, maybe I am not tired. Maybe I'm licked. Maybe I am just not smart enough to grasp these things that go to make up civilization. Maybe I am just too lazy to think hard enough to keep up.

Still, I know my people have many things that civilization has taken from the whites. They know how to give, how to tear one's piece of meat in two and share it with one's brother. They know how to sing—how to make each man his own songs and sing them; for their music they do not have to listen to other men singing over a radio. They know how to make things with their hands, how to shape beads into design and make a thing of beauty from a piece of birch bark.

But we are inferior. It is terrible to have to feel inferior; to have to read reports of intelligence tests, and learn that one's race is behind. It is terrible to sit in classes and hear men tell you that your people worship sticks of wood—that your gods are all false, that the Manitou forgot your people and did not write them a book.

I am tired. I want to walk again among the ghost-birches. I want to see the leaves turn in autumn, the smoke rise from the lodgehouses, and to feel the blue winds. I want to hear the drums; I want to hear the drums and feel the blue whispering winds.

There is a train wailing into the night. The trains go across the mountains. It would be easy to catch a freight. They will say he has gone back to the blanket; I don't care. The dance at Christmas...

A bunch of bums warming at a tiny fire talk politics and women and joke about the Relief and the WPA and smoke cigarettes. These men in caps and overcoats and dirty overalls living on the outskirts of civilization are free, but they pay the price of being free in civilization. They are outcasts. I remember a sociology professor lecturing on adjustment to society; hobos and prostitutes and criminals are individuals who never adjusted, he said. He could learn a lot if he came and listened to a bunch of bums talk. He would learn that work and a woman and a place to hang his hat are all the ordinary man wants. These are all he wants, but other men are not content to let him want only these. He must be taught to want radios and automobiles and a new suit every spring. Progress would stop if he did not want these things. I listen to hear if there is any talk of communism or socialism in the hobo jungles. There is none. At best there is a sort of disgusted philosophy about life. They seem to think there should be a better distribution of wealth, or more work, or something. But they are not rabid about it. The radicals live in the cities.

I find a fellow headed for Albuquerque, and talk road-talk with him. "It is hard to ride fruit cars. Bums break in. Better to wait for a cattle car going back to the Middle West, and ride that." We catch the next east-bound and walk the tops until we find a cattle car. Inside, we crouch near the forward wall, huddle, and try to sleep. I feel peaceful and content at last. I am going home. The cattle car rocks. I sleep.

Morning and the desert. Noon and the Salton Sea, lying more lifeless than a mirage under a somber sun in a pale sky. Skeleton mountains rearing on the skyline, thrusting out of the desert floor, all rock and shadow and edges. Desert. Good country for an Indian reservation...

Yuma and the muddy Colorado. Night again, and I wait shivering for the dawn.

Phoenix. Pima country. Mountains that look like cardboard sets on a forgotten stage. Tucson. Papago country. Giant cacti that look like petrified hitchhikers along the highways. Apache country. At El Paso my road-buddy decides to go on to Houston. I leave him, and head north to the mesa country. Las Cruces and the terrible Organ Mountains, jagged peaks that instill fear and wondering. Albuquerque. Pueblos along the Rio Grande. On the boardwalk there are some Indian women in colored sashes selling bits of pottery. The stone age offering its arts to the twentieth century. They hold up a piece and fix the tourists with black eyes until, embarrassed, he buys or turns away. I feel suddenly angry that my people should have to do such things for a living...

Santa Fe trains are fast, and they keep them pretty clean of bums. I decide to hurry and ride passenger coal tenders. Hide in the dark, judge the speed of the train as it leaves, and then dash out, and catch it. I hug the cold steel wall of the tender and think of the roaring fire in the engine ahead, and of the passengers back in the dining car reading their papers over hot coffee. Beneath me there is a blur of rails. Death would come quick if my hands should freeze and I fall. Up over the Sangre De Cristo range, around cliffs and through canyons to Denver. Bitter cold here, and I must watch out for Denver Bob. He is a railroad bull who has thrown bums from fast freights. I miss him. It is too cold, I suppose. On north to the Sioux country.

Small towns lit for the coming Christmas. On the streets of one I see a beam-shouldered young farmer gazing into a window filled with shining silver toasters. He is tall and wears a blue shirt, buttoned, with no tie. His young wife by his side looks at him hopefully. He wants decorations for his place to hang his hat to please his woman...

Northward again. Minnesota, and great white fields of snow; frozen lakes, and dawn running into dusk without noon. Long forests wearing white. Bitter cold, and one night the northern light. I am nearing home.

I reach Woodruff at midnight. Suddenly I am afraid, now that I am twenty miles from home. Afraid of what my father will say, afraid of being looked on as a stranger by my own people. I sit by a fire and think about myself and all the other young Indians. We just don't seem to fit in anywhere—certainly not among the whites, and not among the older people. I think again about the learned sociology professor and his professing. So many things seem to be clear now that I am away from school and do not have to worry about some man's opinion of my ideas. It is easy to think while looking at dancing flames.

Morning, I spend the day cleaning up, and buying some presents for my family with what is left of my money. Nothing much, but a gift is a gift, if a man buys it with his last quarter. I wait until evening, then start up the track toward home.

Christmas Eve comes in on a north wind. Snow clouds hang over the pines, and the night comes early. Walking along the railroad bed, I feel the calm peace of snowbound forests on either side of me. I take my time; I am back in a world where time does not mean so much now. I am alone; alone but not nearly so lonely as I was back on the campus at school. Those are never lonely who love the snow and the pines; never lonely when the pines are wearing white shawls and snow crunches coldly underfoot. In the woods I know there are the track of deer and rabbit; I know that if I leave the rails and go into the woods I shall find them. I walk along feeling glad because my legs are light and my feet seem to know that they are home. A deer comes out of the woods just ahead of me, and stands silhouetted on the rails. The North, I feel, has welcomed me home. I watch him and am glad that I do not wish for a gun. He goes into the woods quietly, leaving only the designs of his tracks in the snow. I walk on. Now and then I pass a field, white under the night sky, with houses at the far end. Smoke comes from the chimneys of the houses, and I try to tell what sort of wood each is burning by the smoke; some burn pine, others aspen, others tamarack. There is one from which comes black coal smoke that rises lazily and drifts out over the tops of the trees. I like to watch houses and try to imagine what might be happening in them.

Just as light snow begins to fall, I cross the reservation boundary; somehow it seems as though I have stepped into another world. Deep woods in a white-and-black winter night. A faint trail leading to the village.

The railroad on which I stand comes from a city sprawled by a lake—a city with a million people who walk around without seeing one another; a city sucking the life from all the country around; a city with stores and police and intellectuals and criminals and movies and apartment houses; a city with its politics and libraries and zoos.

Laughing, I go into the woods. As I cross a frozen lake, I begin to hear the drums. Soft in the night the drums beat. It is like the pulse beat of the world. The white line of the lake ends at a black forest, and above the trees the blue winds are dancing.

I come to the outlying houses of the village. Simple box houses, etched black in the night. From one or two windows soft lamp light falls on the snow. Christmas here, too, but it does not mean much; not much in the way of parties and presents. Joe Sky will get drunk. Alex Bodidash will buy his children red mittens and a new sled. Alex is a Carisle man, and tries to keep his home up to white standards. White standards. Funny that my people should be ever falling farther behind. The more they try to imitate whites, the more tragic the result. Yet they want us to be imitation white men. About all we imitate well are their vices.

The village is not a sight to instill pride, yet I am not ashamed; one can never be ashamed of his own people when he knows they have dreams as beautiful as white snow on a tall pine.

Father and my brother and sister are seated around the table as I walk in. Father stares at me for a moment, then I am in his arms, crying on his shoulder. I give them the presents I have brought, and my throat tightens as I watch my sister save carefully bits of red string from the packages. I hide my feelings by wrestling with my brother when he strikes my shoulder in token of affection. Father looks at me, and I know he has many questions, but he seems to know why I have come. He tells me to go on alone to the lodge, and he will follow.

I walk along the trail to the lodge, watching the northern lights forming in the heavens. White waving ribbons that seem to pulsate with the rhythm of the drums. Clean snow creaks beneath my feet, and a soft wind sighs through the trees, singing to me. Everything seems to say "Be happy! You are home now—you are free. You are among friends—we are your friends; we, the trees, and the snow, and the lights." I follow the trail to the lodge. My feet are light, my heart seems to sing to the music, and I hold my head high. Across white snow fields blue winds are dancing.

Before the lodge door I stop, afraid. I wonder if my people will remember me. I wonder—"Am I Indian, or am I white?" I stand before the door a long time. I hear the ice groan on the lake, and remember the story of the old woman who is under the ice, trying to get out, so she can punish some runaways lovers. I think to myself, "If I am a white I will not believe that story; if I am Indian, I will know that there is an old woman under the ice." I listen for a while, and I know that there is an old woman under the ice. I look again at the lights, and go in.

Inside the lodge there are many Indians. Some sit on benches around the walls, other dance in the center of the floor around a drum. Nobody seems to notice me. It seems as though I were among a people I have never seen before. Heavy women with long black hair. Women with children on their knees—small children that watch with intent black eyes the movements of the dancers, whose small faces are solemn and serene. The faces of the old people are serene, too, and their eyes are merry and bright. I look at the old men. Straight, dressed in dark trousers and beaded velvet vests, wearing soft moccasins. Dark, lined faces intent on the music. I wonder if I am at all like them. They dance on, lifting their feet to the rhythm of the drums, swaying lightly, looking upward. I look at their eyes, and am startled at the rapt attention to the rhythm of the music.

The dance stops. The men walk back to the wall, and talk in low tones or with their hands. There is little conversation, yet everyone seems to be sharing some secret. A woman looks at a small boy wandering away, and he comes back to her.

Strange. I think, and then remember. These people are not sharing words—they are sharing a mood. Everyone is happy. I am so used to white people that it seems strange so many people could be together without someone talking. These Indians are happy because they are together, and because the night is beautiful outside, and the music is beautiful. I try hard to forget school and white people, and be one of these—my people. I try to forget everything but the night, and it is a part of me; that I am one with the my people and we are all a part of something universal. I watch eyes, and see now that the old people are speaking to me. They nod slightly, imperceptibly, and their eyes laugh into mine. I look around the room. All the eyes are friendly; they all laugh. No one questions my being here. The drums begin to beat again, and I catch the invitation in the eyes of the old men. My feet begin to lift to the rhythm, and I look out beyond the walls into the night and see the lights. I am happy. It is beautiful. I am home.

Thomas Whitecloud

Sweet Summer
by Bebe Moore Campbell

Grade Level
For Middle School ,
High School, and College

Thinking Level
Application

Writing Domain
Sensory/Descriptive
Imaginative/Narrative

Materials Needed
• Yellow highlighter pens

**Suggested
Supplementary
Reading**
Pilgrim at Tinker Creek
by Annie Dillard

The Saturation Recall Paper:
Capturing Your Experience
In and Of a Place

by Carol Booth Olson

Overview

After reading an excerpt from *Sweet Summer: Growing Up with and without My Dad*, students will recall a place that made a strong impression and how they came to be there, and then recreate their experience in a narrative, showing, not telling, description.

Objectives

THINKING SKILLS

Students will:

- *apply* Campbell's account of an experience in a special place by thinking of a place that made a strong impression on them;
- *recall* the sights, sounds, smells, textures, etc., of that place as well as how they came to be there;
- *recreate* the essence of their experience in and of that place by dramatizing the event;
- *illustrate* how that place made them feel;
- *create* a "you are there" feeling in the reader.

WRITING SKILLS

Students will:

- *write* in narrative form—beginning (with an attention-getting opening), middle, and end—conveying a sequence of events and a sense of plot line;
- *use* first person point of view;
- *choose* past or present tense and use it consistently;
- *use* vivid sensory/descriptive language and figurative expressions to paint a picture in words;
- *use* narrative techniques such as dialogue, interior monologue, flashback to dramatize the experience and engage the reader;
- *show*, rather than tell, how this place makes them feel;
- *follow* the conventions of standard written English (including following the rules for using dialogue).

The Process

This lesson relies heavily upon two other sources—The Saturation Report as described by Ruby Bernstein in *Practical Ideas for Teaching Writing as a Process* (ed. Carol Booth Olson, Sacramento, CA: California State Department of Education, 1987) and "On the Nose," a lesson in sensory/ descriptive writing designed by Shari Lockman in *Thinking/Writing: Fostering Critical Thinking Through Writing* (ed. Carol Booth Olson, New York: HarperCollins Publishers, 1992).

 PREWRITING

Prewriting Step 1: *Introduction to Sensory Details*

Introduce the use of sensory description by having students volunteer how something smells. Start by asking a volunteer, in the abstract, to describe how perfume smells. Most likely, his or her response will be vague and overly general.

Example: (without sensory details)	nice perfume sweet perfume strong perfume

Now, spray perfume on that person's wrist. Ask him/her to smell the scent and to come up with additional descriptions of perfume.

Example: (without sensory details)	fragrant perfume gardenia-scented perfume makes me think of an English garden.

Combine these responses into a sentence.

Sample Sentence:	A whiff of the fragrant, gardenia-scented perfume conjured up images of lacy flowers in an English garden.

Repeat this process with one or two other items: ammonia, tuna fish, and sweaty gym clothes are examples (although you can tell students you'll spare them from the actual sample of the latter).

Example: (without sensory details)	smelly gym clothes gross gym clothes stinky gym clothes
(with sensory details)	pungent gym clothes musty gym clothes crusty, like cardboard gym clothes
Sample Sentence:	When she opened the bag, the pungent, musty aroma of the gym clothes assaulted her senses, but having to unravel the crusty, cardboardlike socks was even more unpleasant.

Note: Steps 1–3 in this lesson are directly adapted from Shari Lockman's "On the Nose" lesson.

Explain to students that our six senses (taste, touch, smell, sight, sound, and movement) are ways that our brain receives information about the world around us and that, as writers, if we want to help the reader be there—to see what we saw and feel what we felt—then we must create concrete, vivid, and detailed descriptions that appeal to our reader's senses.

Prewriting Step 2: *Sniff-Around*

Start by raiding spices and locating as many "smells" as you can find. Wrap each in brown paper, number, and write an Answer Key so that you'll remember which number is which spice. Supplement spices with other items. For example, popcorn, barbecue sauce, gardenia, and crushed pine needles may evoke responses in certain students. Some will need to be "disguised" and in numbered paper bags, and students will need to be told to close their eyes when opening the bags.

Explain that the class will be experiencing a kind of guessing game in order to 1) generate descriptive language and 2) connect certain smells with memories of places, people, and events.

Pass out the Sniff Sheet on the next page and read the instructions. Now, pass out the spices and items. Have students sniff in pairs. In Shari Lockman's original "On the Nose" lesson, students take a full class period to smell all the items. For this lesson, twenty minutes to smell several samples (say, six) and react to them will suffice. *Note: If students want to go longer and you have the time, include a break during the middle of this activity lest some students get dizzy.*

Once you call time, select some of the numbers (#3, #6, #8, #11, #14, #15, for example), ask who smelled that scent, note down the descriptive words, the guesses of what the item is, and the memories it evoked, if any.

Example:	Scent	Descriptive Words	What I Think It Is	Memory It Evokes
	#6	earthy	?	N/A
		pungent	oregano	Grandma's kitchen
		grassy	parsley	N/A
		Italian	oregano	An Italian restaurant
	#12	fragrant	flower	N/A
		delicate	perfume	N/A
		flowery	gardenia	A friend's wedding
		heavy	wisteria	Summer in the south

As you discuss each item, you may want to unwrap it to reveal what it really is. Shari has found that students respond almost as if it were Christmas. Again, her lesson involves discussing and unwrapping each scent. For the purposes of this lesson, one can generate quite a list of descriptive words and connect some of those words to memories without discussing every mystery item.

Name: _____

Period: _____

Sniff Sheet

After you have smelled each of the secret spices and assorted mystery items, write down one or more concrete words that describe its scent in the first column and, if you have one, a guess of what the item you're smelling is, in the second column. Then, if that scent reminds you of a person, place, or event, write down the memory it evokes in the third column. Be sure your responses on the Sniff Sheet correspond with the number on the mystery item, since you will not be smelling them in order.

Scent	Descriptive Words	What I think It Is	Memory It Evokes
1			
2			
3			
4			
5			
6			
7			
8			
9			
10			
11			
12			
13			
14			
15			
16			

The Saturation Recall Paper

NONFICTION

Prewriting Step 3: *Thesaurus Page*

Using the words that surfaced during the prior discussion, begin to construct a Thesaurus Page.

An example might be:

Thesaurus Page		
acrid	fragrant	woodsy
bitter	grassy	Italian
delicate	heavy	leathery
earthy	pungent	peppery
flowery	spicy	

Prewriting Step 4: *Clustering*

Ask students to cluster places they associate with the sense of smell and, off those cluster words, to cluster descriptive words they associate with those places.

An example might look like this:

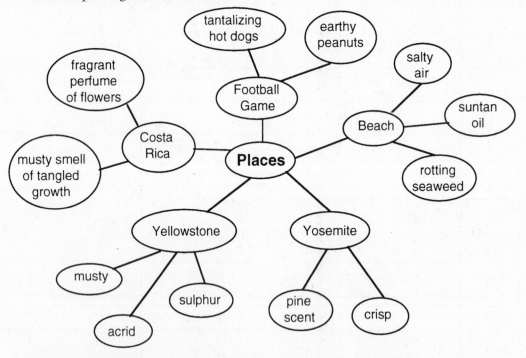

Prewriting Step 5: *Quickwrite*

Ask students to select one of the places on their cluster. Give them three minutes to continue clustering sensory/descriptive words—not just of smells but of other senses. Then, give them fifteen minutes to do a quickwrite about that place.

Two sample quickwrites follow:

> As my knees hit the rich, dark soil and my fingers wove through the blossoming petals of leaf lettuce and young tomato plants, the simple sweet scent of lily-of-the-valley beckoned me to stop what I was doing and lay my head down on the fresh mown grass still damp from the morning dew and watch the morning sun rise through the spindly branches of the crab apple tree. The dainty white, bell-shaped blossoms of grandma's lilies drooping lightly over my face always transported me away from the everyday world to an ethereal netherland. As I closed my eyes and inhaled their sweet scent, all was supremely tranquil—as if I were floating on a puffy white cloud above grandma's garden.

> *Kristin Battaglia—University of California, Irvine*

> The night was filled with anxiety and anticipation. I had already been "pre-warned" about the types of people who frequented this discotheque and could barely harness my excitement to finally replace my mental image with real beings.

> Inside, it was loud and smoky. Laser beams and colored lights flashed on the dance floor. The music had a tribal beat that made people on the dance floor seem as if they were moving in a trance. Sex was in the air, so heavy that I could almost taste it. Sweet, sultry perfume lingered behind every girl that passed me by, and heavy musk leaped off the grinning men.

> As I felt the vibrations of the music tingle my feet through the floor, I felt myself being pulled into this same tribal trance. All my judgments and prejudices had vanished from my mind with the constant boom, boom of the bass. I was now just one of them, in their world, accepting them as they had me.

> *Cindy Steffen—University of California, Irvine*

Prewriting Step 6: *Finding the Golden Lines*

Pass out yellow highlighter pens and, in partners, have students find the "golden lines" (the memorable words, phrases and sentences) in each other's quickwrites. Before students return their partner's paper, ask them to write down descriptive words to add to the Thesaurus Page. After papers have been returned, ask students to volunteer some of their words and add them to the Thesaurus Page (keep this posted throughout the lesson). Note that the words will now encompass not just the sense of smell but all the senses.

Prewriting Step 7: *Reading Excerpt from* Sweet Summer

Read the excerpt below aloud to the class.

From *Sweet Summer: Growing Up with and without My Dad*
by Bebe Moore Campbell

We drove for hours, eating chicken wings and thighs, nibbling on the cake and the Baby Ruth and drinking cold sodas as well as the lemonade in the thermos Nana had packed. After a while I took off my shoes and socks and tossed them onto the floor in the back. Daddy unbuttoned his top two shirt buttons, pulled a rag from behind his seat and began swiping at his damp neck. I read aloud to Daddy from *The Story of Harriet Tubman*, and then we listened to the radio until the station started crackling like dried-up fall leaves. As the day wore on, the June breeze turned silky; it was like a gentle pat across our faces. All the while we drove, Daddy and I had our hands on each other. My daddy's arm rested on my shoulder; I held his wrist. We were on the edge of summer.

It was almost dusk when we reached Route 17. I could smell summer on that road. The lush, heavy oak trees on either side of the one-lane highway grew so thick their branches stretched across the road to each other in an embrace, making a dark leafy tunnel of the road. "Look, Daddy, the trees are kissing," I said. He laughed. To our far right, beyond the dense leaves and branches, the murky waters of Dismal Swamp lay still and foreboding. Grandma once told me that before the Civil War slaves swam across the swamp to escape north, and I thought of the runaways as the stronger night breeze whistled and rattled against our windows. Maybe their ghosts came out at night, as haunting as the Turtle Lady, the green phantom who lurked in North Philly looking for children to eat. But I didn't see any ghosts, just water. The night air held a chill and Daddy and I rolled our windows all the way up. The trees loomed alongside us as tall as dark giants. All of a sudden I saw fading daylight again as the kissing trees thinned out. There in the clearing the words, "Welcome to North Carolina" and below that, in smaller letters, "The Tar Heel State" blazed out in blue and red. Almost summer. My bladder filled immediately.

"I gotta, I have to go to the bathroom."

"Can't you wait? We'll be there in fifteen or twenty minutes."

"I gotta go now, Daddy."

The car slowed and he pulled over to the side of the road near a deserted picnic table surrounded by a grove of pine trees. "Lookahere. Go duck behind that first tree. And Bebe, uh, uh, you better pull your shorts, I mean your panties, else you're gonna wet yourself." He laughed a little. His eyes crinkled up. From the prickly, thin sound of his laughter I knew he was embarrassed. I went behind a tree, about twenty feet away from the car. I heard Daddy yelling. "Lookahere. Watch where you step. Might be a snake in there." I peed fast. When I got back to the car I could hear a trickling sound. . . . "Might as well go too," he said.

The sky turned inky and crickets began to sing their brittle nighttime lullaby. Route 17 went right into Route 58, the heart of South Mills. The town was a collection of a few houses, a post office and a justice of the peace. My cousin Ruby, Aunt Lela's daughter, and her family lived there. We stopped at her house for a split second, long enough for my plump, pretty cousin to hug me and for Daddy to shoot the breeze with her husband, Snoodlum, and drink a great big glass of water while I raced around the yard in the dark with their two sons, Johnny and Jimmy. Then we had to go, because I was getting antsy. Summer was the up the road apiece, waiting for me.

From Ruby's I could have walked to Grandma's blindfolded, the land around me was so familiar. I could have followed the smell of the country night air so weighted with watermelons, roses and the potent stench from the hog pens. We crossed the bridge running over the canal that bordered South Mills. A sign announced that we had entered Pasquotank County. On either side of us, spread out like an open fan, were fields of corn, soybeans, peanuts and melons. White and brick frame houses broke up the landscape. Some belonged to white folks, some to colored. We reached Morgan's Corner and my stomach started quivering. It was where I bought my Baby Ruths and comic books! As my father's car slowed, my eyes scanned the fields of corn and soybeans for the opening to Grandma's. There it was! The car nearly stopped and we slowly turned into the narrow dirt lane. We jostled and bounced over the muddy ruts, the motor churning and sputtering as the tires attempted to plod through water-logged ditches, a result of the last rain. Daddy drove slowly and carefully. "Sure don't wanna get stuck up this lane," he muttered. My stomach was churning just as desperately as the wheels on my father's Pontiac. We lurched out of a deep gulley and glided into the front yard. Finally it was summer.

Grandma Mary was sitting on the porch waiting for us, as I knew she would be. She could outwait anybody. She told me having babies gave you patience. Grandma had had twelve children; one baby died at birth; "You have to wait for the pains to start, then wait for them to go, all that waiting with nothing but a rag to bite down on," she said. She stood up when we drove into the yard. "Hey," she called, walking toward us. My father had barely parked before I was scrambling out of the car and Grandma caught me up in her fat ole arms, hugging and squeezing me. She had a smell, deep in her bosom, like biscuits and flowers and I don't know what all else. That's what washed over me. I turned around to see my daddy pulling his wheelchair out of the back of the car and placing it between his open car door and his seat. He gave a huge lunge and hopped from the driver's seat into the chair. Then he pulled out the pillow he sat on, hoisted up his body and stuffed the pillow under his behind. He rolled over to the ramp in front of the house, pulled himself up and went inside, yelling, "Hey," to Mr. Abe, Grandma's second husband, and "Hey there, girl," to Bunnie, my Aunt Susie's teenage daughter; Aunt Susie had died a few years earlier. I heard Mr. Abe answering back. Mr. Abe had been singing, some old gospel song that only he sang and nobody else. I hadn't heard that song in a year, a whole year. As soon as he answered my father, he started up with his song again. I stood on the porch with Grandma, soaking up Mr. Abe's song, trying to hear it not as last year's song, but as a song of this summer. I stood on Grandma's porch and listened hard. Mr. Abe's song was my bridge; if I could cross that bridge I was back home. I started humming.

Prewriting Step 8: *Quickwrite*

Ask students to write a response to the excerpt they just heard. Tell them they will have three minutes to write their first impressions of the text. For example:

> I felt like I was really there with Bebe and her dad in the car. I could feel the heat—how you start sticking to the seat—and see those trees in their leafy embrace. Bebe's writing is so lyrical. It's like her own kind of song. I liked the image of the bridge at the end and how she wanted to cross that bridge to reconnect with her past.

Then, ask students to quickwrite for three minutes about any personal memories which the piece conjured up for them. For example:

> I remember the car trips when we'd drive across the country to Chautauqua, New York. Once, in Death Valley, the air conditioning went out in the car and we were all putting ice cubes in our T-shirts to keep cool. When we got to the motel, we plunged into the pool before we noticed it was full of crickets! I guess Chautauqua is my summer memory like North Carolina is for Bebe.

 **PROMPT**

Saturation Recall Paper:
Capturing Your Experience In and Of a Place

Think of a place that has made a strong impression on you—one that has created a lasting memory. Then, transport yourself back to that place in your memory. *Saturate* yourself in the sights, sounds, smells, tastes and textures (whichever senses apply) of that place. Recall how you came to be there and whom you were with. Recreate your experience in and of that place by painting a picture of it in words. Your goal is to render your place so descriptively that you create a "you are there" feeling in your reader.

You may organize your paper in a scene-by-scene account and describe several aspects of the place almost as if viewing it from different camera angles or you may write a continuous narrative. Weave yourself into the piece through the first person ("I") point of view. You may write your piece in present tense, as if it were happening now, or in past tense, as a recollection. <u>Show rather than tell about how this place makes you feel.</u> You may also need to introduce other characters into your paper and use them to help the reader *experience* what you saw, did, and felt in your place.

Your paper will combine sensory/descriptive and imaginative/narrative writing. Your goal is to saturate the reader in the description of a place and to tell a story of your experience in and of that place. This story may focus exclusively on your experience of and reaction to the place itself or may include descriptions of characters and events which are central to the essence of your memory of that place.

Your paper should have a sense of a beginning which makes the reader want to continue on, a middle, and some sense of an ending. Use rich, descriptive, showing writing to help the reader experience the place as you did. Some writing techniques you may want to consider are: figurative language, (simile, metaphor, imagery, symbol), strong action verbs, interior monologue, dialogue, flashback, and so forth.

Suggested length: Approximately 4–5 pages

The most successful papers will:

- Demonstrate that the reader has saturated himself/herself in the memory of a place;
- Capture that memory so vividly that it creates a "you are there" feeling in the reader.
- Draw the reader into the piece with an attention-getting opening;
- Paint a vivid picture (using sensory/descriptive and imaginative/ narrative writing strategies) that taps the senses (sight, smell, sound, taste, touch, movement) which convey the essence of your experience of the place.
- Show not just tell how the place makes the writer feel;
- Contain an appropriate closure.

 # PRECOMPOSING

Precomposing Step 1: *Finding the Golden Lines*

After reviewing the prompt, pass out yellow highlighter pens and have students reread the excerpt from *Sweet Summer* silently and find the golden lines. *(Note: This can be done as homework.)*

Precomposing Step 2: *Clustering Sensory Descriptions*

Ask students to volunteer their favorite golden lines (words, phrases, or sentences). As students share their golden lines, cluster these words according to the sensory impressions they convey.

A sample cluster might look like the one on the next page:

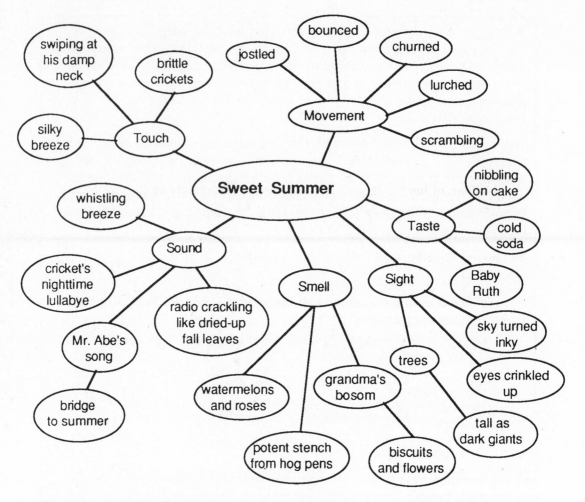

Precomposing Step 3: *Class Discussion*

After you complete the cluster, you may want to ask some questions that connect the students' golden lines to the prompt. These might include:

- **What makes you feel like you are there?**
  Students will point to the wealth of concrete detail, to the richness of sensory impressions, and to Campbell's use of figurative language (for example, how she describes the static on the radio: "we listened to the radio until the station started crackling like dried up fall leaves.")

- **How old do you think Bebe was at the time?**
  Students will guess anywhere from about five to twelve. It is important to ask them why they have this impression. They may point to the fact that she refers to her father as "Daddy," that she's wearing socks and shoes, that she can't wait to get to a bathroom, that she gets "antsy," etc.

  Note: At this point, you might want to explain that Bebe was seven at the time and that, every summer, her father came north to Philadelphia, where she lived with her mother, to take her south to North Carolina. As a child of divorce, Bebe's encounters with her father were limited by custody agreements and distances, a division that she says left her "lopsided and lonely." At that age, nine months can seem like a lifetime. And so, when

Bebe's father would come for her, there was also great anticipation but also some anxiety on both sides. The drive south in Daddy's green car was always a time and place to reconnect.

- **Why has this place made a lasting impression on her?**

  Students will point out that it's more than just a place or time of year; it's a time of belonging, connecting. They will also point out the love that surrounds this childhood memory.

- **How does Bebe show us instead of tell us how she feels?**

  Students will mention the body language of getting "antsy," having a full bladder, of her stomach "churning just as desperately as the wheels of my father's Pontiac," and of how she hums when she's finally home.

- **Can you feel a sense of organization in this excerpt?**
  - **What would you identify as the opening hook?**

    Students will point to the line, "We were on the edge of summer," and how that metaphor is used throughout the piece.
  - **What gives you a sense of closure?**

    Students will point to the bridge metaphor at the end of the story and how Uncle Abe's song is the bridge that leads her home.

Tell students that they will have an opportunity to recreate a rich memory that made a lasting impression on them just as Bebe has done in this excerpt and that they should let ideas for what to write about "simmer" in their heads.

Precomposing Step 4: *Brainstorming Ideas for Writing*

Ask students to get out a piece of paper and to simply jot down any ideas that pop into their heads as you read the following questions. Read slowly so that people have some think time:

- Think of a place that you have been that was of great scenic beauty. Picture that place in your mind and jot something down about it.
- Think of a place where you had a miserable but memorable experience. Where and what was it?

  Think of a place that you associate with a person. What and who comes to mind?
- Think of a place where something happened that caused a change in your life or where you learned something important. Where and what was it?
- Think of a place where you had an adventure. What kind of adventure was it?
- Think of a place that reminds you of your childhood. Where does your memory take you back to?
- Think of a place that you have mixed feelings about. What comes to mind?

- Think of a place that was hard to be in or to look at. What impression did it make on you?
- Think of a place that turned out to be better than you expected. What did you anticipate and what did you actually find?
- Think of a place that is special to you that might seem ordinary to someone else. What makes it special?

Precomposing Step 5: *Drawing*

After students have decided upon the place they want to write about, ask them to draw a picture of that place—visually recreating their mental picture of it. Stress that artistic ability is unimportant. This is simply a strategy for recollecting the place and generating sensory details. A sample drawing for the Teacher Model on Manuel Antonio (appended to this lesson) follows:

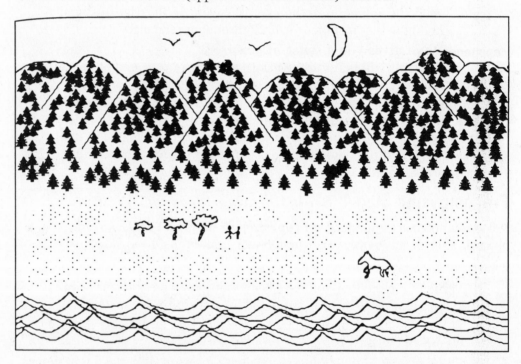

This place makes me feel like saying, "Ahh . . . paradise"

Once students have completed their drawings, ask them to write on the bottom of their paper a telling sentence about how this place makes them feel.

Precomposing Step 6: *Clustering*

Ask students to cluster their place around the six senses. Remind them of how you modeled this earlier with the excerpt from *Sweet Summer*.

A sample cluster for the Teacher Model on Manuel Antonio follows:

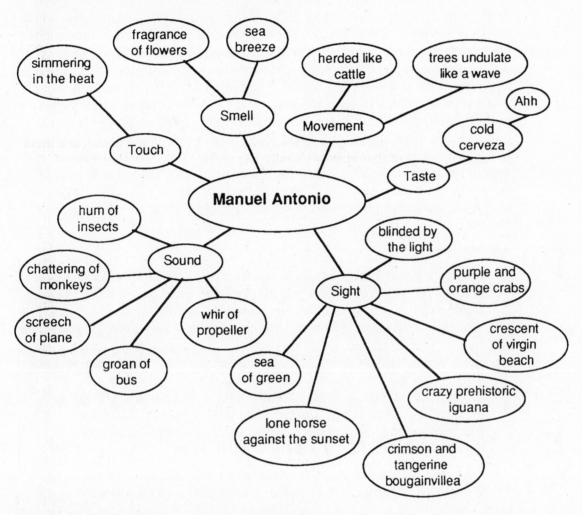

Precomposing Step 7: *Teacher Model*

When teaching this lesson for the first time, I would suggest writing to this prompt, in stages, along with the class. The piece I wrote on Manuel Antonio, along with my class at the University of California, Irvine, is appended to this lesson. While Campbell's piece is written in past tense, as a recollection, and relies heavily on sensory description and dialogue, my piece can be used to model writing in the present tense, as if it were happening now, and to introduce what interior monologue is. Both Campbell's excerpt and my piece are narratives that begin in transit. To demonstrate that one need not be in transit to begin a Saturation Recall Paper, I recommend having the students read pages 2 through 13 of Annie Dillard's Pulitzer Prize-winning *Pilgrim at Tinker Creek*. This is an account of a walk to the creek on a blustery January morning that includes a recollection of an earlier visit when Dillard witnessed the spirit vanishing from a frog as his life was "snuffed" out by a water bug. It is starkly but superbly written and is a wonderful example of observing closely and painting a picture in words. The student model appended to this lesson is another strong example of how vivid description can bring a memory to life.

Precomposing Step 8: *Practice in Showing, Not Telling*

Remind students how Bebe Moore Campbell shows us rather than tells us how she feels about her trip south and her arrival at Grandma's house: through her body language, through her repetition of the metaphor of summer ("summer was up the road apiece"), through her comparison of her feelings with the churning of the wheels of her father's car, and through her response to Mr. Abe's song. Explain that they, too, must show how their place makes them feel in their Saturation Recall Paper. To practice the art of showing, not telling, give the class a telling sentence to practice. An example might be: *The sight of her teenage son's room made her extremely angry.* Ask the class to volunteer what mom might have seen in her son's room and how they, as a class, could show and not tell her reaction. Once you have generated a list of words on the board, ask the class to help you construct a paragraph that shows the telling sentence.

An example might be:

> When she opened the door, she froze, as if suspended in time, and her jaw dropped. Reeling from the stench of unwashed socks, she grabbed the door handle to steady herself. Then, she took a shallow breath and surveyed the damage. A half-eaten sandwich and the remains of two crumpled coke cans lay on the unmade bed. Dirty socks and underwear formed a trail to the closet where wet towels lay molding in a heap. Papers of abandoned homework and pages torn from *Low Rider Magazine* formed a carpet on the carpet. And only the waste basket was left empty of debris. She grabbed the doorknob more tightly and her body began to shake. A volcano was brewing and brewing until finally, she threw her hands up in the air and fumed, "God, I'm going to kill that kid!"

After the class has constructed this paragraph, ask students to go back to the telling sentence underneath their pictures and practice writing some showing description.

 # WRITING

Writing Step 1: *Writing the Opening Scene*

The following opening scenes from Saturation Recall Papers can be shared with the class before they start writing their own. Ask students to read them and to discuss what catches their attention in each.

Student Model

How About Some Eel?

The fragrant combination of basil leaves, barbecuing lobster, and marinated steaks remind me that it is summertime. The welcoming shade of willow trees that encircle our backyard like a forestal half-moon provide relief from the sweltering New Jersey heat. Even the trees watch attentively as my father takes his place at the weathered wooden barbecue table and leads the family in the ritual of slowly turning the photo album pages. My mother, brother, and I gather around him to recall the memories frozen on each page. My eyes fix on a yellowing photograph of my Aunt Ray and me. We had just returned to my grandmother's house after picking up the last needed ingredient for her famous summer family reunion feast. Aunt Ray stood by the kitchen door smiling and clutching a brown paper bag while I stood, a bewildered eight year old, not fully aware that a picture had just been taken.

"Hey," my Dad says, "Look at you and Aunt Ray. You look like you had just seen a ghost."

"Pretty close," I agreed as my mind wandered, and I found myself briefly unlocking a distant memory that only I hold.

* * * * *

I sat in the sticky leather front seat of Aunt Ray's Cadillac. The humid New York City air filled the car, with only hopeful signs of a breeze from the racing trains above us on Liberty Avenue intermittently wisping into the car. I relied on the uncomfortable weather and the thundering roar of the trains as an excuse to fidget in my seat, peeling my bare legs off the rawhide upholstery, while Ray obliviously and silently drove to our destination. I noticed the massive woman next to me with calculated and inconspicuous glances. And I kept wondering how her tousled sun-ray golden curls, piled high on her head like yellow cotton candy, could remain motionless while we hit every pothole in the city of Queens. Each curl was another's clone with stiff curls framing her heavily matted full face. Ray was such a tiny name for a person who seemed larger than life.

Margaret Montemorra—University of California, Irvine

Notice how Peggy uses the barbecue and ritual review of family photo to set up a flashback to the occasion of the photo with Aunt Ray.

Student Model

Beauty and the Beach

Brrring....Brring....Brring....Brring.... Click— "Hi!" booms a voice filled with laughter over some background U2 music, "You've reached 961-2177. We're sorry we missed your call—leave us your name, number, and a brief message an we'll get back to you. Oh! If this is mom and dad, I'm at the library studying up a storm. But if this is Rebecca, I'll meet you down at East Beach to bask in the sun. Meet me there; I've gotta run! Don't forget to leave us a message after the tone. Beeeeeeeeep!"

As I pulled into the parking lot, my little, red Tercel bounced over the yellow striped speed bumps and maneuvered its way down the aisles of cars, dodging scavenging seagulls and clumsy tourists as if it had a mind of its own. The minute crotchety, old Professor Wilson dismissed us from Zoology 25, my brain had shut off. As I arrived at the shore in a dream-like state, I smiled from ear to ear and let out a sigh of relief. My hectic week was over and it was finally time for me to play.

"That was the Doors with 'Light My Fire' and this is 99.9 K-T-Y-D. Weatherman says it's gonna be a hot one so head to the beach and keep us in reach cuz we'll be bringing you the best of the rest with America's coast-to-coast top 40 countdown. But first, I've got a request from Brian James of Isla Vista, John Cougar Mellencamp's 'Hurt So'" —click.

As the caffeineated speech of the disc jockey jolted me out of my real life dream sequence, I pulled into a parking spot dusted with sand. While gazing out beyond the beach onto the white-capped water, a city sign in the foreground caught my eye. It read, "Welcome to East Beach."

Nicolle Hall—University of California, Irvine

Notice how Nicolle gets our attention immediately with her message on her telephone answering machine. This will become a unifying device in her paper, which concludes with the lines, "Back at our dorm room, the messages played on. . . . . 'Nicolle?. . . Nicolle Diane, this is your father speaking. . . .'"

Student Model

The Longest Ride of My Life

My family slowly started disappearing from my view. I looked frantically around, but no one was in sight. My eyes grew larger with fear and my heart pounded as if it was going to burst right through my stiff body as I froze in silence. Then they were gone.

"Mommy, Daddy!" I screamed while pounding at the cold, big, silver door.

"Mommy, Daddy!" "Mommy, Daddy!" "M o m m y. . ." My hoarse voice trailed. I knew they could not hear my weakened cry for help.

What am I gonna do? What should I do? What am I gonna do?

I jumped up and down, the weight of my body shifting left to right. My stomach felt funny.

I'm gonna wet my pants! Oh no!!

My mouth grew dry and my forehead glistened with moisture. The cold walls surrounding me seemed to get closer by the minute. My reflection bounced off the four, closing, enormous mirrors. The air within my enclosure grew stale and muggy. Quickly, I jumped up to press the number 9. It was illuminated as if to tease me with the thought of never seeing my family again. I knew the 9 meant something. That was the floor we were on.

Maybe if I get back to the floor, Mommy and Daddy will still be there. Yeah, it's all okay now. But... HEY!... I'm going down. 9 is up. Oh no! What am I gonna do? What am I gonna do? Quick, push another one. Hurry, HURRY! Oh no... I gotta go potty again. What am I gonna do?

Katy Kwok—University of California, Irvine

Notice Katy uses interior monologue to convey the panic a child (Katy) feels when left behind in a terrifying place—the elevator.

Writing Step 2: *Drafting the Opening Scene*

Have students write a rough draft of their opening scene and bring it to class for sharing and feedback before completing an entire rough draft. Students seem more willing to craft their papers when given the time and opportunity to write in installments.

 ## SHARING

Sharing Step 1: *Finding Golden Lines in Opening Scenes*

Ask students to find partners and another set of partners to exchange papers. Allow fifteen minutes per paper to read all four papers and find the golden lines.

On a separate sheet of paper, they should write the following:

_____ **To the author of** _____

What we liked best about your Saturation Recall Paper so far is. . . .

We think you are ☐ are not ☐ off to a good start because. . . .

One suggestion we have for you is. . . .

As you continue to write your paper, you might want to consider. . . .

After students complete their peer response, convene groups of four and allow five minutes each for discussion. Then, ask the class for descriptive words from golden lines to add to the Thesaurus Page.

 ## WRITING, CONTINUED

Writing Step 3: *Writing the Rough Draft*

Before students write their rough draft, have them consult the Evaluation Scoring Guide criteria. Once you have taught this lesson once, I recommend putting four student papers (representing a range of responses) into a holistic scoring training packet for individual scoring by students and class discussion. This helps students distinguish an exemplary Saturation Recall Paper from ones less effective.

After reviewing the scoring guide, students should write their rough drafts.

 ## SHARING, CONTINUED

Sharing Step 2: *Scoring the Rough Draft*

Have groups of four reform with different pairs of partners. Pass out the Scoring Guide for the Saturation Recall Paper (see Evaluation) and review the scoring criteria. Allow twenty to thirty minutes per paper to give each student an *in progress* score and to fill out the Peer Response Sheet.

Stress that the point of the reading is to help everyone in the class improve and that progress scores are for the students' use only.

Sharing Step 3: *Responding to the Rough Draft*

As students score partners' rough drafts, they should also record responses onto those students' texts as well as fill out a Peer Response Sheet using the following guidelines.

Directions for Responding to the Saturation Recall Paper
(These annotations go directly on the text.)

Pointing

- Use yellow highlighter to point to the writer's golden lines.

Telling

Tell how you are reacting to the piece. For example:

- We thought this was really funny.
- Wow! We loved this scene.
- This kept us in suspense.
- We were with you here.

Summarizing

- Summarize what you think the writer was trying to convey at the bottom of the response page.

Other Helpful Notations:

?—Put this where you are confused as readers.
Show more—Put this where the writer could use more showing writing.
Too much—Put this where the paper is overwritten and where paring descriptive language will highlight effective words, phrases.

Also make suggestions like:

Try to dialogue here; add details; try a metaphor; flashback; etc.

Peer Response Sheet

Responders: _____

_____

To the Author of: _____

We gave your paper an in-progress score of:

We feel the strengths of your paper are:

Our favorite part was:

We felt/didn't feel we were there with you because:

As you revise your paper to hand in for evaluation, we would suggest:

In terms of your handling of the conventions of written English (spelling, grammar, sentence structure, etc.), your paper appeared to:

❑ Have many errors   ❑ Have a few errors   ❑ Be error free

Overall, we thought what you were trying to show was:

Sharing Step 4: *Peer Partner Conferences*

Once students have scored and responded to each other's papers, they need five to ten minutes per person for an oral presentation of the written feedback. This gives students the chance to hear what has been said and to ask for clarification.

 ## REVISING

Students should revise their papers based upon their partners' feedback. Making times available for student-teacher conferences is also recommended. I have found students who receive scores that are lower than they anticipated are quick to seek the teacher's assistance. Allow students ample time to revise their papers at home or provide in-class time for revision.

 ## EDITING

Students have already received feedback on the correctness elements of their papers on their rough draft. Nevertheless, you may want to give them an opportunity to review their paper with a partner for correct spelling, punctuation, consistent verb tenses, and sentence structure. Additionally, you may want to pass out the rules for using dialogue (appended to this lesson) and have students check their use of dialogue in their drafts to ensure that they have used dialogue form appropriately.

 ## EVALUATION

Evaluation Step 1: *Scoring Guide*

The following scoring guide may be used both for student scoring and for the teacher's score.

Scoring Guide

9 This paper will do most or all of the following well:

- Demonstrate that the writer has saturated himself/herself in the memory of a place;

- Bring that place to life by capturing it so vividly that it creates a "you are there" feeling in the reader;

- Draw the reader into the piece with an attention-getting opening, develop a middle section, and come to some sense of closure in the conclusion;

- Paint a vivid picture using sensory/descriptive and imaginative/narrative writing strategies that tap the senses and convey the *essence* of the writer's experience of the place.

Sensory/Descriptive techniques include:

— Concrete, descriptive details

— Sensory words relating to relevant senses (*sight, sound, smell, taste, touch, movement*)

— Strong action verbs

— Showing, not telling, language

— Some figurative language (*similes, metaphors, analogies*)

— Possible symbolism, imagery, etc.

Imaginative/Narrative techniques include:

— First person narrative

— Sense of plot line

— Sequence of events

— Portrayal of character or characters

— Possible dialogue or interior monologue

— Possible flashback

— Possible dramatic pacing

- *Shows* rather than just tells about how the place makes the writer feel;

- Few, if any errors in the conventions of written English (spelling, punctuation, grammar, syntax, etc.);

8   This paper is still impressive and well written but may lack the impact that a 9 paper has on the reader. An 8 paper will do most or all of the following well:

- Demonstrate that the writer has *saturated* himself/herself in the memory of a place;

- Bring that place to life by capturing it vividly, creating a "you are there" feeling in the reader but one that is not as intense as in a 9 paper;

- Draw the reader into the piece with an attention-getting opening, develop a middle section, and come to some sense of closure in the conclusion;

- For the most part, paint a vivid picture using sensory/descriptive and imaginative/narrative writing strategies that tap the senses and convey the *essence* of the writer's experience of the place but do so less impressively than a 9 paper.

Sensory/Descriptive techniques include:

— Concrete, descriptive details

— Sensory words relating to relevant senses (*sight, sound, smell, taste, touch, movement*)

— Strong action verbs

— Showing, not telling, language

— Some figurative language (*similes, metaphors, analogies*)

— Possible symbolism, imagery, etc.

Imaginative/Narrative techniques include:

— First person narrative

— Sense of plot line

— Sequence of events

— Portrayal of character or characters

— Possible dialogue or interior monologue

— Possible flashback

— Possible dramatic pacing

- Shows rather than just tells about how the place makes the writer feel, but does not do so as effectively as a 9 paper;

- Few, if any errors in the conventions of written English (spelling, punctuation, grammar, syntax, etc.).

7　This paper is more than adequately written but it lacks the overall impressiveness of an 8 or 9 paper. A 7 paper will do most or all of the following well:

- Demonstrate that the writer has made a solid attempt to *saturate* himself/herself in the memory of a place;

- Bring that place to life (at least partially) by capturing it reasonably vividly. The "you are there" feeling in the reader is not as distinct as in an 8 or 9 paper;

- Draw the reader into the piece with an attempt at an attention-getting opening, develop a middle section, and come to some sense of closure in the conclusion, although this may be weaker than in an 8 or 9 paper;

- Paint a picture using sensory/descriptive and imaginative/narrative writing strategies that tap the senses and convey some *essence* of the writer's experience of the place. However, this picture is not as vivid as in an 8 or 9 paper;

Sensory/Descriptive techniques include:

— Some concrete, descriptive details

— Some sensory words relating to relevant senses *(sight, sound, smell, taste, touch, movement)*

— Action verbs, but not as strong as in an 8 or 9 paper.

— At least some attempt at showing, not telling, language

— Some figurative language *(similes, metaphors, analogies)*

— Possible symbolism, imagery, etc.

Imaginative/Narrative techniques include:

— First person narrative

— Some sense of plot line

— Attempt at a sequence of events

— Portrayal of character or characters

— Possible weak dialogue or interior monologue

— Possible flashback but not as effective as an 8 or 9 paper

— Little dramatic pacing

- Sometimes tells about how the place makes the writer feel, when it could show.

- Some errors in the conventions of written English (spelling, punctuation, grammar, syntax, etc.) but none that interfere with the writer's message.

6–5　This paper will satisfy the requirements of the prompt but in a marginal way. A 6–5 paper will do most or all of the following:

- Barely demonstrate that the writer has saturated himself/herself in the memory of a place;

- Inadequately bring that place to life by failing to capture it vividly enough to create a "you are there" feeling in the reader;

- Fail to draw the reader into the piece with an attention-getting opening. Paper development and conclusion may also be weak.

- Paint a less than vivid picture using sensory/descriptive and imaginative/narrative writing strategies. Does not adequately tap the senses and convey the *essence* of the writer's experience of the place.

Sensory/Descriptive techniques include:

— Few concrete, descriptive details

— Not enough sensory words relating to relevant senses (sight, sound, smell, taste, touch, movement)

— Few action verbs

— Telling rather than showing language

— Few uses of figurative language (similes, metaphors, analogies)

— Possible symbolism, imagery, etc.

Imaginative/Narrative techniques include:

— First person narrative

— Sense of plot line may be weak

— Sequence of events may be hard to follow

— Portrayal of character or characters may be weak

— Possible weak dialogue or interior monologue

— Possible flashback but not as effective as an 8–9 paper

— Little dramatic pacing

- Tell about how the place makes the writer feel, rather than show;

- Many errors in the conventions of written English (spelling, punctuation, grammar, syntax, etc.), some of which may interfere with the writer's message.

Scores ranging from 5–1 are for papers with serious problems that prevent the paper from meeting the requirements of the prompt.

5–4   These scores are reserved for serious attempts at meeting the requirements, even though the paper falls short in almost all categories.

3–1   These should be given to papers that make only a token attempt to fulfill the requirements of the prompt, are too short to evaluate, are off task, or have so many technical errors that the paper cannot be understood.

The Saturation Recall Paper

NONFICTION

Evaluation Step 2: *Response Form*

Some teachers may also find the following Response Form useful in making their written comments.

Saturation Recall Paper Response Form

Overall comment:

Demonstrates that the writer has saturated himself/herself in the place:

Creates a "you are there" feeling in the reader:

Use of sensory/descriptive and imaginative/narrative techniques:

Saturation Recall Paper

Development: beginning, middle, and end:

Way the place itself is conveyed and/or the event occurring within the place is conveyed:

Use of showing, not telling:

Conventions of written English:

Final comments:

Score _____

Manuel Antonio

As I listen to the whir of the propeller, I can imagine the hum of insects in the sea of green below. Like a wave, it undulates—this canopy of trees. With a flick of the channel, my mind shifts to black and white, and I am ten again, camped out in front of the TV, mesmerized by some "B" movie in which a crash landing in the remote recesses of the jungle holds me spellbound. *Come to think of it, where is the clearing? Seems like we should be about there by now.* Suddenly, with not so much as "fasten your seat belt" or a "prepare for land- ing," the plane descends abruptly. My stomach does the same. As we approach our destination, the shimmering white heat of the airfield rises to greet us. In a matter of minutes, we begin to simmer in this tin oven as we screech to a halt in a cloud of dust, scattering a welcoming party of pigs and chickens into the tall weeds that line the runway. With a creak, the plane door opens, and, wip- ing off the rivulets of sweat with the backs of our hands, we disembark, blinded and dazed by the reflection of the afternoon sun.

"First impressions can be deceiving, you know guys," I say optimistically.

"Let's hope so," Todd whines. "It's hotter than hell here."

We are herded on to an old city bus and huddle together, glued one to the other by the heat. I fish out the travel guide just to reassure myself. "The word paradise does not do justice to Manuel Antonio," it says. *We'll see*, I say to myself, and add *Let us pray* since the whole trip was my idea.

The bus meanders through the narrow streets of the outskirts of town in the heart of siesta time when even the dogs sleep fitfully in what little shade there is. But as we wend our way up a steep hill, the bus gears groaning in protest, a hint of a breeze brings the promise of relief.

"Are we almost there, Mom?" Tyler asks, peering over the seat, his eyes imploring.

"I don't know, sweetie. Probably pretty soon."

Simmer turns to boil as the bus inches its way up the winding road. Travel brochures, check books, and passports become fans as we all struggle to remain cheerful—or at least conscious. The strangest sort of *uh-oh* is forming in my stomach.

"You sure we got tickets to the right place?" Todd asks.

"Don't be silly," I say, clutching my well-worn *Explore Costa Rica*, and turn- ing to the Post-it marked page one more time when no one is looking. Just when I am about to plead guilty for blowing it, a genuine gust of coolish air creeps through the open windows, causing an audible "ahhh" to arise from the partially reviving passengers.

"Feel that, Mom?" Tyler asks.

"Yes, honey."

"I bet we're almost there" he says with conviction. The bus seems to agree. Reaching the crest of the hill, it picks up speed and chugs along.

Over the rise, dust-laden shrubs and errant weeds begin to give way to the green fans of banana trees and coconut palms. Crimson and tangerine-colored bougainvillea spill into the roadsides and giant pothos, their broad leaves looking like elephant ears, climb the trunks of trees. The further we go, the deeper and more intricate the tangle of growth and fusion of colors before us.

Suddenly, I see Tyler scramble over Evan to usurp the window seat. "Mom, look" he says, bobbing up and down and pointing. Between the trees, I see a sliver of blue ocean, sparkling in the sunlight. *Yes,* I whisper to myself. Having been so unceremoniously torn away from the latest rap by Ice Tea, Evan unplugs himself from his portable CD player and tunes into the panorama.

"Cool," he says, giving Tyler a pinch. "But don't tromp over me again, bud, or you're in deep trouble."

After stopping at a number of luxurious hillside resorts, where we let assorted passengers disembark, the bus plunges down a steep driveway and drops us at the Arboleda, where the accommodations are more spartan, we have been told, but you can't beat the scenery. While Todd and I try to unstick ourselves from the seats and stumble up the aisle, our duffel bags in tow, the boys fly out the door and down a cascade of stairs.

Our room—our hut, actually—is nestled against the hillside and offers a red tile floor, bed covered by a single sheet, a ceiling fan, doorless shower, and large wicker chairs on a cobblestone patio, overlooking the sea. What more could we ask for? Oh, yes—our own iguana, his craggy, prehistoric head peering out from his niche in our palm-thatched roof to view the newest group of intruders.

In the midst of unpacking, Tyler and Evan reappear, breathless and panting.

"Oh man," Ev says, shaking his head, and sporting a wall-to-wall grin, "you should see the beach!"

"And wait till you see the crabs," Tyler says, doing a little jig.

"What about them, hon?" I ask.

"We'll, they're sorta purple and orange, and they live in the dirt and they kinda skitter in and out of their holes when you walk by."

"C' mon you guys'" Ev pleads, "you have all evening to unpack. Besides, we won't need anything here but a bathing suit."

Single file, we begin the trek down what seems like a thousand stairs as the crabs, precisely on cue, run for cover. I am aware of a chattering noise in the trees above. Hoping to see a flock of toucans, I look high up in the lacy patches of green. Although the branches bob and sway, the authors of this cacophony are nowhere to be seen. Nevertheless, the invisible chattering follows us as we descend.

And as we emerge into the clearing at the base of the stairs, they emerge as well, tiny brown monkeys, fifty or more of them, leaping from tree branch to tree branch, all converging on one particular spot, where, in unison, they strike up a terrific racket. Having been summoned, the chef from the beachside cafe rushes out the door with an assortment of bananas, mangoes and papayas which he sets along various ledges towards the base of the trunk. When he is a safe distance away, it's open season, and the mad dash for dinner begins. As I look into the tiny faces of these primates and watch them run down the tree trunk, their slender fingers grabbing for the prize, and smile as they scamper back up to higher ground, I notice even tinier human faces on the babies clinging to their backs. No sooner do these contestants reach a comfortable limb and chance a nibble of their delicacies, than larger, more rotund-looking monkeys swoop down from their perches and swipe the coveted prizes right out of their hands. As their bereft partners stew and scold, they glare menacingly.

"Men," I say under my breath, chuckling to myself.

"What?" Todd asks.

"Oh, never mind," I respond.

The beach beckons, so we continue our exploration. Up until now, our view of the ocean has been partially obstructed by the dense lushness of the hillside vegetation. But, as we venture out on the sand, the seascape gently unfolds, and we collectively hold our breath. Before us is a huge crescent of virgin beach with a long finger of jungle at the far end, pointing into the sea. The tide is out, and several hundred yards of glassy sand extend out to the water's edge where the sky is turning a shade of pale peach. As we walk, our shadows dance in the last rays of the sunlight. Evan and Tyler rush out to greet the surf and return with a question written all over their faces.

"Can we?" Ev finally asks.

"Sure, why not," Todd says. "I guess you'll dry off fast enough in this weather."

With that, the boys let out a whoop and plunge into the cresting waves, fully clothed.

"It's like a bathtub, Mom," Ty reports.

As we continue our stroll, Todd says rather wistfully, "You know, the only thing that would make this more perfect is a cerveza."

Pale peach has turned to crimson as we make Todd's wish a reality. Sitting under a palapa, we watch the moon rise above the rainforest behind us and catch a glimpse of a macaw, its scarlet and vermilion hues as brilliant as the final blaze of sunset. I watch its flight and soar as well—lazy and luxuriant. As the boys' laughter floats in on the tide, we see a lone horse silhouetted against the hushed embers of the dying sun. A peacefulness descends as darkness envelopes us. Todd takes a long sip of his beer, lets out an "ahh" and, after a few seconds, proclaims, "Paradise!"

"Yep, I agree" I say, as a smile lights up my face. Just like the book said it would be.

Carol Booth Olson—University of California, Irvine

Student Model

Autumn Gallop

I wrenched my red, rusted bike out of the wooden shed which brimmed with garden rakes, shovels, old chipped plant pots, and the lawn mower which barely worked anymore. The bike squeaked as I wheeled it out to the driveway. Stashing my hard black riding hat in its crooked basket, I climbed onto the high padded seat. The bike glided down the smooth driveway onto the main street below and I began pedaling fast. Early morning frost lay in patches on the roofs and gardens of the homes that lined the street. I could see my breath steaming like a dragon or a movie star smoking a long white cigarette. The neighborhood was asleep and the only sounds came from the whir of my tires, the sweet singing of unseen birds, and my heavy breath as I pedaled on towards the stables.

The sky was a pale, cold blue and was streaked with clouds. There was no sign of the rain which had pelted down all day yesterday and had kept me locked in my house playing "Tiddly-winks" with my little sister. My bike splashed through the puddles which were the only remains of yesterday's storm and I turned back to see the wet tracks they made on the road. My face was flushed with the exercise and with the crisp morning chill which numbed the end of my nose and the tips of my ears. I pulled the sleeves of my cozy knitted sweater over my hands to keep them warm.

I came to the end of my street and turned down towards the little village of Cockington. As the bike flew down the hills, I daringly lifted my hands off the handle bars and soared like a bird downward. The cold wind burned my face and my long dark hair escaped the hold of a small barrette and danced behind me. My bike hit the cobblestones of Cockington's main street with a jolt. The bumpity-bumps rattled my bicycle bell and it tinkled as my riding hat jostled around in the basket. I passed fields where cows, muddy from yesterday's rain, dozed in the morning sun. Small, quaint cottages shone in the light and billows of smoke from an early fire crowned their chimneys. My stomach rumbled deeply, as the salty, sizzling smell of bacon caught my attention. The hedges grew high and succulent blackberries hung heavily in their midst. Tempted by their juiciness, I stopped to pick some, being careful not to get their dark lusty purple stains on my newly washed jodhpurs.

A gust of cold wind carried with it the fresh, pungent smell of manure and I clambered back onto my bike and anxiously pedaled towards the stable. I turned off the main street onto a narrow, twisty lane lined with trees which made it dark and cool. The air was thick and musty. Wet leaves of crimson, gold and brown carpeted the surface. Tree roots which weaved underneath the lane made my bike clang noisily as it flew towards the stable. The smell of manure was growing steadily stronger and sweeter as I drew closer to my destination. I was tired from the hectic pace I had set and my face glowed with excitement. Gradually, the trees thinned out, allowing streams of light to filter into the dim corridor. At the end of the lane, the morning sunshine glowed with its full intensity down onto the gray stone wall which surrounded the stables. I hopped off my bike and carelessly leaned it against the mossy wall, grabbing my riding hat from the basket.

While Cockington had been quiet—just awaking—the stables bustled with life. Three low, gray, stone buildings made up the stables. Ivy clung to their sides and thick green moss grew in the gaps between stones. Dogs yapped loudly, chasing each other across the courtyard. After a breakfast of fresh milk, cats lay lazily in the sun watching sarcastically the rush of activity around them while a bevy of annoyed chickens pecked anxiously for their morning grain.

In a corner, a stable hand washed two horses who stood patiently dozing in the morning sun as a long green hose washed their thick coats. The water trickled across the cobbled courtyard and down the steep entrance way. I nimbly jumped over the shimmering stream and ran across the courtyard, being careful to avoid the small piles of steaming manure which dotted the way. I climbed up two steep steps and opened the heavy wooden door which led to the office in the main building. "Good Morning Jo," beamed Mrs. Fawkes who ran the stables, "Are you here to take Rory out for a ride?" She was sitting perched on a high stool checking the riding bookings for that day. The horses were rented out to tourists in the summer months and to avid horse lovers throughout the year.

"Yep. Okay if I take him into the fields today?" I asked.

"Sure, he'll enjoy the ride after being stuck inside all day yesterday."

"Me too!" I exclaimed as I headed into the tack room which adjoined the small office. The deep and masculine smell of leather met me. Heavy saddles were straddled across splintered beams and piled on top of each other. Some were well worn and their leather soft. Others were new and hard and would need working in. From a dusty wooden cabinet which stored bottles of cleaning oils, hoof polish, and other potions, I grabbed a hard bristle brush and a sharp hoof pick and tossed them into my upturned hat. I heaved a saddle across my left arm and with my free hand, plucked a worn bridle with its shiny metal bit from a rusted nail, carelessly knocked into the wall and bent upwards to form a rough hook.

I hobbled slowly under the weight of the saddle down the steps and around to the entrance of the main stable. Large wooden double doors stood wide open, helping to illuminate the dimly lit, murky interior. The stable smelled musty from the warm bodies and the scent of hay tickled my nose. Heads turned eagerly and heavy hooves clomped anxiously as I slowly walked down the row of stables towards the end stall.

There he was, his ears pricked forward; there was Rory. I heaved the saddle over the stable door and hung the bridle on a high hook.

"Hi, Rory," I murmured as he gently nuzzled my cheek with his soft velvet nose. His large brown eyes gazed at me hopefully as I dug a carrot out of the pocket of my jodhpurs. His bristly lips tickled as he gently took the gift from my hand and began to chomp contentedly with long yellow teeth. While he was occupied, I took the hard bristle brush to his dirty coat and transformed it to a glow of chestnut finery. Next, I lifted each of his heavy legs and propped them on my thigh as I picked out the muck which was stuck in his hooves. Once he was clean, I threw the heavy saddle across his back and fastened the straps tightly. Rory chomped on his bit as I slipped it into his mouth and fastened the bridle behind his ears. Finally, I pulled my long hair into a low ponytail and yanked my hat down tightly over my head, making sure that the chin strap fit snugly.

Taking Rory gently by the reins close to his bit, I led him down the long corridor out into the courtyard. His hoofs clip-clopped and wobbled awkwardly on the cobbled ground. I put my left boot into the metal stirrup and hoisted my body up and over. I sat up, tall, straight and proud. My heart pounded with anticipation and my hands shook nervously as I gathered the reins tightly in my hands and gently nudged Rory forward. His powerful body strode down the steep entrance way. I guided this massive strength towards the open fields which lay next to the stables. Green hills rolled into valleys and valleys gave way to wide open fields. Brown, wooden fences zig-zagged across the huge expanse joining together a patchwork quilt of green. I leaned down to push open the gate which separated Rory and I from the freedom of the fields.

Wrapping my hands around Rory's neck and pressing my cheek against his dark spiky mane, I whispered, "O.K. boy, let's go." We took off with a rush of power. His strong body sprung out beneath me and his legs lengthened into a fast gallop. The wind burned my face as I moved rhythmically with Rory's huge strides. When I turned to look back, the stable, sheltered in a cozy nook of trees, had almost disappeared from view. "Let's never go back," I shouted. But my words were lost in the wind.

Joanna Hockins—University of California, Irvine

Some Rules for Using Dialogue

1. Use separate paragraphs for each speaker's words.

   Example: Larry spooned a generous portion onto his plate, speared a piece of beef, and lifted it to his mouth.

   "How is it?" asked Polly.

   "Pretty good," Larry said.

   "Only pretty good?"

   "I mean, it's fantastic!" he said, taking another bite and smacking his lips.

2. Don't put unspoken thoughts in quotation marks.

3. Put quotation marks only around dialogue and not around your introductions or explanations.

   Example: I could hear her yelling from the other side of the door, "I'll be there in a minute."

4. Commas and periods go inside quotation marks.

   Semicolons and colons go outside quotation marks.

   Dashes, question marks, and exclamation points go inside quotation marks when they apply directly to the dialogue, and outside the quotation marks when they apply to the whole sentence.

   Example: She said, "When are we leaving?"
   Did she just say, "Let's go"?

5. Most dialogue is set off by commas. Dialogue may be interrupted with an explanation or reference to the speaker and then resumed again.

   Example: "There is no point in going any further," he admitted, his frustration clearly evident, "when we've lost the trail."

6. Use a colon to introduce dialogue only when your introduction is a complete sentence.

   Example: His parting words made me wonder if I'd ever see him again: "Well, it's been nice knowing you."

7. Use single quotation marks to enclose a quotation within dialogue.

   Example: "Just remember the old saying," Jane scolded as the kids picked at their meal, "'Waste not, want not.'"

8. Use ellipsis to suggest that the dialogue trails off or stops abruptly.

   Example: "I'd really like to help you, but. . ."

When Clay Sings
by Byrd Baylor

Grade Level
For Upper Elementary,
Middle School, and
High School

Thinking Level
Analysis

Writing Domain
Imaginative/Narrative

Materials Needed:
• Butcher paper
• Modeling clay or
  Play-Doh
• Toothpicks for
  etching designs

**Suggested
Supplementary
Readings:**
At the end of this lesson
is a long list of suggested
readings and music that
could accompany this
lesson.

Stories in Clay

by Erline Krebs and Mindy Moffatt

Overview

After reading Byrd Baylor's *When Clay Sings*, students will make and decorate clay pottery based on what is important in their lives. Then, students
will write an analysis of the decorations from the pot's point of view,
which will provide insight into the life of the student who fashioned the pot.

Objectives

THINKING SKILLS

Students will:

- *recall* information about previous cultures and the lives of
  other people through ancient clay pottery after reading
  When Clay Sings;
- *label* symbols that represent important aspects of their own lives;
- *describe* what is important in their lives;
- *imitate* ancient pottery by decorating their own clay pot;
- *draw conclusions* about the lives of the people who made pottery;
- *design* their own clay pot or container;
- *prioritize* meaningful aspects of their lives as they fashion and
  decorate their clay object;
- *analyze* what the symbols they have chosen say about their lives;
- *make inferences* about what the symbols on a classmate's pot say
  about him or her.

WRITING SKILLS

Students will:

- *assume* the persona of a clay pot made by themselves;
- *write* an imaginative/narrative account of how the pot came into
  being;
- *use* sensory/descriptive language to describe the color, shape and
  decorations on the pot;
- *use* analytical/expository language to interpret the symbols on the
  pot and suggest what it "sings" about the potter;
- *logically develop* the narrative account in paragraph form;
- *follow* the conventions of written English.

The Process

This lesson requires several days, depending upon the sophistication of clay work (firing and glazing pots demands more time than using modeling clay or Play-Doh). After building background information from reading *When Clay Sings*, students compare and contrast modern containers with the clay pots described in the book. While students begin to work on making their own pots, vocabulary is developed as they look at their own lives to prioritize what design symbols they should use for decorating their pots. Finally, students write as if they were the pot describing itself and providing insight into the life of the person who made it.

Much depth and richness can be added to this lesson if the teacher has access to pottery that could be displayed in the class. Further, we suggest that the teacher make a pot and write to the prompt along with the class.

 PREWRITING

Prewriting Step 1: *Reading*

Read aloud *When Clay Sings* by Byrd Baylor. *(It is suggested that Native American music such as* Changes: Native American Flute Music *by R. Carlos Nakai, be played softly in the background during the reading and throughout the lesson.)* As you read, be sure to hold up the pages so that the class can see the designs in the book.

Prewriting Step 2: *Clustering — Ancient Pots*

After the reading is completed, as a whole group, cluster on butcher paper with earth-colored marking pens about the clay pots that were described. *(Putting the cluster on butcher paper allows the cluster to remain on display as students add to it during the course of the lesson.)*

Emphasize the following:

- Who made the pots
- What the pots were used for and the various purposes that dictated the shapes
- The colors of the decorations on ancient pots
- The symbols from nature that decorated the pots
- The special qualities attributed to the pots

A sample cluster appears on the following page:

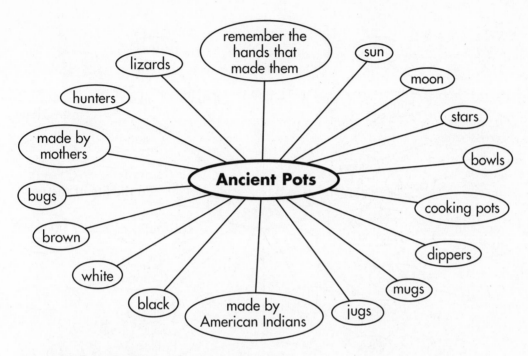

Prewriting Step 3: *Observing*

Invite students to look around the classroom for objects that are containers in order to expand their awareness of the vast array of containers which surround them. *(Allowing quiet, long pauses between responses usually encourages the students to become more creative in their identification of containers and what they contain.)*

Sample responses might include:

- backpack contains books
- chair contains a body
- shoes contain feet
- bodies contain blood and organs
- books contain words
- room contains people
- minds contain thoughts

Prewriting Step 4: *Bringing Objects to Class*

Provide students with the opportunity to bring to class and share objects from their own lives that are used to hold other things. Examples: shoe boxes, eyeglass cases, purses, wallets, cups, backpacks or book bags, sandwich bags, aluminum cans, lockets, pockets, plant hangers and pots, etc.

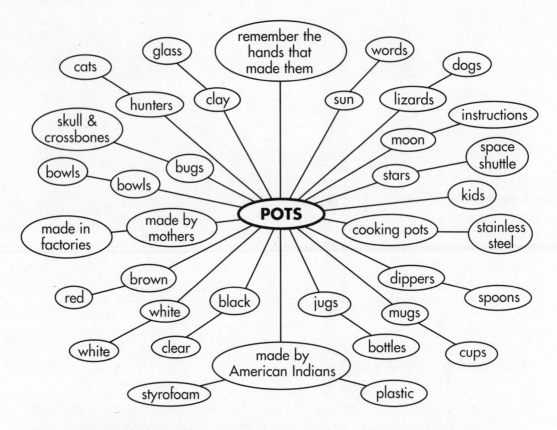

Prewriting Step 5: *Discussion and Clustering—Modern Pots*

Share objects brought to class and add them to the cluster. Use marking pens in colors different from original cluster items to contrast the modern additions on the cluster.

Prewriting Step 6: *Venn Diagram*

As a whole group, make a Venn diagram on another sheet of butcher paper, comparing and contrasting the ancient pots with modern containers. An example appears on the following page.

Prewriting Step 7: *Making Pots*

Give students each a lump of clay to "play" with. As they are pushing, pulling, rolling, and kneading the clay, their pots will take shape. Emphasize to students that their pot must have a practical use in their lives, just as ancient pots all had specific purposes. Allow clay to dry while implementing the next steps. Fire pots if you choose.

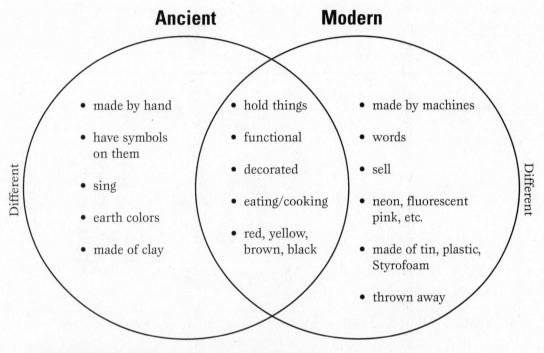

Ancient   **Modern**

Different

- made by hand
- have symbols on them
- sing
- earth colors
- made of clay

- hold things
- functional
- decorated
- eating/cooking
- red, yellow, brown, black

- made by machines
- words
- sell
- neon, fluorescent pink, etc.
- made of tin, plastic, Styrofoam
- thrown away

Different

Prewriting Step 8: *Discussing Designs*

Discuss the designs on the ancient pottery. All of the designs were about the *real* lives of *real* people who made the pots. The designs related what was important to the potter. Refer back to the story.

Prewriting Step 9: *Two-Column Chart—Teacher Modeling*

Once the group diagram is complete, have students make up a personal two-column chart about their lives. *(The teacher models a personal chart for his/her life.)* Attend to the following questions as you model how to fill in the left side of the chart:

- What do you do that is important to you?
  camp (because I like getting away from the city)
- What do you see around you that is an important part of your life?
  outdoors (because I like to tune in to the sounds of nature)
- What people are important to you?
  my family (because they are always there when I need them)
- What is your favorite food? pastime?
  potato chips (because I like the salty taste and the crunchy noise)
  reading and writing (because I like to find our more about the world from reading and share what I know through writing)

Then draw a symbol on the right side of the chart to represent the word on the left.

What is important to me	Symbol
camping outdoors/environment family friends potato chips reading/writing	

Ask student volunteers to come up to the board and draw a symbol that is important to them and explain why it is important.

What is important to me	Symbol
play baseball football my girlfriend pizza music	

Prewriting Step 10: *Choosing Symbols*

Once students' own charts are complete, have students choose three symbols that represent what is most important in their lives right now, which they will eventually paint on or etch into their dried clay pots. Point out the designs on ancient pots to note patterns. If the teacher has examples of Native American pots, discuss repetition in the designs and the abstract symbols. Crosses usually signify the four directions, and circles represent the spiritual, cyclical nature of all life.

Prewriting Step 11: *Drawing Symbols*

Have students draw a picture of their clay object by outlining its shape. Using pictures and words from the chart, have students draw or map three to five designs on their drawing to enable them to see that a story can be told about their lives by the designs they use. Encourage the use of sensory descriptive words mapped on the drawing to build vocabulary as they describe the feelings, thoughts, places, etc., that are triggered while they work on their design. What does the clay "sing" about their own lives?

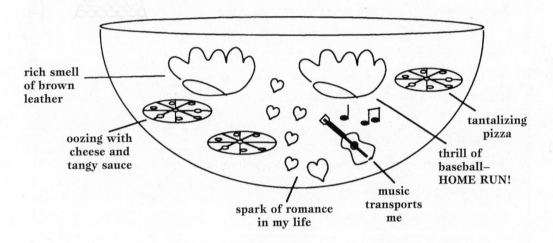

Prewriting Step 12: *Decorate Pots with Selected Symbols*

Now, using toothpicks or other etching tools, paints or glazes, students decorate their own pots using the mapped drawing.

 PROMPT

You have just finished shaping and decorating your own clay pot. If this clay object were to sing about itself, what would it say?

Imagine that you are the clay pot. You will write about yourself (the pot) and tell about the life of the person who made you. Describe yourself: your colors, your shape, your designs, etc. What are you, as the pot, used for? Tell about the person who made you based on the three symbols that decorate the pot. What do these designs "sing" about the potter who made you? Your writing should follow the conventions of standard written English.

 **PRECOMPOSING**

Precomposing Step 1: *Microtheme*

To help students generate ideas for writing, have them fill out the following microtheme guidelines:

Microtheme

Description: Write a five-minute quickwrite in the voice of the pot, describing yourself.

Colors: List three adjectives describing your color. *(Note: Instead of just blue, you might say azure blue, etc.)*

Shape: Write a sentence describing your shape. *(Note: Instead of just round, you might say round as the sun. Instead of just coiled, you might say coiled like a snake.)*

Designs: List the three designs that decorate you.

Use of object: Speaking in the voice of the pot, say what you are used for.

As the voice of the pot, tell about the person who made you.

Sample sentence starts might be:

• The person who made me is

• My potter is

• I was brought into being by

Interpret your designs.

List your designs here.   What these designs say about me is

•   •

•   •

•   •

Freewrite for five minutes to this sentence starter:

Overall, what I want my pot to "sing" about me is

Precomposing Step 2: *Teacher or Student Model*

Before students write, it would be helpful to share a student or teacher model so that the class can see how someone else went about writing to this assignment.

A sample teacher model is included below:

Teacher Model

Here I am. Brown-colored clay like dead autumn leaves is not most people's favorite color, but it's me. It's the way I am. And I bet you didn't immediately dig this shape I'm in or want to put me in some fancy museum. Well, good. I don't belong there. I'm a little too irregular.

My shape looks lumpy and feels bumpy. The hills, valleys, and deep caverns that define my form represent the adventures of my potter's life right now. I have three legs—sturdy little thing, aren't I? But if you aren't careful, I could lose my balance. So, be careful of me, OK? I look a lot more stable than I am sometimes.

The most prominent part of me is flat—like the plains of Nebraska. And in this wide area, there is room for my maker's heart and mind to continue their battle for supremacy. Heart and mind need each other but resent each other because they are trying to occupy the same space at the same time. (They obviously haven't learned to share yet.) So, this almost endless part of me is like a grade school playground when no adult is supervising. It's a wrestling ring....I'm gouged all over.

The money signs dribbled around my base indicate that my maker also wouldn't mind some of the comforts that money can bring. But money doesn't run her life. There are things that money can't buy that she'd rather have.

Way off in one corner a bed is etched in the clay. My maker really longs for that soft, cushy bed at the end of the day. It's her only respite, her only refuge from her life's adventures right now.

So you see, I don't fit any pattern and my maker's life doesn't either. We're two of an irregular kind, my maker and me. But we're also unique.

This second model, by a college student, may inspire students to take risks with the topic. It does a great job of showing and not just telling about what a pot might feel like as it is being created.

Student Model

When Clay Sings

Darkness. I feel lonely and yet there seems to be others of my kind nearby.

Movement. Something has happened. Am I going higher, being lifted?

Light. Blinding. I am blue.

Warmth. I am being caressed by ten long protrusions from pinkness.

Happiness. I am being shaped by someone who feels delight and nostalgic at the sight and touch of me.

Dizziness. I am losing perspective as I twist back and forth between two extremes.

I am being bent in an ever-increasing square so that I am touching myself in an infinite number of places.

Calm. I am being beheld as a treasure. Oh what opulence I've become.

Shape. I have become a square cube made up of myself in a spiral, that has a beginning and an end.

Design. I have been branded by a circle, half of which smiles and shines, the other of which reflects.

Turn. I rotate. A teaching is taking place. I rotate. Love is being shared. I rotate. Security.

Calm. Turn, turn, turn. Design, shape, motion, dizziness, happiness, warmth, light, movement, darkness.

Clay Leeds

Precomposing Step 3: Frame

For students who are having difficulty organizing their writing, you might want to share the following frame:

Note: This frame might inhibit some students who would otherwise take a more creative approach to the topic. But for students who are still unpracticed writers, it will give them a structure to work from. These students should be encouraged once they have a basic, skeletal frame for the writing, to embellish that writing with descriptive language.

Frame Example

I am a _____ (color) pot.

I am shaped like _____.

I am used to hold _____.

The designs on me are _____,

_____,

and _____.

What I like best about me is _____.

The person who made me is _____.

She/he likes _____

because of the _____ design.

_____ is very important to the person who made me.

I know that because of the _____ design.

Finally, the _____ design tells me

that the person who made me likes to _____.

Someday someone may find me who will know that the person who made

me is special because _____

_____

_____

_____.

◆ WRITING

Students write their papers based on what their pot is singing to them.

◆ SHARING

Sharing Step 1: *Interpreting Symbols—Sharing of Pots*

Choose a student partner for yourself. Model how to listen to a pot sing by holding one up and imagining what the pot is singing about itself and its maker. Look at the designs on the pot and talk about what those designs are "singing" to you. What does a particular design mean to you? Listen to it sing. *(A heart may mean love...but combined with other symbols it may mean a love of family or a love of the outdoors.)* What story are the designs telling? As you look at the designs, what meanings do they convey to you? You do not have to be "right" about what the maker meant when decorating the pot; just say what you interpret that the designs mean to you. What story is the pot telling to you?

The partner "listens" to the story that the pot is "singing." The potter is invited to respond by reading any or all of writing, or just responding to the partner's remarks.

Sharing Step 2: *Sharing of Pieces*

Have student partners then fill out the following response sheet:

Response Sheet

Name of Reviewer: _____

You spoke in the voice of your pot: ☐ yes   ☐ no

What I like best about your description of your pot was:

You pot's color(s) was/were:

The pot's shape was:

Your pot was used for:

What I learned about the potter was:

The symbols on your pot said the following about you:

Symbols   What the Symbol Said About You
- •   •
- •   •
- •   •

Overall, the message I got about you from your pot was

My suggestion for revision is to

REVISION

Students revise their writing based on the feedback from sharing so that the writing directly relates to the pot, its designs, and its song.

EDITING

Editing skills for class emphasis and instruction or review are determined by the teacher based on no more than three skills on which the students are to focus. *(The editing skills should be listed in the prompt once the teacher has determined which editing skills will be emphasized.)* With their own papers, students reread their writing looking for examples of the editing skills that need to be improved.

Students fill out the Self-Editing Chart as needed, correcting editing errors on their papers before final evaluation. The Self-Editing Chart is a record of each student's editing work that can become a part of student writing folders and writing conferences.

Self-Editing Chart

Title of Writing:

What I Did Well	What I Need to Work on

EVALUATION

Rubric

5–6   *This writing really sings!* Not only have you covered all of the requirements of the prompt, but also you have written with feeling and emotion. The pot's personality and the potter's personality come alive in your writing. You have written from the pot's point of view. You write about the pot's colors, shape, designs, and use. What is important or valued in the potter's life is evident in your writing. You describe the potter using the design symbols on the pot. The reader knows about the potter and about the pot through your writing. You have few, if any, errors in the conventions of written English.

4   *This writing follows the requirements of the prompt.* You write from the pot's point of view and describe the pot and the potter. However, you have only a few details and sensory descriptions that create a feeling of the personality of the pot and/or the potter. What is important in the potter's life may not be completely clear. The reader may be confused by some of the technical errors of your piece.

3   *This writing is missing some of the requirements of the prompt.* The sense of personality of either the pot or the potter is not evident. Few sensory details are employed and more description is needed to make the writing stronger. Editing skills need much attention.

1–2   *This writing needs additional work with peer partners or teacher conferences.* Your paper does not show an understanding of the writing and thinking skills demanded by this lesson.

Student Models

When Clay Sings

I started out as a lump of mushy gray clay. As my master's soft well worn hands gently sculpted me, thin fragile walls were slowly built with care. My master was thinking at the same time. She would gaze at me with a pondering facial expression, thinking of what I would contain.

My master decided that every morning she would whisper into me what her dream was the previous night. When she whispers, her soft voice echoes through my thin, fragile walls. She often talks of shopping and being at amusement parks.

The symbols she put on my exterior walls were a bushy oak tree to show her immense interest in mother nature, a group of stick people to admire her friends and family, and if you cautiously take a peek inside, you will discover a beautiful engraved picture of our precious earth to show that she realizes she won't be on it forever.

I ended up kind of lopsided, but what matters is that I am an individual artifact. I have feelings just like everything else. People often say I am just a lump of clay, but no, I share what my maker cares about; therefore, I am special in my own unique way.

Meredith Broker—Grade 6

When Clay Sings . . . We Listen

I am fragile, a hardened piece of clay. I sit here in a dingy, misty closet. I am an oval shaped object with designs which interpret my creator's feelings.

On one of my sides there is an inscription of two people holding hands in happiness. This picture describes the maker's hunger for companionship. It's this companionship, with friends and family, which keeps my crafter's insanity intact. There is a picture of lines surrounding a heart on another side. It is this picture, of a glowing heart, that represents the master's need to love and his desire to be loved.

I don't exactly know what I'm used for but I know he hides me in the deepest part of the closet. I think he wants me to stay clean for I know he loves me so.

Garrett Dameron—Grade 8

When Clay Sings

I am a clay pot, small and cone shaped. Money is what I'm filled with, but it's only small change. My maker seemed nice, but he banged me flat.

I'm not sure why he painted me gray, but at least my inside is colored. I think it might be reflective of a book he read, because he scratched a picture of a book on my originally unblemished surface. (The book is *The Hobbit.* In the chapter where Bilbo is making riddles with the Gollum, a riddle comes up. It reads: *A box without hinges or lid, yet golden treasure inside is hid.*)

The next design is a picture of two stick figures holding hands. I can only guess that that means family or friends. The last design is a picture of a tent. Obviously this is a symbol of his love of camping.

Miles Jacob—Grade 6

Learning Log Entries About Working with the Clay

Students were asked to write learning log entries after they had worked with the clay. They were asked to write what they were thinking about while they worked with the clay, what they liked about the activity, and what they would improve about the lesson.

Student Models

What I Was Thinking About . . .

During the day (while working with clay) I felt that I had really gone back for a moment (in time) and I was actually there (with the Navahos) making a pot for our survival. I felt like a young boy helping his mother in her daily tasks. I was feeling this way until brought out of it by someone. But even though I was awakened, my thoughts still kept drifting back, not as if I was there this time but as though it was a real memory (in my past). But now it seems that memory is gone, or though it is only there when working with clay.

Paul Butke—Grade 8

What I Thought About During the Clay Making . . .

I kept thinking will some of my relatives of the future ever find this pot when I'm gone. The clay seemed to have gotten to me because my hands just kept going at the work with no problem. It was like my hands knew what I wanted to make! I only worked with clay once to make a dinosaur in kindergarten, but it seemed like the movement of my hands were just naturally there! This is what was going through my mind while I was working with the clay.

Rose Mary Chavez—Grade 8

RECOMMENDED REFERENCES

Apodaca, Paul. Curator, Bowers Museum, Santa Ana, CA.

Arnold, David. "Pueblo Pottery," *National Geographic*, vol. 162, (November 1982), pp. 593–605.

Babcock, B., et al. *The Pueblo Storyteller: Development of a Figurative Ceramic Tradition.* Tucson: University of Arizona Press, 1986.

Baylor, Byrd. *The Desert Is Theirs;* illustrated by Peter Parnall. New York: Charles Scribner's Sons, 1975.

———*Everybody Needs a Rock.* New York: Macmillan Publishing Co. (Aladdin Books), 1974.

———*Guess Who My Favorite Person Is;* illustrated by Robert Andrew Parker. New York: Charles Scribner's Sons, 1977.

———*Hawk, I'm Your Brother;* illustrated by Peter Parnall. New York: Macmillan Publishing Co., 1976.

———*I'm in Charge of Celebrations;* pictures by Peter Parnall. New York: Charles Scribner's Sons, 1986.

———*Moon Song;* illustrated by Ronald Himler. New York: Charles Scribner's Sons, 1982.

Stories in Clay

NONFICTION

———— *Sometimes I Dance Mountains;* photographs by Bill Sears, drawings by Ken Longtemps. New York: Charles Scribner's Sons, 1973.

———— *The Way to Start a Day;* illustrated by Peter Parnall. New York: Charles Scribner's Sons, 1978.

———— *When Clay Sings;* illustrated by Tom Bahti. New York: Charles Scribner's Sons, 1972.

———— *Your Own Best Secret Place;* illustrated by Peter Parnall. New York: Charles Scribner's Sons, 1979.

Baylor, Byrd, and Peter Parnall. *Desert Voices.* New York: Charles Scribner's Sons, 1981.

———— *If You Are a Hunter of Fossils.* New York: Charles Scribner's Sons, 1980.

———— *The Other Way to Listen.* New York: Charles Scribner's Sons, 1978.

George, Chief Dan. *My Heart Soars;* drawings by Helmut Hirnschall. Canada: Hancock House Publishers Ltd., 1974.

Weitzman, David. *My Backyard History Book.* Boston: Little, Brown Company, 1975.

Native American Music:
The music listed below can be found at such stores as:

- The Indian Store at Hobby City, 1238 S. Beach Blvd., Anaheim, CA 92804 (714) 828-3050
- The Nature Company Stores
- Natural Wonders

Changes: Native American Flute Music by R. Carlos Nakai, distributed by Canyon Records Productions Inc., 4143 N. 16th St., Phoenix, AZ 85016.

Carry the Gift by R. Carlos Nakai and William Eaton, distributed by Canyon Records Productions Inc., 4143 N. 16th St., Phoenix, AZ 85016.

Earth Spirit by R. Carlos Nakai, distributed by Canyon Records Productions Inc., 4143 N. 16th St., Phoenix, AZ 85016.

Landscape by Coyote Oldman Music, 434 Chautauqua, Norman, OK 73069.

Sundance Season by R. Carlos Nakai, distributed by Celestial Harmonies, P.O. Box 30122, Tucson, AZ 85751.

Featured Literature

"Sleep Not Longer, O Choctaws and Chickasaws"
by Tecumseh

Grade Level
For High School and College

Thinking Level
Synthesis and Evaluation

Writing Domain
Analytical/Expository

Materials Needed
No special materials required

Suggested Supplementary Readings
- *Indian Oratory: Famous Speeches by Noted Indian Chieftains* by W. C. Vanderwerth
- *Seeing with a Native Eye: Essays on Native American Religion* edited by Walter Holden Capps
- *God Is Red* by Vine Deloria, Jr.

Writing a Persuasive Speech: Using American Indian Oratory as a Model

by Cristan Greaves

Overview

After reading and analyzing Tecumseh's speech, students will apply their knowledge of American Indian oratory and write a speech attempting to convince a specific audience to believe something or to take a particular course of action about a critical issue or problem.

Objectives

THINKING SKILLS

Students will:

- *identify* persuasive discourse features in Tecumseh's speech;
- *discuss and analyze* Tecumseh's speech as a model of persuasive discourse;
- *create* a persuasive speech by applying their own knowledge of oratory and persuasive discourse;
- *persuade* a specific audience to believe something or to take a particular course of action about a critical issue or problem.

WRITING SKILLS

Students will write a speech in which they:

- *establish* their qualifications as a speaker, that they are like the audience and can speak for them;
- *define* and *address* a critical issue or problem;
- *appeal* to a particular audience;
- *clearly state* what they want their audience to believe or do, and why;
- *use* a tone that is appropriate to the audience and to the occasion;
- *predict* possible objections with logically constructed arguments;
- *utilize* rhetorical questions, repetition of key words and phrases, and figures of speech;
- *demonstrate* proficiency in the standards of written English.

The Process

This lesson assumes that students will have already read and analyzed Patrick Henry's "Speech in the Virginia Convention" or Thomas Paine's "The Crisis, Number 1" or "Common Sense" as models of oratory from the Revolutionary War period. Students will read Tecumseh's "Sleep Not Longer, O Choctaws and Chickasaws," a speech delivered in 1811, as the United States and Britain were on the brink of war. Students will identify and analyze the techniques of oratory and persuasive writing found in this famous speech. The lesson culminates in the writing of a speech in which the students attempt to convince a specific audience to believe something or to take a particular course of action about a critical issue or problem. In this speech, students will be using the techniques of persuasive discourse as modeled in Tecumseh's speech. This lesson should take approximately five–seven days, depending upon the amount of time allotted for writing of a first draft, a revision, and implementation of peer sharing groups. *Note: This lesson has been influenced by Virginia Bergquist's lesson "Persuasive Letters" in* Thinking/Writing: Fostering Critical Thinking Through Writing, *ed. Carol Booth Olson (New York, HarperCollins Publishers, 1992).*

 PREWRITING

Prewriting Step 1: *Guided Imagery*

Ask students to close their eyes and visualize something that is very important to them. It could be a prized possession, a belief, or a special place that in some way has had a profound impact on them.

Create an atmosphere that is conducive to the imaginative task at hand by turning off the lights and using the following questions to guide the students' imagery:

- Close your eyes and relax. You may put your head on your desk or sit back with your eyes closed. The important thing is that you are as comfortable and relaxed as you can be.
- Imagine that all the tension in your body is running down from your head and right through your toes. Picture it evaporating into the air and floating away as lightly as a white cloud. Your whole body is relaxed and you feel calm and peaceful.
- Breathe slowly and deeply, enjoying this calm and peaceful feeling.
- Think of that prized possession, belief, or special place that is very important to you. In fact, it is difficult, if not impossible, for you to imagine living without it. It may be an object that someone gave you which has come to mean a great deal to you. It could be a belief that defines who you are, a belief by which you live. Or it could be a special place that you have been to or can go to reflect or relax.

- You now have that special object, belief, or place in your mind.
  —What is it?   —How do you feel thinking about it?
  —Is it an object?   —What does it mean to you?
  —A belief?   —Why is it important to you?
  —A place?

- Now, imagine that someone is determined to take your special object, belief, or place away from you. Because you feel so strongly about this special object, belief, or place, you feel you must defend it. What will you do to keep it from being taken away from you?

Prewriting Step 2: *Freewriting*

Have students draw and/or write for five–ten minutes about their special thing, about the threat to its existence, and how they would defend it. Ask for volunteers to share their drawings/freewrites.

Prewriting Step 3: *Discuss Context of Tecumseh's Speech*

Before the first reading of Tecumseh's "Sleep Not Longer, O Choctaws and Chickasaws," provide the students with the context for the speech. In their guided imagery, students focused on a particular thing that was vital to them and imagined what their response would be if their special object, belief, or place were to be taken away from them. Similarly, in Tecumseh's speech, Tecumseh identifies a sacred place (the southern part of the United States) and the threat of having that land taken away by the Americans. Tecumseh pleads with the Choctaws and Chickasaws to join his coalition against the "white intruders and tyrants" who threaten to destroy "our homes, our country, bequeathed to us by the Great Spirit, the graves of our dead and everything that is dear and sacred to us. . . ."

In addition, as Jean Molesky-Poz of University of California, Berkeley, has said, it is critical to provide the framework or context of culturally diverse literature when teaching such literature to students. The following information should provide a basic context for Tecumseh's speech and should be available for students as they work in their Jigsaw groups (Prewriting Step 8).

The great Shawnee chief Tecumseh, born in 1768 near the site of present-day Springfield, Ohio, was well known as an outstanding orator and warrior. With his brother Tenskwatawa, the Prophet, Tecumseh was a strong opponent of the advance of American settlers. Tecumseh claimed that the Ohio Valley belonged in common to the tribes that resided there, and that the United States had no right to purchase lands from any single tribe. He made long horseback trips over most of the South, trying to enlist the tribes in his cause. Under Tecumseh's leadership, the Shawnees formed a coalition among the Wyandottes, Delawares, some of the Algonquins, the Chippewas, Nanticokes, Creeks, and Cherokees. During the War of 1812, Tecumseh sided with the British and was made a brigadier general. He commanded a detachment of two thousand Indian warriors from several tribes. He died in 1813 fighting in Ontario against American troops led by William Henry Harrison.

Writing a Persuasive Speech

NONFICTION

In the spring of 1811, when it became apparent that America was headed for a war with England, Tecumseh called for a council with the tribes in the southern part of the country. Accompanied by a party of some thirty Indians, he appeared at a gathering of the Choctaws and Chickasaws. In his speech "Sleep Not Longer, O Choctaws and Chickasaws," Tecumseh pleaded with the two tribes to join in a common effort against the Americans. While it was evident that some of the Choctaws and Chickasaws were sympathetic to Tecumseh's eloquent appeal, the Choctaw chief Pushmataha convinced both tribes that the Americans were their friends, and that if they broke their "sacred treaties" with the Americans, the Great Spirit would punish them. The Americans, however, considered friendship less important, and treaties less sacred, and in the 1830s, the Choctaws and the Chickasaws were forced to leave their homeland and walk the infamous Trail of Tears to Indian territory in Oklahoma.

Prewriting Step 4: *First Reading*

Read "Sleep Not Longer, O Choctaws and Chickasaws" (appended to this lesson) aloud to the class. As the speech is read, have students underline words, phrases, or sentences that particularly appeal to them.

Prewriting Step 5: *Quaker Reading*

Have students read aloud any words, phrases, or sentences they underlined while reading the speech. Anyone may speak at any time. This continues until all the students who wish to share have done so. This technique often brings out the most important ideas in a piece of literature.

Prewriting Step 6: *Reflective Journal*

Hand out a sheet of paper divided into four columns: "What I Learned from This Speech"; "What Questions Do I Still Have"; "How I Felt While Listening to This Speech"; "Overall Response." Have students record their responses. Then, have them share their responses voluntarily either with the class, in peer partners, or in Read-Around groups. The following shows how students might respond to the speech:

What I Learned from This Speech	What Questions Do I Still Have?	How I Felt While Listening to This Speech	Overall Response
That this chief used more complex language than I had expected from the stereotypical close-to-nature simple Indian.	• What language was it originally in? • Who translated it? • Why didn't the speech work?	• It was too long. • I tuned out half way through. • I know he wanted me to die for this cause, but I don't know how—in what kind of war, or whatever.	I wasn't convinced to fight a losing battle.

Prewriting Step 7: *Identifying the Structure of the Speech*

Divide the class into seven groups to identify the structure and content of this seven-paragraph speech. Each groups is to read through their assigned paragraph and have their elected recorder summarize the paragraph's structure and content in a few sentences. Discuss each group's responses and come to a consensus about the structure and content of Tecumseh's speech.

Paragraph 1 Establishes the occasion of the speech; addresses the audience of Choctaws and Chickasaws; begins his argument—it is time for them to stop debating—they must unite and take action against their "merciless oppressors" or be conquered.

Paragraph 2 Begins to anticipate the possible objections of the audience; maintains they must not give in to folly, inactivity, and cowardice; that their land will be taken, too, if they remain passive; that they must unite in "one common cause against the common foe."

Paragraph 3 Anticipates other objections of the audience; they must not give in to "false security and delusive hopes"; states that they have already experienced the oppression of the Americans; poses the question of enslavement—will they meet the same fate as the "black-faces" who are slaves to the "pale-faces"?

Paragraph 4 Reiterates the importance of action and of remembering the Americans' history of taking lands away from Indians; states that Indians must no longer be the "dupes" of the "avaricious American pale faces"; maintains that war or extermination is their only choice.

Paragraph 5 Anticipates other objections of the audience; it is their duty and honor to protect their "endangered country"; to remain passive is "criminal indifference"; reiterates the importance of uniting as "one body, one heart, and defend to the last warrior our country, our homes, our liberty, and the graves of our fathers."

Paragraph 6 Reiterates the Choctaws' and Chickasaws' indolent posture in the face of this threat; reminds them that if they don't join the coalition, they will have failed their friends and their duty; describes the Americans as people "fond of innovations, quick to contrive and quick to put their schemes into effectual execution no matter how great and wrong the injury to us."

Paragraph 7 Reiterates the need to join "our common cause"; that they are bound to the other Indians by "blood"; he finally warns them that if they don't join the coalition, that there will come a day when they will be left "single-handed and alone to the cruel mercy" of their most treacherous foe.

Prewriting Step 8: *Jigsaw*

Through this collaborative learning technique, students will become experts on one portion of the text and share their expertise with their small "home" group.

(See Jigsaws 1 and 2 on pages 228–229.) Form groups A–E to analyze the following: A) the tone of the speech; B) the quality of the proposed argument (is it logical and well-constructed? does it anticipate, state, and refute the opposing argument and develop its own argument?); C) use of rhetorical questions; D) repetition of key points and phrases; and E) use of figures of speech (such as simile, metaphor, personification, and allusion).

Jigsaw 1

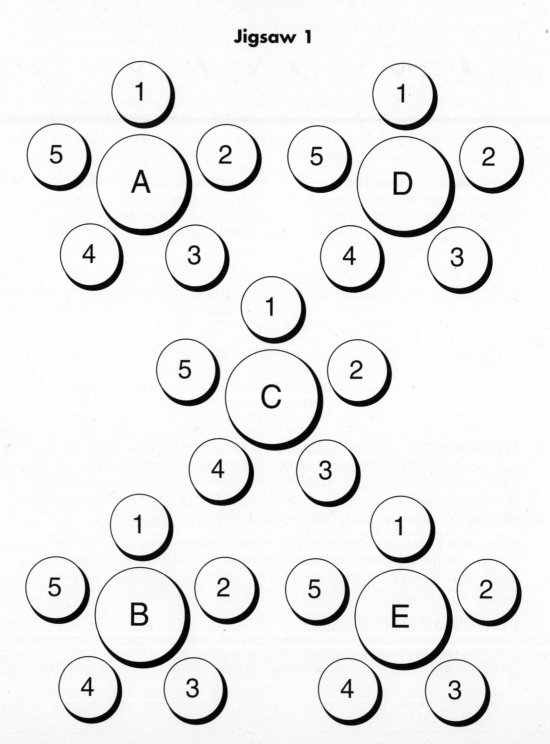

Jigsaw 2

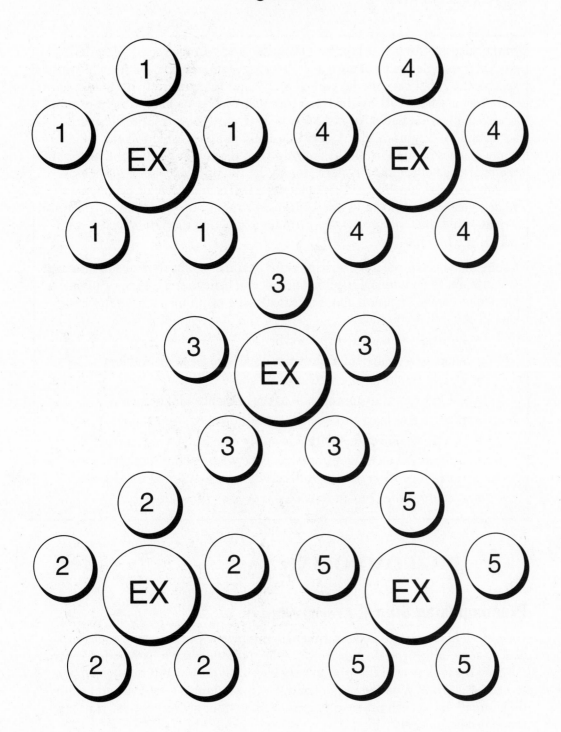

PROMPT

In the speech "Sleep Not Longer, O Choctaws and Chickasaws," Tecumseh tried to persuade the Choctaws and Chickasaws to join the coalition of tribes against the Americans as the United States and England were on the verge of war. Tecumseh had always believed that the Americans had no right to encroach on what had been Indian land for countless years. Furthermore, according to Tecumseh, the Americans could not be trusted to keep their many pledges of support and friendship with the Indians—that the history of the relations between the American and the Indians was one of broken promises and treaties. In his eloquent speech, Tecumseh made an impassioned plea to the Choctaws and Chickasaws to join the coalition of Indian Tribes—that their support was critical for protecting the "endangered country" of the Indians.

Using analytical/expository writing skills, write a persuasive speech in which you attempt to convince a specific audience to believe something or to take a particular course of action about a critical issue or problem. Your speech should show that you have:

- defined and addressed a specific issue or problem
- addressed a particular audience about the issue or problem
- clearly stated what you want and why
- exhibited a tone appropriate to the audience and occasion
- predicted at least three possible objections of your audience
- met those objections with a logically constructed argument
- utilized the techniques of persuasive writing such as rhetorical questions, repetition of key words and phrases, and figures of speech
- edited for the conventions of standard written English.

PRECOMPOSING

Precomposing Step 1: *Freewriting*

Have students freewrite about a time when they tried to persuade someone to believe something or to do something. Whom did they try to persuade? What did they try to persuade the person to believe or do? How did they try to persuade the person? What were the results? Ask students to describe and explain their situations to each other in groups of three–four students each. Have each group produce a chart.

	What	Who	How	Results
1.				
2.				
3.				
4.				

Have each group report to the class the most interesting persuasion. Then, focus the class discussion on the "Who" and "How" columns of the chart. Emphasize the importance of matching audience (Who) and method (How) as a lead-in to the next Precomposing Step. For example, if a student wanted to persuade her parents to use the family car on a Friday night date, she would need to convince them that she was responsible enough to handle the car; that she felt this special privilege had been earned by previous responsible behavior; that this would be an important "step of faith" for her, etc.

Precomposing Step 2: *Cluster*

At this point, students will need to begin exploring issues that are of serious concern to them. They should focus on issues or problems that they believe are critical ones to problem-solve. Have students cluster such issues or problems on the board. A sample cluster may look like this:

Precomposing Step 3: *Problem-Solution Journal*

Have students identify the issues about which they have the strongest feelings. In the Problem-Solution Journal, each student will identify a problem and explore and suggest possible solutions. Using gangs as an example, one can see how this journal exercise should empower students to develop problem-solution strategies as they write to describe new ways to resolve it.

Divide the paper with the following headings:

Problem	Consequences of Failing to Solve the Problem	Possible Solutions
G **A** **N** **G** **S**	**1.** countless numbers of lives lost to gang activity and violence	**a.** gang prevention programs **b.** employment opportunities
	2. more drug trafficking	**a.** stiffer penalties **b.** more police patrol
	3. streets/communities become less safe	**a.** more policing of communities **b.** neighborhood watch programs **c.** provide alternative to criminal activities

Note: To save class time and to allow students unlimited, uninterrupted time for this journal exercise, teachers may want to assign this activity for homework.

Precomposing Step 4: *Predict Objections, Opposing Arguments*

Ask students to choose an audience they believe most needs to hear what they have to say. Ask them what they want their audience to believe or do about the problem or the issue they wrote about in their Problem-Solution Journal. Enter the information in the first columns of the following chart:

Who/Audience	What	Possible Objections of Audience	Possible Argument of Persuaders
The mayor of your city	Fund more gang prevention programs	1. 2. 3.	1. 2. 3.

Have students work in pairs. Have them exchange charts and "dialogue" silently about objections and arguments. The audience (response partner) writes down a possible objection. The persuader (writer) reads the objection and then responds with a possible argument. The chart is passed back and forth in this manner for ten–fifteen minutes.

A completed chart may look like the following:

Who/Audience	What	Possible Objections of Audience	Possible Argument of Persuaders
The mayor of your city	Fund more gang prevention programs	**1.** It will cost too much.	**1.** Local business and community leaders are willing to help fund these programs.
		2. It won't work.	**2.** We have statistics to prove that these programs *do* work.
		3. It would be better to spend the money for more law enforcement personnel.	**3.** In the long run, it's cheaper to fund prevention of gang membership than to rehabilitate gang members.

Then, have students switch roles and do the exercise again so that both students' charts are complete.

Precomposing Step 5: *Role-Playing*

Ask two students to role-play the following situation for the class. One student will be the director of your city's gang prevention program, whose organization's objective is to provide alternatives to gang activity. The other student will be the mayor, who has voiced skepticism about the effectiveness of gang prevention programs. Before they begin, brainstorm characteristics of the audience (the mayor) that will influence the persuader's strategies. Discuss which tones the persuader might use that would be the most effective and why.

Give the following instructions to students:

> Suppose you were the director of your city's gang prevention program and your groups' immediate goal was to persuade the mayor to fund more gang prevention programs in your city. You are concerned that continued gang activity will have a devastating impact on your city. In an effort to gain public support for your cause, you have agreed to meet with the following groups of people to discuss your concerns:
>
> - the mayor of your city
> - concerned citizens in your community
> - law enforcement personnel
> - community leaders (council members, etc.)

Today, you are meeting with the mayor of your city. It is the end of the fiscal year and important budgetary decisions will be made today regarding the continued funding of gang prevention programs in your city.

After the two students have role-played the scenario with the mayor, practice with different audiences and tones by role-playing with the other three audiences with the whole class.

- What words and tone of voice would you use to address each specific audience listed above?
- How would your language and tone differ depending on the audience?
- Choose a word or words to describe the tone you might use with each audience (e.g., objective, sympathetic, accusing, sarcastic, angry, forceful, etc.)

Evaluate the rhetorical effectiveness of the role-plays.

Precomposing Step 6: *Role-Playing (continued)*

Have students decide on a new situation for their role-play and a few different audiences. In pairs, have students role-play their own topics. Then, have them evaluate the rhetorical effectiveness of their role-plays.

Precomposing Step 7: *Practicing Persuasive Discourse*

1. Have students return to Tecumseh's speech "Sleep Not Longer, O Choctaws and Chickasaws" and analyze Tecumseh's use of rhetorical questions and the repetitions of key words and phrases. Have students chart their findings. A sample chart appears below:

Rhetorical Questions	Effect
1. "Are we not...?" 2. "Have we not...?" 3. "Shall it be said...?" 4. "Will we calmly suffer...?" 5. "How long will it be...?" 6. "Which do you choose?"	Each of these questions poses a challenge to the audience. There is a sense of urgency in the questions.
Repeated Key Words	**Effect**
1. "Common" 2. "Nor" 3. "Soon" 4. "Then" 5. "Oppressors, oppression" 6. Words of attack "breading in"; "conquered"; "enslave"; etc.	1. To show the Choctaws and Chickasaws as having the same concerns as Tecumseh 2. Transitions 3. Sense of urgency in Tecumseh's point of view 4. Transitions 5. Americans are tyrants 6. Americans threaten the Indians
Repeated Key Phrases	**Effect**
1. "our country"; "our race"; "our broad domains"; "our lands"; "our lot"; "our eyes"; etc. 2. "Choctaws and Chickasaws" 3. "common cause'" "common danger"; "common fate"; etc. 4. "Every year"	1. They are all in this struggle together 2. Personalizing his audience 3. See comment on #1 4. The threat of the Americans is unending.

With their own topics in mind, have students model Tecumseh's use of rhetorical questions and the repetition of key words and phrases.

2. Have students analyze Tecumseh's use of figures of speech such as similes, metaphors, personifications, and allusions and chart their findings:

Similes	Effect
1. "...We will be... scattered as autumnal leaves before the wind." 2. "They have vanished...as snow before a summer storm." 3. "Your people, too, will soon be as falling leaves and scattering clouds before their blighting breath."	The Americans completely overpower the Indians. The Indians are no match for the Americans' power. Leaves are blown By wind; snow melts in summer, etc.

Metaphors	Effect
1. "one body" 2. "one heart" 3. "mighty forest trees"	1. The coalition must be unified in action. 2. They must be unified in their desires. 3. Traditions of the Indians? Their culture? Their strength?

Personification	Effect
None	None

Allusion	Effect
None	None

With their own topics in mind, have students model Tecumseh's use of figures of speech.

 ## WRITING

Using their Problem-Solution Journals, objections and opposing arguments charts, role-play experiences, and techniques of persuasive discourse models, students should be ready to write a draft of their speech—at home or in class, depending on the level of the group. Encourage students to outline their speech to ensure that they will produce a well-organized first draft.

 ## SHARING/RESPONDING

Sharing Step 1: Partner Response

In pairs, have students share speeches and identify the audience and the occasion of the speech and help each other decide whether the speech would persuade the intended audience. Peer partners should underline what is wanted in yellow; the reasons in red; the objections of the audience in green; arguments to respond to the objections in blue; rhetorical questions and reiterated key words and phrases in brown; and figures of speech in black. Partners should discuss whether the tone is appropriate for the audience and the occasion.

Sharing Step 2: Read-Around Groups

Share papers in Read-Around groups. *(See the Glossary for a description of Read-Around groups.)* Chart the groups' selections of best speeches. Have the writers of the most frequently selected speeches read them aloud to the class.

 # REVISING

Using the feedback received, students should revise their speeches by answering the following questions in writing:

- Have I defined and addressed a specific critical issue or problem?
- Have I addressed a specific audience?
- Is what I want clearly stated?
- Have I stated the reasons why I want it?
- Did the words I chose create a tone that is appropriate for the audience and the occasion?
- Did I include at least three possible objections of the audience?
- Are my arguments against those objections persuasive?
- Have I used a variety of the techniques of persuasive discourse?

 # EDITING

Editing Step 1: Soliciting Feedback

After students have revised their speeches, they may meet in pairs or groups to do the final editing of their papers. Students may request what additional feedback they would like from their peers on the content of the paper as well as a check of the correctness of spelling, punctuation, sentence structure, etc.

Editing Step 2: Final Drafts

Students can then complete the final drafts of their speeches, using the feedback received in the editing session.

EVALUATION

Rubric

6 *This is a paper that is clearly superior: well written, insightful, carefully organized, and technically correct. A 6 paper does all of the following well:*

- Clearly defines and addresses a specific critical issue or problem.

- Addresses a particular audience about the issue or problem.

- Clearly states what the writer wants and why.

- Exhibits a tone that is committed, reasonable, confident, and appropriate to the audience and the occasion.

- Predicts at least three possible objections of the audience and meets those objections with a logically constructed argument.

- Skillfully uses the techniques of persuasive discourse such as rhetorical questions, repetition of key words and phrases, and figures of speech.

- Demonstrates mastery of the conventions of standard written English.

5 *This paper includes all aspects of the assignment but is a thinner version of the 6. It is still well written, carefully organized, and technically correct. It will do all or most of the following:*

- Defines and addresses a specific critical issue or problem.

- Addresses a particular audience about the issue or problem.

- States what the writer wants and why.

- Exhibits a tone that is committed, reasonable, confident, and appropriate but is somewhat less engaging than the 6 paper.

- Anticipates at least three objections of the audience and meets those objections with a logically constructed argument, but not as astutely as the 6 paper.

- Utilizes a variety of techniques of persuasive discourse, but less skillfully than the 6 paper.

- Demonstrates competency in the conventions of standard written English.

4 *This paper includes all aspects of the assignment, but not in as much depth as the 5 or 6 paper. It may exhibit some of the following:*

- Defines and addresses a specific critical issue or problem, but with less sophistication than the 5 or 6 papers.

- Addresses an audience about the issue or problem.

- States what is wanted and gives reasons why, but the reasons are not as clearly explained as in a 5 or 6 paper.

- Uses a tone that is appropriate to the audience and the occasion, but not consistently.

- Anticipates only two objections of the audience and meets them with a logically constructed argument or anticipates three objections but does not meet all three with a logically constructed argument.

- Uses a few of the techniques of persuasive discourse, but less skillfully than the 5 or 6 paper.

- Demonstrates occasional weaknesses in the conventions of standard written English. Errors may be distracting but do not affect reader's understanding.

3 *This paper treats the subject in a superficial way. It exhibits all the weaknesses of the 4 paper:*

- Mentions an issue or problem.

- Mentions an audience to whom the issue or problem will be addressed.

- States what is wanted but does not give reasons why.

- Uses a tone that is not appropriate to the audience or the occasion.

- Anticipates one or more objections but does not meet them with a logically constructed argument.

- Attempts to use one or two of the techniques of persuasive discourse, but less skillfully than the 4 paper.

- Demonstrates frequent errors in the conventions of standard written English. Errors interfere with the flow of the writing.

2 *This paper represents an attempt to write to the prompt. It exhibits all the weaknesses of the 3 paper:*

- Points to an issue or problem.

- Points to an audience to whom the issue or problem will be addressed.

- Does not clearly state what is wanted and why.

- Fails to establish a tone.

- Has a poorly constructed or confusing argument that fails to acknowledge the objections of an audience.

- Uses only one of the techniques of persuasive discourse, but with little skill.

- Demonstrates serious and frequent errors in the conventions of standard written English. These errors distract the reader and lead to confusion.

1 *This paper reveals that the writer may have been unsure of or confused by the prompt. It:*

- Fails to clearly address an issue or problem.

- Does not address a particular audience.

- Does not state what is wanted and why.

- Fails to establish a tone.

- Fails to anticipate any of the possible objections of an audience and meet them with a logically constructed argument.

- Does not attempt to use any of the techniques of persuasiveness discourse.

- Serious errors in almost every sentence interfere with reader understanding.

EXTENSION ACTIVITIES

1. *Make a Speech*

Have students present their speeches aloud in a mock speech contest or debate.

2. *Analyze*

a. Compare and contrast your speech with Tecumseh's speech "Sleep Not Longer, O Choctaws and Chickasaws."

b. Compare and contrast the following speeches:

- Frederick Douglass's "What the Black Man Wants," delivered at the Annual Meeting of the Massachusetts Anti-Slavery Society in Boston, 1865.
- Elizabeth Cady Stanton's "Speech to the First Women's Rights Convention," delivered at the first women's rights convention in Seneca Falls, New York, 1848.
- Chief Seattle's "This Sacred Soil," delivered before signing a treaty yielding the Duwamish tribe's lands to Isaac Stevens, Governor of Washington Territory, 1854.

    Consider how each speaker protests (either directly or by implication) against the way his/her group is treated in America.

c. Using the issue or problem you wrote about in your speech, analyze the belief system and motivations behind your argument. In other words, analyze what makes you feel so strongly about this issue or problem that you have decided is a critical one to problem-solve.

d. Choose a topic being studied in a class, for example, the Civil Rights movement in a history class or an ecological issue in a science class. Have students write a persuasive speech that deals with the topic.

3. *Evaluate*

a. Tecumseh was not successful in persuading the Choctaws and Chickasaws to join his coalition against the Americans. Write a brief speech from Tecumseh's point of view as to why he failed in his attempts.

    b.   Evaluate the effectiveness of Tecumseh's speech. Speculate as to why he failed in his attempts to persuade the Choctaws and Chickasaws to join his coalition.

    c.   Evaluate the effectiveness of your speech.

    d.   Choose one of the speeches listed above (Analyze) written by Frederick Douglass, Elizabeth Cady Stanton, or Chief Seattle. Imagine that you attended the meeting where the speech was delivered. Convince another person that the speaker's protest is justified and that his/her requests must be granted.

POSSIBLE CLASS PROMPTS

1. Autobiographical Incident

    a.   Write about an incident that led you to feel strongly about a particular issue or problem. Use first person point of view and vivid sensory details; order events logically and include the incident's significance to you.

    b.   Write about an incident in which you persuaded someone to believe something or do something that you thought was important. What methods did you use to persuade the person? Use first person point of view and vivid sensory detail; order events logically and include the incident's significance to you.

2. Report of Information

Write a newspaper article that reports the occasion on which your speech was delivered, as well as the outcome. Was your audience persuaded by your speech? Be sure to include a headline.

3. Reflective

Reflect upon what you have learned about the human condition as the result of exploring this critical issue or problem.

Featured Literature

Sleep Not Longer, O Choctaws and Chickasaws

In view of questions of vast importance, have we met together in solemn council tonight. Nor should we here debate whether we have been wronged and injured, but by what measures we should avenge ourselves; for our merciless oppressors, having long since planned out their proceedings, are not about to make, but have and are still making attacks upon our race who have as yet come to no resolution. Nor are we ignorant by what steps, and by what gradual advances, the whites break in upon our neighbors. Imagining themselves to be still undiscovered, they show themselves the less audacious because you are insensible. The whites are already nearly a match for us all united, and too strong for any one tribe alone to resist; so that unless we support one another with our collective and united forces; unless every tribe unanimously combines to give check to the ambition and avarice of the whites, they will soon conquer us apart and disunited and we will be driven away from our native country and scattered as autumnal leaves before the wind.

But have we not courage enough remaining to defend our country and maintain our ancient independence? Will we calmly suffer the white intruders and tyrants to enslave us? Shall it be said of our race that we knew not how to extricate ourselves from the three most dreadful calamities—folly, inactivity and cowardice? But what need is there to speak of the past? It speaks for itself and asks, Where today is the Pequod? Where the Narragansetts, the Mohawks, Pocanokets, and many other once powerful tribes of our race? They have vanished before the avarice and oppression of the white men, as snow before a summer sun. In the vain hope of alone defending their ancient possessions, they have fallen in the wars with the white men. Look abroad over their once beautiful country, and what see you now? Naught but the ravages of the pale face destroyers meet our eyes. So it will be with you Choctaws and Chickasaws! Soon your mighty forest trees, under the shade of whose wide spreading branches you have played in infancy, sported in boyhood, and now rest your wearied limbs after the fatigue of the chase, will be cut down to fence in the land which the white intruders dare to call their own. Soon their broad roads will pass over the grave of your fathers, and the place of their rest will be blotted out forever. The annihilation of our race is at hand unless we unite in one common cause against the common foe. Think not, brave Choctaws and Chickasaws, that you can remain passive and indifferent to the common danger, and thus escape the common fate. Your people, too, will soon be as falling leaves and scattering clouds before their blighting breath. You, too, will be driven away from your native land and ancient domains as leaves are driven before the wintry storms.

Sleep not longer, O Choctaws and Chickasaws, in false security and delusive hopes. Our broad domains are fast escaping from our grasp. Every year our white intruders become more greedy, exacting, oppressive and overbearing. Every year contentions spring up between them and our people and when blood is shed we have to make atonement whether right or wrong, at the cost of the lives of our greatest chiefs, and the yielding up of large tracts of our lands. Before the palefaces came among us, we enjoyed the happiness of unbounded freedom, and were acquainted with neither riches, wants nor oppression. How is it now? Wants and oppression are our lot; for are we not controlled in everything, and dare we move without asking, by your leave? Are we not being stripped day by day of the little that remains of our ancient liberty? Do they not even kick and strike us as they do their black-faces? How long will it be before they will tie us to a post and whip us, and make us work for them in their corn fields as they do them? Shall we wait for that moment or shall we die fighting before submitting to such ignominy?

Have we not for years had before our eyes a sample of their designs, and are they not sufficient harbingers of their future determinations? Will we not soon be driven from our respective countries and the graves of our ancestors? Will not the bones of our dead be plowed up, and their graves be turned into fields? Shall we calmly wait until they become so numerous that we will no longer be able to resist oppression? Will we wait to be destroyed in our turn, without making an effort worthy of our race? Shall we give up our homes, our country, bequeathed to us by the Great Spirit, the graves of our dead, and everything that is dear and sacred to us, without a struggle? I know you will cry with me: Never! Never! Then let us by unity of action destroy them all, which we now can do, or drive them back whence they came. War or extermination is now our only choice. Which do you choose? I know your answer. Therefore, I now call on you, brave Choctaws and Chickasaws, to assist in the just cause of liberating our race from the grasp of our faithless invaders and heartless oppressors. The white usurpation in our common country must be stopped, or we, its rightful owners, be forever destroyed and wiped out as a race of people. I am now at the head of many warriors backed by the strong arm of English soldiers. Choctaws and Chickasaws, you have too long borne with grievous usurpation inflicted by the arrogant Americans. Be no longer their dupes. If there be one here tonight who believes that his rights will not sooner or later be taken from him by the avaricious American pale faces, his ignorance ought to excite pity, for he knows little of the character of our common foe.

And if there be one among you mad enough to undervalue the growing power of the white race among us, let him tremble in considering the fearful woes he will bring down upon our entire race, if by his criminal indifference he assists the designs of our common enemy against our common country. Then listen to the voice of duty, of honor, of nature and of your endangered country. Let us form one body, one heart, and defend to the last warrior our country, our homes, our liberty, and the graves of our fathers.

Choctaws and Chickasaws, you are among the few of our race who sit indolently at ease. You have indeed enjoyed the reputation of being brave, but will you be indebted for it more from report than fact? Will you let the whites encroach upon your domains even to your very door before you will assert your rights in resistance? Let no one in this council imagine that I speak more from malice against the pale face Americans than just grounds of complaint. Complaint is just toward friends who have failed in their duty; accusation is against enemies guilty of injustice. And surely, if any people ever had, we have good and just reasons to believe we have ample grounds to accuse the Americans of injustice; especially when such great acts of injustice have been committed by them upon our race, of which they seem to have no manner of regard, or even to reflect. They are a people fond of innovations, quick to contrive and quick to put their schemes into effectual execution no matter how great the wrong and injury to us; while we are content to preserve what we already have. Their designs are to enlarge their possessions by taking yours in turn; and will you, can you longer dally, O Choctaws and Chickasaws?

Do you imagine that people will not continue longest in the enjoyment of peace who timely prepare to vindicate themselves, and manifest a determined resolution to do themselves right whenever they are wronged? Far otherwise. Then haste to the relief of our common cause, as by consanguinity of blood you are bound; lest the day be not far distant when you will be left single-handed and alone to the cruel mercy of our most inveterate foe.

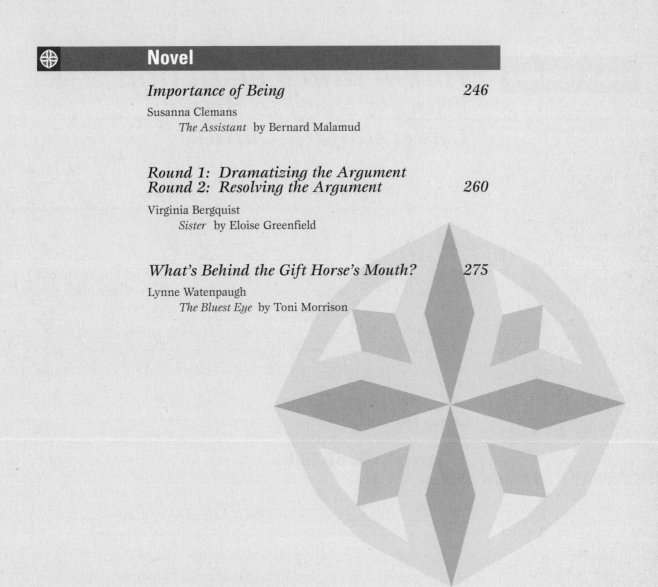

Novel

The Assistant
by Bernard Malamud

Grade Level
For High School
and College

Thinking Level
Analysis

Writing Domain
Analytical/Expository

Materials needed
- Butcher paper
- Colored pens

Suggested Supplementary Readings
- *The Encyclopedia of Judaism* by Geoffrey Wigoder
- *Gateway to Judaism,* vols. I & II. by Albert M. Shulman
- *The International Jewish Encyclopedia* by Ben Isaacson and Deborah Wigoder
- *The New Jewish Encyclopedia* by David Bridger and Samuel Wolk

Importance of Being:
Using a Novel to Better Understand a Culture

by Susanna Clemans

Overview

Using clustering, dialectical journals, freewrites, and other interactive strategies, students will explore the importance of one's roots in defining oneself through studying the novel *The Assistant* by Bernard Malamud.

Students will research and reflect on the origins and significance of Jewish culture. The final product of the lesson is an essay in which students describe how and why Frank rejects his Italian-Catholic culture and adopts the Jewish culture.

Objectives

THINKING SKILLS

Students will:

- *conduct* research on and describe Jewish culture;
- *compare* and *contrast* their culture with Jewish culture;
- *speculate* about how their culture has created them;
- *examine* Frank's complexity and reflect upon the stages of the change process he goes through;
- *comprehend* literary terms: *setting, point of view, structure, pacing, characterization, climax, style, thesis;*
- *hypothesize* about how Frank might have developed as an adult if he had not been an orphan.

WRITING SKILLS

Students will write an expository essay in which they:

- *organize* their information in a comprehensible format: introduction, main body, conclusion;
- *demonstrate* understanding of literary terms discussed in class and apply them to the novel;
- *integrate* textual quotes to support their assertions;
- *give* the reader a keener understanding of the novel and Malamud's "so what" or purpose in writing the story;
- *follow* the conventions of written English.

The Process

 PREWRITING

Prewriting Step 1: *Clustering*

As a class, cluster on a large piece of butcher paper about what students already
know about Jewish culture. (*Save this cluster because there will be additions made
to it later in the lesson.*) A sample cluster might look like this:

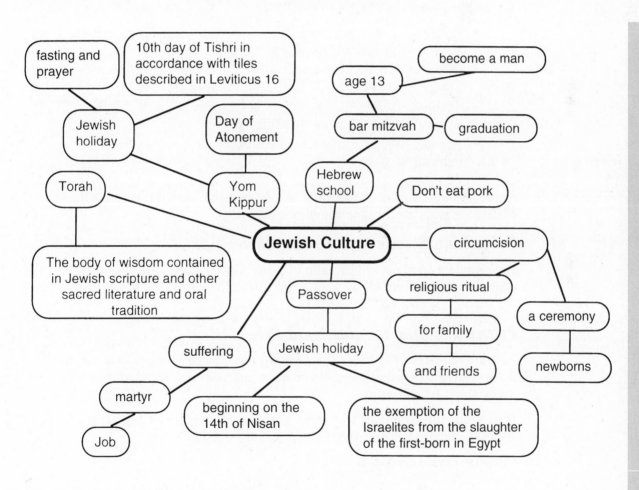

Prewriting Step 2: *Freewrite*

Freewrite about what they know and don't know about Jewish culture.

Prewriting Step 3: *Small Group Work*

Have students share their writing in small groups, create questions to research, and brainstorm people to use as special resources.

Prewriting Step 4: *Research*

Have students conduct research about Jewish culture.

The following are a few good source books:

- Bridger, David, and Samuel Wolk. *The New Jewish Encyclopedia.* New York: Behrman House, 1976.
- Isaacson, Ben, and Deborah Wigoder. *The International Jewish Encyclopedia.* Englewood Cliffs, NJ: Prentice Hall, 1973.
- Shulman, Albert M., *Gateway to Judaism*, vols. I & II. South Brunswick, NJ: Thomas Yoseloff, 1971.
- Wigoder, Geoffrey, *The Encyclopedia of Judaism.* New York: Macmillan Publishing, 1989.

Have students bring in at least one page of research material to share in class. Make sure students document their sources.

Prewriting Step 5: *Additional Clustering*

Have students add new information to the class cluster (see Prewriting Step 1). Add the new information in a different color of pen or chalk to emphasize how the students' knowledge base has been expanding.

Prewriting Step 6: *Additional Freewriting*

Ask students to transfer the class cluster onto a piece of paper they can save. Below the cluster, ask students to do a second freewrite on what they now know about Jewish culture.

Have students share their freewrites within their respective groups. Ask each group to complete the phrase, "What most surprised us was _____ ."

Class discussion could follow.

Prewriting Step 7: *Interviews*

Have students each individually interview a Jewish person. If they don't know anyone, they can contact a synagogue in the area. Devise the interview format as a class.

Possible Interview Questions

- How important is Jewish culture to you?
- Do you feel different or special because you are Jewish?
- How far back can you trace your family's cultural roots?
- Do you follow all the traditions?
- Do you know what they mean?
- Are you more comfortable with people of your own culture? Explain.

Write the interview questions on handout sheets so everyone has the same set.

Have the students bring back their interviews and share their questions in small groups. Students should be encouraged to add any new information to their research notes. For class discussion, each student could share an important new discovery. If time permits, these could be written on the board. Interviews will be collected for credit toward their essays.

Part of Possible Interview:

Question: Are you more comfortable with people of your own culture?

Answer: (*Nineteen-year-old boy*) Most of the time because we have the same interests. My close friends and family all go to Temple. I know everyone there because I've been going my whole life, and it feels right. We celebrate all the same holidays with the same food, especially important during Passover and fasting time. My non-Jewish friends think these customs are stupid. I get tired of explaining them all the time.

Question: Is your girlfriend Jewish?

Answer: Yes, my last one wasn't and it became a problem because she didn't want to join in my activities and I didn't understand hers.

Prewriting Step 8: *Guest Speaker* (Optional)

If time permits, arrange for a guest speaker who is Jewish to come to class. Use questions from the students' other interviews. Have students take notes to add to their research.

Prewriting Step 9: *Synagogue Visit* (Optional for extra credit)

Assign students a synagogue visit for extra credit toward their class grade. Some will not feel comfortable with this while others will enjoy the "real" experience in helping them understand the culture. The experience should be written up and handed in. For additional credit, students could be encouraged to share their experience with the class.

At home, students will write up their reactions and reflections on their synagogue visit and attach it to their earlier freewrites. These will be turned in for credit toward their essay.

Prewriting Step 10: *Reading and Journal Writing*

Students should now read *The Assistant*. Throughout the reading, students should do two journal entries: 1) What I've learned about Jewish culture as a result of reading *The Assistant*; and 2) What I learned about myself and my culture as a result of reading *The Assistant*.

Prewriting Step 11: *Freewriting*

Freewriting at various points in the discussion process in class can help students make connections. Have them do one freewrite in which they fill in their own culture: "What is a _____ *(Example: Chicano)* anyway?"

Prewriting Step 12: *Additional Extra Credit Activities*

- Students could research Malamud's background as an author and give a class presentation for a richer understanding of the novel and its cultural connection.
- Students could read another Malamud novel, make the cultural connections with *The Assistant,* and give a class presentation.
- Students could research other Jewish writers such as Philip Roth, Saul Bellow, and Erica Jong and make connections with Malamud for a class presentation.

PROMPT

Importance of Being

About midway through *The Assistant*, Frank Alpine, an orphaned Italian-Catholic, asks Morris Bober, a displaced Jew, a key question: "What I'd like to know is what is a Jew anyway?" Morris answers in this climactic scene. Because of the honest dialogue, Morris begins to understand Frank, and Frank begins to change his attitude about Morris and his culture. We learn the importance of one's roots, traditions, and spiritual life in defining oneself. We see Frank move toward Morris as "father," his profession as "grocery store owner," and his religion-culture as "Jew."

In a well-organized essay, describe how and why Frank subsequently abandons Italian-Catholicism and embraces Jewish culture, Morris's lifestyle, and Bober family attitudes. The best papers will truly analyze the stages Frank experiences in his metamorphosis and move toward a new identity. Refer to specific images and symbols in the text to support your character analysis. Use applicable direct quotes and follow the conventions of written English. Class discussion and assignment-related exercises should be a part of your paper.

 # PRECOMPOSING

Precomposing Step 1: *Second Reading and Directed Questions*

Have students closely reread *The Assistant,* taking one-fifth at a time. *(Note: Page references are for the 1987 Avon Books edition of* The Assistant.*)*

First section pp. 1–63;
Second section pp. 123–203;
Third section pp. 123–203;

Fourth section pp. 204–258;
Fifth section pp. 259–297.

Students will have a set of questions to answer as a point of departure for each section. These questions need to be answered on paper for credit before the week that class discussion on the section takes place.

The weekly questions can be used a number of ways:

- They can be collected and spot-read for class discussion.
- Students can share questions and answers in small groups and then choose one to three provocative issues for class discussion.
- Several students can work on just one question and present their findings to the class so that each question is covered in depth.
- Students can devise new questions of their own based on small group discussion and present these to the class.

- Students can use the questions to summarize main issues in the section. These can be written on the board and compared to provide insight as to the writer's intent and to promote discussion.

Sample questions for first section, pp. 1–63

1. From whose point of view is this section told? Does it change? When?

2. How would you describe the setting? Does it reflect the characters' situations? If so, how?

3. What do we learn about the neighborhood and Morris's life there?

4. We are introduced to Jewish culture very early in the novel. Discuss different impressions you have about it.

5. Malamud creates a complication on page 23. What does that do for you as a reader?

6. We become very well acquainted with Morris. Describe his character. Does he seem to reflect Jewish culture as you have researched it? Create a cluster, like those that follow, of each person's character traits:

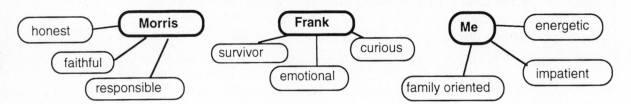

7. After you've created a cluster of Morris, Frank, and you, then create a Venn diagram.

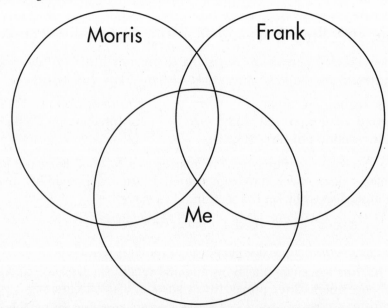

8. We begin to see the relationship between Frank and Morris intensify. "What do you say, Pop?" Frank asked Morris (p. 46). Discuss.

Sample questions for second section, pp. 64–122

1. Frank integrates himself into the Bober family life. How does he do this? Does it seem honest to you?

2. Do you see any prejudice in this section against Jewish culture? for another culture?

3. Although Malamud's style is straightforward, he employs poetic devices at sometimes surprising moments: ". . . and her house dresses guarding her daughter's flower-like panties and restless brassieres" (p. 71). Find another poetic device and discuss how it affects the telling of the story.

4. In this section, we get to know Frank very well. Describe his character, his feelings of alienation.

   Note: You may want to use the character cluster and Venn diagram here instead of in the first section of questions. See Prewriting Steps 6 and 7.

5. Does Frank improve the grocery story? If so, how?

6. How does Frank rationalize his stealing? How do you feel about it?

7. More and more of Jewish culture is addressed. Discuss specific situations and cite page numbers.

   > An example can be found on page 69: "Her expression as she dipped in among the soggy beans pieces of ham from a butt she had cut up caught his eye, and he felt for her repugnance for hating to touch the ham, and some for himself because he had never lived this close to Jews before."

   Choose one situation to freewrite about in your journal.

8. At the end of this section, we see a developing relationship between Helen and Frank. How is each perceiving the other?

Sample questions for third section, pp. 123–203

1. Do you want to tell them how they feel? Why?

2. We learn more about Helen. Describe her character.

3. Does Ida strike you as a "Jewish mother" —someone who needs to control her children's lives? Why or why not?

4. A climactic scene begins on page 148, exactly one-half way through the novel, when Frank asks the question, "What I'd like to know is what is a Jew anyway?" Discuss Morris's reply and the subsequent impact it has on both men.

   Freewrite about this scene and make any personal connections to your own life.

5. Why does Morris deceive Ida? How do you feel about this?

6. What do you learn about Jewish culture in this section? Be specific.

7. By page 203, we see Frank's life crumbling—bad timing, bad luck, faulty thinking. Discuss the reasons you see for his "misfortune."

Try using a chart to help you understand the cause-and-effect relationships.

Example:

Misfortunes	Reasons
1. Loses Helen's love	• misinterprets her feelings • thinks she's beyond his reach • starved and passionate love • endless waiting

Sample questions for fourth section, pp. 204–258

1. Both Helen and Frank undergo changes as a result of their encounter. Describe each one and compare their feelings.

2. Do you feel Frank's anguish, his sense of remorse?

3. On page 231, Frank reads a book about the Jews. Describe his findings. How do they compare to yours?

   Make another journal entry in answer to this question. These entries will be shared in small groups.

4. Morris seems to wallow in self-pity and to become increasingly more downtrodden. Do you see any connections between his feelings and his cultural attitude about life? If so, how?

   Make another journal entry to create your own personal connections to Morris.

5. What's ironic about the end of this section?

Sample questions for fifth section, pp. 259–297

1. Describe the setting that begins the section. Does it reflect the situation? Describe and compare with the first section.

2. Discuss Morris's last act. Does he die happy or sad? Describe his funeral.

3. Does Helen know her father? Be specific.

4. The complexities of the novel all come together in the final pages. If they are resolved, how are they resolved?

5. Do a time line of Frank's change process.

Example:

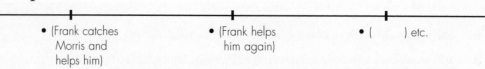

6. The metamorphosis of Frank becomes complete on the last page. Find quotes to document these changes.

7. Discuss the imagery in the last few pages and how it relates to the rest of the novel, concerning culture, identity, and spirituality.

Precomposing Step 2: *Dialectical Journal*

Along with the directed questions, have the students write a two-page dialectical journal (DJ) each week on a scene from the assigned section. This scene will be of their own choosing. The DJs will also need to be completed before the first class meeting of the week and will receive credit. Students will circle one of their quotes and responses to elaborate on with the sharing group. The group will choose one to write on the board for class discussion. Why is the quote important, what does it show, and how does it provide the reader with a deeper understanding of the text?

Model DJ

Note Taking	Note Making
"The early November street was dark though night had ended, but the wind, to the grocer's surprise, already clawed." (p. 1)	The opening makes me feel cold and alone. Strange word, "clawed" —to use for the wind.
"Now the store looked like a long dark tunnel." (p. 3)	What a strong image—makes me think of waiting.
"There he stood in all kinds of weather, drenched in rain, and the snow froze on his head." (p. 4)	Anything, even monotony and discomfort, is better than being out in the cold, taking a chance, for Morris.
"In a store you were entombed." (p. 4)	Shows Morris's perception of his life now, in contrast to his youth.
"Morris is paid cash for the liverwurst; from a German he wanted no favors." (p. 4)	Starting to see Morris as a very narrow, closed-off person. Why?
"He had earned his first cash dollar for the day." (p. 5)	His life is hard and unrewarding. Makes me sad.

Precomposing Step 3: *Review Prompt*

Reread the prompt to the class.

Precomposing Step 4: *Exploring the Prompt Chart*

As part of the preparation for developing their essay, ask students to fill out the following charts:

How and why Frank abandons Catholicism and embraces Judaism	Quotes from the text that support this

Precomposing Step 5: *Writing the Introduction*

Students will come to class with three different introductions that contain their thesis (based on answering questions in the prompt). These introductions will be shared in small groups. Each group will choose one to share with the whole class for discussion. Discuss what makes them work and how they can be improved.

Precomposing Step 6: *Review Timelines*

Ask students to go back to their timelines and label the stages they see Frank go through.

Precomposing Step 7: *Individual Conferences* (Optional)

If time allows, set up individual conferences with each student to approve their introduction and help with their game plan for the body and conclusion. Have them bring their questions and answers, DJs, journals to reinforce all the research they've done. All this will help them write their papers. If there is not enough time, have students work with partners or groups in class.

 **SHARING**

A week before the essay is due, have students share their rough drafts in their sharing groups for feedback, using the response sheet on the next page.

Your Name _____

Response Sheet

To: _____ *(author's name)* _____

The thing you do so well is _____

because _____ .
If I were to describe how and why Frank embraced another culture based upon

your essay, I would say _____
I think you understand the changes Frank goes through because you say _____

_____

_____ .

For me, the most important comment in your paper is _____

_____ because _____ .

I learned more about _____

through reading your paper _____ .

One suggestion I have for you is _____

because _____ .

Checklist   **Yes**   **No**

1. I felt your essay explored all the issues addressed
   in class and through the many assignments.   ____   ____

2. I was immediately immersed in your essay.   ____   ____

3. I was able to follow your thinking easily because of
   your fluid writing style.   ____   ____

4. You made me think because of your insight and
   good textual supports.   ____   ____

5. You showed a keen understanding of literary terms
   and how they applied to the novel.   ____   ____

Students should receive three other students' responses in order to help them rewrite their final papers.

 **EDITING**

Students will exchange papers with peer partners. Using the following editing checklist, they will review each other's work.

Editing Skills

For each item, circle yes or no.

1. You remembered not to punctuate your title.   yes   no

2. You indicated paragraphs by indenting.   yes   no

3. You kept the same verb tense throughout your   yes   no
   essay, unless the content dictated a change.

4. When you used pronouns, it was clear to me that   yes   no
   they referred to a particular noun. I wasn't confused
   about what you meant.

5. When you used prepositional phrases and modifying   yes   no
   clauses, you placed them adjacent to the word(s)
   they modify.

6. You have checked the spelling of every word in your   yes   no
   paper. I found no spelling errors.

7. Your paper follows the conventions of standard   yes   no
   written English.

8. You have organized your paper so that I can follow   yes   no
   your ideas.

 **EVALUATION**

Scoring Guide

For each item, circle the score you assign on the following scoring guide. 5 is high. 1 is low.

1. Your opening is both interesting and explanatory of what your paper will offer. 1 2 3 4 5

2. I was immediately immersed in your paper and felt compelled to read on. 1 2 3 4 5

3. Your paper demonstrated an integration of your research and insightful analysis of the novel. You may have brought in your own personal connections as well. 1 2 3 4 5

4. Your conclusion showed me a wholeness to the paper and your discoveries were brought together for reader understanding. 1 2 3 4 5

5. I was aware of your ability as researcher/analyzer writer. 1 2 3 4 5

6. You used literary terms appropriately as discussed in class. 1 2 3 4 5

7. You used specific data and quotes from the novel to show support. 1 2 3 4 5

EXTENSION ACTIVITIES

Read over all your personal freewrites. Do you see any surprises, things you hadn't known about yourself, things you hadn't known about your family, friends, culture? Are there issues within your freewrites you'd like to explore if you had time? Are there one or two you'd most like to research, do an I-Search paper on? Perhaps you were surprised, for example, to find out how little you knew about the religious history of your church or the village life of your grandparents in Romania or the political climate in Vietnam when your parents fled to America. Create a cluster and freewrite for fifteen minutes before meeting with your group for sharing and discussing. Out of these prewriting exercises will emerge a topic for an I-Search paper on the "Importance of My Being."

Featured Literature

Sister
by Eloise Greenfield

Grade Level
For Middle School

Thinking Level
Application/Evaluation

Writing Domain
Imaginative/Narrative

Materials Needed
- Chart paper
- Marking pens
- Computer lab use (optional)

Suggested Supplementary Readings
- *The Friendship; The Gold Cadillac* by Mildred Taylor
- *Roll of Thunder, Hear My Cry* by Mildred Taylor
- *Words by Heart* by Ouida Sebestyen

Round 1: Dramatizing the Argument
Round 2: Resolving the Argument

by Virginia Bergquist

Overview

Students create an argument scene that they have either actually overheard or which they could have overheard by imitating the scene structure on pages 3–5 of *Sister* by Eloise Greenfield. Students then will write a second scene in which they advise the two people overheard about how to resolve their problems.

Objectives

THINKING SKILLS

Students will:

- *dramatize* an argument they have overheard or could imagine overhearing by imitating a sequence frame from the novel *Sister;*
- *speculate* about how they would feel before, during, and after the argument;
- *compose* a dialogue in which they express these feelings;
- *give advice* and *propose solutions* to the problems they have overheard.

WRITING SKILLS

Students will:

- *dramatize* an argument from the third person point of view;
- *use* vivid dialogue;
- *observe* conventions of dialogue form, including correct use of quotation marks and paragraphing;
- *follow* scene sequence Greenfield establishes before, during, and after the argument.

The Process

 PREWRITING

Prewriting Step 1: *Thumbs Up/Thumbs Down*

Organize students into small groups of five or six. Give each group a sheet of chart paper and a marking pen and ask each group member whether they share a room with a sibling and how they feel about it. Have them list advantages and disadvantages of sharing a room with an older and/or younger sibling on the chart paper. Individual students can list their personal advantages and disadvantages on a "Thumbs Up/Thumbs Down" chart like the one below. To set the mood, play The Beach Boys' song "In My Room" in the background. *(Only children can imagine how they think it might be or relate what they have observed in families other than their own—without mentioning names, of course.)*

- Group charts should be posted around the room and a spokesperson for each group should point out highlights for the entire class. *(Note: Answers can be graphed to integrate mathematics.)*

Sample Chart:

Thumbs Up	Thumbs Down
• You have someone you can talk to when you have a problem. • You can get help on homework. • You can share clothes, the Walkman, skateboard, posters, etc.	• You never have any privacy or get a chance to just be alone. • You can be constantly interrupted and bothered with questions. • They can just take your stuff without asking.

Prewriting Step 2: *Introducing the Book*

Introduce the book *Sister* as a short novel about two sisters who share a room. One loves to escape reality by daydreaming alone in her bedroom. The other has problems coping with reality and is constantly in conflict with others. Read the first fifteen pages of the novel aloud.

Prewriting Step 3: *Dialectical Journal*

Hand out a dialectical journal page (or have students work in their own journals) and direct students to complete the entries.

Dialectical Journal Page

1. Find a passage about Doretha or Alberta that is most like you. Copy it below and explain how the passage is like you in the opposite column.	Why the passage is like me
2. Find a passage about Doretha or Alberta that is most unlike you. Copy it below and explain your choice in the opposite column.	Why the passage is unlike me
3. "After the show, Doretha didn't feel like talking. . . . She wanted to hold onto the feeling and not let the magic go. She wanted to hold onto it forever." (p. 12) Have you ever had a similar feeling?	Response to Question 3
4. "The slamming of the door downstairs jerked Doretha out of her daydream. It was her sister. She heard her mother walk from the kitchen to the front room. She sat up and tried to make her mind a wall to protect herself from the argument that was about to start." (p. 3) What do you think this mind wall was? Have you ever had a similar experience?	Response to Question 4
5. Doretha daydreams to escape her problems, and Alberta argues because of her problems. Do you think either of these is an effective way of dealing with problems?	Response to Question 5

Ask small groups to discuss their five dialectical journal responses, allowing about five minutes for each entry. Then, assign each group one of the five dialectical journal activities/questions and ask each group to appoint a reporter to briefly share a summary of their discussion with the whole class.

Prewriting Step 4: *Reader's Theater*

Choose four students to read the Reader's Theater script of the argument scene shown below (which is adapted from pages 3–5 of the original story). One student is Alberta, another is the mother, and the two other students narrate Doretha's reactions. Repeat the scene twice, asking students in the audience to observe from their own point of view the first time and to observe from Doretha's point of view during the second reading.

Reader's Theater Script

Bam! *(slam a door for sound effect)*

NARRATOR I: The slamming of the door downstairs jerked Doretha out of her daydream. It was her sister. She heard her mother walk from the kitchen to the front room. She sat up and tried to make her mind a wall to protect her from the argument that was about to start.

MRS. FREEMAN: Alberta, do you *have* to slam that door like that?

ALBERTA: I'm sorry.

MRS. FREEMAN: I told you a hundred times not to . . .

ALBERTA: I said I was sorry, Mama! What do you want me to say?

MRS. FREEMAN: Who you think you talking to, Alberta? Just who you think you talking to? You raise your voice at me again, I'll slap you winding.

NARRATOR II: There was a long silence. Doretha could imagine her mother's soft eyes, soft brown heart face, tight and bitter now that Alberta was home. But she knew her mother would never hit anybody, much less slap her own daughter hard enough to send her winding around and around.

MRS. FREEMAN: You look for a job today?

ALBERTA: Yeah.

MRS. FREEMAN: Well?

ALBERTA: I didn't get one.

NARRATOR I: Doretha could hear the worry in her sister's voice even with fourteen steps between them.

MRS. FREEMAN: I told you if you left school you had to get a job and I don't care if it is the summer now, you still not going to just sit around here . . .

ALBERTA: I been looking for a job for two months.

MRS. FREEMAN: You had no business leaving school. Sixteen years old, hanging around the streets all day with those hoodlums...

NARRATOR I: Doretha's mind-wall crumbled. She got up and closed the bedroom door, then went over to look out the open window. Dark summer clouds were growing in the sky, and she should have been setting out the buckets to catch the rain that would drip through the leaks in the roof. But she waited.

(Pause)

NARRATOR II: She leaned on the window sill and tried to slide back into her daydream, but closing the door hadn't shut out what was going on downstairs. She knew what they were saying. She knew it was the same as the time before. And the time before that. And all the other times. Her mother would be holding her slender body still, except for her hands opening and closing in the pockets of her house-dress. Alberta would be sighing and shifting her slight weight in cut-off jeans from one side to the other, her long, thin face longer and her halter top exposing more collarbone than she wanted.

Prewriting Step 5: *Quickwrite*

After the first reading, ask students to quickwrite about their own personal reactions, thoughts, and feelings regarding the argument. Students can share this initial response with a partner. *Note: Students may react to the Reader's Theater by recalling arguments or family squabbles they have overheard. Personal information should remain private and not shared. This first, personal reader response is an acceptable reaction to the text and will actually set the stage for the prompt.*

Prewriting Step 6: *Before, During, and After Chart*

After the second reading, ask the students to chart Doretha's reactions to the argument (i.e. what she is doing, thinking, and feeling). This can be done individually, in small groups, or by the whole class.

Before	During	After
• jerked out of daydream • tries to make a mind-wall to protect her	• imagined mother's soft brown eyes, and face tight and bitter • thinks her mother would never hit anybody • hears the worry in sister's voice	• mind-wall crumpled • closed her door and looked out open window • tries to slide back into daydream

PROMPT

Round I

Just like Doretha in *Sister*, we have all witnessed or overheard arguments between people we care about that have left us feeling uncomfortable or distressed. Create an argument between two people that you have actually overheard *(remember to change names in order to ensure privacy)* or which you could have overheard, or invent an argument between two fictional characters. Like the author, Eloise Greenfield, use third person to write about this argument and weave yourself into the story as the character who overhears the argument. In addition to vividly recreating the dialogue between the two people who are arguing, be sure to describe what you were doing, thinking, and feeling just *before, during* and just *after* the argument.

Round II

Write a second scene in which you confront the two people involved in the argument you just described. Start by writing a transition sentence or sentences that stem from Round I and lead into Round II. Then, tell them how their problems make you feel. Offer them specific advice regarding how they could resolve their problems. Include their reactions to your advice both in terms of what they say and what they do. Conclude by describing how things might be better for all of you if they could get along. Be sure to choose the appropriate tone for your audience, since you want them to be disposed to follow your suggestions and resolve their problem.

Note: Your dialogues are being written to share in class. Please choose a topic and use language that will be appropriate to share at school. Personal information should not be included.

PRECOMPOSING: ROUND I

Precomposing Step 1: *Reread Reader's Theater*

Ask students to silently reread the Reader's Theater script, paying close attention to what Doretha is doing, thinking and feeling while the conflict takes place. Explain that the Reader's Theater excerpt constitutes Round I.

Precomposing Step 2: *Round II Practice–Create Transition*

Now, tell the class to imagine that Doretha actually tells her mother and sister how she feels and to write this dialogue as a group. First, students will need a transition sentence or sentences to get Doretha downstairs so that she can confront her mother and sister. Brainstorm ideas and come up with a sample transition like the one below:

Section A Finally, Doretha thought to herself, *I just can't sit up here and listen to this. I have to do something.* As she slowly descended each of the fourteen stairs, she summoned up the courage to face them and tell them how she felt. When she entered the front room, they both looked surprised. Instantly, they stopped arguing and waited for her to speak.

Precomposing Step 3: *Constructing an Opening Dialogue*

Next, ask students to quickwrite for three minutes, in Doretha's voice—as if she were talking to her mother and sister—telling how their arguing makes her feel. Have several students volunteer to read their prewrites; note vivid phrases on the board. From their responses, construct an opening dialogue like the sample below:

Section B "From the minute I heard the door slam, I knew you two would be at it again. And it just made me feel as dark and cloudy as the weather outside. I tried to build a wall in my mind to shut you out, but I know your argument by heart, so it just kept replaying in my head. Each of your words against each other struck me like a blow. I feel so helpless to make you both stop. Why can't you get along?"

Precomposing Step 4: *Brainstorming Advice*

Then, ask the class to brainstorm specific advice Doretha could give them about what each person might do to help resolve the problem: how one or both might respond to that advice—including objecting to it and/or coming back with an accusation—and how Doretha might overcome their objections, accusations, or denials with reasons why they should get along.

Specific Advice to Solve Problem	How Mother or Sister Might React (What They Might Say or Do)	What Doretha Could Say to Persuade Them
• Alberta shouldn't slam door when she first comes in the house.	• Mother might be more willing to listen to Alberta if she were calmer.	• "Alberta, you know slamming the door upsets Mama. Why not come in quietly and tell her you need to talk?"
• Alberta should go back to school.	• Mother would be so happy.	• "Alberta, Mama's worried about you because she wants you to have a chance in life. You should go back to school."
• They should listen to each other and tell each other "I love you."	• They might listen.	• "I know you both love each other. Talk to each other and listen to each other."

266

Precomposing Step 5: *Reviewing Dialogue Form*

At this point, it might be necessary to review how to write dialogue and examine how dialogue differs from narration. The following graphic taken from Carol Booth Olson's *Thinking/Writing: Fostering Critical Thinking Through Writing.* (HarperCollins Publishers, 1992, p. 291) may be helpful:

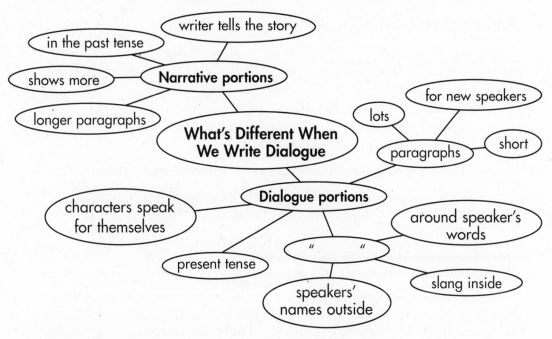

Precomposing Step 6: *Continuation of Dialogue*

Transpose the class chart into dialogue form, asking for additional transitions and narrative sentences to keep the dialogue flowing and show people's physical reactions, as Eloise Greenfield does. Include this as section C on the class model. A sample might look like this:

> **Section C** When Doretha stopped speaking, Alberta jumped in defensively, "This is between Mama and me, Doretha. I'm sorry you're upset, but stay out of it. We don't need your help."

(Whatever opening the students come up with, discuss the importance of the tone Doretha should use with her mother and sister. After all, they are both angry and she wants to help resolve the situation rather than add fuel to the fire. The dialogue might continue this way:)

> "I can't stay out of it, Alberta. I love you both." Doretha watched Alberta for a sign, any kind of sign, but she looked down at the floor. Her mother's lower lip trembled a little, but she clenched her teeth and it stopped.

> "I'm going out," Alberta said.

> "Alberta, Mama's worried about you, that's all. She wants you to have a better life," Doretha said, trying to catch her sister's eyes.

"I know. . ."

"I think Mama's right about going back to school," Doretha said, daring to say more than she ever had before.

"I'm going out," Alberta said; she glanced up at her mother. Her eyes were wet.

Precomposing Step 7: *Concluding the Dialogue*

Finally, ask for suggestions as to what Doretha might say in conclusion that will persuade both her mother and her sister that things will be better for all three of them if they can get along. Add these closing lines as section D.

> **Section D** "Alberta," Mrs. Freeman reached out and touched her daughter's shoulder. "I'll go with you to enroll in school tomorrow, if you want me, too," she said.
>
> "Finishing school will help you have a better life," Doretha said.
>
> Alberta turned and left. Doretha didn't expect an answer, and she didn't get one. But she knew her sister had heard her, maybe for the first time.

The **finished model** would look like this:

Finally, Doretha thought to herself, *I just can't sit up here and listen to this. I have to do something.* As she slowly descended each of the fourteen stairs, she summoned up the courage to face them and tell them how she felt. When she entered the front room, they both looked surprised. Instantly they stopped arguing and waited for her to speak.

"From the minute I heard the door slam, I knew you two would be at it again. And it just made me feel as dark and cloudy as the weather outside. I tried to build a wall in my mind to shut you out, but I know your argument by heart, so it just kept replaying in my head. Each of your words against each other struck me like a blow. I feel so helpless to make you both stop. Why can't you get along?"

When Doretha stopped speaking, Alberta jumped in defensively, "This is between Mama and me, Doretha. I'm sorry you're upset, but stay out of it. We don't need your help."

"I can't stay out of it, Alberta. I love you both." Doretha watched Alberta for a sign, any kind of sign, but she looked down at the floor. Her mother's lower lip trembled a little, but she clenched her teeth and it stopped.

"I'm going out," Alberta said.

"Alberta, Mama's worried about you, that's all. She wants you to have a better life," Doretha said, trying to catch her sister's eyes.

"I know. . ."

"I think Mama's right about going back to school," Doretha said, daring to say more than she ever had before.

"I'm going out," Alberta said; she glanced up at her mother. Her eyes were wet.

"Alberta," Mrs. Freeman said as she reached out and touched her daughter's shoulder. "I'll go with you to enroll in school tomorrow, if you want me too."

"Finishing school will help you have a better life," Doretha said.

Alberta turned and left. Doretha didn't expect an answer, and she didn't get one. But she knew her sister had heard her, maybe for the first time.

Precomposing Step 8: *Brainstorm Overheard Arguments*

In preparation for the students' individual writing, brainstorm with the whole class some arguments they have overheard.

Issue of Argument	People Involved	Your Reactions
• not home on time • using brother's bike without asking • talking behind someone's back	• mother and sister • 2 younger brothers • 2 girlfriends	• scared, worried • disgust • wanted them to stop and be friends

Precomposing Step 9: *Role-Play and Sample Scene*

Next, have students choose a few arguments from the chart and role-play them in front of the whole class. (*Encourage the class to invent names to ensure privacy.*) A sample scene can be transcribed by the teacher on an overhead transparency, or the sample scene included below can be utilized.

Teacher Model

Gail saw the car pull up in front of the house with its lights off. She saw her sister, Lynne, get out of the car. Lynne closed the door with a soft click and waved goodbye without saying anything. She watched her friends drive off. Gail looked out the window at the streetlight. She felt kind of sad and thought, "Why doesn't she just come home on time? It would be so much easier."

Lynne stood under the streetlight for a long time looking at the front door of our house. "She doesn't want to come inside," Gail thought. "She is probably thinking that Dad is waiting for her. She probably thinks he is watching her out the window, but it's just me." Gail heard something and shifted her weight slowly in the darkness to look behind her. The hall light was on again. The light sliced under the door and she saw the shadows of her mother's slippers wearily passing by. She looked out the window again. "She can't stay out there all night," Gail thought. "She doesn't know that Dad isn't home."

Gail slid up to the bedroom door and touched the cold knob. She thought about going out for a second and then decided that she'd better not when she heard the front door creak open. Lynne always said that she figured Dad didn't oil the hinges just so he'd know when she got home at night. Gail slid her feet back toward the bed and held her breath so she could hear it all.

"Where have you been, young lady? It's past midnight!"

"I, uh, we had a flat tire..."

"Why did she use that excuse," Gail thought. "She used that last week."

Her mom's voice broke the silence..."That's a lie! I know it's a lie! You're always telling lies. At least you could think up something more original."

"No! It's the truth. That's what really happened!"

There was another long silence. Gail thought of her sister's face. It was probably beet red. She crept up to the door again and pulled. It wasn't latched so she pulled it open just a crack. Her mother's face looked soft and old. She ran her fingers through her hair and rubbed her pencil-thin eyebrows. Gail thought her mother must have remembered that they had almost this identical conversation last Friday night because she clenched her fist and shook it. Gail ducked her own head and covered her face. But her mother stopped and wrapped her arms around Lynne instead.

"Your father is out looking for you. Laurie's Dad is with him. We've been worried sick." Mom wasn't screaming now, but she was crying.

Dad would be coming home any minute. Just the thought of more angry words made Gail's stomach churn. "Maybe I can do something to make things better before he gets here," she thought.

Resolutions for the argument can be brainstormed, and partners can quickwrite a bit of dialogue giving advice to the people involved in the sample scene argument.

Precomposing Step 10: *Argument Chart*

Finally, give individual students their own chart to complete:

Issue of Argument	People Involved	Your Reactions

Precomposing Step 11: *Reactions Time Line*

Once they have the basic idea for their argument scene, have them map out what they, as the character who overheard the argument, will be doing, thinking, and feeling *before, during,* and *after* the argument.

Before	During	After

 WRITING

Writing Step 1: *Writing Round I*

Have students compose the Round I section of their dialogue. Remind them to write in third person, weave themselves in as the character who overhears the argument, and use both narration and dialogue.

 PRECOMPOSING: ROUND II

Precomposing Step 12: *Microtheme*

To help students prepare to write the Round II section of their papers, ask them to fill out the microtheme chart on the next page.

 WRITING

Writing Step 2: *Role-Playing the Finished Draft of Both Scenes*

Teams of three can role-play each of their dialogues with three other partners. Using the sharing sheet at the top of page 273, each team of partners will give feedback on the criteria for Round I and Round II.

 SHARING

Students should share first drafts with peer response partners or a peer response group. Use the Sharing Sheet opposite for structured feedback.

> **Microtheme**
>
> **Transition** I will use the following sentence or sentences as a transition from my Round I section to my Round II section:
>
> -
> -
> -
>
> **Main Body** I will use the following sentence or sentences to confront the two people arguing:
>
> -
> -
> -
>
> I will use the following sentence or sentences to express how I feel about their arguing:
>
> -
> -
> -
>
> I will propose the following solutions on how everyone can get along:
>
> -
> -
> -
>
> **Conclusion** I will include the following convincing argument about how things will be better if we can all get along:
>
> -
> -
> -

 ## REVISING

Students should be given time for revision of their dialogues based upon the feedback from the partners who viewed their role-play and then silently read their papers.

 ## EDITING

This is an ideal time to take students into a computer lab. Using a word processing program, check spelling, and review punctuation and paragraphing conventions for dialogue with the entire class. Students may work in partners or alone while editing the dialogue section of their piece.

Sharing Sheet

Author's Name _____

Peer Response Partner(s) or Peer Response Group _____

_____

_____

_____

Your Paper: Round 1	Excellent 3	Average 2	Needs Work 1
1. Dramatizes an argument scene that is vividly created through dialogue.			
2. Reflects that you have woven yourself in as the person who overheard the argument throughout the story.			
3. Describes what you are doing, thinking and feeling *before, during,* and *after* the argument.			
4. Is written in third person.			
Round 2			
5. Reflects a second scene in which you confront the two people arguing and propose solutions to their problems.			
6. Expresses how you feel about their arguing.			
7. Proposes solutions on how everyone can get along.			

Round 1/Round 2

NOVEL

273

 **EVALUATION**

Primary Trait Scoring Guide

Round I

3   Your argument scene is vividly created through dialogue and includes descriptive images of what you were doing, thinking, and feeling just before, during, and after the argument.

2   Your dialogue and description of the argument are not as vivid as they could be but you did follow scene sequence of before, during, and after the argument.

1   Your scene does not recreate an argument vividly because you did not include one or more of the following: dialogue and description of what you were doing, thinking, and feeling just before, during, and after the argument.

Round II

3   Your Round II scene includes an effective transition sentence or sentences stemming from Round I. You clearly explain how the arguing of the two people makes you feel. You offer specific advice regarding how they might resolve their problem, respond well to their reactions and objections, conclude with a convincing argument about how things might be better if they could get along, and do all of the above in an appropriate tone.

2   Your Round II scene has a transition sentence or sentences but it does not lead as effectively into Round II as it could. You adequately explain how the arguing of the two other people makes you feel. You offer general advice regarding how they might resolve their problem, respond to at least one or two objections or reactions, have some semblance of a concluding remark, and use a tone which is acceptable.

1   Your Round II scene has a very weak transition or no transition from Round I. Your explanation of how the arguing of the two other people makes you feel is inadequate. You give little, if any, advice about how the problem might be resolved, fail to include reactions or objections, have no discernible concluding remark, and use an inappropriate tone.

Secondary Trait Scoring Guide

3   You wrote your scenes in the third person. You made two or fewer errors in paragraphing and punctuating for dialogue. In addition, your other punctuation, spelling, and grammatical errors are two or fewer.

2   You made three or four errors in paragraphing and punctuating for dialogue and/or you made more than two to four other punctuation, spelling, and grammatical errors.

1   You made more than four errors in paragraphing and punctuating for dialogue and/or you made more than four in other punctuation, spelling, and grammatical errors.

Featured Literature

The Bluest Eye
by Toni Morrison

Grade Level
For Middle School
and High School

Thinking Level
Application
Synthesis

Writing Domain
Imaginative/Narrative
Analytical/Expository

Materials Needed
No special materials
required.

**Suggested
Supplementary
Readings**
- *The Little Colonel*
  (movie)
- "When I Was Growing
  Up" by Nellie Wong

What's Behind the Gift Horse's Mouth?

by Lynne Watenpaugh

Overview

Using an excerpt from Toni Morrison's *The Bluest Eye*, students will speculate about and analyze the possible reasons behind the reaction of the character Claudia to a gift of a baby doll. Students will recall experiences from their own lives and compare their reactions to disappointing gifts with Claudia's. The final product of the lesson will be an autobiographical essay in which students explore their own reactions to a gift from their past.

Objectives

THINKING SKILLS

Students will:

- *discuss* reactions to a film clip;
- *compare* and *contrast* their reactions to those of Toni Morrison's characters;
- *speculate* about possible reasons for Claudia's hostility toward the gift;
- *analyze* the way expectations can be transmitted through gifts;
- *recall* a time in their own lives when they were given a gift they felt did not reflect them;
- *examine* and *reflect* on their feelings about those gifts and what they may have represented.

WRITING SKILLS

Students will write an autobiographical essay in which they:

- *narrate* a significant episode from their own lives;
- *describe* their reactions to an inappropriate gift;
- *use* vivid sensory details to involve their readers;
- *employ* first person narration;
- *follow* the conventions of standard written English.

The Process

 **PREWRITING**

Prewriting Step 1: *Film Clips*

Prepare students for the first excerpt from *The Bluest Eye*. Show them the clip from the movie *The Little Colonel* that the narrator, Claudia, mentions: where Bill "Bojangles" Robinson dances on the staircase with Shirley Temple. This video is available at many video stores.

Prewriting Step 2: *Quickwrite*

After viewing the clip, have students do a five-minute quickwrite about their feelings as they watched the clip. What did they think about Shirley Temple? Bojangles? How did the two of them seem to be getting along?

Have paired students read their freewrites:

Freewrite on *The Little Colonel*

Shirley Temple talks weird. Bojangles loves tapping. He is very good at tapping. My sister loves to tap. Shirley Temple is a very quick learner. To make her more cute she wears a big smile and her cheeks puff up. Sometimes she is giving a puppy dog look. They make a good combination together.

Prewriting Step 3: *Large Group Discussion*

Have students discuss their quickwrites in a large group, focusing in on their feeling toward Shirley Temple. As an audience, did they find themselves identifying with Shirley or Bojangles? Did they envy Shirley Temple?

Prewriting Step 4: *Reading First Excerpt*

Have students read the first excerpt from *The Bluest Eye*. Explain that the narrator, Claudia, and her sister, Frieda, have just greeted their temporary foster sister, Pecola, and are trying to make her feel comfortable.

Featured Literature

Excerpt 1 from *The Bluest Eye*
Toni Morrison

Frieda brought her four graham crackers on a saucer and some milk in a blue-and-white Shirley Temple cup. She was a long time with the milk, and gazed fondly at the silhouette of Shirley Temple's dimpled face. Frieda and she had a loving conversation about how cu-ute Shirley Temple was. I couldn't join them in their adoration because I hated Shirley. Not because she was cute, but because she danced with Bojangles, who was my friend, my uncle, my daddy, and who ought to have been soft-shoeing it and chuckling with me. Instead he was enjoying, sharing, giving a lovely dance thing with one of those little white girls whose socks never slid down under their heels. So I said, "I like Jane Withers."

They gave me a puzzled look, decided I was incomprehensible, and continued their reminiscing about old squint-eyed Shirley.

Prewriting Step 5: *Quickwrites*

Have students respond to the excerpt in three-minute quickwrites to questions:

- What is your first reaction to the excerpt? What feelings did it trigger?

  I didn't understand who was talking. But I understood she hated Shirley Temple while her two friends loved her. I didn't understand if Bojangles was friend, family, relative, or if she just liked him. I like how they described Shirley's dimples.

- What did you see going on in this excerpt? Briefly retell the scene.

  Frieda brought Pecola some milk and crackers and discussed with her how cute Shirley Temple was. Claudia said that she didn't like Shirley and hated that she danced with Bojangles who was her friend.

- What sort of person does the narrator seem to be?

  The narrator seems to be someone who doesn't like hurting friends' feelings. Instead of saying "I hate Shirley Temple," she says, "I like Jane Withers."

Have students share their quickwrite series with a partner.

Prewriting Step 6: *Large Group Sharing*

Ask volunteers to share their quickwrites with the large group. Use the quick-write responses to spark discussion about students' first impressions of Claudia and how their reactions to the scene differed from Claudia's. Encourage students to share any questions they may have formed while reading the text. You may want to list those questions on the board and use them as a point of reference as you teach this lesson. Sample questions might include:

- Why is Claudia envious of Shirley Temple?
- What is so important about Bojangles?
- Are the movies the only thing these girls talk about?
- Who is Jane Withers?

Prewriting Step 7: *Comparison Chart*

With students using both the initial quickwrites about the Shirley Temple clip and the quickwrites following their first encounter with Morrison's text, have them complete the following chart which will help them begin to see the variety of reactions the image of Shirley Temple can evoke.

My thoughts about Shirley Temple's dance with Bojangles	Claudia's thoughts	Frieda's and Pecola's thoughts

Example:

My thoughts about Shirley Temple's dance with Bojangles	Claudia's thoughts	Frieda's and Pecola's thoughts
She was cute. She and Bojangles make a good team.	She hates her. Shirley gets to dance with Bojangles and Claudia seems to be jealous.	They adored her, and think she's "cu-ute." They like to talk about her.

Prewriting Step 8: *Whole Class Chart and List of Reasons*

After students compare their own reactions to the film scene with those of the characters in *The Bluest Eye* (comparison chart), create a whole-class chart of the various reactions to Shirley Temple and Bojangles, with volunteers elaborating on some of the possible reasons for the different reactions.

Student reasons might include:

- Claudia might really wish she could trade places with Shirley Temple.
- Claudia likes to make herself different from Frieda and Pecola.
- Claudia wishes she had someone like Bojangles in her life. Maybe she doesn't like her father.

Prewriting Step 9: *Reading Second Excerpt*

Read the second excerpt out loud to the class. As you read, have students underline any words, phrases, or sentences that appeal or stand out to them.

Excerpt 2 from *The Bluest Eye*

Younger than both Frieda and Pecola, I had not yet arrived at the turning point in the development of my psyche which would allow me to love her. What I felt at that time was unsullied hatred. But before that I had felt a stranger, more frightening thing than hatred for all the Shirley Temples of the world.

It had begun with Christmas and the gift of dolls. The big, the special, the loving gift was always a big, blue-eyed Baby Doll. From the clucking sounds of adults I knew that the doll represented what they thought was my fondest wish. I was bemused with the thing itself, and the way it looked. What was I supposed to do with it? Pretend I was its mother? I had no interest in babies or the concept of motherhood. I was interested only in humans my own age and size, and could not generate any enthusiasm at the prospect of being a mother. Motherhood was old age, and other remote possibilities. I learned quickly, however, what I was expected to do with the doll: rock it, fabricate storied situations around it, even sleep with it. Picture books were full of little girls sleeping with their dolls. Raggedy Ann dolls usually, but they were out of the question. I was physically revolted by and secretly frightened of those round moronic eyes, the pancake face, and orangeworms hair.

The other dolls, which were supposed to bring me great pleasure, succeeded in doing quite the opposite. When I took it to bed, its hard unyielding limbs resisted my flesh—the tapered fingertips on those dimpled hands scratched. If, in sleep, I turned, the bone-cold head collided with my own. It was a most uncomfortable, patently aggressive sleeping companion. To hold it was no more rewarding. The starched gauze or lace on the cotton dress irritated any embrace. I had only one desire: to dismember it. To see of what it was made, to discover the dearness, to find the beauty, the desirability that had escaped me, but apparently only me. Adults, older girls, shops, magazines, newspapers, window signs—all the world had agreed that a blue-eyed, yellow-haired, pink-skinned doll was what every girl child treasured. "Here," they said, "this is beautiful, and if you are on this day 'worthy' you may have it." I fingered the face, wondering at the single-stroke eyebrows; picked at the pearly teeth stuck like two piano keys between red bowline lips. Traced the turned-up nose, poked the glassy blue eyeballs, twisted the yellow hair. I could not love it. But I could examine it to see what it was that all the world said was lovable. Break off the tiny fingers, bend the flat feet, loosen the hair, twist the head around, and the thing made one sound—a sound they said was the sweet and plaintive cry "Mama," but which sounded to me like the bleat of a dying lamb or, more precisely, our icebox door opening on rusty hinges in July. Remove the cold and stupid eyeball, it would bleat still, "Ahhhhhh," take off the head, shake out the sawdust, crack the back against the brass bed rail, it would bleat still. The gauze back would split, and I could see the disk with six holes, the secret of the sound. A mere metal roundness.

What's Behind the Gift Horse's Mouth?

NOVEL

Grown people frowned and fussed: "You-don't-know-how-to-take-care-of-nothing. I-never-had-a-baby-doll-in-my-whole-life-and-used-to-cry-my-eyes-out-for-them. Now-you-got-one-a-beautiful-one-and-you-tear-it-up-what's-the-matter-with-you?"

How strong was their outrage. Tears threatened to erase the aloofness of their authority. The emotion of years of unfulfilled longing preened in their voices. I did not know why I destroyed those dolls. But I did know that nobody ever asked me what I wanted for Christmas. Had any adult with the power to fulfill my desires taken me seriously and asked me what I wanted, they would have known that I did not want to have anything to own, or to possess any object. I wanted rather to feel something on Christmas day. The real question would have been, "Dear Claudia, what experience would you like on Christmas?" I could have spoken up, "I want to sit on the low stool in Big Mama's kitchen with my lap full of lilacs and listen to Big Papa play his violin for me alone." The lowness of the stool made for my body, the security and warmth of Big Mama's kitchen, the smell of the lilacs, the sound of the music, and since it would be good to have all my senses engaged, the taste of a peach, perhaps, afterward.

Instead I tasted and smelled the acridness of tin plates and cups designed for tea parties that bored me. Instead I looked with loathing on new dresses that required a hateful bath in a galvanized zinc tub before wearing. Slipping around on the zinc, no time to play or soak, for the water chilled too fast, no time to enjoy one's nakedness, only time to make curtains of soapy water careen down between the legs. Then the scratchy towels and the dreadful and humiliating absence of dirt. The irritable, unimaginative cleanliness. Gone the ink marks from legs and face, all my creations and accumulations of the day gone, and replaced by goose pimples.

I destroyed white baby dolls.

But the dismembering of dolls was not the true horror. The truly horrifying thing was the transference of the same impulses to little white girls. The indifference with which I could have axed them was shaken only by desire to do so. To discover what eluded me: the secret of the magic they weaved on others. What makes people look at them and say, "Awwww," but not for me? The eye slide of black women as they approached them on the street, and the possessive gentleness of their touch as they handled them.

If I pinched them, their eyes—unlike the crazed glint of the baby doll's eyes— would fold in pain, and their cry would not be the sound of an icebox door, but a fascinating cry of pain. When I learned how repulsive this disinterested violence was, that it was repulsive because it was disinterested, my shame floundered about for refuge. The best hiding place was love. Thus the conversion from pristine sadism to fabricated hatred, to fraudulent love. It was a small step to Shirley Temple. I learned much later to worship her, just as I learned to delight in cleanliness, knowing, even as I learned, that the change was adjustment without improvement.

Prewriting Step 10: *Silent Reading*

Have students reread the excerpt on their own, to jot any questions in the margins, and underline any new words, phrases, or sentences discovered.

Prewriting Step 11: *Dialectical Journal*

Have students start a dialectical journal where they will be given the opportunity to dig more deeply into the text and forge new connections with it. Ask students to add seven more entries to their dialectical journals on their own, using the example below as a model. Have groups of four share their journals.

Quotations from Text	Personal Response	What It Reminds Me of or Makes Me Wonder
"I want to sit on the low stool in Big Mama's kitchen with my lap full of lilacs and listen to Big Papa play his violin for me alone."	She has the selfish desire to have the perfect Christmas. She felt once more as if she had to have everything for herself.	For years now I have wanted the perfect family Christmas. In a way it's similar. I don't want possessions. I want the Christmas spirit.
"Tears threatened to erase the aloofness of their authority."	Her parents felt as though they were making up for their childhood. The doll was more for them than Claudia.	Parents are always trying to make up for what they didn't have and wanted instead of giving their kids what kids want. Why? If they know what it's like, why aren't they more concerned with their own kids?

Prewriting Step 12: *Quickwrite*

Have students do a five-minute quickwrite about Claudia's reaction to the gift doll.

Example:

> She hates the doll. She doesn't understand why anyone would like a doll like this. She's also insulted by the gift. No one has ever asked her what she would like, all of her relatives are running around trying to find the prettiest and most expensive doll there is, while what she wants is very simple and much more worthwhile. She hates the dolls and is very frightened of them. She doesn't like their eyes, faces, ears, fingers, heads, anything. They're all fake to her as well as the stories that she's supposed to create about them (her and the dolls). Everything is fake according to her, and she doesn't understand why grown-ups would want children to do those sorts of things. Everyone around her doesn't understand her, and she doesn't understand them. Or the dolls.

Prewriting Step 13: Class Discussion

As a class, discuss some of the reasons for Claudia's reaction to the doll as well as of some of the reasons the adult world felt she should appreciate it.

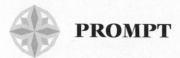 **PROMPT**

Review the following prompt with students.

What's Behind the Gift Horse's Mouth?

Writing Situation

In *The Bluest Eye*, Claudia harbors hostility toward the gift of a "blue-eyed Baby Doll," which she comes to feel represents what adults believed should be her "fondest wish." Claudia feels powerless in a world where "all the world had agreed that a blue-eyed, yellow-haired, pink-skinned doll was what every girl child treasured."

Seeking answers about the mystery behind the rest of "the world's" belief that she ought to love the doll, and everything it represents, Claudia destroys the doll, much to the adult world's displeasure.

Directions for Writing

The act of gift giving can transmit many subtle messages. Sometimes those messages can be about the type of person others believe us to be. Sometimes they may even reflect what others hope we will become.

In an autobiographical essay, recreate an incident from your own life when you received what you felt at the time to be an inappropriate gift. Describe the incident in vivid enough detail so that your reader will be able to experience the event just as you did. Help your reader understand why the gift did not reflect who you were and how receiving the gift made you feel.

The best papers will use first-person narration, use sensory detail to help show people and setting, have people moving, speaking, and acting, and weave in the significance of this event to the writer today.

Note: If you have students who cannot think of a gift they received that was disappointing to them, you might want to consider giving them this alternative to the prompt:

If you cannot think of an incident involving a gift you received that you found disappointing or inappropriate, you may describe some event when you felt as if you were being pressured to conform to someone else's image of who they thought you should be, or to value something they thought you should value.

 **PRECOMPOSING**

Precomposing Step 1: *Selecting an Incident for Storytelling*

Allow students time to reflect back on their own lives to select an incident they would like to write about. It might help to have students cluster their ideas first. After students have gathered their ideas, have them share them with their peer groups through storytelling. Have students volunteer to orally recount past gift experiences when they believe the gift received was an inappropriate one.

Student Model

When I was ten, I became obsessed by Spider Man. I had a Spider Man notebook, a Spider Man lunchbox, even Spider Man underwear. Well, I got it in my head that I wanted to become a cartoonist and all I wanted to do was learn to draw so I'd be able to draw Spider Man. My birthday came and instead of drawing supplies and drawing lessons, I got piano lessons! For three years, I spent every Wednesday afternoon from 3:30 to 5:00 taking piano lessons. I finally talked my parents into letting me quit the piano last year. I never liked playing, and still don't, and I still don't know how to draw.

Ask for volunteers to share their experiences with the class. As students share, help draw out as much vivid detail as possible. Point out that successful autobiographical incidents are grounded in vivid detail.

Precomposing Step 2: *Mapping*

Have students map their incident before writing.

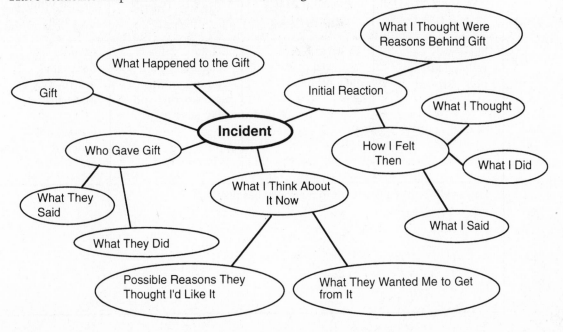

Precomposing Step 3: *Sentence Starter*

Have students complete the following thought:

"When I received my gift I thought _____ but now I think _____ ."

Precomposing Step 4: *Review of Excerpts*

Have students refer back to the excerpts from *The Bluest Eye*. Review and discuss the vivid details in Morrison's writing and emphasize the importance of including similar attention to details in their own autobiographical pieces.

Vivid details students might point out include:

- blue-and-white Shirley Temple cup
- dimpled face
- soft-shoeing it
- clucking sounds
- moronic eyes
- pancake face
- orangeworms hair
- unyielding limbs
- tapered fingertips
- dimpled hands scratched
- bone-cold head
- pearly teeth
- plaintive cry
- bleat of a dying lamb
- frowned and fussed
- etc.

Precomposing Step 5: *Details Chart*

Have students chart some details they will use in their narratives. Here is an example filled in for a portion of excerpt 2 from *The Bluest Eye*:

Sensory/Descriptive Words of What Things Look Like	Details of People Moving/Doing	Details of People Speaking/Sample Dialogue	Details of How People Act/Behave/Feel
blue-eyed yellow-haired pink-skinned	fingered face removed eyeballs take off head etc.	"Here . . . this is beautiful, and if you are on this day 'worthy' you may have it" etc.	Claudia = fascinated, destructive, resentful Grown-ups = shocked, frown and fuss, etc.
This event is still significant to me today because . . .			

WRITING

Review the prompt with the students. Encourage them to refer to the precomposing activities before writing the first drafts of their essays. They might also wish to consult the scoring guide.

SHARING

Have students share drafts with a partner using the following sharing and revising guideline for feedback:

Sharing/Revising Sheet for Gift Horse			
	Great	**OK**	**Need Work**
1. Does the writer use vivid sensory details to help the reader see the people and setting and to experience the event?			
2. Are there people moving, speaking, acting?			
3. Do you know why this particular event was significant to the writer?			
4. Is it written in first person?			
5. My favorite part of your paper was when: _____ _____ _____ _____			
6. You may want to work on: _____ _____ _____			
7. This incident was important to you because:_____ _____ _____			

 **REVISING**

Have students revise their drafts, using the sharing sheets as guides.

 EDITING

Editing Step 1: *Group Editing*

Have students, in groups of four, proof one another's final draft.

Divide the group as follows:

1. Paragraphing, end punctuation
2. Dialogue—proper use of quotation marks and internal punctuation
3. Spelling
4. Verb—proper tenses used and subject verb-agreement

Remind students to make all marks in pencil.

Editing Step 2: *Individual Editing*

Students can now complete the final drafts of their essays, correcting any mechanical errors found by themselves or by their group.

EVALUATION

Rubric

6   This is a superior piece of work. The writer has:

- Related a story from his/her own life about receiving an inappropriate gift;

- Captivated the reader's attention by using vivid language to help show people and setting;

- Had people moving, speaking, and acting;

- Revealed why this particular event was significant;

- Used first person narration;

- Followed the conventions of standard written English.

5   This essay is very well done. The writer included all requirements but failed to elaborate fully on one or more of the criteria. Paper may have a few errors but none that interfere with the writer's message.

4   This essay is enjoyable but fails to go much beyond a basic summary. It may lack enough dialogue, have only a few descriptive details, or offer little discussion of why the event was significant. It may have some correctness problems.

3   This essay is weak. The topic is superficially treated, lacks dialogue or specific detail and wanders away from the prompt. Correctness errors may interfere with the writer's message.

2   This essay is difficult to read, shows little evidence of effort.

1   This paper is unacceptable. Please see the teacher for a conference.

EXTENSION ACTIVITY

Comparison and Contrast

The poem "When I Was Growing Up" by Nellie Wong (in the lesson "Growing Up: A Personal Reflection" elsewhere in this book), has some interesting parallels with the excerpts from *The Bluest Eye* in this lesson. Students can compare the subtle messages Nellie Wong, a Chinese American, was sent about what constitutes beauty with the messages Claudia received and compare the reactions to these messages.

What's Behind the Gift Horse's Mouth?

NOVEL

Poetry

"*On the eve of the quintcentennial celebrating the 'discovery' of the New World by Columbus, we have the opportunity to reflect on the relationship between power and knowledge. The traditional canon of the core curriculum of American education is currently undergoing tremendous pressure for change. At the same time, tremendous resistance is encountered by those efforts intended to include minority and women's perspectives within the curriculum. Our task is to help create a partnership that awakens consciousness through our actions. Our task is also to help create a curriculum that reveals a deeper more complex American reality. We need to help accelerate, to use Michel Foucault's phrase, 'the insurrection of subjugated knowledges.'*"

Manuel Gomez
Associate Vice Chancellor,
Academic Affairs,
University of California, Irvine

Featured Literature

"Be Nobody's
Darling" from
*Revolutionary
Petunias and
Other Poems*
by Alice Walker

Grade Level
For High School

Thinking Level
Application

Writing Domain
Imaginative/Narrative

Materials Needed
Color pens required.

**Suggested
Supplementary
Readings**
• *Self-Reliance*
  by Ralph Waldo Emerson
• *Black Boy*
  by Richard Wright
• *The Scarlet Letter*
  by Nathaniel Hawthorne
• *Their Eyes Were
  Watching God*
  by Zora Neale Hurston

Be an Outcast... Be Pleased to Walk Alone:
Alice Walker's "Be Nobody's Darling"

by Cristan Greaves

Overview

After reading and analyzing Alice Walker's poem "Be Nobody's Darling," students will narrate a significant moment in their lives when they took a stand and, as a result, became an outcast before popular opinion.

Objectives

THINKING SKILLS

Students will:

- *analyze and discuss* the experience of being an outcast as portrayed in Alice Walker's poem "Be Nobody's Darling";
- *select* a significant moment in their own lives when they took a stand and became an outcast before popular opinion;
- *recall and sequence* details that will re–create the moment through narration, description, and dialogue;
- *demonstrate,* either implicitly or explicitly, through the reminiscence the significance of the incident.

WRITING SKILLS

Students will write an autobiographical incident in which they:

- *narrate* a significant moment in their lives;
- *provide* a context for the moment;
- *use* first person point of view;
- *employ* sensory/descriptive details when they delineate people and setting;
- *use* dialogue and/or interior monologue to portray characters;
- *create* a tone that demonstrates the moment's significance;
- *demonstrate* proficiency in the standards of written English.

The Process

This lesson could be used as an "into" or "beyond" activity to American works such as *The Adventures of Huckleberry Finn, The Scarlet Letter, Black Boy,* and *To Kill a Mockingbird* (to name a few), which deal with the "outcast experience." It would also be appropriate as an introduction to transcendentalism or included in a unit on the literature of social protest (Thomas Paine, Martin Luther King, Cesar Chavez, Malcolm X, Frederick Douglass, Jesse Jackson, American Indian orators, Elizabeth Cady Stanton, et al).

The lesson should take approximately three–five days, depending upon the time allotted for the actual writing of a first draft, a revision, and the implementation of peer–sharing groups.

 PREWRITING

Prewriting Step 1: *Cluster Lists*

Write two terms on different sides of the blackboard: *conformist* and *outcast.* As students make associations with these two terms, write their ideas near the appropriate word. Have students come up with examples, people they know of who fit the two categories. This brainstorming is only to help students build a concept of the two terms before examining them in more detail later.

Sample clusters may look like this:

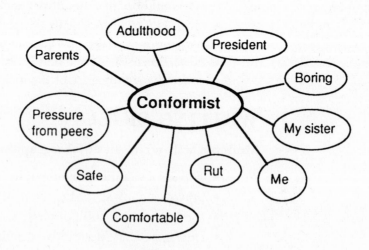

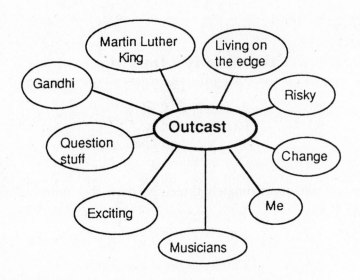

Prewriting Step 2: *Quickwrite Sentence Starters*

To help students begin personalizing the concepts of *outcast* and *conformist,* ask them to write continuously for two minutes, finishing the following open-ended sentence:

I think a conformist is someone who _____ .

Follow the same procedure for each of the following open-ended sentences:

To fit in at this school, a person has to _____ .

I feel like an outcast when I _____ .

I'd rather be a _____ than a _____ because _____ .

Prewriting Step 3: *Introducing the Poem*

Explain that "Be Nobody's Darling" was written by Alice Walker, an African American writer who won the Pulitzer Prize for fiction in 1983 with the publication of her novel *The Color Purple.* "Be Nobody's Darling" is from her collection of poetry *Revolutionary Petunias,* published in 1971. She has stated of this collection that the poems are "about (and for) those few embattled souls who remain painfully committed to beauty and to love even while facing the firing squad."

 READING AND QUICKWRITE

Read the whole poem aloud to the class.

Be Nobody's Darling
for Julius Lester

Be nobody's darling;
Be an outcast.
Take the contradictions
Of your life
And wrap around
You like a shawl,
To parry stones
To keep you warm.

Watch the people succumb
To madness
With ample cheer;
Let them look askance at you
And you askance reply.

Be an outcast;
Be pleased to walk alone
(Uncool)
Or line the crowded
River beds
With other impetuous
Fools.

Make a merry gathering
On the bank
Where thousands perished
For brave hurt words
They said.

Be nobody's darling;
Be an outcast.
Qualified to live
Among your dead.

by Alice Walker

Then, ask students to quickwrite for two minutes on how the poem makes them feel. A sample response might look like this:

I really like what this poem has to say—that it's "uncool" to follow the crowd. Somehow it's better to follow your own conscience even if that means being labeled as an "outcast." I like the line "be pleased to walk alone"—like there's pride involved in going on your way alone. I wonder how many times I've been an outcast in my life. Probably too many to count!

Prewriting Step 4: *Second Reading of the Poem*

Explain that now students will be reading the poem stanza by stanza. As each stanza is read aloud, they will be:

1. underlining key words or images they notice;

2. writing any questions they may want to have answered;

3. recording any personal reactions to the stanza.

(Students should use the same color pen or pencil throughout the first reading because they will be marking in a second color when rereading later in the lesson.)

Read each of the five stanzas aloud. As each stanza is read, pause for two to three minutes as students mark the text.

The following shows how students might mark stanza 1:

What does *darling* mean here? *beloved? favorite?*	Be nobody's <u>darling:</u> Be an <u>outcast</u> Take the <u>contradictions</u>	Being an outcast means being alone.
What are "contradictions"?	Of your life And wrap around You like a <u>shawl,</u>	Hawthorne's Wakefield was the "outcast of the universe."
Warm, comforting—but how can contradictions be that?	To parry <u>stones</u> To keep you <u>warm.</u>	What does *parry* mean?

Prewriting Step 5: *Third Reading*

Ask students to repeat the procedure, reading the poem silently and using a different color pen or pencil for marking the text.

Prewriting Step 6: *Quickwriting*

Have students quickwrite for three to five minutes on how the poem makes them feel now. They may choose to write about ideas that came up when they marked the text (see Step 4). A sample response might look like this:

I can really identify with this poem. This poem energizes me! It's kind of like a national anthem for outcasts. It makes me want to stand up and shout, "I'm proud to be an outcast!" I wonder about the thousands of other outcasts in the world. I think of people who dared to push and to speak. The first who comes to mind is Martin Luther King, Jr.—definitely my personal hero. What he went through to get his ideas across—his house was bombed many times, his life was constantly in danger. But he kept on going. I thought of King especially in stanza 4, for his "brave hurt words." Two of my favorite outcasts in my family are my great-aunt who was a missionary doctor in China in the 1900's (Dad's side of family) and John Ross, Cherokee orator in the 1800's (Mom's side). I hope I can be an outcast, a rebel, who helps others.

Prewriting Step 7: *Class Chart*

In peer groups of four or five, have students volunteer the responses they marked (see Prewriting Step 4) and make a chart. You might want to model possible responses to the first stanza on the board:

Key Words	Questions	Personal Reactions
darling outcast contradictions shawl	• What are "contradictions" of life? • What does *parry* mean? • Why are contradictions seen as positive?	• Being an outcast—being alone • Famous outcasts—Thoreau, King, Gandhi, Huck Finn, Hester Prynne, Antigone

Prewriting Step 8: *Grand Conversation*

Have each group assign a responsibility to its various members:

- **Paraphraser** One who will assign a stanza to each group member and facilitate his or her study of the stanza. Each person should record the paraphrase and report to the group what the speaker is suggesting about what it means to be an outcast. Possible explanations might include these ideas:

    Stanza 1 To face the contradictions in life and try to understand them will make you strong and somehow safe.

    Stanza 2 Those who follow the status quo give in to "madness," and they will regard you with disapproval and suspicion. Don't join their notion of reality.

    Stanza 3 One has a choice—to be an outcast and walk alone (which is socially undesirable) or conform and join the throng of impulsive fools.

    Stanza 4 Join the other outcasts, thousands of them, who died for their brave words, for taking a stand.

    Stanza 5 Take a stand, be an outcast, and be entitled to be a part of the community of outcasts who have come before you.

- **Discussion Leader**   One who will facilitate and encourage comments from all members and keep the discussion relevant to an analysis of the poem.

- **Notetaker**   One who will record topics and issues discussed.

- **Reporter**   One who is responsible for helping the group look for patterns that appear in the recorded responses and who reports the patterns back to the whole class.

Write suggestions for possible discussion topics on the board:

- How are your responses similar to and/or different from one another?
- What questions or issues does the poem give rise to that you would like to discuss?
- What risks do people take to stand against the status quo and for what they believe? Do you admire these people? Why?
- Have you ever consciously made yourself an outcast?
- Is it worth it (for you) to face the "contradictions" of life if doing so means you would become an outcast?
- What images, symbols, and metaphors in the poem stand out for you? Why? How do they help make the poem relevant to you?

At the conclusion of the grand conversation, the leader reports patterns back to the whole class. As each group reports, you should begin a cluster on the board of the kinds of risks people take—especially noting personal examples of risks students have taken.

PROMPT

In Alice Walker's poem "Be Nobody's Darling," the speaker suggests that to face the contradictions, the inconsistencies in life, is a sign of a strong person. Many people would prefer to conform. The outcast, the one who would be "nobody's darling," however, is not alone in his/her journey. There are thousands of people throughout history who have been labeled as outcasts because they uttered "brave hurt words." Finally, the speaker suggests, to be "nobody's darling" is to be a part of the community of all the outcasts who have come before.

Using imaginative/narrative writing skills, relate a moment in your life when you stood up for something you believed in strongly. Because you took a stand and didn't give in to the status quo or the norm, you became an outcast before popular opinion. At the time of the incident, you knew that taking a stand would make you vulnerable to disapproval, suspicion, perhaps even attack, but you were willing to be labeled as an outcast for your beliefs.

Your essay should show that you have:

- narrated a significant moment in your life;
- provided a context or background for that moment;
- used first person point of view;
- employed sensory/descriptive details when you delineate people and setting;
- used dialogue and/or interior monologue to portray characters;
- created a tone that demonstrates the moment's significance;
- demonstrated proficiency in the standards of written English.

Note: If you are unable to think of a time when you took a personal stand, relate a significant moment in your life when you witnessed someone else taking a stand that you admired.

PRECOMPOSING

Precomposing Step 1: *Clustering*

Have students volunteer and cluster more incidents on the board where they have taken a stand for something they believed in and became an outcast.

A sample cluster might look like this:

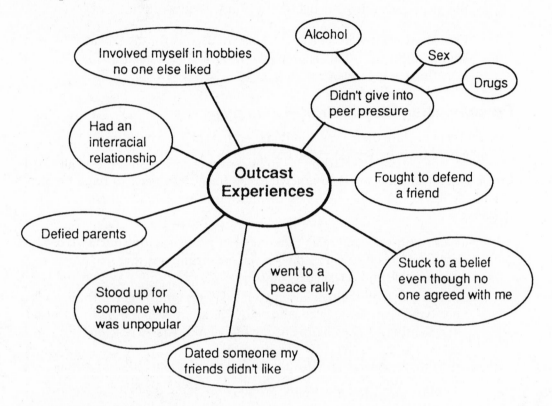

Precomposing Step 2: *Freewrite*

Have students choose an incident from their own lives when they took a stand against the status quo and write for five minutes about why this incident is important to them and why they would like to write about it for their essay.

A sample freewrite follows:

> We lived in a small town in New Jersey when I was in elementary school. In our town, there were mostly Italian and Irish families. Most of my friends were Italian and Irish, but my best friend was Jewish. My other friends hated Rachael—they said she was ugly, shy, and boring. (I didn't know at the time that they hated her because she was Jewish too.) To me, Rachael was sensitive (our family was having so many problems, but I always could talk to Rachael and feel safe), artistic (she could paint, dance, and sing), and fun. One day in 6th grade at recess, I heard my friends talking about how they were going to beat up Rachael after school because she won first place in the school's art contest. I didn't say anything at the time, because I didn't want to give myself away! But after school I made sure that I would protect Rachael. And I did. It was a big scene! My face was burning,

I was so mad. My friends thought I was crazy. I got called into the principal's office for fighting! But it was all worth it.

I stood up against my so-called friends of 5 years for my friendship with Rachael. This is probably the first time I stood up for something really important to me.

Precomposing Step 3: *Guided Imagery*

Ask students to close their eyes and imagine that they are back in the time and setting where their important stand occurred.

Create an atmosphere that is conducive to the imaginative task at hand by turning off the lights and using the following questions to guide the students' imagery:

- Close your eyes and relax. You may put your head on your desk or sit back with your eyes closed. The important thing is that you are as comfortable and relaxed as you can be.
- Imagine that all the tension in your body is running down from your head and right through to your toes. Picture it evaporating into the air and floating away as lightly as a white cloud. Your whole body is relaxed and you feel calm and peaceful.
- Breathe slowly and deeply, enjoying this calm and peaceful feeling.
- Think of the time and setting where your stand against the majority occurred.
  — Where is it?
  — What does it look like there?
  — Who is with you?
  — Why are they there?
  — What are they doing? What are you doing?
  — What are you saying? What are others saying to you?
  — How are you feeling as the moment is being relived?
  — What tones of voice are you hearing?
  — What does this moment mean to you?
- When you have finished experiencing your incident and are ready to return to the classroom, open your eyes. Write or draw for five minutes about the moment you visualized during the guided imagery.

A sample drawing is shown on the next page.

It's weird to think that these people called my "friends" would be hiding by trees waiting to jump on us.

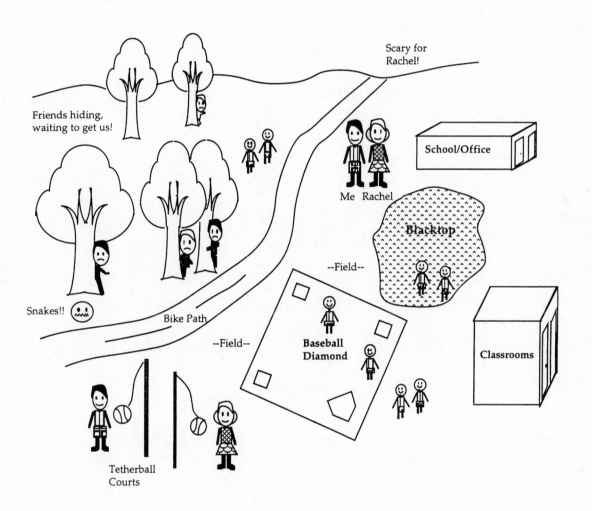

Precomposing Step 4: *Open Mind*

Work to focus on understanding yourself more fully at the time of the incident and your feelings about your role as an outcast. You may write or fill in the Open Mind with symbols, words, phrases, or any combination of writing and drawing that will best represent what you were thinking and feeling about the incident and yourself at the time of the incident.

A sample Open Mind might look like this:

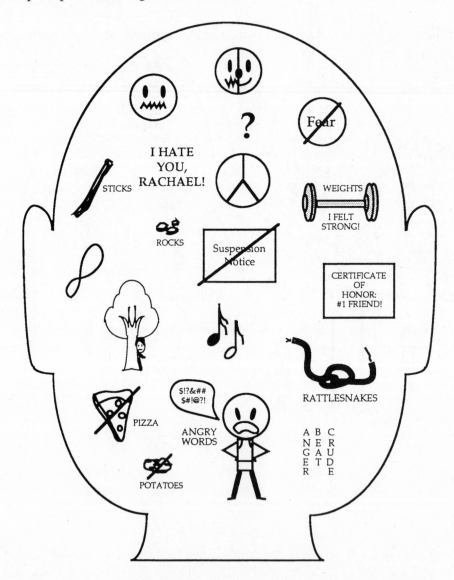

Allow students to share their Open Minds incident and feeling about the incident with their peer group.

Precomposing Step 5: *Detailing*

Pass out details chart.

Have students recall and list in the first column each thing that happened in the incident from beginning to end. Remind students that they are not telling the story of their incident yet. They are just chronologically listing the details of their story.

In order for students to help their readers "see" their experience, have them return to their list of events and complete the relevant columns in the following chart. Remind them that their goal is to create as many vivid details as they can remember or invent.

A sample chart might look like this:

Events	Showing Details	Relevant Images	Relevant Dialogue
"Friends" told me at recess that they were going to beat up Rachael after school.	Their eyes darted at me; their voices were booming; they all formed in a herd and accosted me.	Herd of angry kids; their eyes darted like wild animals' eyes; I felt protective—like Rachael was a small, defenseless animal.	**Mary said,** "We hate Rachael. She's stupid and ugly." **Me:** "Well, she's my friend!" **Laura:** "Well, we hate her and we're gonna get her after school!"
I met Rachael after school.	Rachael was nervous and fidgety; I felt cool and relaxed; confident and loose-limbed.	Rachael seemed like a fawn to me—delicate and quiet and vulnerable; I felt like a bit of a hero, about to right a wrong.	**Rachael:** "Let's just go the short-cut and avoid them." **Me:** "No, We're gonna face them now!"
"Friends" started gathering by the trees. We fought.	Heads peeking around trees; some standing brazenly with sticks and rocks; me pounding their ears with words.	Like rattlesnakes in the grass, they were about to attack. Stand-off in the bike path; kids armed with sticks and rocks.	**Mary:** "Hey ugly, we're gonna kick your _____." **Me:** "Leave her alone!" **Laura:** "Get out of the way!"

 # WRITING

Using their responses and charts on Alice Walker's "Be Nobody's Darling," grand conversation notes, freewrites, clusters, Open Mind, and detail charts, students should now be ready to write.

 # SHARING

Sharing Step 1: *Individual Evaluation*

Before peer sharing, have each writer evaluate his/her own draft, using the Evaluating Your Own Draft handout on the next page.

Sharing Step 2: *Pair Evaluation*

Have students work in pairs to evaluate each other's drafts. Suggest that pairs share their self-evaluations as well, using the Evaluating Another Student's Draft sheet, which follows the Evaluating Your Own Draft handout.

Sharing Step 3: *Read-Around Groups*

Share papers in Read-Around groups. Chart the groups' selections of best papers. Have the writers of the most frequently selected papers read them aloud to the class and discuss. (See the Glossary for a description of Read–Aloud groups.)

 # REVISING

Revising Step 1: *Individual Revision*

Using their own evaluation and the feedback received from their partners, students should revise their paper.

Revising Step 2: *Teacher Conference*

Students may also confer with the teacher after they have completed their Evaluating Your Own Draft handout.

Evaluating Your Own Draft

Now that you have finished a draft of your autobiographical incident, you will want to think about how well you did.

Read your draft. Then answer these questions:

		Circle One	
1.	This essay is mainly about me, not somebody else.	yes	no
2.	This paper is about the incident that happened.	yes	no
3.	I described people, place, time, and objects in my incident.	yes	no
4.	I showed my feelings at the time of the incident.	yes	no
5.	I included conversation .	yes	no
6.	I have focused my incident around the central moment.	yes	no
7.	I gave my essay a title.	yes	no

8. Write down some things you could add to your draft to make it better:

_____

_____

_____

9. Besides these additions, what else will you change in your draft when you revise it?

_____

_____

_____

10. What do you like best about your draft?

_____

_____

_____

11. What specific problems in the draft are you having problems solving?

_____

_____

_____

Evaluating Another Student's Draft

Writer's Name _____

Title of Essay _____

Your Name _____

Help your partner revise his or her draft by answering the questions below. If you need more space, write on the back of this page. Another student will do the same thing for you.

1. As you read the draft the first time, put a straight line under words or phrases that show details most clearly.

2. Put a wavy line under words or phrases you would like to have clarified. In the margin, ask the specific questions you have.

3. Put brackets [ ] around phrases or sentences you couldn't understand. Ask specific questions in the margins.

4. Put an X between sections that seem to have a big gap between them. Is there any place where you are not sure how the writer got from one section of the story to the next? Do any sentences suddenly seem to be about a new subject?

5. In one sentence, summarize the stand the writer took and what you think is the significance of that stand:

   _____

   _____

6. Tell the writer what you liked best about the essay:

   _____

   _____

7. Tell the writer one thing you would like him or her to add to the essay:

   _____

   _____

8. What parts of the essay would you suggest the writer revise? Explain your suggestions clearly:

   _____

   _____

Revising Step 3: *Metacognitive Response*

Ask writers to look at both their draft and their revision and answer the questions on the chart below:

Metacognitive Response

1. What changes did you make from draft to revision?

2. How did these changes improve your revision?

3. What do you like best about your revision?

4. What would you improve if you had still more time?

 EDITING

Editing Step 1: *Pairs Editing*

After students have evaluated their own revisions, they may meet in pairs or groups again to do the final editing of their papers.

Students may request what type of feedback they would like from their peers—either aspects of the content of the paper or the mechanics of the writing. Students generally proofread best when given a few specific things to look for.

Editing Step 2: *Final Revision*

Students can then complete the final drafts of their papers, using the feedback received in the editing session.

 EVALUATION

Papers will be scored on a 1–6 scale according to the following rubric:

6   This is a paper that is clearly superior; well written, insightful, carefully organized, and technically correct. A 6 paper does all of the following well:

- Skillfully narrates one significant moment or incident.
- Skillfully orients readers by providing the context or background for the central incident; context does not dominate the essay at the expense of the incident.
- Consistently uses first person point of view.
- Uses rich sensory/descriptive details for delineating people and setting.
- Skillfully uses dialogue and/or interior monologue to portray characters.

- Creates a tone that clearly demonstrates the moment's significance.
- Clearly communicates the significance of the incident; insights are well integrated into narration.
- Demonstrates mastery of the conventions of standard written English.

5   This paper includes all aspects of the assignment but is a thinner version of the 6. It is still well written, carefully organized, and technically correct. It will do all or most of the following:

- Skillfully narrates one significant moment or incident but in a more predictable or less focused fashion than a 6 paper.
- Skillfully orients readers by providing the context or background for the central incident; context does not dominate the essay.
- Consistently uses first person point of view.
- Uses rich sensory/descriptive details for delineating people and setting.
- Uses dialogue and/or interior monologue to portray characters, but not as skillfully as the 6 paper.
- Creates a tone that clearly demonstrates the moment's significance, but in a less engaging fashion than the 6 paper.
- Clearly communicates the significance of the incident; insights are not as probing and well integrated as in the 6 paper.
- Demonstrates competency in the conventions of standard written English.

4   This paper includes all aspects of the assignment, but not in as much depth as the 5 or 6 paper. It may exhibit some of the following:

- Adequately narrates one significant moment, but may have some digressions.
- Adequately orients readers by providing the context or background for the central incident; balance between context and incident may seem awkward.
- Inconsistently uses first person point of view.
- Uses a variety of sensory/descriptive details for delineating people and setting.
- Exhibits limited use of dialogue and/or interior monologue to portray characters.
- Creates a tone that demonstrates the moment's significance, but not consistently.
- Communicates the significance of the incident; insights may be predictable and/or may seem tacked on.
- Demonstrates occasional weaknesses in the conventions of standard written English. Errors may be distracting but do not affect reader understanding.

3   This paper treats the subject in a superficial way:

- Relates an incident or a series of incidents.
- Inadequately orients readers by providing few details; context may be out of balance and may dominate the essay.

- Inconsistently uses first person point of view.
- Very limited use of sensory/descriptive details for delineating people and setting.
- Very limited use of dialogue and/or interior monologue to portray the characters.
- Creates a tone that does not seem to demonstrate the significance of the moment.
- Briefly states or implies the significance of the incident; insights may be predictable, superficial, or illogical.
- Demonstrates frequent errors in the conventions of standard written English.

2   This paper represents an inadequate attempt to write to the prompt:

- Incompetently and/or briefly narrates an incident or series of incidents.
- Little or no orientation provided to the reader; or context may dominate the essay.
- Fails to use first person point of view
- Minimal use of sensory/descriptive details for delineating people and setting.
- Minimal use of dialogue and/or interior monologue to portray characters.
- Creates a tone that is inconsistent with the significance of the moment; or fails to establish a tone.
- Little or no statement or implication regarding the significance of the incident; insights seem superficial.
- Demonstrates serious and frequent errors in the conventions of standard written English. These errors distract the reader and lead to confusion.

1   This paper reveals that the writer may have been unsure of or confused by the prompt. It:

- Fails to narrate an incident or makes vague reference to an incident within the context.
- Little or no orientation provided to the reader; or context may be so overemphasized that it overshadows the incident.
- Fails to use first person point of view.
- Fails to use sensory/descriptive details for delineating people and setting.
- Fails to use dialogue and/or interior monologue to portray characters.
- Fails to establish a tone.
- Significance may be absent or it may dominate the entire essay; insights (if stated) seem superficial.
- Serious errors in almost every sentence interfere with reader's understanding.

Mirror Mirror
People keep asking me where I come from
says my son.
Trouble is I'm american on the inside
and oriental on the outside.

No Kai.
Turn that outside in.
THIS is what American looks like."

Mitsuye Yamada
Poet and Lecturer;
author, *Camp Notes and Other
Poems* and *Sowing
Ti Leaves: Writings
by Multicultural Women*

Featured Literature

"When I Was Growing Up"
by Nellie Wong from
This Bridge Called My Back: Writings by Radical Women of Color

Grade Level
For Middle School

Thinking Level
Application

Writing Domain
Imaginative/Narrative

Materials Needed
• Colored pens

Suggested Supplementary Readings:
• *"A to Z* in Foods as Metaphors: Or, a Stew Is a Stew Is a Stew" by Mimi Sheraton
• "Charles" or "The Sneaker Crisis" by Shirley Jackson
• "Eleven" by Sandra Cisneros
• "Me & Neesie " by Eloise Greenfield
• "The Moon Lady" by Amy Tan
• "No Gumption" by Russell Baker

Growing Up:
A Personal Reflection

by Meredith Ritner

Overview

Using clustering, quickwrites, organizers, interviews, and drawings, students will explore the topic of growing up. Students will define what growing up is as they read the poem, "When I Was Growing Up" by Nellie Wong and draw from their own experiences with maturing. The final product of this lesson is a personal reflection in which students create a metaphor to describe growing up and develop their ideas with personal experiences, anecdotes, feelings, and quotes from their friends and family members.

Objectives

THINKING SKILLS

Students will:

- *recall* experiences while growing up;
- *reflect* on what growing up means;
- *create* metaphors that illustrate one's attitude toward and experience with growing up.

WRITING SKILLS

Students will:

- *organize* ideas into a reflective essay;
- *develop* a metaphor to describe growing up;
- *use* quotations from personal interviews;
- *write* an effective hook, a well developed main body, and a coherent conclusion to the essay;
- *observe* the conventions of written English.

The Process

 **PREWRITING**

Prewriting Step 1: *Clustering*

Have students cluster "Growing Up."

Prewriting Step 2: *Guided Imagery*

Help your students to reflect upon their experiences while growing up by dimming the lights and using the following statements to focus their thoughts. Leaving pauses for think time, say to them:

- Close your eyes and relax. Rest your head on your desk if you like. Make yourself comfortable without feeling sleepy.
- Take a deep breath in. Quietly let it out. Once more, a deep breath in—and out. Feel your body begin to relax.
- Think about the events and feelings that you have experienced in your life. Visualize and remember:
  — your best day ever; remember the details that made it special for you;
  — the people who have been important to you and why;
  — places that hold special meaning to you;
  — difficult times, maybe when you made a mistake or a poor decision;
  — your special friends—the fun times you've shared and also the hard times when your feelings were hurt;
  — times when you tried something new—like riding a bike, or the first day of a new school year.

Prewriting Step 3: *Quickwrite*

Have individual students do a quickwrite on growing up and then form small groups to share their writing. A sample quickwrite follows:

> I go through ups and downs everyday and sometimes I regret it. I mean like you're having such a great day and then something brings you down. Sometimes, when I go to school, I'll be in a good mood. My friends are there for me to talk to, etc., but when I get home, my sisters and I will quarrel. I think of it as natural because I see other families who are the same way.
>
> What I'm most concerned with about "growing up" is my future. The reason is that I do not know what I want to be. I try to think but there are hardly any choices. I have good grades, but no goals.
>
> I know that lots of people would love to grow up fast because they think it would be better. They'll get to drive and drink and so on. One thing I don't want to do is drive. Well, I know I would need transportation, but I don't want to take the bus or walk. I'm scared to drive right now, but maybe later, my feelings about driving will change.
>
> I've got a lot to say about "growing up" but it's mostly personal. But I've got to tell you one thing, growing up is a lot of responsibility and that's the truth.
>
> *Kelly Vo*

Prewriting Step 4: *Reading the Poem*

Distribute a copy of the poem "When I Was Growing Up" by Nellie Wong.

Featured Literature

When I Was Growing Up
By Nellie Wong

I know now that once I longed to be white.
How? you ask.
Let me tell you the ways.

> when I was growing up, people told me
> I was dark and I believed my own darkness
> in the mirror, in my soul, my own narrow vision
>
> when I was growing up, my sisters with fair skin got praised
> for their beauty, and in the dark
> I fell further, crushed between high walls

when I was growing up, I read magazines
and saw movies, blonde movie stars, white skin,
sensuous lips and to be elevated, to become
a woman, a desirable woman, I began to wear
imaginary pale skin

when I was growing up, I was proud
of my English, my grammar, my spelling
fitting into the group of smart children
smart Chinese children, fitting in,
belonging, getting in line

when I was growing up and went to high school,
I discovered the rich white girls, a few yellow girls,
their imported cotton dresses, their cashmere sweaters,
their curly hair and I thought that I too should have
what these lucky girls had

when I was growing up, I hungered
for American food, American styles,
coded: white and even to me, a child
born of Chinese parents, being Chinese
was feeling foreign, was limiting,
was unAmerican

when I was growing up and a white man wanted
to take me out, I thought I was special,
an exotic gardenia, anxious to fit
the stereotype of an oriental chick

when I was growing up, I felt ashamed
of some yellow men, their small bones,
their frail bodies, their spitting
on the streets, their coughing,
their lying in sunless rooms,
shooting themselves in the arms

when I was growing up, people would ask
if I were Filipino, Polynesian, Portuguese.
They named all colors except white, the shell
of my soul, but not my dark, rough skin

when I was growing up, I felt
dirty. I thought that god made white people clean
and no matter how much I bathed,
I could not change, I could not shed
my skin in the gray water

when I was growing up, I swore
I would run away to purple mountains,
houses by the sea with nothing over
my head, with space to breathe,
uncongested with yellow people in an area
called Chinatown, in an area I later learned
was a ghetto, one of many hearts
of Asian America

I know now that once I longed to be white.
How many more ways? you ask.
Haven't I told you enough?

Give each student a colored pen or pencil. As you read the poem aloud, ask students to underline any words or phrases they do not understand. Ask students to exchange pens with a partner who has a different color of ink and repeat this process. Exchange pens again for a third reading.

In groups of four, ask students to share the underlined parts that they did not understand and try to figure out the meaning of the words or phrases. Have each group record what they discuss on a chart like the following:

What we know . . .	What we're still puzzling over . . .
• She's Chinese • She has dark skin • She doesn't fit in • She likes American food and American styles • She wants to be noticed by white people • Jealous of white girls • Proud of being a good student • She feels dirty and inferior • We know that she wanted to be white but now she likes herself.	• What are the "high walls"? • What does "purple mountains" mean? • "shooting themselves in the arm" • "exotic gardenia" • "anxious to fit the stereotype of an oriental chick"

Record the items students are puzzled about on the board. Invite discussion for the right side of the chart and encourage students to answer one another's questions.

Prewriting Step 5: *Clustering*

As a class, cluster the persona of the poem.

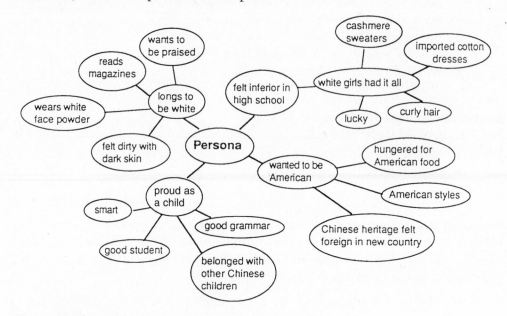

Prewriting Step 6: *Persona Analysis Chart*

Have students complete the chart below to help them analyze the persona.
(Note: Folded white paper works great and saves time at the copy machine.)

Persona Analysis Chart

Thoughts and actions of the persona	What does this tell you about the persona?	What do you think and feel about this behavior?
She wears a false "pale" face.	She doesn't think she's pretty the way she is.	I think she should accept herself and not try to be someone she's not.
She reads American magazines.	She wants to be American and be in style.	I like to do American things too.
She does well in school.	She values education.	She tries to fit in by doing well.
She tries to "shed her skin."	She wants to have new skin, white skin.	She's trying to change who she is.
She wants to "run away to the purple mountains."	She's trying to escape from everyone and everything.	She wants to hide or find freedom.

Prewriting Step 7: *Learning About Metaphors*

Teach students what a metaphor is. The following description may be helpful:

> *A metaphor is a figure of speech in which something is described as though it were something else. A metaphor points out a similarity between two things. An extended metaphor makes more than one point of comparison.*

Have students surface Wong's metaphors for growing up and complete the chart below as a group activity:

Metaphor	What we're still puzzling over . . .
"darkness"	She feels ugly and inferior. Her skin is dark and things that are bad are dark. She feels left out, different, and alone.
"crushed between high walls"	There is no way out of her darkness. She feels trapped. She can't see "the light."
"began to wear imaginary pale skin"	She was pretending to be white.
"exotic gardenia"	She feels beautiful, special, and white.
"could not shed her skin"	She can not grow out of her skin the way a reptile might. She will always be dark.

As a class, determine which metaphor holds the poem together (i.e., the metaphor of darkness).

Prewriting Step 8: *Creating and Extending Metaphors*

Have individual students come up with a metaphor that could be used to describe their experience with growing up. Teach students how to extend their metaphors as a way of explaining how their metaphor pertains to growing up. Students may wish to refer to their clusters and quickwrites as they draw comparisons from their metaphor and personal experience. Create a table to help students generate points of comparison. It is not necessary for students to find points of comparison for each attribute. The purpose is for them to establish what they have in common with their metaphor and to describe similarities. If students have a hard time coming up with something, you may ask them what they would be if they were an animal, a plant, a season, an element of nature, etc. as a means for helping to think of themselves and their experience with growing up in metaphorical terms. *(See the frame for the Coat of Arms in the "My Name, My Self" lesson, elsewhere in this book.)*

Attributes of Metaphor	Comparisons
A rainy day . . .	**Personal experiences . . .**
drops of rain	I feel like a drip.
wet puddles	People step all over me.
cold	My friend talked behind my back.
cloudy	I don't understand people sometimes.
thunder and lightning	I argue with my parents.
stormy	I don't finish my homework.
rainbow	Everything's going my way.
umbrella	A friend stands up for me.
bright yellow raincoats	I got an "A" on my test!

Growing up is like a rainy day. Sometimes I'm like one giant puddle that everyone's waiting to stomp all over. I feel drippy and my life is cloudy and cold—like when my best friend talks about me behind my back or I have an argument with my parents. Talk about thunder and lightning! But I have lots of bright moments also—like getting an "A" on a test that I've studied hard for. I have special friends who act as an umbrella, shielding me from potential storms. The good thing about a rainy day is that there's always a rainbow at the end and I know that if I stay strong, I will see it again. Rainy days help to clear the air. They also help me to appreciate the sunny days—when everything is going my way.

OR

Growing up is like going to Disneyland. There are so many things to see and do. Everything is alive and interesting. One minute I'm so happy and excited that my heart is pounding a million beats per minute—like when you're eeking up the first peak on a rollercoaster and you aren't sure about what's waiting for you on the other side. And then I'm off, riding the dips and curves of life. When I'm at Disneyland, I like to explore new things and I'm curious about what I will find before me. That's what growing up has been for me, an exploration that is fun and exciting.

Have students plan a design or graphic representation to illustrate their metaphor. Mount and display metaphors and illustrations. *(Note: Extended metaphors make great found poems.)*

PROMPT

Writing Situation:
Growing up can mean a lot of different things, according to a person's experiences with maturation. For Nellie Wong, growing up means coming to grips with what it is to be Chinese American. Each of us has a variety of experiences, both positive and negative, that have marked our growing process.

Writing Directions:
Reflect upon what it means to grow up. Introduce your idea with a metaphor and explain what growing up means for you. Allude to your metaphor throughout your piece as a way of tying your ideas together. Discuss ways in which you have already grown up and ways in which you are still growing and changing. Include personal experiences or anecdotes, feelings, and quotes from personal interviews to explain your thoughts.

Begin your paper with an interesting title and hook. Present your ideas, reflections, and anecdotes so that they can be easily understood by the reader. Bring your paper to a conclusion that ties your ideas together and has a sense of completion.

Check your spelling, punctuation, and sentence structure to make your writing as error-free as possible.

PRECOMPOSING

Precomposing Step 1: *Interviewing Relatives*

Have students interview parents, grandparents, aunts, uncles, family friends and older brothers and sisters to learn what others recall about them growing up. Students might ask:

- What do you remember about me when I was little?
- What were my favorite activities?
- Did I get into mischief?
- How did I feel about starting school?
- What memory do you have of me that you will always remember?

Remembrances and anecdotes of the interviewees can be recorded on a chart like the one on the next page:

This is who I interviewed	This is what they remembered about me
Lala (Grandmother)	"I'll never forget the time I took you to the playground. You insisted on going on the slide. I tried to explain to you that it was wet but you wouldn't pay any mind. You darted up the ladder faster than I can run. Then swish! Down you came. The look on your face was priceless. You were so surprised! It makes me laugh just thinking about it."
Dad	One night, my dad says, I had just gotten a haircut from my mom. Apparently, I decided that my doll, Mary Ann, needed one also. So I grabbed the scissors, gathered all of her hair into my hand, and went Chop! Mary Ann had a variation of a mohawk. My dad says that that wasn't the funny part. The funny part was that I couldn't understand why it wouldn't grow back!

Precomposing Step 2: *Creating a Recollection Frame*

Have students complete a frame to help them recall experiences and feelings from their past.

1. When I was growing up, people told me _____.

It made me feel _____ because _____

_____.

2. When I was growing up, my brothers and sisters would _____.

It made me feel _____ because _____

_____.

3. When I was growing up, I would try/try not to act like an adult by _____

_____ because _____.

4. When I was growing up, I was proud of _____

because _____.

5. When I was growing up, I liked/disliked _____

because _____ .

6. When I was growing up, I discovered _____ .

7. When I was growing up, I felt ashamed when _____

because _____ .

8. When I was growing up, I felt special when _____ .

9. When I was growing up, I promised myself that I would always/never ____

because _____ .

10. When I was growing up, the hardest part was _____ .

Precomposing Step 3: *Mapping Their Lives*

Have students create a list of significant events and memories they have. This list may be compiled from their interviews, personal experiences, and memory. Then, ask students to record their age and rank the items on their list as being wonderful (10) or awful (1). For example:

Memories, Events, and Experiences	Age	Rank
• born in Orange County on January 1, 1980	0	5
• Swallowed first tooth at school and got a dollar from the tooth fairy anyway	6	10
• went to the Grand Canyon	10	9
• started kindergarten and cried for the whole first day	5	1
• moved to new neighborhood	11	2
• started talking	1	8
• went to Disneyland	4	10
• sang a solo for the choir	9	8
• shaved my eyebrow off	7	1
• represented my school for spelling bee	12	10

Encourage students to list as many items as possible and then choose one event for each year of their lives. Using graph paper, have students chart and label their experiences. I require students to include a small illustration for each item.

Example:

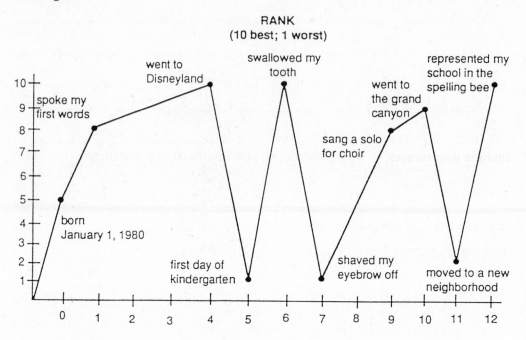

RANK
(10 best; 1 worst)

went to Disneyland

swallowed my tooth

represented my school in the spelling bee

spoke my first words

went to the grand canyon

sang a solo for choir

born January 1, 1980

first day of kindergarten

shaved my eyebrow off

moved to a new neighborhood

Note: You might choose to have students create a bar graph, or give students the choice. A few of my students preferred a pictorial representation, which I also accepted.

Precomposing Step 4: *Creating Metaphors for Growing Up*

Then, ask students to create metaphors that apply to their growing up experience, using the graphic images on their maps. Have students select or create a dominant metaphor. They may use their original metaphors or choose another. Have students select the primary experiences, anecdotes, quotes, and remembrances that they wish to include in their essay. Then, have them create a metaphor chart as they did in Prewriting Step 8 to help them think of ways in which they might extend their metaphors throughout their pieces. They may include more than one metaphor in their essays; however, they should have one dominant metaphor that holds their piece together.

Attributes of Metaphor	Comparisons

Prewriting Step 5: *Organizing a Writing Plan*

Have students use the chart below to organize their ideas.

Pull ideas from your quickwrite on growing up and your extended metaphor.

Introduction

- Elevator metaphor
  (Explain how an elevator is like growing up.)

Include experiences, feelings, anecdotes, and quotes from prewriting and composing activities in the body of your essay.

Experiences While Growing Up

- Born on Christmas Day
- Dropped on floor by sister
- Dressed like a boy—pants and vests

Already Grown Up

- Treated like an adult
- Responsible for keeping the house up, even though my work isn't always appreciated
- Mom always works
- Sister is in college

Still Growing Up

- Act like a kid when I'm with my friends
- Not all the way grown up. Is anybody?

Summarize your ideas about growing up.

Conclusion

- Refer back to elevator metaphor
- We all have a "kid side" to us

Note: This is the chart for Christine Dang's essay, in the Sharing section of this lesson.

 **WRITING**

Have students use their clusters, quickwrites, interview, frame, charts, and drawings to write their first draft.

 SHARING

Sharing Step 1: *Share Cards*

Use the following strategy to teach the class positive frames in which to structure their responses to each other's writing. Make construction paper "share cards" like the ones that follow. Pass the cards out to students in your class. Place the model of the essay that follows on the next page on the overhead and read aloud.

title	dominant metaphor	already grown up	still growing
personal experience	anecdote	additional metaphor	my favorite part is when
quote	this piece makes me feel	I need to know more about	it would help me to understand better if

Have students who are holding cards respond.

Example:

- **Joe** has a "title" card. His response after listening to the essay is, "The title of this piece is _____."
- **Maria** has a "metaphor" card. After listening to the piece, she says, "One metaphor is _____."
- **Patrick** has an "It would help me if..." card. After listening to the essay, he says, "it would help me if _____."

This process enables you, as the teacher, to demonstrate how sharing should occur. It quickly teaches students valuable responses and the importance of positive frames in which to structure their responses. After turning their cards in, organize students into partners or small groups and have them share their writing. You may wish to create a "share sheet" like the one on page 326 to help your students stay on task.

Note: The share card strategy comes from Marty Betzler Moorehead, a UCI Writing Project Teacher/Consultant from Saddleback Valley Unified School District.

Model Essay

Ups and Downs

To me, growing up has lots of ups and downs, just like an elevator. One minute, I am way up high, at the glamorous penthouse, and another minute, I am down at the ground level, in an old, dark, musty, underground parking lot.

My trip on my elevator started when I was born at the Los Alamitos General Hospital, Tuesday, December 25, 1979. Ever since 9:59 a.m. that morning, my elevator started going up. When I came home to Anaheim, the elevator went up even higher. Then, when I was dropped on the floor by my sister, the elevator started heading down—and fast! For the first three years of my life, my mom dressed me like a boy. I had a haircut to match! I was glad when my mom put away the pants and vests. As my life continued, the elevator started bouncing back and forth, like a tennis match, but it stayed mainly in the middle—not terrible and not wonderful, just normal.

Now that I'm almost thirteen (12-25-92), most of the time I feel like I'm already grown up. Although there are still times when I feel like a little kid. When I'm in the "grown-up" stage, of course, I feel like an adult, and I have to keep things in order so that everything runs smoothly. I'm in the "grown-up" stage a lot nowadays because my mom is always at work and my sister is always either at college or work. It's up to me to keep the house nice and neat, and to have everything in order. I'm usually proud of what I do, and when my mom and sister say what a great job I've done, I start floating on a cloud. But sometimes, they really push my buttons and I feel like they just dump everything on me, making me work twice as hard and not noticing what I've done. Not even a single "Thank you," "Wow!" or "That's nice!" They just act like I don't exist or that just because I'm only twelve, I can't do anything. It's always, "Christine, do this, Christine, do that." And what do I get in return? Nothing! I feel like Cinderella with no Fairy Godmother to bail me out.

When I'm around my friends, I like to act like a little kid—giggling, and acting silly, experiencing new things, and just having fun all the time. My best memory is of my sixth grade graduation. That was very fun, and exciting. The dance afterwards was the best ever. Everyone was happy and excited. When I think about that, I feel as though that day was so long ago but really, it has only been six months. Now I feel as if I'm already grown up, but I know I'm not. Not quite.

I'm still growing up—everybody is. Everybody's life is always going up and down, just like an elevator. We're always experiencing something new, being happy, being sad. No one is ever grown up. (Have you ever seen what grown ups do when they think no kids are looking?) So if you think you're grown up, think again because I don't think anyone ever grows up all the way.

Christine Dang

Sharing Sheet

Author's Name _____

Sharing Partner _____

Directions: Have the author read his/her piece to you aloud. Then, respond to the items listed below. When you are finished, discuss your responses with the author.

1. The title of this piece is _____ .

2. The dominant metaphor is _____ .

3. Additional metaphors in the piece are _____ .

4. In some ways, the author is already grown up. I can see this because _____

_____ .

5. In some ways, the author is still growing. I can see this because _____

_____ .

6. One of the personal experiences/anecdotes in this piece is _____

_____ .

7. Another experience/anecdote in this piece is _____

_____ .

8. This piece includes a quote from _____ about _____ .

9. This piece makes me feel _____ .

10. My favorite part is when _____ .

11. It would help me to understand better if _____ .

12. I need to know more about _____ .

REVISING

Revising Step 1: *Revising the First Drafts*

Have students revise their first drafts, referring to the responses and suggestions from their partners.

Revising Step 2: *Showing the Changes*

Have students underline the parts they changed with colored pen or pencil.

EDITING

Editing Step 1: *Reading Aloud*

Have students reread their writing aloud, softly, to themselves. Reading aloud often helps them identify errors in punctuation and grammar because they notice where their voices naturally pause and can listen for what sounds right. Have them make any changes or corrections they want now because they will be sharing their piece in a few minutes. (Make dictionaries available.)

Editing Step 2: *Systematic Editing*

Use a transparency to model the editing process described below.

In groups of four, students will help each other edit. On the first pass to the left, students read for sentence structure and mark any sentences that they think are run-on, incomplete, or awkward. On the second pass to the left, students check for paragraph indentation, when appropriate, and punctuation. On the third and final pass, students check spelling, circling words they think are misspelled. Colored pens or pencils make this activity more interesting to the students and enable them to identify who marked what, should they wish to question an editor.

 **EVALUATION**

Scoring Guide

6   This paper is superior. The writer developed the topic with an organized presentation of ideas. The paper is strong in content, insight, and the conventions of the English language. A person who has written a 6 paper has done most or all of the following well:

- chosen an interesting title

- introduced the subject with a "hook"

- developed a metaphor to describe growing up

- extended the metaphor throughout the essay

- included personal anecdotes to effectively describe experiences with growing up

- included quotations from family, friends, and relatives

- tied ideas together cohesively and brought them to closure

- applied the conventions of written English—spelling, usage, sentence structure, capitalization, punctuation

- written legibly

5   This paper is a thinner version of the 6. The writing is still impressive but the topic is less well handled in terms of the organization, content, insight, and language.

4   A score of 4 applies to papers in the upper-half category that are less well written than a 5. This paper exhibits less clarity of thought, organization, and command of the conventional mechanics of written English. A 4 paper exhibits some of these characteristics:

- includes a metaphor, but it is not extended throughout the piece

- includes personal anecdotes to describe the growing up experience

- includes quotations from family, friends, and relatives

- shows a sense of organization but lacks overall cohesiveness

- contains some errors in mechanics, usage, and sentence structure

- is written legibly

3 A score of 3 applies to a paper that follows the general idea of the writing assignment but is weak in organization, content, thought, and conventions of written English. A 3 paper exhibits several of the following characteristics:

- has no title

- does not include a metaphor

- lacks some clarity and organization

- contains serious errors in spelling, mechanics, usage, and sentence structure

- fails to use personal anecdotes or quotations to support ideas

- is written legibly

2 This score applies to a paper that does not address the topic. The weaknesses in a 3 paper are compounded. A 2 paper is likely to exhibit the following characteristics in addition to the characteristics of a 3 paper:

- does not follow the directions in the prompt

- does not develop ideas

- has gross errors in the conventions of written English

- is written illegibly

1 This score is reserved for any response that ignores the topic.

Addendum

As students are progressing through their writing, you might also have them read:

- "A to Z in Foods as Metaphors: Or, a Stew Is a Stew Is a Stew" by Mimi Sheraton

- "Charles" or "The Sneaker Crisis" by Shirley Jackson

- "Eleven" by Sandra Cisneros

- "Me & Neesie" by Eloise Greenfield

- "The Moon Lady" by Amy Tan

- "No Gumption" by Russell Baker

EXTENSION ACTIVITIES

1. *When I Was Growing Up Book*

Have students create individual "books" to capture their experience with growing up. They might include a personal collage as the cover; information about them such as who their friends are, what they like/dislike, how tall they are, how much they weigh, etc.; a dedication if the book is a gift; extended metaphor written as a found poem and illustrated; graph of life; final piece.

2. *When I Was Growing Up Lecture*

Teach hyperbole and have students write their own "When I was growing up lecture " for their future children.
(When I was your age, I had to . . .)

3. *Film Viewing*

Show the film *Jade Snow Wong,* which is about a Chinese woman who grew up in San Francisco's Chinatown in the 1930s, and compare the film with Nellie Wong's experience.

4. *Reader Response*

Have students write an informal evaluation of Nellie Wong's poem explaining what the author's message is, what they liked or disliked, etc.

"Flower in the Crannied Wall"
by Alfred, Lord Tennyson

"Identity"
by Julio Noboa

"Four Skinny Trees" from *The House on Mango Street*
by Sandra Cisneros

Grade Level
For Middle School and High School

Thinking Level
Analysis/Synthesis

Writing Domain
Sensory/Descriptive

Materials Needed
• Colored pencils

Suggested Supplementary Readings
• *Pilgrim at Tinker Creek* by Annie Dillard
• *Walden* by Henry Thoreau

My Life Through Images

by Pat Clark

Overview

In this lesson, students will explore figurative language in three short pieces of literature and apply what they have learned to their own lives by choosing an appropriate pattern of images or symbols to express who they are and convey their own world view.

Objectives

THINKING SKILLS

Students will:

- *analyze* three literary works for literal and inferential meaning;
- *examine* elements of figurative language in the literature;
- *compare* and *contrast* the world view of each author and how that world view is expressed through language;
- *speculate* about their own lives and their feelings about the world;
- *choose* an appropriate pattern of images or symbols to convey who they are and express their world view.

WRITING SKILLS

Students will:

- *create* metaphors, images, symbols, and other figures of speech in order to describe themselves and their feelings about life;
- *use* action verbs and colorful adjectives as they develop extended metaphors;
- *organize* their information in a logical manner: introduction, main body, conclusion;
- *follow* the conventions of written English.

The Process

This lesson will take approximately eight to ten days, depending on the amount of writing students do at home. Although practice in showing, not telling, is helpful, it is not a prerequisite for this lesson.

 PREWRITING

Prewriting Step 1: *Facts and Inferences*

Poets and other writers often look for reflections of themselves and for meaning in the world around them by personifying nature. In Alfred, Lord Tennyson's "Flower in the Crannied Wall," the poet plucks a flower and speaks to it as if it can hear.

Hand out the poem to the class and read it aloud. Elicit the message of the poem by having students list the facts that the poem reveals. Ask them to put any inferences they draw from these facts in parentheses next to the facts they list.

Feratured Literature

Flower in the Crannied Wall
Alfred, Lord Tennyson

Flower in the crannied wall,
I pluck you out of the crannies,
I hold you here, root and all, in my hand,
Little flower — but *if* I could understand
What you are, root and all, and all in all,
I should know what God and man is.

- The flower is growing in a chink in the wall. (*This is probably a difficult place to grow.*)
- The poet picks the flower. (*It is ironic that he can't find out how it clings to life without destroying it.*)
- He holds the flower and its root in his hand. (*He's trying to make sense of this living thing among walls of stone.*)
- He speaks to the flower and suggests that he does not understand what it is, but if he did, he would understand God and man too. (*He wants to understand, but how can he understand God and man when a simple flower is beyond his comprehension?*)

Prewriting Step 2: *Teaching Figurative Language*

Teach the four most common ways that poets use figurative language: similes, metaphors and extended metaphors, symbolism, and personification.

Figurative Language

Simile

A simile is a figure of speech in which two things that are not at all alike are compared through the use of words such as *like* or *as.*

> **Example:** Her eyes were like deep pools of water; their hidden depths entranced him.

Metaphor

A metaphor is a figure of speech that, again, involves two unlike things; in this instance, however, one thing becomes another.

> **Example:** Her eyes were deep pools of water; their hidden depths entranced him.

Extended Metaphor

An extended metaphor is one that is developed for several lines, a paragraph, or several paragraphs.

> **Example:** Her eyes were deep pools of water; their hidden depths entranced him. He watched the agony and the joys of life reflected in the quiet waters. At times he wished to lose himself by plunging into the warmth that emanated from them, but at other times their icy coldness warned him of the possibility of drowning in those unexplored depths.

Symbol

A symbol is something that stands for itself as well as for something else.

> **Example:** In *The Great Gatsby,* perhaps the most dominant symbol is that of Dr. T. J. Eckleburg's great billboard eyes, not unlike those of a supreme being staring broodingly down on the shoddy actions of his creation, mankind.

Personification

Personification is a figure of speech in which something that is not human is referred to as having human qualities or feelings. In the example below from *The Great Gatsby,* the painted eyes of Dr. Eckleburg on an inanimate billboard are referred to as if they were human eyes—looking down on the narrator, Nick Carroway, and Tom Buchanan, his companion.

> **Example:** I followed him over a low whitewashed railroad fence, and we walked back a hundred yards along the road under Dr. Eckleburg's persistent stare.

Prewriting Step 3: *Analyzing Poetry for Figurative Language*

Tell the class that the first poem they read was written in 1869 by an English poet. Poets today are still engaged with the same theme, exploring nature to understand mankind and the world around them.

Read the poem "Identity" aloud to the class. Tell the students that this poem was written by a youth of Puerto Rican descent in 1949, when he was in eighth grade.

Featured Literature

Identity
Julio Noboa

Let them be as flowers,
always watered, fed, guarded, admired,
but harnessed to a pot of dirt.

I'd rather be a tall, ugly weed,
clinging on cliffs, like an eagle
wind-wavering above high, jagged rocks.

To have broken through the surface of stone,
to live, to feel exposed to the madness
of the vast, eternal sky.
To be swayed by the breezes of an ancient sea,
carrying my soul, my seed, beyond the mountains of time
or into the abyss of the bizarre.

I'd rather be unseen, and if
then shunned by everyone,
than to be a pleasant-smelling flower,
growing in clusters in the fertile valley,
where they're praised, handled, and plucked
by greedy, human hands.

I'd rather smell of musty, green stench
than of sweet, fragrant lilac.
If I could stand alone, strong and free,
I'd rather be a tall, ugly weed.

Give each student a copy of the poem and four colored pencils: red, blue, green, and purple. Tell them to read the poem silently four times while looking for four different types of figurative language. They should use a different color pencil each time they read.

red = simile

blue = metaphor and extended metaphor

green = personification

purple = symbol

Students should share their underlined poems in small groups. When they are sure that they have found all figures of speech, the groups should do a quick-share with the entire class. *(Note: A variation is that different groups might analyze different stanzas. Let them explain why this image is a simile, while another is a metaphor or how one stanza incorporates both metaphor and personification.)*

Prewriting Step 4: *Figures of Speech Chart*

Provide each group with a chart. Have them list the figures of speech, the literal meaning, and the implied meaning.

The Poem: "Identity"

Figure of Speech	Literal Meaning	What You Think the Author Means
Let them be flowers, always watered, fed, guarded, admired, but harnessed to a pot of dirt. (simile)	Humans are like flowers, taken care of but stuck in dirt forever.	If one conforms to an acceptable pattern in life, he/she will be safe but will never make a mark upon the world.

Prewriting Step 5: *Illustrating Quotes from Text*

Have groups select a quotation from the text and illustrate it. Ask them to write the quotation across the top of the drawing. Have them write the message the quotation is trying to convey at the bottom. Let them hang their drawings anywhere in the room.

Example: *"If I could stand alone, strong and free, I'd rather be a tall, ugly weed."*

I'd rather be a nonconformist and make my mark on the world than be one of many.

Prewriting Step 6: *Class Discussion*

Discuss the messages from the previous activity with the whole class. As a class, decide the overall meaning the author is trying to convey. If students have missed anything or do not understand certain images, now is the time to clarify. *(Sample messages might include: One would accept strict conformity if one lived as a flower among many others. If one chose to live as a weed, one would perhaps live dangerously but would be strong and free and able to make choices.)*

Prewriting Step 7: *Exploring Personification*

Give the students copies of Sandra Cisneros's essay "Four Skinny Trees." Cisneros is the daughter of a Mexican father and a Mexican-American mother. This short essay was first published in 1989.

Featured Literature

Four Skinny Trees
Sandra Cisneros

They are the only ones who understand me. I am the only one who understands them. Four skinny trees with skinny necks and pointy elbows like mine. Four who do not belong here but are here. Four raggedy excuses planted by the city. From our room we can hear them, but Nenny just sleeps and doesn't appreciate these things.

Their strength is secret. They send ferocious roots beneath the ground. They grow up and they grow down and grab the earth between their hairy toes and bite the sky with violent teeth and never quit their anger. This is how they keep.

Let one forget his reason for being, they'd all droop like tulips in a glass, each with their arms around the other. Keep, keep, keep, trees say when I sleep. They teach.

When I am too sad and too skinny to keep keeping, when I am a tiny thing against so many bricks, then it is I look at trees. When there is nothing left to look at on this street. Four who grew despite concrete. Four who reach and do not forget to reach. Four whose only reason is to be and be.

If students did not have trouble understanding how an author conveys meaning through figurative language in "Identity," you may wish to skip Prewriting Steps 9–11, which repeat the activities used with Noboa's poem. Instead, involve students in a class discussion. Elicit how Cisneros relies heavily on personification to convey her message. Make sure students notice such stylistic devices as the repetition of the word *keep*, which reiterates the theme of survival and the fact that if the trees did not help one another, they would all perish.

Prewriting Step 8: *Analyzing for Figures of Speech (Optional)*

Repeat Prewriting Steps 3 and 4 with the students. (Have them underline for figurative language and share with the entire class.)

Prewriting Step 9: *Figures of Speech Chart (Optional)*

Provide each group with a chart. Again, have them list the figures of speech, the literal meaning, and the implied meaning.

The Poem: "Four Skinny Trees"

Figure of Speech	Literal Meaning	What You Think the Author Means
They are the only ones who understand me. (personification)	She identifies with the trees because they, too, are skinny and don't belong. They become her friends and empathize with her.	Because they have to struggle in order to survive, they understand and mirror what she faces on a daily basis.

Prewriting Step 10: *Illustrating Quotes from the Text (Optional)*

Have groups repeat Prewriting Steps 5 and 6 in which they illustrate quotations and then decide on overall meaning through class discussion.

Prewriting Step 11: *Three-Way Venn Diagram*

Now, ask students to consider all three pieces of literature. They should, in their groups, delineate the shared characteristics of each piece as well as obvious differences. Give each group a Venn diagram to help them. *(Example is provided on next page.)*

Students may come up with the following shared characteristics:

- All three pieces of literature use nature symbols.
- The flower, the weed, and the trees all grow in places where it is difficult to survive.
- All are personified.

Students may perceive the following differences, among others:

- Tennyson speaks to the flower as a miracle of nature. He feels that true understanding of a tiny flower would be the key to understanding both God and the universe.
- Noboa compares flowers to "the crowd." He compares himself to a weed, wanting to be like one, and not one of the crowd.
- Cisneros speaks of four trees who fight for survival and understand her. These trees help her own fight for survival.

Three-way Venn Diagram

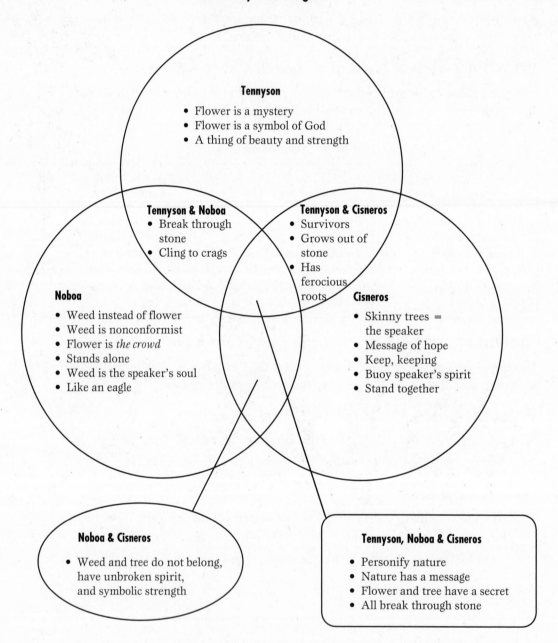

Tennyson

- Flower is a mystery
- Flower is a symbol of God
- A thing of beauty and strength

Tennyson & Noboa
- Break through stone
- Cling to crags

Tennyson & Cisneros
- Survivors
- Grows out of stone
- Has ferocious roots

Noboa

- Weed instead of flower
- Weed is nonconformist
- Flower is *the crowd*
- Stands alone
- Weed is the speaker's soul
- Like an eagle

Cisneros

- Skinny trees = the speaker
- Message of hope
- Keep, keeping
- Buoy speaker's spirit
- Stand together

Noboa & Cisneros

- Weed and tree do not belong, have unbroken spirit, and symbolic strength

Tennyson, Noboa & Cisneros

- Personify nature
- Nature has a message
- Flower and tree have a secret
- All break through stone

Prewriting Step 12: *One-Line Summaries*

Have each student write a one-line summary of what each poet seems to want out of life.

Examples:

Tennyson wants _____ *(to understand God and man)* _____ .

Noboa wants _____ *(to stand out from the crowd)* _____ .

Cisneros wants _____ *(to be strong enough to survive)* _____

Prewriting Step 13: *Listing Effective Verbs and Adjectives*

Students have now examined the literature for meaning conveyed in figurative language. Have them return to it one more time to list effective verbs and adjectives. This will enable them to understand how important simple words can be. You may wish to review the forms of the verb *to be.* Ask students to notice how often it's used, but tell them not to include it in the lists they will be making. Give them a blank chart similar to the one on the next page.

When students have completed their lists, bring out the fact that well-chosen words often make the difference between effective and ineffective writing. Tell them that Tennyson and Cisneros both convey their messages through vivid words and imagery, but that Noboa has added another dimension. He has deliberately used verbs and adjectives that are exact opposites. Example: Flowers are "watered, fed, guarded, admired, praised," but they are also "harnessed, handled, and plucked."

Effective Verbs and Adjectives Chart

	Verbs	Adjectives
Tennyson	pluck hold understand know	crannied
Noboa	watered, fed, guarded admired, (but) harnessed clinging wing-wavering broken live feel swayed carrying shunned growing praised, handled, plucked smell stand	tall, ugly high, jagged vast, eternal ancient pleasant-smelling fertile greedy, human musty, green sweet, fragrant strong and free
Cisneros	understand belong planted hear sleeps send, grow grab, bite quit keep forget droop teach look reach	four skinny pointy four raggedy secret ferocious hairy violent tiny

PROMPT

My Life Through Images

In the literature we have just examined, three different authors use nature symbols and figurative language to express their respective world views.

Write an informal essay in which you choose a symbol to show your own feelings about life and your relationship to the world around you. Make sure that there is a meaningful message about life in your essay.

Although the authors we discussed all chose symbols from nature, you may choose anything that you feel you can relate to. Make sure you use simile, metaphor, and/or personification to show and not just tell what you have discovered about yourself and your world view. Although it is impossible to completely avoid the *to be* verb, use as many action verbs as possible to make your essay come alive. Make sure you incorporate colorful adjectives as you write.

Your paper should be written in paragraph form and have a discernible beginning, middle, and ending. Follow the conventions of written English and strive for a paper as error-free as possible.

PRECOMPOSING

Precomposing Step 1: *Clustering*

Brainstorm with the entire class objects, things, animals, ideas that students can relate to and which they feel personify who they are and convey their world views. Put the words "Just like me" in the center of a cluster and take volunteers from the class to generate comparisons. An example of what a cluster might look like is provided below:

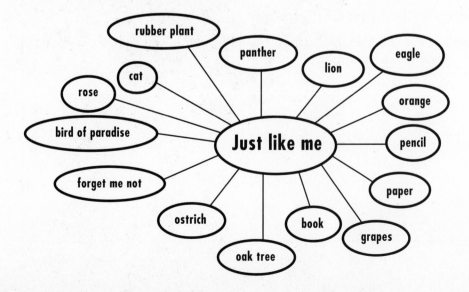

Precomposing Step 2: *Extended Cluster*

After students have clustered all the things they can relate to, they may wish to extend the cluster by listing characteristics next to each item. A few may be done as a whole class to assist those who need more modeling.

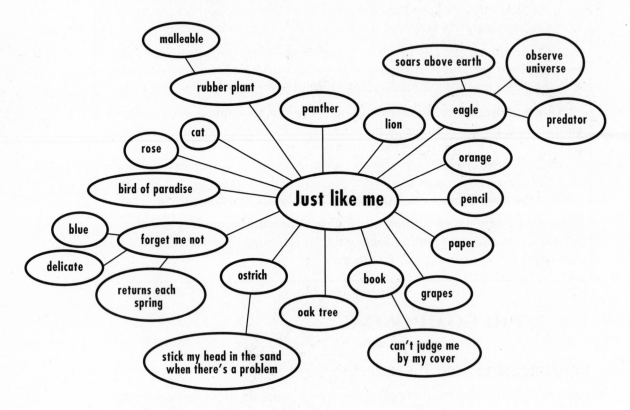

Precomposing Step 3: *Creating Similes*

Have students choose two or three words from the cluster and use them in sentences like the following. (I am like a _____ because _____.)

Example: I am like an eagle because I want to soar above the clouds, looking down on mankind.

Precomposing Step 4: *Similes Chart*

Give students the following chart. Ask them to add to their list of things, objects, etc., that are like them. They may work in groups asking others' opinions, if they wish.

I Am Like This	Because
Lion	I roar when angry, but I am playful.
Pencil	I love to write. I am long and skinny. I want to make my mark on the world.
Book	The cover may not look like much, but there is a lot inside.

Precomposing Step 5: *Developing Extended Metaphors*

Write several of the sentences students have developed on the board. Ask them to choose one, either from the board or from their more extensive lists and take it home to develop into a paragraph. Have them observe the object, animal, etc., that they have chosen, if possible. They should draw a picture of it, consider all the ways they are like it, and develop an extended metaphor.

Precomposing Step 6: *Read-Around*

Ask students to share their paragraphs in a Read-Around within their small groups. Have each group choose the one they like best to read aloud.

Continue with group sharing. Again, do a Read-Around. Ask students as they read to jot down any ideas not shown of the relationship between the author and the object, animal, etc., that the author has described. Return all papers to the author. *(You may wish to give them the following suggestions to help them react to one another's paragraphs.)*

You are also like the _____ for the following reasons:

You are like the *grape* because *you have a semihard shell around you.*

You are like the *grape* because, *despite your shell, inside you are all soft.*

You are like the *grape* because *you like to have a lot of friends around you.*

You are like the *grape* because *storms and bad weather (hard words) can hurt you.*

Precomposing Step 7: *Message to the World*

Now, ask students to consider the message about their lives that they wish to leave in the minds of their readers. Ask them to quickwrite for ten minutes, using the following questions:

- Who am I?
- What is my purpose in life?
- What is my place in the world?

Precomposing Step 8: *Goals-Obstacles-Solutions Chart*

To help students continue their search for meaning, ask them to fill out a chart like the following. Tell them they *do not* need to share the chart. Use this chart as an example of what a finished chart could be:

	Goals	Obstacles	Possible Solutions
Short-Term	Pass algebra	No brain	Get a tutor
Intermediate	Graduate high school	Too many trips to Mexico	Stay with relatives when parents leave
Long-Term	Graduate college	No money; grades too low to try for a scholarship	Work part-time and attend community college

Precomposing Step 9: *Quickwrite*

Students should look at their charts to see what they have written. Have them quickwrite about the themes and issues that emerge as they look at the goals, obstacles, and possible solutions that they have listed. They should consider how these themes and issues are important in life. For instance, the student used as an example in the chart above has had a relatively unsuccessful academic career so far. However, he seems determined to succeed somehow. He may decide that his major message to the reader is that determination is necessary for success in the world we live in.

Precomposing Step 10: *World Goals (Optional)*

Some students will still be undecided about their message to the reader at this point. It may help to have them do a similar chart for World Goals. After they complete a second chart, they will be able to compare the two charts in order to consider their own place in the larger picture.

	Goals	Obstacles	Possible Solutions
Short-Term	Eliminate racial tensions in schools and cities	Insecurities as well as supremacy feelings among different races	Education (King's example of non-violent protest, among others)
Intermediate	Eliminate racial tensions in countries	same as above	Use the media to educate the entire country rather than playing up racial incidents
Long-Term	World Peace	Jealousy among countries	Media/World Conferences

Precomposing Step 11: *Image Personifying World View*

Tell students it is now time to review the object, animal, thing, or idea that they chose to identify with. They should read over their charts, paragraphs, clusters, and any other materials they may have. Tell them that this is the time to change the object, animal, etc., that they have identified with if they are not happy with it—if they do not think it will work as imagery in the writing they are going to do. *(Some students do wish to change at this time.)*

At this point, ask students to complete the following sentence starter.

The image of _____ is a symbol of who I am because

_____ .

It personifies my world view because _____ .

Precomposing Step 12: *Quickwrite*

Ask students to do a quickwrite. They should write for ten minutes and list as many comparisons between them and their object(s), animal, etc., as they can think of.

Ask them to do the following in the quickwrite:

- Use a simile.
- Use personification.
- Use a metaphor. Try to extend it as Noboa did in "Identity."
- Convey a message to the reader.

Example:

> I am a white cloud on a hot summer day. I float across the sky and look down upon the earth. People are able to admire me from below. They watch my changing shapes as I play in the heavens, but they don't understand me. They see my gentleness and serenity, but they don't see the anger I sometimes feel as I observe their constant scurrying motions, heading, like ants, toward nothing.
>
> Floating lazily, I reach a group of friends. We see the turmoil far below us; we see the injustices as each ant strives for recognition; we see all this and we combine.
>
> Now I am one great cloud. I am no longer white. My color is a dark grey, and I pour my angry tears upon the multitudes below me, hoping to drown the wrongs of the world with my weeping.

Precomposing Step 13: *Sharing Quickwrites*

Ask students to share their paragraphs with their groups. They will want group members to answer the following questions:

- What message do you hear in my quickwrite? *(What do you think my purpose in life is?)*
- Do the images I use seem natural, or do they seem contrived? *(How could I improve them?)*
- Are my verbs and adjectives exciting enough to keep the reader interested? *(Please list any you feel I should change.)*

Precomposing Step 14: *Meditating on One's Symbol*

Ask students to think about the object, animal, thing, or idea that they are comparing themselves to. Tell them to write whatever comes into their minds as you read the following questions to them:

- What if _____ were a person?
- One thing _____ would want out of life would be _____.
- One thing _____ would like to do most would be _____.
- If _____ could have one wish, it would be _____.
- _____ would be happiest when _____.
- _____ would be saddest when _____.
- One thing _____ would be afraid of would be _____.
- I _____ could change the world in only one small way, _____ would change the world by _____.

Example:

What if *a book* were a person?

- One thing *a book* would want out of life would be *to be read.*
- One thing *a book* would like to do most would be *to influence those who read it to work for world peace.*
- If *a book* could have one wish, it would be to *be chosen from the thousands of other books to be used in schools so that it could educate many children.*
- *A book* would be happiest when *students and others underline and write notes upon its pages.*
- *A book* would be saddest when *left on the shelf among all the others that make no impression upon the world.*
- One thing *a book* would be afraid of would be *misinterpretation of its ideas.*
- If *a book* could change the world in only one small way, *a book would change the world by influencing all those who read it to work together in harmony for peace among individuals, families, cities, and nations.*

 # WRITING

Tell students that as they begin to write, they must consider their audience.

Ask yourself this question: For whom am I writing? In this instance, your first answer must be, I am writing for myself. I am writing to discover my own feelings about the world. I am attempting to use comparisons that will make my ideas clear to me. This is my primary purpose.

A secondary purpose should be to convey a message to real human beings. After all, writing is also communication. Perhaps by discovering your own ideas about what is important in the world, you can help others decide what is important to them.

Tell students to gather all the quickwrites, clusters, charts and paragraphs they have written while studying Tennyson, Noboa, and Cisneros. Have them reread everything. Tell them that they will probably be able to use much of what they have already written. *(Many students will only need to expand the essay they began in Precomposing Step 12.)*

They now should write a first draft of their essays.

 **SHARING**

Sharing Step 1: *Modeling*

Before students break into pairs to critique one another's essays, you may want to put one of the student samples appended to this lesson on the overhead and have the whole class practice the response sheet.

Sharing Step 2: *Partner Response Sheet*

Students will use the Partner Response Sheet to respond to each other's essays:

Partner Response Sheet

1. This is the message I received from your essay.

    _____

    _____

    _____

2. The symbol to which you compare yourself is a _____ .

3. I see the following figurative language in your essay.

    Similes: _____

    _____

    _____

    Metaphor: (If extended, please write only the first and last sentences.)

    _____

    _____

    Personification: _____

    _____

    _____

4. Verbs: You might try for action verbs or simply more vivid verbs in certain sentences. I have circled the verbs I think you might improve in red. I have written a possible substitution above the circled word.

5. Adjectives: You might try to use a more colorful adjective in certain sentences. I have circled the adjectives I think you might improve in red. I have written a possible substitution above the circled word.

6. You have _____ paragraphs in your essay.

•   The first paragraph introduces your topic and makes me want to keep reading. (Yes/No)

•   The final paragraph concludes your essay and makes me feel that your paper is complete. (Yes/No)

REVISING

Using their Partner Response Sheets, students should revise as necessary.
(Optional) They could write a letter to the teacher, explaining everything they changed in their drafts.

EDITING

Students should edit each other's papers in Read-Around groups. They will want to check for title, paragraphs, correct spelling, complete sentences, and other obvious errors.

EVALUATION

My Life Through Images

There are 96 possible points. Score each essay by circling the proper number and multiplying it by the number listed. Papers will be given four points if they have the correct heading and a title.

1. There is a meaningful message about life in which you express your world view.

   6 5 4 3 2 1 **X 3** = ___

2. You have conveyed this message by choosing an appropriate pattern of images or symbol to compare yourself to.

   6 5 4 3 2 1 **X 3** = ___

3. You have used simile, metaphor, and extended metaphor, and/or personification in conveying your message.

   6 5 4 3 2 1 **X 3** = ___

4. You have used action verbs and colorful adjectives in conveying your message.

   6 5 4 3 2 1 **X 3** = ___

5. Your essay has an introduction, a main body, and a conclusion.

   6 5 4 3 2 1 **X 2** = ___

6. You have observed the conventions of written English.

   6 5 4 3 2 1 **X 2** = ___

EXTENSION ACTIVITY

Have students convert their essays into poems.

Student Models

The Night Owl

I am a cat. I am a furry, cataclysmic, clawing, felonious, feline friend. I am an animal with an ego problem, an attitude, and a bad, short, evil temper; with a silky (smooth as ice) coat. I am better than you and I know it; I have a growl that comes directly from my soul and a fear that grows tired and restless within the cool blanket of forgetfulness which is night.

In that forgetfulness sleep comes quickly and without warning to all, and the snake of fear slithers steadily up through my stomach. It's the snake of society's stench, it's the fear of society's filth; it is the complete obliteration of our only habitat. I am afraid. I am terribly afraid of what I and so many others are doing to this world.

I'm a cat walking through this night, unsleeping and unfeeling. I take what I see and do nothing. Seeing with the eyes in my heart, the eyes in my mind and the eyes in my soul. Allowing these outside extremities to invade me and corrupt my soul.

I'm a cat with many lives and I create lives that never existed and create places that never existed and I breathe life into these beings.

I am a cat that's lost, lost in the rat race of Suburbia U.S.A. A world of perfect people with perfect lives. It's a land of Nutri-Systems, Beverly Hills 90210, muscle tone, tan in a can, and bottle blondes.

It is a land where nobody likes who they are and a land where a cat like me stands out and blends in at the same time.

Just a cat, waiting for that fear, like hot spokes, to fly from my imagination to reality, or from reality to reality? And jut steel wires through my legs, and allow Suburbia U.S.A. to make a house pet out of this night owl.

Robert Ross

A Book

I am a book stationed at a huge library, lost among many. My cover is not exciting, beautiful or ugly. My cover is boring. I am a book, quiet, stationed on the shelves until someone picks me up. I am a book, and if you open me up, you'll find out I'm interesting, full of fiction and non fiction material. I am a book in that I'm going through different stages or chapters as my life goes on. I am a book in that if you judge me by my cover you may never find out how interesting I am. I am a book in that one day there will be an end.

As I sit on the shelves, I see the rest of the books and magazines. It's incredible. I sit and gather dust while people won't let the other more "popular" better looking reading material alone. I just sit, relax, wait and wait, until a person comes and picks me up. This person doesn't flip through my pages for pictures; he reads page by page, day after day, and when he finishes, he is satisfied. He has read my material. He didn't judge my cover. He has found out I'm a pretty good book.

I feel happiness after opening my pages and flipping them for this person who has read me. But the sadness comes back. He puts me back on my old dusty shelf. Once again, people ignore me and pass me by. They go directly to the magazines and books with pictures, my more attractive peers. Yet, somebody discovered me. Perhaps, someday, I'll be discovered again.

Ed Ramirez

Grade Level
For High School
and College

Thinking Level
Synthesis

Writing Domain
Sensory/Descriptive

Materials Needed
• Drawing paper
• Colored markers

**Suggested
Supplementary
Reading**
"XX"
by Jimmy Santiago Baca

Peopling Poems: *Revealing Character Through Images and Narrative*

by Susan Starbuck

Overview

Using Lucille Clifton's "miss rosie," Simon J. Ortiz's "My Father's Song," and Alberto Rios's "Nani" as springboards, students will craft poems revealing characters about whom they have strong feelings.

Objectives

THINKING SKILLS

Students will:

- *analyze* how character is revealed through literal and figurative imagery and narrative;
- *describe* a person in their life, narrate stories about the person, and reflect on what that person means in their life;
- *examine* the use of parallel constructions and repetition to structure free verse;
- *create* a poem.

WRITING SKILLS

Students will:

- *write* a poem of at least twelve lines;
- *use* imagery and/or narration to reveal character;
- *express* strong personal feelings about a specific individual.

The Process

This lesson will take a week to a week and a half. Analyzing the poems should be done in class; the writing assignments may be done as quickwrites shared in class or as homework shared at the beginning of each class.

Since the intent of the lesson is to introduce students to imagery and form in poetry, several different techniques will be offered to ensure a successful experience. Not all students will find all the steps helpful, but most will find at least one step of the assignment essential for them. For this reason, points may be given for completing each step of the process, with the final product "published" on the classroom walls rather than evaluated.

The poems selected for this lesson—"miss rosie" (African American), "My Father's Song" (Native American), and "Nani" (Mexican American)—enable students to view a similar theme from a variety of perspectives. Teachers may want to select additional works to supplement these titles.

 PREWRITING

Prewriting Step 1: *Jot List*

Ask students to think of some people about whom they have strong feelings—positive or negative. These could be people whom they know now (a teacher) or people who are no longer in their lives (former friends). They could be people who are close to them or people they do not know well but have observed often (their bus driver or a neighbor). Have students jot down some of these names.

Explain that, throughout this assignment sequence, they will be writing about one or more of these people or about another person who occurs to them. Their writing will eventually end in a poem.

Prewriting Step 2: *Reading "miss rosie"*

Read and discuss "miss rosie," using the following process:

A. Hand out copies of the poem, telling the students they are free to mark on poems at any time.

B. Read the poem aloud twice.

miss rosie
Lucille Clifton

When I watch you
wrapped up like garbage
sitting, surrounded by the smell
of too old potato peels
or
when I watch you
in your old man's shoes
with the little toe cut out
sitting, waiting for your mind
like next week's grocery
I say
when I watch you
you wet brown bag of a woman
who used to be the best looking gal in Georgia
used to be called the Georgia Rose
I stand up
through your destruction
I stand up

Prewriting Step 3: *Illustrating the Poem*

Ask the students to get into pairs or trios. Have each group read the poem again. Ask them to think about and then to discuss how they would illustrate this poem to share with the class. Have student groups report on their ideas or provide paper and markers so that the students may create a drawing for each group. To decide what symbols to use, they will need to discuss the setting and the clues about the character's condition the poem suggests.

After five to fifteen minutes, have each group share their imaginary or actual illustrations with the class, discussing how they came up with their ideas from the text. After all the groups have shared, discuss the commonalities and differences in their responses.

Prewriting Step 4: *Introducing Imagery*

Now introduce the term *image*—anything in the poem that appeals to the senses. Point out sensory images in their drawings. Have students discuss what senses they experience in this poem— "the smell of too old potato peels," the touch and possible cold of the shoes "with the little toe cut out," the sight of Rosie "wrapped up like garbage," etc.

Now, ask: *What kind of person is Miss Rosie? What words would you use to explain her character?* Cluster or list these on the board or an overhead, asking which of the author's images led to these conclusions. A sample cluster might look like the following:

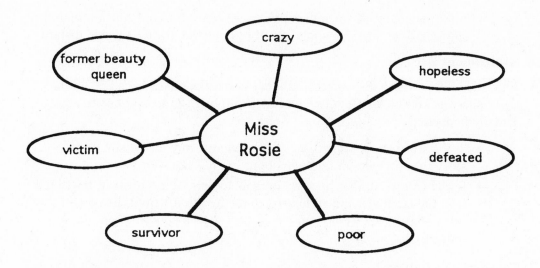

Prewriting Step 5: *Homework Assignments 1 and 2*

Visualization and Storytelling

End this class with the following assignments to be shared the next day. Both may be about the same person or about two different persons. You may wish to model the assignment by writing an example on the overhead as in the sample below or telling in detail what you would write.

Assignment 1

Part of the success of "miss rosie" is how clearly we can visualize her, almost like a photograph. Think of a person from your list of names whom you can imagine vividly.

- If you had a photograph of this person, what feature would stand out?
  - has a body like. . .
  - has hair like. . .
  - has skin like. . .
- What would the person typically be wearing? Think of this in detail. (For example, a torn greasy jeans jacket, a sweat-stained Dodgers' cap, a lace-collared lavender dress.)
- Where would the person be?
- What would the person be doing? What facial expression might you see?

An example might look like this:

> I remember my grandfather standing beside the redwood gate of our house, dressed in a clean dark blue workman's shirt with long sleeves and pants to match. His shiny bald head is fringed with hair like Friar Tuck in the story of Robin Hood. The skin of his jaw is loose and hangs in folds around his mouth. He has gaps between his teeth and,

with the gold caps on some of them, his mouth seems like an unsmiling jack-o-lantern. He spoke gruffly to me and always seemed distant.

Assignment 2

The poem "miss rosie" also suggests a story about the character's life, a time when she was known as the "Georgia Rose," although it does not state what actually happened.

- Tell a story about something that happened to your person or tell a story that the person told you about his/her life.
- If you can remember how the person actually told the story, try to tell it in the language and style used to tell it. What would the person's voice sound like? (For example, a rusty gate, a booming cannon, a butterfly.)

Teacher's Example:

My mother showed me a photograph of my grandfather from World War I and told me that even though his own father and mother were German, he had to go to Europe to fight for America. She didn't tell me what he did in the war, but the picture was actually the front of a postcard that he sent back to my grandmother before they were married. He wrote something silly on it about how handsome he was. In his doughboy uniform, he looked just like the photos in the history books except that there was something so familiar about his face: I have deep-set eyes just like his. It seemed impossible that he could ever have been so young and joking when I knew him as old.

Prewriting Step 6: *Sharing Homework*

Spend a few minutes sharing the homework. (Student groups should remain consistent throughout the rest of the lesson so that group members will be a part of the whole process and will be resources—able to recall vivid or interesting details that may have been discussed but not written down in the same style—for the other writers in the group.) Students should comment on what is particularly interesting in the writing, ask questions about what they don't understand or want to know more about, and make connections to their own lives where possible.

Prewriting Step 7: *Reading "My Father's Song"*

Review for the students how in "miss rosie" they observed Miss Rosie's character from the clues of imagery and the narrative fragments of a life story. Now, they will look at imagery and narrative again.

Hand out "My Father's Song" (reprinted on the following page).

My Father's Song
Simon Ortiz

Wanting to say things,
I miss my father tonight
His voice, the slight catch,
the depth from his thin chest,
the tremble of emotion
in something he has just said
to his son, his song.

We planted corn one spring at Acu—
we planted several times
but this one particular time
I remember the soft damp sand
in my hand.

My father had stopped at one point
to show me an overturned furrow,
the plowshare had unearthed
the burrow nest of a mouse
in the soft moist sand.

Very gently, he scooped tiny pink animals
into the palm of his hand
and told me to touch them.
We took them to the edge
of the field and put them in the shade
of a sand moist clod.

I remember the very softness
of cool and warm sand and tiny alive mice
and my father saying things.

A. Have students read it silently three times, each time underlining a word or phrase that seems most important to them.

B. Have them share their words and why they made these choices with their pairs groups; then ask for sharing in the larger group. Words and phrases might include "song," "sand," "saying things," "tiny alive mice."

C. Add to or summarize the discussion by asking students to consider how the incident at Acu reveals the father's character.

- What kind of person does this incident show the father to be?
- How does the memory of the incident connect with the first stanza?
- How does the title connect with the content of the poem?

Prewriting Step 8: *Homework Assignment 3*

Quickwrite Recalling an Experience

End the class by asking students to do assignment 3—a quickwrite recalling an experience they shared or witnessed involving a person they want to depict.

- Be aware that some students need to talk before they write, so you might allow them to share stories in their pairs/groups before writing. The story needs to be written down, however, because many students will be culling their writing for images for their poems.
- They should try to capture the most memorable images: gestures such as "he scooped tiny pink animals/into the palm of his hands" and senses such as "the very softness/of cool and warm sand and tiny alive mice."
- If they can remember dialogue, they should include that too.

A sample quickwrite might look like this:

> When I was fifteen, we took the train across country from California to Michigan for a white Christmas. At my father's relatives' house, everyone rushed up to us and gave us huge hugs that squeezed the breath out of us and disgusting wet kisses— people we didn't even know. At mother's house in Traverse City, though, it was the exact opposite. Though she hadn't seen them in years, no one came forward to even touch us, even Grandpa and Grandma. I can only remember Grandpa saying, "Hi, Sister," to Mom, who was the only girl with five brothers. I don't remember ever hugging him although Mom said he cuddled me endlessly when I was a newborn before she left with me to join my father on Guam.

Share the incidents in small groups. Have students underline images and tell each other what they think each image and what the story as a whole reveals about the character.

Prewriting Step 9: *Reading "Nani"*

Hand out "Nani" (reprinted on the following page).

A. Read "Nani" aloud to the class twice. This poem is more difficult than the others because it has more metaphor.

Nani
Alberto Alvaro Rios

Sitting at her table, she serves
the sopa de arroz to me
instinctively, and I watch her,
the absolute mamá, and eat words
I might have had to say more
out of embarrassment. To speak,
too, dribble down the mouth as she serves me
albóndigas. No more
than a third are easy to me.
By the stove she does something with words
and looks at me only with her
back. I am full. I tell her
I taste the mint, and watch her speak
smiles at the stove. All my words
make her smile. Nani never serves
herself, she only watches me
with her skin, her hair. I ask for more.

I watch the mamá warming more
tortillas for me. I watch her
fingers in the flame for me.
Near her mouth, I see a wrinkle speak
of a man whose body serves
the ants like she serves me, then more words
from more wrinkles about children, words
about this and that, flowing more easily from these
other mouths. Each serves
as a tremendous string around her,
holding her together. They speak
Nani was this and that to me
and I wonder just how much of me
will die with her, what were the words
I could have been, was. Her insides speak
through a hundred wrinkles, now, more
than she can bear, steel around her,
shouting, then, What is this thing she serves?

She asks me if I want more.
I own no words to stop her.
Even before I speak, she serves.

B. Then, ask the students to read the poem silently three times, underlining the parts they don't understand each time. In their groups, students will discuss the parts they have come to understand through the various readings, and ask others about parts that are still unclear to them.

C. After discussing in small groups, have them turn any unresolved questions, such as the ones below, to the large group for discussion. They will probably want to discuss the images that make the poem so provocative, and so enigmatic ("I see a wrinkle speak/of a man whose body serves/the ants like she serves me," etc.)

Discuss, for example:

- Can a wrinkle speak? How?
- How can a body serve the ants? How can that body be like Nani?

Let the students interpret for each other; it is okay not to reach a consensus on a "right answer." Let the suggestiveness of the text remain open. However, ask each student to explain, if possible, the thinking process for arriving at his/her ideas: what associations did the student make, what "mental" picture came to mind, what story did he or she remember?

D. After some discussion, ask students to stop and to write about what kind of person they feel Nani is and what feelings the speaker seems to have about her. Then discuss as a whole group how the narrative and the imagery in the poems led them to their conclusions.

 PROMPT

Each person in our lives is a poem waiting to be written.

As you read "miss rosie," "My Father's Song," and "Nani," you have seen how poets reveal character through literal and figurative images as well as through narrative. Out of the whole life of the person and the whole history of his or her relationship with those people, a poet selects just a few images and/or an incident to show the heart or spirit of the character.

Write a free verse poem the length of "miss rosie"—or longer if you wish—in which you use imagery and/or narration to reveal the character of a person about whom you have strong feelings. You may find a poem within material from your quickwrites or from ideas sparked by the poems we've read and discussions we've had.

 PRECOMPOSING

Precomposing Step 1: *Analyzing the Structure of Poetry*

Since many students may be unfamiliar or uncomfortable with writing free verse, it will help them to go back to the poems and look for the underlying structures. What holds poems together when they don't rhyme or have a regular pattern or rhythm?

A. Begin by having students look at "miss rosie." Ask them to underline any repeated words.

- Record their responses on a transparency of the poem on the overhead projector. They should notice that "when I watch you" is repeated three times. Likewise "I" acts in "I say" and twice "I" acts in "I stand up."

- Point out for students that "I watch," "I say," and "I stand up" are all examples of parallel grammatical structure. Free verse poets often use repetition and parallel structures to hold their poems together.

- Ask students how these repetitions and parallel structures seem to operate in the poems. What kind of material follows each?

Example:

When I watch you ...
    (This line introduces an image of how she looks and an odor is given.)
            or
(This word is used as a pivot to the next images.)

when I watch you ...
    (Another three images are given.)
           I say
(This seems to be here for emphasis.)

when I watch you ...
    (An image of how Rosie is now is contrasted with what she was.)

I stand up ...

I stand up ...
    (The speaker repeats the action. What might this reveal about his/her attitude toward Rosie?)

B. Explain to students that the above structure, the "bones" of "miss rosie," constitutes a "frame," a possible structure that they might wish to use to begin their own poems. If they feel uncertain about how to form their poem, they can use this option, because it will guarantee sucess. They may use the same words as Clifton does to start lines *("When I watch you,"* etc.), *("When I remember you"* or *"I run away,"* etc.), or just use the idea of watching someone, to get started.

C. For additional possibilities for structuring their poem, have students look at "My Father's Song," again underlining repetition and parallel structures. This time they will notice the following elements:

Wanting to say things ...
    (The first line opens to a memory of the father's voice and to the poem. It will be echoed in the last line.)

I remember the soft damp sand ...
(A specific incident is recalled here in detail.)

I remember the very softness ...
(The sand is repeated, as well as the structure.)

and my father saying things ...
(The poem ends with the father saying. There is a full circle, a rounding off of the piece though the father rather than the speaker is "saying" in the last line.)

D. Finally, look at "Nani." By this time, the students should be good at analyzing structure. Patterns begin to emerge as one observes the first stanza of this poem closely—words and speaking are important, as is serving. Throughout the poem, the parallel structures of "I watch," "I tell," "I taste," and "I ask" hold the poem together, but in this poem these structures do not appear just at the beginnings of lines. The following outline of key words in the three stanzas demonstrates these patterns.

Stanza I

Sitting at her table, she serves ... *("Serves" will be repeated five times and the poem will end with "she serves.")*
...I watch her
...and eat words
...say more
...To speak
...she serves
...with words
...I tell her
...I taste...
...her speak
...All my words
...never serves
...I ask for more.

Stanza II

...I watch...
...I watch her
...I see a wrinkle speak
...then more words
...from more wrinkles...words
...Each serves
...They speak
...I wonder...
...the words
...Her insides speak
...wrinkles...
...What is the thing she serves? *(This stanza continues the parallel structures, references to words and speech, and adds the repeated image of the wrinkles.)*

Stanza III

She asks...
I own no words...
Even before I speak, she serves.

As seen in the other two poems, the last lines of "Nani" also function to tie together the images most prevalent in the poem. Looking at the repetition and parallel structures, students can see how complex, circular, and intricately woven "Nani" is. Every time an image such as "word," "serves," and "wrinkles" recurs, it is used in a slightly different way, resonating more each time because of its previous usage. *(Note: "Nani" is actually a variation of the traditional sestina form.)*

Precomposing Step 2: *Finding a Poem*

After students have examined the structure of the poems, they should have a better sense of how they might structure their own poem. At this point, it is time to focus on images and incidents. One good way to develop images for the poem is for students to go back through their quickwrites and try to "find a poem" that they may have already created (the purpose of the preceding assignments). Many pieces of prose are actually full of images and structures that can be identified and culled to form poems.

A. As homework or in class, ask students to reread all of their quickwrites.

- Students underline the strong images, ones that are emotionally charged or most essential to the feeling of the passages; lines; repetitions; and parallel structures that are already in their work. Since they will not be able to use all of their writing, they need to select the part they like best. One of their previous quickwrites may have everything they want, or a particularly strong image in a particular quickwrite may lead them to isolate that image and work on it alone.

  An example of this process is as follows:

  > I remember my grandfather standing beside the redwood gate of our house dressed in a <u>clean dark blue workman's shirt with long sleeves and pants to match.</u> His <u>shiny bald head is fringed with hair like Friar Tuck in Robin Hood.</u> The <u>skin of his jaw is loose and hangs in folds around his mouth.</u> He has <u>gaps between his teeth</u> and, with the <u>gold caps</u> on some of them, his <u>mouth seems like an unsmiling jack-o'-lantern.</u> He spoke gruffly to me and always seemed distant.

- Or, students who have come up with entirely new subjects or who want to begin fresh may list or cluster possible images as prewriting for their poems. These students might use stimulus words (e.g., "photos," "stories told about or by him/her," "shared or observed experiences," and "feelings") to generate their prewriting.

B. Ask students to share their most vibrant images with their groups, giving and receiving suggestions for language to vivify their poems.

C. Students begin to organize their images into poems. After choosing the best images, words, etc., students should begin to "play" or experiment with the presenting and ordering of them. Several possibilities exist:

- Use the lines for emphasis—separate the images so that you have one strong image per line.
- Place the words you think are most important at the ends of the lines.
- Set off powerful single words on lines by themselves.
- Indent lines that give details for other lines.
- Make a "picture" on the page for the eye to follow as it reads the meaning.
- Use whatever parallel constructions you find in your quickwrite in parallel forms in your poems or create your own parallels. For instance, start all your lines with prepositions, *-ing* words, infinitives ("to work" or "to swim"), or subordinate conjunctions *(when, if, as, et al.)*

WRITING

Students create a draft to share. Usually, they will need three or more drafts to arrive at a first draft they wish to share. Since they are working in a condensed form, the poem, encourage multiple drafts whether or not each draft is shared. "Playing" with images, words, and form is an essential part of what poets do.

Hand students copies of pages 366 and 367, How to Refine a Poem, to use to guide them through drafts of the poem both before and after sharing.

To familiarize them with using the sheet, have them practice applying it to the early and later rough drafts on the next page, which were taken from the preceding quickwrite models. Ask them what could be improved in the early drafts. What has been improved? Where could further revision help? What is still missing?

Teacher's Model Rough Draft

Grandfather
Even now oceans divide us
Taken from you at six months
Never to be held again.

I know you only through stories
Of fox farming and Michigan
And your doughboy photograph to Grandma
A silly boy staring handsome for your girl
With my own deep-set eyes, your legacy.

A blue suited workman with Friar Tuck fringed hair
Standing by our redwood gate
Speaking gruffly to me
I did not hear you laugh.

SHARING

Students share their first drafts with a response partner. Hand out the Sharing Poems Sheet on page 367 and go over the directions with the class.

REVISING

Revising Step 1: *Writing a Revision Plan*

A. Writers now write a Revision Plan stating what they will do to revise. This could be written at the end of the response partner's sheet or on a separate piece of paper.

- It is not sufficient for the writer to say simply, "I will revise according to my response partner's comments." Writers must state specifically what they are going to do to revise—which comments or questions they feel are valid or which suggestions they like.
- If they do not wish to change anything in light of response partner comments, they need to state why they are choosing not to use any of the comments they are given.
- It is possible that the partner did not give quality responses. *(This Revision Plan gives the teacher insight into how partners are working together and serves as a check on affective as well as academic interactions that are occurring.)* If the writer has not received appropriate feedback, writers should state their lack of quality information and go on to state what they will do to revise anyway, since the process itself usually leads the writer to discover something that could be improved in his or her writing.

B. Instruct students to hand in the Revision Statement with the rough draft. They will receive points for each part at the end of the process.

Step 2: Revising *According to the Revision Plan*

The writer revises according to his Revision Plan, looking one last time at his sheet for refining a poem before considering himself finished.

Teacher's Model Second Draft

Grandfather
Those first six months you warmed me
Cuddling me before mother took me
An ocean away

Where you were only a story
Of fox farming through wild, white Michigan winters
And a postcard photo of a doughboy
Staring handsome from a French battlefield
For your girl Tilly
Staring with my own deep-set eyes

On those few visits, I picture you
A worn, blue clothed workman with Friar Tuck fringed hair
Bent over beside our redwood gate
Gruff speaking and aloof
You never warmed me again.

 ## EDITING

Students give their poems to at least two other students in the class to check spelling. Punctuation, if used, should be consistent or purposeful. Editors should also check for effective punctuation.

 ## EVALUATION

All poems are "published" by display on the board or in a book for all students to see.

Points are given for each part of the process:

- Three quickwrites: Assignment 1, Assignment 2, Assignment 3; quickwrites should be marked for images, etc., or a new cluster/list is included
- Rough drafts
- Response Partner's Sheet (points to the writer for including this in the process; points to the response partner for actually doing it)
- Revision statement
- Revision drafts (if there are any)
- Final published poem

Sharing Poems

Writer: _____   Reader: _____

Directions:

Writer reads the poem aloud first. The Response Partner reads it aloud for a second reading. The Response Partner fills out this form, talking through it with the writer.

(Check with your writer. If he/she agrees, you may comment on the following directly on a copy of the poem. If he/she does not want you to write on the poem itself, or if your comments are too lengthy to fit, write on this paper.)

1. The part(s) I like best in your poem is/are
   (Underline and comment or recopy the lines here and comment.)

2. Some words I would use to describe the heart and spirit of this character are

3. The images/narrative fragments that led to my conclusion above are
   (Use arrows on the poem to indicate which parts, or recopy the words and phrases here.)

4. The strongest words/images in this poem are
   (Circle on the poem itself, or recopy the words/images here.)

5. One thing/some things I do not understand in your poem is/are
   (Put a question mark beside these on the draft and explain here.)

6. One thing/some things that confuse/s me about your form is/are
   (Put a question mark beside these on the draft, and explain on the draft or response form.)

How to Refine a Poem

1. Write the first draft just to **get the ideas down on paper.** Do not worry about precise wording. Go for the ideas. Or work to capture the inspiration if you are feeling moved to write.

2. Look back on the poem. Will the reader be able to see the person and to experience the same picture or action that you do?

   - Are you **showing** or telling? Are you giving readers vivid images that they can see or are you telling them? ("He was old and sick" is telling; "bent and frail like a hollow reed, he coughed and hobbled forward" is showing.) Change as much telling to showing as you can.

   - Are you using **specific nouns?** Instead of saying the character is wearing a hat, give a specific type of hat, *a battered Stetson, a velvety fedora, a brand new baseball cap, a moth-eaten sailor's cap*—each presents a completely different picture.

   - Are your verbs pulling their weight? Are they showing the true action? Did the character merely walk, or did he *shuffle, hobble, stride, race?* Avoid lazy verbs like *went,* verbs that really do not do anything.

3. **Look over your poem as if you were an outsider** who did not understand the content. Are the details you are using necessary or confusing? Are they inside jokes or ideas that do not really convey the picture you want to share? Do you need more details?

4. How does your poem **sound?**

   - Do the words themselves seem to echo your meaning? Do you have soft words for soft meanings, harsh ones for harsher meanings?

   - Do some words alliterate, a sound device based on beginning sounds of words that are alike, such as the "sheen and shimmer of silk and sequins"?

   - Do you use onomatopoeia effectively? For example, a word like *whisper* contains the sound of a whisper, just as *buzz* contains the sound of the bee.

5. How does your poem **look** on this page? Some suggestions for form include:

   - Are the lines used for emphasis? Are images separate so that you have one strong image per line?

   - Have you placed the words you think are most important at the ends of the lines or have you organized them in some way?

   - Have you possibly set off powerful single words on lines by themselves to add impact?

   - Have you indented lines that give details for other lines?

   - Did you possibly make a "picture" on the page for the eye to follow as it reads the meaning?

- Have you used parallel constructions or parallel forms in your poem? For instance, did you start all your lines with prepositions, *-ing* words, infinitives, or subordinate conjunctions?
- Are the lines arranged in the best order? Would another arrangement be more dramatic?
- What punctuation and capitalization do you need?

6. Does your **title** work for the poem?

   - Does it draw a reader into the poem?
   - Does it give an insight into the poem?
   - Does it create irony or set a tone in some other way?

7. Does the poem do what you want it to do or has it taken on a new and perhaps even more interesting meaning? Do you want to add anything or delete anything to make the poem more powerful?

"It's much better to celebrate and acknowledge one's culture than to censor and ignore. One's culture is part of the seasons of America. They make America blossom. It is truest democracy, giving to future generations its most important gift via language through literature and poetry. Literature is the tree through which we pass on the most important fruits of culture, nourish the soul, and give it sustenance to dream of a world more humane and loving."

Jimmy Santiago Baca
Author of *Working in the Dark* and *Martin and Meditations on the South Valley*

Featured Literature

"XX" from Martin & Meditations on the South Valley
by Jimmy Santiago Baca

"Warning"
by Jenny Joseph

Grade Level
For Middle School and High School

Thinking Level
Synthesis

Writing Domains
Sensory/Descriptive
Imaginative/Narrative

Materials Needed
• Colored pens
• Highlighters

Suggested Supplementary Readings:
• "History" by Gary Soto
• "miss rosie" by Lucille Clifton
• "My Father's Song" by Simon J. Ortiz
• "My Grandmother Would Rock and Quietly Hum" by Leonard Adame
• "Nani" by Alberto Rios
• "Old Folks" by Maya Angelou
• *When I Am Old, I Shall Wear Purple* edited by Sandra Martz

The Poet Within Us

by Esther Severy

Overview

Students will analyze Jimmy Santiago Baca's poem "XX" in *Martin & Meditations on the South Valley*. Students will closely examine an older person they have encountered in their lives, observe this person's needs, desires and heritage, much as Mr. Baca has done, and then write a poem about this person. Students will use alliteration in their poem.

Objectives

THINKING SKILLS

Students will:

- *recall* details of an older person they have met;
- *comprehend* this person's needs and desires;
- *synthesize* poetic techniques.

WRITING SKILLS

Students will:

- *create* vivid alliteration in an original freeverse poem;
- *develop* appropriate poetic form and organization;
- *identify* and use sensory details.

The Process

 **PREWRITING**

Prewriting Step 1: *Clustering*

Have students cluster the word *old*. A sample cluster may look like this:

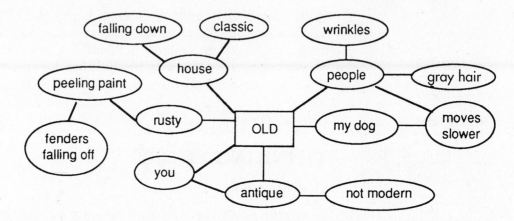

As students begin to focus on those things that are old, point out how the adjectives they choose create a visual image of these old things. These images will be critical to their writing later. This activity also creates the beginnings of a word bank that all students may use later in the lesson.

Now that the students have begun to focus on old, have them get more specific. Have students cluster "old people." A sample cluster may look like this:

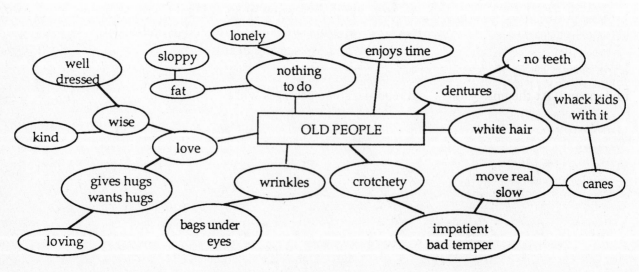

Students now have a descriptive word bank they may use in their writing. Hopefully, they have some fairly clear images of older people. Perhaps the extended cluster has also evoked the image of a particular person in a student's life.

Prewriting Step 2: *Reading*

Tell students that they will be reading a poem about an observation of older men in a neighborhood. The author is from New Mexico, but what he observes about his elderly neighbors is universal. New Mexico becomes our neighborhood. The old men become people we know. Have the students read "XX" from Jimmy Santiago Baca's *Martin and Meditations on the South Valley* silently.

Prewriting Step 3: *Reading in Cooperative Groups*

Using a technique for reading poetry created by Sheridan Blau, Director of the South Coast Writing Project at the University of California, Santa Barbara, read the poem by Jimmy Santiago Baca, "XX," together in cooperative groups. Give each student a different colored pencil or crayon. As you read the poem aloud to the class, each student reads along with you silently and underlines those passages not understood. You, as the reader and teacher, say nothing, except for reading the poem while the students underline those words and passages they do not understand.

At the end of the first reading, have the students exchange colored pencils so that each student now has a different colored pencil. You read the poem a second time as the students follow along, underlining, again, those passages they don't understand.

If the passage they didn't understand in the first reading is still misunderstood in the second reading, they will have two colors under that particular passage. Some passages during this second reading will become clear and, therefore, have only one color under them. Other passages may become unclear during this second reading and have only the second color under it.

Have students exchange colored pencils a third time. Read the poem a third time with the same directions: students underlining those passages they do not understand. At the end of this third reading, some passages will have one color under them, some two, and some three.

XX
Jimmy Santiago Baca

Tengo mucho gusto respeto pa'
los viejos de mi barrio,
They hobble out a creaking door
top hoe and rake their garden plot.
They've survived kill-dem-meskin-days,
retained their humor for a good joke,
and slowly wean themselves
from this life,
and prepare for the next—
 They pull their rosaries out
 and put away their pictures
 of women in bathing suits
they sign their names to church
donor journals,
tear up old phone numbers
of old girlfriends in their wallets,
 strip off the paper
 from their Army suits in closets,
 and no longer stop at Manuel's cantina
 for a drink.
On a stump in their yard,
during the afternoon siesta, they wait
for La Muerte to arrive,
in black cape, red feathered headdress,
red lava face glowing,
jeweled in turquoise and obsidian
from neck to wrists,
black diamond glittering navel,
feet of eagle claws, legs staunch
and furred as a jaguar's,
her voice a blue dark winter dawn,
that slowly numbs them,
until they leave wrinkled bodies of flowers
withering on the stump.

These are the viejos
who endured poverty,
and learned to do
with what they had,
and made a rich dream land
out of a small garden plot.

Ask students, in groups, to discuss those sections of the poem that had two and three colors under them. Ask the groups to discuss the possible answers to the questions that these sections of the poem raise. One recorded peer group discussion went like this:

- "I don't really know what he means when he says, 'Tengo mucho respeto pa' los viejos de mi barrio.' That sounds weird to me. What does it mean? I couldn't figure it out."
- "Dummy. It means that he respects the old people in his neighborhood."
- "Wait a minute, Lupe. She doesn't know Spanish. How's she supposed to know that?"
- "Well, she should have. It's right there, man. The ol' man [Mr. Baca, the author] has a thing for the old ones. Shouldn't anyone know that, man? Even if they don't know the language?"

Prewriting Step 4: *Class Discussion*

After the groups have discussed the poem and tried to answer each other's questions, open the discussion to the whole class, asking whether there was anything that any one group still could not figure out about the poem. As groups ask their questions, ask other groups whether they have possible answers. Some groups will come to some plausible answers; some questions will remain unanswered, and that's okay. Allow the discussion to proceed as students help one another analyze the poem. Some common questions the students ask and potential answers are as follows:

Questions	Potential Answers
1. What does "tengo mucho respeto pa' los viejos de mi barrio" mean?	**1.** I have a lot of respect for the old men in my neighborhood.
2. I don't understand what "kill-dem-meskin-days" means?	**2.** People in the U.S. used to really hate "foreigners," & in some parts of the country, especially Mexicans. There used to be much more prejudice against Mexicans than there is today. These "viejos" survived that era.

Prewriting Step 5: *Viejos Response Chart*

To focus on the personas in the poem, explain that there are two personalities in Baca's poem, the old men, (the *viejos*), and the younger person talking about the *viejos*. In order to focus on the *viejos* more closely, have students fill in the following response chart. Explain that for the *viejo* personality, they should use the exact words of the poem. The responses they give should express the students' feelings, questions, memories, favorite parts or words, places that cause irritations or distress, images—anything that causes some kind of reaction to the text.

Viejos Character and Actions	My Response
"They top hoe and rake their garden plot . . ."	At first I didn't get this. But now I do. Even though they don't walk very fast, they still go out and work in the gardens.
". . . tear up old phone numbers of old girlfriends in their wallets."	It's about time they stop having girlfriends. I respect them for that. They are finally changing their ways.

Prewriting Step 6: *Studying the Poem*

Have students answer the questions on the Response Chart, About the Poem, on page 375. The purpose of this exercise is to get them to focus on the images of the poem, to think about what the author is saying, and to internalize and make more personal Mr. Baca's poem.

Give students an opportunity to share their Response Charts, questions and answers, and pictures in their cooperative groups and with the class.

Prewriting Step 7: *Learning Alliteration*

Explain to the class that some authors use a poetic device called alliteration to lend power to what they have to say. Alliteration is the repetition of beginning sounds of words in a line of poetry or in a sentence of prose. Mr. Baca doesn't use this technique much, but many other authors do. Have students read "My Heritage," which is a teacher-written model for the prompt in this lesson, or "Warning" by Jenny Joseph.

Give students highlighters and have them highlight the words that have repetitious sounds in the poem "My Heritage," and/or "Warning." Have students highlight any alliteration they find in "XX." Have the students reread the poems aloud so that they can better identify the sounds of the words. Alliteration usually is the beginning sounds of words, but can include melodious words that "hang together" because of their sounds.

Give the students time to discuss the poems.

About the Poem

We have just read the poem "XX" by Jimmy Santiago Baca. In your own words, answer the following questions:

1. What is the dramatic setting, the dramatic situation?

2. What literally is going on?

3. What do you see in the poem? *(imagery)*

4. Who is the intended audience? How do you know?

5. What is the tone of the poem? How do you know?

6. What conclusions can you draw about the speaker of the poem?

7. What do you think the message of the poem is?

8. Draw four things you see in this poem. Put the line you are illustrating under each picture you draw.

(Developed by Glenn Patchell, UCI Writing Project Teacher/Consultant, Irvine High School)

My Heritage

I did not understand, and I'm afraid.

Your suffocating, pillowy bosom,
Large, deep-pored nose and toothless grin
With its ready smile
Was enough to make me cringe,
All the while trying to hide it as I
Suffered your loving embrace.

I did not understand, and I'm afraid, Momo.

The musty smell as we opened your door,
The darkness that dwelt within,
The ever-present, closed-in feeling of waiting
Despite the little ray of sunshine
Where you sat with open arms,
What were you waiting for?

I do not understand,
And there's a trembling deep within my soul.

The fading tintype is the me I used to be.
You could have been French, maybe Basque.
Is that the why of the wild, wiry white hair?
The bulbous nose pock-marked with pores
The sagging, suffocating breasts?
The ready smile in the face of life's tragedies?

I'm beginning to understand, and I am terrified.

Will I be like you, Momo? Smiling and giving,
Waiting for love and loved-ones, for death
In my musty, dark and quiet world,
All alone, waiting and smiling my toothless smile
Hoping my laughter will help others
Deal with what life licenses?

Momo, I didn't understand.

E. Severy

Warning
by Jenny Joseph

When I am an old woman I shall wear purple
With a red hat which doesn't go, and doesn't suit me.
And I shall spend my pension on brandy and summer gloves
And satin sandals, and say we've no money for butter.
I shall sit down on the pavement when I am tired
And gobble up samples in shops and press alarm bells
And run my stick along the public railings
And make up for the sobriety of my youth.
I shall go out in my slippers in the rain
And pick the flowers in other people's gardens
And learn to spit.

You can wear terrible shirts and grow more fat
And eat three pounds of sausages at a go
Or only bread and pickle for a week
And hoard pens and pencils and beer mats and things in boxes.

But now we must have clothes that keep us dry
And pay our rent and not swear in the street
And set good example for the children.
We must have friends to dinner and read the papers.
But maybe I ought to practice a little now?
So people who know me are not too shocked and surprised
When suddenly I am old, and start to wear purple.

Prewriting Step 8: *Alliteration Chart*

Transfer these alliterative words to the following chart:

Descriptive word	Adj.	Adj.	Adj.	Participle	Additional
Example: white hair	wiry	wild			

Then, have students add some alliterative words of their own to describe white hair such as *wispy* (adj.) and *waving* (participle).

Ask students to find additional examples of alliteration in the poems and add them to the chart.

Students may want to write sentences using the alliterative words and illustrate them. This encourages risk-taking with language, and students like it.

PROMPT

Give students a copy of the prompt and the rubric. Read both prompt and rubric together. (The rubric is found under Evaluation in this lesson.)

We have read Jimmy Santiago Baca's poem "XX" from his book *Martin and Meditations on the South Valley*. We have discussed old people in general and in particular. Now, think about an older person in your life whom you have either seen, lived with, been associated with, or merely observed. Write a freeverse poem about this person, much as Mr. Baca has done, using descriptive and vivid language to show this person as you see him or her. Use the poetic technique of alliteration as you see it fitting into your poem. Make sure that your freeverse poem has only the essential words in it that lend clarity and power, and that all nonessential words have been deleted. Make sure that your poem makes sense and that it portrays your feelings about this older person.

PRECOMPOSING

Precomposing Step 1: *Guided Imagery*

To focus on a particular older person, have students participate in a guided imagery exercise:

Tell the students that you want them to get as comfortable as they can without falling asleep. You may want to play some soft music for background. Some students will put their heads on their desks, some may stretch their legs out and slouch down in their chairs. Some may want to find a comfortable place on the floor. As they find this spot of comfort, tell them to close their eyes and make sure that the position they are in is comfortable and relaxing. Continue to play the music as the class settles in. Read the following slowly. Give plenty of quiet time between sentences. Add any details that come to your own mind if you wish. The purpose is to allow students to tap a memory bank and, in a relaxed state, really take a close look at some older person in their lives.

Tell them:

> You are now relaxing and are beginning to feel very comfortable. Your eyes are closed and your arms are relaxed. Your toes are relaxed. Your legs don't want to move. You feel your neck drooping down and your brow loosening.

As you begin to feel relaxed and comfortable, the image of some older person floats through your mind. Maybe this older person is someone you know. Perhaps it is someone close to you. Perhaps it is someone you have seen in your neighborhood. Fix the image of this person in your mind.

Observe this older person closely as you relax. Look closely at how this older person is dressed. What he or she looks like. The color of his hair, her skin. Listen to what he says. Look closely at how she moves. How does he feel about things right now? How can you tell? What does she do or say to show these feelings? What's his background? Where do you think she's from? What tells you this? Look closely at this older person. How do you feel about him or her? Look again. Listen again. Fix this person in your mind. Take in all that you can about him. Look.

When you are ready to take one last look, do so, and when you are ready, I want you to open your eyes. When you open your eyes, I want you to cluster or list as many things as you can about this older person you have so closely observed just now. Take one last look, then open your eyes, and list or cluster as much as you can.

Give the students time to come back from this guided imagery as they need. Some may be slower than others, but that's okay. They need the time to fix this person clearly in their minds.

After students have made their lists or clusters from this guided imagery, have them write for ten minutes about this person.

Have them share what they wrote with a partner. If you wish, have some of these quickwrites shared aloud with the whole class.

Precomposing Step 2: *Alliteration Chart*

Have students refer back to their clusters and lists of old people and, using the frame for alliteration chart from Prewriting Step 8, list all the words they can that describe *their* own older person, filling in the columns with words that repeat similar sounds.

Precomposing Step 3: *Cooperative Groups*

Have students take their clusters or the ten-minute quickwrites about the older person in their lives. Using their charts and the word banks of descriptive words, have them, in groups, find where they can add descriptions to make the image of this person more powerful.

Precomposing Step 4: *The "Power" Word*

Demonstrate how an author uses the last word in each line as a "power" word. Articles and conjunctions normally do not end a line of poetry. Students will be able to use this technique of having the last word in a line of poetry in order to make their poems say more.

Example from "My Heritage" (editing to highlight power words):

suffocating, pillowy bosom

Your ~~large and squishy bosom and the~~

Large, deep-pored nose and your toothless grin

With its ready smile

Was enough to made me *cringe*.

Have students highlight the last word in each line of both poems and then, in groups, discuss how they think these words show power. Have each group choose two or three lines from one poem and share with the class what they said about them. What do these words say? How does the placement of the last word affect what the author says to them? How would it be if the author had left a conjunction or an article at the end of the line instead? What does this placement of words on a line of poetry do to the images the poem evokes?

 # WRITING

Have students draft their poems about an older person they have either observed from the neighborhood or one with whom they have had personal contact. Some students may want to use their quickwrites to find words and images for their poems. Some students may want to work from their lists or clusters to draft their poems. Whatever method works for each student is acceptable.

 # SHARING AND REVISING

Sharing and Revising Step 1: *Responding to Partner's Poem*

In pairs, have students complete an "About the Poem" exercise for their partner's poem. (See Prewriting Step 6, *Studying the Poem*.)

Student pairs share their findings, giving each author ideas about where to add, change, and/or delete in order to make the poem say what he or she wants it to say.

In pairs, allow the students to share their images, questions, and comments about each other's poetry. If an image that the author tried to achieve is not noticed, he or she can then ask for suggestions from a partner.

Sharing and Revising Step 2: *Revising the Poem*

Give students time to make revisions.

Sharing and Revising Step 3: *Cooperative Group Response*

Have students in cooperative groups of four or five, each read their poem aloud to the group three times slowly. The group members' responsibility is to listen carefully and complete the following checklist. After the third reading, and the checklist is completed, each member of the group shares his or her findings with the author. These checklists then become the author's to help in the next revision of the poem. This process is repeated until all members of the group have received verbal feedback and checklists from the members of the group.

Poem Response Sheet

Title of the Poem _____

Name of the Author _____

My Name _____ Date _____

This is what I liked about the poem and why:

This is the feeling this poem gave to me:

The older person in this poem seems to be:

This is what I wondered about this poem:

I found this part confusing because:

These are the parts where I found alliteration and they made me feel/think:

Here are the power words I found at the ends of lines:

Here are lines I believe need power endings:

The formatting is/is not effective because:

 **REVISION**

Students may revise their poems from the group's comments.

EDITING

Collect the poems by cooperative group and then pass the entire group's poetry to another, round-robin fashion, until each group has a set of poetry that all belongs to some other group. In these cooperative groups, ask students to use sticky notes to write the misspelled words they find and post their findings to the poem. Ask them, then, to look at all the capital letters at the beginning of the sentences and the punctuation in each sentence and make any corrections on sticky notes, posting these suggestions on the poem. Each member of the group reads each poem given to the group. At the end of the reading, if the groups have four students each, each poem will have been read four times. Return the poems to the authors for editing.

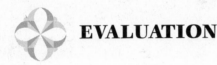

EVALUATION

Rubric

6   This is a well-constructed poem:

- It shows how the author feels about an older person he or she has encountered or been close to.

- It uses descriptive language and creates vivid images for the reader.

- It uses only essential words as well as powerful words to end the lines and to enhance the meaning and beauty of this poem.

- It uses alliteration effectively.

- It follows the conventions of written English.

5   This, too, is a well-constructed poem that shows how the author feels about an older person he or she has encountered or been close to, but not to the polished extent of the 6 poem.

- The language is descriptive and creates vivid images for the reader.

- The use of only essential words, as well as powerful words to end the lines, enhances the meaning and beauty of this poem.

- This poem almost mirrors the 6 poem but is not as polished.

- It uses alliteration effectively.

- This poem follows the conventions of written English with only occasional errors, if any.

4 This poem creates images for the reader but is not as strong as the 5 poem:

- Some nonessential words may remain and begin to detract from the overall message.

- There may be a few words at the ends of the lines that are not the power words discussed during the lesson.

- Alliteration may be missing.

- There may be a few errors in the conventions of written English, but they do not detract from the overall meaning of the poem.

3 The images in this poem are not very clear, but are there.

- There may be many nonessential words.

- There may not be any alliteration.

- The mechanical errors and the formatting of the poem begin to interfere with the message of the poem.

2 This poem is lacking in imagery.

- The image of the older person is either missing or very difficult to see.

- Mechanical errors and nonessential words interfere with the meaning of the poem.

- There is no alliteration.

1 The author did not write a poem.

Have students examine the rubric. Ask them to write an evaluation of their own poem, giving reasons why they believe they deserve a particular score. They can support their reasons by telling what they did in order to reach this final product, describing what their thoughts were at the beginning of this assignment, what they changed, and what they left alone and why. They can also describe how they now feel about this older person they have described and tell whether that feeling is the same or different from when they started, and why they think this is so.

Sample Student Evaluations

For example, one eighth-grade student wrote this self-evaluation for her poem "Myrtle":

Self-Evaluation

The poem I wrote, "Myrtle," was fun to write. I wrote it based on the best and most interesting things about her. It was fun using alliteration. I think it was a good piece, about equal to all of the other stuff I wrote. It was fun cause I had a wide variety of choices and not just a specific thing like, "My Name." I used alliteration and that was different and I like it. I got most of my ideas just by thinking about her and reading what others wrote. I also think I improved since the beginning of the year. On a scale of 1 to 10, I give it a 9.9.

Myrtle

Myrtle had wacky wild
Kool-Aid style hair
that wiggled wonderfully in the whistling wind
Her skin was crinkly
Like my flannel's arms
When I tie it around my waist
Her hands were soft wrinkled and floppy
She had soft pale blue eyes
Myrtle always had a good sense of humor
She had a friendly funky freestyle personality
She used to listen to KROQ with me
Myrtle loved all 8 of her cats
She was sweet and understanding
Even a week before she died
Myrtle was a cool Grandma.

Another eighth-grade student wrote this self-evaluation for her poem,
"My Old Lady":

Self-Evaluation

I decided to write about my grandma because she's one of the people who I love
in this world. I got some of my ideas by trying to remember the good and bad
times we shared together. I think that this poem is the best poem I've done in
this class. I think this way because I show my feelings towards this person and
since I know her real good I had the chance to describe her the way she seems
to me. I copied the part of La Muerte from Mr. Baca's poem because it helped
me to make my poem different from what I have done in the past.

I really liked this poem because I'm proud to have had the chance to write about
my grandma Lupe. I think I did a good job writing this poem about an old person.

My Old Lady

My viejita is my grandma Lupe
She has hair that looks like salt and pepper
She has beautiful eyes
That shimmer and shine like sunshine
She treats plants as if they were fragile
Like a diamond ring
Whenever I visit her
She hugs me tight and tears roll down her cheek
She was born in Jalisco, Mexico
Where the mariachis sing and play
To beautiful Mexican tunes
She has wrinkles on her face

Which make me think
Of flowers when they are dying
And getting wrinkled and old
She sits outside and watches
The sunset go down
And smiles to herself
I always wonder what is on her mind?
Could it be La Muerte she sits
And waits for
Or is it God who she wishes to see?
My pretty old Lady
Who once was young like me
Just sits patiently without any fear
As time goes by
Just waiting for La Muerte to arrive

PUBLICATION

If you have space in your room, post the finished products. Give the students an opportunity to illustrate these poems with pictures if they have them. Or, allow them to search through magazines for pictures that seem appropriate.

If you have a bulletin board or window where student writing might be displayed, post poetry so that the student body can read it.

Send samples to publications that publish student work. Publish poetry in the school's literary anthology. Write to the local newspaper and ask that some of these samples be printed both as student accomplishment and to convey student awareness of others in the community.

EXTENSION ACTIVITIES

1. Have students read and analyze other poems or short stories about older people (see Supplementary Readings) and then compare them to what they have learned from Jimmy Santiago Baca and the writing of their own poetry.

2. Have students write a letter to this older person in their lives, telling how they feel about him or her and why. If they think their poem is appropriate, have them include a copy for this person.

3. Have students write an article for the school newspaper, describing the assignment they did and telling other students about the changes in attitude about, tolerance of, or acceptance of older people that occurred because of this experience.

Reflecting About Our Many Selves

by Julie Simpson

Overview

This lesson takes students through a variety of writing types and facilitates a range of thinking skills to lead them into and through the poem "We Are Many" by the Chilean poet Pablo Neruda. Students move from a concrete, experiential autobiographical incident into a close reading of text to extract ideas for interpretation and reflection.

Objectives

THINKING SKILLS

**Students will run the gamut of thinking skills in this lesson.
They will:**

- *recall* an incident from their past;
- *relate* the incident and *sequence* events;
- *predict* what they will read from knowledge of language;
- *draw* inferences from details;
- *test* inferences against a text;
- *make connections* between ideas;
- *analyze* parts to see how they relate to the whole;
- *synthesize* those parts into an interpretation;
- *apply* that interpretation to their own lives and life in general.

WRITING SKILLS

Students will practice:

- *using* concrete detail;
- *sequencing/organizing* those details;
- *selecting* details to create interest;
- *narrating* a story;
- *predicting* outcomes or consequences;
- *supporting* those inferences with textual details;
- *asserting* a strong interpretation;
- *supporting* that interpretation with interrelated ideas;
- *reflecting* on meaning beyond the confines of the text.

The Process

 **PREWRITING**

Prewriting Step 1: *Class Discussion/Sentence Starters*

To prepare students to read the poem, explain that we are going to look at ourselves to see what kinds of things we do that give us pride or disappoint us in
ourselves. You might begin with "sentence starters." Used in a whole class discussion, they help students think about how they respond to what they do.

A Look at Myself

- I felt a sense of accomplishment when I *(made the cheerleading squad, lost 30 lbs, pressed 200 lbs, learned how to ski, kept the house for a week while my mom was gone, asked so-and-so for a date, went to school for a whole month without cutting)* .

- It was an accomplishment for me because _____ .

- I am proud that I *(keep my promises, don't watch TV, think before I act, don't drive when I've been drinking, don't swear around old people)*

- This makes me proud because _____ .

- I was disappointed in myself when I *(cheated on a test and said my friend volunteered her answers so she would be punished too, didn't concentrate hard enough in the game to play my position well, couldn't think of anything to con- tribute to the list of accomplishments)*

- This disappointed me because _____ .

- I disappoint myself whenever I *(procrastinate, don't study even though I want good grades, lose my temper, worry too much, disappoint others.)* .

- Looking over these things I have written, I can conclude about myself that I _____

- This makes me feel _____ .

A word of warning: *This discussion could raise some sensitive areas for students, so always keep the discussion atmosphere positive and receptive, lest anyone feel confessional or accused.*

Prewriting Step 2: *Autobiographical Incident*

• Writing Exercise

Ask students to write about a time when they did something that didn't live up to their own image of who they are or want to be. It could be something they often do that bothers them, or just a one-time occurrence, but it must be something they can remember as a distinct incident. (Incident = an event that takes place over a short period of time and has a clear beginning, middle, and end.) Let them know that they will be sharing this incident with the rest of the class. They may use invented character names and sign the paper with a four-digit number to maintain anonymity.

(Note: Depending on time and your overall goals for this lesson, you may assign this autobiographical incident as a full writing exercise or as an in-class timed exercise. Detailed suggestions for working with it are included in the Extension Activities.)

• Peer Group Sharing

Have students share their incidents in peer groups of their own choosing. After the groups have listened to one another, ask them to list the similarities and differences in the kinds of things they do that fall short of how they want to see themselves.

• Metaphoric Thinking

While students are still in their groups, ask them to think of the situation they portrayed in terms of a metaphor:

> If your incident were an animal or a plant, what and where would it be? If it were a stereotype, what would it be? Practice by modeling several possibilities as a whole class *(For example, someone who is self-conscious = an insect squirming under a microscope; one who overindulges = an embezzler, an addict; a cheater = thief, packrat, sponge.)*

Explain that metaphoric thinking will prepare them for reading poetry as well as begin to prepare them for the abstractions necessary for reflection. Allow the groups to work together to bounce ideas off one another and to share their metaphors.

Prewriting Step 3: *Speculation*

• Class Discussion

Inform your students that the next thing they are going to do is read a poem. But before you hand it out, you want them to see what they can figure out about it from thinking about the title. *(Note: For suggestions about using this as a full writing exercise in Speculation, see the Extension Activities.)* Ask them what they have to do to be able to make a *prediction*.

- Begin with the known and make guesses or speculations from there about the unknown.
- Write the title "We Are Many" on the board and ask the class to figure out what they know about these words. Suggest that they begin by sticking to the *facts*.
- Discuss a variety of possibilities for the meaning of *many*.

- **Clustering the Title**

As you discuss what they know, listen and record their guesses and speculations and also the *questions* that arise—the things they wonder about concerning the title.

A class cluster might look like this:

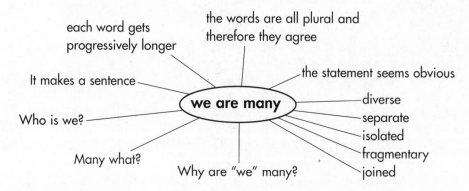

- **Clustering the Subject**

When a mass of knowledge and wonderings has been listed, ask the class to speculate about what the subject of the poem could be. Record these speculations too:

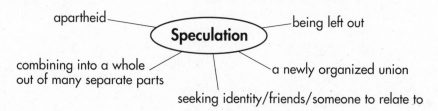

Prewriting Step 4: *Reading/Precomposing*

The following close reading activities prepare students to interpret the poem and get them ready for later reflection.

- **Active Reading**

Read the poem aloud, asking students to underline any words or phrases that stand out for them. They don't have to have a particular reason why their selection strikes them.

We Are Many
by Pablo Neruda *(Translated by Alastair Reid)*

Of the many men who I am, who we are,
I can't find a single one;
they disappear among my clothes,
they have left for another city.

When everything seems to be set
to show me off as intelligent,
the fool I always keep hidden
takes over all that I say.

At other times, I'm asleep
among distinguished people,
and when I look for my brave self,
a coward unknown to me
rushes to cover my skeleton
with a thousand fine excuses.

When a decent house catches fire,
instead of the fireman I summon,
an arsonist bursts on the scene,
and that's me. What can I do?
What can I do to distinguish myself?
How can I pull myself together?

All the books I read
are full of dazzling heroes,
always sure of themselves.
I die with envy of them:
and in films full of wind and bullets,
I goggle at the cowboys,
I even admire the horses.

But when I call for a hero,
out comes my lazy old self;
so I never know who I am,
nor how many I am or will be.
I'd love to be able to touch a bell
and summon the real me,
because if I really need myself,
I mustn't disappear.

While I am writing, I am far away;
and when I come back, I've gone.

I would like to know if others
go through the same things that I do,
have as many selves as I have,
and see themselves similarly;
and when I have exhausted this problem,
I am going to study so hard
that when I explain myself,
I will be talking geography.

• **Second Reading**

Then, ask students to read the poem aloud to themselves and, in a different color of ink, underline any new words or phrases that stand out. They may re-notice something that struck them the first time, or notice something new.

Prewriting Step 5: *Reflective Response Quickwrite*

To allow them to relate their understanding of the poem to their own lives, ask students to quickwrite for five minutes about their many selves, responding to Neruda's question, "I would like to know if others go through the same things that I do."

One student, Julie Ahn, wrote:

> My many selves —there sure are lots of them. But not as many as there used to be. I don't feel as split anymore as I did a couple of years ago
>
> But there isn't exactly unity, either. Like someone (Jennifer) said yesterday—well, no, it isn't like that. So . . . let's shift here. Jennifer was talking about feeling success and how hard it is for some of us to see success in a failure. It's a bit the same with me. Not a failure—just not ever quite good enough. I don't know as if I have ever done something and thought "that's just exactly the way I wanted it to be." I wonder if anyone has . . . Even when I get praised (on those *rare* occasions) I'm not fully satisfied.
>
> But at least I'm not as hung up as the guy in this poem is. He can't see himself anywhere. He's not like me, I think. He thinks he's something he isn't. He needs to take a closer look at himself and see who he is, not live in some dream of who he wants to be.
>
> Since I'm not so split any more, maybe that means that I accept myself more.

When the students finish this writing, let them know that although they're going to set this quickwrite aside while they examine the poem, they will return to it later to reflect upon it.

Prewriting Step 6: *Questioning*

Explain that in beginning to form an interpretation about a piece of literature, it is as important to recognize what *we don't* know about the piece as it is to recognize what we *do know*. In fact, as we come to understand what we don't know, we can often more easily become aware of what we do know.

In the margins of the poem, students should now, as they reread the poem, jot down any questions they have about anything that is not completely clear. They might ask about meaning, about what is going on, about who the speaker is, about things they wonder about, about things they don't understand, etc. They should work to word their questions as specifically as possible.

- **Class Discussion**

Ask students to volunteer their questions in class discussion. As they ask a question, record it on the board, focusing on the questions, not on answers.

—If a question is too vague *(What does this mean? What does "talking geography" have to do with the rest of the poem?),* help the student rephrase it more directly by asking what she really wants to know about "this." *(Why does he only care about a "decent" house? How is he "talking geography" when explaining himself?)*

—You will note that some questions are ones of fact that can be irrefutably answered by defining a term or pointing to a comment in the poem: *What is an arsonist?*

—Other questions are ones of interpretation, which call for an understanding of what the writer might mean by particular parts. To answer them, we would use what we know about the poem: *How can he disappear among his clothes? Why does he say "we" when talking about himself? Why does he say "even" about admiring horses: is he ashamed? What does he mean by "exhausted": is he worn out from his search, or has he worn out all possible answers to himself?*

—Still other questions are outside the realm of the literature and are what we might call personal. We may like to know the answer to them, but there is no information in the poem to help us out. We could perhaps speculate about their possibilities or we could reflect about the meaning of the poem in terms of our own lives. *What heroes does he read about? Who are the distinguished people among whom he sleeps? Why do we have heroes? Why isn't the "real" we good enough?*

- **Examining Questions**

After the board is full of questions, explain about the different kinds of questions that have been asked and have the class answer the factual ones for one another. Explain that all of the questions are important to our understanding of the whole poem.

- **Looking for Connections**

Point to some questions and ask what other questions need to be answered in order to answer those. Help the class to look for connections.

> *They may see, for example, that there are lots of opposites. They may be able to see that if they could answer the connections between these opposites, they might be able to understand how the speaker can be "gone" when he comes "back" from writing.*

In the process of examining questions and finding connections, you will have led an intensive discussion exploring the poem—without ever having had to "give answers." By this point, students will invariably have arrived at their own theories of what Neruda means. To many, even his comment about "talking geography" will no longer be utterly confusing.

- **Imagery Review**

Review the images Neruda uses to portray his speaker's dilemma. Examples:

    —*Himself disappearing in his clothes.*

    —*Becoming an arsonist instead of a fireman.*

In a quickwrite for five to ten minutes, ask students to write about what they now know about the meaning of Neruda's poem. In the process of considering what they do know, they should also consider what they still want to know, and see if they can figure out what they would have to do to come to that understanding. Ask them to work to come up with their own interpretation of why the speaker in the poem will be "talking geography" when he finally understands himself enough to explain himself.

Have students share their writings in their peer groups. Direct them to listen for what ideas are similar and which are different. Have groups report on their findings to the class. Certainly the class will notice that although the interpretations they come up with on their own are similar to one another, each is worded personally and is much more interesting than the stock "Neruda uses the phrase 'talking geography' for many reasons." *(For a full Interpretation prompt, see the Extension Activities.)*

Prewriting Step 7: *Imaging and Responding*

- **Questioning the Reflective Response Quickwrite**

Ask students to return to their Reflective Response quickwrites about their many selves. They should look at them in terms of asking another kind of question. This time they will ask: what question about myself is my writing dealing with? Have them write that question at the end of their quickwrite. The question Julie Ahn wrote was:

> Why is there such a gap between who I want to be and who I am? Do I have lots of different selves, or are they each a side of the same self? Why do I let other people influence me to be something I don't really want to be?

- **Imaging**

Then, ask them to create their own image that best portrays the question their quickwrite deals with. Ask students to sketch the image and then write about it for three minutes. The goal is to think abstractly about an idea.

Here is Julie's image and quickwrite:

> This gap is like a wound. It festers and hurts and is red. I don't know where I got it or how to get rid of it. Salves and creams don't help. I can cover it up with a bandage, but it doesn't go away. I guess the problem is more internal than external. I guess the problem is that I'm not clean on the inside—the wound won't heal unless I decide to work from the inside out rather than from the outside in.

• Peer Partners

Next, have each student find a partner with whom to exchange papers. The goal here will be to extend ideas further. Tell them:

—*Read your partner's "many selves" quickwrite, look at the image, and read the quickwrite about that image.*

—*What can you add to his or her ideas? Write your continuing thoughts about his/her ideas for three minutes.*

Anita responded to Julie:

> So the salves and creams are just the temporary help that might ease the pain—or problem—for a little while, but, in the end, don't actually help the wound improve. They're like makeup, or a wall. They hide the problem, so on the outside, they are helpful. Forces aren't able to come in and cure. Nobody can ever know you're hurting if you always wear a bandage. Bandages are a cover-up that hide the wound or problem so nobody can see it. "Out of sight, out of mind." The bandages and ointments don't help because more is needed. A lot of times, all that is needed is the desire to heal.

Prewriting Step 8: *Moving Toward Reflection*

• Responding to Partner's Response

When the original writers get their papers back, they write for three more minutes in response to their partner's response, still working in the abstract.

Here's Julie:

> Yes. That's the trick—establishing that desire—truly. So many times we <u>say</u> we want to fix ourselves. But it's only words. Something still prevents us from following through with our goals. Maybe it's more like we think we "should" rather than truly believing we want to.

• Comparing Ideas Through a Venn Diagram

At this point, the students have hopefully done some reflecting on themselves and their many lives. Now, ask them to compare what they've written about themselves to how they interpreted Neruda's poem. They should create a Venn diagram to analyze how their own ideas are similar to or different from their idea of Neruda's thinking.

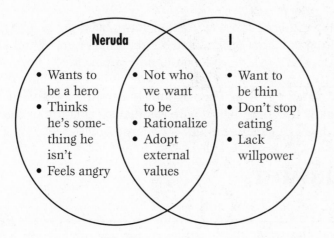

Neruda
- Wants to be a hero
- Thinks he's something he isn't
- Feels angry

- Not who we want to be
- Rationalize
- Adopt external values

I
- Want to be thin
- Don't stop eating
- Lack willpower

- **Coming Up with a Conclusion**

Ask them to write a conclusion about this comparison. Julie's conclusion was:

> I think Neruda doesn't really want to change himself. He seems bogged down in the confusion of not being who he wants to be. The prospect of acceptance doesn't occur to him.

- **Summing Up**

Now it's time to begin putting all their ideas together. Ask that writers look at everything they have written thus far and consider:

> *What do all of these ideas tell you about people in general and how they consist of "many selves"? Why do you suppose people behave this way? Explore whatever ideas come to you as you write. In this type of writing, you do not want to make judgments about how we should be. Rather, your goal is to think about how we are.*

- **Quickwrite**

Ask the class to reflect on this in a five-minute quickwrite. Julie says:

> We are never going to be content with ourselves until we accept us for who we are. As long as we try to be a "dazzling hero"— someone else's image of a great guy—we'll never be happy. Those are the bandages we may apply that do a quick cover up, but don't really cure. Security has to come from the inside and move out. That feeling of being OK with ourselves may involve change, it may not. Maybe I could learn to like myself as a hefty person. It would be better, I suppose than hating myself for it.

To ensure the connection to Neruda, ask if students have tied their ideas back to his. If not, ask them to compare their latest thinking to his. If it's different, what is the difference? If it's similar, how is it similar?

Explain that the thinking and writing they have just done is *reflective,* an informal essay writing in which writers explore their experiences and knowledge about the world, and work to understand how people are. It begins with personal experiences and ends with talking about universal human traits, about what the experience may symbolize. Although carefully organized, it doesn't necessarily follow the strict logical patterns that speculation or interpretation follow. A finished essay may read like a polished quickwrite.

PROMPT

We have been talking and thinking about how and why people have many selves. You have explored your own experience and studied the experience of the poet Pablo Neruda. You have also created images to help look at what these experiences might symbolize in the world. Combine all of these experiences and your thinking into a reflective essay about people and their many selves.

Remember, reflective writing often begins with a specific event and then moves into an abstract reflection about it. One in-depth personal experience or several brief, yet specific, experiences may stimulate the writer to reflect. Reflective writing is personal, often informal, exploratory, perhaps inconclusive. In it you ponder, wonder, and move toward a fresh awareness of a truth about human nature.

Write an essay in which you reflect on people and their many selves. You may want to begin by writing about your own experiences—either literally or in terms of the image you created to represent them—and how they compare to the ideas Neruda wrote about in his poem "We Are Many." Then, explore whatever ideas occur to you as you think about what these kinds of experiences tell us about how people behave and what we can learn about human nature in general from them as examples. Be sure to show the process of your wonderings and ponderings.

WRITING

Instruct the class that they are going to take their various quickwrites and develop them into a draft of a reflective essay, using the above prompt.

Writing Step 1: *Studying Models*

To familiarize students with the open style of reflective writing, have them examine a variety of models. Ask the students to read "Friends Forever," "Lockwood Street," and "A Perfect Self," which are appended to this lesson.

(Note: These are student essays. If you prefer to use professional writers, Joan Didion's "On Self-Respect," Virginia Woolf's "The Death of a Moth," and much from Robert Fulghum and Andy Rooney are good sources.)

You might have the following kind of class discussion:

- Why don't these essays sound like typical essays? Be sure that the class notices the following kinds of characteristics that will be expected in their papers:
  —Even though their style is relaxed, the writers use conventional English.
  —The papers are interesting. They are personal.
  —The writers seem to be thinking as they write.
  —They don't start with a thesis. They move from the concrete to the abstract rather than the abstract to the concrete.
  —You can hear the writer's thinking as it progresses.
  —The incident that incites reflection is clear and interesting, but it doesn't dominate the paper.

Ask students to notice how each reflective essay follows a different pattern of thinking. Look at the various patterns:

Darlene (Friends Forever)	**Chat** (Lockwood Street)	**D. C.** (A Perfect Day)
My brief incident —year book	My extended incident —out for a walk	Situation Watching a movie idol
		How perfect life would be if only
Antigone's situation		
		Flaws in me
My parallel		
		How I'm like Neruda
Wondering about people Me as a representative person	What I realized How life is	
		How society creates our images of perfection
		Why we are self-critical
Reflecting on being honest	End of incident to clinch	How we want to be admired
		Is that good or bad?

Writing Step 2: *Planning a Draft*

Ask students to look through all of their writing thus far and decide what kind of a pattern they would like to use. Then, they should decide what of all their information they want to use and what they want to discard, and figure out a plan for their essay. Have them record this plan in a graph + words in the same way we charted the model papers.

Writing Step 3: *Writing a Draft*

Once their plan is in place, students will be able to complete a draft at home.

 # SHARING

Sharing Step 1: *Scoring Guide*

Pass out drafts of the Scoring Guide for Reflective Essay (see the Evaluation section). Identify any unfamiliar terms and look at the characteristics of a strong 6 in contrast to a 3 or a 4.

Sharing Step 2: *Model Student Paper*

Before students share their drafts, you may want to have them discuss a student model in light of the scoring guide. The complete text of Julie Ahn's reflective essay is appended to this lesson.

Sharing Step 3: *Response Partners*

Ask writers to share drafts with their original dialogue partners. These partners respond to the following:

- Does the paper move from the concrete to the abstract?
- Is the concrete clearly and interestingly shown, without dominating the paper?
- Can you see or hear the writer wondering, pondering, showing the process of turning over an idea?
- Is the thinking process clearly reflective—not just jumping to generalizations or moralizing?

 # REVISING

With input from the scoring guides and their response partners, writers should revise their first drafts.

EDITING

To facilitate a polished, edited final draft, divide students into triads to edit for the conventions of standard written English. Label each group **A** or **B**.

Remind students of the basic mechanics and usage elements that they are expected to have mastered. Triads will be in charge of the following:

Triad A	**Triad B**
• Correct subject-verb agreement	• Clear pronoun references
• Correct use of apostrophes	• Complete sentences
• Correct capitalization	• Correct spelling

Each paper must pass through both groups within a class period, so no one can take more than about five to seven minutes on a paper. It is best to organize this session like a Read-Around, timing each reading so that no one takes too much time. (See the Glossary for a description of the Read-Around.)

Editors make corrections directly on the draft in various colors of ink. Each editor should sign off the paper when he or she finishes with it. If an editor cannot finish within the time period, he can sign the paper off as far as he got.

Writers get their edited papers back at the end of the period to take home to rewrite into a final version.

EVALUATION

Score the papers against the Reflective Scoring Guide.

EXTENSION ACTIVITIES

Following are suggestions for writing prompts that extend the prewriting and precomposing activities begun in the lesson:

1. Autobiographical Incident

- Tell students that for homework you want them to write a story of a time they were disappointed in themselves or felt they had failed. Their challenge is to show the incident so clearly that the reader knows they were disappointed without ever having to say so.

Summary of Rhetorical Effectiveness Scoring Guide for Reflective Essay

Score Points / Criteria	6	5	4	3	2	1

Occasion for Reflection — Something seen, read, overheard, experienced as stimulus for reflection	Occasion presented richly, memorable by using such strategies as
	• extended concrete details
	• sensory language
	• narrative techniques
	  –pacing
	  –dialogue
	  –action
	  –quotations
	May be single incident or web of related experiences or observations
		Occasion presented with extended concrete detail
		
		Lacks only vividness and impact of the 6
			Specific occasion presented
			
			May be lacking the details of a 5
			or
			Presented in such rich detail, that it dominates the reflection
				Occasion
				• may be brief
				  or
				• may dominate
				
				Often will be examples to fit preconceived generalization
					Occasion
					• may be brief
					  or
					• may dominate
					
					May be
					• no occasion
					  or
					• all occasion
						May be
						• lacking
						• brief
						• devoid of specificity

Abstract Reflection	• Thoughtful, convincing, insightful, exploratory • Firmly grounded in occasion Expresses integral connection between experience & idea Explores an abstraction in both personal and general reflections.	Extended, thoughtful, Not as insightful as 6 Firmly grounded in occasion Clear connection between experience and idea Both personal and general reflections	Less well grounded in occasion May be intelligent but predictable, commonplace Connection between experience and idea may seem tangential Personal reflection may dominate but will be some general reflection	May be extended but with little grounding in occasion May seem • additive • meandering • obvious • superficial • moralizing Reflections may be entirely personal or totally general	May be • additive • meandering • unfocused • brief • superficial • moralizing Reflections may be entirely personal or totally general	No reflection May be brief, superficial • attempts at definition • statements of opinion rather than reflection

Writing Situation

All of us, at one time or another, have felt disappointed in ourselves—not necessarily because we have done anything wrong, not necessarily because something horrible has happened. Sometimes we find ourselves doing something that is quite the opposite of what we had hoped for ourselves. These small, personal disappointments can be harder to cope with than major traumas. Think of a time in your own life when your action did not match the expectation you had for yourself and you felt you let yourself down.

Directions for Writing

Write the story of an incident in which you felt disappointed in yourself. Include specific details that will help others see what happened, know what you had expected of yourself, see how that contrasted with your actions, and understand how you felt after the incident was over.

- Depending on the experience your class has had with writing autobiographical incidents, decide how much review of the traits you need to cover. You might just want to review characteristics in class discussion, or to chalk out or photocopy a possible frame for their paper. For example:

  - Set the stage: I always seem to ____ when I should ____ or ____ I want to be ____, but invariably I ____. I remember one time in particular.

  - Show the story of the incident to a reader who doesn't know you:
    Situation/setting
    Problem
    What I wanted to do
    What I did
    Thoughts, feelings, actions, dialogue that occurred

  - Keep the story moving by creating some sort of tension.

  - As you tell the story, choose words to create the feeling of the metaphor that symbolizes the incident.

  - Tie it together with the metaphor: It was as if that night I was a ____. or: I'm like a ____. I always ____.

- To help them get started in their writing, you might ask them to envision the incident as if they were a filmmaker. Ask them to close their eyes and try to see:

  — Where were you? What did it look like? What did it feel like? What did it sound like? How did you feel about where you were?

— Who was there with you? How did you feel about their being there? What did they say? What tone of voice did they say it in? What did you say?

— Run the movie in your head from the beginning of the incident. Stop somewhere in the action and begin writing from that point.

- Have students share their incidents in Read-Around groups.

- After selecting the top papers from the class, discuss what kinds of writing and thinking elements are involved in creating an interesting autobiographical incident. Hopefully, students will see that the writer's purpose is to tell a story and put the reader into the action. They should also see that the most interesting tales are narrow in focus, have no irrelevant details to sidetrack the reader, create tension so that the reader wants to learn of the outcome, use lots of relevant concrete details to put the reader into the action, and choose details that lead the reader into the symbolic significance.

2. Speculation

- Once the class has listed all the things it can think of about the title of the poem, give the following writing task:

    Write one to one and one-half pages in which you predict what a poem entitled "We Are Many" might be about. Base your predictions on what you can speculate from the title. Discuss several possible alternatives and focus on the one you believe is the most logical or feasible. Support your choice with logical reasons for your predictions and speculations.

- Ask students to share their predictions in peer groups. After listening to all papers, groups will discuss what they can tell about the features of speculative writing, answering the following questions:

— How is it different than writing an autobiographical incident? *(It's an essay, not a narrative; it doesn't tell a story; the concrete details are not about what happened.)*

— Are there any specific details? If so, what are they? *(They are the words in the title).*

— How is it organized? *(By ideas or by the words of the title rather than by chronology.)*

- Discuss the groups' findings with the class, noting traits of speculation on the board. Ask:

— Does the writer have to know all the answers to write a speculation? *(No—speculation is the writer's opinion of what might be plausible.)*

- When the poem has been read, questioned, and interpreted, remember to return to these speculations and ask students to reread them to see the connections between what they had speculated and what the poem actually held in store for them. *(Perhaps they had predicted an erroneous subject matter, but they may have sensed the same underlying conflict.)*

3. Interpretation

For an interpretive essay, you might want to use the following prompt:

Writing Situation

Our class has read and carefully analyzed Pablo Neruda's poem "We Are Many." Each of us has arrived at his or her own interpretation of what Neruda means by his image of geography in the last line.

Directions for Writing

Write an essay in which you analyze your theory of what Neruda means when he says, "that when I explain myself,/ I will be talking geography." Write your interpretation clearly enough to convince your reader that it is logical and based on a thoughtful reading and understanding of the poem. Be sure to use evidence from the text to support your theory.

Student Models

Our Unacceptable Selves

The speaker in Pablo Neruda's poem, "We Are Many" has trouble being the person he wants to be. He sees himself as an arsonist rather than a fireman, a fool instead of an intellect, a watcher of heroes who feels so far away from heroism that he envies even the horses the heroes ride. In his misery, he wants to know if he has company, "if others / go through the same things that I do." Well, I'm here to answer, "Yes!" I share his dilemma, in my own way, of course.

Neruda's speaker feels he is a failure. When he wants to be a good guy, he acts like a bad guy. As he says,

> When I call for a hero,
> out comes my lazy old self;
> so I never know who I am,
> nor how many I am or will be.
> I'd love to be able to touch a bell
> and summon the real me,
> because if I really need myself,
> I mustn't disappear.

He talks as if there is a "real" him lying underneath all this failure who disappears when it's called. But it seems to me he thinks he's something that in reality he isn't. If this "real" him never comes forth, maybe it isn't there at all. Maybe it's just an image that he's somehow got of how he "should" be. I think he needs to take a closer look at himself and see who he really is, not continue to live in some dream of who he wants to be. He needs to accept himself more than he does.

For me the situation seems more like a wound. There is often a gap between who I want to be and how I actually behave, and that gap is like a sore that festers and hurts. It's a wound that was created from the inside and has worked its way to the surface; my laziness or my lack of will power infect the sore and prevent it from healing. I may try applying salves or lotions to cure the wound, but they are usually only temporary healers. Unless I alter my attitude, change what is going on inside, all the external ointments can do is cover up how the sore looks to the rest of the world. It's still there. If I can't change the internal me, then the wound will always fester.

Unless I learn to accept that internal me, and take me for better or worse. Then the wound would go away, and it wouldn't hurt anymore.

Take for instance, the issue of weight. Every night when I go to bed, I promise myself that tomorrow I will stick to a diet. I will eat healthily, drink lots of water, avoid all bread and cheese—two of my major downfalls. And I may do pretty well all day—until about 4:00 PM. I get hungry. I eat an apple, but it doesn't fill me right away. So I automatically get out a slice of bread. Before I even realize what I've done, it has been devoured. Because I've eaten it too fast, it hasn't filled me, so I look for something more—some chips, perhaps. Like Neruda's speaker who says his coward "rushes to cover [his] skeleton/with a thousand fine excuses," I begin rationalizing. Well, since I've already blown it today, I might as well make those chips into nachos or something. And suddenly there's another day of eating down the drain.

What I know I need to do is accept that fact that I must really not want the ideal body. If I really wanted to lose weight, I would be more conscious of what went into my mouth, I would not have unhealthy foods around me, and I would develop the will to "just say no." But so far, I haven't done any of those things. So the 'fat wound' still festers.

It's silly, really. Why do people like me and Neruda's character create such agonies for our lives? Life would be so much more comfortable if we could just be whatever self emerged at the moment. We need to follow Emerson's advice and take ourselves for who we are. We don't all look like the ads on television. We're not all models, or heroes. Those are external values that we adopt for whatever reasons. Unless they stem from inside, they will always create wounds. Maybe we can't all be externally perfect, but we can all be nice, warm, loving human beings. Most of us already are. But we don't really value our internal qualities as much as our external ones. Oh, sure, we say we do. But niceness doesn't make us "distinguished." It doesn't "dazzle."

And for some reason or other, we'd rather be thin and dazzling than sturdy and comfortable. It's somehow safer to suffer (to think we're not good enough) than to run the risk of believing we're OK as we are.

Julie Ahn

Reflective Writing Models

Friends Forever?

A chaotic madhouse. These three words describe perfectly what the last couple of days of seventh grade were like. Summer, with its glaring eye upon us each day now, seemed to throw a suffocating blanket of sweltering heat to make all the students restless.

I distinctly remember as school was nearing an end, everyone frantically rushing around trying to get all the signatures possible to fit in that little yearbook. A yearbook with no spaces left to write on was a sign of a "popular" person. And so, of course, in those last days of school, many kids found "long lost friends" or even friends they never knew they <u>had</u> shoving a yearbook and a pen in their faces, giving a sheepish smile, and saying, "Sign my yearbook, please?" And with all the frantic swapping and who knows how many pages signed, it became mechanical for everyone to just sign with "Friends forever," a phone number, and a first name.

Yet now, as I look back in my seventh grade yearbook, I'm amazed at how many friends turned out to be <u>frauds</u> when the going got tough. I discovered my "true" friends when in the eighth grade I got into a fight with a close friend. She had begun to feel the magnetic pull of popularity, and I resented it. We fought. Pretty soon practically the whole junior high was involved in the struggle, and I found that under the pressure, many of my "forever" friends couldn't even last a year! And <u>that</u> is how I discovered the friends who would stick by me, and their words, through thick and thin.

Antigone also loses a friend whose promises of love "forever" die quickly under pressure. When Antigone states, "I love no friend whose love is only words," she is referring to Ismene who only loves their brother Polynices with her mouth, and not with her actions. Ismene won't prove her love by helping her sister, Antigone, bury their brother, and yet she tries to share in the consequences <u>after</u> Antigone buries Polynices. Thus, she wants to become a friend again only when her conscience gets to her for her inaction.

I also found many friends returning after my fight with my friend was reconciled. Yet those friends had not been there when I really needed them, and that's part of friendship. And so, as Antigone said, "I love no friend whose love is only words."

But what prompts people to just <u>say</u> they will be our friends forever, even though they may not make an effort to actually <u>be</u> one? Is it because it's so easy to say without even thinking that our words may sometime soon be tested?

To me, saying I will always be a friend, or that I'll always be around in times of need, comes almost automatically. At the particular moment, I feel that I truly <u>will</u> be a friend forever. And yet sometimes it's also the easiest thing to say to a person because it's what she wants to hear. I don't like to let down the high hopes of a person depending on me. Maybe that's because I'm afraid the person will turn against me or reject me if I let her down, and so I say whatever will comfort her, without thinking of the future.

Many times, I don't even think about the little words such as "forever," even though the <u>other</u> person may notice that word the <u>most</u>. So should I pick my words more carefully? Maybe be more realistic? I suppose so.

Yet reality is hard to comprehend when it deals with the future. Who would want to read a letter signed, "Temporarily friends," or "Friends for now"? It's too pessimistic! But the optimism could result in hurt. I could be more choosy about words also, and just say "Friends." Then maybe I could take friends as they come, and not make any commitments that were not thoroughly thought out.

But which is better: forever or reality? We say we want to hear one, but then we don't like the emptiness of it. When we get an honest word, we don't want to hear it. I suppose it's our choice: to hear an honest feeling and not to get let down in the long run, or to listen to the things we want to hear, and eventually get hurt. It's not always easy, but I'm sure it's better to speak honestly and hear with open minds now rather than to get hurt in the long run.

Darlene Park

Lockwood Street

A glittering coat covered the roofs of every house on Lockwood Street. As the giant yellow furnace descended into the horizon, the wind blew its last shivering breaths, rocking the needles off the Christmas pines. Gentle flurries dropped gracefully onto the snow covered driveways. From each chimney, puffs of grey were released into the dry, cold air. Soon chains of smoke intertwined to surround the perfectly aligned houses, forming a barrier of warmth and comfort.

I eased the front door shut and trampled away from my meadow green house at the far end of Lockwood Street. Leaving the fusses and nags of home, I figured that a maturing eight-year-old deserved a little time alone to himself, and tonight was a positively perfect occasion to carry out my little quest for privacy.

A hush had settled over Lockwood. Lined with only a few antique sedans, the street was drowned in stillness, completely bare of life. I began to whistle, not to amuse myself as much as to break the screaming silence.

The sky had turned a deep scarlet. The emerging stars were now engulfed by scattered winter clouds. As I looked up, the silent snowfall persistently descended onto the ground below. It showed no trace of stopping, no sign of letting up.

I quietly whispered to myself, "Now this is what privacy should be like. I think. At least this is what BIG brother is always asking from Mom and Dad whenever I go into his room. Well, if he thinks he needs it so much, I think I'll want some of it, too."

Across the street, the Pine's home attracted my wandering eyes. The family had switched on a string of flashing lights which outlined the yellow brick house. Their white framed windows were decorated with gold banners expressing a "Merry Christmas" and a "Happy New Year." On the snow covered lawn, three grinning reindeer figures stood greeting any passers by. This scene seemed so undoubtedly perfect. In fact, too perfect.

A grin developed on my face as I bent over and scooped up a handful of crisp, white snow. Giving it the maximum squeeze between my ungloved hands, I transformed the loose pile of flurries into a compact ball of ice. Then I hurled the shiny sphere towards Mr. Pine's bedroom window. The snowball rocked the glass as it splattered into a dripping glop of ice.

A light flickered on inside the bedroom just as I scampered behind a nearby tree. Mr. Pine himself furiously thrust his window open. As he poked his head out into the winter air, his heavy breaths pumped clouds of steam. The middle-aged gentleman searched for his culprit with a sour expression. When he found no trace of anyone outside, he slowly and carefully eased the window shut.

"That was so fun! Come on laugh!" I urged myself but just couldn't find the humor in the silly incident. It just didn't have such a hilarious effect on me when no one was there to appreciate it.

I had begun my walk up Lockwood Street in search of "privacy." Now, the street lamp shone its dull light on my tightly bundled figure and cast a lonely silhouette against the narrow walk. As the silence again emerged, the privacy that I had set out to find was certainly not what I had expected it to be.

True, people need to set aside a portion of their time for themselves. It is during these rare moments that we are able to explore our best qualities whether they be kindness, generosity, or other traits. Privacy takes us away from the nagging mother, the obnoxious friend and the bullying big brother. It shuts out the outside world and gives us a chance to recollect our thoughts. But just as quickly, it takes us out of the reality where we can share these ideas with others.

Separation from others is quite healthy for everyone at times, but it can have a disturbing side effect. Some people carry their privacy over the limit to total isolation. They are completely blocked out of the real world and soon drift to a place where only they exist, like Lockwood Street. Gradually, their "privacy" turns into nothing more than loneliness.

As I pondered these thoughts, I asked myself, "What the heck am I doing here?"

I turned quickly and dashed homeward through the lazy darkness of Lockwood Street.

Chat Chuenrudeemol

A Perfect Self?

Sitting in the movie theatre I lose myself in a world of "anything is possible." Imagining myself as the gorgeous, popular, rich, intelligent teenager, life seems so perfect. Following her script with utmost precision the actress manages to draw me into her character and now I have ultimate control over my life. Within minutes I have solved my problems with family and friends, conquered lifelong fears, and obtained the affection of the most popular guy in the school. Then suddenly I come crashing back to reality as my friend next to me tugs at my shirt saying, "D.C.! C'mon, the movie's over! Let's go!"

As I leave the movie theatre still somewhat in a dream, I begin to think of how perfect life <u>could</u> be. If only ... if only .... Slowly, depressed envy creeps through my body and I feel myself noticing every minute things that could possibly be wrong with me. One of my pinkie fingers is crooked, I'm too short, I'm not smart enough, I always make a fool of myself when it most counts, I procrastinate constantly, and the list goes on!

Pablo Neruda captures my sentiments perfectly in his poem "We are Many" when he states, "I die with envy of them (the dazzling heroes)." Neruda realizes that he is a culmination of many different selves and yet he can't seem to find one self that he likes. Compared to all he admires, Neruda seems to be a fool, a coward, and arsonist, or just a lazy old person.

With all the pressures of society my mind is overflowing with stereotypes and images of the perfect teenager. And I wonder, why am <u>I</u> not even remotely close to my ideal image?

But what makes me think I'm not what I should be? Part of it perhaps is the unrealistic portrayals of T.V. characters as we notice that although the actors may have problems, they are solved within a 30 minute episode and the characters are most always at <u>least</u> half-decent <u>looking</u>. But T.V. programs don't incite me in any way to criticize myself, so why do I?

In several instances I have found myself self conscious about minuscule particularities that no one <u>else</u> seems to notice! Is it easier to criticize myself rather than others? On the contrary, I think it's easier to criticize others rather than myself. Which is why many of us pass judgments on people without seeing some similar faults in ourselves. So why <u>do</u> I have such a low-esteem of myself? Am I afraid that people won't accept the real me? Or am I scared that I <u>myself</u> can't accept the real me?

I think it is human nature to want to be accepted and acknowledged by others, and in <u>some manner</u> to be admired. Thus, we seem to take on a facade of selves in search of the "real" self. Or at least our own personal image of what the true self should be. So whenever a quality or characteristic appears in us that doesn't "fit in" with our unconsciously prepared "perfect" self, we perceive it as unwanted and vile. This self-criticism, is it beneficial or hurtful?

I suppose if it is carried too far it would most likely result in deep depression. Yet in a way, criticizing yourself brings with it incentive for improvement. If I am self-satisfied already I don't feel any need to try much harder, but faults in myself give me areas to work on and improve.

Thus, inevitably I will always admire what is better than me, but I must learn to accept the "good" in me while at the same time concentrating on improving the "bad." A balance? It does appear to be a constant struggle for balance.

D.C. Park

Short Story

Featured Literature

"A Whole Nation and a People"
by Harry Mark Petrakis

Grade Level
For Middle School
High School

Thinking Level
Application

Writing Domain
Imaginative/Narrative
Sensory/Descriptive

Materials Needed
No special materials
required.

**Suggested
Supplementary
Readings**
• "All the Years of Her
  Life" by Morley
  Callaghan
• "A Summer's Reading"
  by Bernard Malamud

Getting in Touch with Your Family's Roots

by Jerry Judd

Overview

After vocabulary development, reading, and discussion of the short story "A Whole Nation and a People" by Harry Mark Petrakis, students will write an autobiographical essay in which they recall an important incident or person in their life that marked a change in their thinking, family situation, personal life, physical condition, or their awareness or acknowledgment of their cultural heritage, background, or traditions.

Objectives

THINKING SKILLS

Students will:

- *read* and *analyze* "A Whole Nation and a People";
- *apply* the story to their own lives by recalling an incident from their past that marked an important change in their life;
- *evaluate* the significance of this incident;
- *compose* an autobiographical paper in which they show how they experienced an important change.

WRITING SKILLS

Students will:

- *write* an autobiographical incident in the imaginative/narrative domain;
- *employ* sensory/descriptive language and concrete details to vividly create the scene;
- *include* dialogue between characters;
- *develop* their incidents with a beginning, middle, and end;
- *follow* the conventions of standard written English, including the correct use of dialogue form.

The Process

 PREWRITING

Prewriting Step 1: *A Journey to My Family's Roots*

One of the techniques used in this lesson to help students organize their writing is a precomposing technique called mapping. The mapping activity encourages students to ask parents, grandparents, and other relatives questions about their family's background, traditions, and genealogical chronology. It also directs students to think about the importance and effect that their family has on their lives. To introduce students to this technique, I ask them to do the following as an initial prewriting activity:

> *I'd like you to plan a trip from California to destinations where you could get in touch with your cultural heritage, background, or family's roots. Draw a map, indicating your starting point and ending point and all the stops you will make in-between. Use words and visual images as you plot your destinations and the things you plan to do on the way.*

You might want to share the model of a student's map on the next page. After students complete the maps, allow time for them to share their maps in small groups. Ask them to put their maps in the center of the table and have the other students group around the maps. Then, have the students narrate their journeys as the other students listen and follow along. At the end, ask the listeners to verbalize one thing they liked about each journey/map.

Student Map

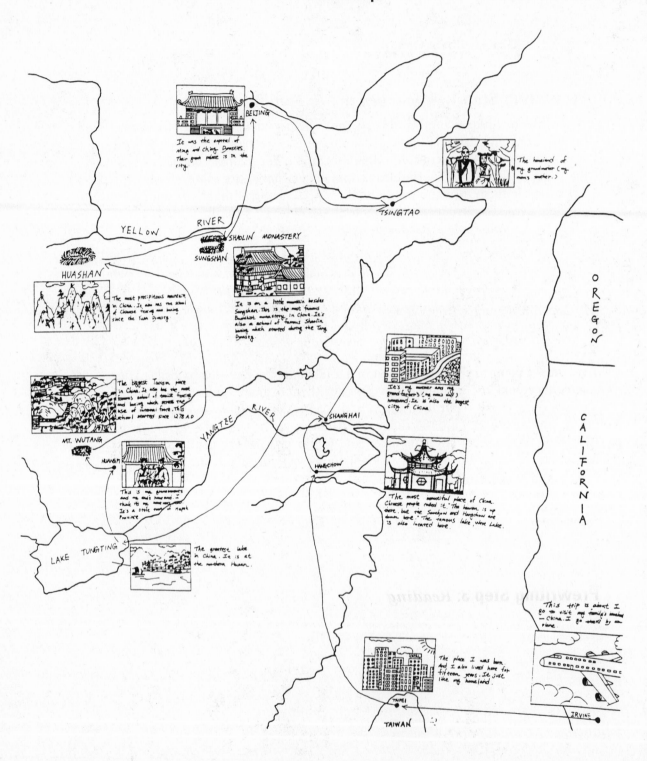

Prewriting Step 2: *Vocabulary Development*

The next step in this lesson, prior to the reading of the short story, is for students to develop the vocabulary base that is a prerequisite to their understanding of the story.

Have students follow these directions for the following vocabulary words:

"A Whole Nation and a People" Vocabulary List

1. motley	8. goaded	15. brusquely
2. ethnic	9. remorse	16. tendrils
3. forays	10. appalled	17. deftly
4. malevolence	11. impudent	18. baleful
5. sinewy	12. apprehensive	19. decrepit
6. epithets	13. grimaced	20. halcyon
7. mettle	14. abysmal	

1. Copy the sentence from the text in which the word appears. Underline the word. *(a)*

2. Give the context clue (part of the sentence) that hints at its meaning. *(b)*

3. Using a dictionary, copy the correct definition for the way the word is used in the story. *(c)*

4. Write an original sentence for at least ten words on the list. Try and put your own context clue in each sentence. *(d)*

Example of a model sentence:

    a. It was shortly before I became ill, spending a good portion of my time with a <u>motley</u> group of varied ethnic ancestry.

    b. group of varied ethnic ancestry

    c. composed of many different and unrelated elements or colors.

    d. A motley crowd of fans poured out of the sports arena.

Prewriting Step 3: *Reading*

Have students read the short story, "A Whole Nation and a People" appended to this lesson.

Prewriting Step 4: *Freewriting*

After students read the story, ask them to record their initial impression in a ten-minute freewrite like the one on the following page.

Getting in Touch with Your Family's Roots

✳ SHORT STORY

417

Example:

This made me think back to my 4th grade year in school. It was a long, difficult, unhappy year. The days went slow, the hours went slower, and the minutes seemed like days, that year in Park Elementary. I would go through so much struggling through every subject, trying my hardest to truly show my efforts. Then suddenly my discomfort began to bother my teacher.

Mr. Alessi was my fourth grade teacher. He was a man of great intelligence, wit, and charm. All his other students were earning A's and B's, but I was unfortunately struggling with a D! When it came to Mr Alessi's attention that I was not doing that well, he stopped being Mr. Perfect and showed me that he cared. That's when it all started.

The hot days, but cool rooms began to please me. Mr. Alessi and I would stay after to try to overcome my misunderstandings.

The days of course got longer because of after school studying. The more time it took, the more bored I got of school, but Mr Alessi would crack jokes and give me snacks and just try so hard to help me.

I guess it took about four to about six months of hard work— many jokes, a cookie every now and then, for me to really benefit from everyone else's understanding and acknowledgements.

When our after school studying was finally over, things that I never knew I began to know more than anyone. Math became a B average for me, Spelling became an A, Reading became an A and so on. I was doing great in school and the funny thing about it was I did not care how long the days were any longer. My stress level was perfect and nothing anyone could say brought me down.

When I had passed to fifth grade, my mother remarried and we moved here to Irvine.

Now that I am in the ninth grade, I can always remember fourth grade. When I look back five years, I'm proud of what I had achieved. Because of those long days and corny jokes, I had a better grasp of things I struggled with before.

I'm very glad I was a student of Mr. Alessi because, to this day, I know him as "the teacher who got me where I am today!"

Have students share their first impressions in small groups.

Prewriting Step 5: *Class Discussion*

Ask the class: *Although the narrator wants the respect of his companions, he feels that the attack on the grocer was a 'hollow victory.' Why?* As students volunteer their responses, write their ideas on the board.

Sample responses:

- He knew what he did was wrong.
- He is feeling guilt and remorse.
- He threw the plum because of peer pressure, not because he wanted to.
- He is feeling an internal conflict as he struggles with doing what the gang wanted him to and with what his parents would have wanted him to do.
- He realizes he isn't getting anything out of what he did.

Prewriting Step 6: *Journal Writing*

Give students the following prompt for a ten-minute journal-writing activity:

Can you identify with the character of Haralambos? If so, describe what personal feelings or incidents come to mind. If you can't identify with this character, explain why.

Sample response:

I can identify with Haralambos because this makes me think about how family relationships are very important. Since the past year, I've been treasuring my time with my family very much. I've been through many crises.

About a year and a half ago, my dad started feeling different towards my mom. He wasn't sure if he loved her anymore. So one night he took me into the room. He sat me down quietly and started to tell me how he was feeling.

Collect these journal entries and, if time permits, write a positive response to each student.

Prewriting Step 7: *Clustering*

Cluster the character and background of Barba Nikos as a class. A sample cluster might look like this:

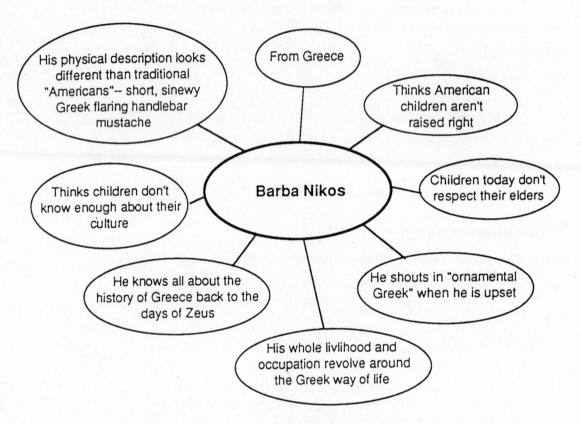

As you cluster, ask the students: *What roles does Greek culture play in Barba Nikos' life? How does the culture shape his values?*

 **PROMPT**

Read over the prompt with the students.

Changes

Writing Situation

Life is full of changes. Your perceptions of yourself and those around you change as you change schools, change teachers, change family situations, or undertake a new job or any number of life's challenges and endeavors. As a result, you and your perceptions change in light of these new circumstances. Often, you can trace back major changes in your life to a small incident, a specific occurrence that took place in a short time, or the influence a particular individual had on you.

Directions for Writing

Recall an incident in which you experienced an important change either in your perception of yourself or those around you. If possible, concentrate on an incident or person, as Petrakis does in "A Whole Nation and a People," which exerted influence over your awareness or acknowledgement of your cultural heritage, background, traditions, or family's roots. The change might involve geographical location, family situation, physical condition, or your personal life. Write about that incident, including details that will help your readers visualize the situation to understand who was involved, what happened, and why it caused an important change in your life. Utilize all the senses: sight, sound, touch, taste, and smell (or as many as possible) as you write about your autobiographical incident. Include dialogue between characters, and interior monologue, if appropriate.

 PRECOMPOSING

Precomposing Step 1: *Autobiographical Incident Writing*

Acquaint students with the characteristics and guidelines for Autobiographical Incident writing. Have students copy them down; then go over the following outline:

Autobiographical Incident Writing

I. Characteristics—about a specific occurrence

    A. Takes place within a discrete period of time (weeks, days, or hours).

    B. Includes sensory details

        1. Touch, taste, sound, smell, sight

    C. Shows clear sequence of the action

        1. Good chronology

    D. States or implies the significance of the event

    E. Evokes feelings in reader

II. Criteria

    A. Focuses on a single incident

    B. Uses specific language and description

        1. Visual details

        2. Includes action

    C. Uses dialogue with correct punctuation and paragraphing

    D. Uses interior monologue *(the inner thoughts of the characters are revealed to the reader)*

        1. Includes feelings and insights

    E. Should be well paced

    F. Should have a central moment (climax or high point of action)

    G. May have suspense, tension, or surprise

    H. May compare or contrast two other people or events

Precomposing Step 2: *Mapping*

Ask students to reread "A Whole Nation and a People" and to make a map of the events of the story. A student model is shown on the next page.

Map of "A Whole Nation and a People"

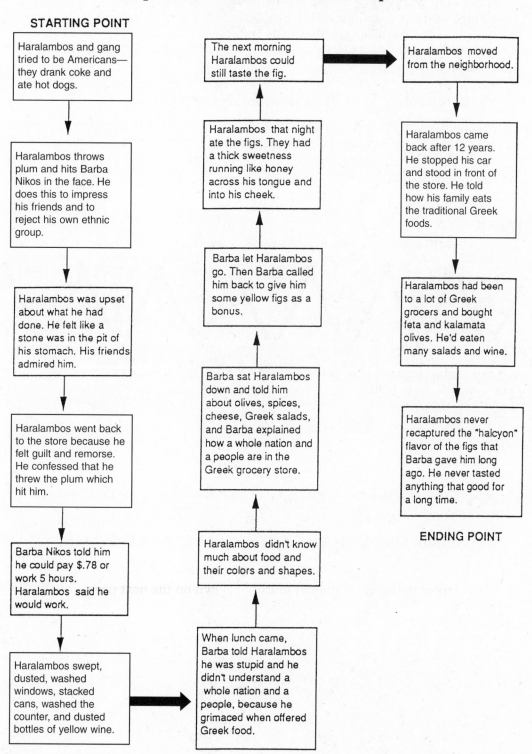

STARTING POINT

Haralambos and gang tried to be Americans—they drank coke and ate hot dogs.

Haralambos throws plum and hits Barba Nikos in the face. He does this to impress his friends and to reject his own ethnic group.

Haralambos was upset about what he had done. He felt like a stone was in the pit of his stomach. His friends admired him.

Haralambos went back to the store because he felt guilt and remorse. He confessed that he threw the plum which hit him.

Barba Nikos told him he could pay $.78 or work 5 hours. Haralambos said he would work.

Haralambos swept, dusted, washed windows, stacked cans, washed the counter, and dusted bottles of yellow wine.

When lunch came, Barba told Haralambos he was stupid and he didn't understand a whole nation and a people, because he grimaced when offered Greek food.

Haralambos didn't know much about food and their colors and shapes.

Barba sat Haralambos down and told him about olives, spices, cheese, Greek salads, and Barba explained how a whole nation and a people are in the Greek grocery store.

Barba let Haralambos go. Then Barba called him back to give him some yellow figs as a bonus.

Haralambos that night ate the figs. They had a thick sweetness running like honey across his tongue and into his cheek.

The next morning Haralambos could still taste the fig.

Haralambos moved from the neighborhood.

Haralambos came back after 12 years. He stopped his car and stood in front of the store. He told how his family eats the traditional Greek foods.

Haralambos had been to a lot of Greek grocers and bought feta and kalamata olives. He'd eaten many salads and wine.

Haralambos never recaptured the "halcyon" flavor of the figs that Barba gave him long ago. He never tasted anything that good for a long time.

ENDING POINT

Once students have completed their maps, ask them (working in pairs) to share their graphs and to star the key events that contribute to creating a change in the perceptions of Haralambos. Ask selected partners to volunteer their insights. If the scene in which Haralambos eats the figs is not discussed, bring this scene to the students' attention and ask them to talk about its significance.

Precomposing Step 3: *Triumphs & Lows Chart*

To help students discover a topic to write about, have them complete a chart of the triumphs and lows they have experienced in their lives. I have them list seven of each and depict each event with words and a visual image. An example might look like this:

Then, have students focus on one event and create a map for this incident. (*See next step.*)

Prrecomposing Step 4: *Autobiographical Incident Map*

Students should then create a map for their autobiographical incident. Have them begin in the center of their paper with the central incident. Then, have students both lead up to the incident and follow up the incident. A student map might look like the following:

MAP OF INCIDENT

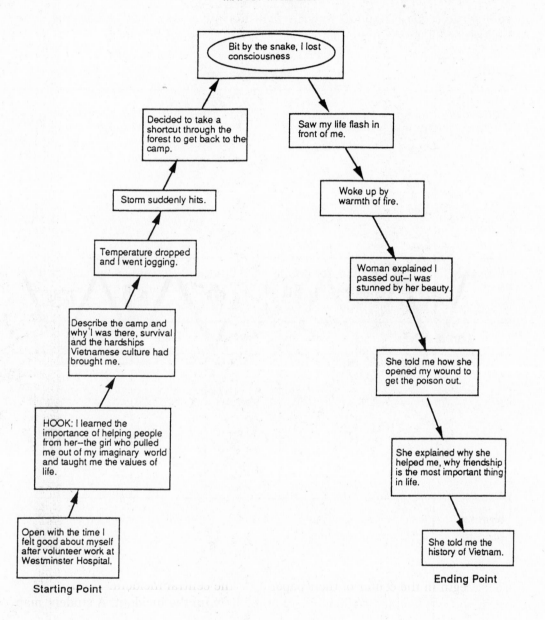

When students have finished their maps, pair them with a partner and have students each explain their graphic. This will enable them to orally rehearse their stories before they put them in writing. Have them also explain to their partners what things that went onto their maps were the most influential in changing their perceptions.

Precomposing Step 5: *Microtheme*

In order to prepare students to write their narratives, ask them to do some brainstorming by creating microtheme notes on the attached form:

Microtheme						
Introduction	Jot down two ideas for opening your paper that will engage your reader's attention: **Idea 1:** **Idea 2:**						
Main Body	List at least four key details you will include in your autobiographical incident and note words, phrases, and images you will use to make your story vivid.						
	Central Details	**Sight**	**Sound**	**Touch**	**Taste**	**Smell**	
	• • • •						
Ideas for Dialogue	Jot down at least four lines of dialogue you will incorporate into your autobiographical incident: " " " "						
Conclusion	Freewrite for five minutes to the following: *The message I would like my reader to take away regarding why this incident was significant to me is...*						

 **WRITING**

Before students begin, they may need to analyze a model to see how the narrative might be structured. Select one of the models appended to this essay and put it on the overhead. Use the Response Sheet below to critique the student model. Write students' comments onto your transparency to reinforce the criteria in the prompt. Then, have students write a first draft of their essays, aiming for fluency and using their microthemes and maps to guide them.

 SHARING

Sharing Step 1: *Responding to a Partner's Essay*

Pair students with a partner to fill out the Response Sheet below. *(Note: Students with a highly personal essay might fill out their own response sheet.)*

Autobiographical Incident Response Sheet			
Does the piece you're reading:	**Yes**	**No**	**Not Sure?**
1. Focus on a single incident?			
2. Have a good, clear sequence of action?			
3. State the significance of the event (or imply its significance)?			
4. Use visual details?			
Use sound details?			
Use smell details?			
Use taste details?			
Use touch details?			
5. Have a good pace?			
6. Have a high point of action or central moment?			
7. Use dialogue effectively?			
8. Begin a new paragraph for each speaker?			
9. Make you want to read on?			
10. Allow you to share the feelings of the writer?			
As you revise your autobiographical incident, you may want to think about ...			

Getting in Touch with Your Family's Roots

SHORT STORY

Sharing Step 2: *Learning Log Activity*

At this point in the writing process, it is appropriate to have students step back from their writing and make a Metacognitive Learning Log entry. Have students write learning log #1 about why No and Not Sure may have been checked on their response sheet. Have them write about how they need to revise their essay and what they need to do to clear up each No and Not Sure. What additional information is needed in the essay? What do you have to do to get this essay into final draft form?

Some student responses might look like this attached sample Learning Log activity:

Student Model (Learning Log)

No's and not sure's may have been marked because the person wasn't sure about something. The no that was marked on my essay response sheet was because the person who checked it was real unsure if I had a good, clear sequence of action. The not sure's that were marked were if I used taste details, if I had a point of action or a central moment because this person wasn't real sure if I described these things.

Something I can do to revise my essay and clear up the no's and not sure's is to add more details where needed in the essay. I can also try to make the sequence of action and make the central moment more clear. Last but not least, I can try to use more taste details.

The additional information I need to add in my essay is the scores of the tennis games. I also need to add information about what the food tasted like. I also need to start a new paragraph every time there is a new speaker. That is all the information I need to add to make my essay more clear.

The information I explained in the previous paragraph is the information I need to correct to get my essay into final draft form. I also need to edit and check for spelling to see if all of it is done right. Another thing I need to do is check the punctuation to see if it is all done the right way. These are the things I need to do to get my essay into final draft form.

 # REVISING

Before students begin to revise their paper, have them split up into peer response partner groups once more. Pass out the Revision Suggestion Sheet that follows and have the peer response partner write out short answers to the questions on the sheet.

When the students now sit down to revise their papers, they have Autobiographical Incident Response Sheets, a Learning Log, and a Revision Suggestion Sheet from which to work.

Revision Suggestion Sheet

1. What else might be said about the incident?

2. Where might more dialogue be useful?

3. How else could the writer convey his/her feelings about the incident?

4. What did you want to know more about?

5. What might be removed from the piece?

6. What could be rearranged for a more effective piece?

7. What else would you change?

8. The paper does/does not fulfill the requirements of the assignment because

9. What confuses or puzzles you?

10. Additional suggestions:

EDITING

During editing, some classes might need to review rules for punctuating dialogue. Partners can check standard rules of mechanics, usage, punctuation, sentence structure, and spelling.

EVALUATION

Use the outline that the students copied down during the prewriting stage as a scoring guide.

Student's Name: _____

Autobiographical Incident Writing

Guide	Evaluation				
	High				Low
	5	4	3	2	1
I. Characteristics—about a specific occurrence **A.** It takes place within a day or two or minutes or hours					
B. Clear sequence of action **1.** Good chronology					
C. Event's significance must be stated or implied					
D. Reader should share feelings of writer.					
II. Criteria **A.** Focuses on a single incident					
B. Uses specific language and description **1.** Visual details **2.** Sounds and smells **3.** Includes taste and feel details (when appropriate)					
C. Dialogue (correct punctuation)					
D. Use interior monologue **1.** The inner thoughts of the character are revealed **a.** Include feelings and insight					
E. Well-paced					
F. Should have a central moment (climax or high point of action)					
G. May have suspense, tension, or surprise					
H. Comparison or contrast to other people or events					
TOTALS	—	—	—	—	—
GRAND TOTALS				_____	

ADDITIONAL RESOURCES

Two other short stories that deal with autobiographical incidents that are successfully taught in conjunction with this writing assignment are "All the Years of Her Life" by Morley Callaghan and "A Summer's Reading" by Bernard Malamud.

Student Models

Here are models of two autobiographical incident essays written by high school students:

A Model to Follow

It was my first time on any camping trip with anyone other than my parents. All around me, kids were displaying their Polish scouting uniforms like mink coats on movie stars. I was the exception. Wherever I went, I would take a sweater or jacket and cover the bright red and white flag which gave away my nationality as if it was a blood stain on a silk blouse. When one of the superiors would tell me to take it off, I would blurt out a "I'm sick," or "I'm very cold." Anything, as long as I didn't have to wear that horrible flag.

Shame wasn't the issue here; it was fright, fright of being laughed at. Fright of being tagged as different from the rest, an alien. As a result, I stayed as far as possible from following the Polish culture. I lied about my place of birth, never spoke the other language in public, and never socialized with people who only spoke Polish.

Until this camp, I was full blooded American. Until one story, I had never cared for Poland. Then the leader began. She was very old and one of the first members of the organization: "We were the young ones. We could not fight for our country because of our age, but that wasn't going to stop us. Hitler's army came through two cities without any trouble and was now in the city where the scouting began." The speaker continued. "The bombs came down like rain. First a high pitched whistle that pierced the ear, then it gradually fell lower and lower until it was a very low hum which shivered the bones, then a moment of silence, and the earth shook. In the background, prayers could be heard thanking the Lord for a miss."

"The younger kids could not fight so they helped with the first aid. Instead of hiding and running for their lives, the first scouts stood their ground. While dodging bullets, they carried the wounded on stretchers made from two sticks and army coats taken from already dead soldiers. They had no guns but had a red and white flag along with a red cross on their jackets. They wore their flags because they wanted to, not because they had to. They walked into half-demolished buildings, pinched their noses to keep out the horrible pungent smell given off from the dead and decapitated bodies, picked up the half living bloodied soldiers, and again through the shower of bullets, raced them to the infirmary, which was no more than a building left standing after the raid from the bombs."

As I sat there by the fire, the thoughts of myself trying to hide my nationality began to disgust me. I was ashamed of being ashamed of my country.

"Many times we threw up as soon as we saw the victims of the war. The bodies automatically brought back memories of science lab and the dissection of fetal pigs that were still full of blood, and mangled arms and legs that stuck out from car doors and from under rubble which was at one time our school. We tried not to think about it and concentrated on the help. We had to rescue our people."

"I still remember the tear gas used by the Germans," someone spoke out. "It was like cutting onions but a thousand times stronger, and it wasn't only in the eyes, it was in the throat. Breathing was impossible. We vomited continuously and were blinded for hours but we kept on going and we were proud to wear the red and white colors that symbolized our country because we were born there, and no matter where we end up, Poland will always be our homeland."

As I heard these words, I felt my shame go away. All of a sudden, I felt I was scared of peoples' laughter more than the truth. All my shame went away and a feeling of pride came in. I was proud of my people no matter how many jokes I heard that degraded them.

Today, even though I might not show it, I pay attention to what happens in Poland and to Polish people. I display my colors proudly like a mink coat, and I don't care who makes jokes about it because I know the true reason why I am wearing the flag and uniform; to pay tribute to the thousands of kids and men who risked their lives and died to save their homeland from being controlled by others.

It only took one story to change the way I looked upon my country and my family's roots, because those first scouts were the ones who helped my grandfather when he served as a soldier and that is why he is still alive today.

Slavek Kasperowicz

Nation Essay

It was raining hard when I returned home from Westminster Hospital. After a productive day of volunteer work, I felt extremely good about myself. Nothing could beat that warm satisfaction you get after nursing hundreds of sick people from their illnesses. I learned this three years ago when I met her in Bataan Refuge Camp in the Philippines. This girl pulled me out from my imaginary world and taught me the values of life. I could never forget that day as long as I live.

It was a cold, gloomy day. Although it was merely noon, there was no light in the sky. It was covered by thick cumulus clouds which extended, like a blanket, from one end of the sky to the other. Now and then a cold, bitter wind would rise and fall behind the dark, solemn valley. The trees for the first time that spring were full of leaves. When the wind blew, soft, dreary murmurs could be heard as the leaves collided softly against each other. Once in a while a truck would roar down the curved, solemn street toward the supply house in the camp.

Like the thousands of others in the camp, I was waiting for permission to leave the Philippines and proceed to the United States. After living in Vietnam for twelve years, I had grown to become a very selfish person. Born in a harsh environment, I had learned to withdraw into my own world and take life one day at a time. I learned that in order to survive, I had to think of no one else but me. I had neither sympathy nor respect for Vietnamese culture, for it had brought me nothing but hardship.

The temperature began to drop as the day got older. Putting on my jeans and shirt, I began my regular jogging. As I ran, the night got even colder. Before I could realize it, a storm had hit the camp. Worried about my health, I stopped and took a short cut home. Instead of following the curved streets, I decided to cut across the forest which laid a few miles from my hut. About half way through the forest, I was out of breath. As I stopped to catch my breath, I became increasingly aware of the fact that there was no light in the forest. A little bit frightened, I walked on with caution. As the rain continued to fall, the ground under me began to disintegrate and slowly turned into thick chunks of mud. I continued to walk on when I suddenly let out a terrible cry. Something had just bitten my foot. I looked down quickly, but I couldn't see anything. It was too dark. The pain was unbearable. I tried to grab my left foot but I couldn't bend down. I tore apart my T-shirt quickly to stop the bleeding, but before I could tie it around my thigh, I suddenly felt a strange dizziness. I saw my life flash in front of me as I fell to the wet, muddy ground.

I woke up by the warmth of the fire.

"Help," I groaned as I tried to help myself up.

"Stay where you are," spoke a strange voice, as a soft, warm hand pushed me back to the dry leaves.

With my head slowly turned toward the direction of the sound, my heart almost stopped at the sight. There she knelt a few feet away from me near the warm fire. Her glistening hair seemed to glow on its own as it rested lightly on her shoulder. Her soft, liquid eyes shined with passion as she stared through the night. Her face was a face of pure innocence. Her figure was so inviting that I had to stop myself from grabbing her.

"You passed out three hours ago by a snake bite," she said as she moved closer to me. So stunned by her beauty, I completely forgot about my pain.

"I wrapped up your wound too," she continued.

I looked down at my foot. It was wrapped with pieces of white cloth that I believe she got from her ragged clothes.

"I had to cut open your wound to get the poison out," she continued in her solemn, innocent voice.

"Why did you help me?" I asked suddenly, for I did not understand why she went through all this trouble to save me.

She looked at me bewilderedly as she stood up to put some more leaves into the fire. "I helped you because you needed help," she said finally.

"In my country, everybody is on his own. I mean, nobody helps anybody," I admitted to her.

"Well, in mine, we always help each other. Even when we are in famine, we still try our best to help each other," she paused. "You see, friendship is the most important thing in life because nobody can live without a friend. We have to stick to each other in order to survive in this world."

Her face became more and more beautiful as she opened up to me. I had never seen such a beautiful face before, for her face was like a delicate rose blooming in the springtime.

"What country are you from?" I asked sincerely.

"Vietnam," she yelled out in a high-spirited voice.

"No!" I exclaimed. "Same here."

For a minute, I was stunned for I could not believe we were talking about the same country.

We spent that whole night talking about VN culture and past. I did not know that VN was at war most of its history. Growing up at the end of Vietnam War, I saw nothing but misery among the Vietnamese people. I realized now that they were suffering because they were trying to do a very big task. Their task was to rebuild VN into a better nation, a nation with thousands of years of glorious history. I know that the task will take a lot of time and effort, but if we stick together, everything is possible.

Quang Nguyen

Featured Literature

A Whole Nation and a People
by Harry Mark Petrakis

There was one storekeeper I remember above all others in my youth. It was shortly before I became ill, spending a good portion of my time with a motley group of varied ethnic ancestry. We contended with one another to deride the customs of the old country. On our Saturday forays into neighborhoods beyond our own, to prove we were really Americans, we ate hot dogs and drank Cokes. If a boy didn't have ten cents for this repast he went hungry, for he dared not bring a sandwich from home made of the spiced meats our families ate.

One of our untamed games was to seek out the owner of a pushcart or a store, unmistakably an immigrant, and bedevil him with a chorus of insults and jeers. To prove allegiance to the gang it was necessary to reserve our fiercest malevolence for a storekeeper or peddler belonging to our own ethnic background.

For that reason I led a raid on the small, shabby grocery of old Barba Nikos, a short, sinewy Greek who walked with a slight limp and sported a flaring, handlebar mustache.

We stood outside his store and dared him to come out. When he emerged to do battle, we plucked a few plums and peaches from the baskets on the sidewalk and retreated across the street to eat them while he watched. He waved a fist and hurled epithets at us in ornamental Greek.

Aware that my mettle was being tested, I raised my arm and threw my half-eaten plum at the old man. My aim was accurate and the plum struck him on the cheek. He shuddered and put his hand to the stain. He stared at me across the street, and although I could not see his eyes, I felt them sear my flesh. He turned and walked silently back into the store. The boys slapped my shoulders in admiration, but it was a hollow victory that rested like a stone in the pit of my stomach.

At twilight, when we disbanded, I passed the grocery alone on my way home. There was a small light burning in the store and the shadow of the old man's body outlined against the glass. Goaded by remorse, I walked to the door and entered.

434

The old man moved from behind the narrow wooden counter and stared at me. I wanted to turn and flee, but by then it was too late. As he motioned for me to come closer, I braced myself for a curse or a blow.

"You were the one," he said, finally, in a harsh voice.

I nodded mutely.

"Why did you come back?"

I stood there unable to answer.

"What's your name?"

"Haralambos," I said, speaking to him in Greek.

He looked at me in shock. "You are Greek!" he cried. "A Greek boy attacking a Greek grocer!" He stood appalled at the immensity of my crime. "All right," he said coldly. "You are here because you wish to make amends." His great mustache bristled in concentration. "Four plums, two peaches," he said. "That makes a total of seventy-eight cents. Call it seventy-five. Do you have seventy-five cents, boy?"

I shook my head.

"Then you will work it off," he said. "Fifteen cents an hour into seventy-five cents makes" —he paused— "five hours of work. Can you come here Saturday morning?"

"Yes," I said.

"Yes, Barba Nikos," he said sternly. "Show respect."

"Yes, Barba Nikos," I said.

"Saturday morning at eight o'clock," he said. "Now go home and say thanks in your prayers that I did not loosen your impudent head with a solid smack on the ear." I needed no further urging and fled.

Saturday morning, still apprehensive, I returned to the store. I began by sweeping, raising clouds of dust in dark and hidden corners. I washed the windows, whipping the squeegee swiftly up and down the glass in a fever of fear that some member of the gang would see me. When I finished I hurried back inside.

For the balance of the morning I stacked cans, washed the counter, and dusted bottles of yellow wine. A few customers entered, and Barba Nikos served them. A little after twelve o'clock he locked the door so he could eat lunch. He cut himself a few slices of sausage, tore a large chunk from a loaf of crisp-crusted bread, and filled a small cup with a dozen black shiny olives floating in brine. He offered me the cup. I could not help myself and grimaced.

"You are a stupid boy," the old man said. "You are not really Greek, are you?"

"Yes, I am."

"You might be," he admitted grudgingly. "But you do not act Greek. Wrinkling your nose at these fine olives. Look around this store for a minute. What do you see?"

"Fruits and vegetables," I said. "Cheese and olives and things like that."

He stared at me with a massive scorn. "That's what I mean," he said. "You are a bonehead. You don't understand that a whole nation and a people are in this store."

I looked uneasily toward the storeroom in the rear, almost expecting someone to emerge.

"What about olives?" he cut the air with a sweep of his arm. "There are olives of many shapes and colors. Pointed black ones from Kalamata, oval ones from Amphissa, pickled green olives and sharp tangy yellow ones. Achilles carried black olives to Troy and after a day of savage battle leading his Myrmidons, he'd rest and eat cheese and ripe black olives such as these right here. You have heard of Achilles, boy, haven't you?"

"Yes," I said.

"Yes, Barba Nikos."

"Yes, Barba Nikos, " I said.

He motioned at the row of jars filled with varied spices. "There is origanon there and basilikon and daphne and sesame and miantanos, all the marvelous flavorings that we have used in our food for thousands of years. The men of Marathon carried small packets of these spices into battle, and the scents reminded them of their homes, their families, and their children."

He rose and tugged his napkin free from around his throat. "Cheese, you said. Cheese! Come closer, boy, and I will educate your abysmal ignorance." He motioned toward a wooden container on the counter. "That glistening white delight is feta, made from goat's milk, packed in wooden buckets to retain the flavor. Alexander the Great demanded it on his table with his casks of wine when he planned his campaigns."

He walked limping from the counter to the window where the piles of tomatoes, celery, and green peppers clustered. "I suppose all you see here are some random vegetables?" He did not wait for me to answer. "You are dumb again. These are some of the ingredients that go to make up a Greek salad. Do you know what a Greek salad really is? A meal in itself, an experience, an emotional involvement. It is created deftly and with grace. First, you place large lettuce leaves in a big, deep bowl." He spread his fingers and moved them slowly, carefully, as if he were arranging the leaves. "The remainder of the lettuce is shredded and piled in a small mound," he said. "Then comes celery, cucumbers, tomatoes sliced lengthwise, green peppers, origanon, green olives, feta, avocado, and anchovies. At the end you dress it with lemon, vinegar, and pure olive oil, glinting golden in the light."

He finished with a heartfelt sigh and for a moment closed his eyes. Then he opened one eye to mark me with a baleful intensity. "The story goes that Zeus himself created the recipe and assembled and mixed the ingredients on Mount Olympus one night when he had invited some of the other gods to dinner."

He turned his back on me and walked slowly again across the store, dragging one foot slightly behind him. I looked uneasily at the clock, which showed that it was a few minutes past one. He turned quickly and startled me. "And everything else in here," he said loudly. "White beans, lentils, garlic, crisp bread, kokoretsi, meatballs, mussels and clams." He paused and drew a deep, long breath. "And the wine," he went on, "wine from Samos, Santorini, and Crete, retsina and mavrodaphne, a taste almost as old as water...and then the fragrant melons, the pastries, yellow diples and golden loukoumades, the honey custard galatobouriko. Everything a part of our history, as much a part as the exquisite sculpture in marble, the bearded warriors, Pan and the oracles and Delphi, and the nymphs dancing in the shadowed groves under Homer's glittering moon." He paused, out of breath again, and coughed harshly. "Do you understand now, boy?"

He watched my face for some response and then grunted. We stood silent for a moment until he cocked his head and stared at the clock. "It's time for you to leave," he motioned brusquely toward the door. "We are square now. Keep it that way."

I decided the old man was crazy and reached behind the counter for my jacket and cap and started for the door. He called me back. From a box he drew out several soft, yellow figs that he placed in a piece of paper. "A bonus because you worked well," he said. "Take them. When you taste them, maybe you will understand what I have been talking about."

I took the figs and he unlocked the door and I hurried from the store. I looked back once and saw him standing in the doorway, watching me, the swirling tendrils of food curling like mist about his head.

I ate the figs late that night. I forgot about them until I was in bed, and then I rose and took the package from my jacket. I nibbled at one, then ate them all. They broke apart between my teeth with a tangy nectar, a thick sweetness running like honey across my tongue and into the pockets of my cheeks. In the morning when I woke, I could still taste and inhale their fragrance.

I never again entered Barba Nikos' store. My spell of illness, which began some months later, lasted two years. When I returned to the streets I had forgotten the old man and the grocery. Shortly afterwards my family moved from the neighborhood.

Some twelve years later, after the war, I drove through the old neighborhood and passed the grocery. I stopped the car and for a moment stood before the store. The windows were stained with dust and grime, the interior bare and desolate, a store in a decrepit group of stores marked for razing so new structures could be built.

I have been in many Greek groceries since then and have often bought the feta and Kalamata olives. I have eaten countless Greek salads and have indeed found them a meal for the gods. On the holidays in our house, my wife and sons and I sit down to a dinner of steaming, buttered pilaf like my mother used to make and lemon-egg avgolemono and roast lamb richly seasoned with cloves of garlic. I drink the red and yellow wines, and for dessert I have come to relish the delicate pastries coated with honey and powdered sugar. Old Barba Nikos would have been pleased.

But I have never been able to recapture the halcyon flavor of those figs he gave me on that day so long ago, although I have bought figs many times. I have found them pleasant to my tongue, but there is something missing. And to this day I am not sure whether it was the figs or the vision and passion of the old grocer that coated the fruit so sweetly I can still recall their savor and fragrance after almost thirty years.

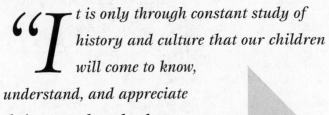

"*It is only through constant study of history and culture that our children will come to know, understand, and appreciate their own cultural values and traditions.*"

Thomas Parham
Director, UCI Counseling Center and Career Planning and Placement Center; coauthor of *The Psychology of Blacks: An African American Perspective*

Featured Literature

"Everyday Use"
from *In Love &
in Trouble*
by Alice Walker

Grade Level
For High School
and College

Thinking Level
Analysis

Writing Domain
Analytical/Expository

Materials Needed
• Colored pens

**Suggested
Supplementary
Readings**
• "My Mother Pieced
  Quilts" by Teresa
  Palomo Acosta
• *Quilting* by Averil Colby
• *The Perfect Patchwork
  Primer* by Beth
  Gutcheon
• *A Quilter's Companion*
  by Dolores Hinson

A Mother's Decision:
Examining a Family's Values and Cultural Heritage

by Scott Edwards

Overview

After closely examining Alice Walker's short story "Everyday Use" to discover details which reveal character, relationships, and cultural values and looking at the factors which lead the mother in the story to give the family quilts to her youngest daughter, students will write an interpretive essay in which they explain this decision. Throughout the lesson, students will be asked to examine situations—both in their own lives and in the literature—and to record facts and make inferences based on these facts.

Objectives

THINKING SKILLS

Students will:

- *distinguish* between facts and inferences;
- *make inferences* about people they know and story characters;
- *identify* their family and characters' attitudes about heritage;
- *identify* the cultural value of quilts;
- *analyze* characters in a short story;
- *interpret* the actions of characters;
- *identify* evidence in support of their interpretations.

WRITING SKILLS

Students will write an essay in which they:

- *provide* a context for their interpretation of the mother's decision;
- *make* a central claim explaining the mother's decision;
- *organize* their paper around a central claim;
- *support* their claim by making inferences from the story;
- *base* inferences on details and specific examples from the text;
- *use* analytical/expository form: introduction, main body, and conclusion;
- *demonstrate* proficiency in the standards of written English.

The Process

"Everyday Use" is usually accessible to older high school students. Characterization is especially strong in the story, allowing students to make substantiated inferences about the characters. The lesson requires about eight days of reading, discussing, and writing, depending on how much time students are given to work in class. Students should already be familiar with the ideas of culture and heritage. (The "My Name, My Self" and "Living in Life's Shadow" lessons, elsewhere in this book, can be helpful precursors to this lesson.) In this lesson, students will examine the value of family objects or heirlooms which symbolize a family's heritage.

 PREWRITING

Prewriting Step 1: *Planning a Skit*

Assign the following situations to two reliable groups of three students. Send them outside to plan a skit. They should plan to use facial expressions, body language, tone of voice, and gestures and actions as well as dialogue (at least six or seven exchanges) to reveal the thoughts and attitudes of the characters they present. *Note: If your students have trouble creating these skits on their own, they can use the sample skit under Prewriting Step 5 as a point of departure, or they can perform that script adding variations of their own. You might also work with the students a day ahead of time to help them prepare for the performance.*

Situation 1: A teenager is tired of the name given to her at birth. She decides to change the name entirely, because it just isn't "her" anymore. She talks to her parents about this and immediately gets into an argument. The parents are proud of the name because it reflects their culture. They are strongly opposed to the name change. What do the teenagers and her parents say to each other? How do they say it? How do they act toward each other?

Your goal in this skit is to reveal the parents' and the teenager's attitude toward their heritage. Plan how you will use facial expressions, body language, tone of voice, and gestures and actions, as well as dialogue to convey your character.

Whoever plays the parents will determine the culture represented in the situation. For example, if the students play Asian parents, then the dialogue should reflect Asian values toward heritage.

Situation 2: A teenager is tired of the name given to her at birth. She decides to change the name entirely, because it just isn't "her" anymore. She decides to tell her parents about her decision. Even though the name reflects the family's culture, the parents are proud of their teenager and they want her to be happy. What do the teenager and her parents say to each other? How do they say it? How do they act toward each other?

Your goal in this skit is to reveal the parents' and the teenager's attitude toward their heritage. Plan how you will use facial expressions, body language, tone of voice, and gestures and actions, as well as dialogue to convey your characters.

Whoever plays the teenager will determine the culture represented in the situation. For example, if the student playing the teenager is Asian, then the dialogue should reflect Asian values toward heritage.

Prewriting Step 2: *Distinguishing Between Facts and Inferences*

While the groups are outside preparing, have your class discuss and practice inferencing skills. To introduce students to the differences between facts and inferences, talk to them about how we get impressions of people and how we make assumptions about them based on these impressions.

How, for example, do we get our first impressions of a class, of a new person we encounter, of a date's parents? *(Students will note that they usually notice the physical aspects of a person first: hair color, height, weight, ethnic features, etc.)* Record student suggestions on the board. As discussion progresses, students will cite many of the following characteristics about people:

A. Clothing, kind of car, neighborhood where a person lives, who the person hangs around with;

B. How the person acts or what the person does—nervous habits (twisting a lock of hair, for example), always carrying a big purse, squinting, never arriving on time, never making a decision;

C. Speech patterns, bad grammar, lisps, accents, gravelly voice, mispronunciations;

D. Direct statements by the person about self ("I detest green olives," or "I am an only child.");

E. Others' reactions to the person—direct statements others make about the person, how people avoid sitting by a person in class, the fact that the person is always chosen for a team, etc.

Distinguish between fact (what is real, true, obvious, provable, clear to everyone, not able to be refuted) and inference (probable, assumption based on fact, educated guess). Discuss: What makes something a fact and something else an inference? Can something be a fact to one person and an inference to another? What makes the difference?

Prewriting Step 3: *Class Practice: Facts and Inferences*

Have students practice distinguishing facts and inferences. In their notes, have them list facts about you in one column, inferences in another. *(If you are not comfortable using yourself as a model, you might use the principal or a well-liked coach.)* You will want to transfer the information to the board, but how you do this will depend on how well you know the class. You may want to collect the lists and read them yourself, selecting the details you feel comfortable with. If you have a comfortable rapport with the group, you may just ask students to orally volunteer items from their lists.

One teacher's list on the board looked like this:

Facts	Inferences
long, curly hair	not conservative
wears glasses	has bad eyes
young	single
lives in Fullerton	lives alone
likes teaching English	intelligent
dresses casually	doesn't care about clothes
doesn't wear a wedding ring	doesn't have a lot of money
drives a dirty Toyota	

Test to see whether the "facts" are factual and the "inferences" can truly be inferred. Note that what is a fact for you may be an inference to your students, and that what is a fact to one student may be inference to another, depending on how well they know you. One student may infer that you are not married because you don't wear a ring on your left hand; another may know it as fact because he heard you mention it. Also, notice the italicized *likes* in the list above. Just because you teach English does not necessarily mean that you like teaching it or even that you like teaching. Be sure to discuss what "facts" led to the inferences the students made. It is a fact that you drive a dirty Toyota; it is an inference, at least from the students' points of view, that you don't have a lot of money. It is a fact that you have long hair, it is an inference that you are not conservative. All inferences are linked to facts, directly or indirectly.

* Note: This idea is taken from Harold Schneider's lesson "Probably Short: Obviously a Democrat" in Thinking/Writing: Fostering Critical Thinking Through Writing, *ed. Carol Booth Olson, (New York: HarperCollins Publishers, 1992).*

Prewriting Step 4: *Distinguishing Facts from Inferences*

Move the discussion now to how we get impressions of characters in a drama.

It might be helpful to show that many of the same methods we use in actual experiences serve us well in our interactions with literature. These methods of characterization may work well to supplement the discussion:

Appearances—(See #2A)
Actions—(#2B)
Speech and tone of voice—(#2C)
Direct statements by the character himself—(#2D)
Reactions of other characters—(#2E)

Prewriting Step 5: *Class Skits*

Now, have the two groups you sent out come in and present their situations to the class. Tell the students that they will have time to record facts and inferences about the presentation. While the students present, the others should watch and listen carefully for facial expressions, body language, tone of voice, and gestures and actions, as well as dialogue. They should give special attention to what these things say about the characters' attitude toward their heritage.

Student Model/Sample

> *(Scene. The Gonzalez household. Luz María sits on a sofa, legs crossed, homework on lap, watching TV. In an adjoining dining room, her mother puts dinner on the table.)*

Mother: Papi, Luz María, ¡vengan se a cenar!
> (The father comes to sit at the table. Luz María doesn't respond.)

Father: Luz María, you heard your mother. Come to the table.
> (Again, she doesn't respond.)

Father: Luz María!

Luz María (under her breath, without looking up): Martie.

Father: What?

Luz María: My name is Martie.

Mother: Your name is Luz María.

Luz María (tossing her homework aside): I'm tired of that name. It's for old ladies.

Mother (shocked, raises her voice): It's a beautiful name. Luz María is the name of your grandmother. We gave you this name to remember her.

Luz María (walking to the table but still not looking at her mother): Why don't you look at some of those pictures you have all over the house if you want to remember her? All the other girls on the softball team have fun names. "Luz María" makes me stand out. It sounds slow.

Mother (taking Luz María by the shoulders and turning her around to face her): Martie is not for a girl of your beauty.
> (Luz María rolls her eyes.)

Martie sounds so . . . so . . . American.

Luz María: I am American. (She breaks out of her mother's grip.)

Father: We know that but you can't forget where you're from.

Luz María: I'm from right here.

Father: But you know how strong our roots in Mexico are.

Mother: Remember the last time you came back from spending the summer with your cousins in Jalisco? You didn't speak English at home again until October.

Luz María: That's at home. At school things are different.

Prewriting Step 6: *Facts and Inferences Chart*

After each presentation, give the student audience a few minutes to record facts and inferences on a two-column chart like the one on the next page:

Facts	Inferences
Luz María avoids eye contact.	She doesn't want to face up to her parents.
LM sounds impatient.	Her parents are bothering her.
Mother takes her by shoulders.	She wants to make her point clear.
Mother mentions grandmother.	Family history is very important for her.

After both groups present, discuss the chart. What did the students list in the fact column? In the inference column? To what facts do they link their inferences? Did the same fact lead to different inferences for different students? What did you notice about the characters' attitudes toward their heritage? How did these attitudes come out? What do you learn about how the child sees himself and his parents? What do you notice about how the parents see themselves and their child?

Prewriting Step 7: *Clustering*

Introduce quilts as artifacts of cultural heritage. Seeing quilts in this way will help students understand the conflict in the story. Find out what students know about quilting by clustering quilts. A class cluster might appear as follows:

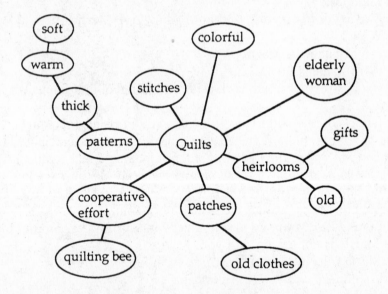

Using pictures in library books and overheads and, if possible, real quilts, discuss the tradition of quilting. Real quilts provide the best focal points for a discussion because students have so many questions about their history, age, etc. Point out how quilting was often a communal activity, involving several people. Often, quilts were sewn from pieces of cloth from old family clothing. Many designs contain symbolism. Quilts were often given on important occasions such as weddings and births.

The following books on quilting are good sources of history as well as colorful illustrations:

Colby, Averil, *Quilting*. New York: Scribners, 1971.

Gutcheon, Beth, *The Perfect Patchwork Primer*. New York: McKay, 1973.

Hinson, Dolores, *A Quilter's Companion*. New York: Arco, 1976.

See also "The Class Quilt" lesson elsewhere in this book for a list of children's books that focus on quilts.

Prewriting Step 8: *Poetry Reading*

If you do not have real quilts to show or if students still need additional orientation to the tradition of quilting, read Theresa Palomo Acosta's poem "My Mother Pieced Quilts," available in many anthologies. Before reading, ask the students to look for indications of how the family's history and heritage are included on the quilts.

After reading the poem aloud, have students reread the poem silently, marking any lines or phrases they find particularly striking. Have students share these lines with the class. To reinforce the previous work the class has done on distinguishing between fact and inference, you might want to consider having the class make inferences about the family described in the poem by Theresa Palomo Acosta, based upon the facts she shares about the quilts.

Facts	Inferences
Dime store velvets	They didn't have much money.
michigan spring faded curtain pieces/santa fe work shirt	Maybe they were migrant workers.
corpus christi noon	They were religious—probably Catholic.

Finally, discuss what the poem shows about how family history and heritage are recorded in the quilts.

Prewriting Step 9: *Family Objects*

To help students relate the concept of heritage to their own lives, have them consider family possessions. After reading the poem, they should be able to think of other objects that could have value to a family and represent an important aspect of its heritage.

Have them think of some family object that they would like to have when they leave home. If for some reason, the family has no objects, what would the student like to have had from the family? This object might be an heirloom or sacred object or even something that they made when they were younger.

Working in pairs, have the students tell what the object is and why they would want to keep it. To help others get ideas, have the students who can think of something tell about it briefly. For example, a student might want an old pair of eyeglasses because they were worn by his/her grandfather and they represent all the hours he spent working, reading through books.

Prewriting Step 10: *Introduction to "Everyday Use"*

Introduce the story "Everyday Use":

- Explain that it presents an African American family in rural Georgia. The mother must decide which of her two daughters should receive the family quilts. On the board, write the names of the sisters and a distinguishing feature of each one so that students can keep them straight while they read:

  Maggie—scarred in a fire, now lives with the mother;
  Dee—returns home to visit, having changed her name to Wangero.

- Identify and define terms:

  heritage: that which has been reserved for one to inherit
  clabber: milk thickened by souring; curds
  dasher: the plunger of a churn
  snuff: a pinch of tobacco

- Explain that the class is going to read the story in sections. (It may be a good idea to hand the story out in the four sections that are appended to this lesson so that students will have to draw inferences as they read instead of after they have read.) That way, they can pay careful attention to what is going on, practice making inferences about the characters, and respond to the story as it develops. As each section is read aloud, students should do the following on the text itself:

  —Underline key words or phrases that they notice;
  —Write any questions that they want to have answered;
  —Record in the margin any inferences they can make.

They should use the same color pen or pencil throughout the first reading because they will be marking in a second color when rereading.

The following shows how students might mark a section of the text:

Why would they want a "wavy" yard?	I will wait for her in the yard that Maggie and I made so clean and wavy yesterday afternoon. A yard like this is more comfortable than most people know. It is not just a yard. <u>It is like an extended living room.</u> When the hard clay is swept clean as a floor and the fine sand around the edges lined with tiny, irregular grooves, anyone can come and sit and <u>look up into the elm tree and wait for the breezes that never come inside the house.</u>	*The family must be poor. Their yard is their living room.* *They take the time to make their home comfortable.* *It seems relaxing in this yard.*

Why is she so nervous?	Maggie will be <u>nervous</u> until after her sister goes: she will stand <u>hopelessly</u> in corners, homely and ashamed of the burn scars down her arms and legs, eyeing her sister <u>with a mixture of envy and awe.</u> She thinks her sister has held life always in the palm of one hand, <u>that "no" is a word the world never learned to say to her.</u>	*How did she get burned?*
		The sister must always get her own way. She sounds spoiled.
Why is Maggie so envious of her sister?		
		The one sister sounds intimidated by the other sister.

Prewriting Step 11: *Reading, Annotation, Discussion*

Read and discuss the story, section by section.

- Read the first two paragraphs of the first section aloud and have students stop to underline what they notice. If they have trouble asking questions and making inferences from this paragraph, you might ask questions like these:
    —What can we infer about the narrator?
    —Where do you suppose they live?
    —Is she an outdoor person or an indoor person?
    —What can we infer about her from her attitude about her yard?

- Students may continue reading the first section on their own or follow along as you read aloud. Again, they should underline, go back to infer, and ask questions. Remind them that they may ask questions about anything that is unclear to them. Have students volunteer their questions and make a list on the board so that as a class you can list as many unanswered issues as possible.

Questions students might want to ask about this section could include:
—How did Maggie get burned?
—Why hasn't the mother ever learned to say "no" to the other daughter?
—Why does the mother think she is not "the way [her] daughter would want [her] to be"?
—Who is the "them" the mother talks to "with one foot raised in flight"?
—Why is Maggie so hesitant when the other sister is so bold?
—Why didn't Dee seem to care that her sister was burning in the first house?
—Why did Dee hate the first house so much?
—Did she set fire to it?
—Why did the mother feel ignorant when Dee read to her?
—Why does the mother think reading is "forcing words, lies, other folks' habits" on her?

—Why does the author have Dee read "without pity" and Maggie read "good-naturedly"?

—Why does the mother throw in that apparently irrelevant comment about cows and milking them the wrong way?

—Why does the mother "deliberately" turn her back on the house now?

—Why does she think Dee will want to tear it down?

—Why did Dee court the boy instead of the boy court her?

Note: When specific, interpretive questions are asked, patterns of inference begin to emerge that will eventually lead to more insightful and supportable interpretive claims.

- The second section begins, "When she comes I will meet—but here they are!" and ends, "It was a beautiful light yellow wood, from a tree that grew in the yard where Big Dee and Stash had lived."

  Questions students might raise about this section could include:
  —Why is Dee so interested in the house when her mother said she hated the one just like it?

  —Why does Dee bring a friend home when she had vowed never to bring her friends home?

  —Why does the mother suddenly describe herself as stout and clumsy just after she has described Dee in the flowing dress?

  —Why does the mother suddenly use bad grammar ("he don't know") when she talks about "Asalama-lakim"?

  —Why does Dee say "She's dead" about herself?

  —Why does Dee reject the heritage of her name?

  —Why is the mother so obliging about Dee's change of name?

  —Why doesn't Hakim-a-barber accept the traditional food?

  —Why is Dee so interested in all her mother's old things?

  —Why does she want remnants of the old culture but not the name, dress, etc.?

  —Why does Dee just want the churn top and not the whole churn?

  —Why doesn't Dee care that her mother might need to use the churn?

  —Why does Dee not appear to care about the history of the dash even though she wants the dash itself?

- After students have finished asking questions and making inferences about this section, ask them to do a two-minute quickwrite about the following question: Do you think Dee/Wangero is real or phony? Discuss answers briefly as a class. You might also have the students recall the skits and compare them to the story and how the family responds to Dee's name change.

- The third section begins, "After dinner Dee (Wangero) went to the trunk" and ends, "'I can 'member Grandma Dee without the quilts.'"

Questions students might pose could include:

—Why does Maggie drop something in the kitchen?

—Why doesn't Dee want her mother to touch the quilts?

—Why does Dee think Maggie won't appreciate the quilts?

—Why does Dee want the quilts now, though she didn't want them when she was offered them?

—Why does Maggie give in so easily?

By this point, students will probably have formulated fairly clear opinions of each of the members of the family, based on the questions they have asked and the inferences they have drawn.

- Before reading the end of the story, ask students to do a five-minute quickwrite predicting who they think will get the quilts. Remind them to base their predictions on the facts and inferences they are now familiar with from the story. *(Note: the question focuses on who will get the quilts, not who may deserve them.)*

- Discuss various predictions before reading the end of the story. Hopefully, there will be a variety of answers such as these:

—Dee will get the quilts because her mother always gives in to her.

—Dee will get the quilts because she knows how to care for them.

—Maggie will get the quilts because she loves them.

—Maggie will get the quilts because she knows how to use them.

—Maggie will get the quilts because she truly cares about the heritage they represent.

- Read the end of the story, underline, infer, and question. Check to be sure the class has noticed important details in this section:

—What the mother becomes aware of just before she decides;

—Dee's sunglasses;

—The snuff in Maggie's bottom lip;

—The snuff the mother asks for;

—The sitting and enjoying at the close of the story.

It is important also in this section to make inferences about the mother: What has she become aware of about herself, her daughters, About her heritage?

PROMPT

Many families keep objects—such as furniture, jewelry, pictures, or decorations—that, because of their special meaning, they pass on from generation to generation. While parents usually bequeath heirlooms according to birth order or gender, they must often decide, according to more subjective standards, who will get a particular object.

In Alice Walker's "Everyday Use," the mother gives the family quilts to her younger daughter, Maggie, even though the older daughter, Dee, demands the quilts for herself. Dee wants to preserve the history of the family as contained in the quilts, and Maggie wants to use them as a part of everyday life. Even though Dee is the only daughter who argues for her right to the quilts, the mother gives them to Maggie. What, then, leads her to do this?

Write an expository essay in which you analyze the mother's final decision to give the quilts to Maggie. Given what you learn about the mother, the history of her relationships with her daughters, and her sense of heritage, why do you think the mother gives the quilts to Maggie?

Base your essay on a central claim that states your understanding of the mother's decision. Support this claim with inferences that you connect to specific details and examples from the story. Your paper should be written in standard analytical/expository form—introduction, main body, conclusion—and should follow the conventions of written English.

PRECOMPOSING

Precomposing Step 1: *Quickwrite*

After questioning and inferring, the class should do a five-minute quickwrite in answer to these questions: Why do you think the mother makes the decision she does? Is it a new awareness she comes to? How do you think she arrives at the awareness she does? The following is a quickwrite that eventually grows into the sample essay by Cooper Christensen, which is appended to this lesson:

> I think the mother decides to give the quilts to Maggie because she has finally become fed up with the way Dee (Wangero) acts. All the time she struts around like she is the most important person in the world. She has never cared about her heritage in the past, but all of a sudden she wants to be a part of it. I think that the mother realizes this only because of Dee's visit. In the

past, she had always given Dee whatever she wanted. Now, when Dee returns, her mother can see how far she has separated herself from her family. She also realizes that Maggie has always been there. Maggie is all she has and she knows it's about time she did something for her. She can't stand to hear Dee put herself before Maggie any longer.

Precomposing Step 2: *Identification of Important Points*

Students should then reread what they wrote and circle the important points they want to make about the mother in their essay. If they left out any important points from their quickwrite, they should add them at the bottom:

I think the mother decides to give the quilts to Maggie because she has finally become fed up with the way Dee (Wangero) acts. All the time she struts around like she is the most important person in the world. She has never cared about her heritage in the past, but all of a sudden she wants to be a part of it. I think that the mother realizes this only because of Dee's visit. In the past, she had always given Dee whatever she wanted. Now, when Dee returns, her mother can see how far she has separated herself from her family. She also realizes that Maggie has always been there. Maggie is all she has and she knows it's about time she did something for her. She can't stand to hear Dee put herself before Maggie any longer.

Additional thoughts:

The mother is like the cow getting milked the wrong way. Dee has really been almost ashamed of her family. The bond between the mother and Maggie has grown while Dee has distanced herself.

Precomposing Step 3: *Sentence Summary*

Finally, have students summarize their quickwrite and additions in one or two sentences. This summary is the students' trial claim, for which they will seek evidence when rereading the story:

The mother in the story decides to let Maggie keep the quilts because she is suddenly pushed too far by Dee's lack of regard for her heritage.

Notice that this thesis may change substantially as students search for evidence and revise their original ideas. In Cooper's paper, although the thesis is never actually stated, it is strongly enough implied that the reader can identify the interpretive stance.

Precomposing Step 4: *Developing Support for Trial Claim*

Have students return to the story and, with a different color of ink, underline facts and inferences that substantiate and develop their trial claim. They should mark in the new color anything that supports their claim, even if they already marked it during the first reading. The following is some of the evidence that Cooper uses to support his claim:

- Dee does nothing when the house burns down. She doesn't care to lose this piece of her heritage.
- She doesn't keep the name that was given to her at birth.
- Her interest in her heritage comes all of a sudden. She wants to possess it—the churn top, the quilts, etc.

Precomposing Step 5: *Revising the Thesis*

After students have reviewed the story, they should revise their claim to reflect any discoveries or interpretive changes they made during the second reading. Students will use this revised thesis to develop a plan for their essay.

Precomposing Step 6: *Planning the Composition*

Students should, at this time, organize support for their claim. Topics to review include thesis (claim), introduction, main body, and conclusion. *Completing a microtheme, such as that used in the "Living in Life's Shadow" lesson elsewhere in this book, may help students to put their ideas in order before they begin to write.*

 WRITING

Students should write a draft of their essay—at home or in class, depending on the level of the group you are teaching.

 SHARING/RESPONDING

Peer Response Sheet

Students will be meeting with a partner or a small group to get feedback on their drafts. Use small groups if students would not receive adequate feedback from just one partner. Partners will be writing on both the draft itself and the peer response sheet on the following page:

Peer Response Sheet

To the author: Give this sheet along with your essay to one or more persons from your writing group. Be sure you get thorough responses that give you solid ideas on how to proceed with revision.

To the reader: Follow the directions below as you read and analyze your classmate's paper. The more specific your comments, the easier the author can make effective revisions.

1. Read the paper silently to yourself. Record your first impression here. You might summarize what you see as the essay's main point, or point out any insights that strike you or places you find confusing.

2. Read the paper again and do the following:

   a. Mark it in two colors as you go: use one color to mark facts and the other to mark inferences.

   b. Ask questions in the margins when you have trouble identifying the connections between facts and inferences, between a number of inferences, or between inferences and the writer's claim.

   c. After rereading, answer the following questions for the writer:

   • What claim does the writer make about the mother's decision?
   • What are the strongest reasons given in support of this claim?
   • What did you find insightful about this paper?
   • What things did you find confusing? How could the writer clarify these things?

REVISING

Revising Step 1: *Metacognitive Log/Revising Plan*

After their partners are finished reviewing their papers, the students should look over their partners' comments and answer the following questions on a metacognitive log.

1. Did your partners identify the claim you want to make about the mother's decision? If not, how can you make your claim more clear?

2. Look at the marks on your paper. How much of the inferences color do you see? How much of the facts color? What does this tell you about how you might need to expand your paper?

3. What other comments and questions did the readers have about your paper? Do you think their comments and questions are valid? Why or why not?

4. Make a plan for revision. What things do you plan to revise? In what order are you going to work on them?

Revising Step 2: *Revising the Draft*

With their partners' comments and their own plan for revision, students are now ready to revise their papers. They can make changes directly on their first drafts or enter changes on a computer. In either case, they should produce a draft that is legible so that their peers can accurately assist them with editing.

 # EDITING

Editing Step 1: *Small Group Editing*

After students have revised their essays, they meet in their writing groups again to do the final editing of their papers. Students generally proofread best when given a few specific things to look for. Choose things—such as spelling, comma usage, sentence structure—according to the needs of your class at the time.

In writing groups, students can proofread the papers one at a time and then pass to the next person until everybody has read each paper. Any student who is unsure of what is correct can ask the other members of the group. A group that is unsure can ask the teacher.

Editing Step 2: *Individual Editing*

Students can then complete final drafts of their essays, correcting any mechanical errors found by themselves or their group.

EVALUATION

Evaluate the papers according to the following rubric:

Rubric

6   The 6 paper is superior in its insight, organization, and use of language. The writer makes an especially perceptive claim about the mother's decision to give the quilts to Maggie. The writer supports his or her claim by making inferences about the mother that connect to specific details and examples from the story. The paper has a clear introduction, main body, and conclusion. In addition, the 6 paper is free from any errors in grammar, punctuation, and spelling that distract the reader or impair understanding.

5   Though still strong, the 5 paper lacks the polish and insight of the 6 paper. Like the writer of the 6 paper, this writer presents a perceptive claim about the mother's decision to give the quilts to Maggie. Though the writer supports his or her claim with inferences about the mother, these inferences are not as carefully connected to details and examples from the story. The paper has a discernible introduction, main body, and conclusion. The 5 paper is also free from any distracting technical errors.

4   The writer provides a less thorough context for his or her interpretation. The writer makes a clear claim, but it may be more predictable than in the 5 and 6 papers. The author uses inferences to support the claim, but they may be more general and lack connections to specific details and examples from the story. Although the paper has an introduction, main body, and conclusion, not all three sections are equally strong. Occasional errors in grammar, punctuation, or spelling may interrupt the flow of reading.

3   The writer presents a perfunctory introduction in which the issues are simply identified. The writer makes a generalized or commonplace claim about the mother's decision. Because the claim is generalized, the writer has difficulty supporting it with inferences based on specific examples. The writer may summarize the story or narrate an event rather than offer support. The paper may lack a clear introduction, main body, or conclusion. Occasional errors in grammar, punctuation, or spelling may interrupt the flow of reading and obscure meaning.

2   The writer may identify the subject of the discussion but fail to identify what he/she plans to interpret. The writer presents no clear claim about the mother's decision, relying on generalizations or summaries. The writer uses no relevant inferences or examples to support his/her ideas. The paper is not written in standard analytical/expository format. Frequent errors in grammar, punctuation, or spelling may interrupt flow of reading and obscure meaning.

1   The writer fails to provide any context for discussion of the mother, presents no claim, and merely summarizes the subject in a few lines. The writer provides no support for his or her ideas. The paper has no identifiable structure and may demonstrate serious weakness in grammar, punctuation, or spelling.

EXTENSION ACTIVITIES

1. If students take an interest in the quilts, you might have them create a quilt design, using cloth or construction paper to depict an important incident or symbol from their lives. *(Note: See "The Class Quilt" lesson elsewhere in this book for guidelines on how to do this project.)*

2. Many of the activities in this lesson might also lead to a reflective essay in which students ponder the importance of possessions or gifts.

Student Model

"Everyday Use"

"Cows are soothing and slow and don't bother you, unless you try to milk them the wrong way." It seems like that should have been written, "I'm calm and patient and don't get mad at anyone, unless I'm pushed to the limit," since that's the image I get from the large, tough-hearted woman who tells the story of "Everyday Use."

The mother in this story has lived a hard, long life, doing the job of a man, never complaining, just doing the things to survive. Then we have her daughter, Dee, who I picture as never having broken a sweat in her life. As a child she hated her house, her living, her culture. When the fire had burnt down the old house, she just sat there in amazement under an old gum tree, as if she wanted to dance in the ashes. She did all this while the mother was carrying Maggie, with arms burnt so bad they were sticking to her, and whose hair was singed and smoking with the foul stench of burning flesh. Why then, if her heritage means so much to her, didn't she lift a finger to save any of the house or items in it? Instead she sat under a tree admiring the disaster that was taking place.

Like the house, her family was of little importance to her. She was ashamed of their lack of knowledge and seemed very much bothered by the poverty in which she lived. In her mind, to be important was to be worldly. To have riches and "style" were what mattered, not her family.

It's ironic how when she was younger she could not wait to get out of her lifestyle, but now she claims her culture is important to her. She even goes through the extent of changing her name since, in her mind, "Dee" was the name given to her by her oppressors when in reality it was the name passed down by her own family. Dee changes her name to Wangero Leewanika Kemanjo, which supposedly goes back to her African roots. The mother passively accepts the change with no argument. She doesn't even say a word when Dee takes the churn top off the butter churner that has milk in it that has already clabbered, and claims it as her own. Dee doesn't even stop to think that it's still in use, just that she wants it and that's that.

The mother's slowly being nudged and pushed; like the cow she doesn't mind! Then Dee demands that she be able to take the two quilts that were made by her grandma. When the mother claims that the quilts were promised to her sister, Maggie, Dee gets furious, stating that Maggie can't appreciate them. She'll ruin them by using them everyday.

Dee is trying to gain a culture that she believes comes from objects like the churner and the quilts. But her idea of culture is as something to be hung on a wall, put on display. She has no idea that culture comes from knowing and living their culture. To them it is a way of life; to Dee, it is the "in" thing to do. I feel that mother finally sees this in Dee and doesn't respect it. So for the first time in the mother's life, the cow was milked the wrong way and had begun to kick. She snatches the quilts out of Dee's hands and throws them into the arms of Maggie. Furiously stomping out of the house Dee shouts, "You don't understand." "What?" exclaims the mother. "Your heritage," Dee responds.

The final words Dee says are, "It's really a new day for us. But from the way you and mama still act you'd never know it." How is it that she doesn't even realize a simple statement? She never has and she never will have this culture. Culture is not all art, it's not something you turn on and off: it's life.

Cooper Christensen High-School Senior

Featured Literature

Everyday Use
for your grandma
by Alice Walker

Section 1

I will wait for her in the yard that Maggie and I made so clean and wavy yesterday afternoon. A yard like this is more comfortable than most people know. It is not just a yard. It is like an extended living room. When the hard clay is swept clean as a floor and the fine sand around the edges lined with tiny, irregular grooves, anyone can come and sit and look up into the elm tree and wait for the breezes that never come inside the house.

Maggie will be nervous until after her sister goes: she will stand hopelessly in corners, homely and ashamed of the burn scars down her arms and legs, eyeing her sister with a mixture of envy and awe. She thinks her sister has held life always in the palm of one hand, that "no" is a word the world never learned to say to her.

You've no doubt seen those TV shows where the child who has "made it" is confronted, as a surprise, by her own mother and father, tottering in weakly from backstage. (A pleasant surprise, of course: What would they do if parent and child came on the show only to curse out and insult each other?) On TV mother and child embrace and smile into each other's faces. Sometimes the mother and father weep, the child wraps them in her arms and leans across the table to tell how she would not have made it without their help. I have seen these programs.

Sometimes I dream a dream in which Dee and I are suddenly brought together on a TV program of this sort. Out of a dark and soft-seated limousine I am ushered into a bright room filled with many people. There I meet a smiling, gray, sporty man like Johnny Carson who shakes my hand and tells me what a fine girl I have. Then we are on the stage and Dee is embracing me with tears in her eyes. She pins on my dress a large orchid, even though she has told me once that she thinks orchids are tacky flowers.

In real life I am a large, big-boned woman with rough, man-working hands. In the winter I wear flannel nightgowns to bed and overalls during the day. I can kill and clean a hog as mercilessly as a man. My fat keeps me hot in zero weather. I can work outside all day, breaking ice to get water for washing; I can eat pork liver cooked over the open fire minutes after it comes steaming from the hog. One winter I knocked a bull calf straight in the brain between the eyes with a sledge hammer and had the meat hung up to chill before nightfall. But of course all this does not show on television. I am the way my daughter would want me to be: a hundred pounds lighter, my skin like an uncooked barley pancake. My hair glistens in the hot bright lights. Johnny Carson has much to do to keep up with my quick and witty tongue.

But that is a mistake. I know even before I wake up. Who ever knew a Johnson with a quick tongue? Who can even imagine me looking a strange white man in the eye? It seems to me I have talked to them always with one foot raised in flight, with my head turned in whichever way is farthest from them. Dee, though. She would always look anyone in the eye. Hesitation was no part of her nature.

"How do I look, Mama?" Maggie says, showing just enough of her thin body enveloped in pink skirt and red blouse for me to know she's there, almost hidden by the door.

"Come out in the yard," I say.

Have you ever seen a lame animal, perhaps a dog run over by some careless person rich enough to own a car, sidle up to someone who is ignorant enough to be kind to him? That is the way my Maggie walks. She has been like this, chin on chest, eyes on ground, feet in shuffle, ever since the fire that burned the other house to the ground.

Dee is lighter than Maggie, with nicer hair and a fuller figure. She's a woman now, though sometimes I forget. How long ago was it that the other house burned? Ten, twelve years? Sometimes I can still hear the flames and feel Maggie's arm sticking to me, her hair smoking and her dress falling off her in little black peppery flakes. Her eyes seemed stretched open, blazed open by the

458

flames reflected in them. And Dee. I see her standing off under the sweet gum tree she used to dig gum out of; a look of concentration on her face as she watched the last dingy gray board of the house fall in toward the red-hot brick chimney. Why don't you do a dance around the ashes? I'd wanted to ask her. She had hated the house that much.

I used to think she hated Maggie, too. But that was before we raised the money, the church and me, to send her to Augusta to school. She used to read to us without pity; forcing words, lies, other folks' habits, whole lives upon us two, sitting trapped and ignorant underneath her voice. She washed us in a river of make-believe, burned us with a lot of knowledge we didn't necessarily need to know. Pressed us to her with the serious way she read, to shove us away at just the moment, like dimwits, we seemed about to understand.

Dee wanted nice things. A yellow organdy dress to wear to her graduation from high school; black pumps to match a green suit she'd made from an old suit somebody gave me. She was determined to stare down any disaster in her efforts. Her eyelids would not flicker for minutes at a time. Often I fought off the temptation to shake her. At sixteen she had a style of her own: and knew what style was.

I never had an education myself. After second grade the school was closed down. Don't ask me why: in 1927 colored asked fewer questions than they do now. Sometimes Maggie reads to me. She stumbles along good-naturedly but can't see well. She knows she is not bright. Like good looks and money, quickness passed her by. She will marry John Thomas (who has mossy teeth in an earnest face) and then I'll be free to sit here and I guess just sing church songs to myself. Although I never was a good singer. Never could carry a tune. I was always better at a man's job. I used to love to milk till I was hooked in the side in '49. Cows are soothing and slow and don't bother you, unless you try to milk them the wrong way.

I have deliberately turned my back on the house. It is three rooms, just like the one that burned, except the roof is tin; they don't make shingle roofs any more. There are no real windows, just some holes cut in the sides, like the portholes in a ship, but not round and not square, with rawhide holding the shutters up on the outside. This house is in a pasture, too, like the other one. No doubt when Dee sees it she will want to tear it down. She wrote me once that no matter where we "choose" to live, she will manage to come see us. But she will never bring her friends. Maggie and I thought about this and Maggie asked me, "Mama, when did Dee ever *have* any friends?"

She had a few. Furtive boys in pink shirts hanging about on washday after school. Nervous girls who never laughed. Impressed with her they worshiped the well-turned phrase, the cute shape, the scalding humor that erupted like bubbles in lye. She read to them.

When she was courting Jimmy T she didn't have much time to pay to us, but turned all her faultfinding power on him. He *flew* to marry a cheap city girl from a family of ignorant flashy people. She hardly had time to recompose herself.

When she comes I will meet—but there they are!

Maggie attempts to make a dash for the house, in her shuffling way, but I stay her with my hand. "Come back here," I say. And she stops and tries to dig a well in the sand with her toe.

It is hard to see them clearly through the strong sun. But even the first glimpse of leg out of the car tell me it is Dee. Her feet were always neat-looking, as if God himself had shaped them with a certain style. From the other side of the car comes a short, stocky man. Hair is all over his head a foot long and hanging from his chin like a kinky mule tail. I hear Maggie suck in her breath. "Uhnnnh," is what it sounds like. Like when you see the wriggling end of a snake just in front of your foot on the road. "Uhnnnh."

Dee next. A dress down to the ground, in this hot weather. A dress so loud it hurts my eyes. There are yellows and oranges enough to throw back the light of the sun. I feel my whole face warming from the heat waves it throws out. Earrings gold, too, and hanging down to her shoulders. Bracelets dangling and making noises when she moves her arm up to shake the folds of the dress out of her armpits. The dress is loose and flows, and as she walks closer, I like it. I hear Maggie go "Uhnnnh" again. It is her sister's hair. It stands straight up like the wool on a sheep. It is black as night and around the edges are two long pigtails that rope about like small lizards disappearing behind her ears.

"Wa-su-zo-Tean-o!" she says, coming on in that gliding way the dress makes her move. The short stocky fellow with the hair to his navel is all grinning and he follows up with "Asalamalakim, my mother and sister!" He moves to hug Maggie but she falls back, right up against the back of my chair. I feel her trembling there and when I look up I see the perspiration falling off her chin.

"Don't get up," says Dee. Since I am stout it takes something of a push. You can see me trying to move a second or two before I make it. She turns, showing white heels through her sandals, and goes back to the car. Out she peeks next with a Polaroid. She stoops down quickly and lines up picture after picture of me sitting there in front of the house with Maggie cowering behind me. She never takes a shot without making sure the house is included. When a cow comes nibbling around the edge of the yard she snaps it and me and Maggie *and* the house. Then she puts the Polaroid in the back seat of the car, and comes up and kisses me on the forehead.

Meanwhile Asalamalakim is going through motions with Maggie's hand. Maggie's hand is as limp as a fish, and probably as cold, despite the sweat, and she keeps trying to pull it back. It looks like Asalamalakim wants to shake hands but wants to do it fancy. Or maybe he don't know how people shake hands. Anyhow, he soon gives up on Maggie.

"Well," I say. "Dee."

"No, Mama," she says. "Not 'Dee,' Wangero Leewanika Kemanjo!"

"What happened to 'Dee'?" I wanted to know.

"She's dead," Wangero said. "I couldn't bear it any longer, being named after the people who oppress me."

"You know as well as me you was named after your aunt Dicie," I said. Dicie is my sister. She named Dee. We called her "Big Dee" after Dee was born.

"But who was *she* named after?" asked Wangero.

"I guess after Grandma Dee," I said.

"And who was she named after?" asked Wangero.

"Her mother," I said, and saw Wangero was getting tired. "That's about as far back as I can trace it," I said. Though, in fact, I probably could have carried it back beyond the Civil War through the branches.

"Well," said Asalamalakim, "there you are."

"Uhnnnh," I heard Maggie say.

"There I was not," I said, "before 'Dicie' cropped up in our family, so why should I try to trace it that far back?"

He just stood there grinning, looking down on me like somebody inspecting a model A car. Every once in a while he and Wangero sent eye signals over my head.

"How do you pronounce this name?" I asked.

"You don't have to call me by it if you don't want to," said Wangero.

"Why shouldn't I?" I asked. "If that's what you want us to call you, we'll call you."

"I know it might sound awkward at first," said Wangero.

"I'll get used to it," I said. "Ream it out again."

Well, soon we got the name out of the way. Asalamalakim had a name twice as long and three times as hard. After I tripped over it two or three times he told me to just call him Hakim-a-barber. I wanted to ask him was he a barber, but I didn't really think he was, so I didn't ask.

"You must belong to those beef-cattle peoples down the road," I said. They said Asalamalakim when they met you, too, but they didn't shake hands. Always too busy: feeding the cattle, fixing the fences, putting up salt-lick shelters, throwing down hay. When the white folks poisoned some of the herd the men stayed up all night with rifles in their hands. I walked a mile and a half just to see the sight.

Hakim-a-barber said, "I accept some of their doctrines, but farming and raising cattle is not my style." (They didn't tell me, and I didn't ask, whether

Wangero (Dee) had really gone and married him.)

We sat down to eat and right away he said he didn't eat collards and pork was unclean. Wangero, though, went on through the chitlins and corn bread, the greens and everything else. She talked a blue streak over the sweet potatoes. Everything delighted her. Even the fact that we still used the benches her daddy made for the table when we couldn't afford to buy chairs. "Oh, Mama!" she cried. Then turned to Hakim-a-barber. "I never knew how lovely these benches are. You can feel the rump prints," she said, running her hands underneath her and along the bench. Then she gave a sigh and her hand closed over Grandma Dee's butter dish. "That's it!" she said. "I knew there was something I wanted to ask you if I could have." She jumped up from the table and went over in the corner where the churn stood, the milk in it clabber by now. She looked at the churn and looked at it.

"This churn top is what I need," she said. "Didn't Uncle Buddy whittle it out of a tree you all used to have?"

"Yes," I said.

"Uh huh," she said happily. "And I want the dasher, too."

"Uncle Buddy whittle that, too?" asked the barber.

Dee (Wangero) looked up at me.

"Aunt Dee's first husband whittled the dash," said Maggie so low you almost couldn't hear her. "His name was Henry, but they called him Stash."

"Maggie's brain is like an elephant's," Wangero said, laughing. "I can use the churn top as a centerpiece for the alcove table," she said, sliding a plate over the churn, "and I'll think of something artistic to do with the dasher."

When she finished wrapping the dasher the handle stuck out. I took it for a moment in my hands. You didn't even have to look close to see where hands pushing the dasher up and down to make butter had left a kind of sink in the wood. In fact, there were a lot of small sinks; you could see where thumbs and fingers had sunk into the wood. It was beautiful light yellow wood, from a tree that grew in the yard where Big Dee and Stash had lived.

Section 3

After dinner Dee (Wangero) went to the trunk at the foot of my bed and started rifling through it. Maggie hung back in the kitchen over the dishpan. Out came Wangero with two quilts. They had been pieced by Grandma Dee and then Big Dee and me had hung them on the quilt frames on the front porch and quilted them. One was in the Lone Star pattern. The other was Walk Around the Mountain. In both of them were scraps of dresses Grandma Dee had worn fifty and more years ago. Bits and pieces of Grandpa Jarrell's Paisley shirts. And one teeny faded blue piece, about the size of a penny matchbox, that was from Great Grandpa Ezra's uniform that he wore in the Civil War.

"Mama," Wangero said sweet as a bird. "Can I have these old quilts?"

I heard something fall in the kitchen, and a minute later the kitchen door slammed.

"Why don't you take one or two of the others?" I asked. "These old things was just done by me and Big Dee from some tops your grandma pieced before she died."

"No," said Wangero. "I don't want those. They are stitched around the borders by machine."

"That'll make them last better," I said.

"That's not the point," said Wangero. "These are all pieces of dresses Grandma used to wear. She did all this stitching by hand. Imagine!" She held the quilts securely in her arms, stroking them.

"Some of the pieces, like those lavender ones, come from old clothes her mother handed down to her," I said, moving up to touch the quilts. Dee (Wangero) moved back just enough so that I couldn't reach the quilts. They already belonged to her.

"Imagine!" she breathed again, clutching them closely to her bosom.

"The truth is," I said, "I promised to give them quilts to Maggie, for when she marries John Thomas."

She gasped like a bee had stung her.

"Maggie can't appreciate these quilts!" she said. "She'd probably be backward enough to put them to everyday use."

"I reckon she would," I said. "God knows I been saving 'em for long enough with nobody using 'em. I hope she will!" I didn't want to bring up how I had offered Dee (Wangero) a quilt when she went away to college. Then she had told me they were old-fashioned, out of style.

"But they're *priceless!*" she was saying now, furiously; for she has a temper. "Maggie would put them on the bed and in five years they'd be in rags. Less than that!"

"She can always make some more," I said. "Maggie knows how to quilt."

Dee (Wangero) looked at me with hatred. "You just will not understand. The point is these quilts, *these* quilts!"

"Well," I said, stumped. "What would *you* do with them?"

"Hang them," she said. As if that was the only thing you *could* do with quilts.

Maggie by now was standing in the door. I could almost hear the sound her feet made as they scraped over each other.

"She can have them, Mama," she said, like somebody used to never winning anything, or having anything reserved for her. "I can 'member Grandma Dee without the quilts."

Section 4

I looked at her hard. She had filled her bottom lip with checkerberry snuff and it gave her face a kind of dopey, hangdog look. It was Grandma Dee and Big Dee who taught her how to quilt herself. She stood there with her scarred hands hidden in the folds of her skirt. She looked at her sister with something like fear but she wasn't mad at her. This was Maggie's portion. This was the way she knew God to work.

When I looked at her like that something hit me in the top of my head and ran down to the soles of my feet. Just like when I'm in church and the spirit of God touches me and I get happy and shout. I did something I never had done before: hugged Maggie to me, then dragged her on into the room, snatched the quilts out of Miss Wangero's hands and dumped them into Maggie's lap. Maggie just sat there on my bed with her mouth open.

"Take one or two of the others," I said to Dee.

But she turned without a word and went out to Hakim-a-barber.

"You just don't understand," she said, as Maggie and I came out to the car.

"What don't I understand?" I wanted to know.

"Your heritage," she said. And then she turned to Maggie, kissed her, and said, "You ought to try to make something of yourself, too, Maggie. It's really a new day for us. But from the way you and Mama still live you'd never know it."

She put on some sunglasses that hid everything above the tip of her nose and her chin.

Maggie smiled; maybe at the sunglasses. But a real smile, not scared. After we watched the car dust settle I asked Maggie to bring me a dip of snuff. And then the two of us sat there just enjoying, until it was time to go in the house and go to bed.

Featured Literature

"Cecilia Rosas"
from the *Collected
Stories of Amado
Muro*
by Amado Muro

Grade Level
For High School

Thinking Level
Analysis and Evaluation

Writing Domain
Analytical/Expository

Materials Needed
• Copies of the story for
each student to mark on
and take home
• Poster boards
• Crayons, colored pencils,
or markers
• Drawing pencils and
erasers
• Sketch pads or plain
white drawing paper
• Scissors
• Tape or glue sticks

**Suggested
Supplementary
Readings:**
• *Great Expectations* by
Charles Dickens
• "The Stolen Party" by
Liliana Heker

Just Another Fool in Love

by Sue Rader Willett

Overview

Students will work in groups to create film proposals based upon the story "Cecilia Rosas" by Amado Muro. Students will also work individually to write persuasive letters defending the importance of their individual scenes.

Objectives

THINKING SKILLS

Students will:

• *comprehend* and *analyze* a story about unrequited adolescent love;
• *adapt* and *organize* scenes from the story into a film proposal;
• *select* essential scenes, actors, and music for their proposed films;
• *defend* a scene's merits by analyzing and evaluating its importance and impact on the film proposal as a whole;
• *evaluate* rough and final drafts by assessing form and content.

WRITING SKILLS

Students will:

• *select, organize,* and *describe* scenes, music and characters for their proposed film versions of the story;
• *present* film proposals in organized, creative formats;
• *write* persuasive letters to change the mind of a chosen audience.
• *revise* rough drafts into polished final drafts;
• *practice* correct business letter form and content.

The Process

 **PREWRITING**

Prewriting Step 1: *Setting the Stage for Reading*

To help students understand the strange and self-destructive behavior of the lovesick protagonist in Amado Muro's "Cecilia Rosas," begin the unit with a discussion of the mysterious ways people behave when they fall madly in love. Students will start this discussion in small groups and will be held accountable for their ideas and participation by completing the Prewriting Discussion Student Worksheet on the next page.

Prewriting Step 2: *Whole Class Sharing*

When all the groups have completed their discussion forms or lists, meet again as a whole class to share some of the interesting people and their changes in behavior or personality because of falling in love. You may be able to draw conclusions about some typical behaviors shared by a few of these people, and you might even be able to assist the transition to the reading of "Cecilia Rosas" by highlighting the behaviors of daydreaming, rebellion against parents, neglecting work or other duties, paying special attention to grooming, etc.—all behaviors exhibited by the protagonist, Amado.

Establish further transition to the reading by explaining that the story the students are about to read tells about a ninth-grade boy's first crush and the problems he faces because of it. In fact, it seems to be an autobiographical account, telling how young Amado tried to deal with his strong attraction, how he prepared for courting Cecilia Rosas, and how he tried to keep his dignity when he felt so much and so out of control.

Name	Date	Points earned:

Prewriting Discussion
Student Worksheet

List the members of your group:

1.   **4.**

2.   **5.**

3.

Note: Your group should be finished by _____ o'clock.

_____

Part One

Directions: Think about lovesick people you have known. Did they always act normally and rationally, or did they do some strange things? How did being in love affect their work, their appearance, their usual habits and their other relationships? List these people below and briefly describe how being in love affected their behavior and personality.

Name the person: Describe the changes in behavior/personality:

1.   **1.**

2.   **2.**

3.   **3.**

Part Two

Directions: Now, recall any characters from books, stories, TV, or movies that exhibited changes in their behavior because they were in love. How did their being in love affect their work, their appearance, their usual habits, and their other relationships? List these characters below and briefly describe how being in love affected their behavior and/or personality.

Name the character: Describe the changes in behavior/personality:

1.   **1.**

2.   **2.**

3.   **3.**

Part Three

After you have filled out this group form, review what is written and decide which real person and which character are the most interesting examples of the strange behavior of people in love. Choose one member of your group to be your spokesperson and have her/him share your results with the whole class. Notify your teacher when your group has finished both parts and when the spokesperson is ready to share with the class.

Prewriting Step 3: *Vocabulary Development*

If you are working with an Honors or accelerated group, you may wish to proceed directly to the reading at this point. If you are working with students who need help with reading skills, you may choose to work with the story's vocabulary before you read.

Listed below are words that an average ninth grade class might find troublesome. You could divide the words among the students and have them complete a Vocabulary Worksheet like the one on the next page. *(There are seventy three words listed in the order they appear in the story.)* Or, you might choose just a few of the words to preview before reading and encourage students to make personal vocabulary lists of words they find troublesome as they read.

Vocabulary List

smock	sapped	admonitions
loathsome	entranced	blustery
stigma	menial	tirades
degrading	refuge	inured
onerous	lolling	rebukes
effeminate	transcended	reveries
compensations	insipid	cunning
alluring	debonair	doggedly
chastely	reveled	comely
obsidian	hubbub	lassitudes
enthralling	brazenly	lissome
raven	quickened	wanly
decorous	somnambulist	bulwarked
furtively	serenity	tenements
effrontery	tranquility	profane
indignant	pygmy	unorthodox
haughty	indiscriminate	grimaced
imperious	voluptuous	renegade
vanity	piquant	serenade
derisively	brusque	mariachis
exemplary	jibed	cantinas
frivolous	austere	bleak
demure	mien	cynically
primly	sordid	
languid	malingering	

Vocabulary Worksheet

Directions: Record the words your teacher assigned you on the blanks labeled Word #1 and Word #2 below. Look up the word in the dictionary and record its meaning (s) and part (s) of speech. Next, find the word in the story and record the sentence in which it appears. After reading and thinking about the sentence, go back to the meaning(s) you listed and underline the meaning that best fits how the word is used in this context. Be prepared to share your words, meanings, and sentences with the class.

Word #1: _____ (found on page _____)

Dictionary: Part (s) of speech _____

Meaning (s) _____

_____

Story context: Sentence _____

_____

_____

Word #2: _____ (found on page _____)

Dictionary: Part (s) of speech _____

Meaning (s) _____

_____

Story context: Sentence _____

_____

_____

Prewriting Step 4: *Relating the Vocabulary to the Text*

The vocabulary study leads nicely into a discussion of the actual language and diction of the piece. Tell students to notice parts of the story that seem artificial or difficult. Ask them whether this sounds like the language of a typical ninth-grade boy. *(No, he is recalling the incident as an adult. The narrative voice is a mature, educated Amado.)* One sensitive reader has noted that Muro's writing almost sounds as if he's trying to be someone he's not—just like the boy!

You might have students underline or highlight passages that interest or puzzle them. These passages may be discussed after everyone has read the story.

Prewriting Step 5: *Reading*

Begin reading the first two to three pages of the story aloud to help the students hear the voice and feel the tone. Continue with student volunteers or assign the rest as homework. If your students need you to read them the whole story, please do so. It is imperative that they read and understand the entire story in order to complete the rest of the unit.

Prewriting Step 6: *Reading Check Quiz*

After reading the story, you may wish to give the students a reading check quiz or a short essay question:

Reading Check Quiz

1. T F   The narrator's name was Amado, just like the author.

2. T F   The narrator's coat-hanging job had two compensations: (1) earning three dollars every Saturday and (2) being out of the house so that his mother didn't nag him.

3. T F   Miss Rosas was the friendliest as well as the most beautiful saleslady in Ladies' Wear.

4. T F   The store managers warned the narrator to improve his work habits or suffer the consequences.

5. T F   The narrator didn't care about anything except Miss Rosas.

6. T F   The narrator spoke Spanish at home to please his family.

7. T F   In spite of his deep love for Cecilia Rosas, the narrator was still attracted to the women he saw on the street.

8. T F   Miss Rosas sincerely liked the narrator and invited him to the movies the following week.

9. T F   The narrator took dancing lessons and learned a romantic song to impress Miss Rosas.

10. T F   The Mariachis were cruel to the young man when his plan to serenade Miss Rosas failed.

Key: 1. T	2. F	3. T	4. T	5. T
6. F	7. F	8. F	9. T	10. F

Short Essay Question

Amado says at one point to his mother, "Mother, why do we always have to eat *sopa, frijoles refritos, mondongo, and pozole?* . . . Can't we ever eat roast beef or ham and eggs like Americans do?" His mother wouldn't speak to him for two days after that, and his Uncle mumbled something about renegade Mexicans.

Why did Amado's request upset his family so much? Why did he speak and act this way , hurting the family he loved? What do you think about his behavior?

Prewriting Step 7: *Sharing Highlighted Passages*

To reinforce understanding of plot, character, and theme, ask the students to share the passages they underlined during their reading. Ask them why they highlighted these passages, and encourage them to ask questions about confusing or puzzling passages.

Prewriting Step 8: *Comprehension Check*

Students may show mastery of the story by exhibiting complete understanding of the following questions. The words printed in block type following each question correspond to levels of critical thinking according to Bloom's Taxonomy.

1. How were Amado's thoughts and behavior at La Feria influenced by his feelings for Miss Rosas? COMPREHENSION

2. How did Amado's feelings for Miss Rosas compare with the feelings of the men who visited the water fountain? ANALYSIS

3. How did Amado feel when men stared at her? COMPREHENSION

4. How did his affection for Miss Rosas affect Amado's feeling about other pretty women? COMPREHENSION

5. How did his feelings for Miss Rosas affect his family relationships? Compare Miss Rosas's view about acting American with his family's beliefs and customs. COMPREHENSION/APPLICATION

6. How did his love for Miss Rosas affect his personal and cultural identity? ANALYSIS

7. How did his love for Miss Rosas enrich his life? COMPREHENSION

8. How did Amado view his future? COMPREHENSION

9. What should have alerted him to the fact that Miss Rosas wasn't romantically interested in him? ANALYSIS

10. What were Miss Sandoval and the other ladies really doing when they talked to him about taking Miss Rosas to the movies? ANALYSIS

11. How did Little Chihuahua appear to Amado after Cecilia spoke to him about going to the movies? COMPREHENSION

12. How did he prepare himself to properly court Miss Rosas? COMPREHENSION

13. Who is Emalina Uribe? Why is she important? KNOWLEDGE/ANALYSIS

14. When and how does Amado finally understand that Miss Rosas sees him as just a foolish young boy? ANALYSIS

15. How does this experience seem to affect Amado in relation to women? ANALYSIS

16. How does the last sentence ("So we serenaded her father instead.") affect you? Why? ANALYSIS

17. In retrospect, which character interested you the most? With whom did you sympathize? Who angered you? Who frustrated you? Why? ANALYSIS

Prewriting Step 9: *Introducing the Production Prompt*

After your students demonstrate mastery of the story, introduce the production prompt. Explain that the class work changes at this point. You are no longer just their teacher. You are also going to play the part of the executive producer of a very successful and internationally acclaimed film company called *Fame and Fortune Enterprises*. They will play the role of talented new film-makers trying to impress you. Their peer group becomes a production company.

 THE PRODUCTION PROMPT

The Situation:

Pretend you have just completed your Master's Degree in Film Production from a prestigious West Coast university. You are anxious about your career and desperately hope to land a contract with a major film company. Today, you received the following letter and are thrilled with the opportunity to prove your talents.

❖❖

Fame and Fortune Enterprises
54321 Movieland Lane
Hollywood, CA 90028

_____
(Today's Date)

Dear _____:
       (Student's Name)

My colleagues and I enjoyed meeting you at the Cinema Industry Awards dinner last spring. It is always a pleasure to become acquainted with talented new filmmakers.

My company is currently seeking proposals for new film projects due to begin production within the year. We would be very interested in seeing you and hearing your ideas concerning a short feature film based on the story "Cecilia Rosas" by Amado Muro. If you are interested in presenting a story board of scenes, a casting list, plus a list of background music, and a theme song, please be able to submit your ideas within the week.

We believe the story lends itself very well to the cinematic medium and look forward to a presentation of your creative vision very soon.

       Sincerely,

_____
Executive Producer   *(Teacher's signature)*

Project Directions

Excited about this creative challenge and a chance for fame and fortune, you eagerly accept the offer from this wealthy, powerful, and highly acclaimed Hollywood producer. You have sent your response, agreeing to present an overview of your proposed film project within two days. In order to complete your proposal and present your film idea to the review committee (which just so happens to be your teacher and fellow classmates), you need to meet with a group to create:

1. Five to seven sketches of individual scenes mounted on a poster board. These scenes will tell Amado's story. Choose scenes that are essential to developing the plot and the theme of your proposed film;

2. Individual summaries of each scene's characters, action, mood, dialogue and merit;

3. A casting list of actors to play each role in your film;

4. A list of background music and a theme song for the film.

Your group of five to seven members will present your film proposal to the review committee (your class) on _____ for _____ points. Plan your presentation to take no more than _____ minutes. Elect a spokesperson or share the speaking duties, but be sure to practice your oral presentation and plan ahead so that the committee and producer will be duly impressed.

 # PRECOMPOSING:

Precomposing Step 1: *Forming Production Groups*

Students should form production company groups of five to seven classmates.

Precomposing Step 2: *Creating a Master List of Scenes*

Production companies should meet to divide the story into essential scenes. Students will need to envision the story as a series of scenes in order to create their story boards. Groups will come up with different numbers of scenes essential to the story. This is fine. Numbers of scenes vary, depending on whether students regard Amado's daydreams as a part of a larger scene or as individual scenes in themselves. Also, since each student is accountable for one scene, groups may divide the story according to the number of members in the group.

Once the students meet in their production companies, distribute the following worksheet to each group member:

Student Worksheet: The Master List of Scenes

Directions: List the names of your production company members.

1. _____ 4. _____

2. _____ 5. _____

3. _____ 6. _____

Please put a * by your name above.

Think about the story as if it were a movie presented in various scenes. Decide where scene breaks would naturally occur. The first scenes have been charted as an example to help you begin. Continue charting the story scenes to the end of the story.

You will need this list later when you choose the scenes for your proposal, so be careful and thorough. Hand in your list when it is complete. Your teacher will give you credit and return it to you. Please ask questions if you need help.

Example:

Scene #	Setting	Characters	What Happens
I	La Feria Ladies' Department	Amado, Miss Rosas, admiring men at the water fountain, salesladies	Amado's admiration of Miss Rosas vs. other men's; Miss Rosas as seen through Amado's eyes; Amado's job.
II	La Feria window ledge on top floor	Amado	Endangering his job; dreaming and smoking; becoming obsessed and irresponsible.
	South El Paso Street	Amado	Escaping the hubbub; no more thought of other women; bleak vision of future
III	Window ledge	Amado	Warning the executive

Student Worksheet: The Master List of Scenes

Scene #	Setting	Characters	What Happens

Precomposing Step 3: *Visualizing the Film*

After students complete their Master List of Scenes, help them begin the transition from seeing the story as a series of literary scenes to visualizing it as a film.

Ask the class:

- Have you ever seen a film based on a story or book you had previously read? Which ones?
- How was the film different from the story or the book?
  —Were the characters like how you had imagined them?
  —Was the setting like how you had imagined it?
  —Was the theme the same?
- Which version did you like better—the book or the film? Why?
- Why do you think the filmmakers changed the original story in the ways they did? Why couldn't they film each and every scene and keep all of the characters and dialogue the same as in the original book?

Just like real filmmakers, your students will have to make choices about what they would keep the same or change in their proposed film versions of "Cecilia Rosas." Tell them that they will be limited in the number of scenes represented on their story boards. Each student in the group will be responsible for one scene from the story. The total number of scenes in the film proposals will equal the number of people in their production company group.

Precomposing Step 4: *Completing Story Board Sketches*

Have the students meet in their groups to determine their scene selections. Remind them that the scenes they select should blend together sequentially to tell Amado's story and to communicate the theme of his personal tragedy.

After the groups reach consensus in determining exactly which scenes will appear on their story board proposals, they should begin their individual sketches. Each student is responsible for one scene sketch and one written summary.

Materials needed to complete scene sketches and the story boards:

- one poster board for each group
- colored markers, colored pencils, or crayons
- drawing pencils and erasers
- large sketch pads or many sheets of blank, white 8 1/2" x 11" paper
- scissors
- tape or glue sticks

Remind your students that you do not expect them to be professional artists. They should focus on capturing one static moment from a dynamic scene to present the story in a series of pictures. Urge them to think of one predominant visual image from their scene and focus on that while being sure to include all significant characters and setting elements. They might wish to include lines of dialogues or label their pictures. A sample story board is shown on the next page.

STORY BOARD FOR "CECILIA ROSAS"

SCENE 1

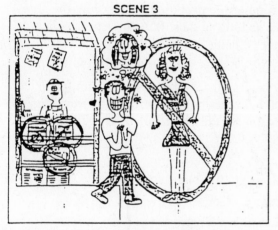

SCENE 2

SCENE 3

SCENE 4

SCENE 5

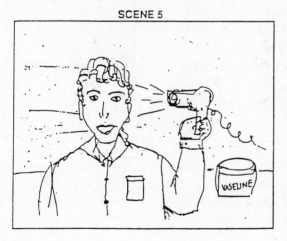

SCENE 6

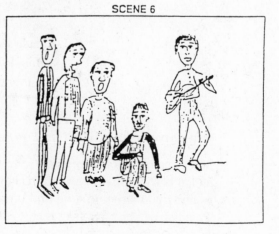

Optional Step You might find it helpful to show photographic stills from well-known movies adapted from works of literature. These should be shown merely as a visual aide to enable students to see how one static moment from a motion picture can communicate an entire scene.

Precomposing Step 5: *Sequencing the Scene Sketches*

After each student finishes her/his scene sketch, the company needs to decide how to place the scenes on the poster board in sequential order to tell the story. Sketches should be firmly affixed to the poster board with glue or tape.

Groups may also include an original title for their film version and decorate the borders of each sketch or other parts of the poster board to add visual interest to their presentations.

Precomposing Step 6: *Creating a Casting List*

Each production company should meet next to determine their casting list. Casting choices often determine the tone of the proposed film. Allow the students to make creative casting choices as long as their film concept is consistent. Some film versions may be rather comedic while others may be terribly tragic. Some students cast their peers while other use professional actors.

Companies will need to present their casting list to the review committee (the class), so encourage the groups to make a visually interesting list. Every major and minor character in the proposed film should be included on the list.

Sample student casting list:

Cast List

Amado Muro — *Lou Diamond Phillips*

Cecilia Rosas — *Gloria Estefan*

Cecilia's Dad — *Ricky Ricardo*

Amado's Uncle — *Tony Danza*

Amado's sister — *Alyssa Milano*

Amado's Mom — *Roseanne*

Johnny — *Johnny Depp*

Precomposing Step 7: *Determining Musical Selections*

Since casting choices often set the tone of the proposed film, they are best completed before musical selections can be made. Now, the companies need to decide upon a theme song and musical selections for each individual scene. This list will also be presented to the review committee.

Sample student music list:

```
┌─────────────────────────────────────────────────────┐
│                    Music List                        │
│   Theme Song — "Cecilia" by Simon & Garfunkel        │
│      Theme from Scene #1 "Nutcracker"                │
│      Scene #3 "Pretty Woman" by Roy Orbison          │
│           Scene #4 "Nutcracker"                      │
│     Scene #6 "Cecilia" by Simon & Garfunkel          │
└─────────────────────────────────────────────────────┘
```

Precomposing Step 8: *Writing Scene Summaries*

In addition to the scene sketch, each student is responsible for her/his individual scene summary. This information may be shared during the oral presentation or may simply serve to inform the evaluator about the selected scene.

Directions to the student: On a piece of 8 1/2" x 11" paper that you will attach to the back of your company's story board, record the following information concerning your individual scene:

1. Which major or minor characters appear in your scene?
2. Where does your scene take place?
3. What happens during your scene?
4. What music is heard during your scene?
5. What is the general mood or prevailing emotion in this scene?
6. What important dialogue takes place during this scene?
7. Why is this scene important to your film version of this story?

Precomposing Step 9: *Formalizing Presentations*

Now it is time for each production company to prepare its presentation. Remind the students that they are competing with one another to make the best impression upon the review committee *(their classmates)* and the executive producer *(you)*. Reread the Production Prompt orally to the class. Allow them a few minutes to formalize their presentations.

When each group is ready, begin your production proposal meeting. Resume your executive producer persona if you are so inclined and:

- Welcome the competing teams to the meeting;
- Thank them for their effort and express your appreciation for their commitment to the project and their creative talents;
- Explain that your company will inform them as soon as possible about your choice of the best proposal and future production details.

Sit down with a note pad and enjoy the group presentations. Students may vote on the best film proposal if you wish, or you may prefer to make positive comments about the best groups. Use your own discretion in judging or grading.

Precomposing Step 10: *Introducing the Writing Prompt*

After all the companies present their film proposals, distribute the following writing prompt.

 **PROMPT**

The Situation:

Your company completed a successful presentation for the Executive Producer of Fame and Fortune Enterprises and its associates. You and your colleagues have anxiously awaited word whether your film proposal has been accepted by the production company. In today's mail you receive the following letter:

❖❖❖

Fame and Fortune Enterprises
54321 Movieland Lane
Hollywood, CA 90028

<u>   </u>
(A Date Last Week)

Dear <u>   </u>:
      (Student's Name)

Congratulations! Your company's film proposal has been accepted by the review committee. We look forward to begin production in the next few weeks. Before we can submit our budget to the financial review committee, however, we need to scale down your vision of the film. With our limited production financing of $7,000,000, it is impossible to include all of the scenes your company has proposed. I am afraid the review committee has suggested that your particular scene needs to be cut from the film.

We appreciate your creative effort and regret this decision, but we are sure you understand that without the funds to produce the scenes, our hands are tied. We look forward to working with your company and to speaking with you at our next production meeting.

                    Sincerely,

                <u>   </u>
                Executive Producer
                (Teacher's signature)

Writing Directions:

Shocked by the prospect that your scene might be cut from the film, you decide to write a persuasive letter to the executive producer explaining why your scene should remain a part of the proposed film.

Write a formal business letter to the executive producer. Be sure to review correct business letter form and refer to the executive producer's letter for the correct name, title and address. Use your own street address and today's date for your heading. The most important part of this letter is the body. If you cannot persuade the executive producer to keep your scene in the proposed film, you may be cut from the project and lose your chance for fame and fortune. Plead a convincing case and use a respectful, businesslike tone. You may wish to include:

1. an opening reference to the producer's last letter;
2. a brief summary of your scene, emphasizing what is accomplished by the action and which main characters are developed;
3. how this scene affects the general mood, tone, or overall emotional impact of the film;
4. what essential quality of the film would be missing if this scene were cut;
5. how the music appearing with this scene is important to the entire film;
6. an expression of your appreciation for considering these arguments for accepting your company's film proposal.

Type your final draft letter or write or print neatly in dark ink.

Your rough draft will be due for peer sharing on _____for_____points.

Your final draft will be due for evaluation on_____for _____points.

 WRITING

If your students know proper business form *(block or modified)*, you may allow them to begin writing their letter in class. If your students seem unsure about proper business letter conventions, it is wise to review the form at this point.

 SHARING AND REVISING

Sharing and Revising Step 1: *Modeling*

Before students evaluate each other's drafts in pairs, distribute the following student sample by Mai Vu or show it on an overhead:

1234 Brookseed Lane
Mission Viejo, CA 92691
December 18, 1991

Ms. Sue R. Willett, Executive Producer
Fame and Fortune Enterprises
54321 Movieland Lane
Hollywood, CA 90028

Dear Ms. Willett:

I just received your letter this morning, and because this matter is so urgent, I felt the need to respond immediately.

I understand because of financial concerns, your company may feel the need to cut certain unnecessary scenes from our film. But I must insist that my scene cannot be one of them! This scene features Amado singing with the mariachis for Mr. Rosas after Cecilia abandoned him for a sleek and sophisticated American.

This scene symbolizes the despair which all lovers suffer at one time or another, and it serves as the sole theme for the entire film. By showing that Amado is capable of befriending the father of the very woman who ignorantly broke his tender heart, one may see the acceptance that must develop in order for a broken heart to mend. In doing so, Amado not only accepts the harsh reality of Cecilia's rejection but also reclaims his faith in his heritage and his true self.

My scene also displays our theme song, "Cecilia" by Simon and Garfunkel. This love song is appropriate not only because Cecilia Rosas is the main character, but also because the lyrics reiterate Amado's blind adoration for her.

In conclusion, my scene is essential to the film because it provides viewers with a resolution. One could say that it represents a clasp that locks all the other scenes together to form a precious strand of pearls. Without it, the other scenes would fall apart. Individually, they would be practically worthless.

I hope your company will reconsider your decision and allow me the opportunity to contribute to this inspirational production. Thank you for your time and consideration. I look forward to your reply.

Sincerely,

Mai Vu

Mai Vu, Capistrano Valley High School
Screenwriter

Note: An additional student model is appended to this lesson.

As a whole class, students will score the paper according to the criteria on the following Peer Sharing Revision Checklist:

Peer Sharing Revision Checklist

Author's name _____ Date _____ Period _____

Sharing partner's name _____

Directions to the sharing partner: Please read the author's letter very carefully. Your evaluation and comments will help her/him during the revision of this rough draft. After you listen to the author read, reread the letter silently to yourself and fill out this checklist. In addition (on the back of this sheet), please write general comments and encouraging remarks to the author about what she/he did well. You will receive

_____ points for completing this activity. It is due at _____ o'clock on

_____. Thank you for your help!

Circle the number that best represents your personal evaluation for each part of this letter. The number symbolizes:

5 = outstanding   4 = very good   3 = good   2 = average   1 = weak   0 = not evident

Body of the letter: How well does the letter include:

1. an opening reference to the executive producer's last letter
5   4   3   2   1   0

2. a brief summary of the scene, emphasizing what is accomplished by the action and which main characters are developed; 5   4   3   2   1   0

3. how this scene affects the general mood, tone or overall emotional impact of the film; 5   4   3   2   1   0

4. how the music appearing with this scene is important to the entire film;
5   4   3   2   1   0

5. what essential quality of the film would be missing if this scene were cut;
5   4   3   2   1   0

6. an expression of your appreciation for considering these arguments for accepting this company's film proposal. 5   4   3   2   1   0

Does the letter exhibit a respectful, businesslike tone? 5   4   3   2   1   0

Is the letter persuasive? Do you think the executive producer will seriously consider its arguments and allow this scene to remain in the film?

   (Yes = 5, 4   Maybe = 3, 2   No = 1, 0)   5   4   3   2   1   0

Form of the letter: Does the letter format include a correct

(Yes = 1 No = 0)

1.	date?	1	0
2.	heading?	1	0
3.	inside address?	1	0
4.	salutation?	1	0
5.	body format?	1	0
6.	closing?	1	0
7.	signature/title?	1	0

Language: Does this writer exhibit effective use of standard formal English by.

1.	using good sentence structure?	5	4	3	2	1	0
2.	using correct spelling?	5	4	3	2	1	0
3.	using correct punctuation?	5	4	3	2	1	0
4.	correctly using subject and verbs?	5	4	3	2	1	0
5.	correctly using pronouns?	5	4	3	2	1	0

Positive Comments:

Sharing and Revising Step 2: *Pair Share*

Now, ask students to meet in pairs to share and evaluate each other's rough drafts. Authors should read their letter aloud to their partner, who reads along silently. Then partners should reread the letter silently to themselves, using the evaluation checklist as a guide for suggesting areas of needed revision.

Sharing and Revising Step 3: *Revising Time*

Give student writers time to ask their partner about their peer evaluation. You may also schedule appointments for students to meet with you individually. Allow students ample time to revise their rough draft.

EVALUATION

Teacher Worksheet
Evaluation Checklist and Grade Report

Evaluate the final drafts of the student letters using this worksheet. Attach your evaluation to the student's final draft and return it to the student.

Student author _____ Period _____ Date _____

Writing Assignment: *Letter to executive producer defending scene inclusion*

Content Evaluation (50%)

5 = outstanding   4 = very good   3 = good   2 = fair   1 = poor   0 = not evident

1. Does the letter clearly explain why the executive producer should keep your scene in the film? (circle one)   5 4 3 2 1 0 **x 2**

2. Does the letter:

   a. briefly summarize the scene?   5 4 3 2 1 0

   b. explain how the setting and mood affect the entire film?   5 4 3 2 1 0

   c. explain how the music in this particular scene advances the mood, theme, and/or plot of the entire film?   5 4 3 2 1 0

   d. explain what essential quality the film would lack if this scene were excluded?   5 4 3 2 1 0

   e. reflect an appropriate tone?   5 4 3 2 1 0

   f. thank the producer for considering your arguments?   5 4 3 2 1 0

3. Is the letter persuasive?   5 4 3 2 1 0 **x 2**

Form Evaluation (20%)

4. Does the letter format include a correct: (*Circle* Yes *or* No)

   a. date?   Yes   No

   b. salutation?   Yes   No

   c. body?   Yes   No

   d. closing?   Yes   No

   e. signature?   Yes   No

   f. printed name and title?   Yes   No

Language Evaluation (30%)

5. Is the language used respectful?   5 4 3 2 1 0

6. Is the language effective by:

   a. using good sentence structure?   5 4 3 2 1 0

   b. using correct spelling?   5 4 3 2 1 0

   c. using correct punctuation?   5 4 3 2 1 0

   d. correctly using subject and verbs?   5 4 3 2 1 0

   e. correctly using pronouns?   5 4 3 2 1 0

Dear _____ *(student's name)*,

I have decided that your letter should receive the following letter grade:

(Circle One)   A   B   C   D   F

This is based on my content evaluation: _____ / 50%

form evaluation: _____ / 20%

language evaluation: _____ / 30%

total evaluation: _____ / 100% = points

If you have any questions about your score or the evaluation process, please feel free to see me privately so that we can discuss your paper.

You also received credit for attaching:

1. your rough draft _____ / _____ points

2. your sharing and revision checklist _____ / _____ points

3. your scene sketch _____ / _____ points

4. your presentation notes _____ / _____ points

In addition, you received _____ / _____ points for sharing your scene with the class during the precomposing segment of this lesson. Thank you!

Sincerely,

_____

Teacher as evaluator   *Date*

EXTENSION ACTIVITIES

1. *Synthesis*

Choose one or more scenes described in your film proposal to develop into a script. If you select only one or two scenes, try to work them into a unified piece, much like a one-act play. Include narration, stage direction, dialogue, and music. Consider submitting your work to the drama department or directing your classmates. Perform the piece live or on videotape for an assembly or school open house.

Make the film version of the story as a group or class project.

2. *Evaluation*

After viewing a classmate's dramatic production, write a review expressing your opinion of the script, acting, and production. (Or, write a review of your own.) Student reviews could be collected and bound or otherwise presented along with student scripts and performances at a school open house or assembly.

3. *Analysis*

- The story of Amado in "Cecilia Rosas" has some parallels with the plight of Pip and his unrequited love for Estella in Charles Dickens's *Great Expectations*. If *Great Expectations* is on your syllabus, you may want to have students compare and contrast the situations of the two characters.

- Another story that has thematic parallels with "Cecilia Rosas" is "The Stolen Party" by Liliana Heker, elsewhere in this book. Set in Argentina, it deals with a young girl who has high hopes for attending a rich friend's birthday party. Her hopes are dashed when she realizes she has been invited as the hired help. Again, students could compare and contrast the characters' loss of innocence in both works.

Student Model

1234 Brookseed Lane
Mission Viejo, CA 92691
December 18, 1991

Ms. Sue R. Willett
Fame and Fortune Enterprise
54321 Movieland Lane
Hollywood, CA 90028

Dear Ms. Willett:

I have just received your letter, and I am delighted that you were able to respond so soon. First of all, I would like to thank you for considering my proposal. It is an honor to be accepted.

I have been thinking about your idea to cut one of the most important scenes from the movie. I understand why you need to consider this, but I must say that if this scene is not included, the movie will be incomplete. The scene in which Miss Rosas is talking to Amado is one of the most important parts of the entire film. Amado is mistaken, and he misinterprets Miss Rosas' joke. In this scene, we see the true Miss Rosas. Everybody thought that Miss Rosas was just as beautiful inside as out, but in this scene we see how she really is. Finally, the song featured in this scene , "Finally, It's Happened to Me" by CeCe Pediston, shows the audience how Amado is feeling inside. It's a fast song, and its rhythm matches Amado's mood and heartbeat.

Just like you wouldn't pull a can from the middle of the stock or else the others would just fall apart, you cannot take out this scene from our production. This is the most important scene!

Forgive me if I have appeared to be too aggressive in my argument. I sincerely hope that you will take my ideas into consideration. Thank you for your time and your consideration, and lastly, thank you for accepting my company's proposal. I look forward to your reply.

Sincerely,

Marie Chau

Marie Chau, Capistrano Valley High School
Producer

Cecilia Rosas
by Amado Muro

When I was in the ninth grade at Bowie High School in El Paso, I got a job hanging up women's coats at La Feria Department Store on Saturdays. It wasn't the kind of job that had much appeal for a Mexican boy or for boys of any other nationality, either. But the work wasn't hard, only boring. Wearing a smock, I stood around the Ladies' Wear Department all day long waiting for women customers to finish trying on coats so I could hang them up.

Having to wear a smock was worse than the work itself. It was an agonizing ordeal. To me it was a loathsome stigma of unmanly toil that made an already degrading job even more so. The work itself I looked on as onerous and effeminate for a boy from a family of miners, shepherds, and ditchdiggers. But working in Ladies' Wear had two compensations: earning three dollars every Saturday was one; being close to the Señorita Cecilia Rosas was the other.

This alluring young woman, the most beautiful I had ever seen, more than made up for my mollycoddle labor and the smock that symbolized it. My chances of looking at her were almost limitless. And like a good Mexican, I made the most of them. But I was only too painfully aware that I wasn't the only one who thought this saleslady gorgeous.

La Feria had water fountains on every one of its eight floors. But men liked best the one on the floor where Miss Rosas worked. So they made special trips to Ladies' Wear all day long to drink water and look at her.

Since I was only fourteen and in love for the first time, I looked at her more chastely than most. The way her romantic lashes fringed her obsidian eyes was especially enthralling to me. Then, too, I never tired of admiring her shining, raven hair, her Cupid's-bow lips, the warmth of her gleaming white smile. Her rich olive skin was almost as dark as mine. Sometimes she wore a San Juan rose in her hair. When she did, she looked so very lovely I forgot all about what La Feria was paying me to do and stood gaping at her instead. My admiration was decorous but complete. I admired her hourglass figure as well as her wonderfully radiant face.

Other men admired her too. They inspected her from the water fountain. Some stared at her boldly, watching her trimly rhythmic hips sway. Others, less frank and open, gazed furtively at her swelling bosom or her shapely calves. Their effrontery made me indignant. I, too, looked at these details of Miss Rosas. But I prided myself on doing so more romantically, far more poetically, than they did, with much more love than desire.

Then, too, Miss Rosas was the friendliest as well as the most beautiful saleslady in Ladies' Wear. But the other salesladies, Mexican girls all, didn't like her. She was so nice to them all they were hard put to justify their dislike. They couldn't very well admit they disliked her because she was pretty. So they all said she was haughty and imperious. Their claim was partly true. Her beauty was Miss Rosas' only obvious vanity. But she had still another. She prided herself on being more American than Mexican because she was born in El Paso. And she did her best to act, dress, and talk the way Americans do. She hated to speak Spanish, disliked her Mexican name. She called herself Cecile Roses instead of Cecilia Rosas. This made the other salesladies smile derisively. They called her La Americana or the Gringa from Xochimilco every time they mentioned her name.

Looking at this beautiful girl was more important than money to me. It was my greatest compensation for doing work that I hated. She was so lovely that a glance at her sweetly expressive face was enough to make me forget my shame at wearing a smock and my dislike for my job with its eternal waiting around.

Miss Rosas was an exemplary saleslady. She could be frivolous, serious or demure, primly efficient too, molding herself to each customer's personality. Her voice matched her exotically mysterious eyes. It was the richest, the softest, I had ever heard. Her husky whisper, gentle as a rain breeze, was like a tender caress. Hearing it made me want to dream, and I did. Romantic thoughts burgeoned up in my mind like rosy billows of hope scented with Miss Rosas' perfume. These thoughts made me so languid at my work that the floor manager, Joe Apple, warned me to show some enthusiasm for it or else suffer the consequences.

But my dreams sapped my will to struggle, making me oblivious to admonitions. I had neither the desire nor the energy to respond to Joe Apple's warnings. Looking at Miss Rosas used up so much of my energy that I had little left for my work. Miss Rosas was twenty, much too old for me, everyone said. But what everyone said didn't matter. So I soldiered on the job and watched her, entranced by her beauty, her grace. While I watched, I dreamed of being a hero. It hurt me to have her see me doing such menial work. But there was no escape from it. I needed the job to stay in school. So more and more I took refuge in dreams.

When I had watched her as much, if not more, than I could safely do without attracting the attention of other alert Mexican salesladies, I slipped out of Ladies' Wear and walked up the stairs to the top floor. There I sat on a window ledge smoking Faro cigarettes looking down at the city's canyons, and best of all, thinking about Miss Rosas and myself.

They say Chihuahua Mexicans are good at dreaming because the mountains are so gigantic and the horizons so vast in Mexico's biggest state that men don't think pygmy thoughts there. I was no exception. Lolling on the ledge, I became what I wanted to be. And what I wanted to be was a handsome American Miss Rosas could love and marry. The dreams I dreamed were imaginative masterpieces, or so I thought. They transcended the insipid realities of a casual relationship, making it vibrantly thrilling and infinitely more romantic. They transformed me from a colorless Mexican boy who put women's coats away into the debonair American, handsome, dashing, and worldly, that I longed to be for her sake. For the first time in my life I reveled in the magic of fantasy. It brought happiness. Reality didn't.

But my window-ledge reveries left me bewildered and shaken. They had a narcotic quality. The more thrillingly romantic fantasies I created, the more I needed to create. It got so I couldn't get enough dreaming time in Ladies' Wear. My kind of dreaming demanded disciplined concentration. And there was just too much hubbub, too much gossiping, too many coats to be put away there.

So I spent less time in Ladies' Wear. My flights to the window ledge became more recklessly frequent. Sometimes I got tired sitting there. When I did, I took the freight elevator down to the street floor and brazenly walked out of the store without so much as punching a time clock. Walking the streets quickened my imagination, gave form and color to my thoughts. It made my brain glow with impossible hopes that seemed incredibly easy to realize. So absorbed was I in thoughts of Miss Rosas and myself that I bumped into Americans, apologizing mechanically in Spanish instead of English, and wandered down South El Paso Street like a somnambulist, without really seeing its street vendors, cafes and arcades, tattoo shops, and shooting galleries at all.

But if there was confusion in these walks, there was some serenity too. Something good did come from the dreams that prompted them. I found I could tramp the streets with a newly won tranquillity, no longer troubled by, or even aware of, girls in tight skirts, overflowing blouses, and drop-stitch stockings. My love for Miss Rosas was my shield against the furtive thoughts and indiscriminate desires that had made me so uneasy for a year or more before I met her.

Then, too, because of her, I no longer looked at the pictures of voluptuous women in the Vea and Vodevil magazines at Zamora's newsstand. The piquant thoughts Mexicans call malos deseos were gone from my mind. I no longer thought about women as I did before I fell in love with Miss Rosas. Instead, I thought about a woman, only one. This clear-cut objective and the serenity that went with it made me understand something of one of the nicest things about love.

I treasured the walks, the window-ledge sittings, and the dreams that I had then. I clung to them just as long as I could. Drab realities closed in on me chokingly just as soon as I gave them up. My future was a time clock with an American Mister telling me what to do, and this I knew only too well. A career as an ice-dock laborer stretched ahead of me. Better said, it dangled over me like a Veracruz machete. My uncle, Rodolfo Avitia, a straw boss on the ice docks, was already training me for it. Every night he took me to the mile-long docks overhanging the Southern Pacific freight yards. There he handed me tongs and made me practice tripping three-hundred pound ice blocks so I could learn how to unload an entire boxcar of ice blocks myself.

Thinking of this bleak future drove me back into my fantasies, made me want to prolong them forever. My imagination was taxed to the breaking point by the heavy strain I put on it.

I thought about every word Miss Rosas had ever said to me, making myself believe she looked at me with unmistakable tenderness when she said them. When she said, "Amado, please hang up this fur coat," I found special meaning in her tone. It was as though she had said, "Amadito, I love you."

When she gave these orders, I pushed into action like a man blazing with a desire to perform epically heroic feats. At such times I felt capable of putting away not one but a thousand fur coats, and would have done so joyously.

Sometimes on the street I caught myself murmuring, "Cecilia, *linda amorcita*, I love you." When these surges swept over me, I walked down empty streets so I could whisper, "Cecilia, *te quiero con toda mi alma*" as much as I wanted to and mumble everything else that I felt. And so I emptied my heart on the street and window ledge while women's coats piled up in Ladies' Wear.

But my absences didn't go unnoticed. Once an executive-looking man, portly, gray, and efficiently brusque, confronted me while I sat on the window ledge with a Faro cigarette pasted to my lips, a cloud of tobacco smoke hanging over my head, and many perfumed dreams inside it. He had a no-nonsense approach that jibed with his austere mien. He asked me what my name was, jotted down my work number, and went off to make a report on what he called "sordid malingering."

Other reports followed his. Gruff warnings, stern admonitions, and blustery tirades developed from them. They came from both major and minor executives. These I was already inured to. They didn't matter anyway. My condition was far too advanced, already much too complex, to be cleared up by mere lectures, fatherly or otherwise. All the threats and rebukes in the world couldn't have made me give up my window-ledge reveries or kept me form roaming city streets with Cecilia Rosas' name on my lips like a prayer.

The reports merely made me more cunning, more doggedly determined to city-slick La Feria out of work hours I owed it. The net result was that I timed my absences more precisely and contrived better lies to explain them. Sometimes I went to the men's room and looked at myself in the mirror for as long as ten minutes at a time. Such self-studies filled me with gloom. The mirror reflected an ordinary Mexican face, more homely than comely. Only my hair gave me hope. It was thick and wavy, deserving a better face to go with it. So I did the best I could with what I had, and combed it over my temples in ringlets just like the poets back in my hometown of Parral, Chihuahua, used to do.

My inefficiency, my dreams, my general lassitude, could have gone on indefinitely, it seemed. My life at the store wavered between bright hope and leaden despair, unrelieved by Miss Rosas' acceptance or rejection of me. Then one day something happened that almost made my overstrained heart stop beating.

It happened on the day Miss Rosas stood behind me while I put a fur coat away, Her heady perfume, the fragrance of her warm healthy body, made me feel faint. She was so close to me I thought about putting my hands around her lissome waist and hugging her as hard as I could. But thoughts of subsequent disgrace deterred me, so instead of hugging her I smiled wanly and asked her in Spanish how she was feeling.

"Amado, speak English," she told me. "And pronounce the words slowly and carefully, so you won't sound like a country Mexican."

Then she looked at me in a way that made me the happiest employee who ever punched La Feria's time clock.

"Amadito," she whispered the way I had always dreamed she would.

"Yes, Señorita Cecilia," I said expectantly.

Her smile was warmly intimate. "Amadito, when are you going to take me to the movies?" she asked.

Other salesladies watched us, all smiling. They made me so nervous I couldn't answer.

"Amadito, you haven't answered me," Miss Rosas said teasingly. "Either you're bashful as a village sweetheart, or else you don't like me at all."

In voluble Spanish, I quickly assured her the latter wasn't the case. I was just getting ready to say, "Señorita Cecilia, I more than like you; I love you" when she frowned and told me to speak English. So I slowed down and tried to smooth out my ruffled thoughts.

"Señorita Cecilia," I said. "I'd love to take you to the movies any time."

Miss Rosas smiled and patted my cheek. "Will you buy me candy and popcorn?" she said.

I nodded, putting my hand against the imprint her warm palm had left on my face.

"And hold my hand?"

I said "yes" so enthusiastically it made her laugh. Other salesladies laughed too. Dazed and numb with happiness. I watched Miss Rosas walk away. How proud and confident she was, how wholesomely clean and feminine. Other salesladies were looking at me and laughing.

Miss Sandoval came over to me. "Ay papacito," she said. "With women you're the divine tortilla."

Miss de la Rosa came over too. "When you take the Americana to the movies, remember not to speak Christian," she said. "And be sure you wear the pants that don't have any patches on them."

What they said made me blush and wonder how they knew what we had been talking about. Miss Arroyo came over to join them. So did Miss Torres.

"Amado, remember women are weak and men aren't made of sweet bread," Miss Arroyo said.

This embarrassed me, but it wasn't altogether unpleasant. Miss Sandoval winked at Miss de la Rosa, then looked back at me.

"Don't go too fast with the Americana, Amado," she said. "Remember the procession is long and the candles are small."

They laughed and slapped me on the back. They all wanted to know when I was going to take Miss Rosas to the movies. "She didn't say, " I blurted out without thinking.

This brought out another burst of laughter. It drove me back up the window ledge, where I got out my package of Faros and thought about the wonderful thing that had happened. But I was too nervous to stay there. So I went to the men's room and looked at myself in the mirror again, wondering why Miss Rosas liked me so well. The mirror made it brutally clear that my looks hadn't influenced her. So it must have been something else, perhaps character. But that didn't seem likely either. John Apple had told me I didn't have much of that. And other store officials had bulwarked his opinion. Still, I had seen homely men walking the streets of El Paso's Little Chihuahua quarter with beautiful Mexican women, and no one could explain that either. Anyway, it was time for another walk. So I took one.

This time I trudged through Little Chihuahua, where both Miss Rosas and I lived. Little Chihuahua looked different to me that day. It was a broken-down Mexican quarter honeycombed with tenements, Mom and Pop groceries, herb shops, cafes, and spindly salt-cedar trees; with howling children running its streets and old Mexican revolutionaries sunning themselves on its curbs like iguanas. But on that clear frosty day it was the world's most romantic place because Cecilia Rosas lived there.

While walking, I reasoned that Miss Rosas might want to go dancing after the movies. So I went to Professor Toribio Ortega's dance studio and made arrangements to take my first lesson. Some neighborhood boys saw me when I came out. They bawled, "Mariquita" and made flutteringly effeminate motions, all vulgar if not obscene. It didn't matter. On my lunch hour I went back and took my first lesson anyway. Professor Ortega danced with me. Softened by weeks of dreaming, I went limp in his arms imagining he was Miss Rosas.

The rest of the day was the same as many others before it. As usual I spent most of it stealing glances at Miss Rosas and slipping up to the window ledge. She looked busy, efficient, not like a woman in love. Her many other admirers trooped to the water fountain to look at the way her black silk dress fitted her curves. Their profane admiration made me scowl even more than I usually did at such times.

When the day's work was done, I plodded home from the store just as dreamily as I had gone to it. Since I had no one else to confide in, I invited my oldest sister, Dulce Nombre de Maria, to go to the movies with me. They were showing Jorge Negrete and María Felix in El Rapto at the Colon Theater. It was a romantic movie, just the kind I wanted to see.

After it was over, I bought Dulce Nombre churros and hot champurrado at the Golden Taco Cafe. And I told my sister all about what had happened to me. She looked at me thoughtfully, then combed my hair back with her fingertips as though trying to soothe me. "Manito," she said softly. "I wouldn't . . ." Then she looked away and shrugged her shoulders.

On Monday I borrowed three dollars from my Uncle without telling him what it was for. Miss Rosas hadn't told me what night she wanted me to take her to the movies. But the way she looked at me made me think that almost any night would do. So I decided on Friday. Waiting for it to come was hard. But I had to keep my mind occupied. So I went to Zamora's newsstand to get the Alma Norteña songbook. Pouring through it for the most romantic song I could find, I decided on "La Cecilia."

All week long I practiced singing it on my way to school and in the shower after basketball practice with the Little Chihuahua Tigers at the Sagrado Corazón gym. But except for singing this song, I tried not to speak Spanish at all. At home I made my mother mad by saying in English, "Please pass the sugar."

My mother looked at me as though she couldn't believe what she had heard. Since my Uncle Rodolfo couldn't say anything more than "hello" and "goodbye" in English, he couldn't tell what I had said. So my sister Consuelo did.

"May the Dark Virgin with the benign look make this boy well enough to speak Christian again," my mother whispered.

This I refused to do. I went on speaking English even though my mother and my uncle did not understand it. This shocked my sisters as well. When they asked me to explain my behavior, I parroted Miss Rosas, saying, "We're living in the United States now."

My rebellion against being a Mexican created an uproar. Such conduct was unorthodox, if not scandalous, in a neighborhood where names like Burciaga, Rodriguez, and Castillo predominated. But it wasn't only the Spanish language that I had lashed out against.

"Mother, why do we always have to eat sopa, frijoles refritos, mondongo, and pozole?" I complained. "Can't we ever eat roast beef or ham and eggs like Americans do?"

My mother didn't speak to me for two days after that. My Uncle Rodolfo grimaced and mumbled something about renegade Mexicans who want to eat ham and eggs even though the Montes packing company turned out the best chorizo this side of Toluca. My sister Consuelo giggled and called me a Rio Grande Irishman, an American Mister, a gringo, and a bolillo. Dulce Nombre looked at me worriedly.

Life at home was almost intolerable. Cruel jokes and mocking laughter made it so. I moped around looking sad as a day without bread. My sister Consuelo suggested I go to the courthouse and change my name to Beloved Wall, which is English for Amado Muro. My mother didn't agree. "If Nuestro Señor had meant for Amadito to be an

American, he would have given him a name like Smeeth or Jonesy," she said. My family was unsympathetic. With a family like mine, how could I ever hope to become an American and win Miss Rosas?

Friday came at last. I put on my only suit, slicked my hair down with liquid Vaseline, and doused myself with Dulce Nombre's perfume.

"Amado's going to serenade that pretty girl everyone calls La Americana," my sister Consuelo told my mother and uncle when I sat down to eat. "Then he's going to take her to the movies."

This made my uncle laugh and my mother scowl.

"Qué pantalones tiene (what nerve that boy's got)," my uncle said, "to serenade a twenty-year-old woman."

"La Americana," my mother said derisively. "That one's Mexican as pulque cured with celery."

They made me so nervous I forgot to take off my cap when I sat down to eat.

"Amado, take off your cap." my mother said. "You're not in La Lagunilla Market."

My uncle frowned. "All this boy thinks about is kissing girls," he said gruffly.

"But my boy's never kissed one," my mother said proudly.

My sister Consuelo laughed. "That's because they won't let him," she said.

This wasn't true. But I couldn't say so in front of my mother. I had already kissed Emalina Uribe from Porfirio Diaz Street not once but twice. Both times I'd kissed her in a darkened doorway less than a block from her home. But the kisses were over so soon we hardly had time to enjoy them. This was because Ema was afraid her big brother, the husky one named Toro, would see us. But if we'd had more time, it would have been better, I knew.

Along about six o'clock the three musicians who called themselves the Mariachis of Tecalitlan came by and whistled for me, just as they had said they would do. They never looked better than they did on that night. They had on black and silver charro uniforms and big black Zapata sombreros.

My mother shook her head when she saw them. "Son, who ever heard of serenading a girl at six o'clock in the evening," she said. "When your father had the mariachis sing for me, it was always at two o'clock in the morning—the only proper time for a six-song gallo."

But I got my Ramirez guitar anyway. I put on my cap and rushed out to give the mariachis the money without even kissing my mother's hand or waiting for her to bless me. Then we headed for Miss Rosas' home. Some boys and girls I knew were out in the street. This made me uncomfortable. They looked at me wonderingly as I led the mariachi band to Miss Rosas' home.

A block away from Miss Rosas' home I could see her father, a grizzled veteran who fought for Pancho Villa, sitting on the curb reading the Juarez newspaper, El Fronterizo.

The sight of him made me slow down a moment. But I got back in stride when I saw Miss Rosas herself.

She smiled and waived at me. "Hello, Amadito," she said.

She looked at the mariachis, then back at me.

"Ay, Amado, you're going to serenade your girl," she said. I didn't reply right away. Then when I was getting ready to say, "Señorita Cecilia, I came to serenade you," I saw the American man sitting in the sports roadster at the curb.

Miss Rosas turned to him. "I'll be right there, Johnny," she said.

She patted my cheek. "I've got to run now, Amado," she said. "Have a real nice time, darling."

I looked at her silken legs as she got into the car. Everything had happened so fast I was dazed. Broken dreams made my head spin. The contrast between myself and the poised American in the sports roadster was so cruel it made me wince.

She was happy with him. That was obvious. She was smiling and laughing, looking forward to a good time. Why had she asked me to take her to the movies if she already had a boyfriend? Then I remembered how the other salesladies had laughed, how I had wondered why they were laughing when they couldn't even hear what we were saying. And I realized it had all been a joke; everyone had known it but me. Neither Miss Rosas nor the other salesladies had ever dreamed I would think she was serious about wanting to take her to the movies.

The American and Miss Rosas drove off. Gloomy thoughts oppressed me. They made me want to cry. To get rid of them I thought of going to one of the "bad death" cantinas in Juarez where tequila starts fights and knives finish them. There I could forget her in Jalisco-state style with mariachis and tequila. Then I remembered I was so young that cantineros wouldn't serve me tequila.

So I thought some more. Emalina Uribe was the only other alternative. If we went over to Porfirio Diaz Street and serenaded her, I could go back to being a Mexican again. She was just as Mexican as I was, Mexican as Chicharrones. I thought about smiling, freckle-faced Ema.

Ema wasn't like the Americana at all. She wore wash dresses that fitted loosely and even ate the melcocha candies Mexicans like so well on the street. On Sundays she wore a Zamora shawl to church, and her mother wouldn't let her use lipstick or let her put on high heels.

But with a brother like Toro, who didn't like me anyway, such a serenade might be more dangerous than romantic. Besides that, my faith in my looks, my character, or whatever it was that made women fall in love with men, was so undermined I could already picture her getting into a car with a handsome American just like Miss Rosas had done.

The Mariachis of Tecalitlan were getting impatient. They had been paid to sing six songs and they wanted to sing them. But they were all sympathetic. None of them laughed at me.

"Amado, don't look sad as I did the day I learned I'd never be a millionaire," the mariachi captain said, putting his arm around me. "If not that girl, then another."

But without Miss Rosas there was no one we could sing "La Cecilia" to. The street seemed bleak and empty now that she was gone. And I didn't want to serenade Ema Uribe, even though she hadn't been faithless, but only lack of opportunity would keep her from getting into a car with an American, I reasoned cynically.

Just about then Miss Rosas' father looked up from his newspaper. He asked the mariachis if they knew how to sing "Cananea Jail." They told him they did. Then they looked at me. I thought it over for a moment. Then I nodded and started strumming the bass strings of my guitar. What had happened made it only too plain I could never trust Miss Rosas again. So we serenaded her father instead.

Featured Literature

"The Moon Lady" from *The Joy Luck Club* by Amy Tan

Grade Level
For High School

Thinking Level
Analysis

Writing Domain
Sensory/Descriptive

Materials Needed
• Colored pens

Suggested Supplementary Readings
• "Mariana" by Pablo Neruda
• "The Stolen Party" by Liliana Heker

Living in Life's Shadow: Amy Tan's "The Moon Lady"

by Pat Clark and Carol Booth Olson

Overview

After reading and analyzing "The Moon Lady" in Amy Tan's *The Joy Luck Club,* students will write an essay in which they describe how the incident at the Moon Festival affects the main character, Ying-ying.

Objectives

THINKING SKILLS

Students will:

- *analyze* the literal and symbolic implications of the term *lost;*
- *trace* the changes in Ying-ying's character before and after the incident at the Moon Festival;
- *make inferences* about the reasons for Ying-ying's transformation;
- *speculate* about how and why Ying-ying allows herself to live in life's shadow.

WRITING SKILLS

Students will:

- *use* sensory/descriptive skills including precise, apt, descriptive, and figurative language to enrich expository writing, to make the interpretation vivid, and to show and not just tell about the character;
- *use* analytical/expository skills to write a well-structured essay (introduction, main body, conclusion) with ample transitions and logical development;
- *correctly follow* the conventions of written English.

The Process

This lesson requires students to immerse themselves in a variety of prewriting and precomposing activities that help them elicit meaning from literature. It familiarizes the students with interpretive writing and with standard expository form. If taught in conjunction with an Asian unit in history classes, it lends itself well to a cross-curricular study of cultural values. In its present form, this lesson will take approximately three weeks to complete. Teachers under strict time constraints should condense as needed.

 PREWRITING

Prewriting Step 1: *Clustering*

Ask students to individually cluster the word *lost* on a piece of paper. Then, cluster the word *lost* on the board with the class. Ask students to suggest anything that comes to mind. Feelings? Associations? Circumstances?

Example:

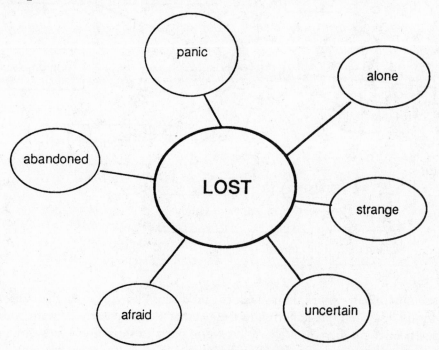

Prewriting Step 2: *First Reading*

Read "The Moon Lady" out loud to the class. *(You may want to break up the story into two parts and read it over two class periods.)* As you read, have students underline any words, phrases, or sentences that particularly appeal to them.

Prewriting Step 3: *Quaker Reading*

Have students read aloud any words, phrases, or sentences they underlined while reading the story. Anyone may speak at any time. This continues until all the students who wish to share have done so. This technique often brings out the most important ideas in a story.

Prewriting Step 4: *Additional Clustering*

Ask students to add to their *lost* cluster, using a different color of ink. A sample cluster might look like this:

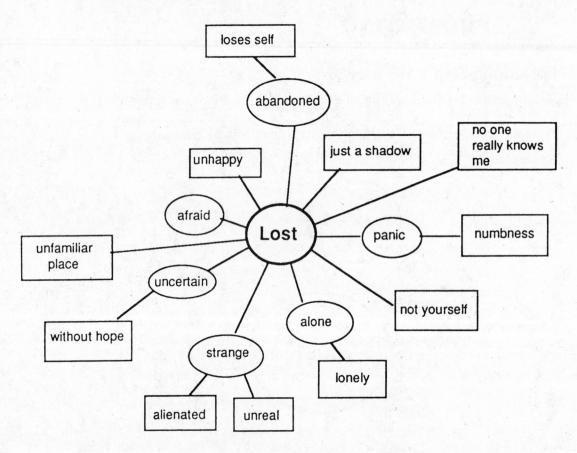

Have students in pairs share their clusters and discuss how hearing the story of "The Moon Lady" and participating in the Quaker Reading gave them an additional perspective on the word *lost*. Ask several pairs to share their new cluster words and to name which words, phrases, or events from the story brought these cluster words to mind. It is hoped that this discussion will bring out the fact that there are two kinds of *lost*—literal and symbolic. *(Note: If students do not point out the phrase from the story, "We are lost, she and I, unseen and not seeing, unheard and not hearing, unknown by others, the teacher might want to bring it to the attention of the class and elicit comments about its meaning.)*

Prewriting Step 5: *Freewriting*

In order to help students relate Ying-ying's plight to their own lives, ask them to freewrite about a time when they felt lost, not literally but symbolically, because people did not know them or see them for who they really are. Point out that Ying-ying most often uses the image of the shadow to describe herself. Ask them what image, if any, do they associate with how they felt. Allow fifteen to twenty minutes for this activity.

Student Model

I Felt Lost

The first day in my new school, I desperately tried to be accepted into a group. Drastically, trying far too hard, I attempted to make my way into the popular "clicks," not letting them into my past, protecting it from the clever, attractive, and husky teenagers the same way a mother cat hides her young from predators. I answered their questions the best way I could, hiding the real me, but hoping I was predestined to be in the group. Feeling a subtle pressure from the teenagers, I began to believe that they were toying with me. Finally, the time came for the word that would deliver me from the alleys of the disliked to the skyscrapers of the approved. I felt myself hurled off the tallest structure. I was rejected, quickly and surely, excluded because no one knew me. Finding out that I was not predestined for popularity was a major fall in my life.

Chris Welle, Freshman

Once students have completed their freewrites, ask them to share what they have written in triads. *(Note: Any students who feel uncomfortable sharing should be given the option to pass.)* After the freewrites have been shared and discussed, ask students to comment in their groups upon whether their experience was like or unlike Ying-ying's and why.

Prewriting Step 6: *Textual Analysis*

Now, ask the students to look back at what they underlined in their Quaker reading and to locate and write down at least four quotes from the text where Amy Tan shows that Ying-ying felt lost. These quotes might include:

- "All these years I kept my true nature hidden, running along like a small shadow so nobody could catch me."
- "I did not lose myself all at once. I rubbed out my face over the years washing away my pain, the same way carvings on stone are worn down by water."
- "I had turned into a beggar girl, lost without my family."
- "In one small moment, we had both lost the world, and there was no way to get it back."

- "On the dock, with the bright moon behind me, I once again saw my shadow. It was shorter this time, shrunken and wild-looking. We ran together over to some bushes along a walkway and hid."
- "But nobody was listening to him, except my shadow and me in the bushes."

Prewriting Step 7: *Found Poetry (Optional)*

One way to help students examine the imagery and symbols in a work of literature is to ask them to translate what they read into another genre. In found poetry, students "find" a poem that is embedded in a work of literature by rearranging the words, phrases, and images that resonate for them.

Ask students to examine both the words they underlined during the Quaker reading and those they wrote down when they identified particular passages where Amy Tan shows that Ying-ying felt lost. Have them make these images their own by "finding" a poem of at least six lines. They should feel free to add new words or change words if they seem cumbersome, but they must base their poem upon actual words and phrases in Tan's story.

For students who are unfamiliar with found poetry, the following example with Edgar Allan Poe's "Ligeia" may be useful to illustrate this technique:

Prose Passage from "Ligeia"
by Edgar Allan Poe

There is one <u>dear topic</u>, however, on which my memory fails me not. It is the person of Ligeia. In <u>stature</u> she was tall, somewhat slender, and, in her latter days, even <u>emaciated</u>. I would in vain attempt to portray the <u>majesty</u>, the <u>quiet ease of her demeanor,</u> or the <u>incomprehensible lightness and elasticity of her footfall</u>. She came and departed as a <u>shadow</u>. I was never made aware of her entrance into my closed study save by the <u>dear music</u> of her low sweet voice, as she placed her <u>marble hand</u> upon my shoulder. In beauty of face no maiden ever equalled her. It was the <u>radiance of an opium-dream</u>—an airy and <u>spirit-lifting</u> vision more <u>wildly divine</u> than the phantasies which hovered about the <u>slumbering souls of the daughters of Delos</u>. Yet her features were not of that regular mould which we have been falsely taught to <u>worship</u> in the classical labors of the heathen. "There is no <u>exquisite beauty</u>," says Bacon, Lord Verulam, speaking truly of all the forms and genera of beauty, "without some strangeness in the proportion."

Note that the sections underlined by the reader in this prose passage are rearranged to form the found poem.

Found Poem

Ligeia

You strange, exquisite beauty
You came and departed
As a shadow
Wildly divine, spirit-lifting
You shimmered in the radiance of an opium dream
Ligeia
He worshipped you
You placed your marble hand
Upon his heart
Awakened his slumbering soul
Became his dear topic
His work of art
Frozen in his memory
An emaciated statue

Allow approximately twenty minutes for this activity. If time permits, students will enjoy meeting in groups and combining their efforts into one composite found poem that includes at least one line from each student. These poems can be posted around the room for students to read.

Found Poetry Example for "The Moon Lady"

Innocence, trust and restlessness,
Wonder, fear and loneliness.
A boy can run and chase dragonflies,
But a girl should stand still,
Unseen and not seeing, unheard and not hearing.
And then, I ceased to be amazed.
I kept my true nature hidden.
If I stood perfectly still,
No one would notice.
For woman is yin, the darkness within,
And man is yang,
Bright truth lighting the mind.
And, I discovered my shadow,
My shadow, this dark side of me.
And I, running along like a small shadow.
But I remember now how I lost myself,
How the Moon Lady looked at me and became a man,
And I remember my wish.
I wished to be found.

 **PROMPT**

Review the following prompt with the class:

In the opening of Amy Tan's short story "The Moon Lady," Ying-ying says that she wants to tell her daughter that they are both lost. She goes on to say, "I did not lose myself all at once." However, a memory which she says she has kept hidden for many years—a childhood memory of becoming lost at the Moon Festival—now comes back to her. This marks the place in her life when she first became lost, both literally and symbolically. In fact, although her parents did find Ying-ying eventually, she never believed her family "found the same girl."

In a well-organized essay, describe how the incident at the Moon Festival affects Ying-ying.

- How and why did she change?
- How did Ying-ying's culture contribute to her transformation?
- How did she allow herself to become lost symbolically?

The best papers will move beyond a factual account of the story to a true analysis of Ying-ying's character, the change in the way she perceives herself, and the way her culture perceives her role in society. Refer to specific images and symbols in the text to support your character analysis. Use direct quotes when applicable.

Your paper should be written in standard expository form (introduction, main body, conclusion). Be sure to use precise, apt, descriptive, and figurative language to show and not just tell about how the incident in Ying-ying's life affected her character. In other words, make your writing as vivid as possible for your reader. Your paper should also correctly follow the conventions of written English, including following the rules for accurately quoting from a text.

Please consult the scoring guide for the criteria by which your paper will be evaluated.

 **PRECOMPOSING**

(Note: The following activities are designed to be given in sequence and completed either individually or by partners; however, in order to save time, teachers may want to assign each activity to a different group and have each group present its findings to the whole class. Teachers electing this option may want to assign the frame for Ying-ying's coat of arms for homework since it helps students generate figurative language about Ying-ying that they may want to use in their essays)

Precomposing Step 1: *Time Line*

Have students reread the story as they create a time line of the significant events in "The Moon Lady," placing events they feel are positive above the line and those that strike them as more negative below the line, as in the example below:

Delight over idea of
Moon Festival

Sees restless
shadow

 Chided by Amah
while being
dressed

Learns it is selfish
to think of own
needs

Have students begin their time line with Ying-ying's retelling of the incident, beginning with the words "In 1918, the year that I was four" *(seventh paragraph)* and return to the beginning of the story only after charting the story through the fifth paragraph from the end (when the Moon Lady becomes a man). Partners will most likely agree about whether events are positive or negative up to the conclusion of the story. However, they may have some healthy disagreement about the opening of the story. Stress that there is no right or wrong answer in creating the time line.

Precomposing Step 2: *Dialectical Journal*

Have students write six quotations from the text—two from the point at which Ying-ying hears of the Moon Festival to the point she becomes lost, two during the time she's lost, and two from the time she is found.

Have them respond to the quotes, using the first two columns of the following dialectical journal format as a model:

Quotation from Text	Personal Response	Further Reflection
"We are lost, she and I, unseen and not seeing, unheard and not hearing, unknown by others."	After hiding her true feelings even from herself, Ying-ying finally realizes that she has lived in a shadow.	

Precomposing Step 3: *Interpretive Questions*

After completing their dialectical journal, partners should go back through the text and write down any questions they have. Tell them their questions will probably be interpretive. That means there will be no right or wrong answers, but there may be some evidence in the story to back up different viewpoints. Students' questions will be used for class discussion.
Some examples follow:

- Why must girls be quiet while boys can be noisy and run and play?
- Why are #2 and #3, the younger sisters, old enough to go on the outing when this is the first year Ying-ying is allowed to go?
- What was the thing that squeezed Ying-ying and tossed her in the boat?
- Why did the Moon Lady's husband open his mouth wide in horror or delight?
- Why were there ten suns, and why did nine suns die?
- Why is woman Yin, the darkness within, and man Yang, bright truth?
- Why did the Moon Lady turn into a man?
- Why did Ying-ying still wish to be found after her parents found her?

Precomposing Step 4: *Discussing Interpretive Questions*

Ask students to form a circle. Start the discussion using your own interpretive questions about the story. Gradually, call on students to ask one of their questions. *(Stress the fact that no answer can be wrong in order to encourage more students to respond.)* Also, ask the students to look for and quote textual evidence in order to lend authenticity to a particular interpretation.

Precomposing Step 5: *More Dialectical Journaling (Optional)*

After a thorough discussion of the interpretive questions, students can go back to their dialectical journals and reflect further about their entries. They can look for connections between entries, expand upon their original responses, add some new insight that has emerged, and/or look for what their quotes and responses tell them about Ying-ying's character and her culture.

Precomposing Step 6: *Frame and Coat of Arms*

Quotation from Text	Personal Response	Further Reflection
"We are lost, she and I, unseen and not seeing, unheard and not hearing, unknown by others."	After hiding her true feelings even from herself, Ying-ying finally realizes that she has lived in a shadow.	Ying-ying has now "found" herself, but is it too late? And what about her daughter? She doesn't know she's invisible.

Have students fill out a frame and then draw a coat of arms for Ying-ying: *(See the "My Name, My Self" lesson elsewhere in this book for a model frame and coat of arms based upon Esperanza in the piece "My Name" by Sandra Cisneros.)*

Frame for Ying-ying's Coat of Arms

1. If Ying-ying were an animal, she would be a _____ because
   _____ .

2. If Ying-ying were a plant, she would be a _____ because
   _____ .

3. If Ying-ying were a season, she would be _____ because
   _____ .

4. If Ying-ying were a time of day, she would be _____ because
   _____ .

5. If Ying-ying were a word, she would be _____ because
   _____ .

6. If Ying-ying were a musical instrument, she would be a _____
   because _____ .

7. If Ying-ying were an object, she would be a _____ because
   _____ .

8. If Ying-ying were a song, she would be _____ because

_____.

9. If Ying-ying were an emotion, she would be _____

because _____.

Draw Ying-ying's coat of arms. Use your frames to help with this activity.

Coat of Arms

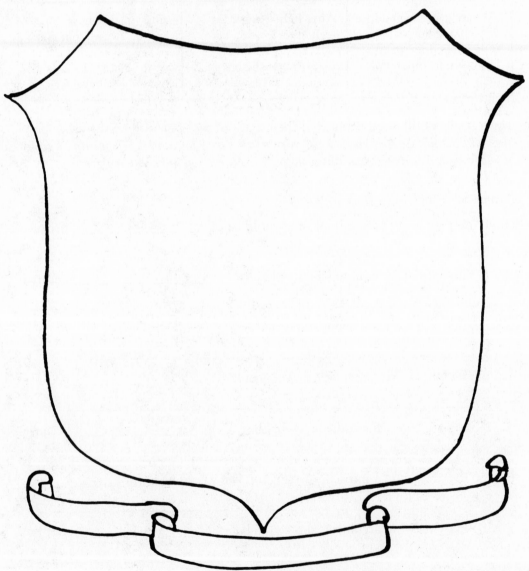

Precomposing Step 7: *Quickwrite*

To help students clarify their ideas before writing, ask them to quickwrite for fifteen minutes on: *How did the Moon Festival experience affect Ying-ying?*

Student Model

It is a world of confusion and beauty, a place where hidden passions lie. This is the Ying-ying zone. It's hard to say why Ying-ying changed her ways.

Was it her culture? Was it her attitude? The mystery of Ying-ying remains unsolved. She is like a set of tinted windows, able to look out, but it is impossible for others to look in.

Ying-ying at first did not see herself as being lost. She did not even think she had changed all that much. But, as the seasons changed, so did Ying-ying. Like the leaves falling slowly from the autumn trees, she said, "I did not lose myself all at once. I rubbed out my face over the years, washing away the pain..." These words may be a clue as to why Ying-ying transformed from a sweet little girl to a lost old woman.

Ying-ying's culture is something that contributed to her confusion and her reasons for hiding from herself. When Ying-ying was young, before the experience at the Moon Festival, she frolicked and played like a boy. But her culture said she should have been really serious and sedate, acting like a "lady." The old ways of the Chinese culture are set in stone. No one tries to change them. But Ying-ying was out to alter that. Unfortunately, she was thwarted, and in later life she paid the price of loneliness.

Matt Carr, Freshman

Give students an opportunity to share their quickwrites in small groups. Then, ask them to spend fifteen minutes specifically discussing these questions:

- How and why did Ying-ying change?
- How did Ying-ying's culture contribute to her transformation?
- How did she allow herself to become lost symbolically and to live in life's shadow?

Ask students to take notes as they discuss and recall passages from the story that would support the view being expressed.

Precomposing Step 8: *Microtheme: Formulate a Writing Plan*

Students are now ready to organize their ideas and information about the change in Ying-ying's character into a writing plan. Enable them to think ahead, to consider how they will proceed, by asking them to create a "microtheme." On a piece of notebook paper, have students write the categories—**Introduction, Main Body, Conclusion.**

Under **Introduction,** ask them to describe three different ways they might begin their paper: quote, anecdote, general analytical statement, description, and so on. *(The packet on introductions appended to this lesson may be useful in making students aware of the number of options they have for writing an opening to their paper, which will orient their readers to their topic and purpose, as well as engage the reader's interest. The examples of "hooks" in the "My Name, My Self" lesson may also be useful to review.)*

Under **Main Body,** ask them to refer back to their prewriting and precomposing activities to brainstorm a list of main points they intend to make, noting the specific references from the text they will use to support those points.

Under **Conclusion,** suggest that they write a sentence in which they describe the predominant feeling, impression, or message that they would like to leave with the reader of their essay.

This microtheme should be viewed only as a point for departure in writing, a guideline for how students will communicate their ideas rather than an outline of precisely what they are going to say.

 **WRITING**

Students should now write their first draft, basing it upon their prewriting and precomposing activities.

Microtheme

Introduction: I could begin my paper in one of the following three ways to "hook" my reader

-

-

-

Main Body

Main points I want to make: to	Specific references from the text support my main point:
• _____	• _____
	• _____
	• _____
	• _____
• _____	• _____
	• _____
	• _____
	• _____
• _____	• _____
	• _____
	• _____
	• _____
• _____	• _____
	• _____
	• _____

Conclusion: A predominant feeling, impression or message that I want to leave with my reader about Ying-ying is

-

-

SHARING

Ask partners or small groups to critique one another's work using the following response sheet, after critiquing the student writing model below.

Student Model

Wild Mustang to Work Horse

As a small child, Ying-ying was like a wild mustang, free to roam, her spirit undaunted. As she became older, her mother, Amah, and the Chinese culture broke her spirit and put the reins of society upon her. Ying-ying became more of a cart horse with blinders than an independent mustang. Instead of ropes, the traditional Chinese culture bound her down. Ying-ying was first encumbered by the heavy ropes of society's expectations when she was six, at the all important Moon Lady Festival. This was the first time that she lost herself.

Before Ying-ying became entangled by the ropes of expectations, she was a carefree happy child. She would run after dragonflies, explore unknown places, and peer wide-eyed at new marvels. Ying-ying was defiant toward the social pressures and didn't worry about what others thought. She did not worry about her place in society. She did not worry about "careless desires" or being subdued and subservient. She did not worry because she was Ying-ying, the wild mustang.

For the first six years of her life, there were often many cowboys trying to lasso Ying-ying into the corral. Amah was always rushing around and scolding Ying-ying for not acting ladylike and running around like a boy. Her mother told her, "A boy can run and chase dragonflies, because that is his nature, but a girl should stand still. If you are still for a very long time, a dragonfly will no longer see you. Then, it will come to you and hide in the comfort of your shadow." And society said, "A woman is yin, the darkness within, where untempered passions lie. A man is yang, bright truth lighting our minds." Ying-ying resisted their ropes until she met the Moon Lady.

When Ying-ying saw the sorrowful tale of the Moon Lady, she began to weep. Ying-ying said, "Even though I did not understand the entire story, I understood her grief. In one small moment we had both lost the world, and there was no way to get it back." While watching the tale, Ying-ying saw all the things that Amah, her mother, and society had warned her about, the careless desires and the untempered passions of mankind. For those few moments, she became the Moon Lady, and her spirit was broken.

As the broken-spirited work horse followed the Moon Lady, the Moon Lady "became a man." To Ying-ying's shock, the wig and dress were carelessly thrown away, along with Ying-ying's independence. The lady she had identified with, who was "flung from the earth by her own wantoness," was a man. This put the final blinders on Ying-ying. The transformation from mustang to work horse was complete.

Nina Alexander, Grade 9

Response Sheet

To the author of _____

Your Paper . . .	Very Well Done	OK	Needs Some Work
Carefully analyzes the way the incident at the Moon Festival affects Ying-ying.			
Offers insights into the character of Ying-ying, discussing how and why she changed.			
Refers to specific images and symbols to show Ying-ying's transformation.			
Considers how Ying-ying's culture contributes to her transformation.			
Considers how Ying-ying allows herself to become lost.			
Is written in standard expository form: • Has a clear introduction with an interesting hook;			
• Well developed main body with adequate transition;			
• Solid conclusion that leaves the reader with a predominant feeling, image, or impression about Ying-ying.			
Uses precise, apt, or descriptive writing (including figurative language) to enrich expository writing, make interpretation vivid, and show and not just tell about Ying-ying's character.			
Is interesting and keeps the reader engaged.			
Has few if any errors in the conventions of written English. Quotes from the text accurately.			
One good point you make about how and why the incident at the Moon Festival changed Ying-ying is . . .			
Our favorite example from the text that you used to support your interpretation is . . .			
Your best use of descriptive language in the paper is . . .			
The main thing we think you mean to say about Ying-ying is . . .			
One thing you may want to work on in your revision is . . .			

REVISING

Students should compare the group response sheet they received from peers with their microtheme statement to see whether the message they intended to get across was received by the readers. They can then revise their essays according to the responses they received on each evaluation criterion.

EDITING

Students will edit their papers for correctness. They will pay particular attention to the rules for quoting accurately from the text, which are appended to this essay.

EVALUATION

Papers will be scored on a 1–6 scale according to the following criteria.

6   This is a paper that is clearly superior: well written, insightful, carefully organized, and technically correct. A 6 paper does most or all of the following well:

- Carefully analyzes the way the incident at the Moon Festival affects Ying-ying.

- Offers insights into the character of Ying-ying and how and why she changed.

- Refers to several specific images and symbols from the text to show Ying-ying's transformation.

- Considers how Ying-ying's culture contributes to her transformation.

- Considers how Ying-ying allows herself to become symbolically lost.

- Is written in standard expository form.

    — Has a clear introduction that has a "hook."

    — Has a well-developed main body with specific references to the text and adequate transition.

    — Has a logical and impressive conclusion that leaves the reader with a predominant feeling, message, or impression about Ying-ying.

- Uses especially precise, apt, descriptive, and figurative language to enrich expository writing, make interpretation vivid, and show and not just tell about Ying-ying's character.

- Maintains a high level of interest and keeps the reader engaged.

- Has few, if any, errors in the conventions of written English. Quotes from the text accurately.

5   This is a strong paper that addresses all of the aspects of the assignment well. It is a thinner version of the 6 paper—still impressive and interesting but less well handled in terms of insight, organization, or language. A 5 paper will do most or all of the following:

- Carefully analyzes the way the incident at the Moon Festival affects Ying-ying but not quite so critically as a 6 paper.

- Offers insights into the character of Ying-ying and into how and why she changed.

- Refers to several specific images and symbols from the text to show Ying-ying's transformation. Interpretation of these references may not be as insightful or as in-depth as the 6 paper.

- Considers how Ying-ying's culture contributes to her transformation.

- Considers how Ying-ying allows herself to become symbolically lost.

- Adheres to standard expository form.

  — Has a clear introduction that has a "hook."

  — Has a reasonably well developed main body with adequate transition.

  — Has a logical conclusion that leaves the reader with a predominant feeling, image, or impression about Ying-ying.

- Uses some precise, apt, descriptive, or figurative writing to enrich expository writing, make interpretations somewhat vivid, and show as well as tell about Ying-ying's character.

- Maintains interest and keeps the reader engaged.

- Has a few errors in the conventions of written English but none that interferes with the writer's message. Quotes from the text accurately (possibly with a few minor exceptions).

4   This is a solid paper that meets most of the criteria of the assignment but does so in less depth than a 6 or 5 paper. A 4 paper may exhibit some of the following:

- Analyzes the way the incident at the Moon Festival affects Ying-ying but less carefully or critically than a 6 or 5 paper.

- Offers a fairly obvious analysis of the character of Ying-ying and of how and why she changed.

- Refers to only a few specific images and symbols from the text to show Ying-ying's transformation and may occasionally neglect to fully interpret their significance.

- Considers how Ying-ying's culture contributes to her transformation but in less depth than a 6 or 5 paper.

- Considers how Ying-ying allows herself to become symbolically lost but in less depth than a 6 or 5 paper.

- Adheres to standard expository form.

  — Has a discernible introduction but one that is not so clear or well stated as a 6 or 5 paper or which does not have an interesting "hook."

  — Has a less well-developed main body with some weaknesses in transition.

  — Has a conclusion that may restate the introduction rather than leave the reader with a predominant image, feeling, or impression about Ying-ying.

- Uses some apt, precise, descriptive, or figurative language but, overall, language is weaker than in a 6 or 5 paper. Tends to tell rather than show.

- Is less interesting than a 6 or 5 paper. Reader can follow the interpretation, but it is less engaging.

- Has some errors in the conventions of written English but none that obscures the writer's message. May have a few errors in quoting from the text.

3 This is a lower-half paper that addresses the assignment superficially and is weak in organization and language. A 3 paper:

- Superficially analyzes the way the incident at the Moon Festival affects Ying-ying.

- Offers few, if any, insights into the character of Ying-ying and into how and why she changed.

- Refers to few, if any, references to the text to support observations. Fails to interpret these references adequately.

- Has weaknesses in the introduction, main body, and/or conclusion of the paper.

- Uses overly general or imprecise language with little, if any, use of descriptive or figurative language. Tells instead of shows.

- Interpretation is hard for the reader to follow.

- Has many errors in the conventions of written English—some of which may interfere with the reader's understanding of what is said. May quote from the text inaccurately, if at all.

2–1 These scores apply to papers that completely fail to analyze the character of Ying-ying or say so little so poorly that the reader cannot understand the writer's interpretation.

EXTENSION ACTIVITIES

1. The following metacognitive questions will provide closure to your students' study of "The Moon Lady":

"The Moon Lady"

1. At the opening of "The Moon Lady," Ying-ying says that she wants to tell her daughter that they are both lost. Think about what you have learned about Ying-ying and possibly about yourself because of reading "The Moon Lady." If you could convey a message to another person that summarized what you learned, what would that message be?

2. What did you learn about the way in which Ying-ying's culture contributed to her feeling of being "lost"?

3. How is Ying-ying's culture like or unlike your culture in its treatment of girls?

4. Is there anything that you see differently, think differently about, or will do differently as a result of reading this story?

---

2. You may be interested in two other works of literature that relate to "The Moon Lady" thematically.

- "Mariana," a poem by Alfred, Lord Tennyson, deals with a character who, like Ying-ying, lives in life's shadow as a result of an incident that leaves her despondent. Students could compare and contrast these two characters and how the respective authors use imagery to show us that each is living in life's shadow. *(Note: "Mariana" is widely anthologized.)*

- "The Stolen Party," a short story by Liliana Heker, also has interesting parallels to "The Moon Lady." Unlike "Mariana," which deals with the despair and withdrawal of a grown woman, "The Stolen Party" focuses on a child named Rosaura, who experiences a major disillusionment at a birthday party, which results in a consequent loss of innocence. Again, students could compare and contrast how Rosaura and Ying-ying have their illusions about who they are and about what life holds for them shattered as a result of a major incident in their childhood.

See "The Stolen Party" in Other Fires: Short Fiction by Latin American Women *(New York: Clarkson & Potts Publishers) and in the lesson "Loss of Innocence" elsewhere in this book.*

Writing an Introduction to an Expository Composition

The introduction to an expository composition orients the reader to the writer's purpose and focus as well as indicates something about what the reader can expect to find in the remainder of the essay. Most introductions contain a thesis statement that communicates the point the writer intends to make—although some writers may choose to let the reader infer what their thesis is or to include it at the end of the composition rather than at the beginning. There are many approaches one can use in writing an introduction. Several of these approaches are described for you below.

Generalization

One way to open a paper is to begin with a generalization about the topic at hand and, in the remainder of the essay, to qualify and support that generalization with specifics. Notice how this paper on birth-order theory begins by offering a generalization about a topic and then supports that generalization with further details.

> According to psychologists, being the first, last, or middle in anything influences people in fairly predictable ways. This is particularly true of the order in which we are born into our families. Since the turn of the century when Freud's student Alfred Adler introduced the concept, psychologists have been exploring the ways in which birth order influences personality traits, and they have noticed that the oldest, only, middle, or youngest children in any family will share certain common tendencies or what Adler called a "lifescript." Despite the general characteristics that often apply, "birth order isn't a simplistic 1-2-3 system that says all first borns are one way, all second children are another, and last borns are always just like this or that," as Dr. Kevin Leman, author of *The Birth Order Book* notes. There are a number of variables in birth order theory that may account for why individuals can and very often do exhibit traits attributed to more than one birth order. "The real point," according to Leman, is that there are "dynamic relationships existing between members of a family." Birth order may help us look at those dynamics and give us "clues as to why people are the way they are."

Notice that although this paragraph begins with a generalization, it ends with the thesis statement, that birth order may help us look at our family dynamics and give us "clues as to why people are the way they are."

Thesis Statement

Many expository compositions begin directly with the thesis statement. The thesis is the key proposition or argument to be supported, advanced, or defended by the writer throughout the remainder of the paper. This paper on *One Flew Over the Cuckoo's Nest* begins directly with the writer's thesis statement about the novel.

The novel *One Flew Over the Cuckoo's Nest* by Ken Kesey is just as much the story of Bromden's recovery as it is of McMurphy's sacrifice. Bromden's progress from a paranoid-schizophrenic posing as a deaf-mute to a liberated man was not because of his treatment in a mental institution, but because of McMurphy's representation of freedom, his leadership, and his self-sacrifice. As a result of McMurphy's losing his sanity, Bromden is able to face reality and becomes aware of his own identity.

Quotation

Quotations from a book, song lyric, poem, etc., are often an attention-getting way of opening a paper. In the paper below, this student uses an especially appropriate quotation from one author to introduce his generalization about the main characters in two other literary works.

> "One sorrow never comes but brings an heir that may succeed as his inheritor."

> This line, written by William Shakespeare, could have been written for Mariana in Tennyson's poem. Surprisingly, it could be applied equally well to Miss Havisham in Dickens's *Great Expectations*. Both women are bitten by the serpent of unrequited love and neither one is able to overcome the effect of its toxicity. Through examining each character's long-standing affliction caused by being abandoned, we can compare and contrast how Tennyson and Dickens reveal the personalities of Mariana and Miss Havisham.

Notice how descriptively this student makes his generalization, using the symbol of the serpent's bite, and then moves from the generalization to a statement of the paper's purpose.

Description

In order to engage your reader's interest, it is often effective to lead into expository writing with a descriptive passage. This is the introduction to a paper on Sylvia Plath's novel *The Bell Jar:*

> She looked as wary as a dog who is kicked every time its owner passes by. Her complexion was a yellowish-color and her hair, limp as seaweed, dripped from her head. She wore this full-type skirt, of an obtrusive pattern, which made your eyes go crazy if you looked at it too long. And her once white blouse was now some color in between grey and khaki, with pale yellow crescents

staining her armpits. Esther Greenwood, former golden girl and winner of countless scholarships and prizes, stood at the door of Dr. Nolan's office, hesitating to take that crucial step inside.

Asking a Question

Opening a paper with a question is another good way to engage a reader's interest. Here is another paper on Sylvia Plath's *The Bell Jar:*

> Why, one wonders, did Sylvia Plath choose only thirty years to live? She was young, beautiful and talented. Seemingly, she had everything to live for. The first stanza from Erica Jong's poem, "The Critics (For everyone who writes about Sylvia Plath including me)," aptly describes some of the torment and promise of Sylvia Plath's short life:
>
> > Because she was clamped in the vise of herself
> > because she was numb
> > because words moved slowly as glaciers
> > because they flowed from her mouth like wine
> > because she was angry
> > & knotted her hair
> > & wore sand in her bra
> > because she had written herself into a corner
> > & then got burned
> > because she invented the stars
> > & watched them fall. . .
>
> Sylvia Plath, the great American poet and novelist, who allowed words to flow from her mouth like wine and then silenced those words by her own hand in 1963, in many ways, remains a mystery.

Notice how this writer moves from a question to a quotation and then concludes with a generalization.

Narration

Very often narration can be used as a framing device for a piece of exposition. Some narrative techniques you might consider are anecdote, dialogue, and interior monologue. Here are examples—all from expository compositions on birth-order theory.

- **Anecdote** An anecdote is a short narrative of an interesting incident or event, often amusing or biographical. This student opens her birth-order essay with a personal reminiscence.

> *Happy Birthday to you*
> *Happy Birthday to you*
> *Happy Birthday, dear Ann*
> *Happy Birthday to you!*

This was the fifth time this song had been sung to me. I just sat there basking in glory, watching the movement of multi-colored, pastel balloons bobbing in bunches from strings everywhere in the patio. My birthday presents had been opened and my wish list had been answered: a baby doll with extra clothing, a china tea set, and a book of paper dolls, complete with a pair of sharp, shiny, silver scissors. Even the cake and ice cream were my favorites—chocolate.

The day had gone perfectly, until shortly after clean-up, when my parents adjourned to the living room with their friends, leaving me and my eight guests alone in the patio. Being the first born child in my family, and naturally gifted with the talents of a leader and entrepreneur, I successfully convinced all eight party-goers that they were in need of a hair cut and for a promissory nickel I would use my new birthday scissors to do the job. My guests were delighted with their new looks, but not so their parents—or mine. I spent the remainder of the day in my room with several clear imprints of my mother's hand on my back end. It was a memorable birthday, but not in the way I had expected.

It was not until I read Dr. Kevin Leman's *The Birth Order Book* that I recognized the influence of birth-order theory on my own life and how I have exhibited classic first-born traits even as a small child.

- **Dialogue** Another element of narrative writing that can lend itself to an expository paper is the use of dialogue. This student took an imaginative approach to his birth order paper by setting up the introduction as if it were the opening scene in a play:

Scene 1

Curtain opens on a rectangular Formica-topped table. A family of five sit engaged in both conversation and dinner: Dad at the head of the table; oldest son at opposite end; mother and youngest to Dad's right; sister across from them.

DAD: *(in a low voice)* Don't reach. You know better than that.

MARK: *(apologetically)* Yes, Dad. *(pause)* Pass the butter please.

MOM: What happened at 4-H, sis?

LAURIE: *(apathetically)* Oh, not much. We learned what to feed the horse and how to groom the mane. She gets so upset if we don't do it just right.

MIKE: *(bouncing up and down smashing vegetables with the fork)* Learned to clean up with the pooper-scooper yet?

LAURIE: *(sarcastically)* Very funny.

MARK: I get to direct the pep band at tonight's basketball game against Monticello. I think we'll win.

DAD: From drummer to conductor, huh? Good for you, son. *(glancing up from his dinner to give a wink of approval)*

MOM: Is the band any good?

MARK: Ah, we're okay. We need more practice. Are my pants clean?

MOM: *(smiling)* Yes, and ironed.

MARK: Great! Thanks, mom. *(exit stage left)*

LAURIE: You iron his jeans? Oh, brother!

MOM: By the way, what took you so long to get home from 4-H?

LAURIE: Julie and some other friends came by and we hung out for awhile.

DAD: I don't know about that group...

MIKE: *(interrupting)* Can I go to the game with Mark?

MOM: You'll have to ask him.

MIKE: *(getting up from the table, calling through a pretend megaphone)* Mark...

How can three children with the same parents in the same house grow up to be so different? Well, according to birth order theory it's relatively simple—just be born!

- **Interior Monologue** An interior monologue is a conversation that goes on inside someone's head. Let's listen to Deedee Hathcock's debate concerning whether she will or won't finish her birth-order paper before taking off for summer vacation:

OLDEST VOICE: No, I have to do the paper tonight.

YOUNGEST VOICE: You are being ridiculous. You have too many things to do for your trip even if you had two full days ahead of you, instead of just tonight.

OLDEST VOICE: I said I would do it, and I will. I can't go back on my word. I must finish what I start.

YOUNGEST VOICE: You will make dumb mistakes. The world can turn without you, you know. Do what is best for you. Two nights of being up until three isn't it.

MIDDLE VOICE: Hang on there. There is always a way. Get up early, but go to bed by twelve. Spend just one more hour on the paper, do the best you can, and finish the rest later.

This argument was bouncing off the inside walls of my brain on the free-way as I rushed home after class yesterday, stopping for two last-minute errands on the way, adding to the overwhelming feeling of drowning because I had not even taken the suitcases out of the closet to pack them for my summer vacation that was due to begin right after class the next day. Suddenly, I realized that here was a living example of the mixture of birth-order traits I had discovered within my personality during this past two weeks. Birth-order theorists have grouped traits most often shared by people born as oldest, youngest, or as a middle child in their families.

Analogy

An analogy is an extended comparison between two things that correspond or resemble each other in some way. In the following paper, the student compares herself to a cinematographer and uses the analogy of the camera lens to repre-sent the reader's perspective of a work of literature. She begins the analogy with the title "What the Lens Reveals." Her opening lines read as follows:

> If I were a cinematographer called upon to delve into the very emotional center of Tennyson's Mariana and Dickens's Miss Havisham, I would surely portray my subjects in quite different lights. Let's let the camera lens reveal to us the plight of the nine-teenth-century lovelorn so indelibly presented to us by a poet and a prose writer.

Note that an analogy must be a sustained comparison. So, the student continues...

> With the widest possible lens and smallest aperture, our camera would first focus on the domicile of Mariana. Here all is black and white. There is no life to portray. All is decay and neglect, with no hope of a living flower arising from the broken flower pot.

Outline of Structure

Very often, introductions present the problem or topic to be discussed and then outline the structure of the essay to follow. Notice how this student combines descriptive language and dialogue to get the reader's attention, then presents the dilemma of which car to buy and then outlines the structure of the essay to follow. As readers, we can and should anticipate that the writer's main body of the essay will cover all three subtopics thoroughly before arriving at a decision.

> Cough, cough, sputter, clank, boom! "Damn it," I screamed. "This is the last straw!" That was three days ago when my 1963 Rambler went to the great salvage yard in the sky. During the past few days, I have narrowed my choices of a new car down to two: a sporty Mazda RX-7 or a functional Datsun pick-up truck. Now the problem is, which to choose. I have to consider styling, practicality, and economy.

These are just a few of the many approaches to writing introductions to expository compositions. You are limited only by your imagination and what kind of approach is suitable for your topic. Consider several options and then choose the one that best fits your topic, your audience and your purpose for writing.

Quoting from the Text

- Make quotations part of your sentence or as independent clauses.

    — Quotations can be woven into sentences without punctuation.
    Example: Ying-ying discovered too late that she "wished to be found."

    — Quotations can be introduced with commas.
    Example: At the beginning of the story, Ying-ying describes her life by stating, "All these years I kept my true nature hidden, running along like a small shadow so that nobody could catch me."

    — Quotations can be an independent clause introduced by a colon.
    Example: The following lines from the story introduce Ying-ying's attachment to her shadow:

    > Standing perfectly still like that, I discovered my shadow. At first it was just a dark spot on the bamboo mats that covered the courtyard bricks. It had short legs and long arms, a dark coiled braid just like mine. When I shook my head, it shook its head. We flapped our arms. We raised one leg. I turned back around quickly and it faced me. I lifted the bamboo mat to see if I could peel off my shadow, but it was under the mat, on the brick. I shrieked with delight at my shadow's own cleverness. I ran to the shade under the tree, watching my shadow chase me. It disappeared. I loved my shadow, this dark side of me that had my same restless nature.

- If a quotation is more than four lines long (as in the example above), indent and single space. Do not use quotation marks. Quotations of fewer than four lines should be placed within quotation marks.

- Commas and periods go inside quotation marks. Semicolons and colons go outside quotation marks.

- Exclamation points and question marks go inside the quotation marks if part of the quoted text and outside the quotation marks if not part of what is being quoted, but rather part of the writer's sentence.

    Examples:

    — Ying-ying is petrified as the men check her over as if she were a piece of merchandise, saying, "Is it too small. Shall we throw it back? Or is it worth some money?"

    — Why is woman "yin, the darkness within, where untempered passions lie, and man yang, bright truth lighting our minds"?

- Don't string quotations in a row. Weave them logically into your own prose.

- Don't pad your essay with quotations. Be selective.

Featured Literature

"The Stolen Party"
by Liliana Heker

Grade Level
For Middle School
Through College

Thinking Level
Analysis

Writing Domain
Analytical/Expository

Materials Needed
- White paper
- Marking pens

Suggested Supplementary Readings
- "Eleven" in *Women Hollering Creek* by Sandra Cisneros
- "The Circuit" by Francisco Jimenez
- "The Garden Party" by Katherine Mansfield

Loss of Innocence:
Liliana Heker's "The Stolen Party"

by Glenn Patchell

Overview

Students will write an analytical/expository essay in which they explain what the main character of "The Stolen Party," Rosaura, learns about herself and society as a result of an incident at a birthday party that made a strong impression on her.

Objectives

THINKING SKILLS

Students will:

- *recall* a favorite birthday party;
- *compare* and *contrast* their experience with Rosaura's;
- *analyze* why the incident at the birthday party made a strong impression on Rosaura;
- *speculate* about what Rosaura learns about herself and society as a result of this experience;
- *predict* the outcome of the story prior to reading it.

WRITING SKILLS

Students will:

- *write* in standard analytical/expository essay format: introduction, main body, conclusion;
- *logically develop* ideas and link ideas with ample transition;
- *use* precise, apt, and descriptive language;
- *support* main ideas with textual references, including direct quotations from the text;
- *follow* the conventions of standard written English.

The Process

 PREWRITING

Prewriting Step 1: *Clustering*

Cluster the phrase "birthday party". An sample cluster might look like this:

Prewriting Step 2: *Freewrite*

Have your students freewrite about a favorite party for about ten minutes. You may wish to prompt them with the following questions:

- When did it happen?
- Where did it take place?
- Who was invited?
- What did you do? (activities)
- What did you eat?
- What do you most remember about the party?
- How did you feel before, during, and after the party?

Student Model

Happy Birthday to you
Happy Birthday to you
Happy Birthday dear Ann
Happy Birthday to you!

This is the fifth time this song had been sung to me. I just sat there basking in glory, watching the movement of multi-colored, pastel balloons bobbing in bunches from strings everywhere in the patio. My birthday presents had been opened and my wish list had been answered: a baby doll with extra clothing, a china tea set, and a book of paper dolls, complete with a pair of sharp, shiny, silver scissors. Even the cake and ice cream were my favorites—chocolate.

The day had gone perfectly, until shortly after clean-up, when my parents adjourned to the living room with their friends, leaving me and my eight guests alone on the patio. Being the first born child in my family, and naturally gifted with the talents of a leader and entrepreneur, I successfully convinced all eight party-goers that they were in need of a hair cut and for a promissory nickel, I used my new birthday scissors to do the job. My guests were delighted with their new looks, but not so their parents-or mine.

I spent the remainder of that day in my room with several clear imprints of my mother's hand on my back end. It was a memorable birthday, but not in the way I had expected.

Ann Jones

Prewriting Step 3: *Read-Around*

Have students share their freewrite with a partner or a small group of four or five. Ask them to look for the way their birthday party memories are similar and the way they are different.

Prewriting Step 4: *Introducing the Story*

Explain that the students are going to read a story entitled "The Stolen Party," about a young girl named Rosaura who is invited to a friend's birthday party. The mother of the friend (Luciana) employs Rosaura's mother as a maid.

- **A.** Have your students predict what will happen in the story. Prompt them to predict the event, attitudes of the character, and outcome of the party for Rosaura.

- **B.** Then, after three to five minutes, call on several students to share their predictions. After two that are similar, you might ask someone to share a prediction that is different.

Examples:

- Rosaura will have something stolen from her at the party.
- Rosaura will be the "hit" of the party and will steal the limelight from the birthday girl.
- Something bad is going to happen—maybe an accident.
- Someone will make fun of Rosaura because her mother is the maid.

Prewriting Step 5: *Reading the Story*

Tell your students to have their Reading Logs at hand. All of the following activities will be done in each student's Reading Log.

- **A.** Read aloud to your students from the beginning of the story to the line, "'I'll die if I don't go,' she whispered, almost without moving her lips."

- Then, ask students to revise their predictions about the story.
- Ask them to write a sentence explaining why they changed.
- Ask students to share their changes; get a variety of predictions.

B. Continue reading to the line, "'See?' said Rosaura to the girl with the bow, and when no one was looking she kicked her in the shin."

- Ask students to write a quick analysis of the girl with the bow and explain Rosaura's reaction to her. *(You might want to have several responses shared or initiate a brief discussion of the attitudes of both girls).*

C. Continue to read to the line, "I helped the magician and he said to me, 'Thank you very much, my little countess.'"

- Have students predict the ending of the story now.
- Again, have students share different endings.
- You might take a vote on the most probable ending for the story.

D. Now, read the rest of the story.

- Have students write about the ending, considering the following:
  — Did you like the ending?
  — Was it expected?
  — How do you think Rosaura felt?
  — How did you feel?
- Have students share their ideas in group of three or four.
- Then, have students share in large group their groups response to the questions.

E. If students have not been given any prior background about the author and setting of the story, they may assume that it takes place in the United Stated and that while Rosaura is Mexican-American, the blond girl with the bow is Anglo. *(They may suspect that Señora Ines and her daughter are of Spanish descent and still make this assumption.)* Share with the class that this story is set in Argentina and that all the characters are Spanish speaking. Ask them what impact knowing this background has on their understanding of the story. *(Students might point out that while the characters are of the same race and nationality, they still differ in terms of social class. Further, the rich family appears to be light-complected and fair-haired while Rosaura is described as dark. So, discrimination on the basis of coloring is also an issue.)*

Prewriting Step 6: *Four-Square Drawing*

Have the students create a four-square drawing in color of what they consider to be four central or key scenes in the story. Assure students that their four-square drawing will be evaluated on detail, not artistic ability. Students may be encouraged to utilize symbolic representations to demonstrate attitude or emotion. These might include:

- The party's setting and Rosaura's arrival
- Rosaura serving the cake
- The magician and monkey performing
- Señores Ines, Herninia, and Rosaura in the final scene

Sample Scene:

Now, have students turn their four-square drawing over and explain the importance or significance of each scene. Then, have students turn in their four-square drawings. If the four-square drawings are evaluated or posted, be sure that attention is not just given to the artistically gifted.

Prewriting Step 7: *Quickwrite*

Have students write for about five minutes about what Rosaura was feeling when Señora Ines handed her the money.

A sample quickwrite might look like this:

> Rosaura must have been feeling shocked at first and then betrayed. The party was all an illusion, a magic trick. She is not an invited guest but, instead, the hired help. She must be feeling so humiliated. But she is also so proud. She stiffens. She's not going to cry—at least not here in front of Señora Ines. She's too proud to show how hurt she is.

PROMPT

In "The Stolen Party" the author, Liliana Heker, describes a significant event in the life of her main character, Rosaura. This event made a strong impression on Rosaura and taught her about life.

Analyze the details, images, attitudes, and sequence of events of the story. Then, write an essay in which you explain what Rosaura learns about herself and society. You will need to describe what Rosaura's attitude was as the story begins, analyze the effects of the events that happen to her during the party, and explain the change that occurs in her attitude after the culminating event of the story.

Your essay should be written in standard analytical/expository form with a clear introduction, a main body with arguments well supported by examples from and references to the text, transition between ideas, and a conclusion that sums up the argument and/or creates a sense of closure. Your paper should also follow all the conventions for standard written English.

PRECOMPOSING

Precomposing Step 1: *Charting the Situation*

Create a chart that outlines Rosaura's attitude before, during, and after the party. Have partners work on these charts in partners and then combine them on the board through a whole class discussion.

A sample chart might look like this:

Attitude Chart

Before	During	After
• Determined to go—"I'll die if I don't go." • Insists she's a real friend • Resistant to her mother's warnings • Envious of the rich	• Admiring of herself • Intrigued by the monkey • Feels special; gets to help • Steals the show; fearless • "My little countess" • Pleased with herself	• Nervous • "The best behaved" • Confides in her mom • Proud—"a marvelous daughter" • A pet—shocked, defiant, hurt, "cold, clear look" in her eyes • Shattered

Precomposing Step 2: *Listing*

List the lines from the story that foreshadow the ending. These might include:

• "She wouldn't have liked to admit that her mother had been right."

- "It's a rich people's party."
- "Listen Rosaura, that one's not your friend."
- "Get away with you, believing any nonsense you're told."
- "That's not being friends. Do you go to school together?"
- "Señora Ines had asked her to help pass the cake around."
- "Her mother suddenly seemed worried."

There are more that should be listed and some lines that students may list that aren't important. But after the list is complete, ask students to identify the five or six most important lines that foreshadow the ending.

Precomposing Step 3: *Character Analysis*

Have students in groups of five, write a character sketch of one of the following characters from the story:

- Rosaura
- Herminia
- Señora Ines
- Luciana
- Blonde girl with the bow

Have each group share their insights about the characters.

Precomposing Step 4: *Class Discussion*

Put the class into groups of three or four. Give each group (of say, ten groups in all) one set of the following questions: Have them create responses to their questions on butcher paper.

Group I
1. What was Rosaura's relationship with her mother?
2. What causes their conflict?
3. What is significant about their relationship at the story's end?

Group II
1. What is the conflict between Rosaura and the blonde girl with the bow in her hair?
2. Why did Rosaura kick the blonde girl?
3. How does the blonde girl represent society?

Group III
1. What is the significance of the monkey?
2. How does Rosaura feel about the monkey?
3. What do you think the monkey symbolically represents?

Group IV
1. What does Rosaura do to help with the party?
2. What reasons are given for her work at the party?
3. How does Rosaura react to helping during the party?

Group V
1. Why was Rosaura asked to help the magician?
2. How does Rosaura react to helping the magician?
3. What is ironic about the magician's calling her "my little countess"?
4. What is ironic about Rosaura's helping the magician?

Group VI	1.	Why are the gifts that Señora Ines gives significant?
	2.	Why didn't Señora Ines offer Rosaura a gift?
	3.	Why did Señora Ines offer Rosaura money?
Group VII	1.	What is the symbolic significance of the cage?
	2.	How is Rosaura like the monkey?
	3.	How is Rosaura similar to the magician?
Group VIII	1.	How is Rosaura different from the others at the party?
	2.	How does Luciana treat her during the party?
	3.	How does Señora Ines treat Rosaura during the party?
Group IX	1.	What kind of a person is the cousin of Luciana?
	2.	Who is most honest: the girl with a the bow or Señora Ines? Explain.
	3.	Describe the relationship between Luciana and Rosaura.
Group X	1.	Why did Rosaura's eyes have "a cold, clear look"?
	2.	What did Rosaura learn from the party?
	3.	How do you think Rosaura will change?

Have each group present its responses to the class.

Precomposing Step 5: *Freewrite*

Have students write a paragraph in response to the question: What does Rosaura learn about herself and her society as a result of her experience at the birthday party?

A sample freewrite might look like this:

> I think Rosaura learns that she has been naive and gullible. She allowed herself to believe that she could "fit in" to Luciana's world despite the fact that her mother worked as Luciana's mother's maid. Now, she knows that for many people in society, it's what you are on the outside — not what you are on the inside — that forms people's impression of you. But I hope that Rosaura will also come to recognize that she is the real one with <u>class.</u> She is beautiful, strong, proud, brave, and resilient. She will bounce back from what seems like a defeat and be the one to triumph.

Precomposing Step 6: *Supporting Details*

Have each student select several details, events, images, or important lines from the story that could be used to reveal what Rosaura learned from her experience.

 # WRITING

The students should now have a good enough understanding of the story to start the composing process. With novice writers, you may wish to direct the first drafting very carefully. With more experienced writers, you may wish to omit the following steps.

Introduction   Introduce the reader to the main events of the story. Present a unifying idea or thesis regarding what Rosaura learns about life.

Main Body   Trace what Rosaura learns about herself and society before, during, and after the party. Cite details, images, and events and use quotations from the text to support your main points. Use transitions words to link ideas.

Conclusion   Sum up or go beyond what's been said to reflect upon Rosaura's lesson, to offer an additional insight, or predict its long-term impact upon her.

 SHARING

Have students pair with a response partner and read their first draft to each other. Each pair should be concerned with content and respond to the following questions:

1. Does the essay explain what Rosaura learns? How?

2. Could what she learns be made more clear? How?

3. What details or events are used for supporting evidence?

4. Is supporting evidence fully explained?

5. What is the strongest part of the essay?

6. How could the strength of the essay be used to better advantage?

7. What needs to be strengthened in the essay?

8. What details or explanations could be added?

9. Does the essay come to a sense of closure? What insight does it offer?

 REVISION

Have students revise for content. Then, group students in triads and fill out the chart on p. 533 for each essay in the group.

 EDITING

Have students find an editing partner. Students will edit for sentence structure, syntax, spelling, vocabulary, and punctuation.

Revision Chart

The Unifying Idea (or Thesis) of the essay is found in these sentences:

1. _____
2. _____
3. _____

The events or details from the story that are used to support the development of the Unifying Idea are:

1. _____   4. _____
2. _____   5. _____
3. _____   6. _____

The following sentences are used to introduce supporting ideas for the Thesis of the essay:

1. _____
2. _____
3. _____
4. _____
5. _____
6. _____

The following are transitional words used to unify the essay:

1. _____   2. _____   3. _____
4. _____   5. _____   6. _____

The following comments reflect what we like about this essay:

1. _____
2. _____
3. _____

The following comments reflect how we think this essay could be improved:

1. _____
2. _____
3. _____

EVALUATION

Scoring Guide: Weighted Trait

Content:

5	4	3	2	1 X 7 = (35 points possible)

Demonstrates a clear understanding of the attitude changes and of the process of learning. Clearly conveys what Rosaura learns.

Adequate understanding of the attitude changes and of the process of learning. Does convey in a general way what is learned.

Fails to convey an understanding of the changes in attitude and of process of learning. Does not convey what is learned.

Analytical/Expository Form:

5	4	3	2	1 X 5 = (25 points possible)

The paper has a clear introduction, a main body with arguments well supported by the text, and a strong conclusion.

The paper has some sense of introduction, a main body with some support from the text for the arguments, and some semblance of a conclusion.

The paper lacks a clear introduction, has few supporting examples for the arguments, and lacks a sense of closure.

Unifying Idea or Thesis:

5	4	3	2	1 X 4 = (20 points possible)

A strong sense of purpose with a clearly defined unifying idea or thesis.

Adequate sense of purpose with a unifying idea or stated thesis.

Seems to have no sense of purpose, no unifying idea, and no clear thesis.

Supporting Evidence:

5	4	3	2	1 X 2 = (10 points possible)

Utilizes details, images, and even quotes from the story to support the thesis. Good elaboration.

Adequate supporting details that are explained in reference to the thesis.

Some facts, details, and references to the story are evidenced, but they do not clearly explain the thesis.

Language:

5	4	3	2	1 X 1 = (5 points possible)

Contains precise, apt and descriptive language.

Contains some precise, apt, and descriptive language.

Contains little or no precise, apt, and descriptive language.

Correctness:

5	4	3	2	1 ✕ 1 = *(5 points possible)*
Few, if any errors; neat and well presented.		Errors do not detract from the meaning of the essay. Neatness adequate.		Errors detract from the meaning of the essay. Not well presented.

Total Score: 100 points possible

Note: This scoring guide could also be used for peer scoring.

EXTENSION ACTIVITY

Analytical/Expository Essay:

- Compare the effects of the learning experience of Rosaura with the young African American boy in the poem, "Baltimore Incident." (A copy of the poem can be found in the anthology *Sound and Sense.*)
- What did Panchito learn from his experience in the short story "The Circuit" by Francisco Jimenez?
- What did Laura learn about herself and life in the story "The Garden Party" by Katherine Mansfield?

Featured Literature

The Stolen Party
by Lilian Heker
translated by Alberto Manguel

As soon as she arrived she went straight to the kitchen to see if the monkey was there. It was: what a relief! She wouldn't have liked to admit that her mother had been right. *Monkeys at a birthday?* her mother had sneered. *Get away with you, believing any nonsense you're told!* She was cross, but not because of the monkey, the girl thought; it's just because of the party.

"I don't like you going," she told her. "It's a rich people's party."

"Rich people go to Heaven too," said the girl, who studied religion at school.

"Get away with Heaven," said the mother. "The problem with you, young lady, is that you like to fart higher than your ass."

The girl didn't approve of the way her mother spoke. She was barely nine, and one of the best in her class.

"I'm going because I've been invited," she said. "And I've been invited because Luciana is my friend. So there."

"Ah yes, your friend," her mother grumbled. She paused. "Listen, Rosaura," she said at last. "That one's not your friend. You know what you are to them? The maid's daughter, that's what."

535

Rosaura blinked hard: she wasn't going to cry. Then she yelled: "Shut up! You know nothing about being friends!"

Every afternoon she used to go to Luciana's house and they would both finish their homework while Rosaura's mother did the cleaning. They had their tea in the kitchen and they told each other secrets. Rosaura loved everything in the big house, and she also loved the people who lived there.

"I'm going because it will be the most lovely party in the whole world, Luciana told me it would. There will be a magician, and he will bring a monkey and everything."

The mother swung around to take a good look at her child, and pompously put her hands on her hips.

"Monkeys at a birthday?" she said, "Get away with you, believing any nonsense you're told!"

Rosaura was deeply offended. She thought it unfair of her mother to accuse other people of being liars simply because they were rich. Rosaura too wanted to be rich, of course. If one day she managed to live in a beautiful palace, would her mother stop loving her? She felt very sad. She wanted to go to that party more than anything else in the world.

"I'll die if I don't go," she whispered, almost without moving her lips.

And she wasn't sure whether she had been heard, but on the morning of the party she discovered that her mother had starched her Christmas dress. And in the afternoon, after washing her hair, her mother rinsed it in apple vinegar so that it would be all nice and shiny. Before going out, Rosaura admired herself in the mirror, with her white dress and glossy hair, and thought she looked terribly pretty.

Señora Ines also seemed to notice. As soon as she saw her, she said:

"How lovely you look today, Rosaura."

Rosaura gave her starched skirt a slight toss with her hands and walked into the party with a firm step. She said hello to Luciana and asked about the monkey. Luciana put on a secretive look and whispered into Rosaura's ear: "He's in the kitchen. But don't tell anyone, because it's a surprise."

Rosaura wanted to make sure. Carefully she entered the kitchen and there she saw it: deep in thought, inside its cage. It looked so funny that the girl stood there for a while, watching it, and later, every so often, she would slip out of the party unseen and go and admire it. Rosaura was the only one allowed into the kitchen. Señora Ines had said: "You yes, but not the others, they're much too boisterous, they might break something." Rosaura had never broken anything. She even managed the jug of orange juice, carrying it from the kitchen into the dining-room. She held it carefully and didn't spill a single drop. And Señora Ines had said: "Are you sure you can manage a jug as big as that?" Of course she could manage. She wasn't a butterfingers, like the others. Like that blonde girl with the bow in her hair. As soon as she saw Rosaura, the girl with the bow had said:

"And you? Who are you?"

"I'm a friend of Luciana," said Rosaura.

"No," said the girl with the bow, "you are not a friend of Luciana because I'm her cousin and I know all her friends. And I don't know you."

"So what," said Rosaura. "I come here every afternoon with my mother and we do our homework together."

"You and your mother do your homework together?" asked the girl, laughing.

"I and Luciana do our homework together," said Rosaura, very seriously.

The girl with the bow shrugged her shoulders.

"That's not being friends," she said. "Do you go to school together?"

"No."

"So where do you know her from?" said the girl, getting impatient.

Rosaura remembered her mother's words perfectly. She took a deep breath.

"I'm the daughter of the employee," she said.

Her mother had said very clearly: "If someone asks, you say you're the daughter of the employee; that's all." She also told her to add: "And proud of it." But Rosaura thought that never in her life would she dare say something of the sort.

"What employee?" said the girl with the bow. "Employee in a shop?"

"No," said Rosaura angrily. "My mother doesn't sell anything in any shop, so there."

"So how come she's an employee?" said the girl with the bow.

Just then Señora Ines arrived saying *shh shh*, and asked Rosaura if she wouldn't mind helping serve out the hot-dogs, as she knew the house so much better than the others.

"See?" said Rosaura to the girl with the bow, and when no one was looking she kicked her in the shin.

Apart from the girl with the bow, all the others were delightful. The one she liked best was Luciana, with her golden birthday crown; and then the boys. Rosaura won the sack race, and nobody managed to catch her when they played tag. When they split into two teams to play charades, all the boys wanted her for their side. Rosaura felt she had never been so happy in all her life.

But the best was still to come. The best came after Luciana blew out the candles. First the cake. Señora Ines had asked her to help pass the cake around, and Rosaura had enjoyed the task immensely, because everyone called out to her, shouting "Me, me!" Rosaura remembered a story in which there was a queen who had the power of life or death over her subjects. She had always loved that, having the power of life or death. To Luciana and the boys she gave the largest pieces, and to the girl with the bow she gave a slice so thin one could see through it.

After the cake came the magician, tall and bony, with a fine red cape. A true magician: he could untie handkerchiefs by blowing on them and make a chain with links that had no openings. He could guess what cards were pulled out from a pack, and the monkey was his assistant. He called the monkey "partner." "Let's see here, partner," he would say, "Turn over a card." And, "Don't run away, partner: time to work now."

The final trick was wonderful. One of the children had to hold the monkey in his arms and the magician said he would make him disappear.

"What, the boy?" they all shouted.

"No, the monkey!" shouted back the magician.

Rosaura thought that this was truly the most amusing party in the whole world.

The magician asked a small fat boy to come and help, but the small fat boy got frightened almost at once and dropped the monkey on the floor. The magician picked him up carefully, whispered something in his ear, and the monkey nodded almost as if he understood.

"You mustn't be so unmanly, my friend," the magician said to the fat boy.

"What's unmanly?" said the fat boy.

The magician turned around as if to look for spies.

"A sissy," said the magician. "Go sit down."

Then he stared at all the faces, one by one. Rosaura felt her heart tremble.

"You, with the Spanish eyes," said the magician. And everyone saw that he was pointing at her.

She wasn't afraid. Neither holding the monkey, nor when the magician made him vanish; not even when, at the end, the magician flung his red cape over Rosaura's head and uttered a few magic words . . . and the monkey reappeared, chattering happily, in her arms.

The children clapped furiously. And before Rosaura returned to her seat, the magician said:

"Thank you very much, my little countess."

She was so pleased with the compliment that a while later, when her mother came to fetch her, that was the first thing she told her.

"I helped the magician and he said to me, 'Thank you very much, my little countess."

It was strange because up to then Rosaura had thought that she was angry with her mother. All along Rosaura had imagined that she would say to her: "See that the monkey wasn't a lie?" But instead she was so thrilled that she told her mother all about the wonderful magician.

Her mother tapped her on the head and said: "So now we're a countess!"

But one could see that she was beaming.

And now they both stood in the entrance, because a moment ago Señora Ines, smiling, had said: "Please wait here a second."

Her mother suddenly seemed worried.

"What is it?" she asked Rosaura.

"What is what?" said Rosaura. "It's nothing: she just wants to get the presents for those who are leaving, see?"

She pointed at the fat boy and at a girl with pigtails who were also waiting there, next to their mothers. And she explained about the presents. She knew, because she had been watching those who left before her. When one of the girls was about to leave, Señora Ines would give her a bracelet. When a boy left, Señora Ines gave him a yo-yo. Rosaura preferred the yo-yo because it sparkled, but she didn't mention that to her mother. Her mother might have said: "So why don't you ask for one, you blockhead?" That's what her mother was like. Rosaura didn't feel like explaining that she'd be horribly ashamed to be the odd one out. Instead she said:

"I was the best-behaved at the party."

And she said no more because Señora Ines came out into the hall with two bags, one pink and one blue.

First she went up to the fat boy, gave him a yo-yo out of the blue bag, and the fat boy left with his mother. Then she went up to the girl and gave her a bracelet out of the pink bag, and the girl with the pigtails left as well.

Finally she came up to Rosaura and her mother. She had a big smile on her face and Rosaura liked that. Señora Ines looked down at her, then looked up at her mother, and then said something that made Rosaura proud:

"What a marvelous daughter you have, Herminia."

For an instant, Rosaura thought that she'd give her two presents: the bracelet and the yo-yo. Señora Ines bent down as if about to look for something. Rosaura also leaned forward, stretching out her arm. But she never completed the movement.

Señora Ines didn't look in the pink bag. Nor did she look in the blue bag. Instead she rummaged in her purse. In her hand appeared two bills.

"You really and truly earned this," she said handing them over. "Thank you for all your help, my pet."

Rosaura felt her arms stiffen, stick close to her body, and then she noticed her mother's hand on her shoulder. Instinctively she pressed herself against her mother's body. That was all. Except her eyes. Rosaura's eyes had a cold, clear look that fixed itself on Señora Ines's face.

Señora Ines, motionless, stood there with her hand out-stretched. As if she didn't dare draw it back. As if the slightest change might shatter an infinitely delicate balance.

The Stolen Party

The short story "The Stolen Party" by Liliana Heker describes an experience that taught a young girl about her life. The girl, Rosaura, wanted to got to a birthday party but her mother didn't want her going because it was a rich people's party. Rosaura's mother was the maid for Sra. Ines whose daughter was the birthday girl; therefore, her social status was very low. But Rosaura's pride made her very ignorant about the situation she was getting into. Through the attitudes, events, and images, Heker shows her readers a painful experience for Rosaura.

Heker first demonstrates Rosaura's character through the conflict she has with her mother. Rosaura's attitude goes through a big change from the beginning of the story to the end. She was very excited to go to this party because "there will be a magician and he will bring a monkey and everything." She even got to the point where she said, "I'll die if I don't go." Rosaura just couldn't understand why her mother didn't want her to go. Rosaura didn't think it would do her any harm because she said, "I'm going because I've been invited. And I've been invited because Luciana is my friend." All Rosaura wanted to do was go to this party and have fun. Through Rosaura's attitude at the beginning of the story, Heker is trying to show the pride that Rosaura has in herself that blinded her to the outside world.

Heker also shows this painful experience through the events that take place in the party. During the party, Rosaura felt very special because Sra. Ines would ask Rosaura, instead of the other kids, to help her out with many things. For example, Sra. Ines "asked Rosaura if she wouldn't mind helping serve out the hot dogs." Also, when "Sra. Ines asked her to pass the cake around, Rosaura had enjoyed the task immensely." All this time, she did not realize what was going on. Because "Rosaura was the only one allowed in the kitchen," she felt so honored; but the reason why she was the only one allowed in the kitchen to see the monkey was because Rosaura didn't matter in this party. The surprise was for the other guests, not for her, and she didn't see that.

Heker also uses symbolism to show the readers Rosaura's blindness. The cage and the monkey are very good symbols for Rosaura's life. As Rosaura saw the monkey "deep in thought, inside its cage," she just stood there and admired it, not knowing what she was seeing. Heker uses the cage of the monkey to symbolize the rich people in Rosaura's life that trap her within her social status. Because of this cage, no matter how hard she tries to be like the others, she will never reach the point where she will be accepted with the rich people. The monkey symbolizes Rosaura herself because they are both there to serve others. Just as the monkey was used by the magician, Rosaura was used by Sra. Ines.

At the end of the story, Rosaura finally comes to realize that she will not be accepted by the rich people. All along, she thought she was an invited guest but as soon as Sra. Ines pulled out the money and said, "Thank you for all your help, my pet," she realized the painful truth. Rosaura finally understood why her mother was trying to stop her from going to this party.

Luis Rhee—Irvine High School

Many Voices, One Heart
Muchas Voces, Un Corazon

by Bill Burns

Overview

In this three-part lesson, students will present selections in a reader's theater format from Edgar Lee Masters's *Spoon River Anthology* and Sandra Cisneros's prose poem-letters in her short story "Little Miracles, Kept Promises." Students will write their own epitaphs in imitation of Masters and reformulate Cisneros's letters into poems and write a found poem of Cisneros's work. Students may culminate their creative efforts with either an analytical or a reflective essay on the works of these two authors if the teacher desires. Prompts for both types of essays are in this lesson.

Objectives

THINKING SKILLS

Students will:

- *examine* the form, character, language, and drama of two works;
- *analyze* the character and tone of the works;
- *make inferences* and *speculate* about the characters' live, hopes, relationships, and values;
- *formulate* their own imitations of Masters;
- *reformulate* a Cisneros letter into a poem;
- *compare* and *contrast* the works of the two authors.

WRITING SKILLS

Students will:

- *use* effective narrative skills to create a free verse epitaph showing a character's life and/or death, not merely telling about it;
- *show* their understanding of poetic form by turning one of Cisneros's letters into a poem;
- *use* analytical and synthesizing skills to write a found poem based on the entire Cisneros story;
- *compare* and *contrast* the two works to develop an analytical essay (optional);
- *correctly use* conventions of written English in poetry and prose.

The Process

This three-part lesson requires students to demonstrate, through oral and written activities, that they understand selected works of two authors, one a part of the traditional canon of literature and one a newer Chicana voice both different and similar in vision. Students will learn about free verse and prose poems as they imitate and also create their own versions of these two authors' works. This lesson can focus on the creative writing of the student or on an expository essay comparing and contrasting the authors. In any case, the teacher will want students to confront the important universals found in these two authors who write from different historical, geographical, and ethnic backgrounds but share a similar love and fascination for human differences.

Part One: Formulating Imitations of Masters's Spoon River Anthology

 **PREWRITING**

Prewriting Step 1: *Reader's Theater Roles*

Several days ahead of time, hand out a different Spoon River character poem to each student. Ask them <u>not</u> to share them with each other until they are read so that they will be a surprise for the whole class. Try to match the poems with each student's gender and some similar or surprisingly dissimilar personality trait. Have fun with these matches. Masters has hundreds of poems and many are connected. *(See the list on the next page for some of the poems I have had success with.)* Tell students they are to prepare to read the poems in a Reader's Theater manner: the poems don't have to be memorized but they have to be read dramatically, with a sense of real character. Explain briefly who Masters was, the name of the book their poems come from, and the circumstances of the poems *(first person narratives, all delivered from characters who are buried in the Spoon River cemetery)*. Explain that they are to know the words in their poem, know any allusions, understand the character's situation, and be ready to respond to questions about their character. Tell them you will be available to answer any questions they might have before the readings. It is a good idea to make a list of who is reading what. You will need to refer to this list of characters when you call upon the students later.

Some suggested poems from Masters's *Spoon River Anthology*:

These are related characters.

Benjamin Pantier
Mrs. Benjamin Pantier
Ruben Pantier
Emily Sparks
Trainor, the Druggist

Dora Williams
Mrs. Williams
Roscoe Purkapile
Mrs. Purkapile

Willard Fluke
Lois Spears
Minerva Jones
"Indignation" Jones
Doctor Meyers
Mrs. Meyers

Knowlt Hoheimer
Lydia Puckett
Lucius Atherton

Elsa Wertman
Hamilton Green

Lillian Stewart
Lambert Hutchins

These are unrelated characters.

Hannah Armstrong
Fiddler Jones
Judge Selah Lively
Lucinda Matlock
Margaret Fuller Slack
"Butch" Weldy
William and Emily
Yee Bow
Constance Hately
Peleg Poague
Walter Simmons
Clarence Fawcett
Eugene Carman

Prewriting Step 2: *Character Guide*

At this time, hand out the character guide found on the next page and direct students to answer the first five questions before their reading. They will answer the second five after everyone has read.

Edgar Lee Masters's
Spoon River Anthology

1. Your character's name: _____

2. Qualities of your character:

    A. What was important to your character?

    B. What values did he/she have?

    C. What, if anything, do you think you character would like to change?

3. What significant events occurred in your character's life?

4. Describe your character.

5. How did you relate or not relate to your character?

THESE QUESTIONS CAN BE ANSWERED AFTER YOU HEAR ABOUT THE OTHER CHARACTERS.

6. What other characters, if any, were connected to yours? How?

7. What other character(s) would your character find sympathetic? Why?

8. What other character(s) would your character find unpleasant or opposite in values? Why?

9. What kinds of characters did Edgar Lee Masters create?

10. What do you think Masters was trying to achieve with his poems?

Prewriting Step 3: *Reader's Theater Performance*

On the selected date, tell students you will call on them in a random order, based mainly on their character and the character's connections to other characters. Begin by reading Masters' opening poem, "The Hill," which is an introduction to the work:

Featured Literature
_____

The Hill
by Edgar Lee Masters

Where are Elmer, Herman, Bert, Tom and Charley,
The weak of will, the strong of arm, the clown, the boozer, the fighter?
All, all, are sleeping on the hill.

One passed in a fever,
One was burned in a mine,
One was killed in a brawl,
One died in a jail,
One fell from a bridge toiling for children and wife—
All, all are sleeping, sleeping, sleeping on the hill.

Where are Ella, Kate, Mag, Lizzie and Edith,
The tender heart, the simple soul, the loud, the proud, the happy one?—
All, all, are sleeping on the hill.

One died in shameful child-birth,
One of a thwarted love,
One at the hands of a brute in a brothel,
One of a broken pride, in the search for heart's desire,
One after life in far-away London and Paris
Was brought to her little space by Ella and Kate and Mag—
All, all are sleeping, sleeping, sleeping on the hill.

Where are Uncle Isaac and Aunt Emily,
And old Towny Kincaid and Sevigne Houghton,
And Major Walker who had talked
With venerable men of the revolution?—
All, all, are sleeping on the hill.

They brought them dead sons from the war,
And daughters whom life had crushed,
And their children fatherless, crying—
All, all are sleeping, sleeping, sleeping on the hill. . . .

Then, begin to call on the students. You can call on them according to their character's relationships (husband-wife, parent-child, lover, employer-employee, etc.). Mix them up. Have fun and be creative. Part of the enjoyment is in the students discovering how their character is related or connected to others.

Prewriting Step 4: *Character Guide*

When the readings are completed, direct students to answer the second five questions from the character guide. This guide will be the main precomposing activity. These guides may be turned in for evaluation and/or they may be used to direct a class discussion of Masters's poems. The last two questions are especially important in order for students to see the "big picture" of the poems and to get themselves ready to write their own imitation.

 PROMPT

Write a poem imitating the form of Masters's poems. The title of the poem will be your own name. You will invent a character to go along with your name. The character can be somewhat autobiographical or entirely make-believe. Masters based his poems on friends, relatives, news stories, and on his own imagination. Your poem can be about a critical moment in the character's life and/or the character's death, just as Masters did. Some characters led happy, positive lives. Some died sensationally; some died ironically. Your poem should be in free verse and no longer than a page.

 PRECOMPOSING

Analyzing Poetic Form

This is a good time to go over the form of Masters's poems. Students need to discover/know that they are all written in the first person. Some students will want to write in the third person, but show them how that is different. It changes the voice of the poem considerably. The poems are free verse. They don't rhyme *(there are a couple of exceptions in the several hundred poems, but they rhyme for a reason)*. Almost always, they are written in one stanza, and they are short—no longer than a page. It will probably be worthwhile to talk about where lines usually break in free verse. Although theoretically lines can break anywhere, usually they break at breathing pauses, punctuation marks, ends of phrases, clauses, natural breaks in language. Give students a couple of practice sentences to divide. Either take one of Masters's poems they haven't read before and give it to them in a paragraph form, or give them some lines from another poet or just some regular prose lines. Here is an example from Masters's poem "Hamlet Micure":

<u>paragraph form:</u>

In a lingering fever many visions come to you: I was in the little house again with its great yard of clover running down to the board-fence, shadowed by the oak tree, where we children had our swing. Yet the little house was a manor hall set in a lawn, and by the lawn was the sea.

<u>original form:</u>

> In a lingering fever many visions come to you:
> I was in the little house again
> With its great yard of clover
> Running down to the board-fence,
> Shadowed by the oak tree,
> Where we children had our swing.
> Yet the little house was a manor hall
> Set in a lawn, and by the lawn was the sea.

You can explain that in free verse there are many ways to arrange the words, but remind students that they are trying to imitate Masters, and he followed a certain pattern, a certain tradition, such as capitalizing the beginning of each line and ending lines at periods.

Tell students that they will be asked to read their poems aloud, just as they read Masters's poems, and they may want to keep that in mind as they write their poems.

WRITING AND SHARING

Students will write their poems and, after the final draft, they will work in pairs to check each other's verse form and content. The following list of questions should help guide them if they need help.

- Does the poem have the student's name for a title?
- Is the poem written in the first person point of view?
- Do the lines break at "normal" places (according to Masters's style)?
- Do the lines begin with capital letters?
- Is the poem unrhymed?
- Does the poem tell of a critical moment in the character's life or describe the situation of the character's death?
- Does the poem create a sense of "character"? (language, voice, irony, humor, suspense, surprise)
- Does the poem follow the conventions of written English?

Student Models

Earnest Wallace

I was the last of seven kids
From two wonderful people named Evelyn and Henry Wallace,
Both of which are dark and lovely.
I was born on September 6, 19—
During my first 18 years of life
I had a lot given to me,
Till my little brother came along and stole all those good things from me.
Then I decided to work and get my own things.
I found a job making $15 an hour
Working 40 hours weekly
With full medical and dental insurance.
I then got married with Julia Roberts and had three kids
Two boys and one girl.
We were married for five years
Until death did us part.

God Bless Earnest Wallace.

Min H. Choi

I lived with four seasons

   Spring with flowers
   Summer with rain
   Fall with higher sky
   Winter with snow
I didn't know seasons with happiness
I didn't know seasons with love
   And I was just me
      I could not smell spring
      I could not hear summer
      I could not feel fall
      I could not touch winter
I was just around them

Now I know that was my season.

Angela Rova

When I was one year old I was left to die.

When I was five I was kidnapped by thieves.

When I was ten I was trapped on a hijacked plane.

When I was eighteen I was hit by a car.

When I was twenty I was captured by the enemy in war.

When I was twenty-one I was slowly tortured as a prisoner of war.

When I was twenty-five I was hung upside down by my toes over
    a scorching fire.

And when I was thirty I was diagnosed as a pathological liar.

 ## REVISING

After working in pairs, have students make any necessary or enhancing changes to their poems. If students have access to computers or typewriters, this would be a good time to have them type them for presentation. I often collect these poems and make copies and bind them so that each student has our own classroom anthology. If students do not have access to print, then have them write very clearly. You could also have them illustrate their poems if you like.

 ## EVALUATION

If you desire to grade these creative writings, use the list they had for revision as your rubric. Form will probably play more importance here than content, which is difficult to assess.

Part Two: Interpreting Cisneros's "Little Miracles, Kept Promises" Through Found Poetry

 **PREWRITING**

Prewriting Step 1: *Reading*

Hand out copies of Sandra Cisneros's short story "Little Miracles, Kept Promises," from her collection of short stories, *Woman Hollering Creek*. Read the first three "letters" aloud in class. Ask students what they see. What are these? Who are the speakers? What level of language is being used? What tone do these have? What more do they need to know?

The first three "letters" are as follows:

Exvoto Donated as Promised,
    On the 20th of December of 1988 we suffered a terrible disaster on the road to Corpus Christi. The bus we were riding skidded and overturned near Robstown and a lady and her little girl were killed. Thanks to La Virgen de Guadalupe we are all alive, all of us miraculously unharmed, and with no visible scars, except we are afraid to ride buses. We dedicate this retablo to La Virgencita with our affection and gratitude and our everlasting faith.

        Familia Arteaga
        Alice, Texas
        G.R. (Gracias Recibido/Thanks Given)

Blessed Santo Niño de Atocha,
    Thank you for helping us when Chapa's truck got stolen. We didn't know how we was going to make it. He needs it to get to work, and this job, well, he's been on probation since we got him to quit drinking. Raquel and the kids are hardly ever afraid of him anymore, and we are proud parents. We don't know how we can repay you for everything you have done for our family. We will light a candle to you every Sunday and never forget you.

        Sidronio Tijerina
        Brenda A. Camacho de Tijerina
        San Angelo, Texas

Dear San Martín de Porres,

    Please send us clothes, furniture, shoes, dishes. We need anything that don't eat. Since the fire we have to start all over again and Lalo's disability check ain't much and don't go far. Zulema would like to finish school but I says she can just forget about it now. She's our oldest and her place is at home helping us out I told her. Please make her see some sense. She's all we got.

        Thanking you,
        Adelfa Vásquez
        Escobas, Texas

Prewriting Step 2: *Analyzing Traditions*

Ask if any students can explain the tradition of *milagritos* (little miracles) in the Catholic Church. Make sure students understand the idea of leaving small charms, tokens, notes pinned to the curtain, vestments, or alter cloth of various saints, giving thanks for a prayer answered or the prayer itself. This is more of a folk custom than a recognized practice in the church.

Prewriting Step 3: *Reader's Theater*

Choose individual students (either assigned or volunteers) to take turns presenting the rest of the letters in a Reader's Theater format or have students work in groups. If you choose groups, divide students into cooperative groups of four to five students who take turns reading the rest of the letters. Each group will write down questions they may have about the letters: vocabulary questions, translation problems (the Spanish words, whole letters in Spanish), and other confusions. If students don't bring it up, ask them why there are double wavy lines in the story. What is their purpose? Help students see that the long section at the end is not a written *retablo* but the thoughts of one character and that the short note at the end written by the same character (Rosario [Chayo] De Leon) is like the rest of the letters. Use student questions to discuss and analyze various letters. Explore why some passages are in all capital letters without punctuation. What inferences can they make about the characters? Why is one passage in code? What does it say? Why are some all in Spanish? Who are all the saints?

Prewriting Step 4: *Organizing the Letters*

When students have read through the entire collection, ask them to organize the letters into groups. They will need to decide what criteria to use. Groupings might be based on length, gender, age, subject, or social status. Have groups report to the whole class how and why they grouped the letters. Dividing the letters into groups allows students to examine the individual letters and their characters from a different angle and provides a way of organizing a seemingly "random" series of letters. This sense of structure will be helpful for completing a writing assignment later.

Prewriting Step 5: *Reformatting the Letters*

In order to prepare the students for the next step, explain to them that Cisneros sees herself as a poet as well as a storyteller. In her novel *House on Mango Street,* although it is written in paragraph form, the short chapters were originally poems. She rewrote the poems into paragraphs in order for her book to be more readable to a large audience. In "Little Miracles, Kept Promises," the "letters" were really first conceived as individual poems. In fact, she first read selections from this story at a public reading before the book was published as if the letters were poems. Remind students of what they learned from studying Masters's form and how lines were broken at particular places. Their task is to take one of the letters that has sufficient length and reformat it so that it looks like a poem. For example, the "letter" from Victor A. Lozano might look like this:

> Saint Sebastian
> Who was persecuted with arrows
> and then survived,
> thank you for answering my prayers!
> All them arrows that had persecuted me—
> my brother-in-law Ernie
>   and my sister Alba
>   and their kids—
> el Junior,
>   la Gloria,
>   and el Skyler—
> all gone.

Prewriting Step 6: *Paragraph Explanation*

At the end of their poetic reconstructions, have students write a paragraph explaining why they divided the lines and spaced the poem in that particular manner.

Prewriting Step 7: *Quaker Reading*

In order to get them ready for the next step, have students share in a Quaker reading, a technique allowing students, in any particular order, to read brief passages from the letters. Passages can be several sentences, one sentence, or even a phrase. They are chosen at random, and students may read after any other student has finished. This continues until the momentum of the reading ceases. Allow time for students to reread the letters and direct students to underline the passages they would like to read aloud. The purpose of this reading is to draw attention to words, phrases, and passages that are memorable, or sound good, funny, sad, dramatic, or powerful. There is a sense of wholeness out of the parts that emerges from such readings. In particular, this is a good technique to prepare students to write a found poem of the entire work, selections from the work, or even one particular letter.

PROMPT

Write a found poem based on the entire collection of letters. With words, phrases, and passages from the Quaker reading as one source, and your own feelings and interpretations, create a poem using the words, phrases, and passages from the collection. Try to capture the feeling, tone, and ideas of "Little Miracles." Add as few of your own words as possible, limiting such additions to connecting words and transitions. Let your structure speak for you.

PRECOMPOSING

The form of the found poem is up to the student. Free verse would be the most likely choice. Explain that found poetry is the rearranging of words, phrases, and images in the collection that stand out for them, that sing and echo to them. Their task is to make Cisneros's words their words, their thoughts, to take ownership of the reading experience. *(Note: Students can refer to the found poetry in the "Living in Life's Shadow" lesson, elsewhere in this book, for a model.)*

WRITING

Students can begin their writing by looking over the underlined places from the Quaker reading and list or cluster the words and images. The most difficult task may be in organizing the lines to connect the images. Suggest that students reexamine the way groups organized the letters (by age, sex, subject) and use this as a structural device. Maybe other motifs, such as male voices, female voices, or wishes and thanks, or formal and informal language, could help organize their poems. There are no right ways, just different ways to see the whole.

SHARING AND REVISION

Students should share and revise their poems using the following criteria:

- Is this in a poetic form?
- Does my collection of words and images have an overall structure?
- Have I accurately copied the words and images from the letters?
- Have I avoided writing my own descriptions/narrations into the poem?
- Have I tried to capture my sense of the whole work? Do I include the ideas, themes, and experiences that give the work its uniqueness?

EVALUATION

Use the above list as a guide to your assessment. A sense of organization and content is probably more important than just form, unlike the evaluation of the poem the student wrote using Masters's form.

Part Three: Comparing and Contrasting Masters with Cisneros

Now that students have read, shared, analyzed, and synthesized the poems and prose of the two writers, they are ready to discuss the similarities and differences between them. Many students do not at first see a connection between Masters and Cisneros, and may express confusion or curiosity as to why they are reading both writers together. If students have these feelings, ask them to do a freewrite about their confusion. Regardless, respond to questions about the connections between the writers.

PREWRITING

Venn Diagram

A Venn diagram can help in visualizing similarities and differences between Masters and Cisneros. Circles represent the work of each author and contain descriptions that summarize the differences. Where the circles overlap are written the similarities. Begin with the differences. Here is a sample:

Spoon River Poems   **Little Miracles Letters**

- Written in 1915
- Author dead white man
- Poetry (free verse)
- Characters speak about lives and death
- Midwest/East
- Written in English
- Not particularly religious
- Characters seem to come from all levels of society

- Little stories of different characters
- Characters represent a variety of people
- Both written in 1st person point of view
- Both written in English
- About all kinds of people who have had many problems and some joys

- Written in 1991
- Author living Chicana woman
- Written in prose (maybe free verse)
- Characters request or give thanks for a prayer. They are about hop and the future.
- West Texas/Tejas
- Bilingual
- Religious
- Characters seem to be mostly lower and middle class

After creating the Venn diagram, discussing the items and where they might be placed, point out to the students that when comparing and contrasting something, there is usually an obvious similarity or dissimilarity. If two items are obviously similar, then they should look for important differences in order to differentiate them. If two items are obviously dissimilar, as they appear to students when they read Masters and Cisneros, then they should look at the important similarities in order to understand them at a level other than the obvious. This is an important aspect of comparing and contrasting and one that students should understand. This also helps to avoid silly similarities or dissimilarities, such as "they both use words," or "they both are literature."

At this point, you can end the lesson, knowing that students have explored both writers from a variety of approaches, mainly through creative writing assignments. However, if you want students to write an expository essay you can use the following prompt to work from to develop precomposing, writing, sharing, revising, editing, and evaluation activities.

 PROMPT

> Write an essay that analyzes the important similarities and differences between Masters's *Spoon River Anthology* and Cisneros's "Little Miracles, Kept Promises." Discuss what qualities are unique to each one and what they have in common. What important differences, if any, are the result of the seventy-two years between them? Consider what might have been the purposes the authors had in writing their poems and letters. Your paper should be in standard analytical/expository form (introduction, main body, conclusion), include comparison/contrast words (such as *similarly, in contrast, like, unlike,* and so forth), and follow the conventions of written English.

EXTENSION ACTIVITY

Note on the *Retablo* Tradition

Students can create a character and, in imitation of Cisneros, write a request for something that character would really desire. Address the note to any saint, god, power, or cosmic force that would be appropriate to the character. These can be put up on the classroom wall, or the teacher's desk, or some other appropriate place, in imitation of the *milagrito* or *retablo* tradition.

Featured Literature

"Eleven" from
*Woman Hollering
Creek*
by Sandra Cisneros

Grade Level
For Middle School

Thinking Level
Application

Writing Domains
Sensory/Descriptive
Imaginative/Narrative

Materials Needed
No special materials
required.

**Suggested
Supplementary
Readings**
"The Stolen Party" by
Liliana Heker

Memories and Metaphors

by Chris Byron

Overview

Using techniques of storytelling, reading, rereading, graphics, and quick-writes, students will explore the short story "Eleven" in *Woman Hollering Creek* by Sandra Cisneros to discover how she uses images to communicate thoughts and feelings. They will also write an autobiographical incident about a memorable birthday in their lives, using images and specific detail to enhance meaning.

Objectives

THINKING SKILLS

Students will:

- *examine* the short story "Eleven";
- *identify* images that communicate thoughts and feelings;
- *recall* a memorable birthday;
- *apply* appropriate images to the birthday incident;
- *narrate* the story of a memorable birthday;
- *sequence* elements into a meaningful order.

WRITING SKILLS

Students will:

- *write* an autobiographical incident about a memorable birthday;
- *hook* their readers with a good beginning;
- *create* images that convey thoughts and feelings;
- *use* specific detail;
- *use* logical development and sequencing;
- *develop* an ending that ties in with the beginning;
- *demonstrate knowledge* of correct mechanics and grammar.

The Process

One of the purposes of reading multicultural literature is to help students develop common understandings, make connections, and validate the individual. Group activities ensure that students listen to the responses others have formulated about a piece. This writing assignment stresses how figurative language can help a writer reach out and "touch human emotion."

PREWRITING

Prewriting Step 1: *Time Line*

Have students make a personal time line by sketching and captioning pictures of memorable birthdays in their lives. Guide them through this activity by asking them to do the following:

- Make a list of as many birthdays as they can remember. If it is difficult to remember birthdays, have them use events that they remember well.
- Give students each a large piece of butcher paper and ask them to divide it into as many sections as there are memorable events. For each event, have them draw a picture (symbol) and caption it. A sample paper might look like this:

Prewriting Step 2: *Storytelling*

Have students select the most significant birthday or other incident that they can remember well—one that has remained in their memory and that they want to share. With peer groups of three or four, instruct them to do the following:

- Recall their event and list as many details as they can to help them remember the story later.
- Tell the story of their significant birthday to their group.
- As a group, select the most interesting story to share with the rest of the class.
- Listen, as a class, to the representative stories from each group.

Prewriting Step 3: *Reading Aloud and Quickwrite*

Read the story aloud to the class. When you finish, ask the students to write for three minutes about their first reactions to the story. They should include any thoughts, questions, opinions, or memories that come to mind from listening to Cisneros's story.

Student Model

That's exactly how I feel. Sometimes I feel like I'm 12, 11, 10, 9, 8, 7, 6, 5, 4, 3, 2, or 1. I act like I'm 9 or 10, but that's how my friends and I communicate. We know each other well enough to act whatever age and share our feelings and still not take everyone seriously.

Jesse Haid

Prewriting Step 4: *Rereading and Annotating*

Ask students now to reread the story to themselves. As they read, have them underline the passages they think are memorable or important and make notes in the right margin of their personal questions and reactions. A sample paper might look like this:

Eleven
by Sandra Cisneros

    What they don't understand about birthdays and what <u>they never tell you is that when you're eleven, you're also ten, and nine, and eight, and seven, and six, and five, and four, and three, and two, and one.</u> And when you wake up on your eleventh birthday you expect to feel eleven, but you don't. You open your eyes and everything's just like yesterday, only it's today. And you don't feel eleven at all. You feel like you're ten. And you are-underneath the year that makes you eleven.

Notes/Reactions

All the ages are inside, all the years, so that by the time you are 20 you have layers of experience. Every birthday I grow older and I don't feel any different.

Like some days you might say something stupid, and that's the part of you that's still ten. Or maybe some days you might need to sit on your mama's lap because you're scared, and that's the part of you that's five. <u>And one day when you're all grown up maybe you will need to cry like if you're three, and that's okay.</u> That's what I tell Mama when she's sad and needs to cry. Maybe she's feeling three.

Because the way you grow old is <u>kind of like an onion or like the rings inside a tree trunk or like those wooden dolls fit one inside the other, each year inside the next one.</u> That's how being eleven years old is.

You don't feel eleven. Not right away. It takes a few days, weeks, sometimes even months before you say eleven when they ask you. And you don't feel smart eleven, not until you're almost twelve. That's the way it is.

Only today I wish I didn't have just eleven years <u>rattling inside me like pennies in a tin Band-Aid box.</u>

If you need to cry it's as if you are 3 years old, and you're really 13. Sometimes I need to cry and I'm a lot older now.

Every birthday I grow another ring and I don't feel it either.

Sort of like you wish you had more experience in life. Sometimes I try to say something, but I can't because I'm afraid I can't say it right.

Prewriting Step 5: *Small Group Discussion*

Have students discuss their thoughts, questions, and the memorable passages they marked in their small groups. After sufficient time, ask for volunteers to share with the class. Take notes about these reactions on a big piece of butcher paper. Some reactions are listed below:

- Is Rachel mute? Why can't she tell the teacher it's NOT HERS!
- I liked the way she described it like cottage cheese and the germs.
- The teacher never believed her.
- She uses great words.
- "Like a waterfall" really gives a good description.
- "All itchy and full of germs" sounds icky.

Prewriting Step 6: *Open Mind*

Below is a diagram of an Open Mind, a way of making a visual representation of what a person might be thinking or feeling at a particular time. Copy this for use in your class; then ask students:

If you could look into Rachel's mind at the time of this incident, what might she have been feeling? Fill in the Open Mind with symbols and images that you think will show her thoughts and feelings.

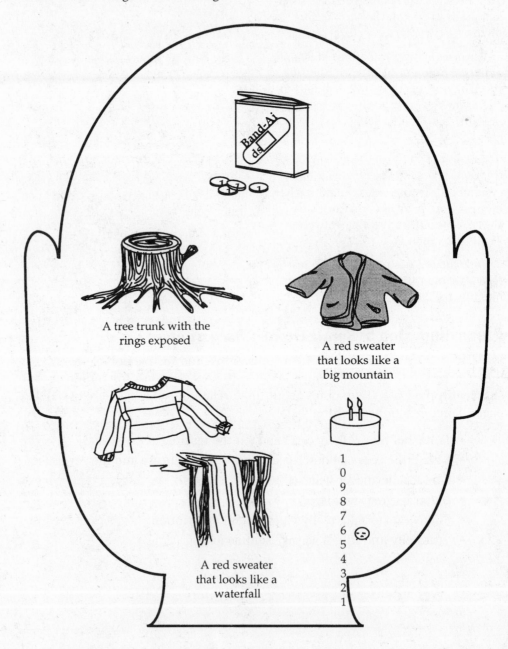

A tree trunk with the rings exposed

A red sweater that looks like a big mountain

A red sweater that looks like a waterfall

Prewriting Step 7: *Image*

For each image they draw, ask students to find a quote from the text showing what the author has to say about that image. As they fill in a chart like the one below, they should record the quotes in the first column. In the second column, they write what they think the quote means; in the third, they explain how they relate to the quote.

Example:

Quote	What It Means to Rachel	How I Relate to It
"Because the way you grow old is kind of like an onion or like the rings inside a tree. . ."	It means that each new year adds to the memories, so that by the time you are ten you have layers of experiences.	I feel that way. Sometimes I can peel away two or three layers and remember an experience I had when I was younger.
"The red sweater's sitting there like a big red mountain."	It's a big obstacle or problem to get over.	It's like when I have a problem that won't go away.
"Only today I wish I didn't have just eleven years rattling inside me like pennies in a tin Band-Aid box."	When you wish you had more experience in life, more than just a little amount.	When I try to say something, but I can't because I'm afraid I can't say it right.

Prewriting Step 8: *Discussion of Significant Images*

With students in peer groups, have them share their Open Minds and charts. After sufficient time, randomly ask one person from each group to share with the class what he or she thought was the most significant image in Cisneros's story. Discuss in class how these images help communicate the author's thoughts and feelings. During discussion, make a list on the board of some of the images.

Example:

- "sleeves all stretched out like you could use it for a jump rope"
- "hanging over the edge like a waterfall"
- "far away like a tiny kite in the sky"
- "I wish I was invisible, but I'm not"

 **PROMPT**

In "Eleven," Sandra Cisneros uses figurative language and the present tense to dramatize an event that ruined the eleventh birthday of the main character, Rachel. Think about a birthday you remember well and have thought about many times—one that evoked strong emotion like the one Cisneros describes. It may have been exciting or disappointing, as long as it was memorable. (*Note: If birthdays do not evoke special memories, then think about some other incident in your life that does.*)

Write about a memorable birthday or incident that has had an effect on you. Use specific details to create mood and setting. Use images and symbols so that your reader can understand how you felt about it. Be sure to include what you learned about yourself or why you consider that particular birthday or incident memorable or important.

Make sure you have a hook at the beginning to engage your reader, a middle that includes specific details, and an ending that ties the piece together. Use the first person point of view and the present tense so that the reader has the sense that your birthday is happening now.

Your piece should be organized into paragraphs, have a logical sequence, and use correct punctuation, paragraphing, and grammar.

 PRECOMPOSING

Precomposing Step 1: *Modeling*

Read the following student model before the students begin to write their pieces.

Student Model

"You can come? Cool!"

"Mom. Jesse can come to my party," I yell as I slam down the phone. "That makes seven of us. Are you sure we can't squeeze any more into the car? Just one more and there would be eight for my eighth birthday."

When the day arrives, I'm so excited that I could pop. Butterflies are doing flips in my stomach just like I'll be doing on Space Mountain. As each of my friends gets dropped off, the presents pile high and my smile gets bigger.

Finally, we load up the mini-van and we're off and running. The car barely comes to a stop when we hop out and charge toward the entrance at Disneyland. "C'mon mom," I scream.

Space Mountain is our first stop. It's like you don't know what's coming in the pitch black. Red and green lights flash as you whirl and drop. My stomach is churning with excitement.

"It's like herding cats," my mom complains as we race toward the next attraction. "Can't you kids stay together?"

While mom tries to count us ONE MORE TIME, we charge into Captain EO and put on those funny 3D glasses. When the movie starts, the characters on the screen float right out into the audience. It's like you could almost touch them. And when the space craft zooms by, we all duck.

As the day is ending, all of a sudden, it's like somebody stuck a pin in my balloon. I feel tears coming and I keep telling myself that I'm eight and only babies cry. So, I wipe my eyes and catch up with my friends.

I still get like that sometimes. Maybe I just don't want good times to end.

Tyler Olson

After reading the piece:

- Discuss the words/phrases that create a mood and show the setting.
- Identify a key image or key images Tyler associates with the memory.
- Ask: why do you think this birthday is still so vivid in Tyler's memory?

Precomposing Step 2: *Looking at Images and Metaphors*

Ask students to return to the significant birthday they shared with their groups. As they look over their lists of details and recall the day, have them think of images and symbols to illustrate their thoughts and feelings as the birthday unfolded. *(Example: loneliness, happiness, anger, joy.)* Then, ask them to fill out their own Open Mind diagram illustrating their day.

Precomposing Step 3: *Index of Feelings*

After students have discussed the feelings they associate with their memorable event, pass out four or five index cards to each student and have them write one of their words on one side of a card and draw something that represents the feeling on the back of it. *(Example: A picture of a caged tiger might represent the feeling of the word* anger *on the other side.)*

When each student has done four or five of these, have the class play a game with the cards in which they show the picture to students in their group who then try to guess the word. Discuss why the images that elicit a correct response are more effective than those that are difficult to guess.

Pick one or two of the more effective images and ask students to suggest a sentence that contains a simile or a metaphor. Write these on the board. *(Example: My little brother was as angry as a caged tiger.)*

Give students an opportunity to draw or finish their Open Mind image.

Precomposing Step 4: *Quickwrite*

Now, students have their birthday details, their Open Mind sketches, and charts of images and meanings they can use to portray their birthdays. Ask them to look over all their information and write for three minutes about the significance of this day in their lives. Share these significances in a class discussion.

Precomposing Step 5: *Time Line*

As a last step, have the students do a time line of the incident or birthday, using pictures if they wish.

Example:

 WRITING

Writing Step 1: *Hooks*

Before they begin their first draft, discuss the way in which Sandra Cisneros and Tyler Olson hooked their readers at the beginning. *(Cisneros pulls her readers in with a general statement about birthdays that most readers will relate to. The student model begins with a telephone call.)* Students might suggest that dialogue is another good way to pull the reader in. The following is the way Kumar McMillan began his piece:

> "It's on fire! It's on fire!" Dad yells. "It is lit up like a bonfire."
> "Get a wet cloth!"
> "My eyebrows!"
> So maybe the sparklers aren't working out on my birthday
> cake, but everything else is going great.

Writing Step 2: *Present Tense*

Finally, discuss the way in which Cisneros uses the present tense to give the reader a sense that the event is happening now. Ask them to reread "Eleven" and underline the verbs.

> "But when the sick feeling <u>goes</u> away and I <u>open</u> my eyes, the red sweater's still <u>sitting</u> there like a big red mountain. I <u>move</u> the red sweater to the corner of my desk with my ruler. I <u>move</u> my pencil and books and eraser as far from it as possible. I even <u>move</u> my chair a little to the right. Not mine, not mine, not mine."

Writing Step 3: *Composing a Draft*

Now that the class has an abundance of information to work with, individuals are ready to write a draft of the story of their significant birthday. Read over the prompt with them, emphasizing the particular elements they should include. Allow a class period (or overnight) to compose a first draft.

Writing Step 4: *Image Chart*

Once they have completed their first draft, ask students to fill in a chart similar to the one they created for "Eleven." Have them look through their own piece and underline the images and metaphors they find. In the first column have them write their own quote that shows an image. In the second they will <u>tell</u> the idea the image means, and in the third they will <u>explain</u> what they were feeling on their birthday or during the memorable incident that inspired the image. If, at this point, some students discover that they have not included any effective images, ask them to read through their pieces to see where they might add information.

Example:

My Quote of Image	Telling What It Means	How I Relate to It
I knew I'd be transformed from an ugly duckling into a swan.	"Sweet 16" birthdays mark the time of being able to go out in the world, not being sheltered anymore.	I had fantastic expectations that my life would change completely. I'd begin living happily ever after.

 SHARING

Peer Group Read-Around

Students now share their full drafts in their peer groups as follows:

1. Have each group of four students pick a leader who collects their drafts and passes them to the leader of the group on their right.

2. When each group has a new set of papers, the leader distributes them so that each student has a draft.

3. All members of the group will read all papers (3 to 4) in the new set. Give them about five to eight minutes to do this.

4. When they have finished, ask each group to pick one paper that uses the most effective images.

5. Collect these and read aloud to the whole class.

6. Have students suggest the best images and write these on the board.

7. Finally, return the papers to their owners.

 **REVISING**

Response Partner Checklist

Pass out the Checklist to students. Explain that each item refers to something the prompt asks them to include in their writing. Have them pick a partner to read their piece, respond according to the list, and suggest an alternative to any no.

Checklist

Yes **No**

___ ___ **1.** You have an interesting title.

___ ___ **2.** You have an opening that hooked my interest.

___ ___ **3.** Your specific details help me picture the incident.

___ ___ **4.** Your paper contains vivid images to convey thoughts and feelings.

___ ___ **5.** Your paper has an ending that ties in with the beginning.

___ ___ **6.** You tell what you learned about yourself and why it's important.

___ ___ **7.** You have used first person point of view.

___ ___ **8.** Your piece is written in the present tense.

___ ___ **9.** Your incident is well written, easy to follow, and interesting.

With the information from the checklist in mind, the students will write a revised draft.

EDITING

Editing Step 1: *Individual Editing*

Have students first edit their own papers using the Editing Guide.

Editing Guide

Yes **No**

___ ___ **1.** All important words in your title are capitalized.

___ ___ **2.** Your paper contains paragraphs, and you have indented.

___ ___ **3.** You have kept present tense consistently throughout your piece.

___ ___ **4.** All words are spelled correctly.

___ ___ **5.** Your periods and capitals are in the right place.

___ ___ **6.** Your paper has a clear beginning, middle, and end.

Editing Step 2: *Group Editing*

Have them work in pairs or groups of three or four to edit a student's paper, using the same guide.

Editing Step 3: *Metacognitive Reflection*

When they have written their final copies, ask students to respond to the questions on the following page.

 # EVALUATION

The holistic scoring rubric should provide the evaluating criteria. Following is a sample rubric:

Scoring Rubric

Papers will be scored on a 1–6 scale according to the following criteria.

6   A **superior paper** is a well-written, well-organized, and technically correct narrative that holds the interest of the reader to the end. It does an excellent job of the following:

- Has a narrative style that is easy to follow;
- Is logically sequenced with a clear beginning, middle, and end;
- Begins with a hook that captures the reader's interest;
- Uses specific detail throughout the piece;
- Contains vivid images that communicate the feelings of the author;
- Tells why the incident is important or memorable;
- Is written in the first person and uses the present tense;
- No errors in the conventions of written English;

5   A **strong** paper is well written, organized, and technically correct. It contains all of the elements listed above; however, the images aren't quite as vivid as in a 6 paper. It has few errors in the conventions of written English.

4   An **adequate** paper contains at least six of the eight elements listed above, but has fewer images that communicate the feelings of the author. Occasional technical errors interrupt the flow of the piece.

3   A **below-average** paper tells a story but has few or no images that help the reader visualize what is happening. It is weak in thought, organization, and language development.

2   An **inadequate** paper contains only the outline of a story and serious errors in conventions that make it difficult to follow.

1   This score is given to papers that show little or no effort on the part of the writer.

Metacognitive Reflection

1. After reading "Eleven" by Sandra Cisneros and completing the writing activity, what did you learn about yourself? What did you learn about your classmates?

2. What surprised you?

3. Evaluate your piece of writing. What was especially good about it? Quote your favorite part. Explain what you intended to convey to the reader when you wrote this.

4. If you had the chance to write another draft, what would you change and why?

5. What did you learn about your writing process?

EXTENSION ACTIVITY

A story that has some striking parallels to "Eleven" is "The Stolen Party" by Liliana Heker, which is reprinted elsewhere in this book. Students could compare and contrast the two characters' expectations about a special birthday versus what really happens.

Featured Literature

Eleven
by Sandra Cisneros

What they don't understand about birthdays and what they never tell you is that when you're eleven, you're also ten, and nine, and eight, and seven, and six, and five, and four, and three, and two, and one. And when you wake up on your eleventh birthday you expect to feel eleven, but you don't. You open your eyes and everything's just like yesterday, only it's today. And you don't even feel eleven at all. You feel like you're still ten. And you are—underneath the year that makes you eleven.

Like some days you might say something stupid, and that's the part of you that's still ten. Or maybe some days you might need to sit on your mom's lap because you're scared, and that's the part of you that's five. And maybe one day when you're all grown up maybe you will need to cry like if you're three, and that's okay. That's what I tell Mama when she's sad and needs to cry. Maybe she's feeling three.

Because the way you grow old is kind of like an onion or like the rings inside a tree trunk or like wooden dolls that fit one inside the other, each year inside the next one. That's how being eleven years old is.

You don't feel eleven. Not right away. It takes a few days, weeks even, sometimes even months before you say Eleven when they ask you. And you don't feel smart eleven, not until you're almost twelve. That's the way it is.

Only today I wish I didn't have only eleven years rattling inside me like pennies in a tin Band-Aid box. Today I wish I was one hundred and two instead of eleven because if I was one hundred and two I'd have known what to say when Mrs. Price put the red sweater on my desk. I would've known how to tell her it wasn't mine instead of just sitting there with that look on my face and nothing coming out of my mouth.

"Whose is this?" Mrs. Price says, and she holds the red sweater up in the air for all the class to see. "Whose? It's been sitting in the coatroom for a month."

"Not mine," says everybody. "Not me."

"It has to belong to somebody," Mrs. Price keeps saying, but nobody can remember. "It's an ugly sweater with red plastic buttons and a collar and sleeves

569

stretched out like you could use it for a jump rope. It's maybe a thousand years old and even if it belonged to me I wouldn't say so.

Maybe because I'm skinny, maybe because she doesn't like me, that stupid Sylvia Saldívar says, "I think it belongs to Rachel." An ugly sweater like that, all raggedy and old, but Mrs. Price believes her. Mrs. Price takes the sweater and puts it right on my desk, but when I open my mouth nothing comes out.

"That's not, I don't, you're not...Not mine," I finally say in a little voice that was maybe when I was four."

"Of course its yours," Mrs. Price says. "I remember you wearing it once." Because she's older and the teacher, she's right and I'm not.

Not mine, not mine, not mine, but Mrs. Price is already turning to page thirty-two, and math problem number four. I don't know why but all of a sudden I'm feeling sick inside, like the part of me that's three wants to come out of my eyes, only I squeeze them shut tight and bite down on my teeth real hard and try to remember today I am eleven, eleven. Mama is making a cake for me for tonight, and when Papa comes home everybody will sing Happy Birthday, happy birthday to you.

But when the sick feeling goes away and I open my eyes, the red sweater's still sitting there like a big red mountain. I move the red sweater to the corner of my desk with my ruler. I move my pencil and books and eraser as far from it as possible. I even move my chair a little to the right. Not mine, not mine, not mine.

In my head I'm thinking how long till lunchtime, how long till I can take the red sweater and throw it over the schoolyard fence, or leave it hanging on a parking meter, or bunch it up into a little ball and toss it in the alley. Except when math period ends Mrs. Price says loud and in front of everybody, "Now, Rachel, that's enough," because she sees I've shoved the red sweater to the tippy-tip corner of my desk and it's hanging all over the edge like a waterfall, but I don't care.

"Rachel," Mrs. Price says. She says it like she's getting mad. "You put that sweater on right now and no more nonsense."

"But it's not—"

"Now!" Mrs. Price says.

This is when I wish I wasn't eleven, because all the years inside of me—ten, nine, eight, seven, six, five, four, three, two, and one—are pushing at the back of my eyes when I put one arm through one sleeve of the sweater that smells like cottage cheese, and then the other arm through the other and stand there with my arms apart like if the sweater hurts me and it does, all itchy and full of germs that aren't even mine.

That's when everything I've been holding in since this morning, since when Mrs. Price put the sweater on my desk, finally lets go, and all of a sudden I'm crying in front of everybody. I wish I was invisible but I'm not. I'm eleven and it's my birthday today and I'm crying like I'm three in front of everybody. I put my head down on the desk and bury my face in my stupid clown-sweater arms. My face all hot and spit coming out of my mouth because I can't stop the little animal noises from coming out of me, until there aren't any more tears in my eyes left, and its just my body shaking like when you have the hiccups, and my whole head hurts like when you drink milk too fast.

But the worst part is right before the bell rings for lunch. That stupid Phyllis Lopez, who is even dumber than Sylvia Saldívar, says she remembers the red sweater is hers! I take it off right away and give it to her, only Mrs. Price pretends like everything's okay.

Today I'm eleven. There's a cake Mama's making for tonight, and when Papa come home from work we'll eat it. There'll be candles and presents and everybody will sing happy birthday, happy birthday to you, Rachel, only it's too late.

I'm eleven today. I'm eleven, ten, nine, eight, seven, six, five, four, three, two, and one, but I wish I was one hundred and two. I wish I was anything but eleven, because I want today to be far away already, far away like a runaway balloon, like a tiny o in the sky, so tiny-tiny you have to close your eyes to see it.

Grade Level
For High School and College

Thinking Level
Evaluation

Writing Domain
Analytical/Expository

Materials Needed
No special materials required.

Suggested Supplementary Readings
- *Agamemmon* by Aeschylus
- *Heart of Darkness* by Joseph Conrad
- "The Lottery" by Shirley Jackson

Mercy or Death

by Sue Ellen Gold

Overview

This lesson is designed to help students explore the power that outside circumstances can exert on characters' actions. Students will infer that characters' actions and motivations occur for a variety of reasons, and they will examine the issue of individual responsibility and the degree to which society has the right to punish individuals for their actions.

Objectives

THINKING SKILLS

Students will:

- *analyze* details of setting and character in "Looking for a Rain God";
- *judge* the characters' levels of responsibility;
- *determine* and *justify* the punishment the characters should face as a consequence of their actions.

WRITING SKILLS

Students will:

- *organize* a written argument with a clear thesis regarding the family's guilt;
- *utilize* textual evidence to support that argument;
- *use* analytical/expository form (introduction, main body, conclusion);
- *demonstrate* proficiency in standard written English.

The Process

PREWRITING

Prewriting Step 1: *Discuss Motivation and Responsibility*

Begin by asking students whether any of them have ever been punished for a misdeed. Of course, almost all will answer yes. Then, ask whether they have ever broken a family rule because they felt they had a good reason? Have the students give examples of their misbehavior and their justification. Examples of such behavior might include breaking curfew to help a friend; lying to their parent to cover up for a sibling; driving a friend's car so that the friend won't drive drunk, etc.

Prewriting Step 2: *Discuss the Idea of Guilt*

Next, introduce the idea of "relative" guilt. In other words, even though a person may commit a crime, the circumstances under which the crime takes place are part of a formula used to determine just how guilty the person is. For example, someone may be hurt in a traffic accident by a driver who is intoxicated; how would perceptions of the accident be changed if the second driver was sober and simply glancing away when traffic suddenly slowed? You may want to discuss why we have a court system that allows a not guilty plea even if the defendant has been caught in the act of a crime.

Prewriting Step 3: *Discuss "Justified" (?) Crimes*

Read each of the following scenarios and have the students discuss whether each crime was "justified" and therefore should not be punished or whether the crime outweighs the circumstances, therefore meriting punishment.

- A sixty-year-old homeless woman is caught pushing a stolen grocery cart into which she has piled her sleeping bag, blankets, and a few possessions. The store wants to prosecute her for stolen goods. Some student responses might include: *She is guilty but shouldn't be prosecuted; she is not guilty because this cart is her home by default.*

- A doctor who has invented a "suicide machine" demonstrates its use to a woman with a terminal disease and then leaves her with the option of using it. She commits suicide. Sample student responses might include: *He is not guilty because she wanted to die; he is guilty because he gave her the idea and means to commit suicide.*

- A woman is told her child has cancer. She cannot afford the treatments, so she breaks into a store to burglarize it and use the money for her child's medicine. Some student responses might be: *She is not guilty because the child's life is more important than the burglary (money); she is guilty because there must be some group that will help pick up payment, so she needs to look further.*

- A gang member discovers that one of his gang brothers has been shot. He stalks and shoots the rival gang member who hurt his friend. Some sample student responses might be: *not guilty because he didn't start it and he has a responsibility to his gang brothers; guilty because he's not doing anything but making the problem worse.*

Prewriting Step 4: *Newspaper Search*

The teacher who wishes can ask the students to look for newspaper or magazine articles that detail crimes. These articles can provide a good basis for classroom discussion of crime and the frequent difficulty of assessing guilt and deciding on an appropriate punishment. *Note: Much has been written about the now-famous trial of Eric and Lyle Menendez (1993–1994), which might suggest a library search and an interesting follow-up discussion.*

Prewriting Step 5: *Story Reading and Freewrite*

After reading the story, have the students freewrite about what they found disturbing in it. Have them share their writing with a partner, and then bring it to a full class discussion. *Warning: It has been my experience that many students may get stuck on the idea that the villagers and the Ramadi family could have just "gone somewhere else" when the weather turned sour. The class may need some background on what it's like to live where all things are not possible.*

 PROMPT

Generally, crimes do not simply occur; there are circumstances that influence people's actions. These circumstances may even force an issue to its conclusion. What we must each decide is to what extent we are to be held responsible for our actions and to what extent society has the right to impose punishment as a consequence of those actions.

Decide whether Ramadi and his father are guilty of first degree murder. If they are not guilty of first degree murder, then how would you classify the crime? Should they suffer the death penalty or a different punishment?

In a multiparagraph essay, argue for your decision. In order to support your choice, you will need to cite specific evidence from the text by:

1. Describing the effect of the landscape and weather;
2. Explaining other factors that influence the family's decision to sacrifice the children;
3. Discussing the reactions of the family and villagers after the deaths.

In each case, the details need to support your decision about the Ramadi family's crime and the necessary punishment.

PRECOMPOSING

Precomposing Step 1: *Tracing Motivation Along a Time Line*

Have each student create a time line of the opening two paragraphs and then compare them in groups. A sample time line might look like this:

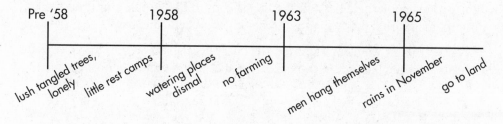

Have students individually create time lines for the rest of the story.

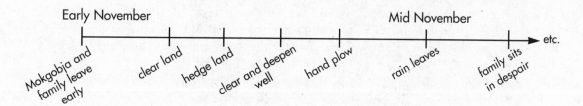

After the students have completed their two time lines, ask them to freewrite on the following question for three to five minutes: *What do the time lines show about how the Ramadi family reaches the decision to sacrifice the children?*

Sample Freewrite:

> Looking at the time line shows that long before the Ramadis decided to kill their children was when the drought started. They had a long time to go insane and be so desperate that they could kill their children for a chance of rain. Also, a lot of other things led up to this point that would make anybody go insane.

Ryan M.—Tenth Grade

Precomposing Step 2: *Charting the Environment*

Have students list all details of nature from their section and then decide which images are positive, which are neutral, and which are negative.

Positive	Neutral	Negative
• lush tangled trees • softened the earth etc.	• vast clearing in the bush • mists cleared a little etc.	• the air . . . burned the skin • deathly silence etc.

Have the groups copy their lists on the board or butcher paper, and then discuss any disagreements that arise as to what belongs in each category.

Instruct each student to select the three strongest descriptive details and freewrite about what they imagine when they read them. Then have them answer the question, *"How did these details of the weather affect the Ramadi family?"*

Student Models

What I see is a tan-colored ground with cracks in it, as the water slowly disappears up into the clouds/sky above. I see little balls of wind tumblers scrambling around as though almost like a country scene from a Billy the Kid movie. I see cactus and weeds springing up everywhere they can, knowing that they won't have water to survive, but still sitting there hoping. Little kids are running, but panting because they are so thirsty, but still having the energy to run around and play with their friends, while their parents hope and pray for the water to magically appear, so they can cool their hot, thirsty, sweaty kids down.

Melissa L.—Tenth Grade

They saw there was some water in the clouds. They thought it would get more or at least stay the same. So they went to the lands. But the light rain was an illusion—no more followed. No rain anymore for the seeds the family set. That meant no vegetables or anything to eat because nothing grows without rain. Without the light rain—the illusion of more rain, they wouldn't have gone out to the lands.

Sandra H.—Tenth Grade

Precomposing Step 3: *Pairing—Looking for Clues*

In pairs, have the students go back to the text and list all the factors except weather that they feel influence Ramadi, Mokgobja, Tiro, and Nesta to sacrifice the girls. Then, together, have them write a brief explanation of each item.

Student Model

Excerpt	Response
plain porridge—milk	They had hopes to eat well again, but having to go back to dry mush was depressing
impossible to plant—sat all day	They got really bored and wondered if their life was ever going to change.

James C.—Tenth Grade

Precomposing Step 4: *Analyzing Reactions*

In pairs, have the students list details of the family adults and other adults after the killing.

Sample List

- terror—extreme and deep
- ashen, terror-stricken faces

Have students freewrite to the following questions: *How does the family feel about the killing after? Why do you think they feel this way? How do the villagers feel? Why?*

Sample Freewrite:

After the killing of the two little girls, they just realized that it was stupid. They were really shocked with what they had done. They went back to the village with a stomach full of guilt. They started to lie to all the villagers that the two girls had died of unknown causes. The two women finally burst in tears with guilt when the police asked to see the grave.

The villagers were desperate for water after seeing some of the men commit suicide because they couldn't handle the drought, the starvation, and the pain. When they saw the Ramadi family come back without the two little girls, some of them might suspect. When the truth finally burst out, I don't think everyone is really that shocked since it could happen to anyone at anytime. They just feel lucky that it didn't happen to them.

Have them share their freewrites in groups of four or five.

Precomposing Step 5: *Questioning Cultural Background*

Ask the students to freewrite on the following: *There are some things our culture views as wrong—e.g., murder. Mokgobja, however, remembers the ceremony from a pre-Christian time. How does that change how you view the murder?*

Student Model

I'm not sure if reading he "remembered" changes my opinion of second-degree murder or not. But it does make me realize that culture can have a lot to do with what people do. I mean we do a lot of things that other people consider weird. But it was still murder.

Anna G.—Tenth Grade

Precomposing Step 6: *Modified Debate*

Many students are aware of different classifications of murder but do not understand the differences. The general classifications were explained to me as follows:

The Classifications of Murder

Murder is the act of killing someone unlawfully with malice, or evil intent.

- **First degree** is a <u>premeditated</u> or planned, "cold-blooded" killing—e.g., a contract killing, a hostage murder, torture, a murder made when "lying in wait," a murder that occurs during a felony.
- **Second degree** is any other murder with "malice aforethought"—a murder in which there was an intention to kill or cause severe bodily damage but which was not premeditated.

Manslaughter is the act of killing someone unlawfully, without malice.

- **Voluntary manslaughter** is a killing that occurs in the heat of passion. If a killer has sufficient time to calm down and think about what he or she is doing, it is murder and not manslaughter.
- **Involuntary manslaughter** is an accidental killing that occurs as a result of either negligent behavior or the commission of a misdemeanor—e.g., shooting someone accidentally while firing a warning shot.
- **Vehicular manslaughter** is the act of killing someone as a result of reckless or drunk driving.

Insanity is a defense that states that the murderer lacked the ability to form an intention to kill and did not understand the consequences of his/her intentions.

After a discussion of these classifications, the students will need to self-select or to be appointed to one of four groups in order to argue the guilt of the family: first degree, second degree, manslaughter, or insanity. *(Caution: There are advantages and disadvantages in each method of forming groups. If students already have a strong feeling about the way they wish to argue the prompt, this exercise will help them strengthen it. If they do not, this will help form their opinion. It is important to have at least one strong student in each group. Otherwise, I generally let them self-select, then divide up the students who have not yet decided upon their stand. Additionally, in my experience, manslaughter is the hardest plea to argue successfully and teachers may eliminate this team if they like.)*

In groups, the students look for evidence to support their assigned or self-selected position. For example: the "first degree" group might argue that the time lapse between Mokgobja's "memory" and the girls' execution shows the act is premeditated and, therefore, first degree. The "insanity" group might argue that this same memory proves that Mokgobja is suffering a lapse from "reality."

Collecting evidence may take anywhere from a half hour to a full class period. I have had best results when the students do this assignment individually and then meet as groups to share ideas. It is important, however, that each member is clear on all the information because each student must participate in the debate.

Each group member fills out the following evidence chart with all of the group information. There must be at least as many points as there are people in the group.

A blank chart for your use is found on the next page.

Example:

The Ramadi family is guilty of *2nd degree* murder because:	
Evidence	**Interpretation**
1. The air was so dry it burned the skin.	The weather was like an enemy and people snapped and hung themselves, not just Ramadis.
2. The women were wailing.	They were emotionally out of control.
3. The children were spanking their dolls.	They were just imitating how they were being treated. This shows the adults were stressed.

Each group writes one statement that summarizes its positions, for example: "The Ramadi family is 'not guilty through insanity' because they were so frightened by the drought they forgot who they were and what they believed."

The Ramadi family is guilty of _____ because:	
Evidence	**Interpretation**

The Debate:

Each team forms one side of a square and elects a team speaker.

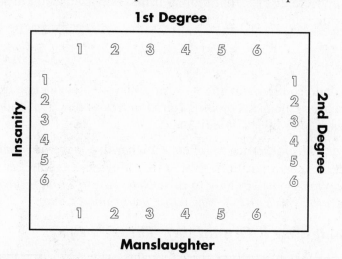

1st Degree

Insanity

2nd Degree

Manslaughter

Beginning with the team arguing for a first degree judgments, each team speaker reads aloud the group's summary statement.

After each statement has been read, the student seated at the head of the first degree team (#1) reads the first bit of evidence and interpretation. The first student on the second degree team must answer this and provide alternate reasoning. If the second degree team already has the same excerpt on their evidence chart, then this step is easy; if their "evidence" or excerpts do not match, then the teams may have one minute to huddle and decide an answer. For example:

Student Models

First degree team member: "The Ramadi family is guilty of first degree murder because although the story says all the other villagers 'knew in their hearts that only a hair's breadth had saved them from sharing a fate similar to that of the Mokgobja family,' none of the rest of them did anything like this. The rest of the villagers knew right from wrong and did not murder, though desperate."

Claire P.

Second degree team member: "It's true that they didn't act on it, but the fact that it was only a hair's breadth shows that the whole thing was desperate and based on emotion."

Marni M.

Manslaughter team member: "The villagers saying that they knew 'only a hair's breadth saved them' from the same fate meant that they believed it was a natural thing to do, that the drought was an accident of nature, and that it made sense to sacrifice to the gods. It was just a shame that someone had to get killed for the ceremony."

John S.

Insanity team member: "What it means is that only a brief moment—'a hair's breadth'—kept them from stepping over the limit themselves, and that the villagers knew they were just barely rational. It makes no sense to kill something to make it rain; therefore it's insanity."—

Tran L.

The statements and counter-statements continue until all evidence from all teams has been heard. Each succeeding round moves to the next student in the group so that each must speak at least once.

Give the students a few minutes to reflect on what they have heard and to freewrite about their own position. What is the Mokgobja family guilty of? What evidence points most strongly to this? *Note: I always find it interesting to poll the students afterwards and see how many have changed sides.*

Precomposing Step 7: *Organizing Through Boxes*

The students are ready to organize their thoughts prior to writing their essays. Since many students find outlining cumbersome or intimidating, I use a cross between an outline and clustering to help them sort out their arguments. You may use the form on the next two pages.

Explain to the students that they may fill in more or fewer reasons than the spaces allotted.

Precomposing Step 8: *Organizing for Transition Thoughts*

Have the students reexamine their box charts and then freewrite for two minutes on the paragraph order that seems most natural.

Ask the students to fill in the chart on the next two pages according to their determined order and then add the transition thoughts.

 ## WRITING

After reviewing the prompt with the students, ask them to use their freewrites, charts, and box outline to write their first draft of the essay.

 ## SHARING

Instruct the students to trade papers to read. Have each student fill out the revision sheet, which follows the Transition Thoughts page.

Organizing Through Boxes

The Ramadi family is guilty of _____ because

_____ .

Effect of Landscape and Weather

Quote: _____

_____

Explanation: _____

_____

Quote: _____

_____

Explanation: _____

_____

Quote: _____

_____

Explanation: _____

_____

Why do these point to your decision? _____

Other Factors That Influence Your Decision

Quote: _____

_____

Explanation: _____

_____

Quote: _____

_____

Explanation: _____

_____

Quote: _____

_____

Explanation: _____

_____

Why do these point to your decision? _____

Organizing Through Boxes

Reactions of Family and Villagers After the Deaths
Quote: _____
_____
Explanation: _____
_____
Quote: _____
_____
Explanation: _____
_____
Quote: _____
_____
Explanation: _____
_____
Why do these point to your decision? _____

Punishment the Family Should Receive Based on Their Crime
Quote: _____
_____
Explanation: _____
_____
Quote: _____
_____
Explanation: _____
_____
Quote: _____
_____
Explanation: _____
_____
What is your final decision? _____

Organizing Through Boxes

THESIS

> The Mokgobja family is guilty of _____
>
> because _____
>
> _____
>
> _____

↓

BOX 1

> Main Idea: _____
>
> _____
>
> This idea connects to the one in the next box because _____
>
> _____

↓

BOX 2

> Main Idea: _____
>
> _____
>
> This idea connects to the one in the next box because _____
>
> _____

↓

BOX 3

> Main Idea: _____
>
> _____
>
> This idea connects to the one in the next box because _____
>
> _____

↓

CONCLUSION

> What punishment should the family be given? _____
>
> _____
>
> _____

Mercy or Death

✳ **SHORT STORY**

Revision Sheet

1. What does the author think that the family is guilty of?

2. List the reasons the author gives for his/her decision.

3. Do you agree with each of these reasons? If yes, why? If not, why not?

    Reason A:

    Reason B:

    Reason C:

4. Does the author of the paper refer to environmental details? What details does he/she use?

    a.

    b.

    c.

    How does the author explain why these details support his/her decision about the family's guilt?

5. Does the author show how other factors influence the family's decision and affect their level of guilt? What reasoning does he/she use?

6. Does the author take into account the various reactions to the deaths? What reactions does he/she cite?

7. Are there any places where the paper or the author's stand was unclear? Where does the author need to add detail or explanation?

REVISION

The students may use the comment sheet to revise and write second drafts.

 ## EDITING

1. Place the students in groups of four.

2. Pick up the drafts from each group and pass them to the next group.

3. Instruct the students that they are to read the papers for correctness only. There are to be no comments other than for punctuation, grammar, or spelling.

4. On the first paper each student reads, they are to look for incorrectly spelled words and circle them.

5. On the second reading, they are to read for sentence completeness. If they think a sentence is a run-on or is incomplete, they put a check in the margin next to the problem sentence.

6. The third reading is for verb tense changes. The students underline any verb that is in the wrong tense.

7. The fourth reading is for correct punctuation of quotes. Wrong punctuation gets an asterisk.

 ## REVISION

The students revise for correctness, checking all the notes made by the peer proofreader.

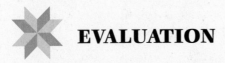 **EVALUATION**

1. Each student brings a third draft to class to be evaluated by a peer group.

2. Each group exchanges papers. It is important that these not be the same papers that have been previously read.

3. All students in each group must read and score each paper according to the scoring guide.

4. The four students in each group must come to consensus on a score for each paper.

 REVISION

All students revise their final draft.

Scoring Guide

I. Chooses a point of view about the family's guilt and supports with specifics:

Does not demonstrate	Argues but needs more specifics	Exceptional	
1 2	3 4	5	X6= _____

II. Demonstrates the importance of landscape and weather, cites specific examples, and explains how details support the decision about the family's guilt:

Does not refer to weather or landscape	Needs more explanation of importance	Exceptional	
1 2	3 4	5	X4= _____

III. Discusses the importance of factors other than landscape and weather:

Does not analyze other factors	Cites other factors, needs more explanation of importance	Exceptional	
1 2	3 4	5	X4= _____

IV. Explains the reactions to the death:

Does not explain reactions to deaths	Refers to reactions, needs more explanation	Exceptional	
1 2	3 4	5	X4= _____

V. Correctness in spelling, punctuation, and grammar:

Errors interrupt meaning	Few errors; author shows grasp of standard grammar, punctuation, and spelling	No errors	
1 2	3 4	5	X2= _____

Total= _____
(100 points possible)

Looking for a Rain God
by Bessie Head

Bessie Head (1937–1986) is considered by some as a South African writer because she was born in South Africa and by others as a Botswanian writer since she chose Botswana as her homeland and became a Botswanian citizen. She escaped South Africa because she would no longer tolerate the conditions of apartheid. Her novels are entitled: *Maru* (1971), *When Rain Clouds Gather* (1969), *A Question of Power* (1974), *The Collector of Treasure* (1977), and *Serowe: Village of the Rain Wind* (1981). The topics of Head's fiction can be classified into two categories: *village life*, which she knew very well, having lived in a small village in Botswana; and the feeling of bitterness that, because of being both black and a woman in an oppressive society, she experienced strongly.

It is lonely at the lands where the people go to plow. These lands are vast clearings in the bush, and the wild bush is lonely too. Nearly all the lands are within walking distance from the village. In some parts of the bush where the underground water is very near the surface, people made little rest camps for themselves and dug shallow wells to quench their thirst while on their journey to their own lands. They experienced all kinds of things once they left the village. They could rest at shady watering places full of lush, tangled trees with delicate pale-gold and purple wildflowers springing up between soft green moss and the children could hunt around for wild figs and any berries that might be in season. But from 1958, a seven-year drought fell upon the land and even the watering places began to look as dismal as the dry open thornbush country; the leaves of the trees curled up and withered; the moss became dry and hard and, under the shade of the tangled trees, the ground turned a powdery black and white, because there was no rain. People said rather humorously that if you tried to catch the rain in a cup it would only fill a teaspoon. Toward the beginning of the seventh year of drought, the summer had become an anguish to live through. The air was so dry and moisture-free that it burned the skin. No one knew what to do to escape the heat and tragedy was in the air. At the beginning of that summer, a number of men just went out of their homes and hung themselves to death from trees. The majority of the people had lived off crops, but for two years past they had all returned from the lands with only their rolled-up skin blankets and cooking utensils. Only the charlatans, incanters, and witch doctors made a pile of money during this time because people were always turning to them in desperation for little talismans and herbs to rub on the plow for the crops to grow and the rain to fall.

The rains were late that year. They came in early November, with a promise of good rain. It wasn't the full, steady downpour of the years of good rain, but thin, scanty, misty rain. It softened the earth and a rich growth of green things sprang up everywhere for the animals to eat. People were called to the village kgotla to hear the proclamation of the beginning of the plowing season; they stirred themselves and whole families began to move off to the lands to plow.

The family of the old man, Mokgobja, were among those who left early for the lands. They had a donkey cart and piled everything onto it, Mokgobja—who was over seventy years old; two little girls, Neo and Boseyong; their mother Tiro and an unmarried sister, Nesta; and the father and supporter of the family, Ramadi, who drove the donkey cart. In the rush of the first hope of rain, the man, Ramadi, and the two women, cleared the land of thornbush and then hedged their vast plowing area with this same thornbush to protect the future crop from the goats they had brought along for milk. They cleared out and deepened the old well with its pool of muddy water and still in this light, misty rain, Ramadi inspanned two oxen and turned the earth over with a hand plow.

The land was ready and plowed, waiting for the crops. At night, the earth was alive with insects singing and rustling about in search of food. But suddenly, by mid-November, the rain fled away; the rain-clouds fled away and left the sky bare. The sun danced dizzily in the sky, with a strange cruelty. Each day the land was covered in a haze of mist as the sun sucked up the last drop of moisture out of the earth. The family sat down in despair, waiting and waiting. Their hopes had run so high; the goats had started producing milk, which they had eagerly poured on their porridge; now they ate plain porridge with no milk. It was impossible to plant the corn, maize, pumpkin and water melon seeds in the dry earth. They sat the whole day in the shadow of the huts and even stopped thinking, for the rain had fled away. Only the children, Neo and Boseyong, were quite happy in their little-girl world. They carried on with their game of making house like their mother and chattered to each other in light, soft tones. They made children from sticks around which they tied rags, and scolded them severely in an exact imitation of their own mother. Their voices could be heard scolding the day long: "You stupid thing, when I send you to draw water, why do you spill half of it out of the bucket!" "You stupid thing! Can't you mind the porridge pot without letting the porridge burn!" And then they would beat the ragdolls on their bottoms with severe expressions.

The adults paid no attention to this; they did not even hear the funny chatter; they sat waiting for rain; their nerves were stretched to breaking point willing the rain to fall out of the sky. Nothing was important, beyond that. All their animals had been sold during the bad years to purchase food, and of all their herd only two goats were left. It was the women of the family who finally broke down under the strain of waiting for rain. It was really the two women who caused the death of the little girls. Each night they started a weird, high pitched wailing that began on a low, mournful note and whipped up to a frenzy. Then they would stamp their feet and shout as though they had lost their heads. The men sat quiet and self-controlled; it was important for men to maintain their self-control at all times but their nerve was breaking too. They knew the women were haunted by the starvation of the coming year.

Finally, an ancient memory stirred in the old man, Mokgobja. When he was very young and the customs of the ancestors still ruled the land, he had been witness to a rainmaking ceremony. And he came alive a little, struggling to recall the details which had been buried by years and years of prayer in a Christian church. As soon as the mists cleared a little, he began consulting in whispers with his young son, Ramadi. There was, he said, a certain rain god who accepted only the sacrifice of the bodies of children. Then the rain would fall; then the crops would grow, he said. He explained the ritual and as he talked, his memory became a conviction and he began to talk with unshakable authority. Ramadi's nerves were smashed by the nightly wailing of the women and soon the two men began whispering with the two women. The children continued their game: "You stupid thing! How could you have lost the money on the way to the shop! You must have been playing again!"

After it was all over and the bodies of the two little girls had been spread across the land, the rain did not fall. Instead, there was a deathly silence at night and the devouring heat of the sun by day. A terror, extreme and deep, overwhelmed the whole family. They packed, rolling up their skin blankets and pots, and fled back to the village.

People in the village soon noted the absence of the two little girls. They had died at the lands and were buried there, the family said. But people noted their ashen, terror-stricken faces and a murmur arose. What had killed the children, they wanted to know? And the family replied that they had just died. And people said amongst themselves that it was strange that the two deaths had occurred at the same time. And there was feeling of great unease at the unnatural looks of the family. Soon the police came around. The family told them the same story of death and burial at the lands. They did not know what the children had died of. So the police asked to see the graves. At this, the mother of the children broke down and told everything.

Throughout that terrible summer the story of the children hung like a dark cloud of sorrow over the village, and the sorrow was not assuaged when the old man and Ramadi were sentenced to death for ritual murder. All they had on the statute books was that ritual murder was against the law and must be stamped out with the death penalty. The subtle story of strain and starvation and breakdown was inadmissible evidence at court; but all the people who lived off crops knew in their hearts that only a hair's breadth had saved them from sharing a fate similar to that of the Mokgobja family. They could have killed something to make the rain fall.

Signs of Death

The land was a pleasant green and the children played with enthusiasm. The village was showered with crops and a plentiful supply of rain, but their happiness would soon end, for a seven-year drought had struck. It left the land dry and the people in anguish. People in the village began to travel to other lands in search of good rain and land, where they could farm their crops and raise their animals. Among those who left was the family of the old man, Mokgobja. Mokgobja and his son, Ramadi, left with two women and two little girls. They, too, had left the village in search of good farming land. Bessie Head, the author of the short story, "Looking For a Rain God," shows how nature can suddenly change when it is least expected. She describes the desperation and need for rain and how it led the Ramadi family into a tragedy that they will never forget. It is a tragedy in which the family is guilty of second degree murder.

Many of the feelings that the Ramadi family got were generated by the environment. They became more and more depressed as they saw that the "leaves of the trees curl up" and "the moss became dry and hard." Their nerves and hope were crushed, for nature itself showed signs of death. "The ground turned a powdery black and white." Time seemed to be running out for the family, for their crops had died and they were forced to sell their animals. Because of these things, the Ramadi family began to weaken and their minds fell behind their actions.

The Ramadi family became tired and hopeless. They could not stand it much longer; the dry and humid climate drove them wild. The women, who gave into the strain, "would stamp their feet and shout as though they had lost their heads." They seemed afraid and lost for "each night they started a weird high-pitched wailing." The family was so desperate for rain that it led them to the point where they would do anything for it. So, when "an ancient memory stirred in the old man," and he told them of an old ritual, they took it as an answer to all their problems. The Ramadi family is guilty of this and should have stayed calm and controlled.

After "the bodies of the two little girls had been spread across the land, the rain did not fall." The family was shocked and afraid, they did not know what to do. "Terror, extreme and deep, overwhelmed the whole family." Unsure of their decision, the Ramadi family quickly "fled back to the village." People in the village who soon noticed the absence of the two girls began to worry about them. They questioned the family and the family told them that the two little girls "had died at the lands." The family could not hide behind their lies, for the village people noticed their "terror-stricken faces." Not long after the arrival of the police, the mother broke down and told everything. "A dark cloud of sorrow" hung over the entire village. The men in the family were sentenced to death. Yet the villagers did not seem to be totally shocked for they "knew in their hearts that only a hair's breadth had saved them from sharing a fate similar to that of the Mokgobja family."

The Ramadi family is guilty of second-degree murder. The reason it is second-degree is because it was not something that the family had planned. They were distracted by the drought and were driven to the point where they had to do something. The family, without thinking about the consequences, took the ritual as a solution to their problems. They would live to regret this for the rest of their lives. The punishment that would fit the crime is a short sentence in prison so that the Ramadi family can think about what they have done and try to straighten out their lives again.

Alex Tu

"*As women, we have learned to listen, rather than speak, causing us, historically, to join with others who maintain we have nothing to say. Only now we are discovering that we do. And those who do not seem interested in knowing our voices are just plain foolish. To limit their knowledge of people, places, culture, and sexes is to live in a narrow, colorless world. It is not only a tragedy, but just plain silly, for only foolish people would not be interested in embracing such knowledge.*"

Helen Viramontes
Author of *The Moths and Other Stories*

Featured Literature

"My Name" from
*The House on
Mango Street*
by Sandra Cisneros

Grade Level
For Middle School and
High School

Thinking Level
Analysis

Writing Domains
Sensory/Descriptive
Imaginative/Narrative
Analytical/Expository

Materials Needed:
No special materials
required.

**Suggested
Supplementary
Readings:**
• "Kizzy" from *Roots* by
  Alex Haley
• "A Pair of Tickets" from
  The Joy Luck Club
  by Amy Tan

My Name, My Self:
Using Name to Explore Identity

by Brenda Borron

Overview

Using clustering, organizers, quickwrites, and graphics, students will explore the relationship between names and identity. After reading "My Name" from *The House on Mango Street* by Sandra Cisneros, students will research and reflect upon the origins, meanings, significance, and effects of names. The final product of the lesson is an essay in which students explore their own names.

Objectives

THINKING SKILLS

Students will function at the analysis level as they:

- *analyze* the short story "My Name" from *The House on Mango Street* by Sandra Cisneros;
- *research* their own names;
- *create* metaphorical equivalents for their names;
- *speculate* about how their names have made them the people they are;
- *hypothesize* about how their lives have given meaning to their names;
- *compare* themselves with others of the same name;
- *examine* and *reflect* upon their feelings about their names and how their names have affected them.

WRITING SKILLS

Students will write a personal essay in which they reflect upon their names.

In this essay, students will:

- *hook* their readers with a provocative opening;
- *create* metaphors for their names;
- *describe* themselves and their feelings about their names;
- *organize* their information in a comprehensible format;
- *demonstrate* their knowledge of opening, body, and closing.

The Process

 **PREWRITING**

Prewriting Step 1: *Reading*

Have students read the short story "My Name" by Sandra Cisneros.

Featured Literature

My Name

In English my name means hope. In Spanish it means too many letters. It means sadness, it means waiting. It is like the number nine. A muddy color. It is the Mexican records my father plays on Sunday mornings when he is shaving, songs like sobbing.

It was my great-grandmother's name and now it is mine. She was a horsewoman too, born like me in the Chinese year of the horse—which is supposed to be bad luck if you're born female—but I think this is a Chinese lie because Chinese, like Mexicans, don't like their women strong.

My great-grandmother I would've liked to have known her, a wild horse of a woman, so wild she wouldn't marry until my great-grandfather threw a sack over her head and carried her off. Just like that, as if she were a fancy chandelier. That's the way he did it.

And the story goes she never forgave him. She looked out the window all her life, the way so many women sit their sadness on an elbow. I wonder if she made the best with what she got or was she sorry because she couldn't be all the things she wanted to be. Esperanza, I have inherited her name, but I don't want to inherit her place by the window.

At school they say my name funny as if the syllables were made out of tin and hurt the roof of your mouth. But in Spanish my name is made out of a softer something like silver, not quite as thick as sister's name Magdalena, which is uglier than mine. Magdalena, who at least can come home and become Nenny. But I am always Esperanza.

I would like to baptize myself under a new name, a name more like the real me, the one nobody sees. Esperanza as Lisandra or Maritza or Zeze the X. Yes. Something like Zeze the X will do.

Note: Teachers who wish to use additional sources of literature involving names and naming will find the "Kizzy" section from Roots *by Alex Haley and "A Pair of Tickets" from* The Joy Luck Club *by Amy Tan useful companion pieces.*

Prewriting Step 2: *Clustering*

As a large group, have students cluster "Esperanza."

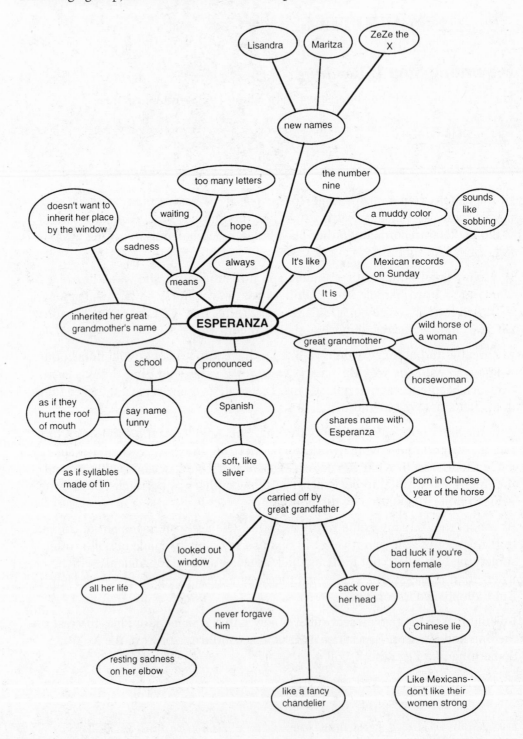

Prewriting Step 3: *Quotation Chart*

As a large group, complete the first two entries for a quotation chart for "My Name."

Quotation from the Story	What the Quotation Tells You	What You Wonder: Understand
1. "It is like the number nine."	Her name is too long.	Is nine the number of letters her name is?
2. "And the story goes she" never forgave him.	She (Esperanza's great grandmother) felt sorry for herself her whole life.	Did she make a mistake?
3.		

Have students individually complete at least ten entries on their charts.

Prewriting Step 4: *Character Frame and Coat of Arms*

Pass out a blank coat of arms and character frame to paired groups. (See forms at end of lesson.) Explain that they are going to think of Esperanza's name in terms of various metaphors. Then, they will create for her a coat of arms, illustrating those metaphors.

Ask various pairs to volunteer their responses for each of the nine questions on the frame. Choose different students for each question to ensure full participation by the class.

Example:

1. If Esperanza's name were an animal, it would be a TURTLE because SHE'S ALWAYS DUCKING BACK INTO HER SHELL.

2. If Esperanza's name were a plant, it would be a WEEPING WILLOW because SHE SWAYS WITH THE WIND; BECAUSE SHE IS NOT SURE WHAT SHE WILL BE BUT SHE WANTS TO BE STRONG.

3. If Esperanza's name were a season, it would be AUTUMN because SHE IS TOO OLD FOR HER AGE; SHE IS BROODING.

4. If Esperanza's name were a time of day, it would be DUSK because SHE IS WAITING UNEASILY; SHE FEELS THE DARK COMING.

5. If Esperanza's name were a word, it would be RUST because SHE IS COLORED BY THE NAME AND LIFE OF ANOTHER.

6. If Esperanza's name were a musical instrument, it would be a PHONOGRAPH because IT PLAYS THE MEXICAN RECORDS THAT ARE HER NAME.

7. If Esperanza's name were an object, it would be an OPEN WINDOW because SHE DOESN'T WANT TO INHERIT HER GREAT-GRANDMOTHER'S PLACE BY A CLOSED ONE.

8. If Esperanza's name were a song, it would be "SEVENTEEN" because EVEN THOUGH SHE IS NOT REALLY SEVENTEEN, THE SONG CAPTURES HER PERSONALITY.

9. If Esperanza's name were an emotion, it would be MELANCHOLY because EVERYTHING SHE FEELS ABOUT HER NAME IS MELANCHOLY, ACHING WITH SADNESS.

Select several of the images, which students volunteer to draw on a transparency of Esperanza's coat of arms.

Example:

Have paired students create a full coat of arms and frame for Esperanza. Ask pairs to share their coats of arms and frames with the large group. Then, have students as a large group chart their information for Esperanza and her name.

Use this frame:

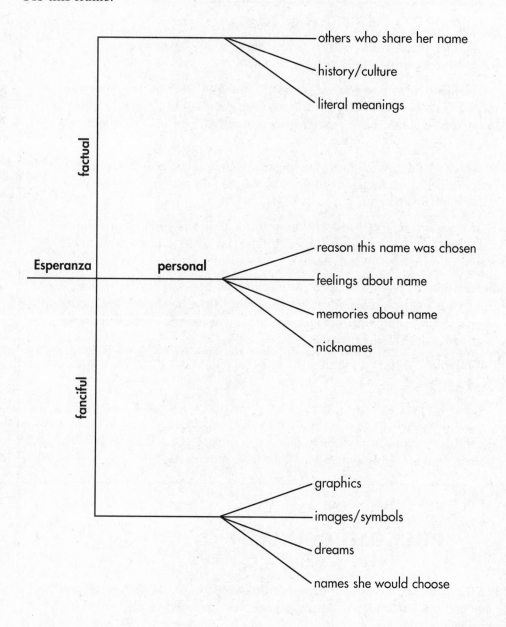

 **PROMPT**

Introduce students to the following prompt:

Who Are You?

A name is just a word. Yet it is more than a word. Names have feelings, memories, meanings, and histories.

We can find meanings for our names in dictionaries, but our names are more than their dictionary meanings. Our names contain our families, our pasts, our feelings, our memories, our dreams. When we explore our names, we are exploring ourselves.

In a personal essay, explore your name. Include facts, personal experiences, fanciful explorations of your name, and an analysis of how your name has affected you.

Here are some suggestions for you to think about as you explore your name. Look at your name as other things. If it were a time of day, what would that time be? Why? A color? A musical instrument? A plant?

Begin your paper with an interesting title and hook (a beginning that captures your reader's attention). Let your ideas flow by carefully structuring your sentences and your paragraphs. Make your paper come full circle: end it so that it feels finished.

Check your spelling, punctuation, and usage to make your work as error-free as possible.

The best papers will move beyond a factual and/or personal exploration of names to a fanciful and imaginative analysis of the relationship between the author's name and identity. They will engage the reader with lively writing that employs images and figurative language.

 PRECOMPOSING

Once the students have been introduced to the prompt, the following precomposing activities will prepare them to generate ideas and to plan for their compositions.

Precomposing Step 1: *Quickwrites*

1. Have students write a five-minute quickwrite about their initial feelings, associations, and memories about their names.

2. Have students take their quickwrites home, read them to their parents, and add any information their parents can contribute about their given name.

3. Have paired students read their quickwrites. A model quickwrite follows:

Student Model

Quickwrite Based on My Name

This is my story. My whole name is "Israel Devora Uvina," but there is a problem with my last name. I actually don't like my last name because "Uvina" is my mom's last name, but in the school they make fun of it. When I used to go to the elementary school the students used to make fun of it like "pineapple, urination," and I didn't like it because the other students used to laugh and I felt sad, put down.

I decided to use just two names Israel and my dad's last name. But some people still can't pronounce my dad's last name and my first name right. Some people call me "Isreal, Ireal, Iseral" and sometimes I don't like being called like that so I have to tell them. Also, too, with my last name, they put me down like "Divora, deBora," and sometimes I just feel sad because the other students laugh at me and I just feel like crying.

Israel Devora Uvina

Precomposing Step 2: *Their Own Coat of Arms*

Have students complete a writing frame and coat of arms for their own names. A sample follows:

1. If my name were an object, it would be a PAINTBRUSH because I COLOR MY LIFE WITH WHAT I DO AND WHAT I PAINT.

2. If my name were a word, it would be "SINGADAMONGA" because IT'S A WORD MY FRIEND MADE UP TO MEAN WHATEVER WE WANT IT TO MEAN.

3. If my name were an emotion, it would be HAPPY because I AM A HAPPY PERSON AND I THINK MY NAME REFLECTS THAT.

4. If my name were a day of the week, it would be FRIDAY because IT'S THE DAY I LIVE FOR.

5. If my name were a color, it would be RED because IT'S FULL OF LIFE AND JOY.

6. If my name were a song, it would be "TAKE ME OUT TO THE BALLGAME" because I LOVE TO PLAY BASEBALL.

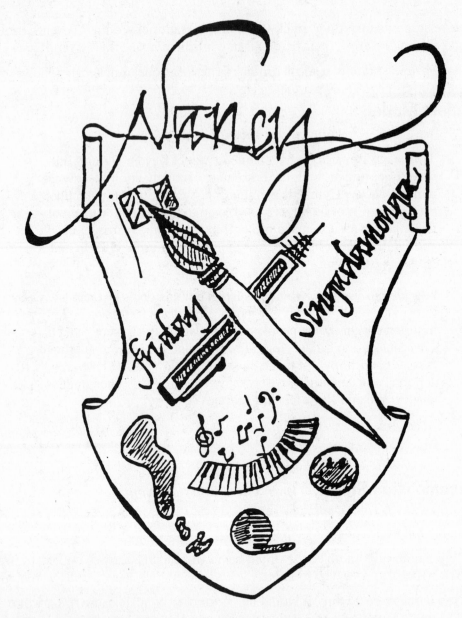

Precomposing Step 3: *Researching Their Names*

Have students research their names. In addition to dictionaries of names, you might want to direct your students to calendars of saints and to the Chinese zodiac, to which Esperanza refers in her story.

THE CHINESE ZODIAC

THE CHINESE ZODIAC consists of a twelve-year cycle, each year of which is named after a different animal that imparts distinct characteristics to its year. Many Chinese believe that the year of a person's birth is the primary factor in determining that person's personality traits, physical and mental attributes, and degree of success and happiness throughout his or her lifetime. To learn about your animal sign, find the year of your birth among the twelve signs. If you were born before 1943 or after 1990, add or subtract 12 to find your year.

1951 1963 1975 1987	**THE RABBIT**	Luckiest of all signs, you are also talented and articulate. Affectionate, yet shy, you seek peace throughout your life. Marry a sheep or a boar. Your opposite is the cock.
1952 1964 1976 1988	**THE DRAGON**	You are eccentric and your life complex. You have a very passionate nature and abundant health. Marry a monkey or rat late in life. Avoid the dog.
1953 1965 1977 1989	**THE SNAKE**	Wise and intense with a tendency toward physical beauty. Vain and high tempered. The boar is your enemy. The cock or ox are your heart signs.
1954 1966 1978 1990	**THE HORSE**	You are popular and attractive to the opposite sex. You are often ostentatious and impatient. You need people. Marry a tiger or a dog early, but never a rat.
1943 1955 1967 1979	**THE SHEEP**	Elegant and creative, you are timid and prefer anonymity. You are most compatible with boars and rabbits but never the ox.
1944 1956 1968 1980	**THE MONKEY**	You are very intelligent and are able to influence people. An enthusiastic achiever, you are easily discouraged and confused. Avoid tigers. Seek a dragon or a rat.
1945 1957 1969 1981	**THE COCK**	A pioneer in spirit, you are devoted to work and quest after knowledge. You are selfish and eccentric. Rabbits are trouble. Snakes and oxen are fine.
1946 1958 1970 1982	**THE DOG**	Loyal and honest, you work well with others. Generous, yet stubborn and often selfish. Look to the horse or the tiger. Watch out for dragons.
1947 1959 1971 1983	**THE BOAR**	Noble and chivalrous, your friends will be lifelong, yet you are prone to marital strife. Avoid other boars. Marry a rabbit or a sheep.
1948 1960 1972 1984	**THE RAT**	You are ambitious yet honest. Prone to spend freely. Seldom make lasting friendships. Most compatible with dragons and monkeys. Least compatible with horses.
1949 1961 1973 1985	**THE OX**	Bright, patient and inspiring to others. You can be happy by yourself, yet you make an outstanding parent. Marry a snake or a cock.
1950 1962 1974 1986	**THE TIGER**	Tiger people are aggressive, courageous, candid and sensitive. Look to the horse and dog for happiness. Beware of the monkey.

SHORT STORY *My Name, My Self*

As they research, have students complete the chart that follows:

Your Name _____		
Derivation of Your Name _____ *(country of origin)*		
Briefly recount how you were named:		
Briefly tell the meaning(s) of your name:		

People Whose Names I Share

	Kind of Person	Description of Each Person	Feelings I Have About Person
Famous			
Family			
School			
Historical			
Literary			

Have students refer to the chart of Esperanza's name in which they examined the factual, personal, and fanciful aspects of her name. Using this as a model, students should now chart their own names. You might want to put the following model up on the board. However, encourage students to invent their own headings as well as leave out those headings that do not apply.

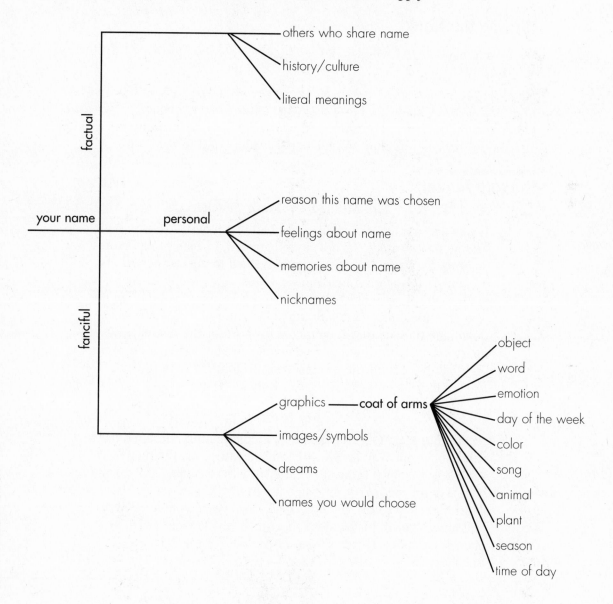

Precomposing Step 4: *Freewrite*

Now ask students to freewrite for five minutes on the following topic: *How My Name Has Affected Me.*

Ask students to share their freewrite with a partner.

WRITING

Have students use their clusters, organizers, quickwrites, and coats of arms to write a draft about their names and their selves.

Writing the Hook

You may want to help them get started by providing the following information about a hook:

Hook—A *hook* is a term writers use when they are talking about the first few lines of a piece. A hook is a bit of dialogue, an unusual statement, an exciting moment from the story, a question, an especially vivid description, or another attention-getting device that will make the reader want to read on.

Student Models

The Messed Up Math Teacher

It was my first day at school, and I had just moved to Santa Ana. I knew no one at all. As my day progressed, I began to feel more comfortable there. I very hesitantly walked to my last period of the day; it was math. I loved math. I was very good at it. As I entered the classroom, the teacher asked for my schedule. Then I gave it to him and stood patiently. He then told me where to sit down and told me that it would be my seat for the rest of the quarter. I then sat down and waited for further instruction. As I was looking around the room getting acquainted with it, the teacher blurted out, "Hey, Barney Rubble."

My Name

In the chill of an October morning, an old man in a tattered black suit hobbles his way up the street. His features are distinctive. A genetic code which seems to be uncanny in its ability to replicate people of his race carry the same inherent characteristics. He is short, but stocky with piercing steel gray eyes. His nose is large and hook beaked; his head is large and oval. He is Jewish. The place is Germany, Circa 1500's. The middle of the great Renaissance.

Rachelle

The R stands tall at the beginning of my name. The R that makes my name unique, unusual and different. "If I could just change that 'Ra' to a 'Mi,'" I would say as a child, "then I could be normal." The theory is people whose names begin with R give selfless service, have a gift of structured communication and are full of brotherly love. I believe this is true of me, and so it is, there is a reason for this R.

Livengood

It was many generations ago when my surname was changed from Liebvengudt to Livengood, only because someone on Ellis Island had trouble pronouncing it. Even though this did not affect me, I can imagine how my ancestors must have felt losing their name. Although I do not know what the old name meant to them, I am sure it was much more beautiful and acceptable than the new one.

SHARING

Have paired students share their drafts. Have partners write three questions and one positive comment at the end of the drafts.

REVISING

Revising Step 1: *Revision Practice Using a Sample Essay*

Refer students to the student model "Flower from God" by Parichat Smittipatana. (See end of lesson.) Read the model aloud as a large group.

Use the Essay Response Sheet on the next page to evaluate the effectiveness of the model. As you go through the items on the response sheet with your class, model the kinds of responses you want them to use for one another's papers in peer response. Explain unfamiliar terms.

Revising Step 2: *Responding to a Partner's Essay*

Have students complete the Essay Response Sheet for partners. Allow partners time to discuss their response sheets.

Revising Step 3: *Evaluating the Title*

Before allowing students time for revision, you might want to give them the following information about titles.

- **Title** Your title gives the reader his first impression of you and your paper. Good titles pique the reader's interest. They cause readers to ask questions, to predict, to make associations. Good titles pull the reader into the paper. After discussing why Parichat selected "Flower from God" as her title, ask students to rethink their own titles as they revise. Will their titles capture the reader's attention and convey something essential about the paper's focus?

- Exchange papers with a partner.
- Complete the content checklist for your partner.
- Discuss your papers and responses.

Name of response partner _____.

Name of author _____.

Essay Response Sheet: Who Are You?

Dear _____.*(insert the author's name)*

The thing I like best about your paper is _____

_____

_____.

If I were to use one word to describe your paper, that would be _____

because _____

_____.

For me, the most effective words in your paper are "_____"

because _____

_____.

Something I learned about you is _____

_____

_____

 **EDITING**

Use a transparency or a class set of model essays to model editing for students, using the editing guide shown below.

Now, have students use the same editing guide to edit one another's papers, either in pairs or in small groups.

Your Name _____

Correctness/Editing Guide

"My Name, My Self"

If the paper you are reading conforms to each statement, check "Good Job!"; if it does not, leave the column blank.

Good Job!

1. You did not punctuate your title either by underlining it or enclosing it in quotations.   _____

2. You indicated new paragraphs by indenting.   _____

3. You kept the same verb tense throughout your essay, unless the content dictated a change.   _____

4. When you used pronouns, it was clear to me that they referred to a particular noun. I wasn't confused about what you meant.   _____

5. When you used prepositional phrases and modifying clauses, you placed them adjacent to the words they modify.   _____

6. You have checked the spelling of every word in your paper. I found no spelling errors.   _____

7. Your paper is neatly written and easy to read.   _____

8. Your paper follows the conventions of written English.   _____

9. You have organized your paper so that I can follow your ideas.   _____

EVALUATION

Use the scoring guide below (or one of your choice) to evaluate your students' papers.

Evaluation: My Name, My Self

For each item, circle the score you assign: 5 is high; 1 is low.

1. Your opening is interesting and provocative.   1 2 3 4 5

2. Your opening (hook) immediately captured my interest.   1 2 3 4 5

3. As I read your paper, I felt a sense of exploration and discovery.   1 2 3 4 5

4. Your paper reflects your individuality, both in content and in voice.   1 2 3 4 5

5. Your paper is grounded in factual information about your name.   1 2 3 4 5

6. Your paper incorporates your personal experiences and how they relate to your name.   1 2 3 4 5

7. Your paper goes beyond factual and personal information to fanciful, imaginative, and reflective associations on that information.   1 2 3 4 5

8. Your paper thoughtfully analyzes how your name has affected you.   1 2 3 4 5

9. Your paper held my attention.   1 2 3 4 5

10. Your paper is filled with images, pictures that appeal to the reader's five senses.   1 2 3 4 5

11. Your paper flows; the ideas follow one another in a comprehensible way.   1 2 3 4 5

12. When I concluded reading your paper, I felt your paper was finished.   1 2 3 4 5

For each item, circle yes or no

1. You remembered not to punctuate your title.   yes   no

2. You indicated paragraphs by indenting.   yes   no

3. You kept the same verb tense throughout your essay, unless the content dictated a change.   yes   no

4. When you used pronouns, it was clear to me that they referred to a particular noun. I wasn't confused about what you meant.   yes   no

5. When you used prepositional phrases and modifying clauses, you placed them adjacent to the word(s) they modified.   yes   no

6. You have checked the spelling of every word in your paper. I found no spelling errors.   yes   no

7. Your paper is neatly written and easy to read.   yes   no

8. Your paper follows the conventions of standard written English.   yes   no

9. You have organized your paper so that I can follow your ideas.   yes   no

Student Models

Flower from God

Parichat is like silk, a very nice gentle sound which just flows through your mouth. If you pronounce it right, Parichat sounds very pretty. It's not too hard, just three simple syllables. You pronounce Par like a pear that you eat, ri with a short i, and then chat like chart without saying the r.

My name means "flower from God" in Thailand. Also, it is the name of a flower you can smell only in the early morning. Most people present this flower to the monks because of its meaning and sweet smell. Only this flower is allowed to decorate the monk's temples.

The flower represents a virgin by its sweet smell and the purity of a lady by its white petals.

It is a tradition in Thailand that when a baby is born, its name is given by the monks who are said to know what the child is going to be like in the future. But my parents weren't just going to settle for any name the monks thought up. My dad wanted to call me "Little Brat" because he knew I was going to be spoiled. My mom wanted to call me "Little Angel" because I was a cute baby. They couldn't decide, so they went to the monks.

When I was born, I weighed seven-and-a-half pounds, so my parents brought seven-and-a-half pounds of parichat flowers to the monks when they took me to be named. That is how I got my name Parichat, as pure as a baby.

I was born in the Chinese year of the ox; that sounds dangerous and wild, but I think it fits me better than "flower of god." I should be sweet, nice, polite, or in other words, ladylike—which I'm not.

Even my nickname was a problem. My dad wanted to call me "Cherry" because when I was born, our cherry tree gave its first fruit. It was small like me and red like my fat cheeks. My mom wanted to call me "nonk" which means "little sister" because I have three older sisters and one older brother. So it was both names for me. I call myself "little sister" and everybody else calls me little sister Cherry. When I turned thirteen years old, Cherry began to sound childish to me, so I changed my nickname to Sherrie because it sounded more mature and it is easier for people to pronounce than my real name.

I used to want to change my name to "Patricia" because I'm an American citizen now. I thought I wanted to have an American name that wouldn't take everyone ten minutes to say. But doing things like Americans, like eating steaks and salad, dressing and talking American makes me homesick sometimes. I want to speak Thai which I can no longer remember. I want to preserve my culture and traditions; that makes me think twice about changing my name. Parichat is unique, one-of-a-kind. It reminds me that part of me is still Thai.

Parichat Smittipatana

Tin, Is Dull and Flat

My Chinese name is Lee Pao Yen. This name my grandmother gave me means only wealth, money and greed. Lee Pao Yen, the name I have grown up with all my Chinese life, stands for everything I hate. The pity I have for my grandmother and her names. This name that poisons me. This name that I will carve away, the shiny stones and leave dull-flat.

Father gave me my English name when mother had me. The Canadian garment buyer asked me to be named after him. "Leon Lee it would be!" he probably said, after the handshake of a business transaction. The business, the transaction and my name; in that order, and in that situation. If father's client had been another, so would have my name? Small talk and big money gave me my name. Leon—the word bridging money to goods and breaking my back.

I see myself in the mirror each morning, with my name plastered on my skull, and many times I see the reflection of grandmother and father behind me, laughing at my resistance. They live within the addiction, and inject greed like heroin into their veins. I want so much to smash the glass and break their stare, but I know it will do no good. They live too deep within the glassy finish to be shaken. This name tag that I've been forced to wear says neither Leon nor Lee Pao Yen, but GREED. Greed people kill with. Greed that massacres morality. Greed is my name.

My grandmother's hands yank at my heels, dragging me down into her grave to lie with her carcass. I seem to have become the gem stone she needed to place on her bony, dead finger. My life, grandmother's void. She waits for me there, and I shall never go. She will have to suffer, just like me.

..........my name is lee pao yen, leon lee if you'd like.

Leon Lee

Jorje

The first day of school is always tough. New teachers and new classmates can make anyone a little nervous. As the teacher begins calling roll, I brace myself for the inevitable. And then it happens, a chill goes up my spine as the teacher calls out, "Is Jorje Chica present?" What's wrong with that, you may ask? Well, if you heard the brutal mispronunciation, you would understand. I find myself saying, "It's just George, with a <u>G</u>." In elementary school, giggles and laughter would follow. This laughter hurt me inside. At that moment, I would wish that I had a normal name. As school went on, my name would take the brunt of much teasing. "Georgie Porgy pudding pie," the other kids would say. And, of course, there's the famous "George of the Jungle, watch out for that tree!"

It's been said that people like to hear their names. Personally, I think it depends on who is saying it. In school and in public, I play it safe by using George. Only at home or with my Hispanic friends am I comfortable with Jorje. Why is this so? I shouldn't have to do this, but hearing my name distorted, accidentally or purposely, hurts inside. I shield myself by settling with the Anglo "George." However, I do like to hear my true name. When my mother or grandmother calls me, my name sounds beautiful. I feel pride for my name, as well as my heritage. However, when someone really screws up on the pronunciation it sounds like a needle being dragged across a record. When this happens, I retreat into my American persona.

I am proud of my name. Either way you say it, it has a long and great history. Jorje comes from the Greek name <u>George</u>. The name <u>George</u> originated from the <u>Georgics</u>, a poetic treatise on agriculture by the Roman poet Virgil. Thus comes the meaning "farmer." In Biblical times, a Roman soldier named George converted a Lybian village to Christianity, after slaying a dragon which victimized the town. He was made a saint, and in the 14th century he was made patron saint of England. This proclamation led to seven British monarchs named George. The name <u>George</u> is also important on American soil. Our first president, George Washington, has been a favorite of Americans for the last 200 years. His popularity will no doubt, ensure the longevity of the name <u>George</u> in the United States.

My name may have a long and celebrated history, but it has more personal meaning to me. It represents a new beginning and a positive future. I'm the first in my family to have the name <u>Jorge</u>, so it's a fresh and unused name. I don't have to live up to the achievements of someone else, just because we share a name. My name is also unique. It differs in spelling from the Spanish Jorge. Another positive aspect of my name is the reason my mother chose it. In Cuba, my parents' homeland, my mother had a friend named <u>Jorge</u>. He had certain qualities that she wanted in her children. She said to me, "He was very noble, and was a good friend." She went on to say, "The name <u>Jorje</u> brings to mind great men and grand achievements. I guess I had great expectations for you."

What use do names have for us? Names perform the public task of separating us from others. But, a number could do the same thing. There has to be more to a name than just a means of differentiating us from our fellow man. Names have to fulfill personal needs, too. My name is a part of who I am. Jorje is a reflection of my heritage. My name influences how I look at myself, and is a part of what I want to be, my own person. My name helps me keep one foot in the past, and the other in the future. By having a Hispanic name, I connect myself with my ancestry, while moving forward in life. Names may have literal meanings, and great histories. But, the personal definitions and histories are usually more interesting, and always more special. I hope to carve out my own personal history, one just as worthy as that of the famous <u>Georges</u> the world has seen.

Jorge Chica

"*It is not the shared experience, but the acceptance of differing human perspectives that inspires the belief that all people are equal.*"

Paul Apodaca
Curator of Native
American Art,
Bowers Museum,
Santa Ana, California

Native American Voices:
Reflecting on Facts and Fallacies

by Bill Burns

Overview

This lesson will help students reexamine their views about Native Americans by analyzing Ernest Hemingway's short story "Indian Camp" and studying several selections of authentic, first-person accounts by American Indians from the last two hundred years. Students will reflect on the nature of bias and stereotypes and how or why persons may change their mind.

Objectives

THINKING SKILLS

Students will:

- *examine* their own stereotypes of Native Americans;
- *compare* and *contrast* them with those of Ernest Hemingway;
- *classify* what categories of behavior their ideas fall into;
- *analyze* whether their ideas are accurate, based on a comparison to the words spoken by Native Americans themselves;
- *draw conclusions* about the nature of their ideas, how these views were formed and how they changed;
- *reflect* on more universal problems of replacing old fallacious ideas with new, more accurate ones.

WRITING SKILLS

Students will:

- *record* and *compare* in a journal their personal perspective with the perspectives of others;
- *write* a reflective essay, following analytical/expository form;
- *employ* direct quotes from both literature and nonfiction speeches of Native Americans;
- *reflect* on their own views of Native Americans, how these views formed, and how they changed.

The Process

This lesson requires students to write in two different modes, first in a journal or "learning log," and secondly in an essay. Students will also read and analyze a short story as well as selections of nonfiction, first person speeches by Native Americans. This lesson is designed to help students examine their own biases and stereotypes of Indians by giving them practice in constructing charts, clusters, and lists to examine ideas. It provides cooperative group activities, opportunities for oral presentations, and practice in drawing generalizations based on specifics and in expressing conclusions drawn from a variety of information sources.

 PREWRITING

You will need to tell students to bring a Learning Log *(a journal)* to class for the start of the lesson. Students will be writing many entries during the lesson, entries that will later provide the foundation for an essay. A Learning Log can be a separate, bound notebook, or a special section in the student's notebook. Decide whether or not these will be given credit. In any case, you should collect them once early in the lesson or make a check in class to verify the student is on task and is making an effort.

Day 1

Prewriting Step 1: *Reading*

Hand out a copy of Ernest Hemingway's short story "Indian Camp," and either read it aloud or have students read it silently.

Prewriting Step 2: *Initial Response*

After reading the story, direct students to write the first entry in their Learning Log, recording their initial feelings about the story. They can write down questions, opinions, surprises, responses to the whole or to parts. The important goal here is **not** to write what happened but to write about what thoughts the story provokes.

Have student volunteers share their responses with the whole class, discuss any questions students might have about the story, and generally "clarify" the story in a class discussion. If any students bring up the presence of the Indians in the story or have questions about their importance, hold off on commenting until the class has completed its discussion. Most likely, student response will focus on the boy, Nick, and the birth and death as in the following example:

I would be really bummed if I went to my Dad's work and saw a dead body. Nick's father was trying to show his son some of the good things he did as a doctor and instead the husband kills himself. Why did he do that? I don't understand that part. I don't think I'd like to see a cesarean birth either. All that blood! But the husband's death is even worse. Instead of seeing life begin, Nick sees a death. I don't think that's what his father wanted him to learn.

Prewriting Step 3: *Discussion*

Next, ask students whether it is important to the story that the action takes place in an Indian camp. Could it just as easily be at some isolated farm or at a logging camp of whites, or perhaps at a campsite of city folk camping in the woods on vacation? After eliciting student responses, explain that it might be easier to answer the question if the class examines Hemingway's use of the Indians.

Prewriting Step 4: *Class Chart*

With the help of the class, construct a chart on the blackboard, or on a transparency, of Indian references. Divide the chart into three columns, labeled "positive images," "neutral images," and "negative images." These images refer to how the reader is made to feel about the Indians. Read through the story again and place every reference to Indians in an appropriate column. Your chart may look like this:

Positive Images	Neutral Images	Negative Images
Young Indian rows faster. Indian blows out lantern, can see in dark. Indians are bark peelers. Women in camp are helping. Young Indian laughs at Uncle.	Two Indians row across lake. Indian Lady is sick.	Indians use quick, choppy strokes. Uncle gives Indians cigars. Indians live in shanties. Dogs running loose. Room smells very bad. Maybe they don't have soap. Husband seems unconcerned.

Students may argue about the placing of some images. Good. You may need to add Nick's father's response to the Indians, such as the directions he gives, the fact that he brings his own soap, won't touch the quilt, and how Uncle George responds. These are part of how we are made to "see" the Indians. Save the chart so that students may refer to it in the next step.

Prewriting Step 5: *Learning Log—Secondary Impressions*

Ask students to return to their Learning Log and, in a second entry, write some generalizations about Hemingway's images of the Indians. Ask them to identify the parts of the chart (such as "positive images," or a particular example from the chart) that supports their generalizations. A sample response may look like this:

> It looks to me like Hemingway thinks the Indians live a pretty primitive life. They live in shanties, it's dirty, and dogs are running around. It just doesn't seem clean. Maybe that's what a doctor would see. The Indians seem to be comfortable there. The Indian men are laughing and the women are helping out. Overall it seems like the Indians are just a backdrop for the father's showing off. They aren't real people. Even the dead husband doesn't seem <u>real</u>.

Day 2

Prewriting Step 6: *Poll*

After students complete their entries, take a poll, either by show of hands or by secret ballot, as to whether Hemingway's portrayal of the Indians is fair or stereotyped. Put the results on the board under the headings Fair/Stereotype. Ask for evidence to support the two stands and put them on the board under the same headings. It isn't important to reach a consensus as a class.

Prewriting Step 7: *Exploring Setting*

Next, ask once again whether students think the setting is an important part of the story. Why? Try to help the students, if they don't see it, that the Indians are an important part of the feeling of the story, of the exoticness, of the feeling that Nick has entered another world and then comes back to a more normal life where he is "quite sure that he would never die." At this time, ask students to explain what they think Hemingway meant when the father says, in response to Nick's question why the Indian killed himself, "I don't know, Nick. He couldn't stand things, I guess." What does Hemingway mean by "things"? *(Nick's question is usually the one that students will most ask in their first log entries.)* The chart ought to be a help in identifying what those "things" are. Some possible responses might be: his wife's screams; the doctor's comments that they don't bother him; the husband's helplessness; his embarrassment at the white men's presence and power.

Ask students whether they think the husband's response and death are peculiarly "Indian"? Does Hemingway present it that way? Do the students still see Hemingway's portrayals of the Indians as fair or as stereotyped?

Prewriting Step 8: *Learning Log*

Have students return to their Learning Logs and reread their first entry. Now, ask them to do a third entry about how their view of the story may have changed as a result of the class discussion. A sample response might look like this:

> I think I have a better idea why the husband killed himself. That really bugged me! Here he is having a son born and he kills himself. What is his wife going to do when she finds out? I didn't really think about whether there were Indians in the story. I can see now that they are an important part. I'm not sure whether Hemingway was prejudiced but there were a lot of negative views of Indians in the story. I wonder what Nick felt about the Indians?

Prewriting Step 9: *Examining Perceptions Through Clustering*

Students have examined Hemingway's Indian images. Next, they will examine the perceptions they and their classmates have about Native Americans.

Clustering: Put the word *Indian* in the middle of a circle and ask students to do the same on a piece of paper of their own. Have them cluster for a few minutes to see what connotations the word *Indian* has for them. Then do a class cluster. It might look something like this:

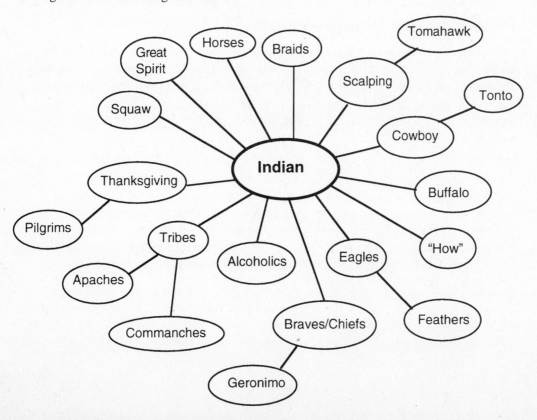

After the cluster is complete, ask students where they got their ideas. For example, where did they learn *how* or think of braids, alcoholics, or Geronimo?

Prewriting Step 10: *Two Column Chart*

In order to provide a different perspective to the class's associative ideas, put a two-column chart on the board with the headings "positive" and "negative." Ask students to place the items from the class cluster on the appropriate side of the positive-negative chart. Have students come to the board, draw a line through a term in the class's cluster, and write it on the chart.

If there are items that don't seem at first to fit clearly either one side or the other, discuss why. The class may need to clarify what a positive and a negative term implies. Is a negative an item that is a stereotype, or is it a generalization that isn't necessarily true? Students may want to add new items on the chart. When the chart is finished, examine whether the number of items on the two sides is equal. If there is inequality, discuss why this might be. A typical chart might look like this:

Positive	Negative
Great Spirt Braves Pilgrims Thanksgiving etc.	Scalping "How" Squaw Braids etc.

Prewriting Step 11: *Learning Logs*

Direct students to turn to their Learning Logs and write down their observations about the cluster and the chart (entry #4). Have them consider the following questions: What conclusions would they make about their own and others' views *(including Ernest Hemingway's)* of Native Americans? What kind of items are on the negative side? on the positive side? From where do these images come?

Day 4

Prewriting Step 12: *Pictures and Oral Presentations*

You are now going to show students some selected pictures of Native Americans. Some of the pictures should be historical pictures of Indians in native dress. Some of the pictures should be pictures of contemporary Indians in modern dress. (Pictures may be found in books about Indians, and newspaper articles. *National Geographic* and *Arizona Highways* are excellent sources for historical and current pictures of Indians.) Divide students into groups of about three or four and give each group one picture. Students will examine their picture and prepare an oral presentation to the class with two responses: first, a physical description of the picture (what do they see?); secondly, what does the picture suggest or evoke (what do they feel?) Have students write in their Learning Logs (entry #5) a summary of what they saw and heard based on all of the class presentations. Have them finish their entries with a conclusion about their own perceptions and the perceptions of others based on the oral presentations and the class discussion. The purpose of this step is to give students a look at their classmates' responses and their own responses to visual examples and to understand that their preconceptions and stereotypes are formed and reinforced by the pictures they have seen of Native Americans.

Day 5

Prewriting Step 13: *Native American Narratives*

So far, students have been examining Native Americans mostly from the perspectives of non-Indians, unless there are students of American Indian heritage in your class. In this step, students will read first person narratives from Native Americans, representing two hundred years of response to the white man. I have arranged the resources appended to this lesson in chronological order.

Divide the students into groups and hand out one or more (depending on the number of groups) examples of Indian speeches. Students are to read the passages, identify where the Indian tribe was and/or is located, and discuss among themselves first, the meaning of the passage, and secondly, what specific topics these passages address (for example, religion, education, marriage, ethics, philosophy, land ownership, politics, etc.). Direct students to write down these topics as they and other students present them, since they will need them later. Give students the rest of the period to work on their presentation.

Day 6

Prewriting Step 14: *Oral Presentations*

Students will do a group oral presentation for the rest of the class. It will consist of the following:

- an oral reading of the passage;
- clarification of terms and identification of the Indian tribe;
- a summary of the passage's topics; and
- a summary of their discussion about the passage and their perceptions about the viewpoint presented.

Group presentations should conclude by asking for comments or questions from the rest of the class. Before the oral presentations begin, give a copy of all the passages to each student so that they may mark and write notations as each passage is read. You may want to evaluate these presentations. If you do, give the groups a rubric from which they will be evaluated. After the class presentations are over, ask students to write another entry (#6) in their Learning Logs, recording their observations about the views presented through the voices of the Native Americans. Were there any particular traits they noticed? Were there any common views shared by the speakers? Were there any surprises? Were there any examples of ideas or attitudes you already expected? A sample student response might look like this:

> After reading these speeches by Indians, I was surprised at how direct they were and how good they spoke. They said what was on their minds without a lot of extra words. They were funny too; they had a sense of humor. There was anger in their speeches but I expected that. They all seem to have had a clear idea of what they had suffered by the white man, how they had been cheated or lied to. Several of them noticed that the whiteman's religion didn't seem to fit their actions and I could see the Indians were religious people too.

This would be a good time to collect the Learning Logs if you intend to give them credit for their precomposing writing. Don't grade on mechanics or form but on whether they completed the assigned number of entries, and on whether they made reasonable efforts to write to the topics.

Day 7

Prewriting Step 15: *Organizing Information*

This step is designed to help students organize the variety of topics discussed and their responses to these topics.

Put on the board or provide a handout of a chart similar to the following one, which includes topics presented by the students in their class presentations on the narratives by Native Americans. You may want to add other topics if you feel some have been omitted. The chart will look somewhat like this:

Topic	What was said? (Examples from the speeches)	When? (Dates)	Your Response (Write student responses here)
Religion **Marriage** **Honor** **Education**			

The students may fill in the chart as a classroom activity and/or as a homework assignment. Since the amount of space needed to complete what the Indians said, and what the student's response is, will vary, remind students that the chart is a guide and that they will need to give themselves enough room between topics.

When the chart activity is finished, give students a copy of the prompt and the rubric for evaluating their essay.

 **PROMPT**

Part of maturing emotionally and intellectually is letting go of old misconceptions, biases, fallacies, and confusions and replacing them with a clearer, more accurate, more discerning viewpoint.

Write a reflective essay about the process of changing viewpoints, focusing specifically on the ideas you had about Native Americans and how they changed and/or expanded. Your essay will include the following:

- Identify and illustrate personal perceptions you had about Native Americans before we began this unit.
- Explain how and why these perceptions changed and/or expanded. Be specific about the topics (remember these from the oral presentations) these perceptions include.
- Use specific references and direct quotes from the works read and discussed in class.
- Reflect on how changes from inappropriate, mistaken, or stereotypical views of people often expand, and how this is an important part of growing.
- Follow standard expository essay form.

 PRECOMPOSING

Precomposing Step 1: *Reviewing*

Have students reread their Learning Logs entries in order to recall their earlier perceptions and how these views changed or expanded. Remind them of the varied approaches examined over the last several days:

- Hemingway's story "Indian Camp"
- Positive, negative images of Native Americans
- Pictures of historical and modern Native Americans
- Narratives of Native Americans
- Native American viewpoints on various topics

Precomposing Step 2: *Clarifying and Comparing*

For a classroom precomposing activity, have students make a list of stereotypes and misconceptions they or others had about Native Americans. Write this list in one column. Opposite, in another column, have students write a revised comment on the first item and what source supports this revised view.

Precomposing Step 3: *Structuring the Essay*

Sterotypes, Misconceptions Regarding Native Americans	Revised, Factual Viewpoint
Indians are always silent, unemotional.	A Blackfoot wife, White Shield, tells how she was abused and vents her anger.
Indians are all similar in culture, language, and housing.	Many different tribes, appearances, and experiences
Indians were always fooled by the white man, not very aware.	Canassatego, Delaware chief in 1782, Chief Joseph
Indians never said much about what happened to them.	Narratives where Indians spoke out angrily and humorously

Think of the essay as a whole made up of parts that fit together *(a very Indian idea)*. The essay can be like a hoop: start with the idea of how ideas change and expand with experience, then develop and illustrate those ideas and their changes, and finally return to the initial idea in a reflection on how the student's specific experiences are also part of the universal experiences of change and expansion of faulty views. *(This is a very Indianlike process.)*

Or the essay may be more linear in structure, starting with an introduction of the topic and each section reflecting the directions in the prompt. For example, the essay "identifies and illustrates personal perceptions" the student had about Native Americans before the unit began. Next, the student explains "how and why these perceptions changed and/or expanded." And finally, the essay concludes with a reflection on "how changes from inappropriate, mistaken, or stereotypical views of people often expand." Each of these sections would consist of at least one and probably several paragraphs.

Remind the students that there are many ways to begin an essay besides repeating the prompt. Since this unit has been so rich in the words of others *(Ernest Hemingway, Native Americans, students),* an effective beginning might use these words to make an exclamation, surprise, or tantalize the reader.

 **WRITING**

Now, students are ready to start writing their first drafts. Give students adequate time to develop a complete first draft of their reflective essay. Remind students to reread the prompt and review the rubric so that they know how their essay will be evaluated.

 SHARING

Sharing Step 1: *Response Groups*

Provide class time for students to meet with response groups or with the teacher to check on progress or answer any questions that might arise as students work on completing a draft of their essay.

Hand out the following checklist:

- Have I identified the topic of my reflective essay near the beginning of the essay?
- Have I presented my views of Native Americans before the lesson began?
- Did I explain what changed or expanded my views?
- Did I make specific references to some of the works read in class in order to support my ideas and provide examples to illustrate my views?
- Did I reflect on how changing and expanding ideas is an important part of growing and maturing?

Sharing Step 2: *Metacognitive Log*

After sharing drafts, have students write a brief reflection in class on their writing problems, successes, and process. This can be shared with groups, or the class as a whole, or read only by the teacher. This is an ungraded metacognition on the student's efforts. A "miniprompt" for this writing would look like this:

> Write about the problems you faced as you wrote this essay, how you resolved some of them and what you think you need to do in revising your paper.

 **REVISING**

Students will revise their essays, considering the comments of the readers, the checklist, the rubric, and their reflection on their writing process.

 EDITING

Students will review and check each other's papers for correct punctuation of quotes and identification of speakers. This is a good time to give a direct teaching lesson on using quotations and other punctuation marks correctly. *(Note: You may want to refer students to the guidelines for correct quotation from text in the "Living in Life's Shadow" lesson, elsewhere in this book.)*

Spelling, accuracy of names, and overall correctness will be checked by student responders.

 EVALUATION

The following rubric is a guideline for you or your students to follow. You can use it to give a letter grade or points. You may want to develop a rubric with the class in order to reinforce their part in evaluation. This rubric can be used for peer evaluation or for teacher evaluation only.

Rubric

A superior paper, an "A" paper, merits a yes to the following questions that appeared on the checklist for sharing:

- Have I identified the topic of my reflective essay near the beginning of the essay?
- Have I presented my views of Native Americans before the lesson began?
- Did I explain what changed or expanded my views?
- Did I make specific references to some of the works read in class in order to support my ideas and provide examples to illustrate my views?
- Did I reflect on how changing and expanding ideas are an important part of growing and maturing?
- Did I choose an appropriate organizational structure for the development of my ideas?

In addition, the superior paper follows the rules of standard English and uses language clearly and effectively.

A good paper, a "B" paper, answers most of the questions and has only a few errors in mechanics and language use.

A satisfactory paper, a "C" paper, answers most of the questions but without many examples or development. More errors in mechanics and language use.

A barely passing paper, a "D" paper, attempts to answer some of the questions but does not provide much development. Contains many errors in mechanics and language use.

A failing paper is any paper that does not address the prompt or has completely missed the point of the essay.

EXTENSION ACTIVITIES

1. Poetry

Have students write a poem about their perceptions of Native Americans.

2. Reader Response

Have students read one of the following novels and discuss, write, or orally present a response to the novel's view of Native Americans:

> *When Legends Die* by Hal Borland
> *Laughing Boy* by Oliver La Farge
> *A Yellow Raft in Blue Water* by Michael Dorris
> *Ceremony* by Leslie Marmon Silko
> *Indian Boyhood* by Charles A. Eastman
> *Crow and Weasel* by Barry Lopez
> *Love Medicine* by Louise Erdrich
> *Talking Leaves: Contemporary Native American Short Stories*
>   edited by Craig Lesley
> Any of the mysteries by Tony Hillerman
> Any of the James Fennimore Cooper novels

3. Comparison/Contrast

Have students make a comparison study of origin in Genesis, and the myths of the ancient Greeks and Native Americans. There are many sources for Indian myths.

4. Book Report

Have students read and report on one of many nonfiction works on Native Americans, such as *Black Elk Speaks* by John G. Neihardt, *Bury My Heart at Wounded Knee* by Dee Brown, or *Rolling Thunder,* an account of a shaman's power and spirituality.

5. Film Critique

Have students watch and respond to the film *Little Big Man,* starring Dustin Hoffman. Other films worth watching for their portrayal of Native Americans are *Jeremiah Johnson, The Searchers, Cheyenne Autumn, and Dances with Wolves.*

Canassatego, Iroquois

In 1744, the Virginia Legislature invited the Six Nations to send six youths to be educated at the College of William and Mary in Williamsburg. This is one reply.

We know you highly esteem the kind of Learning taught in these Colleges, and the maintenance of our young Men, while with you, would be very expensive to you. We are convinced, therefore, that you mean to do us Good by your Proposal; and we thank you heartily. But you who are so wise must know that different Nations have different Conceptions of things; and you will not therefore take it amiss, if our ideas of this kind of Education happens not to be the same with yours. We have had some experience of it. Several of our young People were formerly brought up in the Colleges of the Northern Provinces; they were instructed in all your Sciences; but, when they came back to us, they were bad Runners, ignorant of every means of living in the Woods, unable to bear either Cold or Hunger, knew neither how to build a Cabin, take a deer, or kill an enemy, spoke our language imperfectly, were therefore neither fit for hunters, Warriors, nor Counsellors; they were totally good for nothing. We are however not the less obliged for your kind Offer, tho' we decline accepting it; and to show our grateful Sense of it, if the Gentlemen of Virginia shall send us a Dozen of their Sons, we will take great care of their Education, instruct them in all we know, and make Men of them.

A Delaware chief

This is a response to the Gnadenhutten Massacre, when ninety Christian Indians were slain by 200 whites.

...These white men would be always telling us of their great Book which God had given them. They would persuade us that every man was bad who did not believe in it. They told us a great many things which they said was written in the Book; and wanted us to believe it. We would likely have done so, if we had seen them practice what they pretended to believe—and acted accordingly to the good words which they told us. But no! While they held the big Book in one hand, in the other they held murderous weapons—guns and swords—wherewith to kill us poor Indians. Ah! And they did too. They killed those who believed in their Book as well as those who did not. They made no distinctions.

Native American Voices

✳ SHORT STORY

631

Tecumseh, Shawnee

In 1810 Governor W. H. Harrison listened to Tecumseh's eloquent protest of the land sales of 1805–1806.

Since my residence at Tippecannoe, we have endeavored to level all distinctions, to destroy village chiefs, by whom all mischiefs are done. It is they who sell the land to the Americans. Brother, this land that was sold, and the goods that was given for it, was only done by a few... In the future we are prepared to punish those who propose to sell land to the Americans. If you continue to purchase them, it will make war among the different tribes, and, at last I do not know what will be the consequences among the white people. Brother, I wish you would take pity on the red people and do as I have requested. If you will not give up the land and do cross the boundary of our present settlement, it will be very hard, and produce great trouble between us.

The way, the only way to stop this evil is for the red men to unite in claiming a common and equal right in the land, as it was at first, and should be now—for it was never divided, but belongs to all. No tribe has the right to sell, even to each other, much less to strangers...Sell a country! Why not sell the air, the great sea, as well as the earth? Did the Great Spirit make them all for the use of his children?

How can we have confidence in the white people?

When Jesus Christ came upon the earth you killed Him and nailed him to the cross. You thought he was dead, and you were mistaken. You have Shakers among you and you laugh and make light of their workshop.

Everything I have told you is the truth. The Great Spirit has inspired me.

Daykauray, Winnebago

In 1829, the proposal of Indian agent John H. Kinzie to educate a group of Indian children in the language and habits of civilization received this reply.

Father: the Great Spirit made the white man and the Indian. He did not make them alike. He gave the white man a heart to love peace, and the arts of a quiet life. He taught him to live in town, to build houses, to make books, to learn all the things that would make him happy and prosperous in the way of life appointed him. To the red man the Great Spirit gave a different character. He gave him love of the woods, of a free life of hunting and fishing, of making war with his enemies...The white man does not like to live like the Indian—it is not his nature. Neither does the Indian love to live like the white man—the Great Spirit did not make him so.

We do not wish to do anything contrary to the will of the Great Spirit. If he had made us with white skins and characters like the white man, then we would send our children to this school to be taught like white children.

We think if the Great Spirit had wished us to be like the whites, he would have made us so. We believe he would be displeased with us to try and make ourselves different from what he thought good.

I have nothing more to say. This is what we think. If we change our minds we will let you know.

A Blackfoot wife

On June 10, 1835, members of the Bonneville Expedition recorded this account. They found her lost on the plains, accompanied by a young white trapper.

I was the wife of a Blackfoot warrior, and served him faithfully. Who was so well-served as he? Whose lodge was so well provided, or kept so clean? I brought wood in the morning, and placed water always at hand. I watched for his coming; and he found his food cooked and waiting. If he arose to go forth there was nothing to delay him. I searched the thought that was in his heart, to save him the trouble of speaking. When I went abroad on errands for him, the chiefs and warriors smiled upon me, the braves spoke soft things, in secret; but my feet were in the straight path, and my eyes could see nothing but him.

When he went out hunt, or to war, who aided to equip him but I? When he returned I met him at the door; I took his gun; and he entered without further thought. While he sat and smoked, I unloaded his horses; tied them to stakes, brought in their loads, and was quickly at his feet. If his moccasins were wet I took them off and put on others which were warm and dry. I dressed all the skins that were taken in the chase. He could never say to me, why is it not done? He hunted the deer, and the antelope, and the buffalo, and he watched for the enemy. Everything else was done by me. When our people moved their camp, it was I who packed the horses and led them on the journey. He mounted his horse and rode away, free as though he had fallen from the skies. He had nothing to do with the labour of the camp. When he halted in the evening, he sat with other braves and smoked, it was I who pitched his lodge; and when he came to eat and sleep, his supper and bed were ready.

I served him faithfully; and what was my reward? A cloud was always on his brow, and sharp lightning on his tongue. I was his dog; and not his wife. Who was it scarred and bruised me? It was he.

White Shield, Arikara chief

In 1867, threatened with jail by a government agent unless he signed for goods not received by his people, White Shield refused with these words.

I am old, it is true; but not old enough to fail to see things as they are, and even, as you say, if I am now just an old fool, I still would prefer a hundred times to be a honest red fool than a thieving white scamp like you.

Chief Joseph, Nez Perce

In about 1870 he was asked why churches were not allowed on his reservation.

They will teach us to quarrel about God, as Catholics and Protestants do on the Nez Perce reservation and other places. We do not want to do that. We may quarrel with men sometimes about things on earth, but we never quarrel about the Great Spirit. We do not want to learn that.

Two Plains Indian chiefs

At the 1876 Commission where government representatives listened to Indian complaints, these two chiefs summarized the Indian's point of view.

If you white men had a country which was very valuable, which had always belonged to your people, and which the Great Father [President of U.S.] had promised should be yours forever, and men of another race came to take it away by force, what would your people do? Would they fight?

I am glad to see you, you are our friends, but I hear that you have come to move us. Tell your people that since the Great Father promised that we should never be removed we have been moved five times. I think you had better put the Indians on wheels and you can run them about wherever you wish.

Washakie, chief of the Shoshonis

This is his response in the 1880s to the problem of the white man's keeping his word.

The whiteman's government promised that if we, the Shoshonis, would be content with the little patch allowed us, it would keep us well supplied with everything necessary to comfortable living, and would see that no white man should cross our borders for our game, or for anything that is ours. But it has not kept its word!

The white man kills our game, captures our furs and sometimes feeds his herds upon our meadows. And your great and mighty government...does not protect us in our rights. It leaves us without implements for harvesting our crops, without breeding animals better than ours, without the food we still lack...without the many comforts we cannot produce, without the schools we so much need for our children.

I again say, the government does not keep its word. And so, after all we can get by cultivating the land, and by hunting and fishing, we are sometimes nearly starved, and go half-naked, as you see us! Knowing all this, do you wonder, sir, that we have fits of desperation and think to be avenged?

Later, following the Dawes Allotment Act of 1887, Washakie met in council with Indian Bureau officials to discuss small truck farming (vegetables) for the Indians. For hours he listened to the officials and his minor chiefs discuss the subject. Finally, rising, he cut short the debate with majestic simplicity. (from Look to the Mountain Top, *p. 105)*

God damn a potato!

Four Guns, Oglala Sioux Indian judge

In 1891 he made these remarks at a dinner for anthropologist Clark Wissler.

I have visited the Great Father in Washington. I have attended dinners among white people. Their ways are not our ways. We eat in silence, quietly smoke a pipe and depart. Thus is our host honored. This is not the way of the white man. After his food has been eaten, one is expected to say foolish things. Then the host feels honored. Many of the white man's ways are past our understanding, but now that we have eaten at the white man's table, it is fitting that we honor our host according to the ways of his people.

Our host has filled many notebooks with the saying of our fathers as they came down to us. This is the way of his people; they put great store upon writing; always there is a paper. But we have learned that though there are many papers in Washington upon which are written promises to pay us for our lands, no white man seems to remember them. However, we know our host will not forget what he has written down, and we hope that the white people will read it.

But we are puzzled as to what useful service all this writing serves. Whenever white people come together there is writing. When we go to buy some sugar or tea, we see the white trader busy writing in a book; even the white doctor as he sits beside his patient writes on a piece of paper. The white people must think paper must have some mysterious power to help them on in the world. The Indian needs no writings; words that are true sink deep into his heart where they remain; he never forgets them. On the other hand, if the white man loses his papers, he is helpless. I once heard one of their preachers say that no white man was admitted to heaven unless there were writings about him in a great book.

On December 1, 1927, the Grand Council Fire of American Indian *spoke these memorable words to the mayor of Chicago.*

You tell all white men "America First." We believe in that. We are the only ones, truly, that are 100 percent. We therefore ask you while you are teaching school children about America First, teach them truth about the First Americans.

...History books teach that Indians were murderers—is it murder to fight in self-defense?...White men who rise to protect their property are called patriots—Indians who do the same are called murderers.

White men call Indians treacherous—but no mention is made of broken treaties on the part of the white man...White men called Indians thieves—and yet we lived in frail skin lodges and needed no locks or iron bars. White men call Indian savages. What is civilization? Its marks are a noble religion and philosophy, original arts, stirring music, rich story and legend. We had these...

...Why not teach school children more of the wholesome proverbs and legends of our people? Tell them how we loved all that was beautiful. That we killed game only for food, not for fun. Indians think white men who kill for fun are murderers.

Tell your children of the friendly acts of Indians to the white people who first settled here. Tell them of our leaders and heroes and their deeds. Put in your history books and the Indian's part in the World War. Tell how the Indian fought for a country of which he was not a citizen, for a flag to which he had no claim, and for a people that have treated him unjustly.

We ask this, Chief, to keep sacred the memory of our people.

Note: The text of "Blue Winds Dancing," written by Thomas Whitecloud and published by Scribner's Monthly *in 1938, appears in the lesson "Reflections on Alienation," elsewhere in this book. It fits in well with these selections.*

Patrick Kills Crow and Mary Crazy Thunder, Sioux high school freshmen in Pine Ridge, South Dakota

They write in 1966 about a new course offered in their school.

We've got something really different and exciting at Holy Rosary this year, and our whole class is talking about it. You'll probably be surprised when I say the exciting thing is a New Class, but that's what it is. I never thought that I would look forward to a class period before, but we sure do now...

When Father first came in and put the name of our new course on the board, we couldn't even pronounce it, much less know what it meant. It's called Acculturational Psychology, and it can also be called Modern Indian Psychology. It means a study of how to be a modern Indian. Since we are the same as the old time Indians, except in our way of making a living now, we have to learn two things—how to be like the old time Indians and yet make our living in a different way. Since this can be kind of hard, this thing called adjustment, we have to learn now. And that's what makes the course so interesting. No one ever told us this before. Before this course, we didn't even know that Indians were important or that it is important for us to know Indian history and values and what the old time Indians did hundreds of years ago. Now we can see that it is, and it sure makes you feel good to know that you are a Sioux. It makes you really proud to see all the obstacles the old time Sioux had to overcome and to know that the Indian race is the oldest race on the face of the earth today.

Dog Head Stew (for fifty people)
by Dorothy Pennington

Carefully prepare one medium dog head, removing teeth from jaw bones and hair, putting these aside for future use. Into kettle, add heaping handfuls of camos bulbs and cattail roots. The eggs from two medium-size salmon may be combined with water to cover, and place over fire and bring to boil for three hours.

It is customary to observe the rites of preparation in order to have all present appreciate the dish that will begin the feast.

At the proper moment, using the ceremonial arrow, impale the dog head and bring forth for all to observe the excellence of the dish.

Then allow fifteen to thirty minutes for all whites to excuse themselves and leave for home. Bury stew in back yard and bring forth the roasted turkey with all the trimmings. In this way, a 15 pound turkey will do. The others have been invited to the feast...and the fact they didn't stay is their tough luck.

New Way, Old Way
by Dave Martin Nez

Beauty in the old way of life—
The dwellings they decorated so lovingly;
A drum, a clear voice singing,
And the sound of laughter.

You must want to learn from your mother,
You must listen to old men
   not quite capable of becoming white men.
The white man is not our father.
While we last, we must not die of hunger.
We were a very Indian, strong, competent people,
But the grass had almost stopped growing,
The horses of our pride were near their end.

Indian cowboys and foremen handled Indian herds.
A cowboy's life appealed to them until
   economics and tradition clashed.
No one Indian was equipped to engineer the
   water's flow onto a man's allotment.
Another was helpless to unlock the gate.
The union between a hydro-electric plant and
Respect for the wisdom of the long-haired chiefs
Had to blend to build new enterprises
By Indian labor.

638

Those mighty animals graze once more
    upon the hillside.
At the Fair appear again our ancient costumes.
A full-blooded broadcasts through a microphone
    planned tribal action.
Hope stirs in the tribe,
Drums beat and dancers, old and young step forward.

We shall learn all these devices the white man has,
We shall handle his tools for ourselves.
We shall master his machinery, his inventions,
    his skills, his medicine, his planning;
But we'll retain our beauty
And still be Indians.

Research and References

Research Studies

The Impact of Reading, Thinking, and Writing About Multicultural Literature on Student Performance in Grades 9–12 and Grades 7–9

From 1990 to 1994, the UCI Writing Project had a grant from the California Academic Partnership Program to develop curriculum, deliver staff development training, and conduct teacher research in an effort to enhance the college eligibility of ethnic and linguistic minority students. Using the Thinking/Writing approach to curriculum design previously described in this book, Teacher/Consultants from the project created a wide selection of demonstration lessons that model ways to infuse multicultural literature into the English/language arts curriculum from grade seven through college. These demonstration lessons, in turn, became the framework for three staff-development programs, held monthly throughout the school year, in which teachers not only implemented this curriculum but also developed sample lessons of their own.

A key question during the project was... *Does in-servicing teachers on reading and writing about multicultural literature translate into better thinking and writing by ethnic and linguistic minority students?* The research team that designed the project enlisted as partners a subset of teachers receiving the in-service training. These research partners helped frame a number of questions related to the cognitive and affective impact of multicultural literature on ethnic and linguistic minority students. Then, these teachers participated in semester-long experimental treatment studies to explore those questions and to reflect upon their own attitudes toward English/language arts curriculum and instruction.

Background on 9th–12th Grade Study

During Winter/Spring 1991, the UCI Writing Project conducted two in-service programs for teachers in grades nine through twelve on *Enhancing Student Reading, Thinking and Writing Through the Study of Culturally Diverse Literature* as part of the staff development component of our California Academic Partnership Program grant. These in-service programs were held in two locations—at Saddleback High School in Santa Ana Unified School District and at Irvine High School in Irvine Unified School District—and were open to interested teachers from Garden Grove, Irvine, Santa Ana, and Saddleback Valley Unified School Districts. Of the thirty-nine teachers trained in the in-service component, thirty-two were from schools with high ethnic- and linguistic-minority student populations. Of these thirty-nine teachers, twelve elected to participate in a research study to determine what impact the in-service training on multicultural literature they were receiving was having on the academic growth of their students. Of the twelve, eight completed the study.

The cultural background of their students in the experimental treatment groups who were part of the random sampling for scoring are as follows:

Cultural Background of Students of Teachers Participating in the Study

	American Indian	Asian/ Filipino	Black	Hispanic	Pacific Islander	White	Other (East Indian)	TOTAL
Number	3	68	4	153	5	49	1	283
Percent (%)	1	24	1	54	2	18	0	100

The Research Study

In February, teachers participating in the in-service course administered a timed (fifty minute) pretest to their students. Students either wrote to an interpretive prompt about an excerpt from Dick Gregory's "Shame" or Alice Walker's "Beauty—When the Other Dancer is the Self." These two prompts were mixed so that half the students wrote to one work of literature as the pretest while the remaining students wrote to the other prompt as the pretest. Each experimental (Writing Project inservice) teacher also had a control teacher who taught the same subject area and grade level at the same school site. The criteria for "comparable populations" included the following: 1) grade level; 2) ability level; 3) school site; 4) ethnic makeup; 5) overall GPA; and 6) GPA in English/language arts. The control teachers' students wrote to the same pretest and posttest prompts in the same order as the experimental teachers' students.

In early June, both experimental and control students took the timed posttest. Pretests and posttests were then coded and scored by Fellows in the UCI Writing Project Summer Institute. A fluency count was conducted later by the Writing Project/CAPP Research Team.

Between March and May, the teachers in the experimental group taught three Thinking/Writing lessons based upon works of literature that had been developed by the UCIWP Teacher/Consultants during June–July 1990. Each lesson—one using Sandra Cisneros's "My Name" as a springboard, one analyzing Amy Tan's "The Moon Lady," and one based on Alice Walker's "Everyday Use"—focused on literary interpretation and self-reflection. These lessons were sequenced to build upon one another and were scaffolded so that students received ongoing guided practice in the cognitive task of character analysis and literary interpretation. For example, students analyzed Esperanza, the character in Cisneros's "My Name," by clustering Esperanza's life, examining quotations from the literature through the use of a dialectical journal, and finally using metaphors to establish a frame for Esperanza. A sample entry would be: "If

Esperanza's name were an animal, it would be a *turtle* because *she's always ducking back into her shell.*" Finally, students created for Esperanza a coat of arms illustrating their metaphors. The lesson led students through several more carefully constructed steps until the students were ready to write an essay exploring their own names. Students were then ready to move to the next step—an essay analyzing a character—in this case, the character of Ying-ying in Amy Tan's "The Moon Lady." In this lesson, the clustering centers around how Ying-ying lost herself, both literally and symbolically. The dialectical journal involved her "lostness," and the frame and coat of arms added a further dimension to student analysis. Several activities were added to ensure student success as they prepared to write an in-depth character analysis of Ying-ying and how and why she changed. At this point, students were ready to write an expository essay on an element beyond character in a story. In Alice Walker's "Everyday Use," students learned to distinguish between facts and inferences as they clustered, read, annotated, and discussed the story. The writing task was to analyze the mother's final decision in the story to give her quilts, the family heirlooms, to one daughter instead of the other. Students wrote several drafts of each paper and received feedback from both a peer response group and the teacher. Additionally, each student wrote a metacognitive log that contained both cognitive and affective comments about each work of literature and the writing task itself.

February	March	April	May	June
pretest	Lesson 1 "My Name"	Lesson 2 "The Moon Lady"	Lesson 3 "Everyday Use"	posttest
• timed test	• multiple-draft essay • metacognitive log	• multiple-draft essay • metacognitive log	• multiple-draft essay • metacognitive log	• timed test

Each control teacher taught the English/language arts curriculum delineated by the school and the school district. For example, *Romeo and Juliet* and *Huckleberry Finn* are two of the core readings at grades nine and ten, respectively, in the Santa Ana Unified School District. While the experimental treatment (Writing Project-trained) teachers continued to teach some of the regular course curriculum, they eliminated sections in order to include multicultural literature in the form of the lessons from our study. They allowed ample time frames for the step-by-step approach to writing about literature; they allowed thinking and reflection time; they allowed discussion and sharing time. And because of this "less is more" philosophy of teaching, as well as the type of literature they were using, students responded with enthusiasm for their own cultures, an understanding of other cultures, and insight that the diverse cultures represented in their classrooms are not so very different after all. This awareness of community, along with enhanced writing ability, was the outcome teachers most noted.

Throughout this seventeen-week period, the teachers participating in our study annotated the lessons as they taught them, noting the changes and modifications we encouraged them to make so that the lessons would be tailored to the specific needs of their students. Monthly, the research team met with the teachers to debrief on how the pilot testing was going and to check in with the teachers about their own sense of how the literature-based lessons were influencing their respective classroom environments. At these meetings, teachers shared sample student papers, reflections from the metacognitive logs, and their own "Ahas" about the process of infusing multicultural literature into the curriculum.

Research Results

The results of this study were extremely gratifying:

Anova table for a 3-factor repeated measure Anova.

Source:	df	Sum of Squares	Mean Square	F-test	P value
TEACHER PAIR (A)	7	277.247	39.607	9.144	.0001
Tx (B)	1	20.503	20.503	4.733	.0312
AB	7	43.472	6.21	1.434	.1962
Subjects w groups	144	623.75	4.332	—	—
Repeated Measure (C)	1	17.578	17.578	10.998	.0012
AC	7	21.597	3.085	1.93	.0688
BC	1	7.503	7.503	4.695	.0319
ABC	7	56.672	8.096	5.065	.0001
C x subjects w groups	144	230.15	1.598	—	—

Repeated measure		Pretest	Posttest	Gain
TX	Workshop/ Experimental	80 5.625	80 6.4	.775
	Control	80 5.425	80 5.589	.163
TOTALS		160 5.525	160 5.994	.612

Difference in favor of Experimental Treatment over Control Group

The overall growth from pretest to posttest for the experimental (Writing Project in-service) students was .775 on an 11 point scale (two readings on a 1–6 rubric that yield a combined score of anywhere from 2 *[1 + 1]* to 12 *[6 + 6]*). The overall growth for control group students from pretest to posttest was .163. Therefore, the experimental group outscored the control group by .612. The probability of the occurrence of this difference in gain scores by chance alone is 3 in 100.

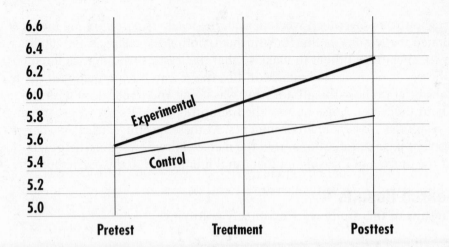

The experimental treatment group also had significant gains on the fluency count. From pretest to posttest, students in the experimental treatment groups gained 109 words—which represents an overall increase of 39%. The probability that this gain could occur by chance alone is 1 in 10,000. In contrast, the control group lost approximately 6 words from pretest to posttest—representing a 2% decrease in fluency.

Anova table for a 3-factor repeated measure Anova.

Source:	df	Sum of Squares	Mean Square	F-test	P value
TEACHER PAIR (A)	7	846,201.488	120,885.927	5.617	.0001
Tx (B)	1	490,627.812	490,627.812	22.797	.0001
AB	7	31,052.887	44,307.555	2.059	.0517
Subjects w groups	144	3,099,058.7	21,521.241	—	—
Repeated Measure (C)	1	212,386.05	212,386.05	20.412	.0001
AC	7	482,082.45	68,868.921	6.619	.0001
BC	1	261,747.2	261,747.2	25.156	.0001
ABC	7	202,415.4	28,916.486	2.779	.0097
C x subjects w groups	144	1,498,312.9	10,404.951	—	—

Repeated measure		Prewords	Postwords	Gain/Loss
TX	Workshop	80 279.025	80 387.75	+ 108.725
	Control	80 257.913	80 252.238	-5.675
	TOTALS	160 268.469	160 319.994	+ 114.4

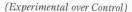

(Experimental over Control)

We also analyzed the data by grade level and ability level. Our findings indicate that grade level (ninth to twelfth grade) was not a significant indicator of growth over time. In other words, no grade level scored appreciably higher than another. But ability level was a factor in indicating growth. Students categorized by their teachers as Remedial, Regular, Basic, or Transitional ESL showed significantly higher gains than students identified as Regular/College Prep, College Prep, or Honors. To quote our Internal Evaluator, Bob Land, "What's interesting here is that the Tx effect seemed stronger for lower ability students. They gained more on pretest to posttest and on fluency. In fact, they ended up with the highest word count gain of any group, gaining 60%!"

Affective Responses

In addition to empirical data, we collected qualitative data on the effectiveness of the Thinking/Writing model and lessons and on the impact of multicultural literature upon both teachers and students alike. These comments, taken from the journals of ninth through twelfth grade teachers in our Research Component, provide feedback on their sense of how these lessons influenced their students—not only cognitively but affectively:

"I know my students became emotionally involved with the stories from the lessons because they felt a common human link, even if the culture was different.... I will be more inclined to seek out literature from other cultures in my teaching."

Kristi Kemp

"My Hispanic students loved 'My Name,' and my Chinese girls related well to 'Moon Lady.' The Anglo students enjoyed the lessons—very puzzled about Ying-Ying.... I will be including more culturally-diverse literature in my curriculum."

Cathey Avis

"I've discovered that my students can have much stronger analytical faculties than I previously was aware of.... We've all learned and are more aware, and hopefully, more sensitive."

Jane Bruckler

Comments from the metacognitive learning logs of the students of these teachers mirror their teachers' observations and serve as eloquent testimony of the fact that the multicultural curriculum materials that have been developed by teachers in the UCI/CAPP Project are not only improving student reading, thinking, and writing ability but are enhancing students' cultural awareness and self-esteem as well:

"I just want to tell you that I really appreciate that you wrote these lessons. If we hadn't gone through these lessons, I don't think I would ever really think seriously about my culture."

Norma Lopez

"The lessons were really full of thought. I really had to think to understand the meaning. So now I appreciate my culture—something that I really didn't appreciate before."

Veronica Gonzales

"'The Moon Lady' lesson helped me appreciate my own culture because I thought about Ying-Ying's culture and my culture. I really looked at how important my culture is and how different and also how valuable."

Raquel Bruno

"The Esperanza [lesson] helped me to appreciate my own culture. Writing about my own name, helped me to understand that my culture has reasons for doing everything that it does. Every Chinese name has a meaning behind it."

Lan Huynh

"I can tell you that it's good to believe in your culture's way; but you should also believe in yourself and your own ideals. If you keep your desires hidden away and don't talk about them, no one will really know you as a person."

Ofelia Valencia

Note: This research study is described in more depth in the Winter 1994 issue of *Multicultural Education.*

Background on the 7th–9th Grade Study

During Winter/Spring 1993, we launched a new study of students in the classes of ten Writing Project Teacher/Consultants in grades seven through nine. The students these teachers serve represent the cultural spectrum of Orange County, from Santiago Middle School in the Orange Unified School District with a slight majority of white students (53%), to Sunny Hills High School in the Fullerton Joint Union High School District, which serves a large percentage of Asian and Pacific Islander students (47%), to McFadden Intermediate School in the Santa Ana Unified School District, where the students are predominantly Chicano and Latino (85%).

The Research Study

In this study, we replicated the experimental treatment we used in our ninth through twelfth grade study in which students took a pretest at the beginning of the semester, went through the Thinking/Writing process with three works of multicultural literature, kept metacognitive logs, and took a posttest at the end of the semester. However, we wrote new pretests and posttests, focusing on "Eleven" by Sandra Cisneros and "The Stolen Party" by Liliana Heker, which called for character analysis and dealt with the theme of being "put in one's place" and the consequent disillusionment and loss of innocence that comes with this experience. Additionally, we had students keep portfolios that included copies of all of their work for the research study and asked them to reflect upon their own learning and assess their own growth over time. The graphic below depicts our research design:

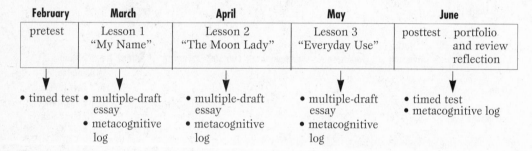

February	March	April	May	June
pretest	Lesson 1 "My Name"	Lesson 2 "The Moon Lady"	Lesson 3 "Everyday Use"	posttest portfolio and review reflection

- timed test
- multiple-draft essay
- metacognitive log
- multiple-draft essay
- metacognitive log
- multiple-draft essay
- metacognitive log
- timed test
- metacognitive log

Teachers of students in the control group (who were selected following the same criteria as for the ninth through twelfth grade study) did not read this multicultural literature or write these essays. Rather, they were exposed to the regular course curriculum for that teacher and grade level. For example, *Call of the Wild* and *Romeo and Juliet* are two of the core readings at grades eight and nine, respectively, in the Santa Ana Unified School District.

Research Results

During the summer of 1993, we conducted a random sample of fourteen pretests and posttests per teacher from both the experimental and control groups for a total of 560 papers and scored them using a six-point rubric. The criteria for a 6 paper from the scoring rubric is as follows:

6 Exceptional Achievement

- Writer provides a context or background of "Eleven" or "The Stolen Party" so that the reader can follow the interpretation he/she offers in response to the prompt;

- Writer carefully considers why the event described in "Eleven" or "The Stolen Party" made such a significant impression on the character of Rachel or Rosaura, respectively;

- Writer presents a perceptive, insightful, or unusual interpretive claim about what the character learns;

- Writer uses evidence from the text skillfully to support this claim;
- Examples aptly describe and explore the character's actions, interactions with other characters, and reactions to what happened;
- Writer interprets authoritatively and advances logically to a conclusion;
- Paper has few errors in the conventions of written English.

The self-identified ethnic backgrounds of the students in the random sample for scoring were as follows:

Ethnic Codes of experimental treatment students in random sample for scoring
Total Number of Sampled Students: 140

	Hispanic	African American	Anglo	Pacific Islander	Vietnamese	Chinese	Korean
Count	32	0	65	3	8	13	6
Percentage (%)	23	0	47	2	6	9	4

	Native American	Japanese	Cambodian	Laotian	Hmong	Other:	1 Afghan
Count	0	1	0	1	2	8	3 Filipino 3 East Indian 1 Hungarian
Percentage (%)	0	1	0	1	1	6	1 Palestinian

Pretests and posttests were then coded and scored by Fellows in the UCI Writing Project Summer Institute who were not participants in the study and who had no familiarity with it.

The results of this study were even more gratifying than our ninth through twelfth grade study in terms of overall gains. As the graph on the next page indicates, the overall growth from pretest to posttest by the experimental group was .971 (as opposed to .775 on our previous study), the equivalent of half a letter grade. The growth of the control group students was a marginal .193. Therefore, the difference between the gains by experimental and control groups was .788 (as opposed to .612 on our previous study.) Because we read more papers, the probability of the occurrence of this gain by chance alone was much lower, 8 in 1000—as opposed to 3 in 100 on our previous study.

Page 1 of the AB Incidence table on Y2: Q-Gain

Tx teacher:	Teacher 1	Teacher 2	Teacher 3	Teacher 4	Teacher 5	Teacher 6
Treatment Group	14	14	14	14	14	14
	.286	1.786	.857	2.429	–.714	.5
Control Group	14	14	14	14	14	14
	.357	.571	–.786	–.214	–357	–.789

Page 2 of the AB Incidence table on Y2: Q-Gain

Tx teacher:	Teacher 7	Teacher 8	Teacher 9	Teacher 10	Totals
Treatment Group	14	14	14	14	140
	1.214	.648	1.786	.929	–.971
Control Group	14	14	14	14	140
	143	1.286	-286	2	.193

Difference in growth between experimental treatment and control students is .788.

We also conducted a fluency count of the word gain between pretest and posttest. Again, the experimental group significantly outgained the control group. On the average, the experimental treatment group gained 57 words, representing an increase of 22%. The control group, in contrast, lost an average of 13 words, representing a 5% decrease overall. The probability of the occurrence of this difference in fluency by chance alone is 1 in 10,000.

Repeated measure	Pre Fluency	Post Fluency	Totals
Treatment Group	140	140	+57
	259.286	312.279	up 22%
Control Group	140	140	–13
	275.093	261.707	Down 5%

The difference in favor of experimental treatment group is 56 words.

An examination of the experimental group's gain in fluency by level reveals that seventh, eighth, and ninth graders gained 17%, 23%, and 28%, respectively, with the ninth graders increasing, on average, 97 words between pretest and posttest. Since students in the ninth through twelfth grade study gained 109 words overall, one might conclude that there is a correlation between growth in fluency, syntactic maturity, and progress through the grade levels.

We were curious to see how the students of nonwhite background would fare as compared with white students. While the numbers of most of the ethnic groups were too small to draw any conclusions, we did find that the two largest groups in the study—students who identified themselves as Hispanic and

students who identified themselves as white—grew comparably. While the white students slightly outscored the Hispanic students on writing quality (1.34 to .969, respectively) the Hispanic students outscored the white students in fluency (54 words to 50 words, respectively).

In the debriefing session in which Teacher/Consultants who participated in the study reviewed the gain scores and fluency counts of their students and read and analyzed a packet of sample pretests and posttests, they identified the following indicators of growth in the students' writing ability:

- Increase in the amount of writing;
- More control of and ease with the language; evidence of more syntactic maturity; some use of figurative language;
- Greater use of supporting evidence from the text, including the use of quotations;
- Evidence of planning and organization; more structured essay format—introduction, development, and conclusion;
- Stronger sense of the personal voice of the writer.

When reviewing the growth in writing ability, Teacher/Consultants also remarked upon the growth in the students' reading and thinking ability. They noticed that many students who had initially relied upon summary and retelling in responding to a text developed, over the seventeen-week period, more analytical strategies for responding to literature.

Overall, Teacher/ Consultants noticed the following shifts in the students' texts:

Reliance on summary and retelling	⟶ More evidence of analysis and interpretation
Emphasis on literal level of the texts	⟶ Ability to discuss symbolic implications of the texts; evidence of inferential reasoning
Often tentative about taking a stance and making a claim	⟶ More confident about taking a stance and making a claim

To summarize, the Teacher/Consultants saw indications in the pretest and posttest writing samples that their students had begun to master the reading/thinking/writing process and could approach a complex work of multicultural literature and a sophisticated writing task with greater confidence and an increased repertoire of critical reading and writing tools.

The following pretest and posttest, written by an eighth grade LEP student from the Santa Ana Unified School District, reproduced *unedited* here, illustrates the kind of growth the teachers identified:

Student Model of Pretest

This story "Eleven" by Sandra Cisneros, is important to me. The same thing happened to me when I was eleven. It was horrible. In Rachels case, I wouldn't want to be in her shoes. It shows you even on your birthday, you can have a bad day.

I feel for Rachel. She plans for the whole day to be perfect with she coming home and getting presents, cake and a whole birthday day. The bad luck starts when Mrs. Price asks who the sweater belongs to. Then Sylvia Soldivar says, "I think it belongs to Rachel." Mrs. Price agrees and gives it to Rachel. Rachel keeps pushing the sweater to the edge of her desk, until Mrs. Price makes her put it on.

After all these happings, Rachel must be feeling awfuling sad and mad. Sad because she has to put on the sweater and mad because knowing its not hers. She begins to cry in front of the whole class. Suddenly, Phyllis Lopez remembers the sweater is hers. All the embarassment for nothing.

Scorer 1 =	2
Scorer 2 =	2
Total =	4
Fluency Count:	179

It goes to show you, even on your birthday, you'll still have a bad day.

Student Model of Posttest

The Little Pet

Has this ever happened to you? When your mother tells you something, and you don't believe what she's saying. Then in the long run, your mother was right. It's hard to admit your mother was right. That is what Rosaura had to do. She had to admit her mother was right.

"It's a rich people's party," the mother said. When the mother said this, she was arguing with Rosaura about going to a party she had been invited to. I don't understand this part. If her daughter has been invited to a party, why did she get all mad? Why doesn't she want her daughter to go to a rich party? The answer is simple. The mother does not want her daughter to go to the party because the mother thinks they see her as the maid's daughter.

"So how come she's an employee?" the little girl with the bow said. Rosaura's mother had always told her to say that she was the daughter of the employee; that's all. I feel that Rosaura wasn't proud of her mom. Her mom was a maid,

and Rosaura didn't like it, I feel. The little girl with the bow asks all these questions about her and her friend Luciana, which was the birthday girl. I think that those questions asked by the girl with the bow were similar to her mother's.

"Thank you for all your help, my pet," Señora Ines said. The key word in this quote is PET. Her mother was right. They only saw her as the daughter of the maid. All day she had been helping with everything from cutting the cake to serving hot dogs. As if she was invited just to work like a slave. All through the day Rosaura thought she was invited because she was a friend. A very good friend to Luciana. She thought she was special. You have to feel for Rosaura. This must have been crushing to a little 9-year old girl.

So her mother had been right all along. Every kid on this earth hates it when their parents are right. But your parents don't do this to embarass you. They do it to warn you. They don't want you to get hurt at the end. They do this because they love you. So next time your parents say something, don't say anything back, just agree with them.

Scorer 1 =	5
Scorer 2 =	5
Total =	10
Fluency Count: 398	

What About the Affective Domain?

It's empirical! The Thinking/Writing model with its carefully scaffolded approach to fostering thinking and writing about multicultural literature had a positive impact upon the performance of ethnic and linguistic minority students and nonminority students as well. But equally as important as pretest, posttest and word-gain scores are the affective responses of teachers and their students.

Our study also yielded a wealth of qualitative data. Once again, we were pleased and often touched by how much affective impact these lessons had on students. A few of their comments, gleaned from individual metacognitive logs and the final portfolio reflection, are included below.

Students' Comments

About the lessons...

> The "Moon Lady" lesson was my favorite because I could relate to that story the most. I remember how frightening it was to get lost as a child. Both Ying-ying and I are in the same position, caught in between Chinese tradition and modernization. It is not very often that I get to study literature about my own culture.
>
> Pauline Lim

> As a person, I believe I have learned the most from the "Everyday Use" lesson. I learned that culture is not merely decorations or pictures, it is a real understanding of your roots.
>
> Hope Chau

My favorite piece of work was the one in which we analyzed our name and what it meant to us. I enjoyed doing this because all my life, people have told me that I'm lucky to have a name that is a combination of both my Indian and American cultures. But I've never thought that it was a good thing. In my essay, I was able to set the record straight, even if it was only to one person. Writing the essay helped me get all my negative and angry feelings off my chest, and I felt that a burden had been lifted off my shoulders.

Sheila Nagaraj

About what they learned cognitively...

First, I would like for everyone at the UCI Writing Project to know that I probably learned more in English this year than any other year in the history of my schooling. I have learned to proof-read papers, edit, revise, use correct punctuation, etc. I have even applied my skills and done intern work for the "Orange County Register." I probably learned the most from "Everyday Use." Even though I had all these enriching writing projects behind me, I was shown again and again that I am ONLY in eighth grade and my writing has a long way to go. Even my final draft for "Everyday Use" has a long way to go still. I had hoped to have it up to my expectations. I think every student would be a better writer if they had the opportunity to participate in this program.

Talline Kojian

I learned to think logically. It was quite a challenge to present my jumble of thoughts in a well-organized essay! From now on, I realized that I have to do a lot more organization before I start writing.

Louise Chen

I learned to make inferences and use quotes along with details, to be able to get my point across

Juan Diaz

I feel that I've really improved. I'm writing more deeply, and thoroughly. I'm explaining not only about the character's outside, but also the inside. I'm also learning, too, about how to look for the thoughts and feelings of the characters, that aren't just said out loud. I'm "reading between the lines."

Christine Dang

In my pre-test I feel that I TOLD the story again instead of really answering
the question, but in my post-test, I feel that I did much better in explaining and giving inferences that are based on fact.

Rebecca Jensvold

About what they took away from this experience affectively...

> *Boy! If I could only put it in writing! I have learned so much from this past year—respect for my fellow classmates, and their cultures, but most of all I sense their respect for my culture. A friend of mine, who I shall refer to as "Madeline" always made fun of my lunch, whenever I had something different from hot dogs and pizza. Now, she sees it and even ventured to ask for a "taste." Unfortunately, now I can't tear her away from my food.*
>
> Talline Kojian

> *I didn't think I was capable of doing such a big job, but now I know I can.*
>
> Malia Ramirez

> *I have found that my race is as valuable as the next. I see that my differences are what make me special. I learned to be proud and have pride in who I am and what I have become today.*
>
> Gabrial Caringal

> *I learned that the best way to preserve my culture is to make my life an example of it. That way, my children will be able to truly understand it and pass it on to their offspring. Material things do not matter. What matters is the person inside and the family.*
>
> Pauline Lim

> *I've always respected and appreciated my culture, but now I realize the beauty of the other cultures around me. This is because I learned that every culture has its way of life and I should respect that.*
>
> Juliet Servin

Teachers' Comments

In our final debriefing session, we asked the teachers participating in the study to review their students' portfolios, paying particular attention to their final metacognitive log entries, and to reflect upon the evidence they saw of the cognitive and affective impact of the lessons upon their students. The portfolios confirmed the teachers' sense that their students had grown significantly in their ability to read, make inferences about, and interpret complex works of literature, and to write thoughtful, well-organized, and logically developed papers. Further, they were pleased and touched by the insights students shared about themselves, their culture, and the culture of their classmates:

> *I enjoyed observing how relatively easy it was for the students to achieve the highest level of writing and thinking that I've ever seen in 8th graders. It has made my English Honors Program go sky high! And I was able to "kill so many birds with the one stone..." collaborative learning, learning about oneself, and responding in an expository fashion to literature. The icing on the cake was the use of the multicultural literature. It was a wonderfully subtle way to show that we can celebrate our diversity as well as our "oneness" with each other.*
>
> Cathie Hunsberger

They willingly tackled each lesson even though the written prompts became more difficult and more analytical. I think they felt more confident with each lesson and more prepared with the knowledge that they would be exploring cultural themes.

Susan Leming

The essays became smoother. Transitions, microthemes, and the use of quotes became more natural. Students also showed evidence of becoming more thoughtful and willing to search out ideas. Challenge students and they will rise to the heights!

Carolee Dunn

To Summarize

The comments of the students and teachers in our studies convince us that increased efforts must be made to infuse multicultural literature into our classrooms, whether those classrooms be language minority or language majority, whether those classrooms be ethnically diverse or ethnically homogeneous. Our work attests to the power of the Thinking/Writing model. Repeatedly, we see that the scaffolded approach this model affords enhances the cognitive abilities of students. We are equally pleased to note that the infusion of multicultural literature has parallel affective results. The pairing of the Thinking/Writing model with the infusion of multicultural literature has not only brought students growth in reading, thinking, and writing, it has also brought students growth in appreciating and understanding their own culture and has engendered cultural awareness, tolerance, and mutual respect for students of diverse cultures.

Note: Our seventh through ninth grade study was selected as the recipient of the First Annual Caddo Gap Press Award for California Education Research. A more detailed version of the study is available in the 1994 Yearbook of California Education Research, edited by Dennis S. Tierney, (San Francisco: Caddo Gap Press, 1994).

Glossary of Terms

Affective Domain

The feelings, interests, attitudes and values that influence learning. For an in-depth discussion of the role of the Affective Domain in writing, see Russ Frank's chapter; "What About the Affective Domain," in *Thinking/Writing: Fostering Critical Thinking Through Writing* ed. Carol Booth Olson, (New York: HarperCollins Publishers, 1992).

Audience

An audience is the reader(s) of the writer's work. Students should write for a variety of audiences in addition to the teacher as evaluator or "giver-of-grades." A proposed hierarchical order of audiences is self, peers, trusted adult, teacher as collaborator, teacher as evaluator, and unknown audiences. It is important for writers to identify their audience so that they may choose the appropriate subject and a suitable way of communicating about it.

Bloom's Taxonomy of the Cognitive Domain

Under the leadership of Benjamin Bloom, a committee of more than thirty educators constructed a taxonomy (classification scheme) of objectives in the cognitive domain that delineates the intended behaviors that relate to mental acts or thinking. The committee conceived of six major classes of educational objectives, arranged in hierarchical order from simple to complex:

- Knowledge
- Comprehension
- Application
- Analysis
- Synthesis
- Evaluation

The KNOWLEDGE level requires such skills as remembering specifics: facts, terminology, events, and relationships. COMPREHENSION encompasses the ability to understand the meaning of the material or ideas contained in it. This stage also involves translation of knowledge from ideas and thought into print. APPLICATION includes the ability to apply what has been learned to new situations and to make appropriate generalizations or to derive principles. ANALYSIS is the breaking down of material into its components parts and the discovery of the relationships and organization of those parts. SYNTHESIS involves composing the parts of the material into something original—a creative act in which elements are put together to form a new whole. EVALUATION refers to making judgments according to set criteria. Evaluation includes rating, ranking, and persuading. See *Taxonomy of Educational Objectives—Handbook I: Cognitive Domain,* ed. Benjamin Bloom (New York: David McKay Company, Inc., 1956.)

Brainstorming
Brainstorming is a generic term given to a wide variety of strategies used for generating ideas. These include listing, clustering, charting, mapping, etc.

CLAS
The California Learning Assessment System has identified a number of writing types for elementary school, middle school, and high school. Use the Chart of Cultures and Writing Types, elsewhere in this book, to determine the writing types for each of the lessons in this book.

Charting
Charting involves organizing words or ideas in columns, list, or chart form to help students categorize information and see relationships. See "The Saturation Recall Paper" lesson for an example of a Memory Chart and the "What's Behind the Gift Horse's Mouth" lesson for an example of a Details Chart. Both lessons are elsewhere in this book.

Checklist
A checklist is a list of things, names, criteria, etc., to be checked off or referred to for verifying, ordering, comparing, etc. See the lesson "My Name, My Self," elsewhere in this book, for the Correctness/Editing Guide, which is a checklist of correctness elements required in the prompt.

Close Reading
Students are to read carefully to determine tone, theme, main idea, characterization, sophisticated inferences, specific facts, and details. Students are often required to do a close reading when preparing for a test on the text or when preparing to write an analytical or critical essay on the text. See the lesson "Peopling Poems," elsewhere in this book, for several strategies for close readings of a text.

Clustering
Developed by Professor Gariele Rico and California State University San Jose, clustering is a nonlinear, brainstorming activity that generates ideas, images, and feelings around a stimulus word until a pattern becomes discernible. As students cluster around a stimulus word, the encircled words rapidly radiate outward until a sudden shift takes place, a sort of "Aha!" that signals an awareness of that tentative whole which allows students to begin writing. It can be done as a class (on the board or on paper) or individually. Clustering is used widely throughout this book. Examples can be found in

"The Class Quilt" lesson, and the "Living in Life's Shadow" lessons, to name a few.

Coat of Arms

A coat of arms is an activity that requires students to determine what symbolic figures they would put on a shield or crest that would represent their ideas or feelings about something. See the "My Name, My Self" lesson, elsewhere in this book, for an example.

Cooperative Learning

Cooperative learning is a process of grouping and building teams for learning content collaboratively, for creatively posing and solving problems, and for practicing and internalizing social skills. One source for cooperative learning strategies is Spencer Kagan's book, *Cooperative Learning Resources for Teachers* (San Juan Capistrano, CA: Resources for Teachers, 1989).

Correctness

Correctness as a goal of writing is the ability to use the conventions of written English—capitalization, punctuation, word choice, grammar, usage, spelling, and penmanship—in order to communicate effectively.

Dialogue

Dialogue is the passages of conversation within a written work. Rules for using dialogue are included in *"The Saturation Recall Paper,"* elsewhere in this book.

Dialectical Journal

The dialectical journal is a double-entry note-taking process that the students can keep while reading literature. It provides the student with two columns that are in dialogue with each other, not only developing a method of critical reading but also encouraging habits of reflective questioning. A sample of a dialectical journal can be found in "The Rules of the Game" lesson, elsewhere in this book.

Domains of Writing

Domains are categories that delineate the purposes of writing and which have a distinctive place in writing and thinking development. The four domains include sensory/descriptive, imaginative/narrative, practical/informative and analytical/ expository. *Sensory/descriptive* writing involves presenting a picture in words, one so vivid that the reader or listener can recapture many of the same perceptions and feelings that the writer has had. The main intent of *imaginative/ narrative* writing is to tell a story—sometimes real, sometimes imaginary. The forms may range widely, but the main idea is to tell what happens. In the *practical/informative* domain, students are required to provide clear information. Finally, the goal of *analytical/expository* writing is to analyze, explain, persuade, and influence.

Editing	Editing is the process in which the writer's concern is with correctness. Like revision, editing occurs continually throughout writing and is automatic for some writers. Revision is actually the reshaping of thought, whereas editing is the polishing of that thought. For most student writers, formal editing takes place immediately before the final evaluation. The goal is for the paper to stand alone without needing interpretation or explanation by the writer because of distraction caused by errors in the conventions of written English.
Evaluation	Evaluation is final feedback given to a writer when a paper is completed—usually in the form of a score or letter grade. It is important that the criteria on which papers will be evaluated be communicated to students early on in the writing process.
Extension Activities	Those activities given at the end of a Thinking/Writing lesson that could be used as natural activities to reinforce the skills taught (or extend) the skills taught in the lesson. Extension activities often provide ideas for writing about the literature in a different domain or for comparing one work of literature with another thematically related work.
Family Tree Chart	A family tree chart is a lineage chart of ancestors. See "The Class Quilt" lesson, elsewhere in this book, for an example of a family tree.
Fluency	Fluency is the ability to express ideas comfortably and easily in writing. Prewriting strategies promote fluency.
Form	In determining the form of a piece of writing, the writer must respond to the requirements of the writing task, work through and choose a shape or format for the piece, execute a plan that fulfills that format, and select the domain and style of writing suited to the audience. The form of any work should be appropriate to its purpose, content, and audience.
Found Poetry	An activity in which the students select words, phrases, or sentences from the text (their own or a literary text) and create a poem that reflects the tone, intent, or theme of the literature. Often, students need to be limited to a set number of lines so that discussion is initiated about the important words, phrases, or sentences from the literature. The number of words in each line may also be restricted. Samples of found poetry exercises appear in the "Peopling Poems" lesson and the "Living in Life's Shadow" lessons, elsewhere in this book.
Four-Square Drawing	Students are asked to draw four images from the story or poem on a sheet of paper that has been divided into four equal squares. Students are told that they will not be evaluated on their artistic ability, but rather on the number of details

they perceive in the text. The students may be asked to draw figurative or symbolic representations of the imagery or create a symbolic representation of the purpose or intent of a scene or image. This activity is especially effective for students who have trouble visualizing scenes or images from literature. See the "Loss of Innocence" lesson, elsewhere in this book, for an example.

Framing

Framing is a way of showing students how to write an assignment by providing a teacher-generated structure. See the framing exercise in the "Stories in Clay" and "Growing Up: A Personal Reflection" lessons, elsewhere in this book, for examples.

Freewriting

Freewriting is nongraded, nonstructured writing. From this "stream of consciousness" writing, a student can sometimes find a topic. Freewriting is also used as an exercise to eliminate self-consciousness and ease the constraints of correctness. See the "I Felt Lost" freewriting exercise in the lesson "Living in Life's Shadows," elsewhere in the book.

Grand Conversation

Grand conversation is a group activity that helps students comprehend a poem. The "paraphraser" will assign a stanza to each group member and facilitate the study of the stanza. Each person should record the paraphrase and report to the group what the speaker is suggesting in the stanza. A "discussion leader" will facilitate and encourage comments from all members and keep the discussion relevant to an analysis of the poem. The "note taker" will record topics and issues discussed, and the "reporter" is responsible for telling the class what the group has discovered about the poem. The "Be an Outcast" lesson, elsewhere in this book, contains a Grand Conversation.

Golden Lines

Finding the golden line is a strategy whereby students, using yellow highlighters, read for the most memorable words and phrases (the golden lines) in each other's papers or in works of literature. Both "A Special Place" and "The Saturation Recall Paper" lessons, elsewhere in this book, include golden lines activities.

Guided Imagery

Guided imagery uses visualization to stimulate writing ideas; the students watch the "movie screens" in their minds. The teacher slowly narrates a setting or story, using sensory detail to elicit impressions or images, pausing often to give students time to develop their own mental pictures of the words they are learning. This method is especially helpful as a prewriting activity for sensory/descriptive and imaginative/narrative writing. The lesson "Writing a Persuasive Speech," elsewhere in this book, contains a guided imagery exercise, as does "The Poet Within Us."

Heterogeneous Grouping

Heterogeneous grouping is the grouping of students of different traits, talents, interests, etc.

Holistic Scoring

When scoring holistically, an evaluator judges a piece of writing based on an overall impression of how well the piece fulfilled the objectives of the assignment. Thus, holistic scoring helps objective evaluation because the scorers follow a rubric of specific traits that should appear in the writing. Examples of these traits might be: (1) complete coverage of the topic, (2) excellent fluency, (3) effective structure, and (4) freedom from mechanical errors. The better the student achieves these traits in a piece of writing, the higher the numerical score received.

Interior Monologue

Interior monologue is writing in which the author presents the ideas within the head of an individual character or within the thoughts of the speaker of the text. The result is a kind of stream of consciousness effect. "The Saturation Recall Paper," elsewhere in this book, contains examples of interior monologue.

Interpretive Questions

Interpretive questions are questions students ask about a text that have neither a right nor wrong answer but which elicit a variety of interpretations. The "Living in Life's Shadows" lesson, elsewhere in this book, contains an interpretive questions activity.

I-Search

The I-Search paper is a nontraditional approach to the research paper based upon the student's own genuine need to know. Developed by author Ken Macrorie, the I-Search paper usually begins with what the student knows, assumes or imagines about a topic, follows with conducting the search, and concludes with what is learned. For an in-depth example of the I-Search paper, see *The I-Search Paper: Revised Edition of Searching Writing* (Portsmouth, NH: Boynton/Cook Publishers, Heinemann, 1988).

Jigsaw

Jigsaw is a cooperative learning activity that has each group become experts on selected topics and report their concepts to the whole class. Also, groups could be assigned certain topics to learn, and the experts move from group to group reporting their findings. The "Persuasive Speech" lesson, elsewhere in this book, contains an example of a jigsaw.

Job Cards

Job cards is another term for share cards.

Journals

Journals are personal writing or notes that a student keeps during the course of the learning experience in a given discipline. Some teachers have students keep journals that are categorized into learning areas, and they check them from time to time for diagnostic purposes. The "Importance of Being" lesson, elsewhere in this book, contains numerous examples of journal writing.

Learning Log

A learning log is a student's informal written response to class information, but is unlike the journal, which usually deals with personal experience. Cognitively, the log is a place for students to think "out loud" on paper—to question, sort through, clarify, or challenge what they are learning; it may be shared with the teacher to enable judging the students' comprehension. Affectively, the log is a place where students can express how they are feeling about the learning experience taking place in the class and share with the teacher as a partner in dialogue rather that as an assessor. The teacher can respond either by addressing the students individually (orally or in writing) or by opening up issues to class discussion.

Mapping

Mapping is a composing method that can best be described as graphic outlining. Rather than organizing primary, secondary, and tertiary ideas in outline form, students choose a geometric shape or simple picture to depict the ideas. This is a more organized form of clustering. Examples of mapping can be found in "A Special Place" and "Reflections on Alienation" lessons, elsewhere in this book.

Metacognition

Metacognition, simply defined, is thinking about thinking. It is a conscious monitoring of one's own thinking. It could be the ability to realize that you do not understand something another person has said. It could be paraphrasing aloud what someone has just told you to determine whether he or she will agree that, in fact, that is exactly what was meant. It could be the realization that someone does not know enough about a particular subject to write effectively and needs to gather more information before beginning to write. A sample metacognitive log can be found in the "Be an Outcast" and "Living in Life's Shadow" lessons, elsewhere in this book.

Microtheme

A microtheme is a minicomposition which allows students to formulate a writing plan. On a 3' x 5' card or piece of 8 1/2' x 11' paper, students can select headings related to both the form and content of their papers and begin to think about where they will be heading in their writing. Examples of microthemes can be found in the "Stories in Clay" and "Living in Life's Shadow" lessons in this book.

Modeling	Through modeling, the teacher provides examples or models, either by other students or by professional writers, for students to emulate so that they may better understand what it is that they are being asked to produce.
Note Taking/ Note Making	Note taking/note making is a strategy to encourage students to think critically about what they are learning—to question, sort through, puzzle over, clarify, or comment on. Students take notes in the left-hand column of their journal and make notes of their reflections in the right-hand column. See the sample Note Taking/Note Making activity in the "Importance of Being" lesson, elsewhere in this book.
Open Mind	An Open Mind involves an outline of a head in which the students may write or draw what a character from a story is thinking. It is a reader response strategy that helps students focus on imagery and symbolism in a text. Sample Open Minds can be found in the "Be An Outcast" and "Memories and Metaphors" lessons, elsewhere in this book.
Peer Editing	Instead of the teacher's marking errors, peers (or classmates) assume the role of editors. By editing one another's writing, students often become more proficient in editing their own writing.
Peer Evaluation/ Peer Scoring	This is a valuable tool to help students internalize the rubric, or scoring guide, as well as the prompt. Students must be given training in holistic scoring and a clear scoring guide to use. Students are placed in random groups of five or six. Each student is given a rubric (scoring guide) and each group is given a consensus chart. Each student reads and scores each essay before any discussion is allowed. Then the scores are recorded for each paper and comments included to justify the score. Individual papers can be coded so that no names are involved.
Peer Partners	A teacher uses peer partnership so that students may help one another through any of the stages of the writing process. Peer partners are particularly useful for giving feedback and differing viewpoints during the sharing and revising stages of the writing process. Students often "hear" better when the critique comes from a peer.
Poetry Response Strategy	Developed by Dr. Sheridan Blau, Director of the South Coast Writing Project, at University of California, Santa Barbara, poetry response is a technique in which students read a text several times, each time underlining with a different color of ink, words and phrases they have trouble understanding. Students then meet in groups to illuminate each other's read-

ings in the text. Examples of this strategy can be found in the lessons "Peopling Poems" and "The Poet Within Us," elsewhere in this book.

Point of View   Point of view is the perspective from which a story is narrated. Point of view includes: *who* (first person, third person, omniscient, and stream of conscious narration); *when* (past, present, future, and flashback); and *where* (from a distant perspective, in the midst of the action, from beyond the grave, and so forth).

Precomposing   Helping students generate ideas for writing is often not enough to enable them to organize and articulate their thoughts. Precomposing activities help students to focus on the specific requirements of the writing assignment as well as to formulate a writing plan. Each of these lessons uses a variety of precomposing activities, depending on the type of writing.

Prewriting   Prewriting generates ideas for writing. Taking a wide range of forms—class discussion, brainstorming, visualizing, freewriting, etc.—prewriting aims to stimulate the free flow of thought. In the writing process, prewriting usually precedes the introduction of the writing assignment (prompt) and may set the stage for thinking and writing about a given topic without specifically addressing it. Each of the lessons uses a variety of prewriting activities, depending on the type of writing.

Primary Traits   In evaluation, the primary traits are those considered to be the most important in a student's writing. Generally, no more than five traits are identified for one assignment. A point system is used to denote a student's grade on each of those traits in the writing assignment. The "Round 1, Round 2" lesson, elsewhere in this book, contains a primary trait scoring guide.

Prompt   The prompt is the writing task or assignment. Effective prompts provide specific directions for the writing task. They not only explain what is required in terms of the content of the final piece of writing, but describe what is required in terms of fluency, form, and correctness. Prompts can be open-ended, allowing for student choice, or structured. The more specific the prompt, the clearer the criteria for evaluation, the better able the student is to respond effectively.

Quaker Reading   A Quaker Reading is a reading of a text in which students read—in random order—words, phrases, and passages that they find particularly striking. Often, the way in which students jump in with their readings can offer students new insights into the text. An example of a Quaker Reading can be found in the "Living in Life's Shadow" lesson, elsewhere in this book.

Quickwriting

Quickwriting is a method of freewriting that helps a writer achieve fluency. The student is asked to write as much as possible without stopping in a limited amount of time. The instructor also emphasizes that the student should not be concerned with correctness. See the lesson "Reflecting About Our Many Selves," elsewhere in this book, for an example for quickwriting.

Read-Around Groups

Created by Jenee Gossard, a Teacher/Consultant for the UCLA Writing Project, read-around groups give students the opportunity to share their own writing, as well as to read and respond to each other's writing anonymously at several stages in the course of any assignment. Students write for a specified amount of time and then place a code number rather than their name on the paper. Then, they form groups (preferably of four) to read all the papers of the other groups of four in the class. At the teacher's signal, the group leader passes the set of papers to another group, who reads them very quickly (usually thirty seconds to one minute per paper.) At the end of the thirty-second to one-minute interval, the teacher signals the readers to pass the paper they have just read to the right. As soon as all the papers have been read, the group must come to consensus on the paper they liked best. In addition to the reader appeal, papers can be read around for beginnings, middle, and/or ending, for language use, for organization, for correctness, or for any other feature specified by the teacher or the class. The lesson "The Rules of the Game," elsewhere in this book, uses Read-Around groups as does the "Be An Outcast" lesson.

Reader Response

Reader response is an approach to responding to literature that values the reader's initial reactions to a text and holds that it is the *transaction* between the reader and the text that enables the reader to construct meaning. See Louise M. Rosenblatt's *Literature as Exploration* (New York: Modern Language Association, 1976) for detailed information.

Recursive

The composing process—prewriting, precomposing, writing, sharing, revising, editing, and evaluation—involves all levels of critical thinking and is a recursive process. It is termed "recursive" because the process is not strictly linear. Writers often "go back to go forward."

Response Forms or Sharing Sheets

Response forms or sharing sheets are forms of written feedback used primarily during the sharing stage of the writing process. The writer receives reactions to his or her work in progress. Sample Response Forms are contained in the lessons

"The Story of Your Maker" and "My Life Through Images," elsewhere in this book.

Revising

Revision not only involves a commitment to fully engage in the challenges of the writing task—to make the effort to discover and articulate our ideas for ourselves—but also the detachment to get enough distance from the writing to appreciate the perspective of the reader. Revising requires a writer both to appraise his or her writing and then to make the necessary changes. The writer examines his or her ideas and then the words chosen to express them and how these words work together in phrases, sentences, and paragraphs to communicate the ideas and the writer then adds, deletes, substitutes, and rearranges to enhance the communication. Revision can occur after a single word written, a total composition, or at any place in between. A teacher can facilitate revision by asking questions that address surface level changes as well as meaning changes. A writer then rereads his or her paper with specific objectives in mind. Each lesson in this book has a variety of revision strategies or activities included.

Role-Playing

In role-playing, students act out specific scenarios created by them or the teacher to dramatize a certain situation. Examples of role-playing can be found in the "Customs and Conflicts" and "Everyday Use" lessons, elsewhere in this book.

Rubric

A rubric is a scale or set of criteria that delineates the key features of a writing task. It often has a numerical scale attached to it that is used as a basis for evaluating the final written product. Rubrics (also called Scoring Guides) are included in all of the lessons in this book.

Scoring Guide

A scoring guide is another term for rubric.

Secondary Traits

In evaluation, the secondary traits are those considered to be of secondary importance in a writing assignment. They are often areas such as format and mechanics. A point system is used to denote a student's grade or success in addressing those requirements. The "Round 1, Round 2" lesson, elsewhere in this book, contains a secondary trait scoring guide.

Share Cards

Developed by Marty Moorehead, a Teacher/Consultant for the UCI Writing Project, share cards are cards that the teacher creates to correspond with the directions in the prompt. Each element of the prompt is included on a separate card (*i.e.,* a card might read: dominant metaphor, personal experience, quote). In the sharing process, these cards focus student response on specific requirements that should be included in the writing. Some share cards might also include cues for personal reactions (i.e. favorite part, I need to know more about...) The lessons "On Growing Up" and "Fifth Chinese Daughter" include an exercise using share cards.

Sharing Groups (Writing Response Group)   Sharing groups are composed of students who are willing to share their own writing as well as respond to the writing of their peers. The goal of sharing groups is to provide the writer with *movies* of people's minds while they hear the writer's words. Sharing group members can play the roles of supportive listener, constructive critic, and editor.

Showing, Not Telling   The concept of showing, not telling, has been popularized by Ribekah Caplan, a Teacher/Consultant from the Bay Area Writing Project. The assumption behind the showing, not telling, technique is that most students have not been trained to show what they mean. Showing, not telling, encourages students to dramatize their writing by "showing" with specific details that paint pictures in the reader's mind. It involves giving students a *telling sentence* such as "The room was vacant" or "The lunch period was too short" and asking them to expand the thought in that sentence into an entire paragraph. Students are challenged not to use the original statement in the paragraph at all. Rather, they must *show* that the room was vacant without making that claim directly. "The Saturation Recall Paper," elsewhere in this book, contains a showing, not telling exercise.

Storyboard   A storyboard is a graphic representation of key scenes in a work of literature. A sample storyboard can be found in the "Just Another Fool in Love" lesson, elsewhere in this book.

Stylistic Imitation   Stylistic imitation involves emulating an author's word choice, uses of figurative language (similes, metaphors, symbols, imagery, analogies, etc.) syntax, rhetorical devices (such as foreshadowing, irony, hyperbole, etc.), tone, and point of view. The "Peopling Poems" lesson, elsewhere in this book, pays attention to the style of several authors and encourages students to emulate those styles in writing their own poems.

Thinking Skills Objectives   The thinking skills objectives are the key cognitive tasks that students practice in a Thinking/Writing lesson. Each lesson in this book provides these at the beginning of the lesson.

Time line   A time line is a graphic representation of a sequence of events or activities. In the study of literature, developing time lines often helps students to reconstruct what happened in the text.

The "Living in Life's Shadow" lesson, elsewhere in this book, contains an example of a timeline.

Tone
Tone is an author's attitude toward his or her subject and is communicated in writing through word choice and phrasing.

Transition
Transition is the word, phrase, sentence, or group of sentences that relates a preceding topic to a succeeding one or that smoothly connects a piece of writing. Please see "The Rules of the Game" lesson, elsewhere in this book, for a list of transitional words.

Venn Diagram
Venn diagrams are overlapping circles often used in mathematics to show relationships between sets. In language arts instruction, Venn diagrams are useful for examining similarities and differences. Sample Venn diagrams can be found in the lessons "Stories in Clay" and "My Life Through Images," elsewhere in this book.

Vocabulary Development
Vocabulary development is the use of textual vocabulary words and context clues to improve a student's reading and writing vocabulary. The "Getting in Touch with Your Family's Roots" lesson, elsewhere in this book, contains an example of a vocabulary development exercise.

Word Walls
Developed by Karin Hess in *Enhancing Writing Through Imagery* (New York: Trillium Press, 1987), word walls are kinesthetic brainstorming lists where students use index cards and group them topically and then paste them to poster board or pin them to the wall. Word walls help students with close textual analysis and comparison and contrast. The "Customs and Conflicts" lesson, elsewhere in this book, contains an example of a word wall.

Writing
During the writing stage of the composing process, students allow their ideas to take shape by putting words to paper. Because writers may lack a conscious awareness of what they specifically want to communicate, writing becomes a process of discovering on the conscious level what they are thinking about the given topic. This movement of an idea to the conscious level allows for spontaneity and creativity and should not be impeded in the first draft by concerns with correctness.

Writing Skills Objective
The writing skills objectives are the key writing strategies that students practice in a Thinking/Writing lesson. These are listed at the beginning of each lesson in this book.

Annotated Bibliography

Lesson: **Be an Outcast . . . Be Pleased to Walk Alone** page 291
Author: Cristan Greaves

Selection: "Be Nobody's Darling," a poem
Book: *Revolutionary Petunias and Other Poems,* a collection of poems by Alice Walker
Publisher: New York: Harcourt Brace Jovanovich
Year: 1973
Culture: African American
Grades: 9 – College

"Be Nobody's Darling "

Revolutionary Petunias and Other Poems is a collection of poetry by Alice Walker. Walker has said that these poems are "about (and for) those few embattled souls who remain painfully committed to beauty and to love even while facing the firing squad." This collection also represents a search for the roots and essence of the African American experience. "Be Nobody's Darling" is a short powerful poem that celebrates the "outcast" experience. The outcast who is "nobody's darling" is unafraid to face the contradictions in life. In doing so, she/he joins a large community of people throughout history who have been labeled as outcasts for uttering "brave hurt words." This collection of poetry lends itself well to all the domains of writing.

Lesson: **The Class Quilt** page 99
Author: Dale Sprowl

Book: *The Keeping Quilt,* a children's story by Patricia Polacco
Publisher: New York: Simon & Schuster Books for Young Readers
Year: 1988
Culture: Russian-Jewish
Grades: K – 3

The Keeping Quilt

After a Russian-Jewish family immigrates to America, the mother and her friends make a quilt from the clothing she brought with them. For four generations, the quilt is passed from mother to daughter. The story portrays the unity and strength of the family together with the changes in their religious and cultural traditions. This story elicits the appreciation of all for the diverse cultural heritages we encounter in everyday life. It lends itself well to autobiographical writing and analytical/expository writing as well as to the making of a class quilt.

Lesson: **Customs and Conflicts** page 33
Author: Maureen Rippee

Book: *Like Water for Chocolate,* a novel by Laura Esquivel and translated by Carol Christensen and Thomas Christensen
Publisher: New York: Doubleday
Year: 1992
Culture: Mexican
Grades: 9 – College

Like Water for Chocolate

The number one bestseller in Mexico in 1990, *Like Water for Chocolate* is a romantic tale of star-crossed lovers, in the tradition of Romeo and Juliet. Prevented from marrying the love of her life because she's the youngest daughter and because tradition dictates that she must devote her life to taking care of her mother, Tita channels her emotions into cooking. Dispersed throughout the book are the succulent recipes that have a magical effect on those who partake of them. *Like Water for Chocolate* lends itself well to a comparison/contrast paper with the customs and conflicts in Shakespeare's *Romeo and Juliet.*

Lesson: **Customs and Conflicts** page 33
Author: Maureen Rippee

Book: *Romeo and Juliet,* a play by William Shakespeare
Publisher: New York: Penguin Books USA (Signet Classic)
Year: 1964
Culture: European-American
Grades: 9 – College

Romeo and Juliet

Shakespeare's first assured success as a writer of tragedy, *Romeo and Juliet* is probably the most famous example of the tragic fate of young lovers when tradition and custom dictate love. When Juliet falls in love with Romeo at first sight, she disregards the custom of arranged marriages. The result is conflict as the youths struggle against the obstacles and unexpected developments generated by custom. The play is an ideal comparison/contrast to the Mexican novel *Like Water for Chocolate* and to the Japanese novel *Spring Snow.*

Lesson: **Fifth Chinese Daughter** page 123
Author: Meredith Ritner

Book: *Fifth Chinese Daughter,* an autobiography by Jade Snow Wong
Publisher: Seattle: University of Washington Press
Year: 1989
Culture: Asian American
Grades: 6 – 12

Fifth Chinese Daughter

Fifth Chinese Daughter is the autobiographical account of the upbringing of Jade Snow Wong in twentieth century America by parents still observing the "nineteenth century standards of Imperial China." While it is Jade Snow's story, it is written in the third person, which follows Chinese literary form, and which reflects "cultural disregard for the individual." *Fifth Chinese Daughter* will appeal to students who are immigrants or children of immigrants to the United States and who are caught between two cultures and trying to define themselves. It lends itself well to comparison/contrast and reflective writing.

Lesson: **Getting in Touch with Your Family's Roots** page 414
Author: Jerry Judd

Selection: "A Whole Nation and a People," a story by Harry Mark Petrakis
Book: *Adventures in Reading,* an anthology
Publisher: Harcourt Brace Jovanovich
Culture: Greek-American
Grades: 7 – 10

"A Whole Nation and a People"

To reject his own ethnic background and prove allegiance to the gang of boys he runs around with, a young Greek-American boy throws a plum and hits a Greek grocer in the face. Haunted by remorse, the boy returns later to the grocer to face up to the consequences. The grocer then proceeds to teach the boy about his Greek past, Greek mythology, Greek foods, and the importance of remembering one's cultural past. This incident makes a lasting impression and forever changes the young boy. This story elicits excellent autobiographical writing.

Lesson: **Growing Up: A Personal Reflection** page 311
Author: Meredith Ritner
Selection: "When I Was Growing Up," a poem by Nellie Wong
Book: *This Bridge Called My Back: Writings by Radical Women of Color*
Publisher: New York: Kitchen Table, Women of Color Press
Year: 1983, 1981
Culture: Chinese American
Grades: 7 – 12

"When I Was Growing Up"

Nellie Wong's poem "When I Was Growing Up" captures the conflict of a Chinese-American teenager who is caught between two cultures. Set in Chinatown, it tells the story of a girl who yearns to fit in but cannot find a place where her Chinese heritage and American dreams can merge. This poem lends itself to a reflection upon one's own story of maturation, a story which so often begins with the phrase, "When I was growing up. . . ."

Lesson: **Importance of Being** page 246
Author: Susanna Clemans
Book: *The Assistant*, a novel by Bernard Malamud
Publisher: New York: Avon
Year: 1957
Culture: Jewish American
Grades: 9 – College

The Assistant

The Assistant is a rich, spare novel of only 297 pages brimming over with the struggles of immigrants who grasp for the American dream during the 1940s. Within a small Brooklyn neighborhood, the reader becomes a part of the Jewish Bober family, grocery store proprietors—Ida and Morris—and their 23-year-old daughter, Helen, a secretary. By unusual means, Frank Alpine, an orphaned Italian American, becomes a part of their family. The reader watches each of these lonely characters search for his/her "importance of being." The Jewish culture is stressed throughout the novel, yet connections are continually made by anyone who has felt alienated, not a part of a close-knit family or community. Therefore, the novel is ideal for autobiographical writing, for analysis, and research writing.

Lesson: **Just Another Fool in Love** page 465
Author: Sue Rader Willett
Selection: "Cecilia Rosas," a story by Amado Muro
Book: *The Collected Stories of Amado Muro,* short story anthology
Publisher: Austin, TX: Thorp Spring Press
Year: 1979
Culture: Mexican American
Grades: 9 – 12

"Cecilia Rosas"

"Cecilia Rosas" is a touching story about a ninth-grade boy from the El Paso barrio who falls in love with an older woman. Young Amado suffers through jealousy, confusion, daydreams, and elaborate preparations for wooing Miss Rosas. At one point, he even alienates his Mexican family by insisting upon speaking, eating, and acting "like Americans." Everything comes to naught, however, when Amado realizes his own foolishness as Miss Rosas drives off with her American, Johnny. He loses his love but regains his heritage. Students enjoy this story and identify with Amado. It lends itself well to many different discussions, role-playing, and a variety of writing assignments.

Lesson: **Many Voices, One Heart** page 541
Author: Bill Burns
Selection: "The Hill" & "Hamlet Micure"
Book: *Spoon River Anthology* by Edgar Lee Masters
Publisher: New York: The MacMillan Company
Year: 1915
Culture: European American
Grades: 9 – College

"The Hill" & "Hamlet Micure"

Spoon River Anthology is a collection of short, first-person, mostly narrative, freeverse poems. Each poem, titled with a character's name, is about the essence of that character's life, death, or moment of discovery. The poems are microcosms of life, timeless and universal, funny, sad, shocking, and ultimately, revealing.

Lesson: **Memories and Metaphors** page 556
Author: Chris Byron
Selection: "Eleven," a story
Book: *Woman Hollering Creek*, a collection of stories by Sandra Cisneros
Publisher: New York: Vintage Books, a division of Random Books
Year: 1992
Culture: Mexican American
Grades: 6 – 12

"Eleven"

"Eleven" is the short story of a young girl whose birthday turns out to be anything but the happy day the girl had imagined. Using metaphor and imagery, Cisneros paints a vivid picture of the young girl's thoughts and feelings as she reviews the day. This story is excellent for eliciting the autobiographical incident.

Lesson: **Mercy or Death** page 572
Author: Sue Ellen Gold
Selection: "Looking for the Rain God," a short story by Bessie Head from the book, *The Collector of Treasures*
Publisher: London: Heineman Educational
Year: 1977
Culture: African
Grades: 9 – 12

"Looking for the Rain God"

"The drought was in its eighth year. This year there was a promise of good rain and many families left the village to move to the land to grow. But the rains left. There was no food. The women broke first; then the men. Then the civilized faith. The old man remembered an ancient ceremony—a rain-making ceremony, a sacrifice. The sacrifice was made; the rain did not come. Terror, extreme and deep, overwhelmed the whole family." They sacrificed their own children to save lives and it didn't work. This powerful story shows vividly the problems the tribal communities face in trying to live off the African land. It is a powerful introduction to *Cry, the Beloved Country*. On another level, it is an interesting parallel to "The Lottery."

Lesson: **My Life Through Images** page 331
Author: Pat Clark

> **Selection:** "Four Skinny Trees," a vignette
> **Book:** *The House on Mango Street* by Sandra Cisneros
> **Publisher:** New York: 1st Vintage Contemporaries: A Division of Random House, Inc.
> **Year:** 1991
> **Culture:** Mexican American
> **Grades:** 7 – 12

"Four Skinny Trees"

"Four Skinny Trees" is most likely autobiographical in nature as Cisneros learns a lesson in survival by observing four trees growing out of concrete in the middle of a city. This vignette lends itself to both sensory/descriptive and interpretive writing as one discovers the lessons to be learned from objects in nature.

Lesson: **My Life Through Images** page 331
Author: Pat Clark

> **Selection:** "Identity," a poem by Julio Noboa
> **Book:** *Prentice Hall Literature: Silver*, an anthology
> **Publisher:** Prentice Hall
> **Culture:** Puerto Rican American
> **Grades:** 7 – 12

"Identity"

"Identity" is a five-stanza poem written by Noboa in 1949 when he was in the eighth grade. It uses nature symbolism to state what the poet wants out of life. The poem lends itself to sensory/ descriptive writing; it elicits comparisons between oneself and nature as one makes one's way through today's world.

Lesson: **My Name, My Self** page 596
Author: Brenda Borron

> **Selection:** "My Name," a vignette
> **Book:** *The House on Mango Street* by Sandra Cisneros
> **Publisher:** New York: 1st Vintage Contemporaries: A Division of Random House, Inc.
> **Year:** 1991
> **Culture:** Mexican American
> **Grades:** Middle School – College

"My Name"

The *House on Mango Street* is a series of vignettes which appear to be autobiographical in nature. The book is the story of a young Mexican American girl growing up in a run-down section of Chicago. "My Name" is one of the most lyrical and rewarding vignettes to use in the classroom as it causes students to reflect on their own names and cultures. It leads to excellent autobiographical writing.

Lesson: **Native American Voices: Reflecting on Facts and Fallacies** page 617

Author: **Bill Burns**

Selection: "Indian Camp," a short story by Ernest Hemingway

Book: *In Our Time*

Publisher: New York: Charles Scribner's Sons

Year: 1958

Culture: European American

Grades: 9 – 12

"Indian Camp"

Hemingway's short story appears at first to be a "coming-of-age" story of a young Nick Adams, who accompanies his doctor-father to an Indian camp where his father is called to help a pregnant woman having a difficult birth. The father has brought his son to see what he does for a living, but the birth turns out to require a Caesarean and Nick sees far more than he wants to. Nick also sees the bloody body of the pregnant woman's husband, who kills himself out of shame and grief. Hemingway's portrayal of the Indian provides an interesting subtext to this story and may reveal more about the stereotypes Indians have been given than about what Nick has learned. This story can be used to help students examine their own stereotypes about another culture.

Lesson: **Native American Voices: Reflecting on Facts and Fallacies** page 617

Author: **Bill Burns**

Selection: "Speaking for My People," a speech by Robert L. Jacopi

Book: *Look to the Mountain Top,* a nonfiction book

Publisher: San Jose, CA: H.M. Gousha Publications

Year: 1972

Culture: Native American

Grades: 9 – 12

"Speaking for My People"

This book is a resource of information about Native Americans, including history, politics, religion, and literature, that focuses on commonalities rather than on the great diversities among Native American peoples. Among the useful information is a selection of first-person narratives from a wide selection, historically and geographically, of Native Americans. These narratives are taken from Virginia Armstrong's *I Have Spoken: American History Through the Voices of the Indian,* published by Swallow Press, Chicago, 1971. These nonfiction pieces create a counterpoint to European American perceptions of American Indians and can be useful in a comparison/contrast essay.

Lesson: **Native American Voices: Reflecting on Facts and Fallacies** page 617

Author: Bill Burns

Selection: "New Way, Old Way," a poem by Dave Martin Nez

Book: *The Way: An Anthology of American Indian Literature*

Publisher: New York: Vintage Books

Year: 1972

Culture: Native American

Grades: 9 – 12

"New Way, Old Way" Nez's poem reflects the blend of tradition and change found in Native American lives. He explores the "beauty in the old way of life" and the changes wrought when "economics and traditions clashed." He suggests that Indians will regain their "beauty" when they learn and master the tools of modern society.

Lesson: **Peopling Poems: Revealing Character Through Images and Narrative** page 352

Author: Susan Starbuck

Selection: "miss rosie," a poem by Lucille Clifton

Book: *Good Woman, Poems and a Memoir 1969-1980,* by Lucille Clifton

Publisher: Brockport NY: BOA Editions Ltd.

Year: 1987

Culture: African American

Grades: 9 – College

"miss rosie"

Selection: "My Father's Song," by Simon J. Ortiz

Book: *Harper's Anthology of 20th Century Native American Poetry*

Publisher: Harper and Row

Culture: Native American

Grades: 9 – College

"My Father's Song"

Selection: "Name," by Alberto Alvaro Rios

Book: *Whispering to Fool the Wind: Poems by Alberto Alvaro Rios*

Publisher: NY: Sheep Meadow Press

Year: 1982

Culture: Mexican American

Grades: 9 – College

"Name" All three of these poems reveal character through imagery and symbol and, in each case, the subject of the poem is someone who has made a strong impression on the author. Students can easily emulate these poems by describing a person in their lives, reflecting upon what that person means in their lives, and creating a poem that captures the essence of who that person is and the lasting impression he or she has made on the writer.

Lesson: **The Poet Within Us** page 371
Author: Esther Severy

Selection: "XX," a poem
Book: *Martin & Meditations on the South Valley* by Jimmy Santiago Baca
Publisher: NY: A New Directions Book
Year: 1987
Culture: Mexican American
Grades: 6 – College

"XX"

Martin & Meditations on the South Valley by Jimmy Santiago Baca is a narrative poem about a man who, recently released from prison, really takes a look at his native land, New Mexico. Baca, in this 99-page narrative poem, paints pictures that allow the reader to experience the realities of everyday life in small-town New Mexico. He portrays his feelings for the older generation of the village, their hopes and dreams, their preparations for death. In the section entitled "Meditations," Baca further divides the poem into sections I through XXVIII. "XX" is in this portion of the poem. The poetry lends itself to both analysis and evaluation as students see how acceptance of death and the accompanying preparations are simply a part of living in the Latino community. The poem also serves as a model and a springboard for creating one's own poetry.

Lesson: **The Poet Within Us** page 371
Author: Esther Severy

Selection: "Warning," a poem
Book: *Selected Poems* by Jenny Joseph
Publisher: Newcastle upon Tyne: Bloodaxe Books
Year: 1992
Culture: English
Grades: 6 – College

"Warning"

This poem is about an older woman who starts thinking about all the fun things she can do when she is older and doesn't have all the responsibilities she has now. But then she starts thinking she should start practicing all the crazy things things she wants to do now so that people won't be too shocked. This is a tongue-in-cheek, fun poem.

Lesson: **Reflecting About Our Many Selves** page 388
Author: Julie Simpson

Selection: "We Are Many," a poem by Pablo Neruda
Book: *Five Decades: A Selection (Poems 1925-1970),*
edited and translated by Ben Belitt
Publisher: NY: Grove Wedenfield
Year: 1974
Culture: Latin American (Chilean)
Grades: 10 – 12

"We Are Many"

The speaker in this poem is troubled by his inability to control the various sides of his personality. He is continuously disappointed in himself. The poem is particularly suitable for discussing expectations versus reality, for analyzing imagery, for reflecting about how people are.

Lesson: **Reflections on Alienation** page 147
Author: Shari Lockman
Selection: "Blue Winds Dancing," a short story by Thomas S. Whitecloud
Book: *Literature and Life* and *The Heath Anthology of American Literature*
Publisher: Scribner's Magazine, Volume 103 (February 1938)
Year: 1938
Culture: Chippewa (Native American)
Grades: 7 – college

"Blue Winds Dancing"

"Blue Winds Dancing" is a moving account of a Chippewa college student's search for identity as he tries to walk in the white world while still maintaining his traditional values and his culture. The story is told in the first person point-of-view and uses rich sensory images to describe the difference between Whitecloud's two worlds as well as his cross-country journey to return to the Chippewa reservation. The story paints a true picture of the reservation as a place of material poverty, but spiritual strength. It enhances a non-Indian reader's understanding of Native American culture. It is a wonderful example of showing writing and autobiographical incident. It also lends itself to reflective thinking and writing.

Lesson: **Round 1: Dramatizing the Argument Scene**
Round 2: Resolving the Argument page 260
Author: Virginia Bergquist
Selection: *Sister,* a novel by Eloise Greenfield
Publisher: New York: Crowell
Year: 1974
Culture: African American
Grades: 6 – 9

Sister

An ALA Notable Children's Book and *New York Times* Outstanding Book of the Year, *Sister* gives insight into a thirteen-year-old and her struggles growing up. The main character began keeping a journal when she was nine and now at age thirteen she rereads it and recalls the good times and the bad times. She realizes at the end that these events are what give her strength. This book could be used with the *Diary of Anne Frank* or any diary or journal activity.

Lesson: **The Rules of the Game** page 67
Author: Michael O'Brien
Book: *Romeo and Juliet,* a play by William Shakespeare
Publisher: New York: Penguin Books USA (Signet Classic)
Year: 1964
Culture: European American
Grades: 9 – College

Romeo and Juliet

See description under the lesson, "Customs and Conflicts" by Maureen Rippee.

Lesson: **The Rules of the Game** page 67
Author: Michael O'Brien
Book: *Spring Snow*, a novel by Yukio Mishima and translated by Michael Gallagher
Publisher: NY: 1st Vintage International
Year: 1990
Culture: Japanese
Grades: 11 – College

Spring Snow

Mishima's novel somewhat parallels *Romeo and Juliet*, but is set in Imperial Japan in 1912. Kiyoaki of the ambitious Matsugae family has a love-hate relationship with Satoko of the ancient, aristocratic Ayakura and family. Only after she is betrothed to a prince of the Royal Family does Kiyoaki finally decide he truly loves her. The two lovers then begin the dangerous game of meeting secretly. Mishima explores issues of social class and the psychology of love and desire. The last few chapters are haunting for their beauty.

Lesson: **The Saturation Recall Paper** page 172
Author: Carol Booth Olson
Book: *Sweet Summer: Growing Up With and Without My Dad*, an autobiography by Bebe Moore Campbell
Publisher: NY: G. P. Putnam's Sons
Year: 1989
Culture: African American
Grades: 6 – College

Sweet Summer: Growing Up With and Without My Dad

Sweet Summer is an autobiographical account of Bebe Moore Campbell's childhood and coming of age and her rich and complex relationship with her father, from whom she was separated nine months of each year by divorce. Written in vivid, lyrical prose, Campbell's book is a wonderful example of sensory description and imaginative narrative writing. It lends itself to the teaching of autobiographical incident and more extended memoirs.

Lesson: **A Special Place** page 82
Author: Mindy Moffatt
Selection: "Letter to the U.S. Government," a nonfiction work by Chief Seattle
Book: *Prentice Hall Literature: Copper Edition*, an anthology
Publisher: Prentice Hall
Culture: Native American
Grades: 6 – 12

"Letter to the U.S. Government"

Although the authorship of this literature has recently been disputed, the message remains:

- How can you buy or sell the sky, the warmth of the land?
- The idea is strange to us.

In striking images which expose the thoughts and feelings of Native Americans, Chief Seattle presents a view of the Earth contrasted with the view taken by white settlers. By expressing the value of the Earth in Native American terms and also by acknowledging how white men view the Earth, the point of view taken by Chief Seattle makes a persuasive argument in the "Letter to the U.S. Government." This piece lends itself well to sensory/descriptive writing about nature and to using sensory/descriptive language in persuasive writing.

Lesson: **Writing a Persuasive Speech: Using American Indian Oratory as a Model** page 223

Author: Cristan Greaves

Selection: "Sleep Not Longer, O Choctaws and Chickasaws" by Tecumseh

Book: *Indian Oratory,* a collection of speeches by W.C. Vanderwerth with a foreword by William K. Carmack

Publisher: Norman, OK: University of Oklahoma Press

Year: 1971

Culture: Native American

Grades: 9 – 12

"Sleep Not Longer, O Choctaws and Chickasaws"

Indian Oratory is W.C. Vanderwerth's classic collection of the finest American Indian oratory of the "mid-18th to early 20th centuries." The speeches featured in this collection vary in purpose, from intertribal pleas for unification to treaty signing speeches. There are also numerous surrender speeches, the most famous being Chief Joseph's "I Will Fight No More Forever." To date, this collection is the most comprehensive in the field of American Indian oratory. This book offers a unique perspective of early American history and Native American history. It also provides the reader with excellent models of persuasive discourse.

Text Credits

"Be Nobody's Darling" from *Revolutionary Petunias & Other Poems,* copyright © 1972 by Alice Walker, reprinted by permission of Harcourt Brace & Company.

"Blue Winds Dancing" by Thomas Whitecloud is reprinted with the permission of Scribner, an imprint of Simon & Schuster, Inc. from *Scribner's Magazine,* 103, February 1938 issue. Copyright 1938 Charles Scribner's Sons; copyright renewed

Excerpt from *The Bluest Eye* by Toni Morrison. Copyright © 1970 by Toni Morrison. Reprinted by permission of International Creative Management, Inc.

"Cecilia Rosas" by Amado Muro. From *Collected stories of Amado Muro.* Reprinted with permission of Thorp Springs Press.

"Dog Head Stew" (for fifty people) by Dorothy Pennington.

"Eleven" by Sandra Cisneros. From *Woman Hollering Creek.* Copyright © 1991 by Sandra Cisneros. Published in the United States by Vintage Books, a division of Random House, Inc., New York. Originally published in hardcover by Random House, Inc., New York, in 1991. Reprinted by permission of Susan Bergholz Literary Services.

"Everyday Use" from *In Love and Trouble: Stories of Black Women,* copyright © 1973 by Alice Walker, reprinted by permission of Harcourt Brace & Company.

From *Fifth Chinese Daughter* by Jade Snow Wong, copyright 1945/1978 Jade Snow Wong. Reprinted with permission of University of Washington Press.

"Four Skinny Trees" by Sandra Cisneros. From *The House on Mango Street.* Copyright © 1984 by Sandra Cisneros. Published in the United States by Vintage Books, a division of Random House, Inc., New York. Reprinted by permission of Susan Bergholz Literary Services.

"The Hill" and "Hamlet Micure" from *The Spoon River Anthology* by Edgar Lee Masters. Originally published by the Macmillan Co. Permission by Ellen C. Masters.

"Identity" by Julio Noboa. Reprinted by permission of the author.

From *Like Water for Chocolate* by Laura Esquivel. Copyright Translation © 1992 by Doubleday, a division of Bantam, Doubleday, Dell Publishing Group Inc. Used by permission of Doubleday, a division of Bantam, Doubleday, Dell Publishing Group Inc.

From "Little Miracles, Kept Promises" by Sandra Cisneros. From *Woman Hollering Creek.* Copyright © 1991 by Sandra Cisneros. Published in the United States by Vintage Books, a division of Random House, Inc., New York. Originally published in hardcover by Random House, Inc., New York, in 1991. Reprinted by permission of Susan Bergholz Literary Services.

Excerpt from *Look to the Mountain Top* by Patrick Kills Crows and Mary Crazy Thunder. Reprinted by permission of The Times Books, a division of Random House, Inc.

"Looking for a Rain God" by Bessie Head. Copyright © The Estate of Bessie Head. From *The Collector of Treasures,* Heinemann Educational Books, African Writer Series, 1977. Permission granted by John Johnson Ltd., London.

Lucille Clifton. "miss rosie," copyright © 1987 by Lucille Clifton. Reprinted from *Good Woman: Poems and a Memoir 1969–1980,* by Lucille Clifton, with the permission of BOA Editions, Ltd., 260 East Avenue, Rochester, NY 14604.

"My Father's Song" by Simon J. Ortiz. Permission granted by author, Simon J. Ortiz.

"My Name" by Sandra Cisneros. From *The House on Mango Street.* Copyright © 1984 by Sandra Cisneros. Published in the United States by Vintage Books, a division of Random House, Inc., New York. Reprinted by permission of Susan Bergholz Literary Services.